Teach Yourself®
Visual Basic® 6

Teach Yourself®
Visual Basic® 6

Patricia Hartman

Wiley Publishing, Inc.

Teach Yourself® Visual Basic® 6

Published by

Wiley Publishing, Inc.

909 Third Avenue

New York, NY 10022

www.wiley.com

Copyright © 2000 by Wiley Publishing, Inc., Indianapolis, Indiana

Published by Wiley Publishing, Inc., Indianapolis, Indiana

No part of this publication may be reproduced, stored in a retrieval system or transmitted in any form or by any means, electronic, mechanical, photocopying, recording, scanning or otherwise, except as permitted under Sections 107 or 108 of the 1976 United States Copyright Act, without either the prior written permission of the Publisher, or authorization through payment of the appropriate per-copy fee to the Copyright Clearance Center, 222 Rosewood Drive, Danvers, MA 01923, (978) 750-8400, fax (978) 750-4744. Requests to the Publisher for permission should be addressed to the Legal Department, Wiley Publishing, Inc., 10475 Crosspoint Blvd., Indianapolis, IN 46256, (317) 572-3447, fax (317) 572-4447, e-mail: permcoordinator@wiley.com.

Trademarks: Wiley, the Wiley Publishing logo, and related trade dress are trademarks or registered trademarks of Wiley Publishing, Inc., in the United States and other countries, and may not be used without written permission. PowerPoint and Windows are registered trademarks of Microsoft Corporation. Include additional trademark info here. All other trademarks are the property of their respective owners. Wiley Publishing, Inc., is not associated with any product or vendor mentioned in this book.

For general information on our other products and services or to obtain technical support, please contact our Customer Care Department within the U.S. at 800-762-2974, outside the U.S. at 317-572-3993, or fax 317-572-4002.

Wiley also publishes its books in a variety of electronic formats. Some content that appears in print may not be available in electronic books.

ISBN: 0-7645-7516-3

Manufactured in the United States of America

10 9 8 7 6 5 4 3

About the Author

Patricia A. Hartman has written a number of books related to computer databases as well as having worked in a civil service environment where she supervised a computer network support staff and developed applications in Basic and database languages. Dr. Hartman holds graduate degrees from the University of Minnesota and has taught at state universities in Minnesota and California. She is a Certified Netware Engineer and is currently consulting in networking and Web design services, as well as authoring books and other publications. She lives in North San Diego County with her husband, two Rottweilers, a cat, and their computer network.

Credits

Acquisitions Editor
Debra Williams Cauley

Project Editors
Barbra Guerra
Laura Brown

Technical Editor
Christopher Stone

Copy Editors
Robert Campbell
Marcia Baker

Project Coordinator
Amanda Foxworth

Graphics and Production Specialists
Amy Adrian
Jill Piscitelli
Jacque Schneider
Janet Seib
Brian Torwelle
Mary Jo Weis
Dan Whetstine
Erin Zeltner

Quality Control Specialists
Laura Albert
Corey Bowen

Book Designers
Daniel Ziegler Design
Cátálin Dulfu
Kurt Krames

Proofreading and Indexing
York Production Services

To my husband, William Rupp, and my family —
Mark, Craig, Karina, Deborah, Kent, Serena, Laurissa,
Ryan, Sam, Giovanna, Deanna, Laithe, and Aunt Florence —
whose patience and understanding helped me along the way.

Welcome to
Teach Yourself

Welcome to *Teach Yourself*, a series read and trusted by millions for a decade. Although you may have seen the *Teach Yourself* name on other books, ours is the original. In addition, no *Teach Yourself* series has ever delivered more on the promise of its name than this series. That's because IDG Books Worldwide has transformed *Teach Yourself* into a new cutting-edge format that gives you all the information you need to learn quickly and easily.

Readers have told us that they want to learn by doing and that they want to learn as much as they can in as short a time as possible. We listened to you and believe that our new task-by-task format and suite of learning tools deliver the book you need to successfully teach yourself any technology topic. Features such as our Personal Workbook, which lets you practice and reinforce the skills you've just learned, help ensure that you get full value out of the time you invest in your learning. Handy cross-references to related topics and online sites broaden your knowledge and give you control over the kind of information you want, when you want it.

More Answers . . .

In designing the latest incarnation of this series, we started with the premise that people like you, who are beginning to intermediate computer users, want to take control of your own learning. To do this, you need the proper tools to find answers to questions so you can solve problems now.

In designing a series of books that provide such tools, we created a unique and concise visual format. The added bonus: *Teach Yourself* books actually pack more information into their pages than other books written on the same subjects. Skill for skill, you typically get much more information in a *Teach Yourself* book. In fact, *Teach Yourself* books, on average, cover twice the skills covered by other computer books — as many as 125 skills per book — so they're more likely to address your specific needs.

...In Less Time

We know you don't want to spend twice the time to get all this great information, so we provide lots of time-saving features:

- ▶ A modular task-by-task organization of information: any task you want to perform is easy to find and includes simple-to-follow steps
- ▶ A larger size than standard makes the book easy to read and convenient to use at a computer workstation. The large format also enables us to include many more illustrations — 500 screen illustrations show you how to get everything done!
- ▶ A Personal Workbook at the end of each chapter reinforces learning with extra practice, real-world applications for your learning, and questions and answers to test your knowledge
- ▶ Cross-references appearing at the bottom of each task page refer you to related information, providing a path through the book for learning particular aspects of the software thoroughly

- ▶ A Find It Online feature offers valuable ideas on where to go on the Internet to get more information or to download useful files
- ▶ Take Note sidebars provide added-value information from our expert authors for more in-depth learning
- ▶ An attractive, consistent organization of information helps you quickly find and learn the skills you need

These *Teach Yourself* features are designed to help you learn the essential skills about a technology in the least amount of time, with the most benefit. We've placed these features consistently throughout the book, so you quickly learn where to go to find just the information you need — whether you work through the book from cover to cover or use it later to solve a new problem.

You will find a *Teach Yourself* book on almost any technology subject — from the Internet to Windows to Microsoft Office. Take control of your learning today, with the *Teach Yourself* series.

Teach Yourself
More Answers in Less Time

Go to this area if you want special tips, cautions, and notes that provide added insight into the current task.

Search through the task headings to find the topic you want right away. To learn a new skill, search the contents, chapter opener, or the extensive index to find what you need. Then find — at a glance — the clear task heading that matches it.

Learning More about Windows

Stated as simply as possible, a window is a rectangular area in which coding and form design take place, and in which properties and projects are selected. The window environment is a place where you can design forms, implement controls, add properties, and write code.

Windows Collection

The Windows collection is made up of Window objects. In Visual Basic these include the Project Explorer; the Properties, Object Browser, Code, and Designer windows; and the development environment.

When you open a new window, you add a new member to the Windows collection. When you close a window, the action removes a window from the collection. If you close a permanent development environment window, the window will become invisible, but the object will not be removed.

Linked Windows Collection

The Linked Windows collection is all of the currently linked windows. Code windows, the Object Browser, and Designer windows are not by default linked to other windows or docked to the Main window, but their docking options can be changed from the Tools ⇨ Options menu. The Add and the Remove methods can be used to add and remove windows from the currently linked Windows collection.

The Window object may be displayed, hidden, or positioned. The Close method causes different actions when it is applied to different window types. Close, used with the Code and Designer windows, actually closes these windows. Used with the Project Explorer or Properties

windows, it renders these windows invisible. Closing the Project and Properties windows has the same effect as setting the Visible property to False for the Code and Designer windows. SetFocus can be used to change the focus of a window.

The Windows API

The Windows Application Programming Interface (API) includes all the tools to which you have access under Microsoft Windows. Using code, you can call API functions from Windows. The Windows API includes thousands of procedures, functions, subs, constants, and types that you can declare. You can translate the DLLs, but it is easier to use the declares predefined in Visual Basic.

The file Win32api.txt contains the declarations for many Windows API procedures used in Visual Basic. You can copy the code and paste it into your module. As a convenience, bring up the API text viewer from the Microsoft Visual Basic 6.0 Tools option on the Windows 95/98 Start menu.

Learn the concepts behind the task at hand and, more important, learn how the task is relevant in the real world. Time-saving suggestions and advice show you how to make the most of each skill.

TAKE NOTE

▶ **THE WINDOW MENU**

You also can rearrange your development environment quickly by using the Window menu. You can split the code window into two panes, tile horizontally or vertically, or cascade the windows in your application. In addition, you can switch between windows by selecting the desired project from the open projects list.

After you learn the task at hand, you may have more questions, or you may want to read about other tasks related to the topic. Use the cross-references to find different tasks to make your learning more efficient.

CROSS-REFERENCE

Chapter 1 also discusses windows.

32

FIND IT ONLINE

Try http://msdn.microsoft.com/vbasic/technical/pasttips.asp# 2-23-98 for terrific tips on Windows API and lots of other topics.

Use the Find It Online element to locate Internet resources that provide more background, take you on interesting side trips, and offer additional tools for mastering and using the skills you need. (Occasionally you'll find a handy shortcut here.)

Welcome to Teach Yourself

The current chapter name and number always appear in the top right-hand corner of every task spread, so you always know exactly where you are in the book.

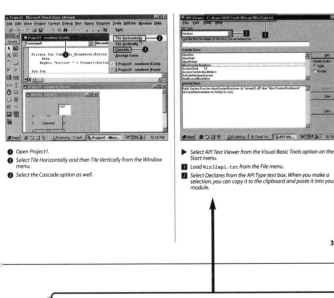

Learning More about the IDE

CHAPTER 2

Table 2-1: WINDOW TYPES

Window Type	Can Be Docked	Can Be Closed
Code windows	NO	YES
Design window	NO	YES
Project Explorer	YES	NO (hidden)
Properties window	YES	NO (hidden)
Object Browser	YES	YES
Form Layout window	YES	YES

❶ Open Project1.

❷ Select Tile Horizontally and then Tile Vertically from the Window menu.

❸ Select the Cascade option as well.

▶ Select API Text Viewer from the Visual Basic Tools option on the Start menu.

1 Load Win32api.txt from the File menu.

2 Select Declares from the API Type text box. When you make a selection, you can copy it to the clipboard and paste it into your module.

33

Ultimately, people learn by doing. Follow the clear, illustrated steps presented with every task to complete a procedure. The detailed callouts for each step show you exactly where to go and what to do to complete the task.

Who This Book Is For

This book is written for you, a beginning to intermediate PC user who isn't afraid to take charge of his or her own learning experience. You don't want a lot of technical jargon; you *do* want to learn as much about PC technology as you can in a limited amount of time. You need a book that is straightforward, easy to follow, and logically organized, so you can find answers to your questions easily. And, you appreciate simple-to-use tools such as handy cross-references and visual step-by-step procedures that help you make the most of your learning. We have created the unique *Teach Yourself* format specifically to meet your needs.

Personal Workbook

It's a well-known fact that much of what we learn is lost soon after we learn it if we don't reinforce our newly acquired skills with practice and repetition. That's why each *Teach Yourself* chapter ends with your own Personal Workbook. Here's where you can get extra practice, test your knowledge, and discover ideas for using what you've learned in the real world. There's even a Visual Quiz to help you remember your way around the topic's software environment.

Personal Workbook

Q&A

1 A Visual Basic object is unique in that it combines both_____ and _____.

2 How can you add new controls to the toolbox?

3 What value do you modify to change the tab order on the form?

4 What does the Windows collection contain?

5 How can you find the value of a variable as the program executes?

6 How can you add a new command to a menu on the menu bar?

7 Will Visual Basic 6 run on a Pentium 120MHz running Windows 98 with 16MB RAM?

8 What is the best way to get online help?

ANSWERS: PAGE 519

42

After working through the tasks in each chapter, you can test your progress and reinforce your learning by answering the questions in the Q&A section. Then check your answers in the Personal Workbook Answers appendix at the back of the book.

Another practical way to reinforce your skills is to do additional exercises on the same skills you just learned without the benefit of the chapter's visual steps. If you struggle with any of these exercises, it's a good idea to refer to the chapter's tasks to be sure you've mastered them.

Learning More about the IDE

CHAPTER 2

EXTRA PRACTICE

1. Select the newform form and then select Project ➪ Components to select a tool library. See how this changes the toolbox. Pass the mouse over the new controls. What are they? Place one of the controls on the form.

2. Change the captions on the Command buttons.

3. Place a new CommandButton on the form. Give it a new name and caption.

4. Practice docking and undocking the windows.

5. Create a new project. Imagine this is a project to demonstrate different sizes of command buttons. Give the project an appropriate name beginning with "Proj." Give the form an appropriate name beginning with "Frm" and a caption appropriate to your project.

REAL-WORLD APPLICATIONS

✔ Your company wants to create a multimedia application. Make a list of factors that would influence your design of the project in general and the forms in particular for the project.

✔ You continually get a compile error when you try to run your application. What are the factors that might be causing the error? How would you approach debugging it?

✔ Your client, Joe Schmoe, needs to update an old Visual Basic employee database application. He is looking to spiff up forms and add some new toolbars. Make an outline of the features you would add to his project and give him reasons for adding each.

Read the list of Real-World Applications to get ideas on how you can use the skills you've just learned in your everyday life. Understanding a process can be simple; knowing how to use that process to make you more productive is the key to successful learning.

Visual Quiz

Which of these options shown will give you online help?

_____

_____

_____

_____

_____

_____

_____

43

Take the Visual Quiz to see how well you're learning your way around the technology. Learning about computers is often as much about how to find a button or menu as it is about memorizing definitions. Our Visual Quiz helps you find your way.

Acknowledgments

When I considered whom and how many to thank for their help in this project, I decided that the person primarily responsible for the launching of the project deserves special thanks. This person is my agent, David Fugate, of Waterside Productions. He has been encouraging as well as a good listener throughout this project.

Debra Williams Cauley was also extremely reassuring when I first began. Both she and my editors, Laura Brown and Barbra Guerra, have been most helpful. A special thanks goes to Barbra Guerra, since it is she who toiled along with me through most of the book. Ms. Guerra has always been very understanding and accepting of the many little problems that keep cropping up in an endeavor as complex as this one.

Also, I appreciate very much having such a great technical editor as Christopher Stone, who provided that security every technical author needs.

Thanks, also, to all of those behind-the-scene people at IDG Books who worked to produce *Teach Yourself Visual Basic 6* and to make it succeed.

Patricia Hartman
Pat@hitekdesigns.com

Contents

CONTENTS

Contents

CONTENTS

CONTENTS

Contents

Teach Yourself®
Visual Basic® 6

PART

I

Contents of 'Desktop'

Name

My Computer

Network Neigh

Internet Explor

Microsoft Outloo

Recycle Bin

My Briefcase

3252-9

3259-6

3261-8

3262-6

3281-2

3286-3

DE Phone List

Device Manager

In

Iomega Tools

Introduction to Visual Basic

You must gain some understanding of underlying concepts in order to develop applications in any computer language. Further, you must couple this understanding with practice actually creating projects. It is this combination of understanding and practice that results in developing the skills necessary to create useful applications. The best way to approach the learning process, especially if you are teaching yourself, is to begin by taking small but consistent steps.

The first step is to learn about the working environment. Visual Basic provides you with a visual interface (naturally). You are provided with a design window area in which to work. This design window comes complete with a toolbox, toolbars, and menus.

The first thing you will do when you launch Visual Basic is decide whether you want to begin a new project or open an existing one. If you have never used Visual Basic, you will need to begin a new project. When you begin a Standard EXE project (a good beginning point), a form will appear in the design window. That is because you are going to begin your new project by designing and adding objects to the form.

During the process, you will be able to use the tools provided on the menus, toolbar, and toolbox. The objects that appear as icons in the Toolbox are called "controls." These controls can be added to your form to interact with users. The form controls can be buttons to be pressed, picture boxes to display graphics, boxes to hold text user input, lists from which the user can choose items, and many other possibilities.

The first and most important step in the learning process is to master the Integrated Development Environment (IDE). This means becoming familiar with the menus and toolbox controls. It is worth spending several hours, or even several days, opening and closing windows and dialog boxes, adding new items from the View menu, and checking the properties of different objects you have added to your form. It also means learning about concepts such as "object" and "event." In the next five chapters, you will develop an understanding about the objects that comprise a project and the environment in which you will work.

After you have acquired skill in manipulating the IDE, you will learn about variables, constants, and data types. You will learn to write procedures, attaching them to forms and modules. You will gain experience in making decisions and selections using code.

Finally, you will gain experience responding to and anticipating events generated by the application and by the application's users. At that point, you will be ready to further enhance your knowledge of forms, menus, and controls.

CHAPTER 1

MASTER THESE SKILLS

- ▶ **Learning about the Windows Environment**
- ▶ **Understanding Events**
- ▶ **Identifying Menus**
- ▶ **Using Toolbars**
- ▶ **Learning to Use the Toolbox**
- ▶ **Managing Projects with the Project Explorer**
- ▶ **Understanding the Properties Window**

Understanding Visual Basic's Integrated Development Environment

The Microsoft Windows environment is visual. Some of you began your computing career prior to the introduction of Windows, using DOS programs. A few people even may be nostalgic about that memorable black screen with the white letters displaying the familiar text operating system prompt (`c:\`). If you are not familiar with the DOS environment, you can get the flavor by going to the DOS prompt from the Windows Start menu.

Even the early versions of Microsoft Windows were vast improvements in ease of use. Windows 95 was the first graphic interface on DOS machines that really broke away from the 80-column, 24-line interface.

"What has all this done for us?" you might ask. The major impact has been to make computers easier for most folks to use. Perhaps the most important thing for programmers is that their way of writing computer programs vastly changed. Programs used to be written from the top down, with the user interface either built into the code or nonexistent.

Now, with Visual Basic 6, not only are the old problems solved, but the many built-in routines and programmer's aids mean not much is left from the past. Not only does Visual Basic provide an excellent code editor, but pop-up menus offer prompts for possible keywords as code is being typed.

New features of increasing importance in Version 6 are ActiveX controls, documents, and projects. There are new controls, properties, and events.

The new Data Aware controls and OLE DB concepts offer a more seamless way to access and manage databases. The Component Object Model (COM), which provides objects with the capability to use multiple interfaces, goes a long way to maintain compatibility with both new and old versions of applications.

The Integrated Development Environment is the working setting for creating Visual Basic applications. It includes designers, menu options, tools, add-ins, and all the resources available in each of the editions purchased by the user. The IDE manages projects from their inception through the addition of objects and procedures to compiling and packaging the completed applications.

Learning about the Windows Environment

All Visual Basic development requires a choice about interface type. The options are Single Document Interface (SDI) or Multiple Document Interface(MDI). This is true of all Windows programs as well.

Visual Basic's Extensibility Object Model can be used to go beyond the fundamental options provided while staying within the Integrated Development Environment. That is because the basis for extending the IDE is an integral part of it. Extensibility objects can be used to create new ActiveX components that provide new functionality to the environment. These new components (add-ins) can even be used outside the Visual Basic IDE.

SDI programs are much like the DOS programs of the past in the sense that they do not stack documents on different levels. Windows are not cascaded. You can switch from one form or document to another and move windows anywhere on screen, but they will remain on top of other applications only while Visual Basic is the active window.

MDI programs cover the majority of applications developed for Windows. For example, word processing and spreadsheet programs are MDI applications. All windows are enclosed in the MDI parent window.

Windows can be anchored by clicking and dragging. This is called *docking*. You can also specify which windows can be docked by selecting Options from the Tools menu and then checking or unchecking the various windows on the list.

Other Environment Options

The Editor and Editor Format options customize settings. You can modify options such as code settings, indentation, window settings, font, and colors.

Within the General tab, you can modify the defaults for Error Trapping, Compiling, Grid display settings, and ToolTips display options.

Under the Environment tab of the Tools ⇨ Options menu, you can change the defaults for prompting when Visual Basic starts and when a program starts, as well as determine the objects for which templates are displayed.

Related Development Tools

Visual Basic for Applications (VBA) comes with many Microsoft products and also is licensed and distributed with other vendors' product lines. It uses the Visual Basic engine but is not as powerful as the Professional edition of Visual Basic. Most code is portable to Visual Basic but should be checked for specific application elements required on the host machine. VBA's forms and controls are displayed in the Object Browser by selecting the VBA library.

Visual Basic Scripting Edition, or VBScript, is a less substantial programming tool than Visual Basic. It is used across platforms, probably most commonly on the Internet. The language syntax is close to that of VBA, but there is no Interface like the IDE. You can write code in the Visual Basic Editor, but you cannot test or run it.

JScript is derived from languages C++ and Java. JScript is a high-performance scripting language used to link objects on Web pages. Using JScript, you can generate your own code. JScript is not recognized by all browsers, nor is VBScript.

Continued

TAKE NOTE

▶ **EXTENDING THE VISUAL BASIC ENVIRONMENT**

You can extend the Visual Basic environment with tools called *add-ins* you create as part of the extensibility model. Add-ins can be visible or invisible and can work in the foreground or the background. They can operate in response to an event, such as moving and resizing windows for the end user.

CROSS-REFERENCE

Chapter 2 explores the Integrated Development Environment further.

FIND IT ONLINE

Joe Garrick's site is a great place for beginners to start: **http://www.citilink.com/~jgarrick/vbasic/resources/books.html**.

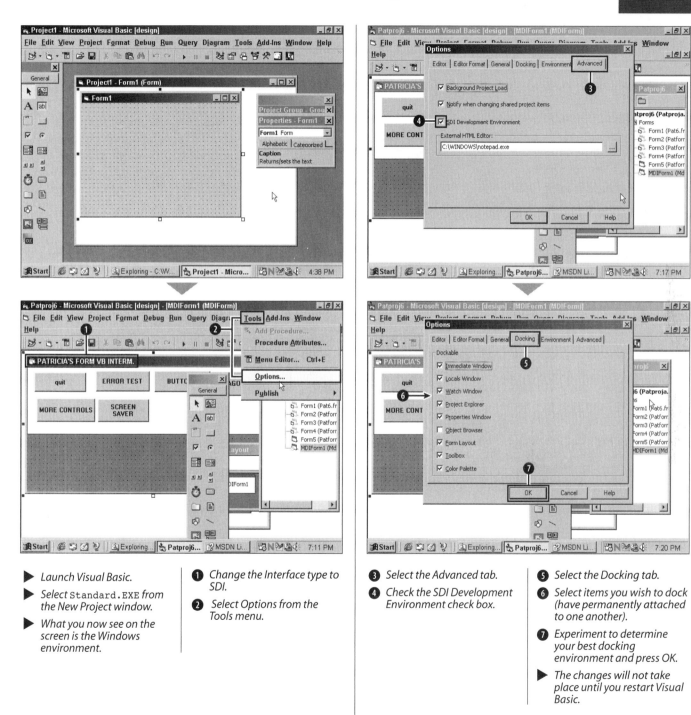

▶ *Launch Visual Basic.*

▶ *Select* Standard.EXE *from the New Project window.*

▶ *What you now see on the screen is the Windows environment.*

❶ *Change the Interface type to SDI.*

❷ *Select Options from the Tools menu.*

❸ *Select the Advanced tab.*

❹ *Check the SDI Development Environment check box.*

❺ *Select the Docking tab.*

❻ *Select items you wish to dock (have permanently attached to one another).*

❼ *Experiment to determine your best docking environment and press OK.*

▶ *The changes will not take place until you restart Visual Basic.*

Learning about the Windows Environment *Continued*

Elements of the IDE

These elements include menus and toolbars with their icons that include all the objects available to you in the development environment.

Menus are lists (usually pull-down or pop-up) of options to choose for particular tasks. The toolboxes and toolbars usually feature icons rather than text to symbolize the options you are selecting. Icons produce ToolTip text when you pass the mouse cursor over them.

Context menus are displayed when you right-click an object in use. The dialog box that pops up is a context menu. When you click a command button and then right-click, you will be able to Cut, Copy, Paste, Delete, change stacking order, View Code, Align to Grid, or view the Properties.

The default position of the Standard toolbar is immediately below the menu bar, at the top of the screen. It can be moved, like most of the tools and menus in the Visual Basic Integrated Development Environment. Other toolbars are: Debug, Form Editor, and Edit. These toolbars can be docked, or they can float.

Visual Basic powers up with a default set of controls in the toolbox, but you can add controls to the Standard toolbox by selecting Components from the Project menu and then clicking the Controls tab to add new controls. You can add new ActiveX controls to the Standard toolbox by choosing specific Component controls. Libraries of Component controls are shipped with Visual Basic (only a few come with the Learning edition) and also can be obtained from third party vendors. As you will see in Chapter 20, you can create your own ActiveX controls and add them to the ToolBox.

Once you have saved your project after adding new controls to the Standard ToolBox, the project will be reopened with the custom toolbox in the previously saved state. For example, if you added a Datagrid and ADO control to a project before saving it, you would see those controls in the ToolBox (as well as the Standard Controls) upon opening the same project in the future.

The most commonly used windows and dialog boxes in Visual Basic are the New Project dialog box, the Project Explorer, the Properties window, the Code Editor, the Form Layout window, the Form Designer window, and the Object Browser window.

The Properties window opens with the default properties assigned to a new form. For example, properties include size, name, color, caption; all those features that can be assigned to each object. As you add controls and methods to the form, you can change the properties accordingly.

The Code Editor is the area in which you write your code. This is done by double-clicking an object to which you want to attach code. The Code Editor at once pops up on the screen. You can then select an object at the top left and an event from the scrollbars at the top of the window.

The Form Layout window looks like a little monitor, only it displays a small representation of any or all forms that are open.

The Form Designer window is the first window you will be likely to notice when you first launch the IDE. It is a box with a grid of dots, which you will use to position controls selected from the toolbox.

The Object Browser window lists the contents of the Visual Basic and other libraries and shows the Classes and Members of the selected class.

TAKE NOTE

TO DOCK OR NOT TO DOCK

You can change your environment at any time by deciding which windows should be floating and which should be docked. Select the Docking tab from the Tools ⇨ Options menu and check the boxes next to the windows you wish to dock or deselect the one you want undocked.

CROSS-REFERENCE

Chapter 6 offers additional info on the IDE.

FIND IT ONLINE

Gary Beene's Visual Basic World at **http://web2.airmail.net/ gbeene/tutor.html** has VB tutorials for beginners.

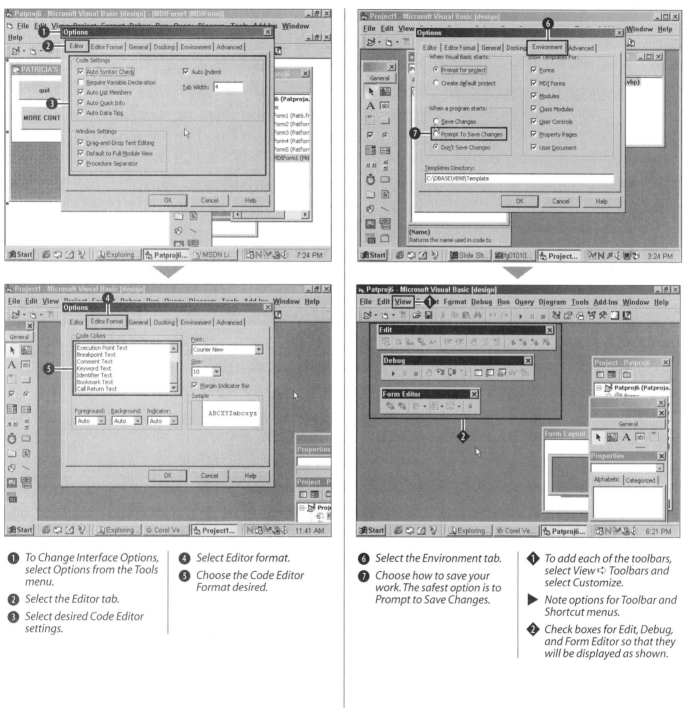

❶ To Change Interface Options, select Options from the Tools menu.

❷ Select the Editor tab.

❸ Select desired Code Editor settings.

❹ Select Editor format.

❺ Choose the Code Editor Format desired.

❻ Select the Environment tab.

❼ Choose how to save your work. The safest option is to Prompt to Save Changes.

❶ To add each of the toolbars, select View ⇨ Toolbars and select Customize.

▶ Note options for Toolbar and Shortcut menus.

❷ Check boxes for Edit, Debug, and Form Editor so that they will be displayed as shown.

Understanding Events

An event can be a cause or an effect. That is, the event may occur as a result of a prior action, or it may, itself, cause a different action. In the simplest terms, an event is something happening. The usual event is a mouse click on a form button. This is an event initiated by the user. At that point, the event will likely trigger another event, such as opening a form or performing a calculation. If a second event occurs in response to a mouse click, this is because the programmer has provided an event handler.

Event Handlers

An event handler is the code attached to the button that was mouse-clicked to trigger the event. The second event can trigger a third event and so on. If there are no subsequent event handlers after the action triggered, then the action is said to "bubble up" to the next event handler.

This means that the event continues moving up the hierarchy. The process is complex, and if you are not careful, your code may not execute the way you expect. You can terminate the process of continuing to move up the "bubble" to parent commands by using `cancelBubble`.

Event Objects

All event handlers can manipulate the event object. This is language independent and means that an object can be used by VBScript and JScript, as well as Visual Basic. In fact, a lot of event handling is done using VBScript and JScript.

Inline event handlers can assign specific properties to event objects and associate an event handler to an element. Keyboard events include `KeyPress`, `KeyDown`, and `KeyUp`. The `KeyPress` event occurs when the user presses an ASCII key with any character code. The `KeyPress` event tests for any key that represents an ASCII code value. The ASCII character set is the American Standard Code for Information Interchange. It includes the characters on the standard keyboard. The first 128 characters are the numbers and letters of the alphabet. The second 128 characters are special characters and symbols. `KeyDown` and `KeyUp` occur when the key changes state, from up to down and down to up.

The `MouseDown` event occurs when the mouse button is pressed on an object that has the focus. *Focus* means the object is selected. The `MouseUp` event is associated with the user release of the mouse button on an object under focus. The `MouseMove` event results when the user moves the mouse. `MousePointer` returns or sets the type of pointer displayed when on an object. The `Click` event occurs in response to pressing and releasing the mouse button when over an object. The `DragOver` event results when a drag-drop action has been completed. `DragDrop` takes place when the click, drag, and release operation is completed.

Selection and Focus Events

The `Selection` event occurs when the user selects an object by pressing a key or clicking the mouse button.

The `GotFocus` event occurs as a result of the focus shifting to a specific object. When the focus moves off the object, the `LostFocus` event takes place. `SetFocus` moves the focus to a specific object. Whether or not an object can be selected depends upon the tab order of objects on a form. A `TextBox` will not accept user input if it does not have the focus. Some controls are known as the *lightweight controls* because they cannot receive focus.

TAKE NOTE

EVENT CYCLES

There is a cycle to any event. The first element is that the user clicks a button, the event handler registers this state, the code associated with the mouse click event is executed, and the event handler returns to the source. The source in this case is the button. The next event specified in the code is carried out, and the event handler returns to the source.

CROSS-REFERENCE

Chapters 4 and 5 offer a more extensive discussion of the event process.

FIND IT ONLINE

Carl and Gary's beginner's links at **http://www.cgvb.com/links/lpage.boa/beginner** offer more rich material from Joe Garrick's site. This deals with event-driven programming specifics.

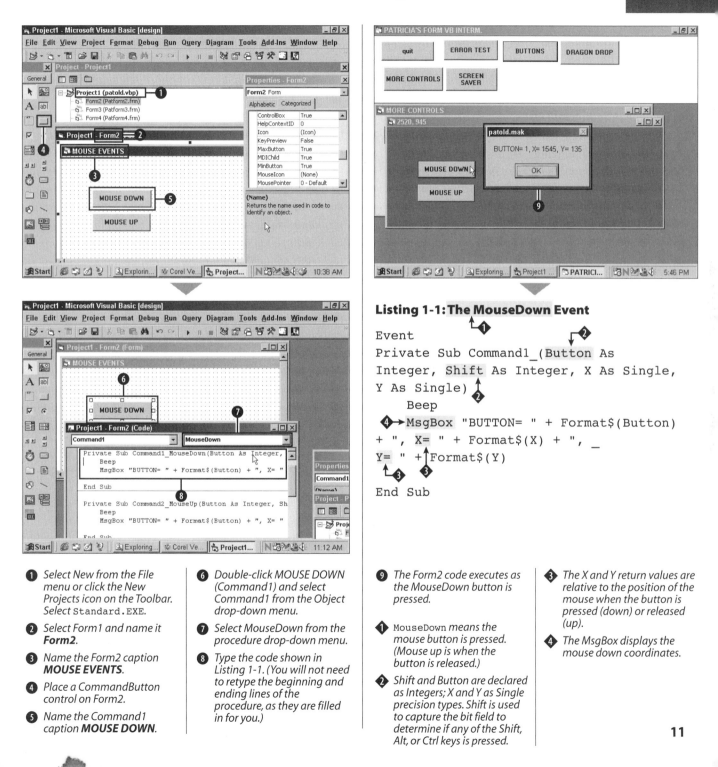

Listing 1-1: The MouseDown Event

```
Event
Private Sub Command1_(Button As
Integer, Shift As Integer, X As Single,
Y As Single)
    Beep
    MsgBox "BUTTON= " + Format$(Button)
+ ", X= " + Format$(X) + ", _
Y= " + Format$(Y)

End Sub
```

❶ Select New from the File menu or click the New Projects icon on the Toolbar. Select `Standard.EXE`.

❷ Select Form1 and name it **Form2**.

❸ Name the Form2 caption **MOUSE EVENTS**.

❹ Place a CommandButton control on Form2.

❺ Name the Command1 caption **MOUSE DOWN**.

❻ Double-click MOUSE DOWN (Command1) and select Command1 from the Object drop-down menu.

❼ Select MouseDown from the procedure drop-down menu.

❽ Type the code shown in Listing 1-1. (You will not need to retype the beginning and ending lines of the procedure, as they are filled in for you.)

❾ The Form2 code executes as the MouseDown button is pressed.

➊ MouseDown means the mouse button is pressed. (Mouse up is when the button is released.)

➋ Shift and Button are declared as Integers; X and Y as Single precision types. Shift is used to capture the bit field to determine if any of the Shift, Alt, or Ctrl keys is pressed.

➌ The X and Y return values are relative to the position of the mouse when the button is pressed (down) or released (up).

➍ The MsgBox displays the mouse down coordinates.

11

Identifying Menus

The menus provided by the IDE are displayed across the top of the screen. They are: File, Edit, View, Project, Format, Debug, Run, Query, Diagram, Tools, Add-Ins, Window, and Help.

File Menu

The File menu exists in nearly all Windows programs. It is universally used to start a New project, Open, Save and Save As, Print, and handle Print Setup. In Visual Basic, as in all Windows programs, some of the menu options are tailored for operations specific to that application. These include Make Project, and Recent Files List.

New Project appears at the top of the menu options and begins a new project. Select it and you're prompted to Save your open project. The keyboard shortcut is Ctrl+N.

The Open Project command prompts you to save your open projects. The shortcut command is Ctrl+O.

If you have one or more projects open, the Add Project command opens an additional project and creates a *project group*, that is, more than one project saved together. If you already have a project group, your new project will become part of that group. An in-process project, once referenced, appears in the References dialog box and is stored in the project file.

When you remove a project, you will be prompted to Save changes to your files. If a project having a reference to any of the executable files in the project group is removed, it is marked as missing.

You can save Project Groups, Forms, and Selections. Saving Project Groups closes all files and saves the work. Saving as a new filename or path presents the folder from which the project was originally loaded, and you will be able to move up levels or down levels, clicking the up one level icon in order to select a new path if desired.

You also can click the New Folder icon to create a new folder if none exists where you want to save. You also may save your project with a different extension, rather than the default, .vbp. The keyboard shortcut is Ctrl+S.

When you select the Print option from the File menu, you will first view the Print Setup menu, displaying the current default printer. You can select Setup to modify the properties of the current printer, or you can click the down arrow beside the printer name and select a different printer. Next, a dialog box pops up with options on range and what to print. The keyboard command is Ctrl+P. The Toolbar shortcut under the menu uses the printer icon.

The Make Project option enables you to build a project in .exe, .dll, or .ocx format. You can also pull down the Project menu, select Project Properties, and click the Make tab to construct the project according to the options supplied.

You can have one main project, but you can add other projects to the group. Or you can select Make Project Group, which enables you to save separate .exe files for each project in the group.

The Recent Files list contains the four most recent projects you have opened. This is a shortcut to enable you to retrieve a file previously used, rather than opening the file from the Files List dialog box.

Exit enables you to quit the program but always prompts you to save before closing. The keyboard shortcut is Alt+Q.

Continued

TAKE NOTE

▶ PRINTING OPTIONS

Visual Basic printer options are very different from most applications, including word processors. You can determine whether to print the form itself or the code. You can also opt to print the form as text. The Range option specifies what part of the current project to print. You can print a portion that is selected, the current module, or the entire project.

CROSS-REFERENCE

Chapter 2 deals with the use of the interface menus as well.

FIND IT ONLINE

View **http://www.Vbonline.com/vb-mag/** for more information about Visual Basic.

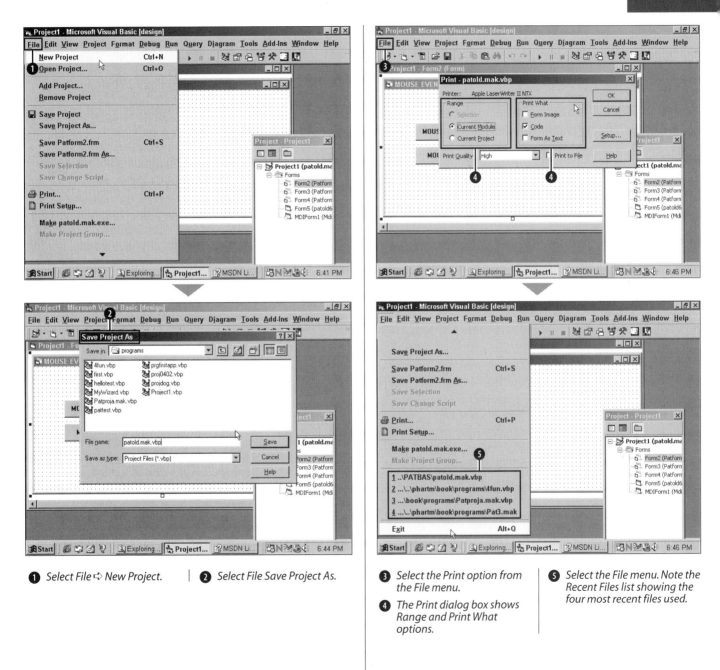

1 Select File ➪ New Project.

2 Select File Save Project As.

3 Select the Print option from the File menu.

4 The Print dialog box shows Range and Print What options.

5 Select the File menu. Note the Recent Files list showing the four most recent files used.

Identifying Menus
Continued

The Edit Menu

Options offered by the Edit menu include Undo, Redo, Cut, Copy, Paste (Link), Remove, Delete, Select (All) (All Columns), Table, Find (Next), Replace, Indent, Outdent, Insert File, List Properties/Methods, List Constants, Quick Info, Parameter Info, Complete Word, Go to (Row), Bookmarks.

The View Menu

You can switch between the Code view and the Object (form) view. This is similar to switching between different objects on the Window menu. Other options in the View menu enable you to view the other windows. For example, this menu is the one to access to restore the Object Browser, Project Explorer, Properties, Form Layout, Immediate, Toolbox, Toolbars, Color Palette, Data View, and Visual Component Manager.

The Project Menu

The Project menu lets you add Forms, Modules, User Controls, Property Pages, Data Reports, WebClasses (only in DLL files), References to Control Libraries, Add File, Remove specific Form, and Project Properties.

The Format Menu

Some of the Format menu options include Alignment, Grid options, Horizontal and Vertical Spacing, Stacking Order options (To Back and Front), and Locking Controls.

The Debug Menu

You can Step Into (execute code a line at a time), Step Over (execute the next line of code even if it calls another procedure), Run to Cursor (click your cursor at a place in the code, then execute until that place is reached). The menu Adds Watch variables, Toggles Breakpoints (controls where the program will stop when running), and Clears Breakpoints (reinitializes the stopping points in programs during the debug process).

The Run Menu

One of the shortest menus is the Run menu. It controls the runtime process, including Starting the program, Compiling the code, Breaking at specific points, and Ending and Restarting the runtime process.

The Query Menu

The Query menu is used for SQL commands in database projects. More will be said about this topic in the database section of the book.

Tools Menu

The most frequently used submenu of the Tools menu is the Options submenu, which we discussed earlier.

The Window Menu

This is much like that in other Windows applications, in that it arranges your application desktop. You can tile or cascade windows and toggle between forms you are working on.

The Help Menu

The Help menu enables you to look at the Contents of Help, check the Index, or Search for a topic. There is some additional information, such as Technical Support and Microsoft on the Web. Finally, About Microsoft Visual Basic gives you the product ID number.

TAKE NOTE

FINDING HELP

Excellent Technical Support is found on the Microsoft Developer Network Library Visual Studio CD that is offered with the Professional and Enterprise Editions of Visual Basic. Also, the help available at microsoft.com is very good.

CROSS-REFERENCE

Chapter 7 deals with menus.

FIND IT ONLINE

View **http://www.extreme-vb.net/e2/** for some tutorials.

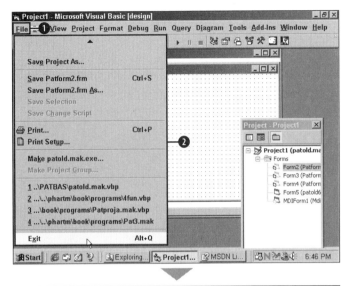

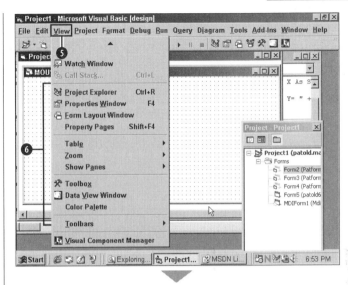

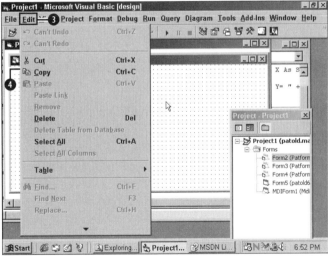

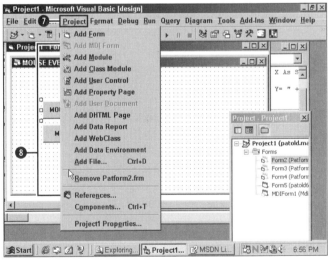

① Select the File menu.
② View the options.

③ Select the Edit menu.
④ View the options.

⑤ Click the View menu.
⑥ View the options.

⑦ Click the Project menu.
⑧ View the options.

Using Toolbars

The Toolbars function as shortcuts to the regular menu options. The IDE Standard toolbar is by default directly under the menu at the top of the screen. The toolbar can be customized, and other toolbars can be added or displayed alongside the Standard toolbar.

Toolbars can be docked or not, as you wish. To change the docking properties of any toolbar, click and drag it to the new location. The Docking tab under the Tools ⇨ Options does not control docking for the Toolbars.

The Standard toolbar is displayed by default when Visual Basic is launched. Unlike the menus, it uses icon buttons instead of text.

The options offered by the Standard toolbar combine options from the major portions of the menu bar. Specifically, they include:

▶ Add Project and Add Form from the File menu.
▶ Menu Editor, Open, Save, Cut, Copy, Paste, Find, Undo, and Redo from the Edit menu.
▶ Start, Break, and End from the Run menu.
▶ Project Explorer, Properties window, Form Layout window, Object Browser, Toolbox, Data View window, and Data Component Manager from the View menu.

The icons on the Debug toolbar enable you to Start your application, Break the execution of the program at a selected point, and End the program and return to the design mode. Also, you can Toggle the Breakpoint on or off at the current line, Step Into or Over each statement in the code, and Step Out (continues function through remaining code).

The other options display the Locals, Immediate, Watch and Quick Watch windows. The Call Stack option lists the procedure calls currently active.

The Edit toolbar is a quick reference for code editing. The first icon lists Properties/Methods available for the object currently selected, lists Constants that will be valid for an object, and provides Quick Info on syntax for specific action and Parameter Info for functions currently highlighted.

Other options on the Edit toolbar include Complete Word with a pop-up menu of similarly spelled keywords, Indent, which shifts lines to the next tab stop, and Outdent, which shifts selected lines to the previous tab stop. You also can Toggle Breakpoint as in the Debug menu.

The Comment Block option adds comment characters to each line of selected text, and Uncomment Block removes the comment characters.

Bookmark toggles the bookmark on and off at the cursor, Next Bookmark moves the focus to the next bookmark, Previous Bookmark moves the focus back to the prior bookmark, and Clear Bookmarks removes all bookmarks.

The Form Editor toolbar functions very much like the Format menu. You can perform alignment functions, change the horizontal and vertical spacing, center, and modify stacking order.

TAKE NOTE

▶ CUSTOMIZING AND SHORTCUTS

The View ⇨ Toolbars menu offers additional Debug, Edit, and Form Editor toolbars. Clicking each one in turn will add a window for each to the desktop. The View ⇨ Toolbars ⇨ Customize menu enables you to tailor the toolbars to your specifications. Also, you can add shortcut menus to your environment by checking the Shortcut box. Shortcut menus will pop up contextually whenever you right-click.

CROSS-REFERENCE

Chapter 8 has references regarding the use of toolbars.

FIND IT ONLINE

Vbnet has routines on Windows programming issues: http://www.mvps.org/vbnet/.

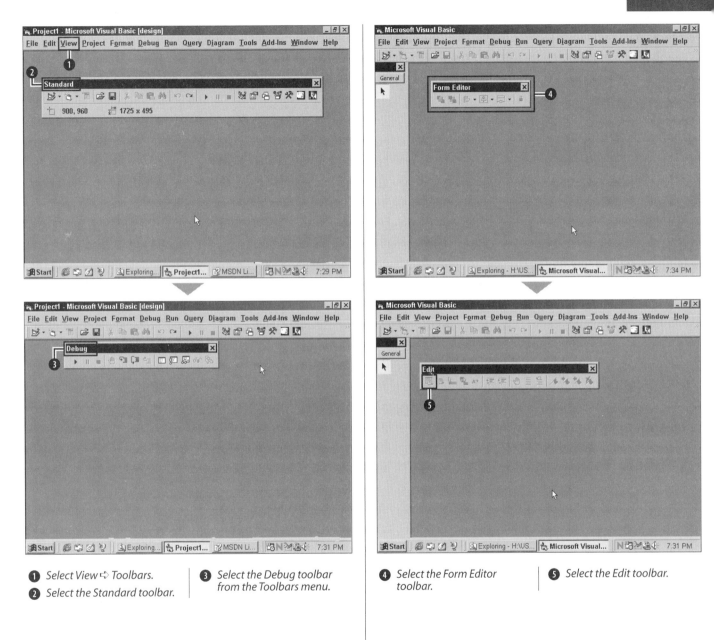

① *Select View ➪ Toolbars.*

② *Select the Standard toolbar.*

③ *Select the Debug toolbar from the Toolbars menu.*

④ *Select the Form Editor toolbar.*

⑤ *Select the Edit toolbar.*

Learning to Use the Toolbox

The Standard toolbox contains all the tools necessary to place controls on your forms. You can add components to the toolbox from the libraries by selecting Components from the Project menu. When you slide the mouse pointer over the toolbox icons, the various controls are identified. The major controls are listed next.

The Pointer is the only element in the toolbox that is not used to create a control. The PictureBox serves as a container for graphics you display on a form. The Label is for writing text labels on a form. The TextBox is primarily used to accept user input.

The Frame also serves as a container to hold other controls in a group. This enables you to move the entire frame and move all the controls at the same time. The CommandButton lets you draw a button on a form, which serves as a push button. Event and function code is attached to the BCommandButton.

The CheckBox is for checked or blank responses. That is, the user either checks the box or leaves it blank. The OptionButton is to obtain user input for multiple choice where one response only is allowed.

The ComboBox combines an option box and a list box. Your user can fill in the blank or select one of the options listed in the drop-down menu.

The user selects an item from those in the ListBox. The Horizontal (HscrollBar) and Vertical (VscrollBar)

controls enable the addition of scrollbars in the event that the graphic or data items will not fit on the form.

The Timer enables events to fire at specific intervals.

The DriveListBox, DirListBox, and FileListBox all display drives, directories, files, and paths.

The Shape and Line tools are for drawing shapes and straight lines on the form in the design mode.

The Image tool is similar to the PictureBox, except that it is only able to display a specific bitmap and is not interactive.

The Data tool accesses data in databases.

The OLE tool enables linking and embedding of objects from other applications.

TAKE NOTE

TOOLBOX KEYBOARD COMMANDS

In addition to the Standard toolbox, toolboxes are available that will add tools for different purposes. For example, the Forms objects library adds a SpinButton and a TabStrip. Each library you add tools from will add them to the toolbox icons. Pressing the End key will jump to the last tool in the toolbox, and Home will go to the first tool (the Pointer). Finally, Alt+F4 closes the toolbox.

CROSS-REFERENCE

Chapters 6 and 8 contain more information about the toolbox.

FIND IT ONLINE

Gary Beene's site at **http://web2.airmail.net/gbeene/tutor.html** has excellent tutorials, as well as references and links.

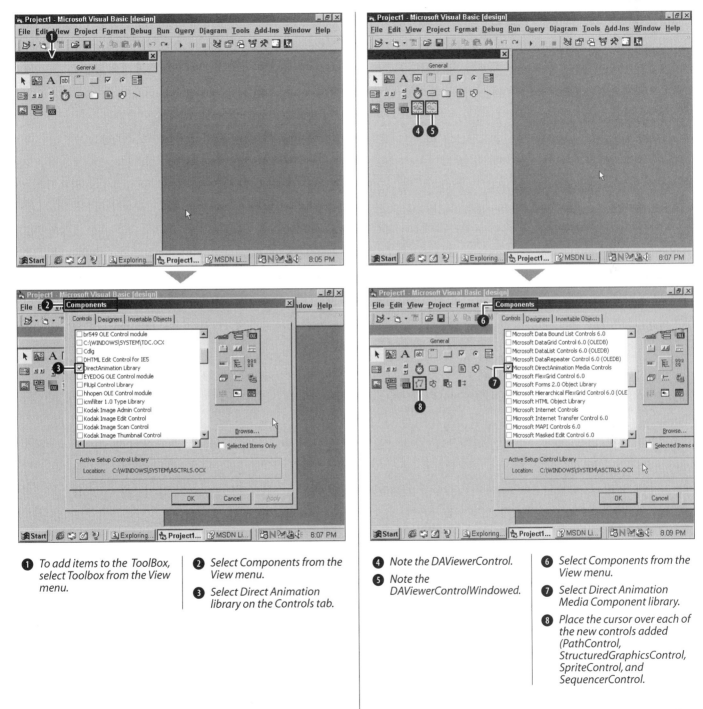

❶ To add items to the ToolBox, select Toolbox from the View menu.

❷ Select Components from the View menu.

❸ Select Direct Animation library on the Controls tab.

❹ Note the DAViewerControl.

❺ Note the DAViewerControlWindowed.

❻ Select Components from the View menu.

❼ Select Direct Animation Media Component library.

❽ Place the cursor over each of the new controls added (PathControl, StructuredGraphicsControl, SpriteControl, and SequencerControl).

Managing Projects with the Project Explorer

When you create a project, you must give it a name. The project name cannot contain periods or spaces, it cannot have more than 37 characters, and it must begin with a letter.

Visual Basic manages all the files and resources for you. Your project files may consist of seven or more files, each having a different extension, indicating the file type.

Visual Basic Project (.vbp) files maintain a list of all the objects and files in the project. *Form files* (.frm) are the actual forms, while the .frx files contain information about *form controls*. They are generated when the form contains binary data, such as a picture. *Class modules files* have the .cls extension. The *standard module* has a .bas extension and is like the code file for DOS versions of Basic. *ActiveX files* have the .ocx extension. *Resource files* have the .res extension.

In addition, there are *ActiveX Designer files* (.dsr), *Property pages* (.pag), and *Document objects* (.dob).

Using the Project Explorer

The View Code and View Object icons let you toggle between viewing the form or other object and viewing the code attached to that object. When you click the View Object icon, the Registry is searched for the document type and the appropriate open command is executed.

The folder icon toggles between hiding and displaying the project folders. Hiding the folders does not hide the current object or its code.

The List window shows a tree view of the projects and all their objects: all the Form files, Modules, standard modules, Class Modules, Controls, Documents, property pages, ActiveX Designers, Document Objects, and all other related documents to which you want pointers.

When your project is complete, the project files are used to produce an executable (.exe) file.

Using the Project Explorer with Databases

You can manage database queries and SQL scripts from the Project Explorer. As with all other project files, queries and scripts become part of your project. The Project Explorer displays these queries and scripts under the database to which they belong.

You can open, create, and edit queries from the Project Explorer by the usual click-and-drag process.

CROSS-REFERENCE

Chapters 2, 10, and 11 contain more information on using the Project Explorer.

FIND IT ONLINE

See http://www.vbits99.com/ — this site is a developer's exchange.

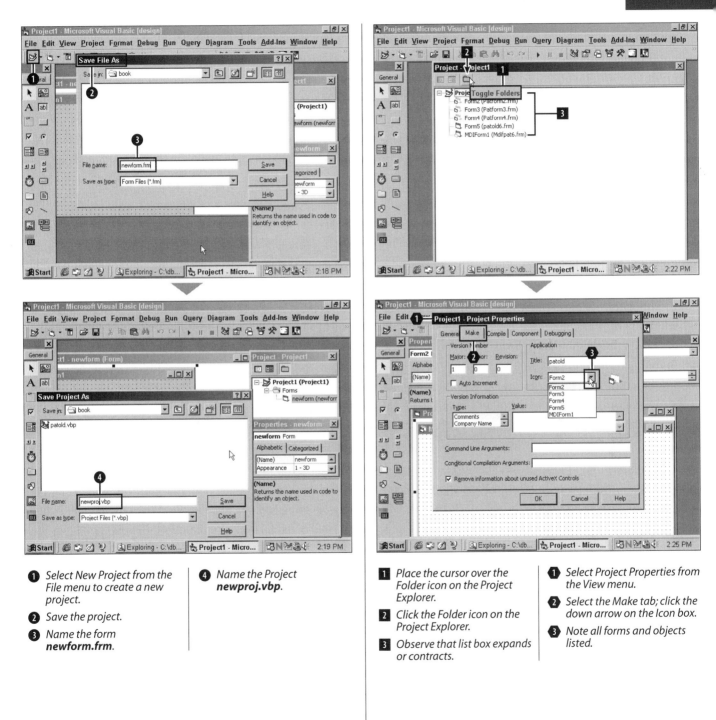

1 Select New Project from the File menu to create a new project.

2 Save the project.

3 Name the form **newform.frm**.

4 Name the Project **newproj.vbp**.

1 Place the cursor over the Folder icon on the Project Explorer.

2 Click the Folder icon on the Project Explorer.

3 Observe that list box expands or contracts.

1 Select Project Properties from the View menu.

2 Select the Make tab; click the down arrow on the Icon box.

3 Note all forms and objects listed.

Understanding the Properties Window

The Properties window lists the properties for all objects in the design mode. When you are working on a project, (writing code and adding controls to a form), you are in design mode. The parts of the window are the Object box at the top of the window, the List tabs, and the Description pane. The Object box displays the object class and the name of the selected object. The List tabs list the currently selected object alphabetically and categorically.

The categories are based on types of objects. Appearance, behavior, scale, position, DDE, Font, and Miscellaneous are the categories. Color, Caption, and BorderStyle are some of the properties in the Appearance category. Most of the time, it is probably easier to find the desired property by alphabet.

Different objects will obviously have different properties defined, although all objects are assigned default properties. Some objects will have BorderStyle and some not. BackColor and ForeColor colors are properties that can be redefined for different objects. Perhaps you want to emulate functions on an existing application. In that case, you may want to also make your control properties similar.

Visual Basic assigns a procedure ID to all standard properties. If you set up your own properties, you should also assign a procedure ID to these properties.

Setting properties is a practice made easy by using the Properties Window.

To begin, you select the object and then right-click to view the pop up menu. Selecting the form or other object on the screen allows you to change the caption or any other of the object's properties from the Properties Window. If you wish to change the name of the form from the Properties Window, type the new name of the form in the right hand column (pane) of the Properties window.

In many cases, you will select the property from a drop-down list by clicking the down arrow to the right of the listed property. You can see which properties listed have options by clicking once in the right-hand pane. If there are options to select, a down arrow will appear. You can explore the choices by clicking the down arrow.

For example, the BackColor property offers a large selection of objects for which you can change the background color. You can change the background color of the menu text, the menu bar, the active border, the inactive border, etc. You also can change other form properties, but you won't see them until you add those controls to the form.

TAKE NOTE

▶ PROPERTIES ON MULTIPLE CONTROLS

When you select multiple controls, the Properties window contains a list of the properties common to all the selected controls. Thus, if you select both a CommandButton and a ComboBox on a form, your property list will only include those properties that are possessed by both objects. This will narrow down your list of possible properties.

CROSS-REFERENCE

Chapter 6 contains more examples on assigning properties to objects on forms.

FIND IT ONLINE

The site at **http://www.teleport.com/~pweber/vbtips.shtml** has Visual Basic tips.

Understanding Visual Basic's Integrated Development Environment

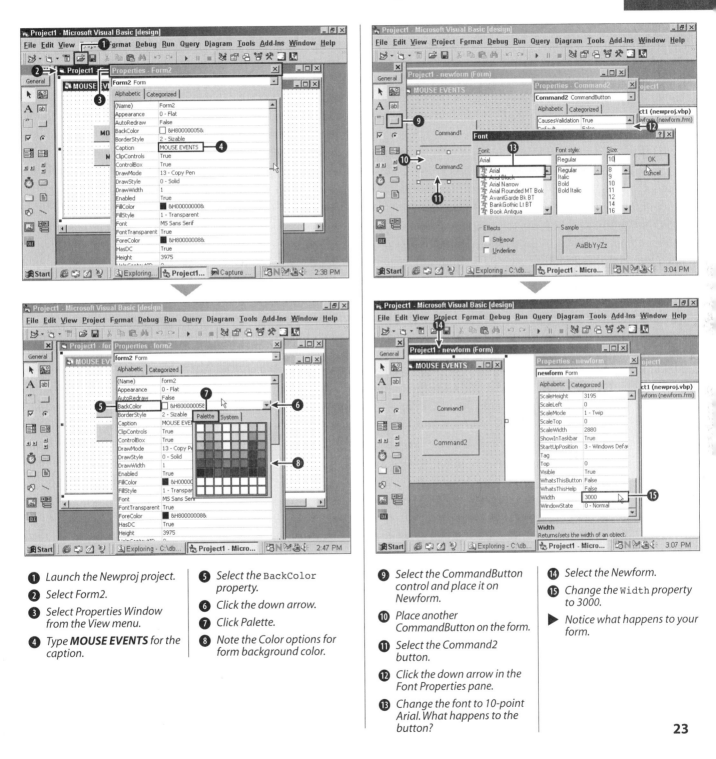

① Launch the Newproj project.

② Select Form2.

③ Select Properties Window from the View menu.

④ Type **MOUSE EVENTS** for the caption.

⑤ Select the BackColor property.

⑥ Click the down arrow.

⑦ Click Palette.

⑧ Note the Color options for form background color.

⑨ Select the CommandButton control and place it on Newform.

⑩ Place another CommandButton on the form.

⑪ Select the Command2 button.

⑫ Click the down arrow in the Font Properties pane.

⑬ Change the font to 10-point Arial. What happens to the button?

⑭ Select the Newform.

⑮ Change the Width property to 3000.

▶ Notice what happens to your form.

Personal Workbook

Q&A

1 What has Windows got that DOS didn't have?

_____

_____

_____

2 What are the two options for a Windows interface type?

_____

_____

_____

3 What term is used for the process of anchoring windows to a part of the application window?

_____

_____

_____

4 What development tools are related to Visual Basic?

_____

_____

5 What is an event handler?

_____

_____

_____

6 On which menu do you find the Project Explorer and the Properties window?

_____

_____

_____

7 How do you change your environment to customize your Editor and Docking options?

_____

_____

_____

8 How can you add controls to the toolbox?

_____

_____

_____

ANSWERS: PAGE 519

24

EXTRA PRACTICE

1. Add a form to the Newproj project, and customize it by changing the BackColor, Font on the Command buttons, and form caption.

2. Customize your environment options by changing your windows docking options.

3. Customize your Code Editor options according to what works best for you.

4. Practice viewing your project using the Project Explorer, the Properties window, and the Object Browser. Try to identify the objects in your project.

5. Pull down each of the Visual Basic menus. Look at all of the options. Familiarize yourself with the programming environment.

REAL-WORLD APPLICATIONS

✔ You have been asked to design a form to incorporate a variety of controls to get user input to calculate mortgage interest payments. The form should be well designed and colorful.

✔ You are working on the job of converting an old DOS Basic program to Visual Basic. You must change the character-based interface to that of two forms for data collection.

✔ Cousin Rolph has a mail order business and is eager to automate it. He doesn't know the first thing about computers, and because he knows you are an "expert," he asks you to advise him. Where would you begin?

Visual Quiz

The form shown at the right has a problem. How can you fix it?

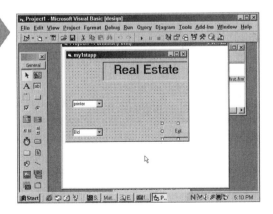

_____

_____

_____

_____

_____

_____

CHAPTER **2**

Learning More about the IDE

As you saw in the first chapter, the Visual Basic environment is a highly sophisticated one. The work space includes designers, tools, menus, and other special environments. Because Visual Basic is built around objects, you will take a look at the objects in the IDE.

As you probably have realized, the many windows, icons, menus, and submenus can be very confusing. The best way to deal with the complexity is to explore, explore, and then explore some more. There is simply no way you can read your way through the maze of the IDE. You must experience it or you will not retain all the details.

The best way to do this is to create some practice projects. Make up names for the projects, forms, and controls. Save the results in a practice directory or folder on your hard drive. You can come back to these projects later if you find yourself stumped in a subsequent project. Perhaps you will have learned something that helps you understand future problems encountered. Saving successes is particularly worthwhile. Sometimes you will create applications that seem to work almost by accident. The important thing is that with each practice exercise you will learn something. That something can come in handy at times and can ultimately turn out to be quite valuable.

You begin this topic by examining the nature of objects. What is an object? You have heard so much about object-oriented programming and have undoubtedly wondered what is meant by an object. The Object Browser is an excellent place to begin finding out about objects in Visual Basic.

Another puzzling fact about visual programming is the multitude of burgeoning windows. Sometimes windows pop up, sometimes they drop down, and sometimes they come from everywhere at once. How many are there and what are they all needed for? These questions and their answers will be discussed in the chapter.

How do you find errors, and more important, how do you fix them once they are found? The debugging windows will be introduced here only to explain the IDE; real debugging won't be probed in depth until Chapter 11.

The chapter finishes with a discussion of how to customize the IDE to your needs, an outline of program limitations, and last, but very important, how to use the Help features.

Browsing Objects

It is no secret that Windows applications are object based, because Windows itself is based on objects.

The Nature of Objects

Objects are entities you can create and use in the process of developing a Windows application. An *object* in Visual Basic can be virtually anything that becomes part of the application. In your project, there will be `Form` objects, `CommandButton` objects, `ListBox` objects, `TextBox` objects — all sorts of objects. Objects help organize and structure your project.

You manipulate objects in the course of a project, usually in conjunction with *events*. Objects are inextricably linked with events. In this way, events and objects will interact to produce your intended outcome. The method or program is how you tell the object what to do. The event is what the object really does.

Perhaps the most interesting feature of objects in Visual Basic is they incorporate both data and code. This combining of data and program code is one big difference between object-based programming and procedural programming.

When you package a form button with code that tells the button to give you information when the mouse is clicked, the entire entity becomes an object. When you create a form button, it is a great deal more than a square drawn on a background because it includes the square along with whatever functions it is able to perform under what conditions. Objects are also bound together with object variables. Objects have attributes, called *properties*.

The Object Browser

Visual Basic objects are created from *classes*. An object is said to be a member of a class. The class determines what an object is capable of. It also establishes the interface, as well as what attributes the object can have. When you create an object, you can view its class and members in the Object Browser.

The Object Browser can be selected from the View menu. You can view your newly created form in the Object Browser by selecting the project from the Project/Library box at the top of the Object Browser. The form, which is part of the project, will be displayed in the Classes box. All the elements of the members of that class (`Form` in this case) will be shown in the Members box in the right pane. Your selected form will cause the members of the form to be bolded in the Members box. If you have added a `CommandButton` control to your form, the name of the button and its procedure will be shown in bold type on the right.

When you select the `CommandButton` member, the partial code listing will be displayed in the Details pane below along with the name of the project and form. If you click the `Form` name in the Details pane below, you see the project name, and clicking that name displays the path where the project is stored.

TAKE NOTE

▶ SEARCHING THE OBJECT BROWSER

You can search for a specific string in the Object Browser by typing the search text in the Search Text box and then clicking the binocular icon to carry out the search. The search results are shown in the Search Results pane. You can search for an element of the members of a class or any part of the class object. The search is done on the library or project selected in the Project/Library text box.

CROSS-REFERENCE

Chapter 4 also provides information on objects.

FIND IT ONLINE

Go to **http://msdn.microsoft.com/library/sdkdoc/sql/sqlole/src/ sqlole02_965v.htm** for a discussion of Visual Basic's elementary principles.

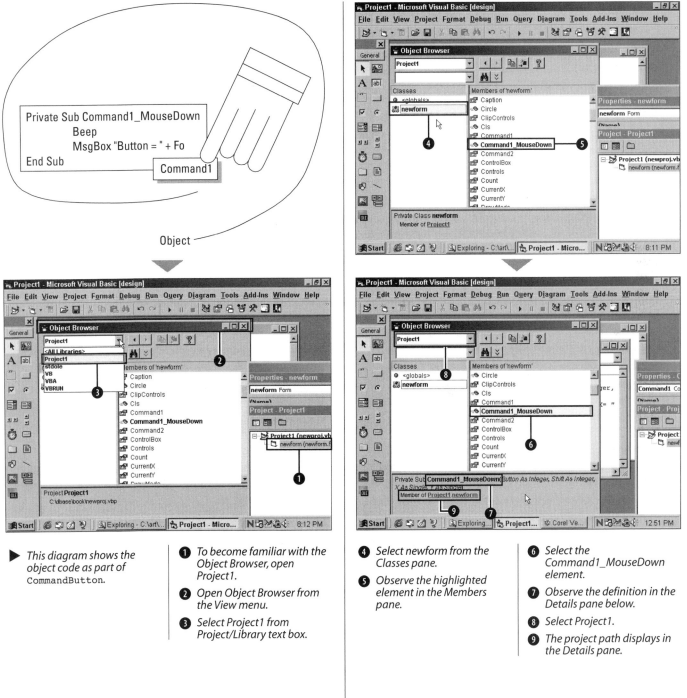

```
Private Sub Command1_MouseDown
        Beep
        MsgBox "Button = " + Fo
End Sub
```

Command1

Object

▶ *This diagram shows the object code as part of* `CommandButton`*.*

❶ *To become familiar with the Object Browser, open Project1.*

❷ *Open Object Browser from the View menu.*

❸ *Select Project1 from Project/Library text box.*

❹ *Select newform from the Classes pane.*

❺ *Observe the highlighted element in the Members pane.*

❻ *Select the Command1_MouseDown element.*

❼ *Observe the definition in the Details pane below.*

❽ *Select Project1.*

❾ *The project path displays in the Details pane.*

Learning about Form Controls

The beginning of any Visual Basic project involves building an interface. This interface is engineered to benefit users, whether only yourself, the staff at a large company, or the general public.

The interface starts with a *form*. The form is the basis for the events that will be taking place when the user interacts with the application. When Visual Basic is launched, you are always prompted to begin a Standard .exe project, open an existing project, or use a recent one.

By default, a project is created for you and you are instantly presented with a form in the Windows environment. The project will be given the names Project1 and Form1. If you do not change these names, your project will be saved with them. The form is an object, just as its controls and other entities in Visual Basic are objects. It has properties, events, and methods. The properties are appearance attributes of the object. Form events establish their interaction with the user, and methods identify these interactions.

Once created, the form is then populated by placing controls found in the toolbox. The General toolbox contains the necessary controls for most forms. You can add controls from component libraries found by selecting Components from the Project menu. In addition to `CommandButtons`, there are controls to set up images, picture boxes, list boxes, text boxes, check boxes, frames, labels, scroll bars, combo boxes, and so on.

Form controls also are objects. They too have properties, events, and methods that determine their behavior. Properties that are appropriate for one object may not be appropriate or available for another. The kind of action your form needs will determine which controls you select and what their properties will be.

The General Toolbox controls fit into several functional categories. They are buttons that carry out actions, boxes that enable user choices between alternatives, boxes that enable text to be displayed and input, controls that show graphics. Other controls enable data access, file system access, ActiveX, object linking, and timer functions.

The more familiar controls are those that enable the user to press a button and cause something to happen, enter data onto the form, select items from a list, and make containers for other controls on the form.

When several controls are placed on a form, the user only may interact with the particular control that currently has the *focus*. Not all objects can be selected (have the focus), however, because settings will ultimately manage which objects can have the focus at any particular moment. The focus is controlled by keyboard key presses or mouse movements and clicks. Focus can also be controlled in the code. Moving the focus to the first `TextBox` on the form upon initially loading the form is an example of this. Some objects (frame control, image control, label control, line control, and shape control) cannot have the focus. The `GotFocus`, `LostFocus`, and `SetFocus` methods control the focus.

Another important navigating feature to know about is the *tab order*. This is the order in which the Tab key moves through the controls on the form. By default, the first box or button has the focus when the form is opened. You can then move from one control to another by pressing Tab. This order can be changed by changing the `TabIndex` value. By default, the first control created has the lowest `TabIndex` value, 0. Each subsequent control will have one integer higher. In order to change the tab order, you change the `TabIndex` value.

TAKE NOTE

▶ FOCUS AND TAB ORDER

There are some controls for which focus cannot be set, (Labels, Images, Lines, and Frames). These controls cannot have a `TabIndex` value. Neither are they included in the tab order. These objects are bypassed when the user presses Tab.

CROSS-REFERENCE

Chapter 6 goes into further detail about form controls.

FIND IT ONLINE

The Technical FAQ at **http://msdn.microsoft.com/vbasic/ technical/techfaq.asp** has information on many basic concepts.

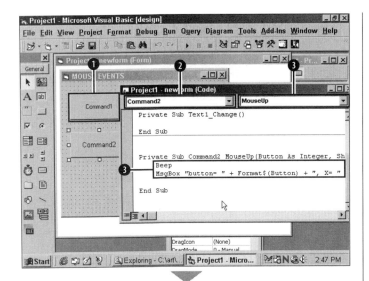

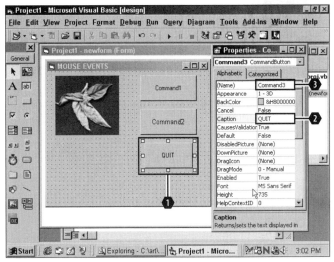

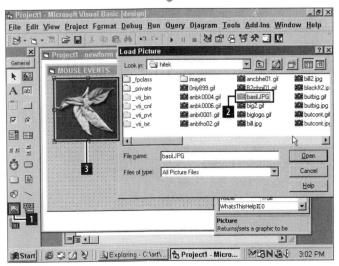

Listing 2-1: MouseUp Event

```
MouseUp Event
Private Sub Command1_MouseUp(Button As Integer,_
Shift As Integer, X As Single, Y As Single)
    Beep
    MsgBox "BUTTON= " + Format$(Button) + ", X=
"_ + Format$(X) + ", Y= " + Format$(Y)

End Sub
```

① Select the CommandButton control from the toolbox and place it on the form under the Command1 button.

② Double-click Command2 (the new button).

③ Copy the lines beginning with Beep and MsgBox from the MouseUp procedure and paste into the Command2 procedure.

1 Select Image control and place it on the form.

2 Double-click the Picture property in the Properties window and select a bitmap on your hard drive. It must have a .bmp, .jpg, or .gif extension. If you pick a large file, it will not fit on the form.

3 View the picture that appears on your form.

① Place a new button under the Command1 and Command2 buttons.

② Make the caption QUIT. The label will change from Command3 to QUIT.

③ Select Command3 Object and the Click Procedure.

▶ Add the word **End** to stop execution.

Learning More about Windows

Stated as simply as possible, a window is a rectangular area in which coding and form design take place, and in which properties and projects are selected. The window environment is a place where you can design forms, implement controls, add properties, and write code.

Windows Collection

The Windows collection is made up of Window objects. In Visual Basic these include the Project Explorer; the Properties, Object Browser, Code, and Designer windows; and the development environment.

When you open a new window, you add a new member to the Windows collection. When you close a window, the action removes a window from the collection. If you close a permanent development environment window, the window will become invisible, but the object will not be removed.

Linked Windows Collection

The Linked Windows collection is all of the currently linked windows. Code windows, the Object Browser, and Designer windows are not by default linked to other windows or docked to the Main window, but their docking options can be changed from the Tools ⇨ Options menu. The `Add` and the `Remove` methods can be used to add and remove windows from the currently linked Windows collection.

The `Window` object may be displayed, hidden, or positioned. The `Close` method causes different actions when it is applied to different window types. `Close`, used with the Code and Designer windows, actually closes these windows. Used with the Project Explorer or Properties

windows, it renders these windows invisible. Closing the Project and Properties windows has the same effect as setting the Visible property to False for the Code and Designer windows. `SetFocus` can be used to change the focus of a window.

The Windows API

The Windows Application Programming Interface (API) includes all the tools to which you have access under Microsoft Windows. Using code, you can call API functions from Windows. The Windows API includes thousands of procedures, functions, subs, constants, and types that you can declare. You can translate the DLLs, but it is easier to use the declares predefined in Visual Basic.

The file `Win32api.txt` contains the declarations for many Windows API procedures used in Visual Basic. You can copy the code and paste it into your module. As a convenience, bring up the API text viewer from the Microsoft Visual Basic 6.0 Tools option on the Windows 95/98 Start menu.

TAKE NOTE

THE WINDOW MENU

You also can rearrange your development environment quickly by using the Window menu. You can split the code window into two panes, tile horizontally or vertically, or cascade the windows in your application. In addition, you can switch between windows by selecting the desired project from the open projects list.

CROSS-REFERENCE
Chapter 1 also discusses windows.

FIND IT ONLINE
Try **http://msdn.microsoft.com/vbasic/technical/pasttips.asp# 2-23-98** for terrific tips on Windows API and lots of other topics.

Table 2-1: WINDOW TYPES

Window Type	Can Be Docked	Can Be Closed
Code windows	NO	YES
Design window	NO	YES
Project Explorer	YES	NO (hidden)
Properties window	YES	NO (hidden)
Object Browser	YES	YES
Form Layout window	YES	YES

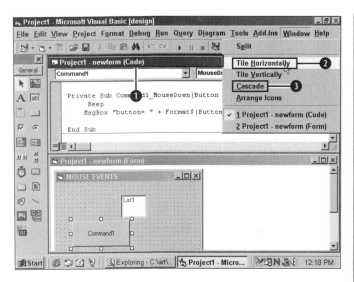

① Open Project1.

② Select Tile Horizontally and then Tile Vertically from the Window menu.

③ Select the Cascade option as well.

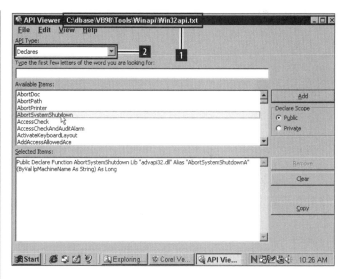

▶ Select API Text Viewer from the Visual Basic Tools option on the Start menu.

1 Load Win32api.txt from the File menu.

2 Select Declares from the API Type text box. When you make a selection, you can copy it to the clipboard and paste it into your module.

Using the Debugging Windows

Visual Basic provides tools you use to debug your projects. The debugging process is one in which you try systematically to eliminate the syntax errors, type mismatches, or whatever is producing the errors. The windowing arena in which you carry out debugging tasks includes the Immediate window, the Watch window, and the Locals window. These windows let you observe the changes in variable values while the procedure is executing.

The Immediate window displays what happens as a result of adding debugging statements to your code.

For example, if you wish to know the value of a variable, you can type **Print X** in the Immediate window. When the procedure executes, the value of X will be displayed in the window. If you have written a For-Next loop in which the variable X is incremented by the value of 1 each time the code proceeds through the loop, you can actually watch what happens to the value of X on each pass through the loop.

You can use the Watch window to display the value of a variable as you step through the code. That is, you can set a value of X in the Watch window and then step through the loop (using the F8 key) a line at a time. The Watch window will show at what point the value of X matches the value you entered. This would be a good debugging tool when you have the For-Next loop shown below.

```
Private Sub Image1_click()
X=0
For X = 1 to 10
  X = X + 1
  MsgBox "X = " + Str(X)
Next
End Sub
```

This procedure, when run, displays a message box with the value of X each time you click, after you initially click the image. The problem is that X seems to increment by 2 each time through the loop. You can determine the reason by adding a variable expression in the Watch window. As you step through the procedure, you can observe when X has an odd numbered value (because the MsgBox only shows even numbered values from 2 to 10). You also can enter a Break expression, causing the procedure to break its execution when the value is reached.

You can view variable values within the scope of the current procedure in the Locals window, accessed from the View menu. The Locals window routinely displays the names, values, and types of all variables declared in the currently running procedure. The window is updated when the state changes from Break mode to Run mode.

The first column shows the variable currently being accessed, the system variable Me, which refers to a class module. In standard modules, the first variable shown in the upper left is the name of the current module.

The second column displays the value of the expression, and the last column displays the data type of the variable. The first variable listed beside a plus sign is the module variable. You can resize the columns by clicking and dragging.

You can edit the value in the Value column by clicking, retyping, and then clicking to validate the new value. If the new value is invalid, you will get an error message. You can cancel your changes by pressing the Esc key.

TAKE NOTE

▶ DATA TIPS

When you are in Break mode, you can pass the mouse over a variable value in the Immediate window and its current value will be displayed. This is a feature of Data Tips and is available only for variables in the scope of the current procedure.

CROSS-REFERENCE

Chapter 11 probes further into debugging techniques.

FIND IT ONLINE

See this site for beginning **help.http://.visualbasic. about.com/**

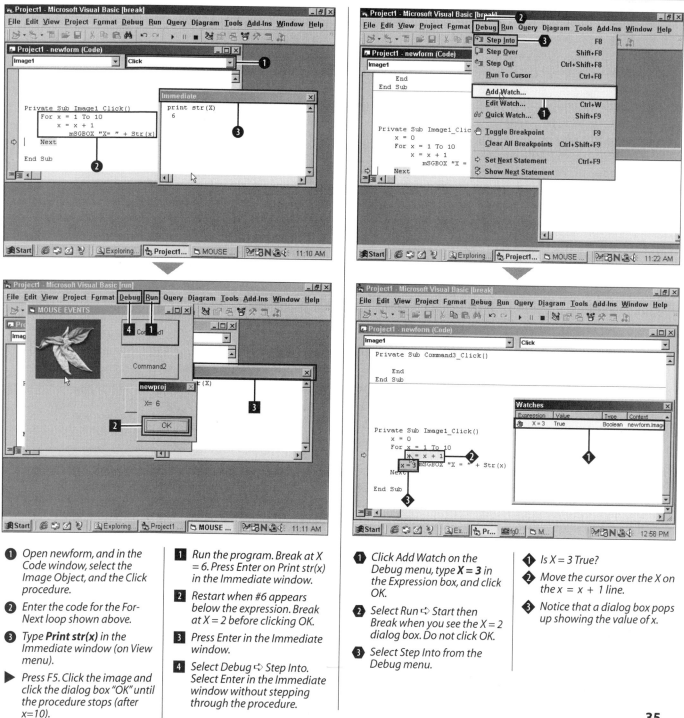

① Open newform, and in the Code window, select the Image Object, and the Click procedure.

② Enter the code for the For-Next loop shown above.

③ Type **Print str(x)** in the Immediate window (on View menu).

▶ Press F5. Click the image and click the dialog box "OK" until the procedure stops (after x=10).

❶ Run the program. Break at X = 6. Press Enter on Print str(x) in the Immediate window.

❷ Restart when #6 appears below the expression. Break at X = 2 before clicking OK.

❸ Press Enter in the Immediate window.

❹ Select Debug ⇨ Step Into. Select Enter in the Immediate window without stepping through the procedure.

① Click Add Watch on the Debug menu, type **X = 3** in the Expression box, and click OK.

② Select Run ⇨ Start then Break when you see the X = 2 dialog box. Do not click OK.

③ Select Step Into from the Debug menu.

◆ Is X = 3 True?

❷ Move the cursor over the X on the x = x + 1 line.

❸ Notice that a dialog box pops up showing the value of x.

Customizing the IDE

Found on the View menu, the Customize dialog box lets you make changes in settings for Toolbars, Commands, and Options.

You can modify and delete existing toolbars, create new ones, and reset to the defaults. Toolbars currently displayed are shown with check marks in the check boxes.

A new toolbar can be named from the View ⇨ Toolbars ⇨ Customize menu. When you do this, the new toolbar will be added to the list of toolbars. The Rename option enables you to rename a previously defined toolbar. You may not rename any of the system toolbars; only those you have defined.

You can develop your toolbar by placing a `PictureBox` on a form and then selecting controls from the toolbox representing the functions of the toolbar buttons.

The Delete option lets you delete only a toolbar you have defined for your project. This option will be deselected if you have not created any user-defined toolbars.

The Reset option eliminates any changes to the system toolbars. This does not pertain to those you defined.

The Commands tab lists all of the categories for menu and toolbars.

Commands lists the controls available for the category you select in the Categories list. You can drag the command to the toolbar where you want the command to reside. To add the command to a menu, drag it from the Customize dialog box to the menu bar to the menu item where you want to move the command. Drag it over the menu's title and then into the desired location when the menu drops down.

The Options selection enables you to change icons, show ScreenTips on toolbars, and display shortcut keys in ScreenTips. There also is an option to select menu animations.

You can customize your projects by setting properties. Select Project Properties from the Project menu. When you complete your changes, they are saved with the `.vbp` file extension.

You can customize the startup object, which is the first form that Visual Basic displays at runtime. The Project name must be under 37 characters, begin with an alphabetic character, and not contain periods or spaces. This name is documented in code. The Project Description, on the other hand, is user-friendly. The Project Help Context ID and the Help file may be tailored.

Windows 95/98 ships with many features making Windows accessible to individuals who might otherwise have difficulty using a computer. These features assist those who have difficulty using a mouse, typing with the QWERTY keyboard, hearing, or reading a screen. These aids can be installed during setup, or at any time. You can search on "accessibility" under Windows Help for information on installation. Optionally, you can download these files from the Internet by going to **www.microsoft.com**.

TAKE NOTE

► **MORE CUSTOMIZING**

Menus and windows can be customized, just as can the toolbars and projects. The Project Explorer; Properties window; toolbox; Form Layout window; color palette; and Immediate, Locals, and Watch windows can be moved freely on the screen without being anchored, or they can be attached to other windows or the edge of the screen.

CROSS-REFERENCE

Chapter 1 also has a lot of information on customizing the environment.

FIND IT ONLINE

The VB Beginner's corner at **http://www.citilink.com/~jgarrick/ vbasic/beginners/resources.html** has a great discussion of the IDE.

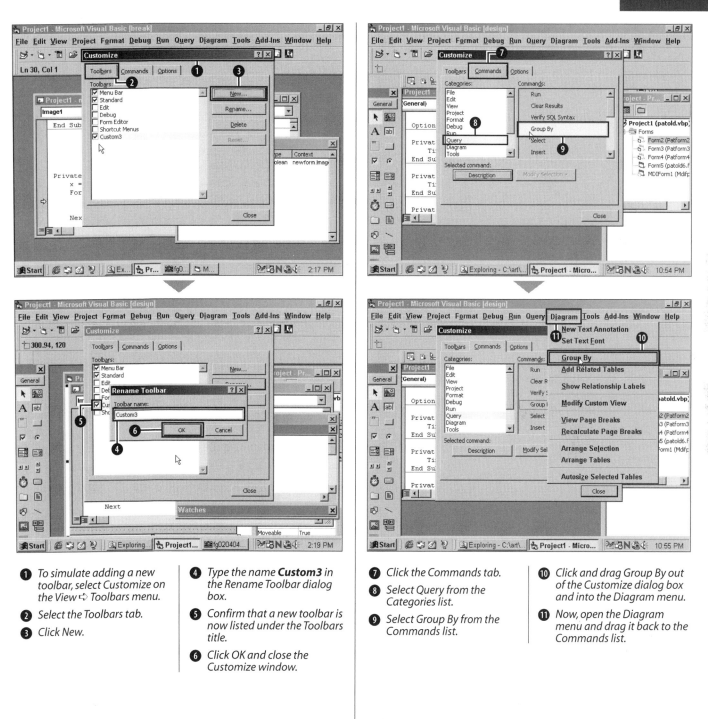

1 To simulate adding a new toolbar, select Customize on the View ➪ Toolbars menu.

2 Select the Toolbars tab.

3 Click New.

4 Type the name **Custom3** in the Rename Toolbar dialog box.

5 Confirm that a new toolbar is now listed under the Toolbars title.

6 Click OK and close the Customize window.

7 Click the Commands tab.

8 Select Query from the Categories list.

9 Select Group By from the Commands list.

10 Click and drag Group By out of the Customize dialog box and into the Diagram menu.

11 Now, open the Diagram menu and drag it back to the Commands list.

Program Limitations

As is the case with all software systems, there are system requirements in order for the application to function properly.

The following software and hardware items are mandatory in order to install and use Visual Basic 6.

- ▶ A Pentium 90MHz or higher microprocessor
- ▶ A VGA 640 by 480 monitor supported by Microsoft Windows (higher resolution is recommended)
- ▶ 24MB RAM for Windows 95, 32MB for Windows NT
- ▶ 64MB RAM for Windows 95/98 or NT will greatly improve system performance.
- ▶ Microsoft Windows NT 3.51 or later, or Microsoft Windows 95 or later
- ▶ Microsoft Internet Explorer version 4.01 or later (version 4.01 Service Pack 1 or later for DHTML application developers, and 4.x for end users of these applications)
- ▶ Disk space requirements: *Standard Edition* requires typical installation 48MB, full installation 80MB; *Professional Edition* requires typical installation 48MB, full installation 80MB; and *Enterprise Edition* requires typical installation 128MB, full installation 147MB
- ▶ Additional components (if required): MSDN (for documentation): 67MB, Internet Explorer 4.x: approximately 66MB
- ▶ CD-ROM (no MS-DOS support assumed)

Project Limitations

There is a general limitation of 32,000 nonreserved keywords, and a specific limitation that is dependent upon machine memory. The restriction of 32,000 identifiers includes objects, forms, controls, modules, procedures, variables, constants, and functions.

Visual Basic restricts variable names to 255 characters, and the names of forms, controls, modules, and classes to 40 characters. There is no limit on the number of separate objects in a given project.

All nongraphic controls use windows. Since each window uses system resources, the limit is dependent upon the user's system memory.

The `Line`, `Shape`, and `Image` controls use less memory than the `PictureBox` control. The maximum number of controls on any single form again depends upon the individual machine memory. However, there only may be 254 control names. All the elements in an array share the same name, so declaring array variables is one way to get around this constraint. You can have no more than 25 levels of nested controls.

Code Limitations

No form, class, or module can have more than 65,534 lines of code, and each line of code must be no more than 1,023 bytes. You can have as many as 256 blank spaces preceding text on one line.

Procedures

You can have any number of procedures per module, and each procedure can have up to 64K in code. You will get a compile-time error if this is exceeded. The idea is to break

CROSS-REFERENCE

Chapters 10 and 12 address issues with limitations.

FIND IT ONLINE

The site **http://support.microsoft.com/support/kb/articles/ q229/7/56.asp** has info on control limitations and references to other limitations.

big procedures into a number of smaller procedures, or to move out module-level declarations.

Visual Basic uses tables to store the names of identifiers (variables, procedures, constants, and so on) in your code. Each table is limited to 64K.

System Tables

Form and code modules use tables that contain structures identifying a DLL entry point. Each structure uses approximately 40 bytes, for a total restricted size of 64K, and about 1,500 declarations are allowed per module.

The project name table contains all names, including constants, variables, any user-defined types, modules, and DLLs. It is not limited in size but may have only 32K unique entries.

The import table includes every reference to an identifier in a different module. Each such entry is between 24 bytes and 64K.

The module-entries table allows 125 bytes per module, totaling 64K and about 400 modules per project.

Stack Space

The *stack* refers to available memory in the Visual Basic environment. It is ultimately dependent upon the total MB of RAM on your PC, but the particular modules you are running can affect it. The stack grows and shrinks, depending upon the number of functions, subroutines, or procedure calls in your project. When the stack runs low on memory, Visual Basic returns the error "Out of Stack Space (Error 28)."

To rectify the problem, you can reduce the number of functions and subroutines, reduce the number of layers of nested procedures, and declare some variables at the module

level. These measures will release stack space because module and static variables do not use stack space, and variables and expressions in procedures use stack space at runtime.

Windows System Resources

The Windows interface has certain limitations in terms of memory allocation. Each open window uses these system resources. In order to determine the status of memory resources, select About Windows 98 or 95 from the Help menu in the Windows Explorer.

TAKE NOTE

▶ **AVAILABLE DISK SPACE**

Needless to say, there should be ample disk space remaining after installation to carry out programming and other tasks. Disk space can be monitored by right-clicking the C: drive in the Windows Explorer and checking Properties on the drop-down menu. Disk space should not be allowed to drop below 100MB.

▶ **INDIVIDUAL LIMITATIONS**

The IDE has set limitations on the number of variable names, keywords, code, procedures, and so on. It is more common for Windows system resources and individual machine memory to restrict processing than it is for the Visual Basic IDE limits to be reached.

Using Online Help

There are six options on the Help menu. The first four options run the MSDN Library Visual Studio. The Contents option displays the Contents tab. The Index displays the Index tab. Search displays the Search tab. The Technical Support option prompts you to insert the CD-ROM disc labeled "MSDN VS 6.0 CD2 in drive X:"

The Microsoft on the Web option goes to the URL **msdn.microsoft.com/vbasic/technical/** and displays a menu of support options.

The About Microsoft Visual Basic option shows a dialog box with the version number, a copyright notice, and the amount of available memory.

The CD that is shipped with the Professional and Enterprise versions includes the MSDN Library Visual Studio help.

Microsoft Developer Network

The Microsoft Developer Network, MSDN, is the indispensable developer reference for Microsoft development tools to create applications for Windows and Internet platforms. The Library contains over 1GB of programming information, including coding examples, the Knowledge Base, all Visual Studio documentation, technical articles, and technical specifications. You can visit the MSDN Web site at **http://www.microsoft.com/msdn/**.

You can select the Microsoft on the Web option or use the MSDN CD to obtain help using the system.

Microsoft on the Web

When you click the Microsoft on the Web option, your current Web browser will be launched and you will be connected to Internet, depending upon how your dial-up networking is configured. If you do not have a default browser, you will need to connect first.

Once online, the Microsoft on the Web option takes you directly to the Product Support site. You can select Knowledge Base from the Product Support menu. You will be prompted for the Product Name to search on. Then you can choose to search by Keywords, Article, downloadable file, troubleshooting tool, what's new in the past 1–30 days. You can even ask a question using the Natural Language search.

Just as you can go directly to MSDN Online, you can go there from the Microsoft on the Web option as well. From the initial Product Support area, use this URL: **msdn. microsoft.com/vbasic/technical/support.ast**.

Select MSDN Online from the menu bar and then select Libraries to go to the MSDN Online Libraries. Here you will find some of the same information that is included on the CD for the Professional and Enterprise products. As of July 1999, the documentation online and on CD was updated. If you purchased Visual Basic 6 prior to July 1999, you should view the documentation online, or download the more recent documentation.

Web Workshop is another important area on the Online Web. Here you can get the latest information about Internet technologies. Once there, you can choose sections on Component Development, Data Access and Databases, Design, Networking protocols, and much more.

> **TAKE NOTE**
>
> **ONLINE BONANZA**
>
> The online information is so rich with material covering every conceivable topic related to Visual Basic that you really must explore it for yourself. There is no way to list even 10 percent of the topics and options waiting for you online. The menus and instructions are clear and easy to follow, so it is not easy to get lost. So much is available that you may want to bookmark your finds.

> **CROSS-REFERENCE**
>
> Chapter 21 covers some topics dealing with online help.

> **FIND IT ONLINE**
>
> Check out **http://msdn.microsoft.com/library/** as a place to begin learning about Visual Basic.

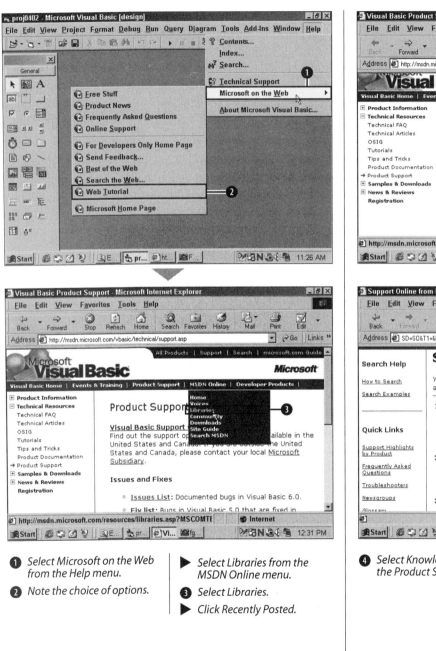

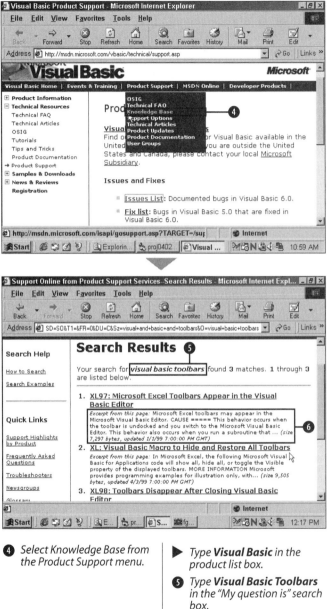

❶ Select Microsoft on the Web from the Help menu.

❷ Note the choice of options.

▶ Select Libraries from the MSDN Online menu.

❸ Select Libraries.

▶ Click Recently Posted.

❹ Select Knowledge Base from the Product Support menu.

▶ Type **Visual Basic** in the product list box.

❺ Type **Visual Basic Toolbars** in the "My question is" search box.

❻ Do your results look like this?

Personal Workbook

Q&A

1 A Visual Basic object is unique in that it combines both_____ and _____.

_____

_____

_____

2 How can you add new controls to the toolbox?

_____

_____

_____

3 What value do you modify to change the tab order on the form?

_____

_____

_____

4 What does the Windows collection contain?

_____

_____

_____

5 How can you find the value of a variable as the program executes?

_____

_____

_____

6 How can you add a new command to a menu on the menu bar?

_____

_____

_____

7 Will Visual Basic 6 run on a Pentium 120MHz running Windows 98 with 16MB RAM?

_____

_____

_____

8 What is the best way to get online help?

_____

_____

_____

ANSWERS: PAGE 519

Learning More about the IDE

CHAPTER 2

EXTRA PRACTICE

1. Select the newform form and then select Project ⇨ Components to select a tool library. See how this changes the toolbox. Pass the mouse over the new controls. What are they? Place one of the controls on the form.

2. Change the captions on the Command buttons.

3. Place a new `CommandButton` on the form. Give it a new name and caption.

4. Practice docking and undocking the windows.

5. Create a new project. Imagine this is a project to demonstrate different sizes of command buttons. Give the project an appropriate name beginning with "Proj." Give the form an appropriate name beginning with "Frm" and a caption appropriate to your project.

REAL-WORLD APPLICATIONS

✔ Your company wants to create a multimedia application. Make a list of factors that would influence your design of the project in general and the forms in particular for the project.

✔ You continually get a compile error when you try to run your application. What are the factors that might be causing the error? How would you approach debugging it?

✔ Your client, Joe Schmoe, needs to update an old Visual Basic employee database application. He is looking to spiff up forms and add some new toolbars. Make an outline of the features you would add to his project and give him reasons for adding each.

Visual Quiz

Which of these options shown will give you online help?

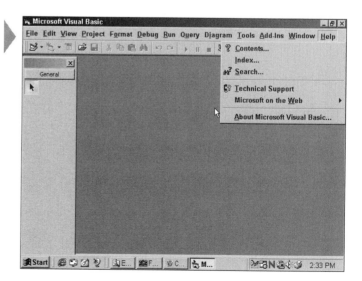

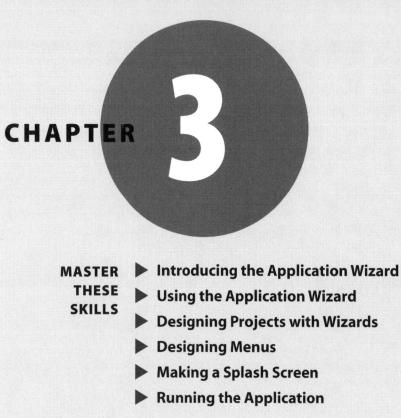

CHAPTER 3

MASTER
THESE
SKILLS

▶ Introducing the Application Wizard
▶ Using the Application Wizard
▶ Designing Projects with Wizards
▶ Designing Menus
▶ Making a Splash Screen
▶ Running the Application

Using the Application Wizard

It is important to realize that you need not necessarily write code to create an application in Visual Basic. The Application Wizard, along with the other Visual Basic 6 wizards, makes the job of application development possible to do without any programming. But it is unlikely that you will not want to modify the generated code, or that the generated application will entirely suit your needs.

The best use of the Application Wizard is to give you a starting point and ideas for enhancement. If a feature doesn't seem to work, you can examine the code and compare it with other applications that do work. Some people learn by example this way, and some learn better when presented with theory. If you learn by example, the Application Wizard is for you.

Some new wizards shipped with version 6 are the Package and Deployment Wizard, Data Object Wizard, Add-In Designer, Class Builder Utility, Toolbar Wizard, and Data Form Wizard. View **http://support.microsoft.com/support/kb/articles/ q191/0/37.asp** to find which wizards are available in each edition of Visual Basic 6.

One of the most exciting features of the Application Wizard is the capability to create an Internet Web browser. This is especially fun because you can adapt it to your own needs just as you can the other features. You can jump to any Web site and use it just as you would the commercial browsers, Netscape and Internet Explorer.

To run the browser, you must have Internet Explorer, version 3.0 or higher, installed on your system. Also, those running the application must have an Internet service provider and dial-up networking or direct access installed.

You can now save your settings in files called *profiles* for later use. This saves time by letting you reuse a format in several applications. The Data Form Wizard and the Toolbar Wizard can be accessed from the Application Wizard. The Wizard also automates toolbars and menus.

Introducing the Application Wizard

The Application Wizard generates a full-blown interface for using a database. You can use it with a Microsoft Access database or with any Remote ODBC database for which you have a driver. Open Database Connectivity (ODBC) is the older way (the newer way is via OLE DB) to connect with remote databases via drivers installed in Windows. Provided that you own the proprietary driver, ODBC is an open way to seamlessly access data stored in different formats and by different database engines. If you choose the Remote ODBC option, you must be able to furnish the connect data on the Data Form Wizard. For practice, it is better to use the Access option.

When you create a project with the Application Wizard, you will be able to read, edit, add, delete, browse, and update records in your database. This is a powerful program with so many features that you may not realize how much sophistication and capability you are producing when you move through its menus.

The Application Wizard makes creating the database surprisingly simple, but it is by no means foolproof. Some potential bugs can be difficult to figure out without help. Fortunately, the Microsoft MSDN comes to the rescue. Again, the Microsoft Developer Network is an indispensable resource, both in terms of volume and timeliness of information.

Application Wizard enables you to choose between the SDI, MDI, or Explorer interfaces when generating your application. It also creates a toolbar and a status bar by default. The default looks like the Microsoft Office toolbar. It consists of the New, Open, Save, Print, Cut, Copy, Paste, Bold, Italic, Underline, Align Left, Align Right, and Center buttons.

The applications using the Explorer interface have a toolbar with Navigation, Cut, Copy, Paste, Delete, Properties, View Large Icon, View Small Icon, View List, and View Details buttons. Of course, you can add or subtract the various functions to customize the toolbar. The status bar displays the status of the application and the date and time.

The magic of the Application Wizard is you can get started very quickly and learn by examining the generated code, and use the knowledge to develop other applications. Also, when you become a seasoned Visual Basic developer, you may use the Application Wizard to create applications with similar interfaces. You can save your settings to a profile and use them to create similar-looking applications.

All code generated by the Application Wizard is fully commented to help you understand how the application functions. You can use this understanding to enhance the project.

An exciting feature of the Application Wizard is that you can offer your users Internet access. You can build an application that will, on launching, go directly to your Web site. This means you can offer your users a help page or tips and tricks at your Web site, so you can provide a constant source of new information. The only requirement is that the users' browser be Internet Explorer 3.0 or later and that they have an Internet service provider. This feature requires the Internet Explorer in order to work, because the HTML support is provided through that product.

TAKE NOTE

RESOURCE FILES

The Resource file (`.res`) lets you change the data it contains without modifying the actual code. Text strings (such as captions) that will be used repetitively can be stored in a separate file and called from one location. Using a Resource file can help organize your code and eliminate redundancy.

CROSS-REFERENCE

Chapter 13 gives more detail about database connectivity.

FIND IT ONLINE

The article at **http://support.microsoft.com/support/kb/articles/ q220/8/16.asp** discusses a common error in the Learning edition.

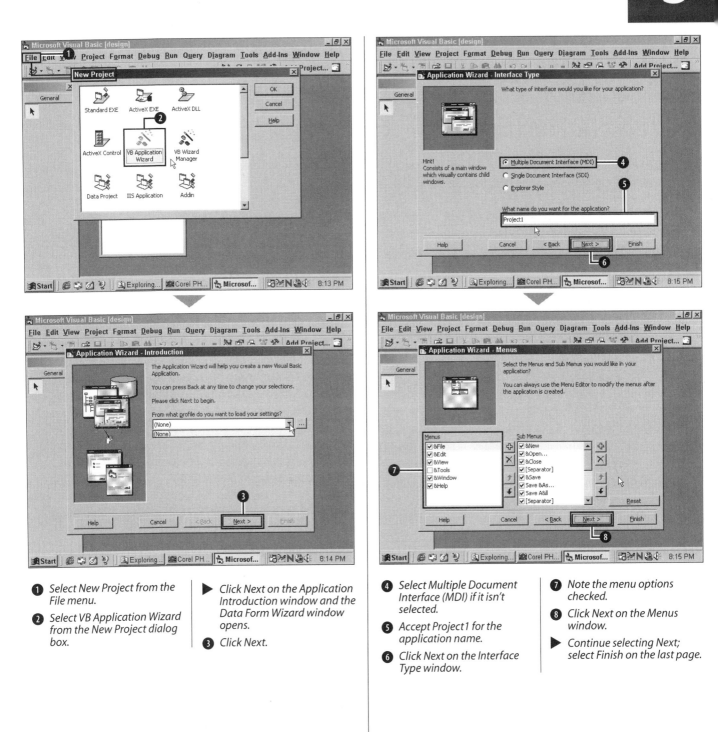

① Select New Project from the File menu.

② Select VB Application Wizard from the New Project dialog box.

▶ Click Next on the Application Introduction window and the Data Form Wizard window opens.

③ Click Next.

④ Select Multiple Document Interface (MDI) if it isn't selected.

⑤ Accept Project1 for the application name.

⑥ Click Next on the Interface Type window.

⑦ Note the menu options checked.

⑧ Click Next on the Menus window.

▶ Continue selecting Next; select Finish on the last page.

Using the Application Wizard

I n using the Application Wizard, you follow the Next arrows through a series of windows, each with options to select. First, you are prompted to load your settings from a previously saved profile. The following screens request you to select the Interface type, Menus, Toolbars, creating a Resource file, Internet Connectivity, Standard Forms, Data Access Forms, then Finish.

The profile is a file containing the settings you previously saved. The options for Interface are the MDI, SDI, or Explorer-style interfaces from which all applications must choose. The menus and toolbars have, as options, the standard options featured in the application environment. The Resource file can be used in order to store strings to be used in captions. Internet connectivity will enable users to use their Internet service provider accounts to connect and possibly access a Web site set up for them as support for the application. The Standard Forms screen gives you a chance to decide between several form types. Data Access Forms give you the choice of creating a new form for using a database.

New Features

In previous versions, you could not save your settings and reuse them later. Other wizards (Data Form and Toolbar) can be opened from the Application Wizard. The Toolbar Wizard opens when you add a new toolbar to a form. You can then customize your toolbars and create forms. It is now possible to customize the menus as well. You also have the capability to construct forms in which the controls are not bound to a data control and can use ActiveX Data Objects (ADO) code. The ADO data access technology and OLE DB data provider give you consistent access to many different kinds of data. OLE DB is a broad set of Component Object Model (COM) interfaces that can provide uniform access to data stored by various information sources. This is a jump ahead of the older Open Database Connectivity (ODBC) technology.

The Data Form Wizard in the Professional and Enterprise Editions now gives you the ability to build code-only forms where controls are not bound to a data control. It allows you to use ADO code.

ADO Reference

As useful and impressive as the Application Wizard is, it has some bugs. A difficult bug to troubleshoot is the omission of the ADO Reference in an application created in the Application Wizard.

This error occurs when you create forms via the Data Form Wizard. The Application Wizard should automatically add an ADO reference to the project. When you select the option to create a data form and choose the ADO control, you get a compile error on running the application, such as this:

```
Compile error: User-defined type not defined.
```

The error occurs because the Application Wizard did not add the ADO data control to the application. Adding a reference to ADO solves the problem. The library containing the correct control is found under Project ⇨ References and is called Microsoft ActiveX Data Objects 2.0 Library.

You also can avoid the problem by not selecting the Create New Form option and then using the Data Form Wizard to add data forms.

> **TAKE NOTE**
>
> ▶ **DATA FORMS WIZARD**
>
> The Data Forms Wizard creates child forms if you select the Create New Form option in the Application Wizard Data Form window. In addition, it adds a menu for you if none exists. If there is already a menu, it adds new commands to your existing menu.

CROSS-REFERENCE

Chapter 21 offers additional uses for the Application Wizard.

FIND IT ONLINE

View **http://support.microsoft.com/support/kb/articles/ q193/3/26.asp** for information on the user-defined type not defined error.

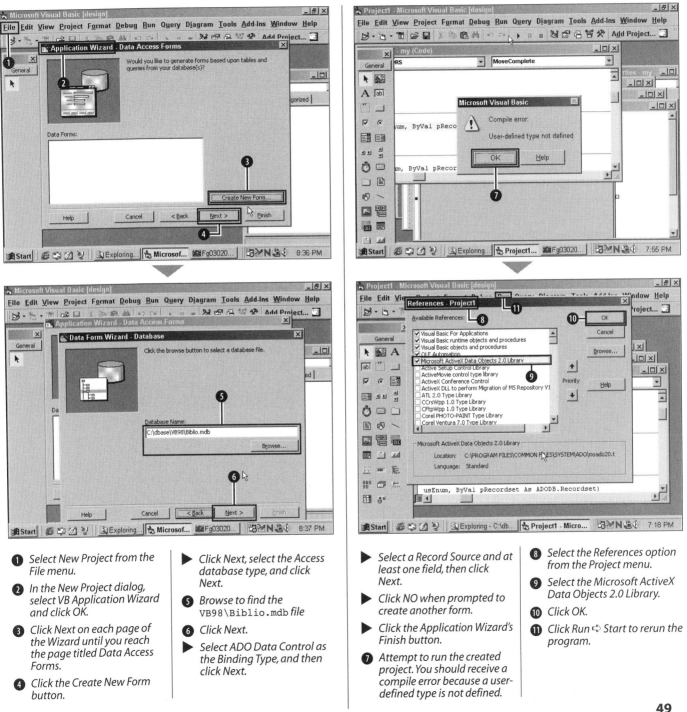

1. Select New Project from the File menu.

2. In the New Project dialog, select VB Application Wizard and click OK.

3. Click Next on each page of the Wizard until you reach the page titled Data Access Forms.

4. Click the Create New Form button.

▶ Click Next, select the Access database type, and click Next.

5. Browse to find the VB98\Biblio.mdb file

6. Click Next.

▶ Select ADO Data Control as the Binding Type, and then click Next.

▶ Select a Record Source and at least one field, then click Next.

▶ Click NO when prompted to create another form.

▶ Click the Application Wizard's Finish button.

7. Attempt to run the created project. You should receive a compile error because a user-defined type is not defined.

8. Select the References option from the Project menu.

9. Select the Microsoft ActiveX Data Objects 2.0 Library.

10. Click OK.

11. Click Run ➪ Start to rerun the program.

Designing Projects with Wizards

In addition to the Application Wizard, a number of other wizards help to speed application development. These include the Data Form Wizard, Toolbar Wizard, Property Page Wizard, Data Object Wizard, Class Builder, Built-In Designer, ActiveX Control Interface Wizard, ActiveX Document Migration Wizard. There is even a Wizard Manager to help you create your own wizard.

The Add-In Manager

When you want to use a wizard but do not want to access it from the Application Wizard, you can load it from the Add-In Manager on the Add-In menu. For example, if you do not have the Application Wizard loaded, you can load it by selecting it from the Add-In Manager on the Add-In menu. It will then display in the New Project window.

The Data Form Wizard

When you run the Data Form Wizard, whether from within the Application Wizard or added to the New Project window via the Add-In menu, you will have several opportunities to customize your form. You also can select the Data Form Wizard directly from the Add-In menu.

The Single record form displays database information one record per screen. The Grid format is similar to a table or tabular format, except that it scrolls up, down, and sideways.

The Master/Detail form is used where there are one-to-many relationships between tables in the database. For example, a customer table might have one record for each customer, whereas the orders table would link many orders to each customer. Thus, the customer table would be the Master and the orders table would be called the Detail. If you wish, the Data Form Wizard will construct a form with the Orders Records displayed on the Customer form. You are prompted to select the record source and fields you want from each record on the form.

The MS Chart format displays data on a chart and requires at least one numeric field to be selected from the Record Source window. You must decide which field is to be the X axis (along the bottom of the graph) and which the Y axis (left side of graph). The Z axis is optional. You can select your chart's text, its captions, and even the style. Styles range from pie to line or bar and also can be two or three dimensional. In addition, you can choose the function used to compute the chart relationships. Examples of aggregate functions are average, count, and sum.

The MS HFlex Grid shows data in a table format and has many options. The Data Form Wizard offers a choice for style (Classic, Professional, Contemporary, and Win32 application). You can opt to allow column dragging to change column width and to sort by changing the position of columns. Finally, you can add captions for your column headers, instead of displaying the field names.

Continued

TAKE NOTE

OPEN DATABASE CONNECTIVITY

The second window encountered in the Data Form Wizard, Database Type, forces a choice between Access and Remote (ODBC). ODBC refers to Open Database Connectivity. Using ODBC, you can build access to tables in any database for which you have drivers. This is done through the Windows Control Panel, ODBC Data Sources (32bit) menu. An icon in the Control Panel represents this.

CROSS-REFERENCE
Chapter 13 continues the discussion of databases in greater detail.

FIND IT ONLINE
Find the latest on bug issues and fixes at **http://msdn. microsoft.com/vbasic/technical/support.asp.**

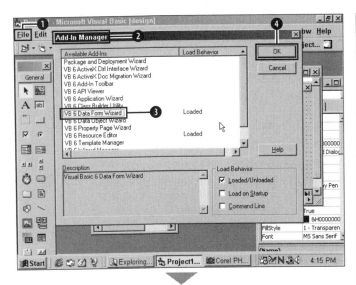

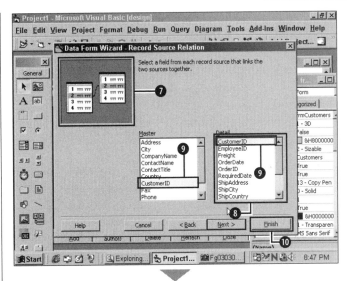

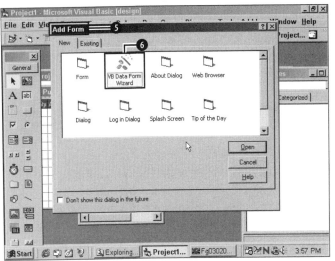

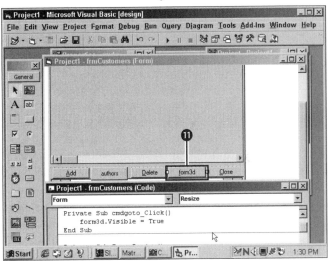

① *Click the Open icon on the toolbar to open the Newproj project.*

② *Select Add-In Manager from the Add-In menu.*

③ *Double-click the VB 6 Data Form Wizard option.*

④ *Click OK and pull down the Add-Ins menu to see the Data Form Wizard option.*

⑤ *Select Add Form from the Project menu.*

⑥ *Click the Data Form Wizard in the Add Form window.*

▶ *Select the defaults on each screen until you come to the Database name request. Select Nwind.mdb and name the form Form3d.*

▶ *Select the Master/Detail layout and the Customers for the Master record source. Select all fields.*

⑦ *Use the arrows near each pane to place Available fields in the Selected fields box.*

⑧ *Select Orders for the Detail record source. Select all fields. (Clicking the double-arrow icon selects all fields.)*

⑨ *Select CustomerID from both the Master and Detail tables as the field to link both.*

⑩ *Complete the selections and click Finish to create the form.*

⑪ *Place a* CommandButton *named cmdgoto on the Customers form. Set the caption properties to read "Form 3d."*

▶ *Double-click the new (cmdgoto) button and add this code to open the new form:*

Form3d.visible = true

▶ *Run the program and click the new button.*

51

Designing Projects with Wizards

Continued

Add-In Designer

The Add-In Designer helps speed development by letting you determine the default features of the selected add-in. These attributes are load behavior, name, target application, and version, as well as other properties.

Data Object Wizard

The Data Object Wizard is set up to create classes and user controls bound to the classes. However, you cannot create the user controls until you have first created the classes.

You should use this add-in if you want to create User controls, generate code regarding data relationships, and use text to improve user understanding.

Toolbar Wizard

If you have the Professional or Enterprise editions, you can use the Toolbar Wizard to create custom toolbars on forms. The Toolbar Wizard works by using the `Toolbar` control in the toolbox or through the Application Wizard.

You can place a toolbar on a form by selecting the `Toolbar` control from the toolbox. The `Toolbar` control must be installed in the toolbox. This is done from the Project menu by selecting the Components option and then selecting the Microsoft Windows Common Controls check box. Once selected, the Toolbar icon will appear on the toolbox. When you select the `Toolbar` control and place it on your form, it will be blank. You right-click and select properties to get the Toolbar menu. You can select the Buttons tab and fill in the appropriate information.

If you do not have the Professional or Enterprise edition of Visual Basic, you can create your own custom toolbar manually. You do this by selecting the `Image` control and

filling it with a bitmap selected from the Properties window Picture property. You then add code to make the function happen. You also can select the PictureBox tool from the toolbox. Then select controls from the toolbox, placing them inside the PictureBox.

A good reason to present the user with a graphic button is to quickly indicate what the button does. ToolTips can also be used to display the button's function. ToolTips can be generated automatically from the Property pages in the Toolbar Wizard, by typing in the text you want to be displayed.

Alternatively, if you cannot use the Toolbar Wizard, you can create the button with the `Image` control and set the ToolTipText property for the button to create the ToolTips you want.

Another way to populate your Wizard-created toolbar buttons with icons indicating their purposes is to use the `ImageList` control. This can be done quite easily by loading the toolbar bitmaps into the ImageList Property pages and then associating the ImageList with the properties on the toolbar.

TAKE NOTE

▶ CUSTOM TOOLTIPS

You can determine whether ToolTips are displayed when you move the mouse pointer over a toolbar button. ToolTips = Yes will cause them to be displayed. You also can set a variable using the Show ToolTips check box with the Customize Toolbar command on the Tools menu.

CROSS-REFERENCE

Chapter 23 provides further information on wizards with the Packaging and Deployment Wizard.

FIND IT ONLINE

View **http://support.microsoft.com/support/kb/articles/q190/1/12.asp** for more bug reports on wizards.

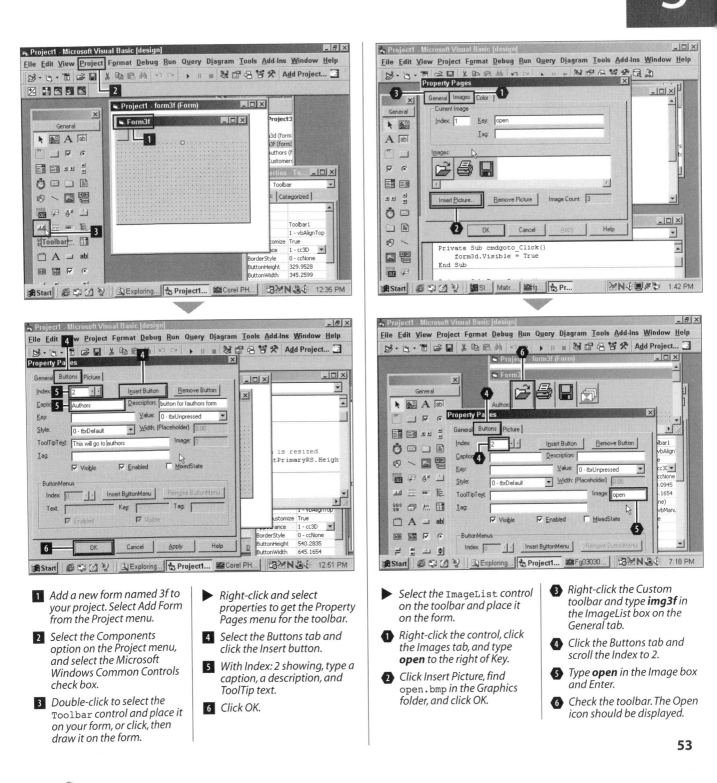

1. Add a new form named 3f to your project. Select Add Form from the Project menu.

2. Select the Components option on the Project menu, and select the Microsoft Windows Common Controls check box.

3. Double-click to select the Toolbar control and place it on your form, or click, then draw it on the form.

▶ Right-click and select properties to get the Property Pages menu for the toolbar.

4. Select the Buttons tab and click the Insert button.

5. With Index: 2 showing, type a caption, a description, and ToolTip text.

6. Click OK.

▶ Select the ImageList control on the toolbar and place it on the form.

1. Right-click the control, click the Images tab, and type **open** to the right of Key.

2. Click Insert Picture, find open.bmp in the Graphics folder, and click OK.

3. Right-click the Custom toolbar and type **img3f** in the ImageList box on the General tab.

4. Click the Buttons tab and scroll the Index to 2.

5. Type **open** in the Image box and Enter.

6. Check the toolbar. The Open icon should be displayed.

Designing Menus

The Application Wizard offers you customization for menus and submenus for your application. These menus, which you create by responding to prompts, contain working code. The menus you create can later be edited using the Menu Editor.

Menu Options

When you move through the Application Wizard screens, the third screen you encounter is the Menu and Submenu selection. Here, you either check or uncheck menu options.

The File menu is different for Explorer and SDI/MDI applications. The Single Document Interface (SDI) and Multiple Document Interface (MDI) are the two basic types of Windows interfaces. The SDI presents only one window or form to the user (WordPad is an example), whereas the MDI presents multiple windows to the user. Basically, the MDI applications allow more than one document to be open at any one time. This has come to represent the idea of the Windows environment. Excel and Word are examples of the MDI.

Explorer applications' menus are like those in the Windows Explorer. They include Open, Find, Send To, New, Delete, Rename, Properties, and Close.

The File menus for the SDI and MDI applications offer New, Open, Close, Save, Save As, Save All, Properties, Page Setup, Print Preview, Print, Send, and Exit.

All styles include a Most Recently Used list, with the files that have been most recently opened.

All types of applications have the options on the Edit menu to Undo, Cut, Copy, Paste, and Paste Special. Explorer-type applications may also use Select All and Invert Selection.

The View menu includes Toolbar, Status Bar, and Refresh and Options. Also included here is the Web Browser option to list Internet features you may add.

In addition, the Explorer-type applications have ListView Mode and Arrange Icons. The Arrange Icons command has a cascading menu that contains the by Date, by Name, by Type, and by Size commands.

The Tools menu is not checked by default. You will have to check the check box if you want it. It contains only the Options command.

The Window menu is available for all types of applications and includes New Window, Cascade, Tile Horizontal, Tile Vertical, and Arrange Icons commands as well as the list of open windows in the application.

The Help menu is available for all application styles and contains the Contents, Search for Help On, and About commands.

Menu Editor

In addition to these built-in menus, you can use the Menu Editor to create custom menus for your application. You select the Menu Editor from the Tools menu. The Menu Editor dialog box is similar to other dialog boxes in that it has text boxes to fill in with specifications tailored to your applications' needs.

The text you type in the Caption box will appear as the menu option titles on your form. The name will not appear on the form. The Index is for use with an array and does not reflect the order of the option. The arrow keys are to move your menu options around in the directions the keys indicate.

TAKE NOTE

ADDING NEW MENU OPTIONS

You can replace submenu items or add new ones by clicking the Plus sign at the right of the Menus window. When the dialog box pops up, type in your new submenu item's caption and Name you want to display on the menu. You can choose to make the item a separator (grouping line).

CROSS-REFERENCE

You will find more examples in Chapter 7.

FIND IT ONLINE

View **http://support.microsoft.com/support/kb/articles/ q191/0/37.asp** for features offered by each edition.

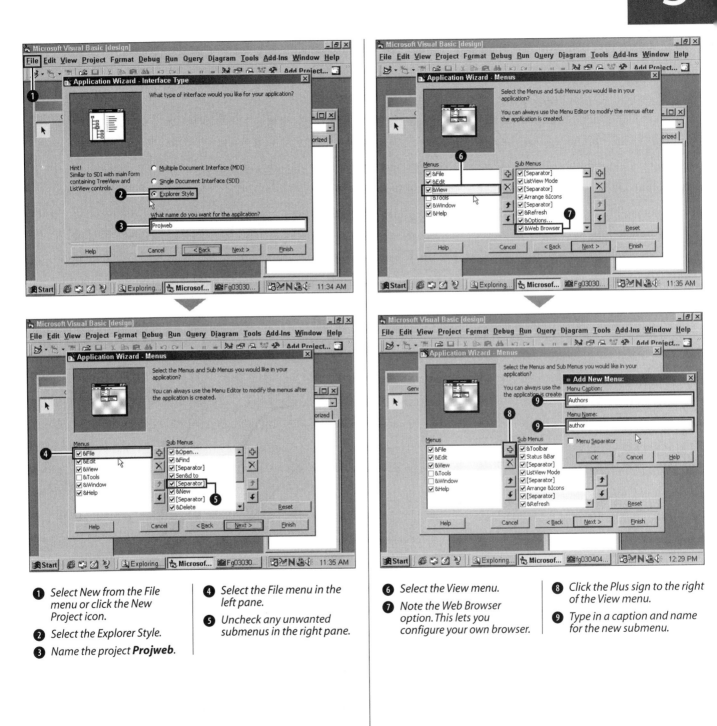

1. Select New from the File menu or click the New Project icon.

2. Select the Explorer Style.

3. Name the project **Projweb**.

4. Select the File menu in the left pane.

5. Uncheck any unwanted submenus in the right pane.

6. Select the View menu.

7. Note the Web Browser option. This lets you configure your own browser.

8. Click the Plus sign to the right of the View menu.

9. Type in a caption and name for the new submenu.

Making a Splash Screen

When you create your Application Wizard–generated project, you have the option of creating a Splash screen. The Splash screen is the window that greets you when you first launch an application. The company logo and any other important information not presented in the About form can be here. More often, the Splash screen is used to entertain users while the application is loading. Some companies get crazy with sound and graphics and some just use the screen to display the software title.

The Standard Forms window offers the options of creating a Splash screen, a Login dialog box, an Options dialog box for custom settings, and an About box. The Login dialog box requests a User Name and password from the user in order to proceed. The Options box has tabs that you can rename, add, or remove. The About box displays information about the version number and description.

The Splash screen will load first and display the company logo in the form of a bitmap, the company name, version, copyright, license, and anything else you want displayed on launching.

When you click Finish to complete the project, your forms will be displayed (except for those you did not choose). You can then select the Splash screen form and begin customizing it.

You will want to change the properties of each object so as to display your company, version number, copyright, and bitmap in the `PictureBox`. You do this by selecting each of the objects in turn and changing the captions in the Properties window. To save steps, you can select the object, right-click, and select Properties to pop up the Properties window.

When you change the text on the Splash screen form, you also can change any of its properties. With the object selected, you right-click and make the changes you want in the Properties window. Properties you can change are the `BackColor`, `ForeColor`, `Font`, `ToolTipText`, or anything on the property list. Of course, it may not make sense to change some properties, such as `Visible`, from true to false. To save steps, you can select multiple objects and change the properties for all of them at once, provided they share the same property. An example of this would be each text object on your Splash screen. When you select the `PictureBox`, you can select Picture on the property list. Click in the description area to the right of Picture, and then the box with the dots. This will bring up the Load Picture dialog box, which is actually the directory list box. You can go up levels or down until you find a picture you want for your logo.

If you do not have many pictures on your hard drive, you can go into the `VB98\graphics\bitmaps folder` and select one of the bitmaps there. Most of them are too small to fit into the default `PictureBox` the Application Wizard constructs for you, but you can resize the box. You can type a smaller number in the Properties Height and Width area or just click and drag it smaller.

If you selected a nice graphic for your `PictureBox`, you may notice that the gray background of the form does nothing for your logo. You may want to change the `BackColor` to match the logo. Continue modifying the Splash Screen to conform to your taste. As you can see, you can do a lot of customizing to your Wizard-generated application.

TAKE NOTE

▶ SAVING AND RETRIEVING THE PROFILE

Once you click Finish, you cannot go back and edit your project using the Application Wizard. You can retrieve a saved profile to guide future Application Wizard projects. The settings you can save in the profile are mainly the toolbar and menu selections. The profile file has the `.rwp` extension. When you run the Application Wizard next, you can use the previous settings.

CROSS-REFERENCE
Chapter 6 has more information on form development.

FIND IT ONLINE
For a great site about Splash screens, see **http://web2. airmail.net/gbeene/tut-samp.html#splash**.

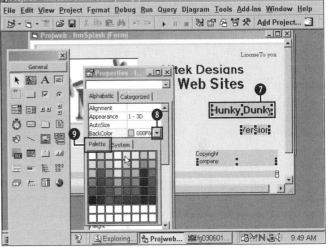

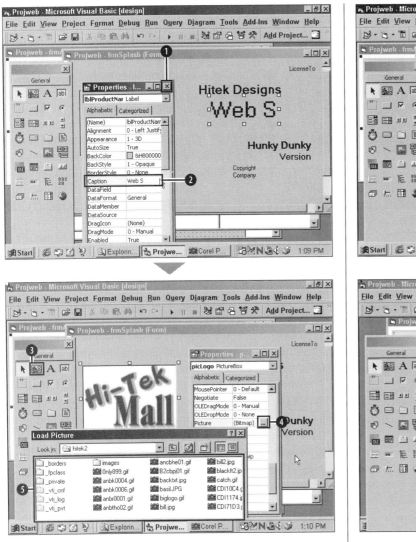

▶ When you are using the Application Wizard to create this application, be sure you check the box for Splash screen before you click Finish.

❶ Select the lblProductName Label and right-click to get the Properties window.

❷ Type in a new caption with your product name (Web S is pictured).

❸ Select the PictureBox and right-click for the Properties window.

❹ Click the area to the right of Picture properties and click the dots next to (Bitmap).

❺ Select a bitmap from the Load Picture window (hidropb2.jpg) that you copied from the **hi-tekmall.com** Web site.

❻ Select the rest of the text on the form and change it for your company, version, and copyright information.

❼ To change the BackColor property, first select each text object on the Splash screen form.

❽ Click the gray box and then the down arrow.

❾ Click the Palette tab and select a color to match your logo.

Running the Application

The ability to create an application without writing code is an impressive feat, but you probably will not want to stop there. There are many improvements you can make, while using what has already been done.

Enhancing the Splash Screen

If you run the application, you may find your new Splash screen can hardly be seen, because it flashes on and off so quickly.

You can fix that easily. The Application Wizard creates a Sub Main routine to control the order of form loading. This is how the first form can be displayed briefly and then the main form can be loaded. When you have multiple forms, Visual Basic must know which form is the Start Up form. Usually this is taken care of by having a Sub Main.

The Sub Main is found in the Project Explorer window under the Modules heading. You can select the Module and open it in the code window. You can edit the Sub Main and set up a pause that will allow the Splash screen to be seen before the Main form is loaded and displayed. The Sub Main module is used when there is no appropriate form to use as the application startup object. There must be a startup object that is first presented to the user. The Application Wizard automatically creates a Sub Main module, which you may use as is or modify according to your needs.

Putting on Finishing Touches

In addition to the Splash screen, you have three forms: an About form, the Browser, and the Main form. The Sub Main module loads the Main form after the Splash screen is unloaded. You can make similar modifications to the About form, tailoring it to your needs.

When you run the application, you will view the Splash screen, then the Main form. The buttons on the Main form toolbar will need to be completed. The code for the Main form has remarks that indicate which portions of the code

are incomplete. The remark statements are preceded by a single quotation mark. They also are displayed in green, as opposed to the executable code shown in blue or black by default.

The remark statements tell you what needs to be added to make the toolbar or menu fully functioning. For example, on the Main form, a ToDo remark statement says to "Add Forward button code" immediately following the Select Case "Forward." Also, a MsgBox advises you when you click that you need to "Add Forward button code."

Running the Web Browser

When you run the application, you can click the View menu and then select the Web Browser. This launches the Web Browser form, which was created as part of the Standard forms in the Application Wizard.

Now you can see what you have done! You have made your own Web browser. If you are connected to the Internet via a service provider, you will by default go to microsoft.com. If you click the Home icon, you will go to the Home site that you have designated when you configured your browser. You can move Forward and Back, Stop, Refresh, go Home, and Search. You also can click the Help menu and select the About option to view the About form.

TAKE NOTE

GENERATED CODE

Select the About option on the Help menu on the Main form to view the About form. Though it looks simple, there is a lot of code behind it. Use the View Code option by right-clicking the form. There is a lot of functionality in this apparently simple form. Click System Info to view all you ever wanted to know about your computer system.

CROSS-REFERENCE

Chapter 21 contains more information on Web programming.

FIND IT ONLINE

View **http://msdn.microsoft.com/library/devprods/vs6/vb/html/ vbwizapplicationwizardtheinternet** for a good discussion of the Wizard on the Internet.

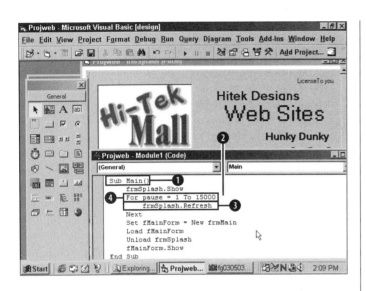

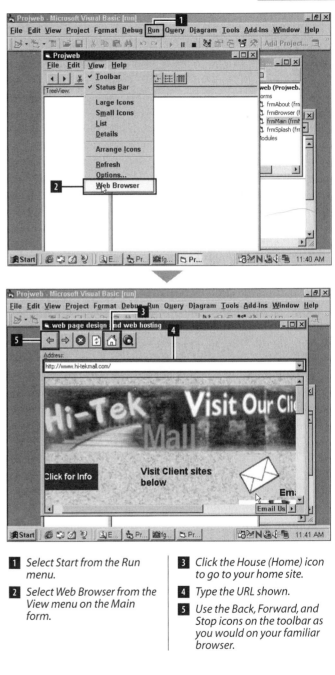

① *Double-click the module in the Project Explorer to view the code window and scroll to the Sub Main routine.*

② *Insert the code **For pause = 1 to 15000** after the second line. Be sure to place a Next after the For in the loop.*

③ *Type the line **frmSplash.Refresh** between the* For *and the* Next *lines.*

④ *If the form stays too long on the screen, you can use a smaller number than 15000.*

Listing 3-1: The Pause Loop

```
Attribute VB_Name = "Module1"
Public fMainForm As frmMain

Sub Main()
    frmSplash.Show
    frmSplash.Refresh
    Set fMainForm = New frmMain
    Load fMainForm
    Unload frmSplash

fMainForm.Show
End Sub
```

1 *Select Start from the Run menu.*

2 *Select Web Browser from the View menu on the Main form.*

3 *Click the House (Home) icon to go to your home site.*

4 *Type the URL shown.*

5 *Use the Back, Forward, and Stop icons on the toolbar as you would on your familiar browser.*

Personal Workbook

Q&A

1 What is a wizard?

_____

_____

_____

2 What is the best use of the Application Wizard?

_____

_____

_____

3 What is the difference between the Standard forms and those created by the Data Forms Wizard?

_____

_____

_____

4 What is the purpose of icons on the toolbar?

_____

_____

_____

5 How would you display a toolbar button's function in text?

_____

_____

_____

6 How do you add new menu items to the default menus in the Application Wizard?

_____

_____

_____

7 What is a good reason to have a Splash screen?

_____

_____

_____

8 What does the About form offer?

_____

_____

_____

ANSWERS: PAGE 520

EXTRA PRACTICE

1 Make an application in Application Wizard and select all the Standard forms. Customize each menu with new options.

2 Do the preceding, and edit the toolbar options in the toolbar Property pages, changing the ToolTips text on the buttons. Then run the application and drag the mouse over the buttons.

3 Make your own toolbar using the `PictureBox` and `ImageList` controls.

4 Create a new project in the Application Wizard, selecting the Splash Screen option. Customize the screen to be as flamboyant as possible.

5 Design a project for Application Wizard. This time, carefully select the menus, submenus, and forms you will use. Make sure there is a rationale for using them.

REAL-WORLD APPLICATIONS

✔ Your mother has a database recording all her dogs' visits to the veterinarian. She currently has no way to access the data, as she doesn't have the program used to create the database. She asks you to set up a Visual Basic application so that she can view the data.

✔ Your boss wants to set up a Web browser for her staff to use. She does not want them to use the existing browsers, as she needs them to have a custom menu without toolbar buttons to move backward and forward.

✔ Your client was given an Access mailing list, but he doesn't have Access nor does he know how to use a database program. He is hiring you to set up an application to view and print his database records. Design the application.

Visual Quiz

How and where does the form on the right display the URL?

_____

_____

_____

_____

_____

_____

_____

CHAPTER 4

Understanding Basic Concepts

Most programmers would agree that the purpose of programming in the first place is to extend your control over your application environment. The wide range of tools available in this environment facilitates creating programs with Visual Basic 6. It is likely that programmers of the past, using older procedural languages, might have wished they had it so good.

With Visual Basic, you can create a user interface by placing control objects on a form that allows the user to carry out some action. These objects are placed with a mouse click. You also can set properties (characteristics) for each object placed. For example, the button you place on the form will have characteristics, such as a label, a caption, and dimensions.

The Graphic User Interface is the powerful attribute of Visual Basic that makes it completely innovative and divergent from past languages. Using Visual Basic and the Integrated Development Environment (IDE) has more in common with drawing a schematic of all the functions you want your application to have than it has with traditional procedural languages. It is more like painting a picture than writing a story. Perhaps one way to sum up object-based programming is to say that the focus has shifted from the program to the user. Users command the environment. Here, the user is in charge, and the language is offered as an extension of the medium. Conventional languages force the programmer to conform to its structure.

However, the objects belonging on a form will ultimately need code attached to them in order to carry out the intended functions and activities. It is not enough to create the look; you must also create the feel. In order to make these objects and controls come to life, it is important to learn some traditional programming concepts and see how they relate to Visual Basic.

Recognizing Objects

Visual Basic is object based. Much has been written about the Microsoft Windows object-based languages. How does an object-based language differ from a traditional procedural language? In a traditional language you are focused on carrying out functions in a top-down, stepwise manner. In object-based languages, you build the code around *objects*. The programmer is oriented toward an object on a form. In that scenario, a user does something with the object (mouse click). This event triggers other occurrences depending upon the code. Thus, objects are entities that you invent and use to accomplish the purpose of your application.

The object metaphor is used to emulate the way people are believed to view the world. People are visually oriented, so object-based languages are also visually based. Rather than imposing the logical and highly structured way of thinking on their users, object-based languages make an appeal to those new to programming, who have no preconceived notions about how programs should be constructed. In this way, object-based languages, including Visual Basic, are designed to be convenient for people to learn and use.

Of course, this does not mean that visual, object-based languages throw logic out the window. The major change is in how the language manages the applications you create.

Every object has a *class*. In fact, objects are classes. The proper designation of an object is class. The properties and methods of an object are contained in its Class. A Class also functions as a template for creating other objects. If this definition seems circular, remember that objects can themselves contain other objects. Classes combine data and procedures into a unit. For example, when you create and name a form, it becomes a class of its own.

Every object also has a name. For example, if you place a `ComboBox` on a form, you must give the box a name, or Visual Basic will name it for you. Visual Basic names it `Combo1` if it is the first `ComboBox` you have placed on the form. You may not want it named in numerical order, so you can also name it yourself.

The root object at the base of the object model is the object that contains all the other objects in the model. Even though they are the foundation for all objects in the object model, root objects can be created. For example, the root object of an inventory system might have a product collection. Each product object in the collection might contain a price collection, so that you could access a particular price object by referring to it as being in the product container, which is within the inventory container. For example, `Root.inventory.product.price`.

The concept of containership extends beyond Windows applications into other areas of mathematics, computers and even philosophy. The idea is that you can associate some things with other things by advancing a hierarchy of ownership. If you can associate one item with another by seeing that it belongs to the other because it is contained by that object, then you have a practical way of manipulating large numbers of objects.

TAKE NOTE

▶ **WHAT ARE OBJECTS?**

Objects include both code and data. They have properties, events, and methods. *Properties* are characteristics of the object. *Events* are the things the objects actually do. *Methods* are used to cause the objects to do something. Objects must be created from *classes*. Objects are always specific occurrences of a class. Visual Basic stores an internal identification number for each and every object defined in an application.

CROSS-REFERENCE

Chapter 2 discusses browsing objects in the Object Browser.

FIND IT ONLINE

Elementary concepts covered at **http://msdn. microsoft.com/library/devprods/vs6/vb/html/ vbcontheoneminuteterminologist.htm**.

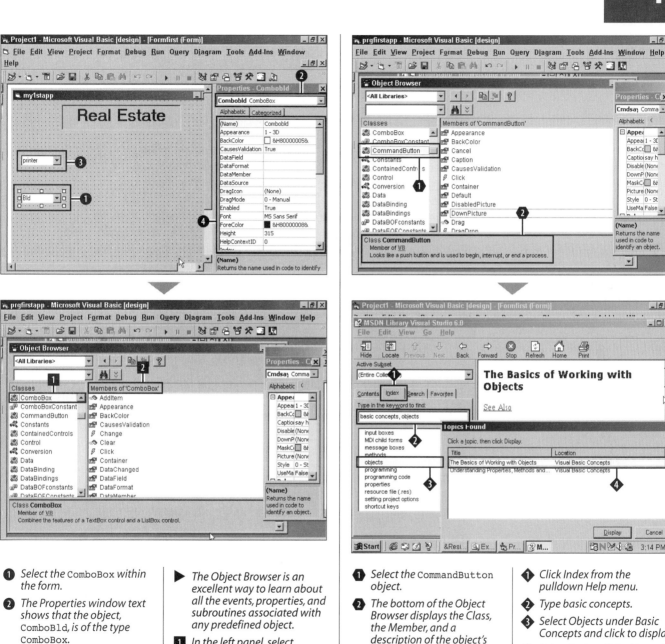

① Select the ComboBox within the form.

② The Properties window text shows that the object, ComboBld, is of the type ComboBox.

③ The properties of each ComboBox may be different, but they are both ComboBoxes.

④ Each object has a list of properties, shown in the Property box and in the Object Browser.

▶ The Object Browser is an excellent way to learn about all the events, properties, and subroutines associated with any predefined object.

■ In the left panel, select ComboBox.

② The Members of ComboBox are shown in the right panel. "Members" includes properties, events, and subroutines.

① Select the CommandButton object.

② The bottom of the Object Browser displays the Class, the Member, and a description of the object's functions.

① Click Index from the pulldown Help menu.

② Type basic concepts.

③ Select Objects under Basic Concepts and click to display.

④ Select Basics of Working with Objects.

65

Using Variables

Theoretically, a variable is anything that has two or more categories. For example, the variable Sex or (Gender) has two subclasses, Male and Female. In this manner, a program might refer to a variable called `Name`, which can hold any value. Without knowing the exact contents, the `Name` variable can be used in different ways.

The ability to work with variables is one of the most useful feature of computers. Computers work with specific values, but you in your programming do not. The idea of variables is important to understanding the way programs work. When a variable is assigned a certain value, the value is contained in the variable until either it is replaced with a new value or the program ends, whichever comes first. The values of a variable can change during the course of a program, depending upon conditions and events occurring in the program. Variables can also be assigned values, much like constants. Variables can be as simple as:

```
A = 1
B = 2
```

Or variables can be more complex:

```
D1 = INT(D / 10000)
D2 = INT((D - D1 * 10000) / 100
D3 = INT(D - (D1 * 100 + D2) * 100)
FF = 27 + D1
```

Declaring variables at the start of a program is highly recommended. For example:

```
Dim A As Integer
```

Variables defined in the course of the program, such as

```
A1 = A1 - N1 * 1000
    N1 = INT(A1 / 100)
```

are called Implicit variable declarations. This is the default in Visual Basic, and the variables will be automatically created on the fly. Being able to locate variables definitely helps the debugging process. Defining variables implicitly means that you may have difficulty remembering where each of your variables is defined or how they are spelled. In order to have the Visual Basic system monitor the declaration of variables up front, you use the command:

```
Option Explicit
```

This way, Visual Basic won't let you define a variable that has not been declared first. Another good reason for using the `Option Explicit` command is that variables that are not assigned types will be automatically assigned the type *Variant*. Although Variant types are flexible, they reduce an application's performance. Variants may hold any type of data and automatically convert to the needed data type when used in an expression.

The Dim statement is used to declare variables in Visual Basic.

```
Dim Variablename [As datatype]
```

You can declare several variables at the same time, but the type must be restated after each variable, or the type will revert to Variant. For example, use:

```
Dim A As integer, B As Integer
```

rather than

```
Dim A, B As Integer
```

In this example, A will become a Variant type.

TAKE NOTE

▶ INTEGER TYPE VERSUS VARIANT

In `Dim Age As Integer`, Age is declared as an integer data type. This is more efficient because integers require fewer bytes for storage than the Variant type.

In `Age = 95`, Age is not declared, so it becomes a Variant data type. This is less efficient because more storage space will be required in memory and on disk.

CROSS-REFERENCE

Chapters 10 and 11 delve further into the use of variables.

FIND IT ONLINE

See **http://msdn.microsoft.com/library/conf/html/sa95f.htm** for more information on variables.

All variable names begin with an alphabetic character and are a maximum of 255 characters. There cannot be an embedded period (.) in the name. Variable names are unique within the scope of the procedure. That is, you are allowed to have more than one variable of the same name if they are each contained within a specific form or procedure. However, it is a good policy to give each variable in a project a unique name. Troubleshooting will be greatly aided when you can readily identify all variable names in the project.

Listing 4-3: More Variable Calculations

```
FOR X = 4 TO 12
PCT(X) = 100 * ((ROW(X) / (ROW(1))))
NEXT
IF PRIM1 = 2 AND PRIM2 = 1 THEN ROW(28) =
ROW(28) + 1
IF PRIM1 = 2 AND PRIM2 = 2 THEN ROW(29) =
ROW(29) + 1
IF PRIM1 = 3 AND PRIM2 = 1 THEN ROW(30) =
ROW(30) + 1
IF PRIM1 = 3 AND PRIM2 = 2 THEN ROW(31) =
ROW(31) + 1
```

Listing 4-1: A Simple Variable Declaration

```
Dim Sex As Integer
Dim Sexname As String
```

Listing 4-2: A Variable in Calculation

```
Dim Birthyear As Integer
Dim Curryear As Integer
Age  = Curryear — Birthyear
```

Listing 4-4: Explicit and Implicit Variable Definitions

```
Dim myvariable as String
    Myvariabl2="You pushed my button"
```

❶ Sex *is declared as an integer with the idea that it has two categories: 1=male and 2=female.*

❷ Sexname *is declared as a* String *in order to enable names (male and female) to be used as variable categories.*

■ Birthyear *and* Curryear *are both defined as integer variables.*

■ Age *is defined as an integer and results from subtracting* Birthyear *from* Curryear.

▶ *This example might also have declared* Birthdate *and* Currdate *as date types. The subtraction would have yielded an exact age, rather than one rounded to years. In that case,* Age *should have been returned in days.*

❶ *The variables* Row(x) *are used to hold values based upon the values of* Prim1 *and* Prim2.

❷ *The* ROW(x) = ROW(X) + 1 *routine is used to continue incrementing a value that the variables are used to contain.*

❸ *Each time a line of code is executed, the row variables are incremented by 1.*

◆ myvariable *is declared explicitly.*

◆ Myvariabl2 *is declared implicitly.*

Learning about Constants

Another way values can be used in a Visual Basic application is by entering the value itself in the statement. This type of value is called a *constant* and cannot be manipulated by the program. A constant is inserted directly into the expression in which it is to be used. For example, the calculation that is necessary to convert Fahrenheit temperatures into Celsius temperatures is

```
Cel=5/9 * (Fah-32)
```

In this expression, the `Cel` and the `Fah` are variables because their values can change. The 32, 5, and 9 are constants, because their values never change.

Constants are simply entities with assigned values that do not change in the course of the program's execution.

User-Defined Constants

Constants may also be user defined to hold specific values for use in an application. These user-defined constants are prefaced by the keyword `Const`, as in this example:

```
Public Const Blue = "4"
```

Names of constants are typically in upper- and lowercase, with the prefix representing the object library defining the constant. The Visual Basic library constants are prefaced with the letters `vb` so as to avoid conflict with those in other libraries.

If you wish a constant to be used within one procedure and not available to other procedures, then it should be declared within that procedure. If a constant is declared in the Declaration section of the program module, it will be available to all its procedures.

Defining your constants within the program makes much more understandable code than simply repeating the value for the constant each time it must be referenced.

```
Dim Fah As Integer
Dim Cel As Integer
Public Const confahcel As  Integer = 32
```

```
Public Const concelfahdiv As Integer = 9
Public Const concelfahvalu As Integer = 5
```

The formula would then read:

```
Cel=concelfahvalu/concelfahdiv * (Fah -
confahcel)
```

System-Defined Constants

Visual Basic also provides system constants that can replace actual values. Opening the Object Browser window and listing the contents of the Visual Basic library shows the built-in constants in Visual Basic.

For example, the function `DateDiff` qualifies as a constant, simplifying date calculations:

```
DateDiff(interval, firstdate, seconddate[,
firstdayofweek[, firstweekofyear]])
```

`Calendar`, `Color`, `Date Format`, `File attribute`, `File`, and `Directory I/O` are some of the Visual Basic System Constants providing functions. As an example, the vb constant can be substituted for the actual value of the color:

```
ForeColor = vbRed
```

TAKE NOTE

ASSIGNMENT STATEMENTS

In a mathematical expression, the equal sign is used to show equality between the left and right sides of the equation. In a computer language, this is called an assignment statement and does not express equality. It tells the computer to take the value expressed on the right side of the statement and place it into the variable on the left side.

CROSS-REFERENCE
Chapters 10 and 11 are further references for using constants in expressions.

FIND IT ONLINE
See the intrinsic constant definition: http://msdn.microsoft.com/library/devprods/vs6/vb/html/vbdefinstrinsicconstant.htm.

▶ From the Start menu, select Microsoft Visual Basic 6.0 Tools, then API Text Viewer.

❶ Select Load Text File (Win32api.txt) from the File menu.

❷ Select Constants from the API Type drop-down box.

❸ Select the desired Constant from available items.

❹ Declare scope as Public or Private.

❺ Click Add to add Windows procedures to Visual Basic programs.

Table 4-1: COLOR CONSTANTS

Constant	Value	Description
vbBlack	0x0	Black
vbRed	0xFF	Red
vbGreen	0xFF00	Green
vbYellow	0xFFFF	Yellow
vbBlue	0xFF0000	Blue
vbMagenta	0xFF00FF	Magenta
vbCyan	0xFFFF00	Cyan
vbWhite	0xFFFFFF	White

Understanding Data Types

As outlined previously, in the "Variables" and "Constants" sections, both variables and constants have data types. In addition, functions and values assigned to properties have data types. Generally, in Visual Basic, all entities dealing with data have data types.

The data type identifier determines how the value of the variable or constant is stored in computer memory or on disk. Numeric data types require less space than string data types. Of the numeric types, integers require less space than single precision (single). Single precision requires less space than double precision (double).

Integer Type

If your data will always be expressed in whole numbers, your data type should be `Integer` or `Long` integer.

`Integers` must be within the range of −32,768 to +32,767. This type is stored in only two bytes of memory or disk space and is 16 bit. This type would work if you were storing a person's age in whole years, rather than as years, months, and days. It would also work for hours worked, number of pencils sold, or anything that does not use fractions and always has a value no higher than 32,767.

Long Integer Type

`Long` integers are 32-bit numbers and may contain higher numbered integers (values from −2,147,483,648 to +2,147,483,647). This type requires four bytes for storage, compared with two bytes for `Integer`. For example, if a zip code is to be stored, it must not be `Integer` type, since even five-digit codes are greater than 32767. Of course, if a zip code has a hyphen after the first five digits, it must be stored as a `String` type.

Floating Point

Floating-point values have higher ranges than `Integer`, `Long` integer, or `Currency` types but also are subject to small rounding errors.

`Single` precision types are used when you have fractions (numbers with decimal places) to store. The highest positive value of this type is 3.402823E+38, or 3.4 times 10 to the 38th power. If you were storing weight in pounds for commodities, you might use the `Single` type. This type is stored in memory using the 32-bit IEEE format (four bytes).

The `Double` Precision type is commonly used for extremely large numbers with many positions to the right of the decimal point. The highest positive value of a `Double` data type is 1.79769313486232D+308. D as used here to separate the mantissa and exponent in a numeric literal causes the value to be treated as a `Double` data type. Likewise, using E in the same fashion treats the value as `Single` data as just shown. Scientific or financial work often uses this type. `Double` Precision was formerly used for large budget calculations prior to the advent of the `Currency` type.

TAKE NOTE

REGIONAL SETTINGS IN WINDOWS

Modifying your Regional settings on the `Windows Control Panel` is important. You should choose the `Short` date style (`MM/dd/yyyy`). Otherwise, you will not have Y2K compliance and you will be unable to do date calculations across the century. The date argument here is dependent upon the Regional settings. For `DateDiff`, to calculate the number of days between first and second dates, use either Day of year (y) or Day (d). When interval is Weekday (w), `DateDiff` returns the number of weeks between the two dates.

CROSS-REFERENCE

Chapter 10 discusses data types.

FIND IT ONLINE

Chuck Eastom's site gives a summary of data types.
http://www.geocities.com/~chuckeastom/vb/vb.htm.

Currency

As the name implies, `Currency` is used to store monetary values. In Visual Basic, `Currency` is stored as 64-bit numbers in eight bytes of space. Unlike the floating-point types, this type provides a fixed point with 15 places to the left of the decimal point and 4 digits to the right of the decimal. This type is used for financial calculations, such as budgets.

Byte Type

The `Byte` type is used to store binary data and has the range 0–255. It cannot be used for negative numbers. It should be used to read and write from files when converting data from one file type to another. Using `Byte` variables to store binary data preserves it during format conversions. When `String` variables are converted between ANSI and Unicode formats, any binary data in the variable is corrupted.

String Type

`String` variables usually contain letters but may contain any numeric or nonnumeric character. The data are stored with each character in one byte. While `String` variables can contain numbers, you cannot do calculations on them without first converting them to numbers.

You can specify fixed-length `Strings`, using the format:

```
Dim FirstName As  String * 20
```

This results in the variable or database field allocating 20 spaces for `FirstName`. Since first names vary in size, the space will be filled with blanks if the name is shorter than 20 characters. If the first name is Amy, then the variable will be padded with 17 blank spaces at the end of "Amy." If the name exceeds 20 characters, it will be truncated to 20. The default for `Strings` is to be variable, so that the space allocated changes depending upon the size required by the data entered.

`Strings` can be converted to numbers in order to carry out calculations. The `String` data can be converted to numbers with the `Val` function and back to `String` with the `Str` function.

You also can use the `ReDim` command to change the type of a variable. The `Set` command is used to assign objects to variables and convert variables into arrays.

Variant Type

The Variant type is automatically assigned to any variable that is not declared using the `Dim` statement. In a sense, it lets you off the hook, because you don't have to know what type you want to assign. On the other hand, if you are doing numeric calculations, it will not be efficient, either in the execution of the program or in maximizing storage space. In addition, you may experience errors when adding or subtracting Variant type variables.

A Variant variable type is a type that can change its type on the fly, depending upon what is required, rather than it is a variable of no type.

When you concatenate strings, you must use the & operator instead of the + operator. Variants can also contain three special values: `Empty`, `Null`, and `Error`.

Continued

> ### TAKE NOTE
>
> #### ▶ OPTIMIZING THE SPEED OF APPLICATIONS
>
> The Variant is the default data type in Visual Basic. This works where processing speed is not an issue. If you want to optimize the real speed of your application, you should avoid Variant variables. Because Visual Basic converts Variants to the actual data type at run time, operations involving other simple data types eliminate this step and are faster than their Variant equivalents.

Understanding Data Types
Continued

Boolean Type

The `Boolean` type is declared for a 0/1- or Yes/No-type variable. It is used for storing variable values such as changing an event from `off` to on or on to `off`. The example that follows shows how a `Boolean` might be used to set a flag when some condition has been met:

```
Dim Flag As Boolean
   If FlagMode = 1 Then
   Flag = True
End if
```

Date Type

Date values may be stored and date calculations may be carried out on them, without writing special algorithms to add and subtract dates. The calculation of age by subtracting birth date from the current date is a common practice in order to obtain age. With the `Date` type, this need not be difficult.

Numeric values can be converted to `Date`. When this is done, values to the left of the decimal represent date information, while values to the right of the decimal represent time. Midnight is 0, and midday is 0.5. Negative whole numbers represent dates before December 30, 1899.

Object Type

The `Object` type is used to declare objects within an application. They are stored in 32-bit (four-byte) format. Variables declared as `Object` type can later be assigned (using the `Set` statement) to refer to an actual object.

```
Dim objDb As Object
Set objDb = OpenDatabase("c:\Vb5\Biblio.mdb")
```

Object type variables should be specified as definite classes (`TextBox` or `ComboBox`) and not merely generic objects.

TAKE NOTE

VARIANT TYPES

When you do not assign a type, Variant is assigned by default. There are pitfalls with this. More space in memory and disk is required. For example, Variants use 16 bytes of space, regardless how much you store. If you store only numbers 1–9 or letters A–Z, each uses 16 bytes of space. This will make a huge difference if you have a large file.

CROSS-REFERENCE
Chapter 10 also discusses data types.

FIND IT ONLINE
View Data Types at **http://msdn.microsoft.com/library/books/techlang/dnjet/apa_body_4.htm**.

Table 4-2: DATA TYPES AND USES

Data Type	Description
Integer	Whole numbers within the range of –32,768 to +32,767. Stored in 2 bytes; 16 bits.
Long	Whole numbers stored as 32-bit numbers that may contain higher numbered integers (values from –2,147,483.648 to +2,147,483,647). Requires 4 bytes.
Single	For fractional values. Highest positive value of this type is 3.402823E+38.
Double	The highest positive value of a Double data type is 1.79769313486232D+308.
Currency	Provides a fixed point with 15 places to the left of the decimal point and 4 digits to the right of the decimal. Used for financial data.
String	Usually contains letters, but may contain any numeric or nonnumeric character. Stored with each character in one byte.
Date	Used to store date values. Allows date additions and subtraction without special algorithms.
Byte	The Byte type is used to store binary data and has the range 0–255. Not for negative numbers. Used to read and write from files.
Boolean	Used for 0/1- or Yes/No-type variables.
Object	Used to declare objects within an application. Stored in 32-bit (4-byte) format.
Variant	Assigned to any variable that is not declared using the Dim statement.

Learning about Operators

Operators are symbols used in arithmetic and string expressions. Expressions are combinations of variables, constants, or any object used to calculate a value. The simplest of expressions might be 1 + 1 = 2. In this example, the plus and equal signs are operators.

Operators are not limited to those involving arithmetic calculations. Operators can be used on text and numeric variables, making comparisons between variables.

The arithmetic operators are the plus (+), minus (-), multiplication sign (*) and the division sign (/).

Along with these familiar operators, there are operators used for comparing variables, such as the equal sign (=), symbols for not equal (<>), less than (<), greater than (>), less than or equal (<=) and greater than or equal (>=).

```
A< = B, B > = C, A <> B, C = D
```

The `Like` operator is used for pattern matching and the Is operator for verification of object references.

`Not`, `And`, `Or`, `Xor`, `Eqv`, and `Imp` are logical operators used on integer-level data that evaluate the binary form of a number.

Operators in text expressions are used to concatenate variables. The most typical example is one of combining first and last name in an address book. If `firstname` and `lastname` are separate variables and if they need to be combined into one variable to print mailing labels, you can use an expression like:

```
Fullname = firstname + " " + lastname
```

In this example, the quotation marks are to produce a space between the two names. A street address is another familiar use of concatenation.

```
Address   =  City + ", " + State + " " + Zip
```

This example will print a comma followed by a space after `City` and a space between `State` and `Zip`.

In addition to their use in expressions, it is important to understand the use of operator precedence. There is an order in which calculations are made. If the operators are of equal precedence, they are evaluated from left to right.

Multiplication and division take precedence over addition and subtraction, so the evaluation of an expression depends upon which operators are given and in what order. For example, if you are summing a series of scores and then dividing the result by the number of scores to obtain an average, you will not get the result you want if the expression is like this:

```
ScoreAverage = 12 + 14 + 10 / 3
```

This will not work the way you expect because the division will be carried out on the value 10 before the three scores are summed. You would need to enclose the expression in parentheses to ensure that the three scores are summed prior to dividing. The expression would look like this:

```
ScoreAverage = (12 + 14 + 10) / 3
```

This expression makes sure that the addition is done before the division.

Greater complexity in an expression requires a good understanding of operator precedence, as the following example shows:

```
ScoreAverage = ((12 + 14 + 10) * 2) / 3
```

Here, the sum of scores is multiplied by 2, then divided by 3. Two sets of parentheses are used to first sum the three scores, then multiply, then carry out the division on the product.

CROSS-REFERENCE

Chapter 10 deals with operators and expressions. Chapter 13 covers operators in the course of database functions.

FIND IT ONLINE

View more about Visual Basic operators: **http://msdn.microsoft.com/library/officedev/ access/d1 /s1228b.htm.**

TAKE NOTE

▶ **OPERATOR PRECEDENCE**

In expressions with several types of operators, arithmetic operators are evaluated first, comparison operators are evaluated next, and logical operators are evaluated last. If all operators are of the same type, they will be evaluated left to right. However, parentheses will supersede this priority and result in specific parts of the expression being evaluated first. Even though parentheses ensure the priority of expressions inside them, operator precedence is maintained within parentheses.

Table 4-3: NUMERIC OPERATORS

Operator	Meaning
+, –	Unary positive, negative
+	Addition
–	Subtraction
*	Multiplication
/	Division

Table 4-4: ORDER OF PRECEDENCE

Arithmetic	Comparison	Logical
Exponentiation (^)	Equality (=)	Not
Negation (–)	Inequality (<>)	And
Multiplication and division (*, /)	Less than (<)	Or
Integer division (\)	Greater than (>)	Xor
Modulus arithmetic (Mod)	Less than or equal to (<=)	Eqv
Addition and subtraction (+, –)	Greater than or equal to (>=)	Imp
String concatenation (&)	Like	Is

Using Procedures

Modules and procedures are ways of organizing code in a program. A *module* contains the procedures and functions that put the code into operation.

Procedures are self-contained routines within a larger program that carry out specific tasks. Procedures should be used when you need to repeat the same process over and over in a program. The procedure can be called many times but appears in the code once. The format for the procedure is:

```
Sub ProcWhatEver (Argument)
    commands
End Sub
```

To create a procedure, you select the object on the form to which you wish to attach code. You double-click the object to access the Code window. Then select the corresponding object in the left scroll bar. Then select a template in the Code Editor, selecting a procedure from the Procedure box.

After you select the procedure, you should select the Name property of your controls before you start writing event procedures for them. You must remember to change the name of the procedure to match the new name of the control if you change the name of a control after attaching a procedure to it. If this is not done, the control will not be matched to the procedure.

For example, suppose we select an object called Command1, a button on a form. Double-click the object, Command1. When you see the Code window, Command1 will be selected in the Object box (because you selected it). Click the down arrow on the right drop-down menu (the Procedure box) to select the procedure type you want. In this case, it will be the Click procedure. The Procedure syntax is then filled in for you. Whatever you select in the Procedure box will be placed in the code attached to your selected object.

At that point, all you need to do is type in the commands you wish to carry out in response to the click event. Let us suppose you want to say "Hello" to your user. This is how your procedure might look when viewed in the Code window:

```
Sub Command1_Click ()
    Dim msg As String
    msg = "Hello-"
    MsgBox msg
End Sub
```

Here the object is Command1 and the event procedure is Command1_Click (). The variable msg is created in order to display the String "Hello" when the button is clicked.

TAKE NOTE

▶ NAMING RULES

There are rules to be followed in naming objects in procedures. Procedures complete names are shown in the Code window with the object and procedure name separated by an underscore. In the preceding example, Command1_Click () combines the name of the object with the event name. The underscore separates the object and event. In order to distinguish the object further, it might be named cmd-hello, by typing in the new name in the Properties window in the right column beside the (Name) prompt. If a form were the selected object, the event procedure would include the word Form, followed by an underscore and the event name.

CROSS-REFERENCE

There is further discussion on events and procedures in Chapters 5, 10, and 11.

FIND IT ONLINE

View Event Procedure at http://www.itlibrary.com/reference/library/0672310643/htm/ch05.htm#Heading11.

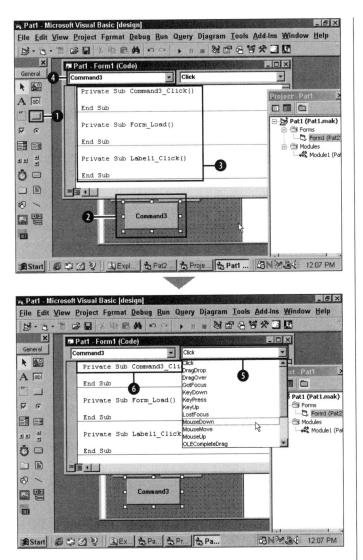

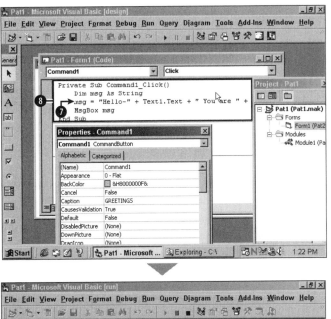

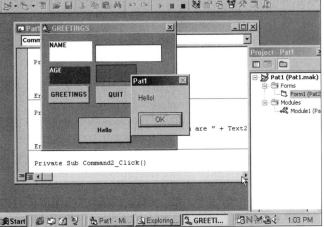

❶ To create a new project, draw a command button on the form.

❷ Name the object Command3.

❸ Select Command3 and double-click it.

❹ Command3 will be selected in the Object box (because you selected it).

❺ Press the down arrow on the Procedure box in the code window and choose the Click procedure.

❻ When you see the Code window, the Procedure syntax is then filled in for you.

❼ You want to say "Hello" to your user when the Hello key is pressed.

❽ Type in the commands you wish to carry out in response to the click event.

▶ This is how your procedure might look when viewed in the Code window.

▶ This is how the procedure will look when run.

Making Decisions

It is difficult to imagine a computer program in which there are no decisions to be made. This is because programming involves testing to see if certain conditions are met, and then taking action depending upon the status of events occurring in the program. Programs are decision-makers.

Statements

Statements are complete units using expressions to describe an action, make a declaration, or identify an object. Statements usually take up a single line.

The If Statement

The `If` statement and the `If` command block are perhaps the most often used decision-making technique in the history of programming. In its simplest form, the `If` statement tests for specific conditions, for ranges of conditions, or for the lack of certain conditions. It can be expressed as a single line of code.

```
If A = 1 then B = 0:C = D
```

This means that given A has a value of 1, B will take the value of 0 and C will take the value of D. In Visual Basic 6, however, the single-line statement is seldom used. More often the code will look like this:

```
If A = 1 then
        B = 0
        C = D
End if
```

When used as a block statement, `If` must be terminated with `End if`.

If-Then-Else-End If

Single line statements must not contain the keyword, `Else`. This statement cannot be expressed in a single line but must be written in a block:

```
If A = 1 Then
        B = 0
ElseIf A = 2 Then
        B = 2
Else
        B = 3
End If
```

The statements are evaluated and the condition immediately following the `If` is tested. If the condition exists (true), the statements following `Then` are executed. In the event that the condition does not exist (false), the `ElseIf` conditions are evaluated. Under the `ElseIf` conditions, each condition is tested to see if it exists (is true). If none of these conditions is found to be true, then the testing moves on to the `Else` statements. Finally, after each process is completed, in a top-down manner, the program execution continues with statements following the `End if` statement.

TAKE NOTE

AN ALTERNATIVE TO IF

If you have a number of conditions to test for, it may be helpful to consider using `Select Case` instead. If there are going to be several occurrences of one test, `Select Case` will use less code and will be easier to read and debug than `If...Then...Else...End if`.

CROSS-REFERENCE

Chapter 10 gives more intensive examples of branching statements.

FIND IT ONLINE

For more information on making decisions, see http://www.itlibrary.com/reference/library/0672310643/htm/ch07.htm#Heading6.

Listing 4-5: The If Statement

```
Dim Bedcat As Integer, Level As String,
Colm As Integer ◄①
If Bedcat = 1 And Level = "1" Then
              Colm = Colm + 1
End If
```
①
②
③

Listing 4-6: The If-Then-Else-End if Command Block

```
Dim Oldname As String, Newname As String,
Bc As Integer, X As Integer
If Newname = Oldname Then
          Bc = Bc + 1 ◄❶
Else
          X = X + 1 ◄❷
End if
```

▶ Bedcat *is the number of hospital bed categories.* level *is the level of care given.*

① *The variable* Colm *is used to increment a counter as the values of* Bedcat *and* Level *are tested.*

② *Each time a data record is read, the test is made for the specific values.*

③ *When both conditions are true, the counter is incremented by* 1.

❶ *Here, a counter (*Bc*) is incremented when* Newname *matches* Oldname.

❷ *If* Newname *and* Oldname *are not the same, a different counter (*x*) is incremented.*

▶ *If* Newname *and* Oldname *are the same, then one action is taken, and if they are not, then a different action will be carried out.*

Listing 4-7: If- Elseif-End if

```
If Age = "1" Then ◄①
              A17 = A17 + 1 ②
          Elseif Age = "2" Then
              A59 = A59 + 1 ③
          Elseif Age = "3" Then
              Aover = Aover + 1
End If
```
①

① *If* Age *has the value "*1*", counter A17 is incremented by 1.*

② *If* Age *equals "*2*", then counter* A59 *is incremented by 1.*

③ *If* Age *equals "*3*", then counter* Aover *is incremented by 1.*

▶ *This results in age categories for a specific government-funded program.*

▶ *In this example,* Select Case *wouldn't be a good alternative choice, because the test is only for several values of* Age. *If there were more categories of* Age, *then* Select Case *would be a better choice than the* If *block.*

Making Selections

There are several ways for the program to handle decision making for options offered in the application besides the If-End If command block.

Select Case

The Select Case statement enables a multiple choice in which the first case that matches the criterion is performed. In Select Case, a number of conditions are tested for one object, whereas in the If command block, there can be nested If statements, Else statements, and Else if statements.

Select Case structures test one expression, comparing the result of this expression with the values for each Case in the structure. A block of code is executed if there is a match. If there is no match, the execution falls to the next Case.

A common use of Select Case is to provide menu options. For example, you might have a menu with ten options. Rather than using a series of If statements to test for each of the ten conditions, you could more easily code the menu using the Case structure.

This is much easier to read and debug than the alternative using If statements.

```
If Moption = 0 then
   Text1.text = "Zero"
End if
If Moption = 1 then
   Text2.text = "One"
End if
```

You cannot use Else with Case, but you can use multiple conditions and ranges of conditions on one line as here:

```
Case 1 To 4, 7 To 9, 11, 13, Is > MaxNumber
```

Switch Function

In addition to Case structures, selections can be made with Switch. Switch makes a "switch" between items that are paired in some association, much like the Data statement in older versions of Basic. The expressions are evaluated from left to right, and the value associated with the first expression is returned. A Null value is returned if none of the expressions is true or the value is null.

Choose Function

Choose can be used to look up a value from a list of options. The operation is based upon the index value. If the numeric value of the index is 1, then the first choice is returned and so on, until the last index value.

The MsgBox function should not be used to display the choice, because it will display each option evaluated, and not only the selection. This is because Choose evaluates every choice in the list, even though it returns only one.

> **TAKE NOTE**
>
> ▶ **IF VERSUS SELECT CASE**
>
> You can replace an If...Then...Else structure with a Select Case structure only if the If statement and each ElseIf statement evaluate the same expression. Select Case evaluates an expression once at the top of the structure, rather than evaluating a different expression for each ElseIf statement as the If...Then...Else structure does.

CROSS-REFERENCE

Chapter 10 has information regarding decision structures.

FIND IT ONLINE

For more information on making selections, see
http://www.itlibrary.com/reference/library/
0672310643/htm/ch07.htm#Heading11.

Listing 4-8: Select Case

```
Select Case Index
  Case 1
    Text1.text = "One"
  Case 2
    Text2.text = "Two"
...
  Case 10
    Text10.text = "Ten"
End Select
```

▶ *The text displayed in the text box is determined by the index number.*

Listing 4-9: Switch Function

```
Function dogs (Breed As String)
    dogs = Switch(Breed = "Rottweiler", "working", Breed _
               = "Golden Retriever", "hunting", Breed = "Poodle", "show")

End Function
```

▶ *The Switch function allows certain traits to be associated with the breed of dog in this example.*

Controlling Program Flow

The decision structures (`If` and `Select Case`) offer many options in making decisions and data selection. They do not provide control over program execution in the way that some of the other options do.

The Do-While Statement

This statement enables program execution to continue until some condition is met. In this way, the number of iterations can be specified, such as:

```
Do While X > 0
Statements
Loop
```

If `X = 0`, then execution will stop.

The general syntax is, `Do While` some condition exists. The program execution can continue by reiterating the sequence until the condition no longer exists.

The While-Wend Loop

The `While-Wend` loop continues to be executed as long as the statements are true. While [a condition] exists, statements are evaluated and calculations are carried out. When that condition no longer exists, the `Wend` statement terminates execution.

```
While X < 2000
  A = A + 1
Wend
```

As long as X is less than 2000, `A` will continue to be incremented by 1 each time execution continues through the loop. At the time when X = 2000, the `Wend` statement is encountered and execution falls to the next statement.

The For Loop

The `For` loop is perhaps a type of program flow that goes back to the earliest days of programming. At its most basic, it consists of code like this:

```
N = 10
For I = 1 to N
  Print "Hello"
Next
```

This code will cause the word "Hello" to be printed on the form 10 times.

When loops are nested, subsequent variables must be named, such that they should be designated as Next X, Next Y, and so on.

TAKE NOTE

▶ **LOOPING EFFICIENCY**

`Do` loops are used when you do not know how many times the program should iterate the loop. They are often used for reading through records in a file when the exact number of records is not known. If you know how many times the loop must execute, a `For` loop is more efficient, because it uses a counter that changes in value during each iteration of the loop.

CROSS-REFERENCE

Chapter 10 covers expressions, control structures, and more advanced program flow.

FIND IT ONLINE

See Visual Basic looping at **http://www.itlibrary .com/reference/library/0672310643/htm/ch08.htm**.

Listing 4-10: The Do While Statement

```
X = 1
    Do While X < 5
        If Bedcat = X And Level = "1" Then
            Colm(X,2) = Colm(X,2) + 1
        End If
        If Bedcat = X And Level = "2" Then
            Colm(X,3) = Colm(X,3) + 1
        End If
        X = X + 1
    Loop
```

❶ The variable Bedcat *represents four categories of hospital beds based upon level of patient care.*

❷ The variable Level *represents two levels of patient care.*

❸ *There will be continuous loops through the procedure as long as the value of* X *is under 5.*

❹ *The value of* X *will be incremented in the array elements of* Colm *each time through the loop.*

▶ *This is an efficient way to create a kind of spreadsheet or cross-tabulation report with columns showing values for different levels, depending upon type of beds.*

Listing 4-11: The While-Wend Loop

```
While Field1 = "Total"
    Lcount = Lcount + 1
Wend
```

▶ *This loop will continue until Field1 no longer contains the string "Total."*

Listing 4-12: The For Loop

```
FOR V = 1 TO 12
  For J = 1 To 10        1
        For K = 1 To 10   2
        MsgBox = "Hi"
        Next K
    Next J
NEXT
```

▶ V, J, *and* K *are nested loops.*

1 *Each pass through the loop causes commands to be executed once for* V *and 10 times for* J.

2 *Each pass for* J *causes commands to be run 10 times for* K.

▶ *Each pass through the entire loop results in one count for* V, *10 counts for* J, *and 100 counts for* K.

Personal Workbook

Q&A

1 What is an *object* in Visual Basic?

_____

_____

_____

2 What is an *event?*

_____

_____

_____

3 How is a variable distinguished from a constant?

_____

_____

_____

4 Would you use the default Variant type to define a variable that you intend to use as a counter, which gets incremented by 1 each time the execution loops? Why or why not?

_____

_____

_____

5 How many "Hi's" will you get from the example in Listing 4-12?

_____

_____

_____

6 What data type would you select for a five-digit zip code?

_____

_____

_____

7 Which would you choose to test for 10 different age categories, with different events taking place for each possible category, the `If` command block or the `Select Case` structure?

_____

_____

_____

8 What is the significant difference between the `Do-While` and the `For-Next` loops?

_____

_____

_____

ANSWERS: PAGE 521

EXTRA PRACTICE

1. Design a decision-making procedure to test for user input of any number from 1 to 10, giving a different option for each possible input. Is the `If` command block best for this?

2. Write the correct expression for calculating an average of the scores 345, 495, and 1025.

3. An application requires the user to enter a letter (A, B or C) as a response. If the user enters A in the text box, the number 1 is returned, and so on.

4. Use `If-Else-End If` to make decisions for the letters above, returning different values (1, 2 or 3) in response to each letter entered.

5. Use `Select Case` in the above example to return the same values. How does the logic differ?

REAL-WORLD APPLICATIONS

✔ Your company is designing a telephone and address database. You have been assigned the job of identifying the variables for which values will be stored and accessed. Use the `Dim` statement to declare your variables and assign them each the appropriate data type.

✔ You are assigned the job of converting an old DOS Basic program to Visual Basic. Your first task is to identify the variables in the old program and determine the appropriate data types for the new program.

✔ You are writing a procedure to offer users menu options for a database project. You need to Add records, Edit records, Save records, Search records, End, and Cancel. Design your selection criteria.

Visual Quiz

The code shown on the right has an obvious flaw. What is it?

_____

_____

_____

_____

_____

_____

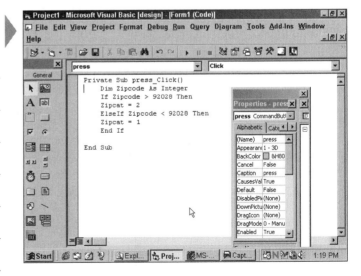

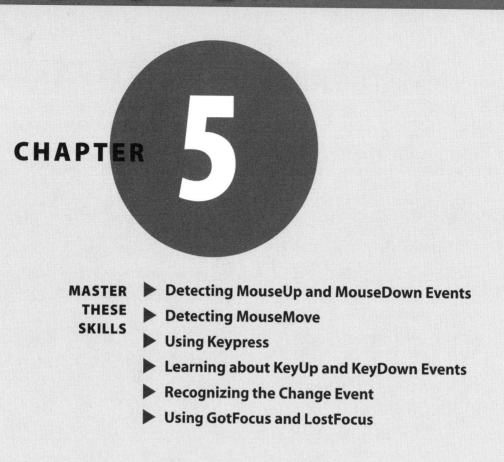

CHAPTER 5

MASTER
THESE
SKILLS

▶ **Detecting MouseUp and MouseDown Events**

▶ **Detecting MouseMove**

▶ **Using Keypress**

▶ **Learning about KeyUp and KeyDown Events**

▶ **Recognizing the Change Event**

▶ **Using GotFocus and LostFocus**

Interpreting Events

An *event* is any action that is associated in a causal manner with an object. Key presses and mouse clicks are examples of user actions that initiate events. An event is an action recognized by a form or control. Event-driven applications execute Basic code in response to an event. Each form and control in Visual Basic has a predefined set of events. If one of these events occurs and there is code in the associated event procedure, Visual Basic invokes that code.

Objects are set up to be aware of preset events, but your code will determine whether or how a specific object will respond to a particular event. You will write event procedures to make that determination. An event procedure is one in which a user, program code, or the system starts an action and event procedures are written to address events. You write code as a plan for controlling the responses to events.

Possibly, the most familiar event is the mouse click. Something is supposed to happen when the user clicks a command button. The code you write to address that event is an event procedure. Sometimes the user does not precipitate the event directly. A user can trigger one event that initiates a different event. Also, events can be controlled by the program itself, as is the case with the `Timer` control.

The process of deciding which events will trigger other events can be quite complex. Good design is important in orchestrating the interaction between objects and events. It is also the challenge and the fun to write an application that functions smoothly and has quality functionality.

Detecting MouseUp and MouseDown Events

Since the advent of Windows, the mouse has been the pointing tool of choice. You can write applications that recognize pressing, releasing, double-clicking, and dragging, as well as dragging and dropping. Just how Visual Basic treats these activities and how you learn to treat them is the subject of this task.

If the database application development possibilities in the Application Wizard were impressive, you will be even more pleasantly surprised by what you can achieve in just a few lines of writing you own code. The capability of mouse movements in Visual Basic is truly amazing. You can give locations of the mouse coordinates wherever the mouse is pressed. You can even create your own draw program.

If you tend to think of applications as primarily a front end on a database, you will find the other possibilities exciting as well.

There is a good way to learn to program and that is by programming. So, go ahead and do it! You are going to demonstrate what mouse pointer movement procedures can do.

Mouse States

You use the arguments `button` and `shift` with the `MouseDown`, `MouseUp`, and `MouseMove` event procedures. The mouse button state is determined by the bit value returned.

The state of the mouse is represented in a bit-field argument in which each mouse button is represented by one of the three least significant bits. Binary and decimal values and a constant are assigned to each mouse button (left, right, and middle), These values are expressed as integers 1, 2, and 4 for the left, right, and middle buttons.

The `Shift` argument is also a bit-field argument in which the three least-significant bits give the status of the Shift, Ctrl, and Alt keys.

The Project

Start by creating a new project named `Projevents`. Name the form `frmevents`. Add a new form named `frmouse`.

Add a new module named `modulemouse`. This project will have a form that lets you draw pictures and also load the other form, `frmouse`. The `frmouse` form will give you coordinate locations of the mouse when the button is pressed (down) and released (up). The `frmevents` form will feature a drawing program to let you do free-form line drawing.

Because you have more than one form in your project, you must have a way of loading one or the other first. The easiest way to do this is to have a module with a `Sub Main` procedure. A module is a file with a `.bas` extension containing code. It is the closest to the older DOS versions of Basic of anything remaining in Visual Basic. The DOS Basic programming used only modules. There were no forms or other objects to which code could be attached. You just wrote the code in one long file and then saved and executed it.

You write the code for the `modulemouse` module by double-clicking it to get to the Code window, and then filling in these two lines:

```
FrmEvents.Show
FrmEvents.Refresh
```

This instructs the program to display the first form. Now, you can go ahead and set up the forms.

Continued

TAKE NOTE

PROCEDURE AND FULL MODULE VIEWS

If you click a form or form object that has been coded, you may notice that all the associated code is displayed. You can try this with the project in the previous chapter, `Projweb`. If you wish to see only the code related to one object, you can select the little square on the bottom left of the Code window. The right square is for viewing the entire form's code.

CROSS-REFERENCE

Chapter 1 began the discussion of events.

FIND IT ONLINE

Check out **http://users.quake.net/obrien/vb/** for a wealth of programs to download.

Table 5-1: THE MOUSE STATES

Event	Description
MouseDown	Any mouse button is pressed.
MouseUp	Any mouse button is released.
MouseMove	The mouse pointer is moved to a new point on the screen.

① *Create a new project named* `Projevents`.

② *Add a new module named* `modulemouse`.

③ *Create the* `frmEvents` *form.*

④ *Place 2* CommandButtons *on the form.*

⑤ *Name captions* **mouse form** *and* **quit**.

⑥ *Double-click the Mouse Form button.*

⑦ *Enter the code* "`frmouse.Visible = True`" *in the Code window.*

Detecting MouseUp and MouseDown Events *Continued*

Place two `CommandButtons` at the bottom of the `frmevents` form, leaving a large space above them. Name the buttons `cmdoform` with a caption "mouse form" and `cmdquit` with the caption "quit."

You want to show the `frmouse` form when the `cmdoform` button is pressed. So you enter the code to make the `frmouse` form visible. Select `cmdoform` from the object list, then select the `click_procedure`. Enter the following code inside the subroutine:

`Frmouse.Visible = True`

So that you can stop the program executing, add the `End` command to the Quit button. Select `cmdquit` from the object list, and then the `click_procedure`. Then add `End` inside the procedure.

The Mouse Events form, `frmouse`, needs two buttons, one for `MouseUp` and one for `MouseDown`. Place the `CommandButtons` on the form, giving them captions, MOUSE UP and MOUSE DOWN. You can leave the default `CommandButton` names (Command1 and Command2) if you wish.

The `MouseUp` event occurs when the mouse button has been pressed and is released. The button comes back up when released, hence `MouseUp`. You want to write a routine that will show the locations of the mouse when pressed and released.

When you select the Command2 `CommandButton` in the `frmouse` Code window, you have a selection of several procedures. You should select the `MouseUp` procedure. When you do this, the `Private Sub Command2_MouseUp` procedure definition is filled in for you. You have only to complete the code within the `Private Sub` and `End Sub` lines.

The variables (`button`, `Shift`, X, and Y) are already declared for you. The Format expression provides a string format for the values of button, X, and Y. The title is not given here, so the default title (the project name) will be displayed on the title bar.

The `Beep` is an unnecessary enhancement. The sound will be based upon whatever sound theme is installed on the user's computer. With Windows 98, there are many themes, plus add-ons with Windows 95 and Windows 98 to give you interesting sounds like jungle birds and cars honking. In any case, the `Beep` will take on those characteristics.

The `MsgBox` will display the word "BUTTON" followed by X and its current position when the button is released. Likewise, the position of Y upon release will be shown in the dialog box. Try pressing the right and middle mouse buttons and see if the BUTTON value changes.

The `MouseDown` event occurs when any mouse button is pressed, not when it is released. When you double-click the MOUSE DOWN button and select the `Command1` object, select the `MouseDown` procedure from the procedure list on the right.

This time you won't need to type the code. You can copy it to the clipboard from the Code window on the other button, or if you use the module view, you can copy and paste it in the same window. Just remember to copy the `MsgBox` line from the `MouseUp` procedure and paste it in the `MouseDown` procedure. This works because the procedures for `MouseUp` and `MouseDown` are already built into the interface. That is, the system knows whether to monitor the press or the release based upon the procedure name.

TAKE NOTE

THE MSGBOX DIALOG BOX

The `MsgBox` function is used to display a dialog box to enable the user to acknowledge some action. Here it is used to display the positions of the button coordinates. The default user response is OK, and this box uses the default. The prompt is "Button =" followed by the values of each button. The title is not entered, so the project name is shown on the title bar.

```
MsgBox(prompt[, buttons] [, title] [,
helpfile, context])
```

CROSS-REFERENCE

Chapter 6 returns to the interface issues.

FIND IT ONLINE

The **http://www.codearchive.com/** site is a source of many downloadable procedures.

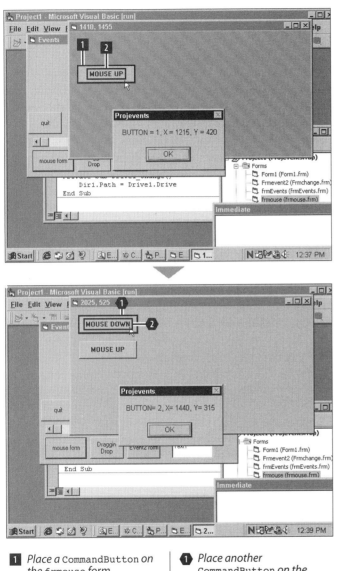

Listing 5-1: MouseUp procedure

```
Private Sub Command2_MouseUp(Button As _
Integer,
Shift As Integer, X As Single, Y As Single)
    Beep
    MsgBox  "BUTTON = " + Format(Button) + ", _
X = " + Format(X) + ", Y = " + Format(Y)

End Sub
```

Listing 5-2: MouseDown procedure

```
Private Sub Command1_MouseDown(Button As
Integer, Shift As Integer, X As Single, Y As _
Single)
    Beep
    MsgBox  "BUTTON= " + Format (Button) + ", _
X= " + Format (X) + ", Y= " + Format$(Y)

End Sub
```

1 *Place a* CommandButton *on the* frmouse *form.*

2 *Make the caption "MOUSE UP."*

▶ *Enter the code in Listing 5-1. Click the form and click "MOUSE UP" using the right button. Note it shows "button 2."*

❶ *Place another* CommandButton *on the* frmouse *form.*

❷ *Make the caption "MOUSE DOWN."*

▶ *Enter the code in Listing 5-2. Click the form and tnen click "MOUSE DOWN."*

Detecting MouseMove

You have been exploring the uses of the `MouseUp` and `MouseDown` procedures. The `MouseMove` procedure is an ongoing series of events that don't stop until the user stops moving the mouse. As long as the pointer is being moved, it generates this continual series.

You may wonder just how many points of movement are plotted as the mouse moves across a form. A `MouseMove` event is not necessarily generated for each pixel point that the mouse moves over. Only so many mouse messages can be generated each second.

The operating environment generates a limited number of mouse messages per second. As you move the mouse at increasing speed, fewer mouse messages will be recorded.

You can try almost an infinite number of great examples of `MouseMove` to test this function. One exercise that is easy to understand but fun to do changes the background color on the fly.

Rainbow Forms

This is another quick exercise that goes a long way to illustrate the kinds of things you can do with a little code. For this you will use the `frmouse` form also. Double-click the form. In the Code window, select the `Form` object from the Object drop-down list, then select the `MouseMove` procedure from the Procedure box.

Here, you need only type one word:

```
Randomize
```

The syntax for this statement is

```
Randomize[number]
```

The number you state here initializes the random number generator and gives it a seed. If there is no number in the statement, the system timer value is used as the seed. The seed is the place where the random numbers begin. You also can state a range of numbers to randomize.

To add the rainbow colors to the form, scroll down a line or two. Again select the `Form` object from the object list, then select `MouseMove` from the procedure list.

The code that drives this function includes the creation of a caption and the randomization of the background color. The purpose of the caption is to show the location of the mouse as it moves around. This is similar to the `MsgBox` in the `MouseUp` and `MouseDown` routines. In this case, a caption displaying the mouse position will be placed on the title bar of the form, changing as the mouse moves.

The other action in the procedure is to generate random numbers based upon the selection of an integer between 1 and 32,000. The result depends upon the user's display settings. If a computer is set to display 256 colors, then the colors displayed will be different from one that has high (16-bit) or true (24-bit) or true (32-bit) color. With 256 colors, you will get a lot of patterns, rather than solid colors.

If the system can display high color or true color, then you can increase the value. Try increasing it to 10,000,000. And notice that the colors are much prettier. High color is 16,000,000 colors, so you could increase it to that and see what happens. If your user is not expected to have high color settings, then you may want to adjust your algorithm accordingly.

TAKE NOTE

DISPLAY SETTINGS

The best way to determine appropriate settings is to experiment by changing the settings on your own system, and then changing the code. It is a good idea to save your work before experimenting, though, as your system may well need to be reset when you change the settings.

CROSS-REFERENCE

Chapter 9 covers some of the same topics.

FIND IT ONLINE

This site has a download program to fill make **MsgBox** run in unattended mode: **http://www.codesmiths.com/VB/**.

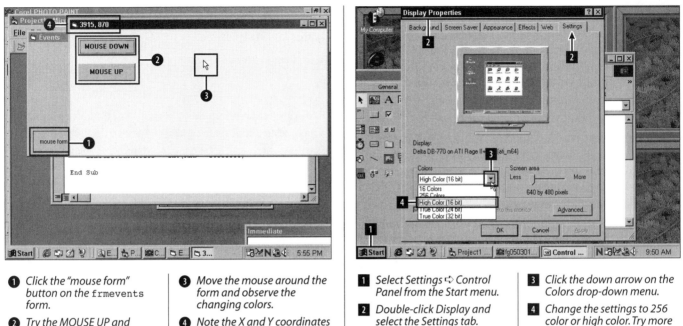

① *Click the "mouse form" button on the* frmevents *form.*

② *Try the MOUSE UP and MOUSE DOWN buttons.*

③ *Move the mouse around the form and observe the changing colors.*

④ *Note the X and Y coordinates shown on the Form title bar.*

1 *Select Settings ⇨ Control Panel from the Start menu.*

2 *Double-click Display and select the Settings tab.*

3 *Click the down arrow on the Colors drop-down menu.*

4 *Change the settings to 256 color or high color. Try more than one setting.*

Listing 5-3: The Rainbow Form

```
Private Sub Form_Load()     Randomize
End Sub

Private Sub Form_MouseMove(Button As Integer, Shift As Integer, X As Single, Y As Single)
    frmouse.Caption = Format(X) + ", " + Format(Y)
    frmouse.BackColor = Int(Rnd * 16000000)

End Sub
```

Artwork Form

The Rainbow Forms exercise gives an example of what you can do with Visual Basic. You have seen examples of database access and Web browser development, but the possibilities that mouse event programming offer, appeal to the imagination and pique curiosity. Because mouse event programming promises the chance to do something for fun, as well as something useful, it may appeal to your artistic side.

You will have a chance to find out about your artistic ability when you write the next procedure. This procedure uses all three mouse event procedures; MouseUp, MouseDown, and MouseMove.

This procedure will use the frmevents form. This time you double-click the form to get the Code window. In the declarations area at the top of the Code window, you declare a variable called artwork. Artwork could just as well have any other name you want to give it.

Make artwork Boolean. Remember, Boolean has only two values (true or false, 0 or 1). Scroll past the procedures for the two CommandButtons (cmdquit and cmdofrm). Select the Form object from the object list, then the MouseDown procedure. Because you will likely want to do your artwork when the mouse button is down, or pressed, set artwork equal to true.

```
Artwork = True
```

Once that procedure is complete, select the Form object again, then the MouseUp procedure. This time add the statement:

```
Artwork = False
```

This will turn off the artwork function when the mouse button is released.

Once again, select the Form object on the object list. This time, select the MouseMove procedure. Because you want the mouse to draw a line when the mouse is moved, that code goes in this procedure. If the artwork variable is true, then you want the line to be drawn. You learned

about conditional statements in Chapter 4, and you can apply that knowledge here.

```
If artwork Then
Line —(X,Y)
End If
```

You could state "If artwork = true," but there is no need to include "true" in your expression as its existence will be assumed. The X and Y coordinates determine the location or the line to be drawn. The routine is ready to try. You can select Run ➪ Start from the menu and then hold down the mouse button and drag the mouse around the form. If you try to run the program now, you will notice that each time you lift the mouse button, move the mouse, and begin again, a straight line is drawn between the last drawing point and the new one. This can be remedied.

Go back into the Code window and move to the MouseDown procedure. Directly under the artwork = true line, insert these lines:

```
CurrentX = X
CurrentY = Y
```

Now run the program again. Did you notice the difference? This time, the starting point value is reset, rather than beginning where you left off.

TAKE NOTE

▶ OBJECTS AND MOUSE EVENTS

Placing mouse event code on a form enables the form to recognize the event when the mouse pointer is on any part of the form where there are no controls. This recognition occurs when the user holds down a mouse button. When the pointer is moved off the object, it continues to recognize the mouse moves until the button has been released.

CROSS-REFERENCE
Chapter 16 deals more with drawing and other graphic issues.

FIND IT ONLINE
This site belongs to a 14-year-old programmer and has some better tips than many other sites: **http://members.aol.com/damiac14/index.html**.

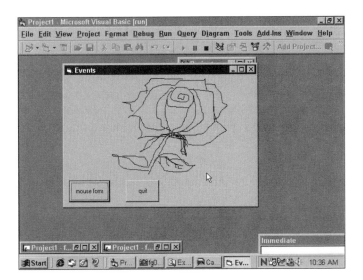 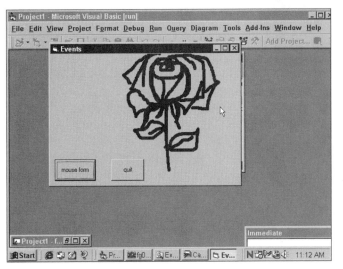

Listing 5-4: The Artwork Form

```
Dim artwork As Boolean
Private Sub Form_MouseDown(Button As Integer, Shift As Integer, X As Single, Y As Single)
    artwork = True
    CurrentX = X
    CurrentY = Y
End Sub


Private Sub Form_MouseUp(Button As Integer, Shift As Integer, X As Single, Y As Single)
    artwork = False
End Sub


Private Sub Form_MouseMove(Button As Integer, Shift As Integer, X As Single, Y As Single)
    If artwork Then
        Line -(X, Y)
    End If
    DrawWidth = 6
End Sub
```

Using Drag and Drop

At its simplest, the drag and drop operations combine a number of features set up to enable dragging an object while holding down the mouse button and dropping it onto another object by releasing the mouse button.

You can drag and drop files from the Windows Explorer into a control, such as a TextBox or PictureBox.

How you set up the response to the drag and drop is dependent upon your implementation of the process. If you are setting up a drag and drop to enable the user to drag data by default, you can set the OLEDropMode property of the control to Automatic.

The Draggin' Drop

Add a new form to your projevents project. Name the form Form3 and make the caption DRAGGIN DROP. Size the form by changing the height and width properties to accommodate several controls. Place a PictureBox control on the right side of the form. Size the PictureBox about 4000 (4000 twips, using the Property window.

To the left of the PictureBox, place four labels in one column. Place a CommandButton beneath the labels at the bottom of the form. Change the caption to Quit. Double-click the Quit button to get the Code window. Select the Command1 object, select the Click procedure, and insert the End statement within the procedure, as you did before.

Now, you need to do some investigating. Check your hard drive for some .bmp files, that is, bitmaps with the .bmp (for Windows bitmap) extension. The most likely place to find these is the Windows folder. You can choose View Files and Arrange by Type to see the .bmp files in one group. You probably have a Clouds.bmp, Forest.bmp, or Setup.bmp, but if you don't, just find any such file. Those with a file size of under 10K are probably too small to be very exciting, so look for bigger ones.

Going back to the form, select the first label, right-click for the Property window, and type in a caption to match the path for your first bitmap. Do the same for the other labels. It will help to make the BackColor of the label light and the ForeColor dark, or vice versa, to give some contrast on the label.

Now for the fun part. Double-click the PictureBox. Select Picture1 from the object list, the DragDrop from the procedure list. Notice again that the procedure is pretty much built in, in the sense it does some declarations for you. Type in the following line between the Private Sub and End Sub lines:

```
Private Sub Picture1_DragDrop(Source As _
Control, X As Single, Y As Single) _
    Picture1.Picture =
LoadPicture(Source.Caption)
End Sub
```

This says to load a picture in the PictureBox using the label Caption as the source path. This seems quite simple. Will it work? Test it. Another enhancement you might add is setting the ToolTipText property. You could perhaps have it state, "DRAG ME." That way, when you run the program and pass the cursor over the labels, you will get the message to drag the label to the PictureBox.

> **TAKE NOTE**

> ### DRAGDROP MECHANICS

> When an object is dragged and dropped, several events belong to the source (object dragged) and the target (destination). The source events include OLEStartDrag, OLESetData, OLEGiveFeedback, OLECompleteDrag. The target events are OLDDragDrop and OLEDragOver. At each point along the way, different events are triggered. For example, the OLEFeedBack event is triggered by the target's indication of the drop effect that will take place. The way these events work to produce the intended effect can be simple or complex, depending upon the goal.

CROSS-REFERENCE

Chapters 10 and 17 require knowledge of event procedures.

FIND IT ONLINE

This site has some interesting sample code on such topics as creating a gradient background: **http://www.mvps.org/vbnet/**.

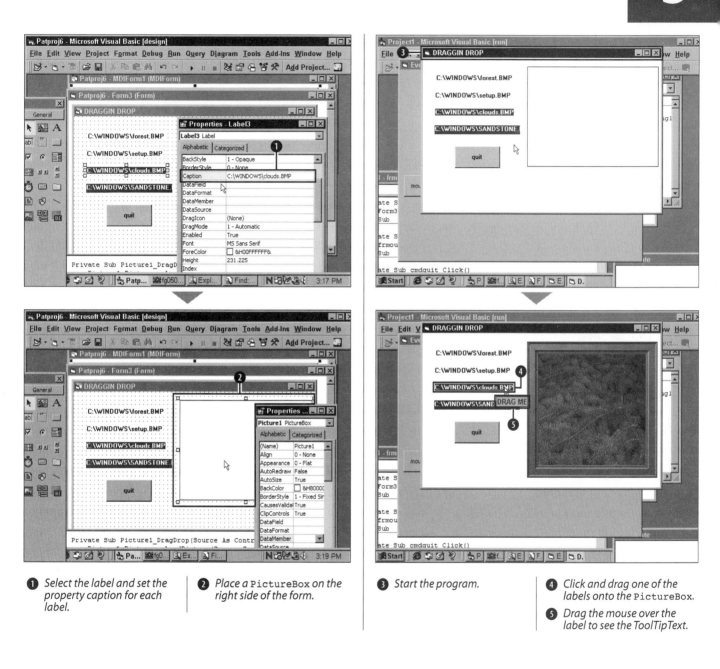

① Select the label and set the property caption for each label.

② Place a PictureBox on the right side of the form.

③ Start the program.

④ Click and drag one of the labels onto the PictureBox.

⑤ Drag the mouse over the label to see the ToolTipText.

Using KeyPress

The `KeyPress` event tests for any key that represents an ASCII code value. The ASCII character set is the American Standard Code for Information Interchange. It includes the characters on the standard keyboard. The first 128 characters are the numbers and letters of the alphabet. The second 128 characters are special characters and symbols.

The `KeyPress` event does not identify navigation keys, as they are perceived by the `KeyDown` and `KeyUp` events. The `KeyPress` event does recognize the Enter, Tab, and Backspace keys.

The `KeyPress` event occurs when a key that has an ASCII character equivalent is pressed. You can use the `KeyPress` event in numerous ways. For example, you might want to collect data from users only in uppercase or lowercase. You can write a routine to convert the text entered by users to the correct case.

Open your `ProjEvents` project and select the `frmEvents` form. Add a `TextBox` to the right of the three `CommandButtons` (Mouse Form, Draggin Drop, and quit). Double-click the form object to get the code view. Enter the following code.

```
Private Sub Text1_KeyPress(KeyAscii As _
Integer)
    KeyAscii = Asc(UCase(Chr(KeyAscii)))
End Sub
```

This procedure converts the ASCII character code to the equivalent text character and then uses `Ucase` to convert the character to uppercase.

There are many `KeyPress` options you can test for. To do that, though, you will need to have a handy ASCII chart to reference. If you don't have a chart, you can make your own in the Immediate window.

Select the Immediate window from the View menu and then type the next line of code. Remember, because this code will execute when you press Enter, you must keep it all on one line. You can separate the statements with a colon.

```
For i=1 to 128:Print Chr(i);i:Next
```

Try it and you will see what a nice tool the Immediate window is. By checking the character equivalents for the codes, you can set up expressions to trap the characters you don't want users to type.

Suppose you decide that you don't want users to type slashes (backslash and forward slash). You can take care of that very easily by adding this line of code to your `KeyPress` procedure.

```
If KeyAscii = 92 Or KeyAscii = 47 Then MsgBox _
"You pressed the BACK OR FORWARD slash key."
```

ASCII characters 47 and 92 are the codes for the forward and backslash keys.

You also can check for ranges of codes. For example, since the codes between 33 and 47 are nonalphabetic and nonnumeric characters, you might not want them typed in the text box. You can handle that problem by adding this line to your procedure:

```
If KeyAscii > 32 And KeyAscii < 48 Then MsgBox _
"You pressed an illegal character."
```

As you gain experience, you will be able to think of many applications for similar procedures.

TAKE NOTE

THE ASCII CHARACTERS

If you did the experiment in the Immediate window, you will have noticed that the first 30 codes did not appear, or had squares next to the numbers. That is because many of them are control characters or key combinations. Some are keys like the Enter key (13). You can trap for these as well, just by using the ASCII code.

CROSS-REFERENCE

Chapter 9 touches on some of the same material.

FIND IT ONLINE

The site at **http://www.vbexplorer.com/** is a great site for links to newsgroups for beginners.

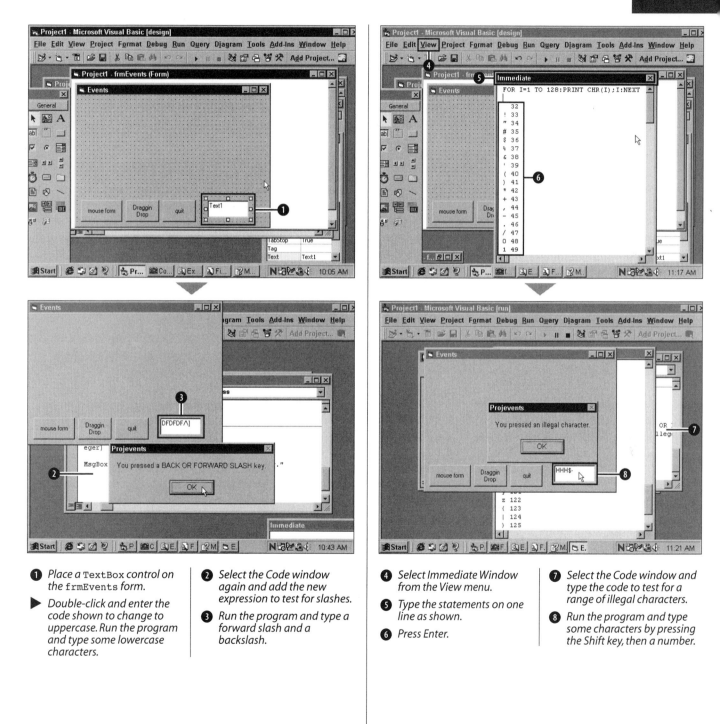

① Place a TextBox control on the frmEvents form.

▶ Double-click and enter the code shown to change to uppercase. Run the program and type some lowercase characters.

② Select the Code window again and add the new expression to test for slashes.

③ Run the program and type a forward slash and a backslash.

④ Select Immediate Window from the View menu.

⑤ Type the statements on one line as shown.

⑥ Press Enter.

⑦ Select the Code window and type the code to test for a range of illegal characters.

⑧ Run the program and type some characters by pressing the Shift key, then a number.

Learning KeyDown and KeyUp Events

The `KeyDown` and `KeyUp` events contrast with `KeyPress`. `KeyDown` and `KeyUp` detect the state of the actual key that is pressed, rather than the ASCII or ANSI code. This means that a lowercase and an uppercase letter would have the same value in `KeyDown` and `KeyUp` but have different codes in ASCII. It is the physical key on the keyboard that `KeyDown` and `KeyUp` detect.

The `KeyDown` and `KeyUp` events should be used for determining keys pressed that cannot be detected by `KeyPress`. Also, `KeyDown` and `KeyUp` are used when you want to detect the pressing and releasing of a key, as opposed to only pressing a key.

`KeyDown` and `KeyUp` test for Shift, Ctrl, Alt, Page Up, Page Down, and function keys. The Enter, Esc, and Tab keys are not tested by `KeyDown` and `KeyUp`.

Writing code to detect keyboard events is easier to do with `KeyPress`, so `KeyDown`/`KeyUp` should be reserved for events that `KeyPress` won't detect.

You can test for the `Shift` argument by using the `Shift` constants that determine specific values for the Shift, Ctrl, and Alt keys. Just as the mouse buttons share the least bit pattern, so does the `Shift` argument. The mouse button clicks return the values of 1, 2, and 4 for the left, right, and middle buttons, and the `Shift` argument returns the same integer values of 1, 2 and 4 for the Shift, Ctrl and Alt keys, respectively.

The `Shift` constants are bit masks for the Shift, Ctrl, and Alt states. This means they enable you to assign a resulting value to an integer variable and then compare the bit mask with each of the `Shift` constants.

```
vbShiftMask (tests for the Shift key) value=1
VbCtrlMask (tests for the Ctrl key) value=2
VbAltMask (tests for the Alt key) value=4
```

You can use these `Shift` constants to test for several keys by using `Select Case` to handle the three options of `Shift`, `Ctrl`, and `Alt`. Begin by creating another `TextBox` (`Text2`) on the `frmEvents` form, and then select `Text2` from the object list and `KeyDown` from the procedure list.

You must define your variable that will hold the values for the three `KeyDown` options. This is done in the Declarations section at the top of the form module. You will give your variable a name and declare it as the integer type. Next, set your variable equal to `Shift And 7`. This reflects the key value combination of 1 + 2 + 4 for each of the three keys. If you wish to detect only the Shift key, you can set the value of your variable (`Whichkey` in this case) to 1. The value for the Ctrl key is 2 and for Alt, 4.

`Select Case` matches the value of your variable against each of the three constants. If there is a match, the corresponding `MsgBox` is displayed.

TAKE NOTE

▶ KEYCODE

You can use the `Keycode` argument to recognize a key from its ASCII value. However, this only applies to uppercase letters, as "A" and "a" are the same. The 1 on the keypad is not the same as 1 on the main keyboard. That is because the codes represent the keys, not the key combinations expressed by the Shift key and some other key. To get the code for a Shift key and a number key, you need to use the `Shift` argument.

CROSS-REFERENCE

Chapter 14 discusses user input also.

FIND IT ONLINE

The site **http://www.thebestweb.com/vb/codesnippets.htm** is a good place for beginners to learn Visual Basic.

Listing 5-5: Using KeyDown to Detect Shift + Ctrl + Alt

```
Dim WhichKey As Integer
Private Sub Text2_KeyDown(KeyCode As Integer, Shift As Integer)
    WhichKey = Shift And 7
  Select Case WhichKey
    Case vbShiftMask
       MsgBox  "You pressed the SHIFT key."
    Case vbCtrlMask
       MsgBox  "You pressed the CTRL key."
    Case vbAltMask
       MsgBox  "You pressed the ALT key."
  End Select
End Sub
```

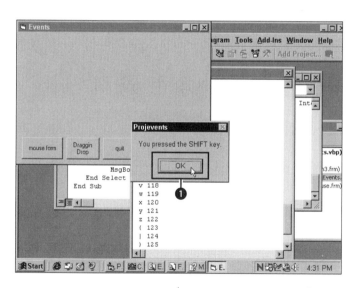

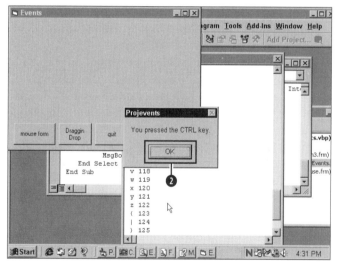

▶ *Place a* `TextBox` *on the* `frmEvents` *form.*

▶ *Select Text2 from the object list and the* `KeyDown` *procedure.*

▶ *Declare the* `Whichkey` *variable in the declarations area and enter the code in Listing 5-5.*

❶ *Run the program and press the Shift key.*

❷ *Run the program again and hold down the Ctrl key.*

Recognizing the Change Event

The Change event indicates that a value has changed. The event actually occurs when the value property of an object changes. The Change event is specific to each control.

When the user enters text in the `ComboBox`, it causes a Change event. The Change event also will occur if you change the text property setting in your code.

For the `DirListBox` control, the change occurs when the user changes directories, or you can change the path property in your code.

Similar to the `DirListBox`, the `DriveListBox` control Change event occurs when a new drive is chosen. You also can code the change in the drive.

The horizontal and vertical scroll bars (`HScrollBar` and `VscrollBar`) Change event takes place when the user scrolls from one side the other. The Change event also occurs through code.

The `Label`, `TextBox`, and `PictureBox` Change events occur when a Dynamic Data Exchange updates the text in the `TextBox,` on the `Label` or the picture in the `PictureBox`. They also can be changed through code.

Your procedure can use the Change event to change the display on other controls. For example, you can use the `Hscroll` value to change the form caption, depending upon where you are in the scrolling range. It is not recommended to use a `MsgBox` statement with `HScrollBar` and `VScrollBar`.

The Change event can be used to update other MDI child forms as well. The Change event is very useful in the `DirListBox`, `DriveListBox`, and `FileListBox` controls. It is a common experience in just about every application to be asked to select a file from the file system. The drive list is usually displayed first, with the directory and file list placed subsequently. This is a typical application of the Change event.

The Flashing Scroll Bar

It is a good idea to practice something new you have just learned by making the lesson memorable. One of the typical examples of the Change event is the change that takes place when you move a scroll bar from side to side (or top to bottom). It helps you to remember just how this works when you add a touch of drama.

The object here is to use the value generated by the scrolling position to display on the form caption. As you move the scroll bar, the number associated with the position will change. To add that touch of drama, you will again have the moving scroll bar change the form's background color.

TAKE NOTE

▶ **CHANGE EVENT CAVEAT**

Beware of creating a Change event procedure that changes the elements of the control. The danger is that further changes may try to take place as the change in progress. Also, you probably don't want controls whose Change event procedures impact each other. An example would be two controls that update each other at the same time.

CROSS-REFERENCE

Chapter 8 has more information about control Change events.

FIND IT ONLINE

This site has good info on event procedures: **http://www. thebestweb.com/vbarticles/vbpropertieseventsmethods.htm.**

Listing 5-6: The Flashing Scroll Bar

```
Private Sub HScroll1_Change()
    frmEvents.Caption = Format(HScroll1.Value)
    frmEvents.BackColor = HScroll1.Value + 100000
 End Sub
```

▶ *Start by placing a Horizontal Scroll Bar on the* frmEvents *form.*

▶ *Select* Hscroll *from the object list, then Change from the procedure list.*

▶ *Enter the code within* Private Sub *and* End Sub.

▶ *How would you display a toolbar button's function in text?*

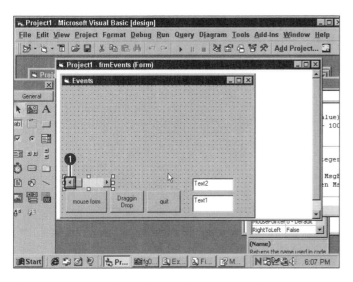

❶ *Place a Horizontal Scroll Bar on the* frmEvents *form.*

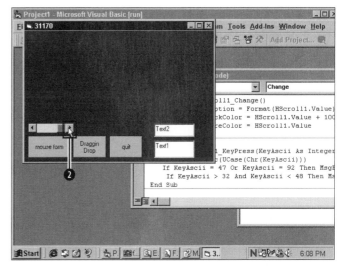

❷ *Run the program and move the scroll bar.*

Understanding Focus

Focus bestows on an object the ability to accept user input via keyboard or mouse. Focus means the object is selected. Whether or not the object can be selected depends upon the tab order of objects on a form. A TextBox will not accept user input if it does not have the focus.

Some controls are known as the lightweight controls. They cannot receive focus. They are: Frame, Image, Label, Line, Shape and the Timer control. The timer control is not visible at runtime, so it cannot receive focus.

Using GotFocus and LostFocus

The GotFocus and LostFocus events happen when an object obtains or loses focus. Focus is set at runtime by selecting the object. The SetFocus method can be written in code.

Objects with focus are highlighted. If an object's Enabled and Visible properties are set to True, it can receive focus. Forms can only receive focus if they don't have controls set to acquire focus.

An example best illustrates the uses of GotFocus and LostFocus. You are going to set up a project to demonstrate the meaning and uses of GotFocus and LostFocus. What you want to do is to devise a situation in which something on the form changes to indicate the change in focus. If the form has a TextBox that can change color depending upon whether it has the focus (GotFocus) or not (LostFocus), then it will be easy to see the change in focus. Also, if there is a label to display a message indicating that the focus has shifted, that will be even more helpful. Because there are only two controls on the form, it will be effective to add another control so that you have something to aid you in changing the focus.

Create a new form called FrmEvent2. Place a TextBox and a Label on the form. Add an OptionButton beside the TextBox. Double-click the TextBox and select Text1 from the object list and GotFocus from the procedure list. Because you want to make the change in the TextBox noticeable, change the BackColor to yellow when the object has focus. Further, you want to display the text in the Label, "Text1 has the focus." Now you will have no trouble in telling which object has the focus.

Select Text1 from the object list again, then select LostFocus from the procedure list. This time, you want the background color to be different from Yellow, to be easily discernable from the Yellow associated with GotFocus, so you make it black. You want the text message to change also, so you make the caption "Text1 does not have the focus."

Now, when you run the program, you should see the TextBox change to yellow and see the first message on the Label. When you press the OptionButton, the TextBox will lose the focus, so the color will change to black and the message on the Label will change also.

> ### TAKE NOTE
>
> #### SETFOCUS
>
> Setfocus is used to move the focus to a visible control or another form. SetFocus will not move the focus unless the form is currently visible. Neither will SetFocus work if the Enabled property is False. This can be used for selecting a different form as if the user has click the title bar. The object used to SetFocus must be a Form, MDIForm, or control that is capable of receiving the focus.

CROSS-REFERENCE

Chapter 6 continues in the same vein.

FIND IT ONLINE

This site contains a lot of reference material for beginners as well as others: **http://www.thebestweb. com/classcatalog/meetvbhugebook.htm**.

LISTING 5-7: The GotFocus and LostFocus Events

```
Private Sub Text1_GotFocus()
    ' Show focus with yellow.
  Text1.BackColor = RGB(255, 255, 0)
  Label1.Caption = "Text1 has the focus."

End Sub

Private Sub Text1_LostFocus()
    ' Show loss of focus with black.
  Text1.BackColor = RGB(0, 0, 0)
  Label1.Caption = "Text1 does not have the focus."
End Sub
```

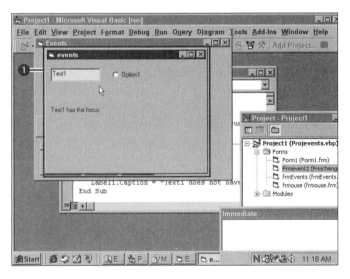

❶ Click Text1 TextBox.

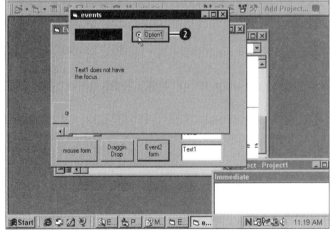

❷ Click OptionButton.

Personal Workbook

Q&A

1 What is the purpose of the `Sub Main` procedure?

_____

_____

_____

2 What is the difference between `MouseUp` and `MouseDown`?

_____

_____

_____

3 When would you use `MouseMove` rather than `MouseUp`?

_____

_____

_____

4 What is a good application for drag and drop?

_____

_____

_____

5 How can you use the Immediate window?

_____

_____

_____

6 How can you utilize the values generated by the Change event?

_____

_____

_____

7 What do `GotFocus` and `LostFocus` do?

_____

_____

_____

8 What does it mean to have the focus?

_____

_____

_____

ANSWERS: PAGE 521

EXTRA PRACTICE

1 Write a procedure to enable the user to drag and drop the contents of a Label into a PictureBox.

2 Write a procedure that uses MouseMove to display the mouse coordinate position in a Label box as the mouse is moved.

3 Repeat these steps, this time using a TextBox.

REAL-WORLD APPLICATIONS

✔ You are working on a data collection application. Your boss tells you to make sure users are kept from entering nonalphabetic characters on the data collection form. How can you do this using KeyPress?

✔ You are designing a project that will implement a screen saver using specific bitmap files. Set up a procedure to enable the users to select files from their hard drives that they would like to display.

✔ Joe Blow, your client, wants his application to enable the users to use key combinations such as the Shift key, Ctrl key, and Alt key pressed with number keys. Design a form with TextBoxes to collect data and check for all to see which key events are occurring.

Visual Quiz

What does this code do?

_____

_____

_____

_____

_____

_____

```
Private Sub Form_MouseMove(Button As Integer, _
Shift As Integer, X As Single, Y_ As Single)
    Form2.BackColor = Int(Rnd * 32000)
    Label1.Caption = Format(X) + ", " + _ Format(Y)
    Text1.Text = Format(X) + ", " + Format(Y)
End Sub
```

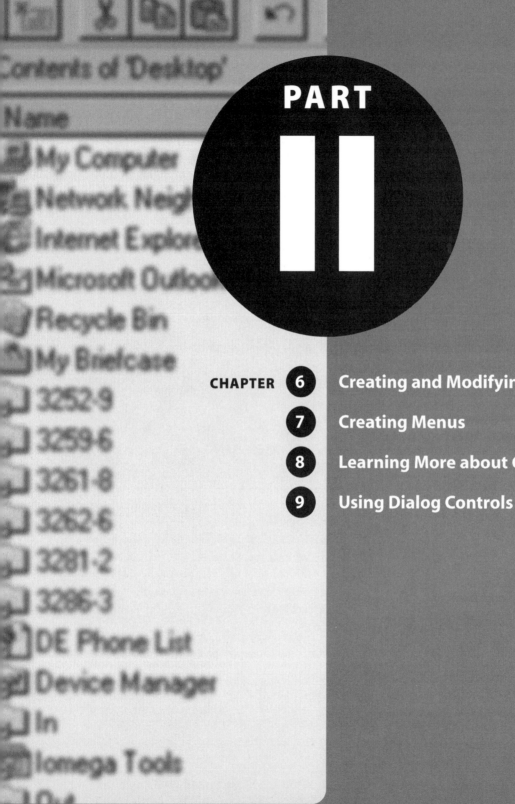

PART

II

Working with Forms and Controls

I n this Part we move on from the basic topics regarding the Integrated Development Environment toward gaining skills in forms, menus, and controls.

The previous chapters laid the groundwork to understanding the basic concepts and introducing the interface. But you have already been working with forms, controls, and menus in the process of exploring the Integrated Development Environment because these are the elements that make up the IDE.

Now that you have practiced using the IDE — including the Wizards — it is time to get more intensive experience with the key players making up the IDE. It is because forms, menus, and controls are so apparent that they represent the program to the user. Their visibility explains why they are so different from most other objects available in Visual Basic.

The goal of a programmer in any project should be to provide an environment for users that allows them to use an application to the best advantage. Therefore, the time and effort taken to provide a good interface should not be underrated. The best way to insure the interface works to the advantage of the user and the program developers is to master the construction of these integral parts of the environment.

In making decisions about placement of controls on forms, maintaining clarity in menus and toolbars, and writing code to respond to events, you can determine the usefulness of an application. The basis of these decisions is design. The design of a project is critical to its success. Success can only be achieved if sufficient resources are allocated to the design phase of a project.

The judgments made in the design determine how forms' properties, menus, dialog boxes, methods, and events are defined. Mistakes made in the design portion of development may haunt the entire lifetime of the project, and may even insure its demise.

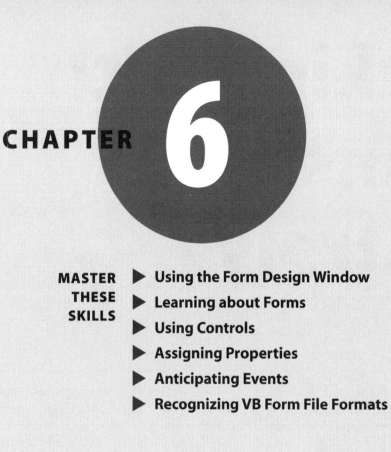

CHAPTER **6**

MASTER
THESE
SKILLS

▶ **Using the Form Design Window**
▶ **Learning about Forms**
▶ **Using Controls**
▶ **Assigning Properties**
▶ **Anticipating Events**
▶ **Recognizing VB Form File Formats**

Creating and Modifying Forms

The *form* is the keystone of any graphical user interface (GUI). That is because the form is the basis of communication between the user and the application. Everything is built around the form. The code is attached to the form and its objects. Properties are set for controls and other objects on the form. All construction proceeds from this basic object. Most of the other objects in the project are contained within it.

All forms pass through several phases. First, the form is created. Before it is loaded, it is in the created and not-loaded state. Next, it is in the loaded but not-shown state (that is, until it becomes shown). It can next be shown and available for the user. Finally, the form can be unloaded and all the references reset to zero. Even when unloaded, the form can still be resident in memory if a variable or other object on it is referenced.

As you can see from the Form Design window and the Code window, the form really has two parts: the code and the visual form. Whether or not the form is loaded, the code portion is in memory and you can call its procedures without making the form visible.

Many types of forms are used in Visual Basic. The Standard forms include the splash screen, About box, Web browser, login dialog, options dialog, Multiple Document Interface (MDI), and Single Document Interface (SDI). In addition to these, you can set up data forms and virtually any custom form you wish.

The thing to keep in mind is that everything in Visual Basic starts with the creation of a form. In fact, when you select File ⇨ New Project ⇨ Standard EXE, a Form1 is automatically created. This new form is your *tabula rasa*. You can do anything you wish to do in the application, but you must first add controls and code to the form. You can also load an existing form into a new application. You are then free to modify and customize that form as well as the default form created with the project.

The purpose of the form is to provide a backbone for the project. The form is the user interface. The steps in developing an application are to create a form, populate it with controls from the toolbox, set properties for the objects, and then write code to manage the events taking place in the execution of the program.

Using the Form Design Window

When you first open a new project, Visual Basic creates a form, Form1, for you automatically. This form then becomes the default startup form for the project. The form is there for you to build on; you may set up several forms in the process of developing your application.

The Form Design window presents you with a form with a gray grid background. Of course, you can change the color and size of the form. In fact, you can change just everything about it, including the name on the title bar. When you set or change the default attributes, that is called setting the *properties*. This you do from the Properties window.

The Form window contains Minimize, Maximize, and Close buttons, just as virtually all Windows applications do. You have many options in creating forms: fixed, movable, small dialog box-sized, large, with various background and foreground colors, and so on. Controls are placed on the form by selecting them in the toolbox. The Form Layout window lets you arrange the layout of your forms on a window that looks like a tiny monitor.

Form Properties

Having seen the new form, you will next set the properties for the form. Usually the first property to set is the `Name` property. You need to give each form a specialized name; otherwise, you will be very confused if every form in every project is called Form1, Form2, and so on.

The naming convention for objects is to use the first three characters of the object and then customize the name to fit its place in your project. For example, Form1 in a Web Browsing application might become `frmWeb`, or `frmBrow`.

The Properties Window

The Properties window displays the property list as either Alphabetic or Categorized. You select one of these options by clicking the respective tab. The categories are: Appearance, Behavior, Dynamic Data Exchange, Font, Misc, Position, and Scale.

The Appearance properties are those dealing with color, caption, picture, border, and so on. Behavior properties control Drawing mode, style and width, visibility, and enable mode. DDE has to do with linking. The Font category has only one property (Font). Misc has a number of properties, such as Tag, Icon, minimize, and maximize. The Position and Scale categories deal with the placement and sizing options for the form.

The best way to discover the meaning of each property is to select Properties Window from the View menu and then scroll down the list, selecting each property. Each time you highlight a property, its definition is displayed in the detail box at the bottom of the Properties window.

Setting Properties

Typical properties you are likely to want to set are the `Caption`, `Height`, `Width`, `Left`, and `Top` properties. The `Height` and `Width` establish the form's original size, and the `Left` and `Top` properties determine the form's location on the screen. Using the `BorderStyle` property, you can manage the form's appearance. By setting the value to zero, you can eliminate the border. You can prevent the form from being minimized and maximized by changing those values as well. If you want, you can set the `WindowState` property to start in the minimized state.

Continued

TAKE NOTE

▶ **FORMS ARE OBJECTS**

Forms are objects and participate in and respond to events. When a form is resized, the resize event is precipitated. The `Activate` event occurs when a form is displayed, using the `Visible =`, `True`, or `Show` statements. The `deActivate` event is brought on when another form is made active.

CROSS-REFERENCE

Chapter 2 introduced the form concept.

FIND IT ONLINE

The site **http://www.citilink.com/~jgarrick/vbasic/beginners/resources.html** is a good place to find resources.

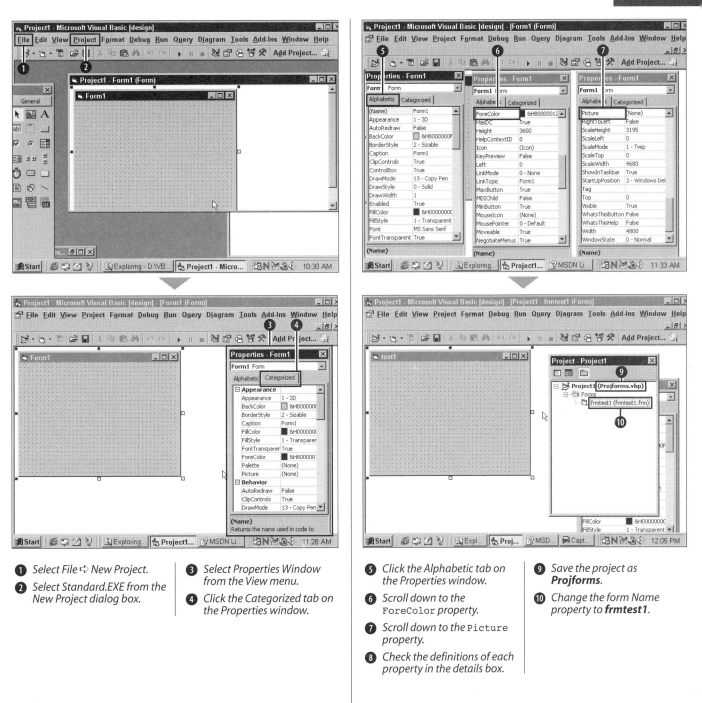

① Select File ➪ New Project.

② Select Standard.EXE from the New Project dialog box.

③ Select Properties Window from the View menu.

④ Click the Categorized tab on the Properties window.

⑤ Click the Alphabetic tab on the Properties window.

⑥ Scroll down to the ForeColor property.

⑦ Scroll down to the Picture property.

⑧ Check the definitions of each property in the details box.

⑨ Save the project as **Projforms**.

⑩ Change the form Name property to **frmtest1**.

Using the Form Design Window
Continued

One of the easiest and most important properties to change is the `Caption`, which displays on the form's title bar. To do this, select the form and type a new title in the space to the right of the Caption property in the Properties window.

When you first start a new project and a default form is created, you have created a class. This is because when the form is first created, Visual Basic creates a hidden, global object variable. You can verify the creation of this form class by selecting the Object Browser from the View menu. Select `frmtest1` from the Classes list, and then note the information in the detail pane. You will see that `frmtest1` is listed under Classes.

To see how the object variable works, add a `CommandButton` control to the `frmtest1` form, and then double-click to launch the Code window. Select `Command1` from the object list and `Click` from the procedure list. Declare a new variable `f6` as a new `frmtest1`. Then enter this code to show the new form variable:

```
Private Sub Command1_Click()
    Dim f6 As New frmtest1
    f6.Visible = True
End Sub
```

Run the procedure. How many copies of the form can you make by clicking the `CommandButton`? The first copy of the `frmtest1` form is the only one that stayed in memory after the initial display of the form copy. Each went out of memory as soon as it was displayed. The original will stay in memory, because it was automatically declared as a Public variable. This points up the fact that after the form is unloaded, all form variables should be initialized to nothing to free memory when not used.

When you added the `Command1` button to the form, you added a member to that class. Using the `New` statement created a duplicate copy of the original form. This is a way to create another form with the same properties as the original.

A forms collection is each loaded form in a project. This includes MDI forms, child forms, and all form objects.

If you are concerned about running into memory limitations and/or want to speed up your application, there are a number of factors to look at. As a rule of thumb, all objects should be unloaded when not in use.

One idea is to limit graphics or to change the way you are using them. The `PictureBox` uses more memory than the `Image` control. The `PictureBox` should be used for DDE and as a container for other controls, such as forming the basis for a toolbar. The `Image` control uses far less resources and should be used when you are just displaying a picture or clicking and dragging.

You also can store pictures and call them using `LoadResPicture` when you are ready to display them, instead of loading them with the form. Another way to economize is to load a picture one time and then share it, rather than using `LoadPicture` several times. When you are finished using a picture, you should set its value to `Nothing`.

A fact about graphics that every Web developer learns about is the difference in size of various bitmaps. For example, a Tagged Image Format (TIF) file or Windows Bitmap (BMP) file will use many times the memory and storage that a Joint Photographic Experts Group (JPEG) or Graphics Interchange Format (GIF) uses. This is because the JPEGs and GIFs are compressed. Though the default is a BMP, that does not mean that is the best for all situations.

TAKE NOTE

▶ UNDERSTANDING INTERFACE DESIGN

The key to a good interface design is one that aids the use of the application. It is helpful to look at highly successful programs. The basic rule is that you want users to feel the application is intuitive in the sense of controls and menus being where expected for ease of use. Forms should be designed so that there is white space, and colors are easy on the eyes, making for successful reading.

CROSS-REFERENCE

Chapters 2 and 8 cover similar topics.

FIND IT ONLINE

Check **http://www.citilink.com/~jgarrick/vbasic/beginners/optimize.html** for speed.

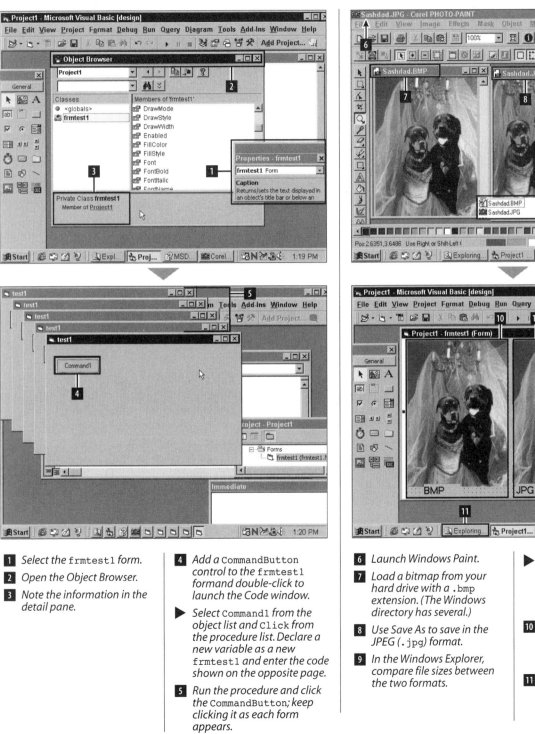

1. *Select the* `frmtest1` *form.*

2. *Open the Object Browser.*

3. *Note the information in the detail pane.*

4. *Add a* `CommandButton` *control to the* `frmtest1` *formand double-click to launch the Code window.*

▶ *Select* `Command1` *from the object list and* `Click` *from the procedure list. Declare a new variable as a new* `frmtest1` *and enter the code shown on the opposite page.*

5. *Run the procedure and click the* `CommandButton;` *keep clicking it as each form appears.*

6. *Launch Windows Paint.*

7. *Load a bitmap from your hard drive with a* `.bmp` *extension. (The Windows directory has several.)*

8. *Use Save As to save in the JPEG (*`.jpg`*) format.*

9. *In the Windows Explorer, compare file sizes between the two formats.*

▶ *Add two* `Image` *controls to* `frmtest1`*. From the Properties window, double-click the dots next to the Picture property.*

10. *Load the picture you just loaded into Paint and the JPEG you saved in Paint into the two* `Image` *boxes.*

11. *Make sure the* `Image` *controls are the same size. Compare the quality of the two pictures.*

115

Learning about Form Types

The Interface types in Visual Basic are Multiple Document Interface, Single Document Interface, and Explorer Style. The form types follow the interface styles. There are Multiple Document Interface (MDI) forms and Standard forms in Visual Basic. You can have many standard forms with one start-up form without creating any MDI forms.

Multiple Document Interface

Multiple Document Interface forms enable you to maintain multiple forms within the same form container. Multiple documents can be displayed at the same time, and each MDI form has its own window.

The child forms are displayed within the parent form's workspace at runtime. When you minimize the MDI application, the child forms are all minimized along with the parent form, but only the parent form displays an icon. MDI forms can only have controls placed that have an `Align` property or are not visible on the form. You are allowed to have only one MDI form per application, but of course you can have multiple child forms.

You cannot place most controls directly on the MDI form. For the most part, only `PictureBoxes` and `ToolBars` and menus can be placed directly onto the form. If you need `CommandButtons`, `Textboxes`, `ListBoxes`, and such, you can first place a `PictureBox` on the form and place the other controls inside that. When you add component libraries (select Components from the Project menu), you can add other controls that may have the `Align` property, enabling them to be placed on MDI forms. The `Data` control is an example of a control you can add that has the `Align` property and can be placed on an MDI form.

The MDI form will not accept a control that requires a user to take action to move the focus. This is called *modality*. A unique characteristic of MDI forms is that all child forms are contained within them at runtime. All controls belong to the MDI parent, and when the child form is active, the child's menu replaces the MDI form's menu.

To experiment with the MDI features, create a new application called `Projmdi1`. Create a new MDI form called `MDIFrmtest` by selecting Add MDI Form from the Project menu. You can use Remove Form from the Project menu to remove the default form. Load two of the forms from your last project, frmouse and Form3. Name Form3 **frmdraggin**.

You can use these with the new MDI form, but first use Save As to save the old forms in the same directory with the new MDI form. If your old forms have different names, then rename them in the Properties window first. It is a good idea to keep the project objects together so that you avoid overwriting old forms and also keep projects organized.

Add a new `CommandButton` to each of the old forms (`frmdraggin` and `frmouse`). Name the button on the `frmouse` form **cmdreturnm**. Name the button on the `frmdraggin` **cmdreturn2**. Give the buttons on both forms the same caption, **Return**. You will also need to write the code to make these forms "return" to the MDI form.

Finally, select each form in turn and set its `MDIChild` property to True. If you wish, you can finish the program and run it before you change this property. That way, you can see the difference in performance with and without designating the old forms as child forms.

TAKE NOTE

▶ **EXPLORER-STYLE FORMS**

The Explorer-style form is a Web Browser form. It looks much like the Internet Explorer browser interface. Its purpose is to browse the Internet, but can also be used to browse drives, folders, and files, as with the Windows Explorer.

CROSS-REFERENCE

Chapters 2 and 3 introduce the topic of forms.

FIND IT ONLINE

The site **http://msdn.microsoft.com/library/devprods/vs6/vb/html/vbobjformsx.htm** has a forms collection example.

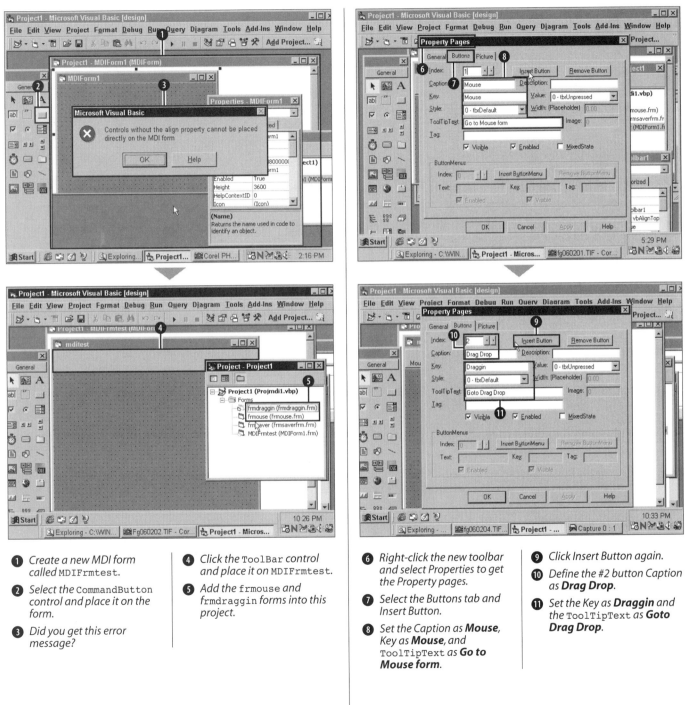

① Create a new MDI form called MDIFrmtest.

② Select the CommandButton control and place it on the form.

③ Did you get this error message?

④ Click the ToolBar control and place it on MDIFrmtest.

⑤ Add the frmmouse and frmdraggin forms into this project.

⑥ Right-click the new toolbar and select Properties to get the Property pages.

⑦ Select the Buttons tab and Insert Button.

⑧ Set the Caption as **Mouse**, Key as **Mouse**, and ToolTipText as **Go to Mouse form**.

⑨ Click Insert Button again.

⑩ Define the #2 button Caption as **Drag Drop**.

⑪ Set the Key as **Draggin** and the ToolTipText as **Goto Drag Drop**.

Using Controls

Controls are essentially small windows on a form. The icons you see in the `ToolBox` represent the controls around which you will build event procedures.

Control Types

The three types of controls are: Intrinsic controls, ActiveX controls, and insertable objects.

The Standard controls installed by default when you first launch Visual Basic should be somewhat familiar to you by now. They include the `CommandButton`, `TextBox`, `ListBox`, `PictureBox`, `Frame`, `Label`, `ComboBox`, `OptionButton`, `CheckBox`, `Image`, `DirListBox`, `DriveListBox`, `FileListBox`, `ScrollBars`, `Shape`, `Line`, `Timer`, `ImageList`, `Data`, and `OLE`.

Some of the controls are used to obtain user input; display data, images, and files; trigger events; allow selections; and so on. All of the controls have properties, methods, and events. These controls are also referred to as Intrinsic controls, because they always appear in the `ToolBox` and they are included in the executable file upon compiling.

These controls must be added via the selection of Components from the Project menu. Some components are available only in the Professional and Enterprise editions. Many are available to be added when you are creating your applications. Each set of controls is on the Components list and is contained within a file having the `.ocx` extension. You can add a set of controls from a third-party vendor as well as those shipped with Visual Basic.

You also can create your own ActiveX controls. You can use a paint program to draw the control, or make a new control from two or more existing controls. If you make a new control, you can distribute it with your application, requiring a license for the users to install it. This feature is especially useful for Internet applications.

The insertable objects feature enables you to insert objects from other applications, such as spreadsheets and scheduler files. These become controls once they are added to your project. You then have the ability to address these other applications from your project.

New Controls

In addition to the controls available in older versions of Visual Basic, there are a number of new controls in version 6. A few of these are described in the sections that follow.

The `Data` control lets you create a relationship between controls with a `DataSource` property and data sources written to OLE DB specifications. It provides a graphic scroll forward and back.

The `Coolbar` is found only in the Professional and Enterprise Editions. It can be used to create Internet Explorer–type toolbars.

The `DataGrid` control works in conjunction with the ADO Data control and enables you to display data (including databases) in a spreadsheet format.

The `DataList` and `DataCombo` controls look like list boxes, but their lists can be filled in from a database source. They can function as lookups to different tables in the same application.

Continued

TAKE NOTE

▶ OLDER VERSIONS

The ADO control is more flexible than the data controls in previous versions of Visual Basic. These old versions included the RDC and the intrinsic `Data` control. These are still available in the current version for backward compatibility, but they are not recommended for new applications.

CROSS-REFERENCE

Chapters 9 and 10 explore further the topic of controls.

FIND IT ONLINE

The page **http://msdn.microsoft.com/library/ devprods/vs6/vb/html/vbconformscontrolsmenus. htm** has examples of form controls.

Table 6-1: STANDARD CONTROLS

Controls	Description	Controls	Description
PictureBox	Displays graphics, acts as object container	VscrollBar	Provides vertical scrolling when not automatic
Label	Label that can't be changed by user	Timer	Executes events at specified time intervals
TextBox	Displays information input by user at runtime	DriveListBox	Allows user to select system drives
Frame	Groups other controls together	DirListBox	Allows user to select directories
CommandButton	Carries out a process when clicked	FileListBox	Allows user to select files
CheckBox	Can be used in groups for multiple choice	Shape	Draws shapes on forms, frames, or picture boxes
OptionButton	Displays options in groups or singly	Line	Draws lines on forms, frames, or picture boxes
ComboBox	Combines TextBox and ListBox	Image	Displays icons, bitmaps, metafiles
ListBox	Shows list of items for user choice	Data	Accesses data with minimum programming
HscrollBar	Provides horizontal scrolling when not automatic	OLE	Allows data use/changing in other applications

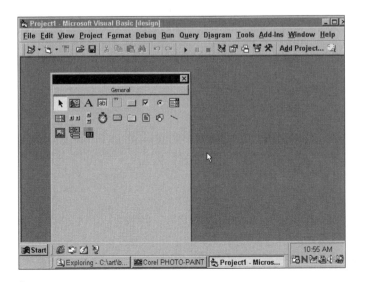

▶ The Standard ToolBox

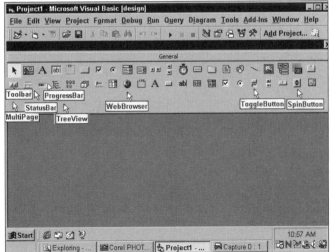

▶ The ToolBox with additional controls

Using Controls

Continued

The DateTimePicker control, which is in only the Professional and Enterprise Editions, provides a drop-down calendar for user selection of data and/or time.

The `FlatScrollbar` control gives a more chic look to the scroll bars but is available only in the Professional and Enterprise Editions.

The `ImageCombo` control is similar to the `ComboBox` but lets you add images to the list.

In addition to the new controls, some of the older controls have been enhanced. The `ImageList` is one example. It now supports GIF and JPG files.

Adding Controls to ProjMDI1

In the previous topic, you placed a `ToolBar` control on the MDI form (MDItest) and then made a custom toolbar for your application. The buttons on the toolbar can be added in the Property pages by inserting buttons from the Buttons tab. Because you have already added the Mouse and Drag Drop buttons to the custom toolbar, you need to add the Quit option. If you had a menu on this form, you might use the File menu and place an Exit option there.

Select the toolbar and then right-click for the Property pages. Scroll to button three by clicking the right arrow in the Index box. Use Quit for the caption and the Key. Type **Quit Program** for the `ToolTipText` if you wish. Click OK.

You know from your previous experience that you can end the program by using the keyword `End` in the `Command_Click` procedure. Because you want to go back to the MDI form here, rather than ending the program, you must take other measures.

When you wanted to display a new form to the users, you used the `Visible = True` or `Show` statements. That way, the desired form would be displayed on top of the other windows. If you simply make the other form Visible,

it will have no effect, because the MDI form is already visible. What you need to do then is to `Hide` your `frmouse` form. Add this line of code to the `Click` procedure for the `cmdreturnm` object:

```
Me.Hide
```

This will hide the current form and make it seem that you have returned to the MDI form. This works well as long as all the forms are loaded with the project. What happens here is that all the forms are available and the previous form has suddenly come to the front.

If you find that one or both of the forms do not "return," check to see whether their property values for the `MDIChild` property are set to True. If not, they will not return to the MDI form. Experiment by resetting the `MDIChild` property to False and run the program. What difference does it make? Notice that the forms are resized so that they fit into the MDI form. If you were to add menus to each of these forms, you would find that the parent form's menu is replaced with each child form's menu when each of the child forms has the focus.

TAKE NOTE

▶ **ALIGNING CONTROLS**

When you created the toolbar example, it was aligned to the top of the form. You can change the `Align` property of the toolbar. Click to the right of the `Align` property in the Properties window and then select one of the options other than `vbAlignTop`. If you want the control to appear correctly, you should plan ahead, as the `vbAlignRight` might not display a button with a text caption correctly.

CROSS-REFERENCE

Chapter 16 pursues the topic of graphic controls further.

FIND IT ONLINE

Check out **http://msdn.microsoft.com/library/devprods/vs6/ vb/html/vbconunderstandingpropertiesmethodsevents.htm**.

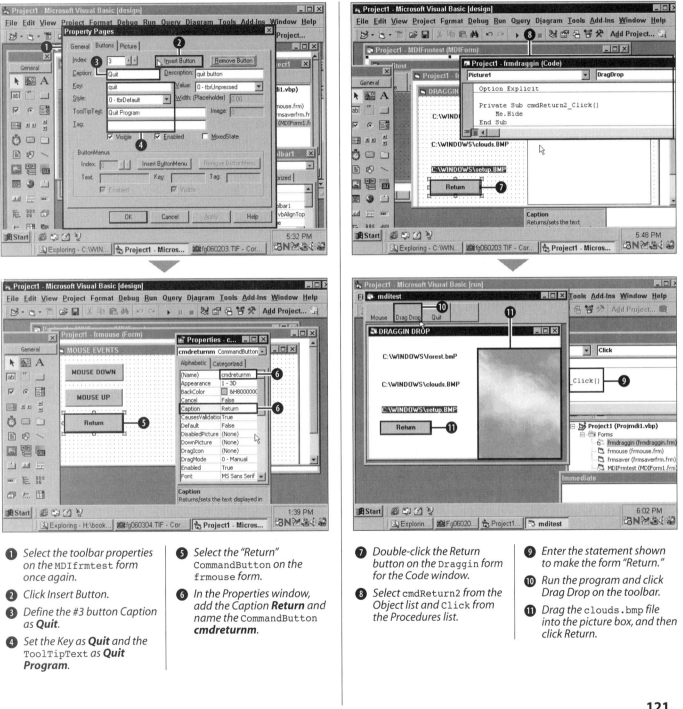

① Select the toolbar properties on the MDIfrmtest form once again.

② Click Insert Button.

③ Define the #3 button Caption as **Quit**.

④ Set the Key as **Quit** and the ToolTipText as **Quit Program**.

⑤ Select the "Return" CommandButton on the frmouse form.

⑥ In the Properties window, add the Caption **Return** and name the CommandButton **cmdreturnm**.

⑦ Double-click the Return button on the Draggin form for the Code window.

⑧ Select cmdReturn2 from the Object list and Click from the Procedures list.

⑨ Enter the statement shown to make the form "Return."

⑩ Run the program and click Drag Drop on the toolbar.

⑪ Drag the clouds.bmp file into the picture box, and then click Return.

Assigning Properties

You have been exploring property assignments for controls in several chapters. Properties you should assign are those dealing with appearance (`ForeColor`, `BackColor`, `BorderStyle`, `Enabled`, `Font`, `Name`, and `Caption`. In addition, you should consider properties assigned to objects in other applications providing similar functionality to yours.

For example, if you are adding a child form to an MDI form, you should set the `MDIChild` property of the child form to True. The `AutoShowChildren` property of the MDI form should be set to `True` as well. If you have a `PictureBox` that will display a screen saver box and you have large bitmaps that you want to fill the page, you may wish to change the Align property to Bottom. Otherwise, you may want it set to None.

Properties Collection

Every property in the Properties window is an object. Every property provided for an existing control is displayed in the Properties window.

Ambient Properties

Before you assign properties to a control, note that the control has certain assumptions regarding properties appropriate to specific containers. These are called *ambient properties*. Ambient properties are available to your ActiveX controls through the `AmbientProperties` object. In case your control's container does not have ambient properties, properties will be provided by default.

For example, a custom toolbar control on a form will have information regarding the properties of the form, so that the properties of the control will be consistent with those of the form. Ambient properties are also defined by containers. These will not be displayed in the Object Browser, because they are not in the Type Library.

Saving Properties

When you assign properties to your controls, they are saved in a separate file. This file has an `.frx` or `.frm` extension for a form or a `.ctl` or `.ctx` extension for a user control. If you create an ActiveX control, you need to write code specifically to save and retrieve the property values. You can use the `PropertyBag` object to carry out this task.

Property Pages

Property pages provide an additional way to view properties for ActiveX controls. Property pages have tabs for setting different properties. The tabs are specific to each type of control; for instance, you only have a Buttons tab when your control can have buttons. When you used the `ToolBar` control you set the properties for the buttons in the Property pages. You can still view the properties in the Properties window, but in order to create and configure the individual buttons, you must use the Property pages.

Continued

TAKE NOTE

▶ SCALING THE FORM

Using the `ScaleLeft` and `ScaleTop` properties, you can set up coordinates with both positive and negative coordinates. These `Scale` properties interact with the `ScaleMode` property by resetting the `ScaleMode` property to zero if any other scale property is given a value. If you set the `ScaleMode` property to a positive number, the `ScaleHeight`, `ScaleWidth`, `CurrentY`, and `CurrentX` values are set to the new unit of measurement. `ScaleLeft` and `ScaleTop` are set to zero.

CROSS-REFERENCE

Chapter 16 has more usage of controls and properties.

FIND IT ONLINE

See **http://msdn.microsoft.com/library/devprods/vs6/vb/html/ vbcondesigningform.htm** for information on form design.

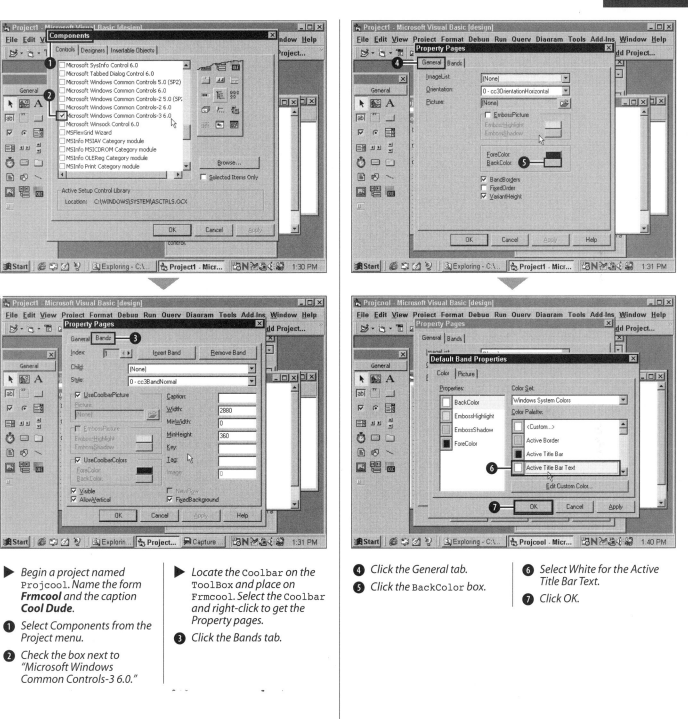

▶ *Begin a project named* Projcool. *Name the form* ***Frmcool*** *and the caption* ***Cool Dude***.

❶ *Select Components from the Project menu.*

❷ *Check the box next to "Microsoft Windows Common Controls-3 6.0."*

▶ *Locate the* Coolbar *on the* ToolBox *and place on* Frmcool. *Select the* Coolbar *and right-click to get the Property pages.*

❸ *Click the Bands tab.*

❹ *Click the General tab.*

❺ *Click the* BackColor *box.*

❻ *Select White for the Active Title Bar Text.*

❼ *Click OK.*

Assigning Properties

Continued

Properties are specific to the type of control or other object. Forms have properties other objects don't have, and other objects may have properties not available to forms.

Most objects have the `Appearance` of flat or three-dimensional.

`BackColor` or `ForeColor` color is set by using the System color scheme options, or making a selection from the RGB Palette.

`FillColor` is available for filling shapes created with the Shape control, but `FillStyle` must be not be set to transparent or the `FillColor` will not show.

`BorderStyle` has the following options: None (no border), Fixed single (only resizable with Minimize and Maximize buttons), Sizable (resizable using Minimize and Maximize buttons, or clicking and dragging), Fixed dialog (doesn't have minimize and maximize buttons), Fixed `ToolWindow` (not resizable), Sizable `ToolWindow` (resizable).

Typing the text in the `Caption` property box sets the form caption property.

Setting the `Palette` property controls the `ForeColor` and `BackColor` properties.

The `Picture` property can be set to a bitmap. Try setting this property by using a large bitmap, such as `Clouds.bmp` in the Windows directory.

The various properties categorized as Behavior concern the drawing, modal, enablement, and visibility display context features.

`AutoReDraw` is used in conjunction with `ClipControls` to produce varying effects in the way graphical controls and methods paint on the screen.

The `DrawMode`, `DrawStyle`, and `DrawWidth` control the tool, type of line, and width of the pen, respectively.

The `DDE` properties deal with linking and exchanging data. The `LinkTopic` property consists of a string that supplies part of the information necessary to set up either a destination link or a source link.

The `LinkMode` property controls the communication between the destination form and a data source.

Along with the font selection, this enables selection of typeface, font style, effects, and size.

The miscellaneous category includes more than any other. This category includes some of the most important properties. The `Name` property is one of these, along with the `MDIChild` property. If `MinButton` or `MaxButton` is set to false, that button will appear grayed out on the form at runtime. The `MouseIcon` displays an icon of your selection when the form is minimized. The `MousePointer` property lets you change the default cursor for variations.

The `WindowState` may be normal, maximized, or minimized.

The `Position` and `Scale` properties pertain to forms. The `Height` and `Width` properties determine the number of twips that will be required for the dimensions of the form. The `Left` and `Top` properties determine the form's relationship to the screen. The `Moveable` property may be true or false. The `StartUpPosition` determines the placement in relation to the workspace.

If the `Left` and `Top` properties are given values, the `StartUpPosition` reverts to Manual. The `ScaleMode` may be changed to other units of measure, such as the pixel.

CROSS-REFERENCE

Chapters 2 and 8 have more to say on form properties.

FIND IT ONLINE

The site **http://msdn.microsoft.com/library/devprods/vs6/vb/html/ vbcondisplayingenteringtext.htm** has material on text controls.

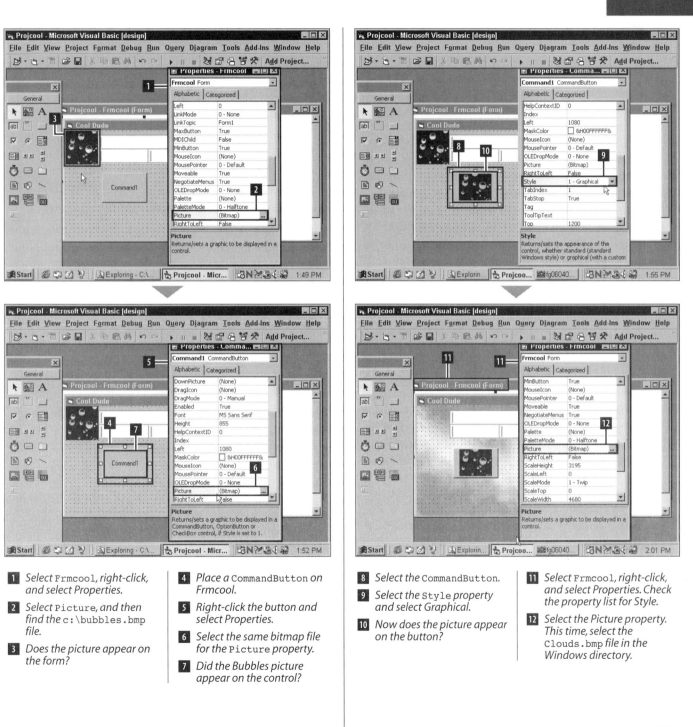

1. Select Frmcool, right-click, and select Properties.

2. Select Picture, and then find the c:\bubbles.bmp file.

3. Does the picture appear on the form?

4. Place a CommandButton on Frmcool.

5. Right-click the button and select Properties.

6. Select the same bitmap file for the Picture property.

7. Did the Bubbles picture appear on the control?

8. Select the CommandButton.

9. Select the Style property and select Graphical.

10. Now does the picture appear on the button?

11. Select Frmcool, right-click, and select Properties. Check the property list for Style.

12. Select the Picture property. This time, select the Clouds.bmp file in the Windows directory.

Recognizing Project File Formats

Visual Basic stores project data in files with specific extensions when you create a project. The various formats are done at design time, miscellaneous development, and runtime.

The design files are the building blocks of your project: basic modules (`.bas`) and form modules (`.frm`).

Form (`.frm`) and project (`.vbp`) files are saved in ASCII format, but some of the files in a Visual Basic project are saved in binary format and are not readable as text. The ASCII files are readable in a text viewer (Notepad for instance). Form (`.frm`) files are created and saved in ASCII format. The form file contains the version number, a text description, form attributes, the code in the form.

Some form controls have binary data values due to bitmaps they contain. An additional form file will be saved with the same name, but with an .FRX extension. The .FRX file is a proprietary format and should be distributed with the .FRM form files. Your project will not work without all including all of the files.

Project File Formats

When you save your project, the project is updated. The project file (`.vbp`) includes the files shown in the Project Explorer, where they are grouped according to type. You also can view the files in the Windows Explorer providing you remember the names you gave each form and module. Project files, however, contain other references besides forms and modules.

When you add a file to your project, you are simply adding a reference to that file, not the file itself. When you remove a file within Visual Basic, the reference to the file is removed, but if you delete a file in the Windows Explorer, Visual Basic cannot remove the reference to the file. If you wish to save a file without saving it as part of the project, select File ⇨ Save and then type the filename.

Visual Basic displays multiple projects in the Project window in a hierarchical view. Each project appears at the top level, with the project's forms, modules, controls, Property pages, or document objects grouped under it in the hierarchical view.

You can also import files into the Code window. Just move the cursor to the place where you want the new file inserted and then select Insert from the Edit menu and select the filename of the file you want to insert and click Open.

When a project is complete, you can compile and create an `.exe` file. You do this by selecting `Make.exe` from the File menu. If you have the Professional or Enterprise Edition of Visual Basic, you can create dynamic linked libraries (`.dll`) files or ActiveX files (`.ocx`).

Table 6-1: DESIGN-TIME FILE TYPES

File Extension	Purpose	File Extension	Purpose
.bas	Basic module	.oca	Control TypeLib cache
.cls	Class module	.pag	Property page
.ctl	User Control	.pgx	Binary Property page
.ctx	User Control binary file	.res	Resource
.ddf	Package and Deployment Wizard CAB	.tlb	Remote Automation TypeLib
.dep	Package and Deployment Wizard	.vbg	Visual Basic group project
.dob	ActiveX document form file	.vbl	Control licensing
.dox	ActiveX document binary form file	.vbp	Visual Basic project
.dsr	Active Designer file	.vbr	Remote Automation registration
.dsx	Active Designer binary file	.vbw	Visual Basic project workspace
.frm	Form	.vbz	Wizard launch
.frx	Binary form	.wct	WebClass HTML template
.log	Log file for load errors		

Table 6-2: RUNTIME FILE TYPES

File Extension	Purpose
.dll	Dynamic link library (ActiveX component in process)
.exe	Executable or ActiveX component
.ocx	ActiveX control
.vbd	ActiveX document state

Personal Workbook

Q&A

1 How do you change the startup form in a project?

_____

_____

_____

2 What name would you give form1 in the project "Projmoney?"

_____

_____

_____

3 What are the most important properties to set for a form?

_____

_____

_____

4 What is a forms collection?

_____

_____

_____

5 What is one thing you can do to reduce memory overhead?

_____

_____

_____

6 What is an MDI form?

_____

_____

_____

7 What control can you place directly on an MDI form?

_____

_____

_____

8 What are ActiveX controls?

_____

_____

_____

ANSWERS PAGE: 522

EXTRA PRACTICE

1 Create an application that has an MDI form and four child forms.

2 Practice adding controls from different component libraries to your project.

3 Start a project with an MDI form and add a custom toolbar to it.

REAL-WORLD APPLICATIONS

✔ You have been asked to design a project with an MDI form and child forms. The client wants the main form to have a toolbar with such options as Open, Save, Print, access form2, access form3. Design the project.

✔ You are designing a project at the request of your boss, who wants all the forms to have only Close buttons, not Minimize or Maximize buttons. Design the project and specify the forms' properties.

✔ Joe Schmoe, your client, wants his application to have a bitmap background on the Main form. He also wants at least one form to feature custom shapes and buttons with pictures on them. How can you do this?

Visual Quiz

What property is being set in the picture on the right? What object is the property being set for?

_____

_____

_____

_____

_____

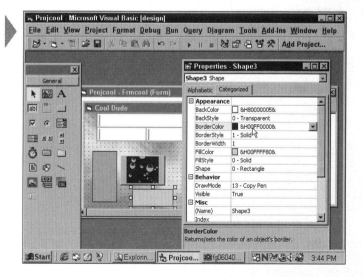

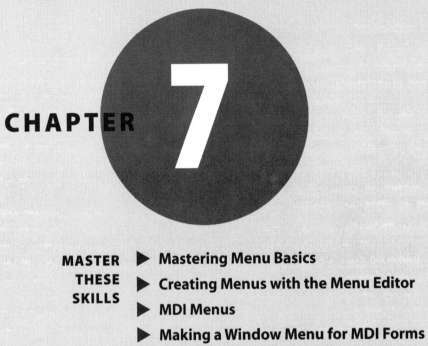

CHAPTER 7

Creating Menus

Menus, together with forms and controls, are an integral part of the Visual Basic environment. Menus guide the user through the application. They are a convenient way to give the user choices and options and enable you to organize the options into logical groupings. For example, a word processor might offer font options under the Format menu, while a database program might place reports under the Format menu.

Nearly all Windows applications offer File, Edit, View, Tools, Window, and Help menus. Any other menus usually fall between the View and Window menus. These additional menus follow the guidelines determined by the type of application and its functions. The Tools menu for Microsoft Word offers such options as Spelling and Thesaurus, while the Visual Basic Tools menu provides options for the Menu Editor and further options.

The critical part of an application for users is what they see and use. No matter how great the programming techniques, the optimization and skill, if you stint on the user interface you will limit the application's usability.

The issue of how to make a good user interface points up the importance of menus. For the menus reflect the organization of the application. When you design your application, you should give a great deal of thought about all of the features and functions that it must encompass. If the design is complete, then the menus (and the interface) will be appropriate.

An application that is used to access and process database files would dictate a different menus system than one that is designed to be a draw and paint program. There still would be a File menu for the paint program, but there might also be Layout and Effects menus. Other features of the application that would affect the menu system are the number of different functions and how these functions are grouped. For example, a report designing function might be better placed on the Tools menu of the main form. Alternatively, a special form might be needed if the report design aspect had many parts and functions.

Another factor to consider is what types of users will use the application. The users' job descriptions and experience will dictate the structure and design of the menus. The reality of application development usually involves many interactions with the users and the users' supervisors. The greater the amount of time you spend in conference with the users, the less time you will need to use making revisions.

Mastering Menu Basics

As you saw in Chapter 3 there are certain default menus you get when you create an automated application.

At the very top of the form is a *title bar.* Immediately below that is the *menu bar.* Selecting the items on the menu bar produces a *drop-down menu,* usually with more than one option. Some of the menu options produce subsequent drop-down menus with further options. Other menu options provide a direct command that is executed, rather than accessing another menu. The Exit option on the File menu is one example. Menu objects also often have spaces between the various menus, called *separator bars.*

As with all other Visual Basic controls, menu controls also are objects. You can set the same properties to other controls. Menus have only one event, however. That is the `click` event, which is initiated either by mouse click or keypress.

Menu Names

Menus should have unique names within the same form. You can use the same or similar names for menu options with similar functions as long as they appear on different forms. Menu item names may be multiple words but should follow the general naming convention of Visual Basic objects.

The first three characters of an object's name indicate the object type. Thus, `frm` are the first three characters in the name of a form, and Command buttons all begin with `cmd`. For management of files and resources, object names should be as brief as possible. The naming standard for Menus is the prefix `mnu`.

Command Bars

Command bars combine the functions of the menu bar and the toolbar into one object. Command bars are seen by Visual Basic as essentially the same as menu bars and toolbars. That is, they are in the same object library.

Coding Menus

Once you create a menu, whether in the Menu Editor or using a predefined menu, such as in the Application Wizard, you will need to write the supporting procedures for the menu options. Because the menus only support the `Click` procedures, coding may be simpler than in writing other procedures you have examined so far.

Just as you have written code to carry out the `Click` procedures for command buttons, you need to set up procedures for each menu and submenu option. You can use this same code to carry out similar functions for the menu options.

For example, when you created the Projmdi1 project, you set up a procedure to return to the `mdifrmtest` form from the `frmouse` form. Although this was code attached to a `CommandButton`, you can use the same code for the same function on a menu bar. You used this procedure to respond to the `click` event on a toolbar button on the `mdifrmtest` form.

TAKE NOTE

► **ADDING AN ABOUT FORM**

A user new to your application may not understand what it is all about. Therefore, you should consider adding an About menu and form to your project. This will provide the information needed about the application name, description, when created, version and system info. You can do this from the Project menu, selecting Add Form, then the About icon on the Add Form dialog box.

CROSS-REFERENCE

There are good parallels in Chapter 2 and Chapter 3.

FIND IT ONLINE

Gary Beene's site is chock full of menu info: **http://web2. airmail.net/gbeene/tut-samp.html#menus.**

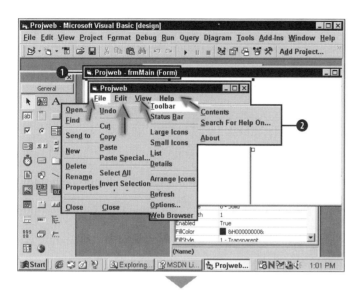

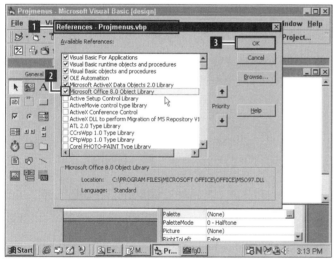

Listing 7-1: Click Procedures for CommandButtons

```
Private Sub cmdreturnm_Click()
    Me.Hide
End Sub


Private Sub Cmdmouse_Click()
    Form2.Show
End Sub
```

Listing 7-2: Click Procedures for Menu Options

```
Private Sub mnumouse_Click()
    frmouse.Show
End Sub


Private Sub mnusaver_Click()
    frmsaver.Show
End Sub
```

① Open the Projweb project from Chapter 3.

② Click each of the menus on the frmMain form.

▶ Observe the menu options.

1 Select References from the Project menu.

2 Check the box for the Microsoft Office 8.0 Object Library.

3 Click OK.

Creating Menus with the Menu Editor

The Menu Editor enables you to create custom menus for your application. Select the Menu Editor from the Tools menu. The Menu Editor dialog box has text boxes for name and caption.

The text you type in the Caption box will appear as the menu option titles on your form. The name will not appear on the form. The Index is for use with an array and does not reflect the order of the option. The arrow keys are there to enable you to change the positions of your menu options.

Menu Editor Commands

The Caption text box is where you enter the name of the menu you want shown on the title bar. If you want the users to be able to pull down the menu with a keypress, you should type an ampersand in front of the letter that will be the key for them to press. An underscore character designates the items that will accept a keypress.

If you would like to have a line separating menu items (called a separator bar), you can do this by inserting an item and then typing a hyphen in the caption box.

The Name box will contain a control name for the menu option. This will not appear anywhere on your menu, but you will refer to it when you write the code to carry out the menu item's procedure.

The Index box is used for arrays.

A Shortcut key provides a key combination for access to the option. You can see the options by clicking the down arrow on the right side of the Shortcut box. There is quite a large selection of key combinations.

If you have a help file associated with the menu option, you should place the ID value in the HelpContextID box.

The NegotiatePosition box determines the position of the option on a form.

The Checked box lets you show whether the item is currently turned on or deselected.

The Enabled option is the way to control whether menu options are shown bolded or grayed out (not available). For example, if you have nothing on the clipboard, you cannot copy or paste, so that item would not normally show as bolded or available for selection.

An item that has Visible unchecked will not appear on the menu title.

The WindowList option is for use in an MDI application.

The Arrows control the placement of the menu options as well as the level of menu. The right arrow moves the selection down to a submenu level, while the left arrow moves the option up to a parent level. The up and down arrows move the options up and down on the list within the same menu level.

The List box shows the listed options as you create them. It is empty until you start adding menu items. Next moves to the next line. Insert adds a line above the current line and is the way you add new menu options. Delete removes the currently selected line.

Continued

TAKE NOTE

DIMMING OR GRAYING OUT OPTIONS

Perhaps you haven't gotten around to defining all your menu options but want them on the menu bar anyway. If you wish to make them appear dimmed, so they can't be selected, this is an option at design time. You can just remove the check in the Enabled box. This will permanently deselect the items. If you want to dim the options only at run-time (the users can't paste because there is nothing on the clipboard to paste), you will need to write an event procedure.

CROSS-REFERENCE

Chapter 6 deals with toolbars and menus.

FIND IT ONLINE

Here is further info on runtime menus: **http://msdn. microsoft.com/library/devprods/vs6/vb/html/ vbconcreatingmodifyingmenusatruntime.htm.**

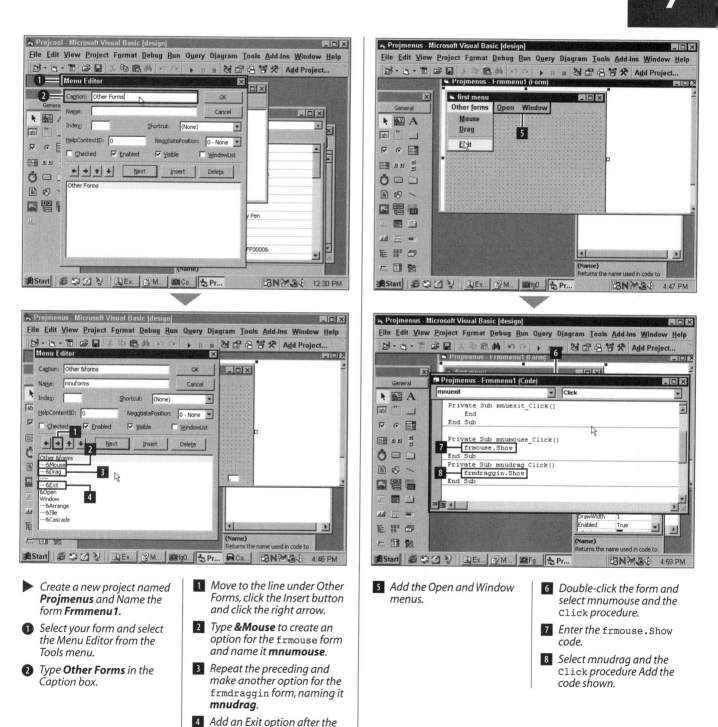

▶ Create a new project named **Projmenus** and Name the form **Frmmenu1**.

① Select your form and select the Menu Editor from the Tools menu.

② Type **Other Forms** in the Caption box.

1 Move to the line under Other Forms, click the Insert button and click the right arrow.

2 Type **&Mouse** to create an option for the frmouse form and name it **mnumouse**.

3 Repeat the preceding and make another option for the frmdraggin form, naming it **mnudrag**.

4 Add an Exit option after the Mouse and Drag options.

5 Add the Open and Window menus.

6 Double-click the form and select mnumouse and the Click procedure.

7 Enter the frmouse.Show code.

8 Select mnudrag and the Click procedure Add the code shown.

Creating Menus with the Menu Editor *Continued*

Now that you have made a menu with some options, you need to explore the way to make the options work. When you add the options to menus and submenus, the Menu Editor adds nothing to make them operate.

When you created the Projweb project in Chapter 3, the Application Wizard made the menus for you and made some of the options work. You will remember that selecting an option (File New) presented a dialog box saying, "Add the `mnuFileNew_Click_code`." The menus created in the Menu Editor do not produce any code for options. The Menu Editor sets up the structure and the appearance of menus only.

The Projmenus Project

The new project name is Projmenus. The main form is named `Frmmenu1`. You must import the `frmmouse` form and the `frmdraggin` form you used in subsequent chapters. If you do not have these forms, you can recreate them following the instructions in Chapter 5 or Chapter 6. The `frmdraggin` form was named "Form3" in Chapter 5. Add the Form3 form in Chapter 5; name it **frmdraggin** now.

In the last exercise, you wrote the code for the Other Forms menu items so that this selection would display either the `frmmouse` or the `frmdraggin` forms. Once you add the previous forms to your work, you should run the application and test the part that displays these two forms. The forms should be displayed and return to the main form. If they do not have return buttons, you can add these according to the instructions in Chapter 5 or Chapter 6. It is important that you test the menu procedures that you just set up.

The menu options should be named as in the examples unless you want to change your code from that shown. The first menu, "Other forms," is named "mnuforms." Mnuforms has three options, "Mouse," "Drag," and "Exit." The Mouse option is named "mnumouse" and the Drag item is named "mnudrag." Exit is named "mnuexit." The Open menu has no options and is named "mnuopen." The Window menu, "mnuwindo," has three options. They are Arrange, "mnuarrange," Tile, "mnutile," and Cascade, "mnucasc."

The next step is to write the procedures for the Exit option and the Open menu.

Exit

The code to Exit is the same as the procedure you wrote to quit the program in previous projects:

```
Private Sub mnuexit_Click()
    End
End Sub
```

In this exercise, the only difference is that of the object. It is the `mnuexit` object, rather than the `CommandButton` object. This procedure stops program execution, rather than unloading or hiding the form.

Open

Before you get started writing some code for the Open procedure, you may wonder what it is supposed to open. The answer is that there is a planned function, namely, to bring a file into a text editor. We need to carry out some preliminary work before the Open menu makes any sense.

TAKE NOTE

TOP-LEVEL MENUS VERSUS SUBMENUS

Different rules apply to top-level menus than for submenus. When you add submenus, you can control the status of a menu by selecting or deselecting the Checked box, the Enabled box, and the Visible box. This will render the options either bolded (Enabled), made visible, or made invisible. You also can separate submenus with separator bars. Top-level menus cannot be checked or separated, but they can be disabled and made invisible.

FIND IT ONLINE

Here is info regarding the Menu Editor: **http://msdn. microsoft.com/library/devprods/vs6/vb/html/ vbconcreatingmenuswithmenueditor.htm.**

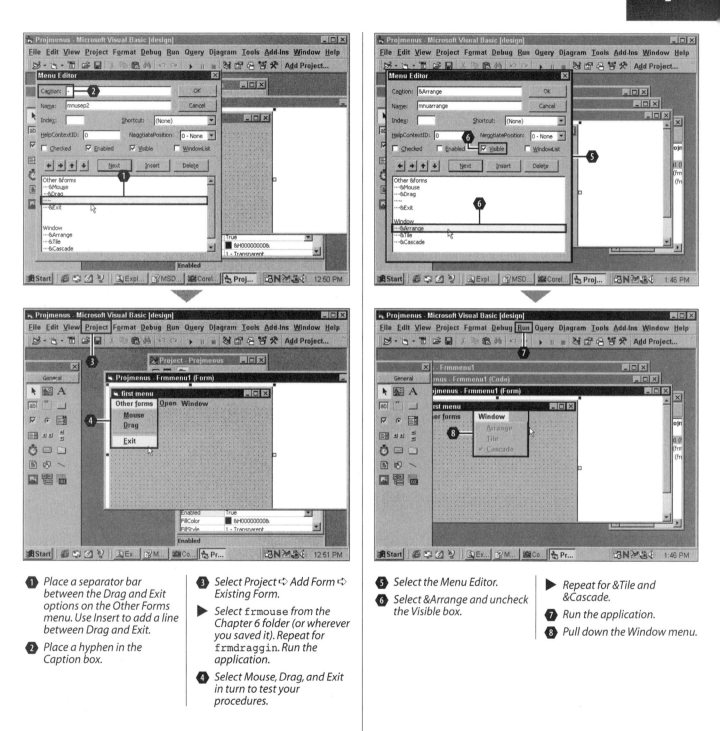

① Place a separator bar between the Drag and Exit options on the Other Forms menu. Use Insert to add a line between Drag and Exit.

② Place a hyphen in the Caption box.

③ Select Project ⇨ Add Form ⇨ Existing Form.

▶ Select frmouse from the Chapter 6 folder (or wherever you saved it). Repeat for frmdraggin. Run the application.

④ Select Mouse, Drag, and Exit in turn to test your procedures.

⑤ Select the Menu Editor.

⑥ Select &Arrange and uncheck the Visible box.

▶ Repeat for &Tile and &Cascade.

⑦ Run the application.

⑧ Pull down the Window menu.

Adding Controls to the Frmmenu Form

The `RichTextBox` control is available from a control library on the Projects ⇨ Components menu. It enables you to format ASCII text files and rich text files. You can use many formatting options similar to those offered by standard word processors. For example, you can change text to bold or italic, change its color, and create superscripts and subscripts.

Return to the Project menu, select Components, and check the box next to Microsoft Rich Textbox control 6.0. Click OK. You should see a new control in your toolbox. When you run the mouse cursor over it, it will display "RichTextBox."

At this point you should make sure you have a rich text file. These files have the `.rtf` extension, so you can use the Find option on the Start menu to look for one. If you don't have one, you can go to any word processor, retrieve a document, and select Save As to save it in the `.rtf` format. This will enable you to retrieve it for your lesson.

Place the `RichTextBox` on the `Frmmenu1` form. Drag it to at least half the size of the form, so you have enough room to edit the file. Name the file **rchTestText**. When you right-click and select Properties (with rchTestText selected) you will access the Property Pages dialog box. There is space at the top of the window to type in a specific filename.

The `CommonDialog` control includes a set of dialog boxes designed for several types of operations: opening and saving files, selecting print options, selecting colors and fonts. It also can access the Windows Help engine to display help. This control uses routines in the Microsoft Windows dynamic link library `Commdlg.dll`. Make sure that file is in your `Windows\System` directory to use this control.

Another preparatory action you must take is to place the `CommonDialog` control on your form. You will find this control on the Components option on the Projects menu. Select the Controls tab, then place a check in the box next to Microsoft Common Dialog Control 6.0.

Once you place the `CommonDialog` control on your form, it will only be visible at design time. At runtime, the control takes the form of the method used with it. For example, the `ShowOpen` method will show an open file dialog box. If the `ShowHelp` method is invoked, context-sensitive help will be available.

The `CommonDialog` control should be named "dlgTestOpen." When you right-click the control and access the property pages, you should give it a title, specify the filename (according to where you put it and what you named it), and type *****.rtf** in the Filter box. When you click OK on the Property Pages and go to the Property window, you will now see that those items appear.

If you double-click the `CommonDialog` control, you will get the Code window. Select the `mnuopen` object and the `Click` procedure. `Click` is the only procedure available for menus and options.

The `RichTextBox` and the `CommonDialog` control are often used together. In this exercise, the `CommonDialog` control, `dlgTestOpen` object will display the Open File dialog box and filter the file selection to that of Rich Text files. The `rchTestText` object will load the file into the text box.

TAKE NOTE

▶ **HELP WITH THE COMMONDIALOG CONTROL**

You can provide users of your application with help by accessing the Windows Help engine through the `CommonDialog` control. When you invoke the `ShowHelp` method, `WINHLP32.EXE` is launched and displays a help file that is set by the `HelpFile` property. You must specify `HelpFile`, `HelpContext`, and/or `HelpCommand` property. You can set up context-sensitive help or specific help, but you must specify the help you are requesting.

CROSS-REFERENCE

Chapter 8 has more examples of controls.

FIND IT ONLINE

This site has info on menu basics: **http://msdn.microsoft.com/ library/devprods/vs6/vb/html/vbconmenubasics.htm**.

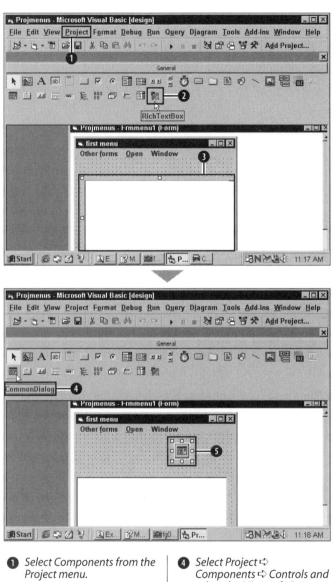

Listing 7-3: The Menu Open Procedure

```
Private Sub mnuopen_Click()
    dlgTestOpen.Filter = "Rich Text Format _
files|*.rtf"
    dlgTestOpen.ShowOpen
    rchTestText.LoadFile dlgTestOpen.FileName,
rtfRTF

End Sub
```

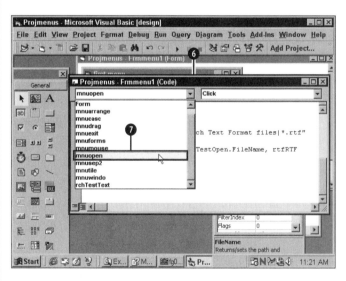

① *Select Components from the Project menu.*

② *Select the Microsoft Rich TextBox control 6.0.*

③ *Select the RichTextBox from the toolbox and place on the form.*

④ *Select Project ➪ Components ➪ Controls and select the Microsoft Common Dialog Control 6.0.*

⑤ *Place the* CommonDialog *control on your form.*

⑥ *Double-click to select the Code window.*

⑦ *Select the* mnuopen *object. The* Click *procedure is the only procedure available.*

MDI Menus

There are a number of differences between applications that use MDI forms and those that don't. Child menus typically display on the MDI form instead of the MDI form's menu when the child form has the focus. For example, when you make a selection to go to another form, then choose a command from the child form, you will see that the child menu is displayed on the MDI form.

When you set up the menus on MDI applications, you should remember how the menus are displayed. Because the child menus are displayed as if they were actually on the parent (MDI) form, you may wish to create the child menus with this fact in mind. Also, remember that the child form is displayed as if contained within the MDI form. This will be the case only after you change the `MDIChild` property to true. Because the default is false, you will need to make the change after adding the new child form to the MDI project.

You can use the previously created MDI project (Projmdi1) if you wish, but your learning will benefit best if you organize your projects into folders with a naming convention best suited to your memory capabilities. For example, you might have a folder named "book," with subfolders named for each chapter in the book. In this case, the instructions will follow that convention.

Create a new project named "Projmdi2." Use Project ⇨ Add Form to add a new MDI form. Name this form **MDIfrmtest2**. Now you will need some child forms in order to set up menus and options for the `MDIfrmtest2` form. One way to do this is to replicate what we did in previous projects. So use the Project ⇨ Add Form menu to add the forms in the previous project, `frmmouse` and `frmdraggin`.

After you have all the forms showing in the Project window, you should use File ⇨ Save As to save the project and each form to your current directory. Because you undoubtedly added the two child forms from the last lesson's directory, you should resave them in a new working directory as you will change them significantly. Use the Save `frmmouse.frm` As and Save `frmdraggin.frm` As options on the File menu to save each form in turn.

Select your new MDI form and run the Menu Editor from the Tools menu. Make an Applications menu with options Mouse, Draggin, and Exit. Make Window and Help menus and uncheck the Visible option for these menus. That will keep them from being displayed until you can write procedures for them.

Set up the options for the Applications menu as you did for the previous MDI project. Click the Applications menu and select the Mouse option. In the Code window, inside the `mnumouse_Click` procedure, enter:

```
Frmmouse.Show
```

Back to the Applications menu, click Draggin. In the Code window, enter:

```
Frmdraggin.Show
```

Within the `mnudrag_Click` procedure. When you click the menu option, you are transported directly into the procedure where the code belongs. This time, you do not even need to select the object, and `Click` is the only procedure available for menu items. The Exit option is done similarly. This time, you type **End** within the `mnuexit_Click` procedure.

CROSS-REFERENCE

Look for more menu controls in Chapter 8.

FIND IT ONLINE

There is info at this site on MDI application menus:
http://msdn.microsoft.com/library/devprods/vs6/vb/html/vbconmenusinmdiapplications.htm.

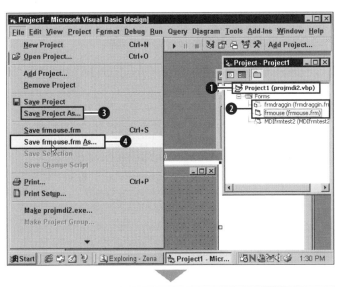

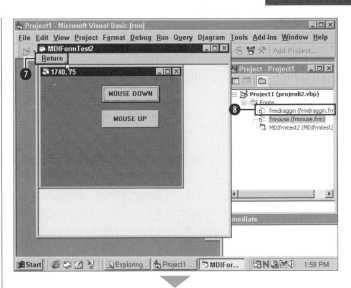

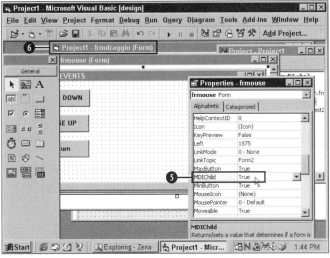

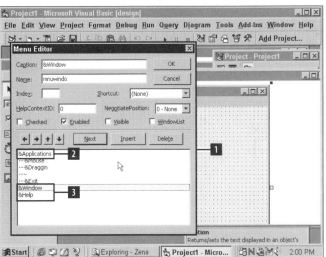

① *Create the Projmdi2 project.*

② *Use Add Form from the Project menu to add* frmouse *and* frmdraggin.

③ *Use Save Project As to save your project in a new folder.*

④ *Use Save As to save each of the forms.*

⑤ *Select* frmouse *and change the MDIChild property to True.*

⑥ *Select* frmdraggin *and repeat the preceding step.*

▶ *Enter the Menu Editor with the* frmouse *form selected.*

⑦ *Add a Return menu. Name it* **mnuretn***. Click the Return option of* frmouse *and add the code* Me.Hide *inside the* mnuretn_Click *procedure.*

⑧ *Repeat the preceding with* frmdraggin *and Exit.*

1 *Select MDIfrmtest2 and enter the Menu Editor.*

2 *Add the Applications menu and Mouse and Draggin options.*

▶ *Click the Applications menu and enter the code to show each form.*

3 *Add a Window menu and a Help menu at the top level.*

141

Making a Window Menu for MDI Forms

A Window menu only makes sense for an MDI application. That is because you cannot move between several open documents in any other type of document interface. All menus in an MDI project can display a list of all open child forms. This is done from the Menu Editor by placing a checkmark in the WindowList box for a particular menu. The list of open windows is shown at runtime when the window menu is pulled down. A checkmark is next to the window most recently opened, and a separator bar appears between the window list and the other window options, such as Tile and Cascade.

Working out a coordinated menu system for MDI projects is well worth the trouble. In fact, it is truly amazing how easy it is to give your application that authentic Windows look. Here is a situation where the planning is essential to getting the application to do what you intend. It is best if you break the task into a separate part for each form.

Begin by entering the Menu Editor with the MDIfrmtest2 form selected. Check the Visible and Enabled boxes on the Window menu. You are going to make the Window option active. Now check the WindowList box. This will cause Visual Basic to monitor the open windows and display them on the menu. Add Tile and Cascade options under the Window menu by clicking the right arrow above the List box, then adding each option. You can insert an option above the cursor by clicking Insert.

You follow the general process you did previously to add the Applications menu with its Mouse and Draggin options that open each of those forms.

Now you can add the code to make these options work. Click the Window menu and select the Tile option. Your cursor will land inside the mnutile_Click procedure. Here, you will reference the MDIfrmtest2 form and use the intrinsic constant vbTileHorizontal to respond to the event.

```
Private Sub mnutile_Click()
    MDIfrmtest2.Arrange vbTileHorizontal
End Sub
```

The procedure for Cascade is similar, except it uses the vbCascade constant.

```
Private Sub mnucasc_Click()
    MDIfrmtest2.Arrange vbCascade
End Sub
```

Make a Window menu with Cascade and Tile options in the Menu Editor. Check the WindowList option for the Window menu. Set up the Tile and Cascade procedures just as you did on the MDI form. The code is the same, unless you named the menus different names from the MDI form menus. If you did not, the procedures will look the same.

Add a top-level menu to the Mouse form. Call it Draggin and name it **mnudrag**. This is the same name you used on the Applications menu, but menu names in a project may be the same as long as they are on different menus. Access this option in the Code window and use the Show command to display the frmdraggin form.

Add the same Window menu and options to the frmdraggin form. Use the same procedures to Tile and Cascade. Also, check the WindowList Box for the top-level Window menu. Give this form a Mouse menu, just as you gave the Mouse menu a Draggin menu.

Run the application. Try all the menu options. You can open both Mouse and Draggin forms from the MDI form, then tile and cascade them. You can switch back and forth by clicking the forms in the WindowList. Click Return twice to get back to the MDI form and Exit.

TAKE NOTE

USING THE INTRINSIC CONSTANTS

To make your menus respond appropriately to the menu and submenu options, use the existing click event procedures for the menu controls. These procedures use the intrinsic constants (preceded by vb) vbTileVertical, vbTileHorizontal, vbArrange, vbCascade.

CROSS-REFERENCE

Chapter 8 continues using coding examples. Also, Chapter 10 deals with similar material.

FIND IT ONLINE

This site has info on shortcut menus and toolbars: http://msdn.microsoft.com/library/officedev/access/BldApps/chapters/ba01_6.htm.

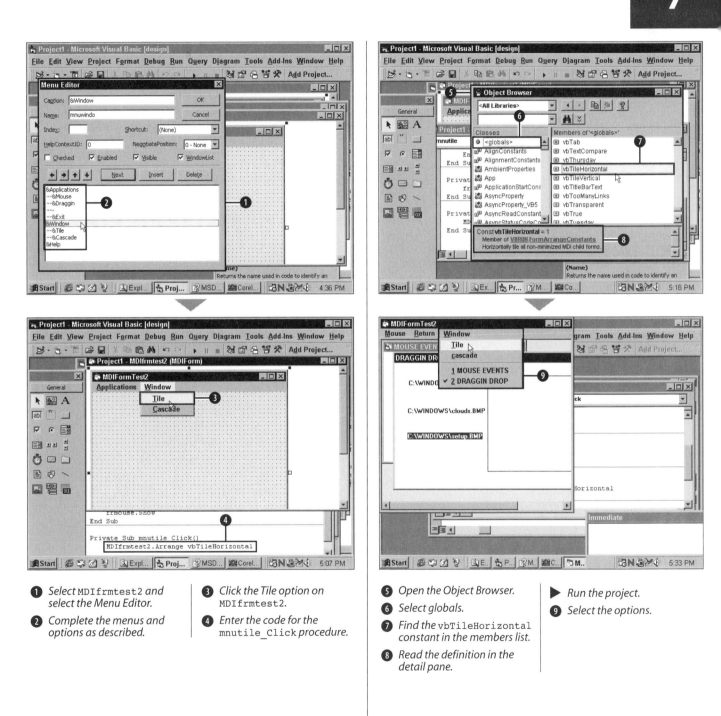

① Select MDIfrmtest2 and select the Menu Editor.

② Complete the menus and options as described.

③ Click the Tile option on MDIfrmtest2.

④ Enter the code for the mnutile_Click procedure.

⑤ Open the Object Browser.

⑥ Select globals.

⑦ Find the vbTileHorizontal constant in the members list.

⑧ Read the definition in the detail pane.

▶ Run the project.

⑨ Select the options.

Modifying Menus at Runtime

You may realize that setting certain properties at design time does not reflect what may be happening at runtime. If you toggled the Checked property on when you designed the Window menus for `frmouse` and `frmdraggin`, you will note that the Tile and Cascade options always display checkmarks. This is not likely to be what you had in mind. The point of having a checkmark next to an option is to show that item is currently selected. Having the item either permanently checked or permanently unchecked is misleading.

How do you arrange for the checkmark to be placed next to an option only when it is currently selected? The answer is to write code to execute the changes at runtime, depending upon the conditions encountered. In other words, you must tailor your application to respond to events. In this case, the event will be the current selection of either Tile or Cascade, but not both. Of course, if neither is selected, then neither option displays a checkmark.

Because you want to make the checkmarks conditional on the selected status, you must either create a new procedure or modify an existing one. Click the `frmouse` form in design mode and choose Tile from the Window menu. You will find your cursor placed on the `mnutile_Click` procedure. Note that your existing code carries out the Horizontal Tile process. If appropriate, you can add to that procedure. Here you want to cause the checkmark to appear when the Tile option has been clicked. Because this is a `Click` procedure (as all menu options are), you can add your `Click` event code here.

The two menu options in question are mnutile and mnucasc. Type **mnucasc.** under the existing code for the `mnutile_Click` procedure. When you type the period, the pop-up menu will offer you a selection of properties. Select the Checked option. Type an equal sign and select False from the pop-up menu. The statement says that when the Tile option is clicked, the mnucasc `Checked` status is false. That is, when the user selects the Tile option, the Cascade option does not show a checkmark.

Add a line below the one just completed. This time you want to give the Tile option a checkmark, so you make the `Checked` status True:

```
Private Sub mnutile_Click()
    MDIfrmtest2.Arrange vbTileHorizontal
    mnucasc.Checked = False
    mnutile.Checked = True
End
```

You now need to apply these statements to the `mnucasc_Click` procedure. Find that procedure on the `frmouse` form. Add the two lines of code to the procedure. This time, the mnutile `Checked` status is False, because the Cascade checkmark should be turned off when the Tile selection is current.

```
Private Sub mnucasc_Click()
    MDIfrmtest2.Arrange vbCascade
    mnucasc.Checked = True
    mnutile.Checked = False
End Sub
```

This process must be repeated for the `mnucasc_Click` and `mnutile_Click` procedures on the `frmdraggin` form. Replicate it for the `frmdraggin` form. The code will remain the same, because the logic is the same. You are simply repeating this exercise because the child menus will be shown as if they were on the MDI form when each of the child forms has the focus.

TAKE NOTE

▶ RIGHT-TO-LEFT ORDER ON MENUS

The Menu Editor supports menus with options going from right to left for non-European languages. To do this, you use the RightToLeft property setting for the parent form. Setting the RTL property to True will correctly align the menu and options from right to left, rather than the default left to right.

CROSS-REFERENCE

Chapter 9 pursues these methods also.

FIND IT ONLINE

This is a directory of other good sites: **http://www. citilink.com/~jgarrick/vbasic/resources/#WebSites.**

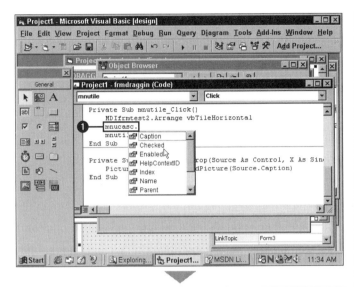

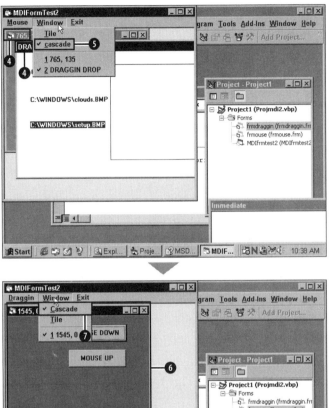

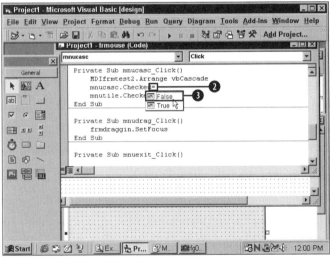

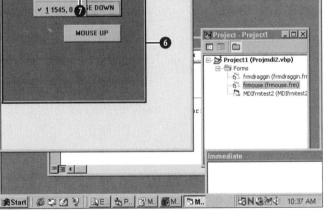

▶ Select the Tile option on the frmdraggin form.

1 Type **mnucasc**. Then select the Checked property on the pop-up menu.

2 Type an equal sign.

3 Select False from the pop-up menu.

4 Run the program.

▶ Click Mouse, then Draggin.

5 Select the Cascade option from the Window menu.

6 Select the Mouse form.

7 Click the Window menu to see Cascade checkmarked.

Changing the Focus

If you complete the code for the Checked property and then run the project, you will find that some of the options do not work properly. The checkmarks should work as intended. That is, the Tile and Cascade options are checkmarked when selected. On the other hand, the menu options for Mouse and Draggin leave something to be desired.

Run the program and select Mouse and Draggin each in turn. What happened? Neither form stays on the screen when you select the other. How can you fix this? In the last chapter, you learned that you could "hide" one form in order to return to a previous form. The problem here is that it is impossible to load both forms at once. The offending statement you used was Me.Hide. You also used another statement on these forms. The statements form.Visible = True and form.Show are ways of displaying forms.

Try changing the Me.Hide to frmmouse.Show and frmdraggin.Show in each of the forms' menu click procedures.

```
Private Sub mnumouse_Click()
    frmmouse.Show
End Sub
Private Sub mnumouse_Click()
    frmmouse.Show
End Sub
```

Run the program and click the Mouse option. So far so good. Now, select the Draggin option. Again, so far so good. Click the Mouse option again. The Draggin form stays on top, even though you can see it behind the Draggin window. You can change the focus by clicking each form in turn, and you also can switch between the forms by selecting them from the list of forms on the Window menu.

Selecting the forms from the Window menu seems to work as long as they are both loaded. But maybe this should be built into the code.

You will remember the exercise in Chapter 5 on understanding focus. There, we covered GotFocus and LostFocus in terms of reporting the status of objects getting or losing focus. SetFocus is another type of event that will help solve the dilemma. SetFocus can bring each of the desired forms into focus. Focus means that the object is selected. Thus, if each of our forms has focus, they will each, at the desired point, have an active bar, be on top, and be ready to accept input.

On the frmdraggin form in the mnumouse_Click procedure, set the focus of the frmmouse form:

```
Private Sub mnumouse_Click()
    frmmouse.SetFocus
End Sub
```

Do the same on the frmmouse form in the mnudrag_Click procedure:

```
Private Sub mnudrag_Click()
    frmdraggin.SetFocus
End Sub
```

Now the menus should work on all the forms. Try them and the Tile and Cascade options on the Window menu.

CROSS-REFERENCE

Chapter 9 carries the tasks further.

FIND IT ONLINE

This site also has download code for menus: **http://www.mvps.org/vbnet/code/_acc/ndxmenus.htm**.

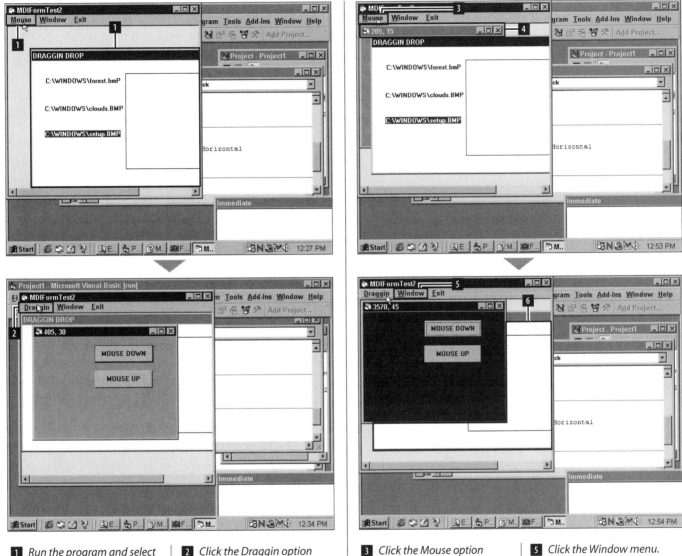

1 Run the program and select the Draggin option, then the Mouse option.

2 Click the Draggin option again.

3 Click the Mouse option again.

4 The Mouse form stays behind.

5 Click the Window menu.

6 The Draggin form has the focus.

147

Using Pop-Up Menus

Pop-up menus are those menus usually offering you help when you click the right mouse button in some area. Sometimes they pop up by themselves due to the context of what you are doing. They are also called *context menus*. You had some experience with the context menu provided by Visual Basic in the last topic and nearly every chapter as well. When you enter code in the Code window, menus pop up depending upon what you are doing.

For example, when you type the name of an object followed by a period, the menu pops up with property suggestions. You can select one of these properties (if appropriate) by double-clicking the selection. When you type an equal sign, another pop-up menu offers you `True` or `False` options. Entering code this way may or may not be helpful to you, but it is often an option in applications.

Usually, right-clicking accesses the pop-up menus, but you can also set them up to use the left or middle mouse button. In the chapter on events (Chapter 5), you learned that the mouse button state is determined by the bit value returned. Binary and decimal values and a constant are assigned to each mouse button (left, right, and middle). These values are expressed as integers 1, 2, and 4 for the left, right, and middle buttons. Thus, the right button has an integer value of 2.

To create the pop-up menu, you need to have a menu and at least one submenu. Whatever items are on the submenu show on the pop-up. First you will need to add a menu option to your Window menu on the `frmdraggin` form. Open the Menu Editor and insert a new option under the Window menu. Call this option **mnupop**. Then add three submenus under mnupop. Call the submenus **mnupopme**, **mnupopme2**, and **mnupopme3**. You can make the captions anything you desire.

Exit the Menu Editor and enter the Code window for `frmdraggin`. Because you are expecting the menu to pop up anywhere on the form, you need to associate it with the form object. Select the form object from the object box, and then select the `MouseDown` procedure.

You are going to want users to use the right mouse button, so you will need to write a procedure conditional on the clicking of button 2. You want the action to take place when button equals 2, so enter the code:

```
Private Sub Form_MouseDown(Button As Integer,
Shift As Integer, X As Single, Y As Single)
    If Button = 2 Then
        PopupMenu mnupop
    End If
End Sub
```

This seems pretty straightforward, so go ahead and try it. Run the program, and then select Draggin. Cruise around the form and right-click at some point. The menu should appear on the spot.

TAKE NOTE

MAKING THE POP-UP INVISIBLE

It seems likely that you will not want users to see the pop-up menu and submenu items on the menu bar at runtime. Because the menu bar is simply a place to store the pop-up list, it would not look good with the other menu items. This is particularly true if it's on the Window menu, because it clearly doesn't belong there. You can prevent it from showing in the Menu Editor. Select the mnupop (or whatever you named your top level pop-up) and uncheck the Visible property. That way it will work as a pop-up but not show on the menu bar.

CROSS-REFERENCE

Chapter 9 covers similar material.

FIND IT ONLINE

This site has downloadable files for pop-up menus: **http://www.codearchive.com/**.

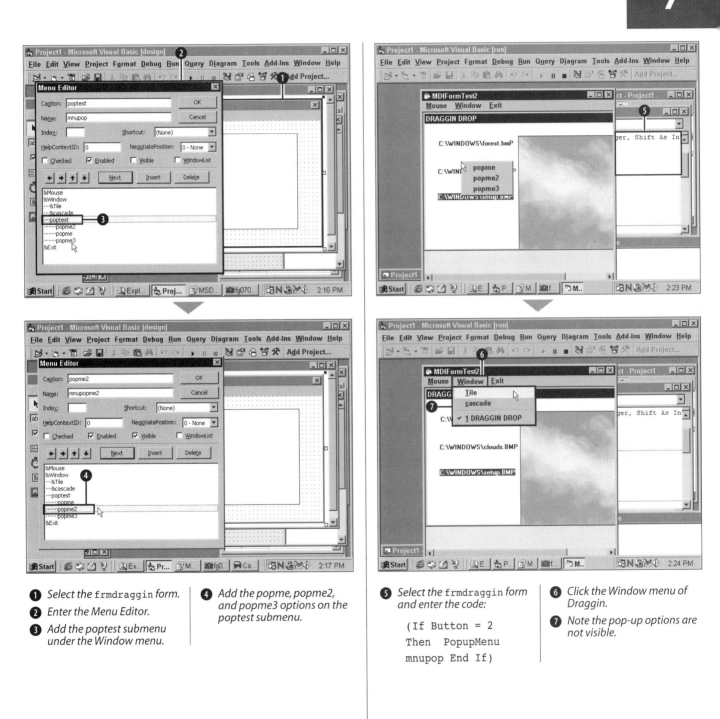

1 Select the frmdraggin form.

2 Enter the Menu Editor.

3 Add the poptest submenu under the Window menu.

4 Add the popme, popme2, and popme3 options on the poptest submenu.

5 Select the frmdraggin form and enter the code:

```
(If Button = 2
Then  PopupMenu
mnupop End If)
```

6 Click the Window menu of Draggin.

7 Note the pop-up options are not visible.

Personal Workbook

Q&A

1 What would be a good name for the main menu in an accounting application?

_____

_____

_____

2 Does the Menu Editor generate code for you?

_____

_____

_____

3 Which is the menu caption, "mnucaption" or "Tools"?

_____

_____

_____

4 How do you make sure a menu option indicates it is ready for selection?

_____

_____

_____

5 For what type of interface is the `WindowList` property applicable?

_____

_____

_____

6 What actions do you take to make submenus in the Menu Editor?

_____

_____

_____

7 If you wanted to view an ASCII text file, what control could you place on your form?

_____

_____

_____

8 What control is commonly used to open and save files?

_____

_____

_____

ANSWERS: PAGE 523

EXTRA PRACTICE

1 Create a form and place a `RichTextBox` on it. Add a `CommonDialog` control and write the procedures to open an ASCII text file.

2 Create a new menu and submenus on an existing form.

3 Add two new forms to your mditest2 project and check the `WindowList` property for all of them.

4 Plan a new project with several menus and submenus. Practice naming and giving captions for each menu.

5 Practice toggling the `Enabled` property on and off for several menu options.

6 Create a pop-up menu on one of your menus and make the option invisible.

REAL-WORLD APPLICATIONS

✔ You have just begun your fifth type of treatment for your dog's fleas. Because it is becoming hard to remember how long each treatment protected your dog from fleas, you decide to set up an application to track each treatment's efficacy. Design the forms and menus for the application.

✔ One of your company's clients is desperate for a program that would display menus and options from right to left. You have been given the job of designing the application. Where would you begin?

✔ Your client, Joe B., asks you to design a project that will enable him to right-click and get a context menu depending upon the location of the cursor on the form. Design a context menu for him.

Visual Quiz

Select the menu name that doesn't belong.

```
mnulog
mnuopen1
menfile1
mnuup
```

CHAPTER 8

MASTER THESE SKILLS

▶ Using TextBoxes and ListBoxes

▶ Adding a Label Control

▶ Using the ComboBox Control

▶ Changing Objects with Scrollbars

▶ Modifying Controls at Runtime

▶ Using the Image Control

▶ Utilizing the Timer Control

▶ Using Drive, Directory, and File Controls

Learning More about Controls

In the process of covering the material in the first seven chapters, you have learned quite a bit about controls. You have used controls in the context of learning about forms, menus, events, and application development. In this chapter, you will learn about some of the controls either you have not yet covered or for which important aspects remain to be considered.

Controls in Visual Basic fall into three categories: intrinsic, ActiveX, and insertable objects.

Intrinsic controls are those that are always displayed in the Standard toolbox. They are shipped with Visual Basic and are part of the Basic executable file. They are the essential controls that are always available in all editions of Visual Basic.

ActiveX controls, which you have already used, are added as components from the Project menu. Also, they can be user-created or purchased from a third party. One example of an ActiveX control you have used is the `ToolBar` control. Some additional ActiveX controls are included with the Professional and Enterprise Editions. When you add these controls to your toolbox, you import a file with the `.ocx` extension. This file extension is shown in the list of libraries on the Components option on the Project menu.

Insertable objects are actually documents or data from another application. Examples are spreadsheets, database tables, calendars, or documents from Microsoft products. You can add these objects to the toolbox, and some of them can be controlled from Visual Basic procedures.

In the exercises that follow you will create a form to learn about several different controls that will interact with each other to carry out tasks. The form will use the `TextBox`, `ListBox` and `ComboBox` to add names to a list, make selections of names from a `ComboBox`, and rotate names in a `Label` box. Further exercises utilize the horizontal and vertical scrollbars to change the size of a `CommandButton` and to change background and foreground colors.

Using TextBoxes and ListBoxes

The **TextBox** control is typically used to collect user input. It usually allows the data to be edited, but you can make it read only. The default amount of text you can enter is 2048 characters, but with the **MultiLine** property True, you can enter up to 32K. The text will wrap unless you set the **ScrollBar**'s property to **Horizontal**, in which case the text will not wrap but scroll to the right.

You also can control the characters the user may enter by using the **KeyPress** event as discussed in Chapter 5.

The **ListBox** control is used to enable users to select items from a list. If the list is longer that the number of items that will fit in the box, a scrollbar will be added to the box.

The first item in the list has an index value of zero, the second has an index value of 1, and so on. If no item is selected, the index value is –1. Adding items to the **ListBox** is done using the **AddItem** method. Removing items is done with the **RemoveItem** method. You use the **ListIndex** property to enable the user to use items on the list.

In the following project, you are going to use the **TextBox** to enter a name to add to a list in the **ListBox**. When you click the ADD button, the **ListBox** will then display the new name. You also can use the **Label** to display a name when selected in the **ListBox**.

Create a new project named "Projcontrol." Name the form "frmcontrol," with the **Caption**, "More Controls." In this project you are going to work with **TextBox**, **Label**, **ListBox**, **ComboBox**, **CommandButtons**, and **Scrollbars**.

Begin by placing the **TextBox** control in the upper-left corner on the form. Place a **CommandButton** named Cmdadd and the **Caption** "ADD" under the **TextBox**. Place a **ListBox** control under the ADD button.

The items in the **ListBox** should be displayed at runtime, so the items on the list must be added using the **Form_Load** procedure.

The **AddItem** method is used to fill a **ListBox** with items. You can name the items in the code so that they display at runtime, or you can allow the user to input items at runtime. **AddItem** requires an object (in this case, **List1**) and a string expression. The **AddItem** method is not supported if the control object is bound to a data control, but here that does not present a problem.

For example,

```
For X = 1 to 10
        List1.AddItem Items
Next X
```

would give your user the option of entering the code at runtime, in which case, nothing is displayed in the **ListBox** at runtime until the user enters it.

In this exercise, we will add the items on the list via code in the procedure. Double-click the **frmcontrol** form and select the **Form** object in the Code window. Select the **Load** procedure. Because the object in the **ListBox** is named **List1**, you should apply the **AddItem** method to the **ListBox** object.

TAKE NOTE

▶ **ADDING ITEMS TO THE LISTBOX**

In the syntax, "*object*.AddItem *item, index*," if *index* is omitted the item added will be in sort order if **Sorted** is True and at the end if **Sorted** is False. Thus, if you set the **List1** Sorted property to True and then type a name in the **TextBox** beginning with the letter "A," the name will be inserted at the top of the **ListBox**. If the **Sorted** property is set to False, any name will be inserted at the end of the names in the **ListBox**.

CROSS-REFERENCE

Chapter 9 and Chapter 6 both discuss controls.

FIND IT ONLINE

The site **http://www.mvps.org/vbnet/code/listapi/ combolistdropdown.htm** has downloadable list box routines from the Vbnet code library.

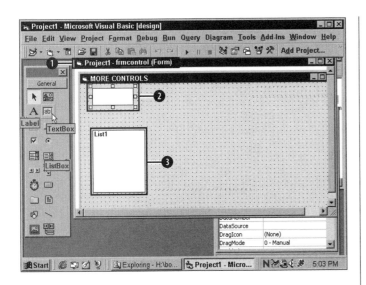

① Select the frmcontrol form.

② Place a TextBox upper left.

③ Place a ListBox below the TextBox.

Listing 8-1: Adding an Item to the ListBox

```
Private Sub Form_Load()
    List1.AddItem "Betty"
    List1.AddItem "Bobby"
    List1.AddItem "Gary"
    List1.AddItem "Brenda"
    List1.AddItem "Germaine"
End Sub
```

▶ Enter this code in the Form_Load procedure.

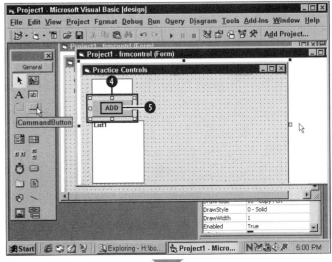

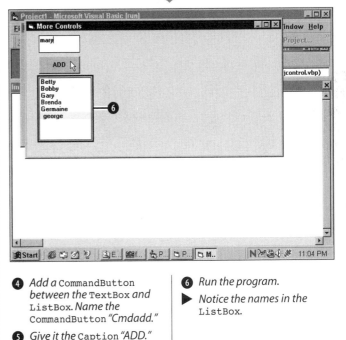

④ Add a CommandButton between the TextBox and ListBox. Name the CommandButton "Cmdadd."

⑤ Give it the Caption "ADD."

⑥ Run the program.

▶ Notice the names in the ListBox.

Adding a Label Control

The Label control is generally used to display labels adjacent to other objects they are describing. They may also be used to provide instructions to the user, but they cannot be edited at runtime. An interesting and functional use for the Label is to have its Caption change at runtime, based upon the change of the value of some other object. Labels also can be used to create key combinations to move the focus to the next control. In this exercise, you will use the Label control to show the text typed into the Text1 TextBox. Labels used to display text will wrap the text unless the AutoSize property is True, in which case the label will grow horizontally to accommodate the text.

For this part of the application, you need to attach code to the Label and the ADD CommandButton. You have just seen the way the AddItem method works to add items to the list. Now that you have a list of names in List1 and have added the ADD button and the Label box, there are some new features that will enhance your project.

You have many options in terms of what you can do with the list of names. You could offer the user multiple item selection. You can use the ListIndex property to keep track of the position of the currently selected item in the list. In this case, you are going to display the selected item from the ListBox in the Label1 box. If you wished to remove all items in the list, you would use the syntax:

```
List1.Clear
```

Add this statement to the List1 list shown in Listing 8-1. Run the program. What happened to the names? The Clear method removes those items from memory.

The Label control can be used to display time and date, as well as just about anything the user cannot change, except the contents of a data field. One interesting thing you can do with the Label control is to change the Caption at runtime. You are going to change the caption on the label by replacing it with the contents of the currently selected name in the ListBox. Enter this code in the List1_Click procedure:

```
Private Sub List1_Click()
    Label1.Caption = List1.List(List1.ListIndex)
End Sub
```

The List property (Object.List(index) [=String]) returns the string value of each element in the list. This list here is the List1 list. The index is the position of the item in the list. You can display each item in the list as it is currently selected by setting the Label Caption to the value of the item in the string array.

The ADD button is used to add a name to the ListBox below the ADD button. By clicking ADD, the user causes the name typed in the TextBox to drop down into the ListBox. Just as you used the AddItem method to fill the string array of List1 with names, you can use the same method to add the new item to the list.

This time, the List1.AddItem is set to Text1.Text (the value of the text in the TextBox). If you add this line to the Click procedure for Cmdadd, run the program, then type a new name, and click ADD, you will find the new name appearing on the list below. You may notice that you encounter a new problem if you continue to enter names. That is, the name you just typed stays in the TextBox. You need to add this code to clear the box:

```
Text1.Text = ""
```

This statement places a null (empty) string in the box. Finally, if you wish the focus to return to the TextBox so that you can add more names, then include this statement to return the focus to the TextBox:

```
Text1.SetFocus
```

This completes the section on the Label and ADD button controls.

CROSS-REFERENCE

Chapter 16 discusses controls further.

FIND IT ONLINE

The site **http://web2.airmail.net/gbeene/tut-std.html** is from Gary Beene's site and is a tutorial on intrinsic controls.

TAKE NOTE

CHANGING THE LABEL CAPTION SIZE

Because the Caption property of the Label control has unlimited size, you can increase the size of the label by setting the AutoSize property to True. Then the label caption will increase its size as necessary. When you change the AutoSize property to True at design time, the label immediately becomes a minimum size. At runtime, it shifts size according to the length of the Label Caption.

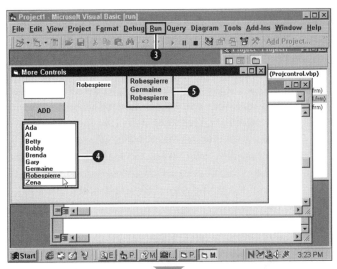

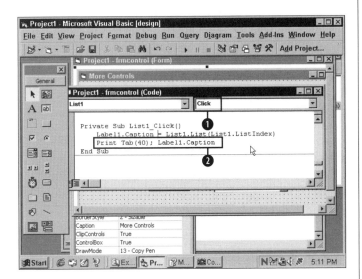

1 Double-click the List1 box and enter a new line in the Click procedure.

2 Print Tab(40); Label1.Caption.

Listing 8-2: The ADD Click Procedure

```
Private Sub Cmdadd_Click()
    List1.AddItem Text1.Text
    Text1.Text = ""
    Text1.SetFocus
End Sub
```

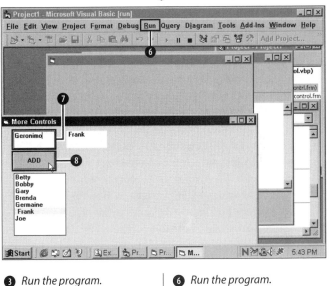

3 Run the program.

4 Click each of the names in the ListBox.

5 Note that the elements in the array are printed on the form.

6 Run the program.

7 Type a name in the TextBox.

8 Click ADD to insert it in the ListBox.

Using the ComboBox Control

The ComboBox control is so called because it is a combination of the ListBox and the TextBox. Like the ListBox, the ComboBox uses the AddItem method to add items to the box. ScrollBars will be added to the ComboBox when all the items cannot be shown in the box without scrolling.

ComboBoxes are used when there is a range of recommended selections but the user is able to compose a new item, because the ComboBox includes an edit box. Also, the ComboBox typically does not drop down until the user clicks the arrow, so it does not require as much space as a TextBox might.

There are several types of ComboBoxes. The styles are *simple combo, drop-down list,* and *drop-down combo.* The simple combo does not pop up or drop down, so you must make the box large enough to hold all entries or they will not all show at runtime. The drop-down list is similar to a list box and looks the same as the drop-down combo, except that the user cannot type text into it. The drop-down combo appears as a drop-down list, and you can type new entries into it as well. You can change the Combo style in the Properties window.

You can change the Sorted property to true to sort the lists in either the ListBox or the ComboBox.

You can fill the ComboBox list at design time by entering code, as you did with the ListBox. Or you can enter new names in the Properties window by adding them to the List property. In this exercise, you will use the AddItem method to add the same names to the Combo1 ComboBox at design time just as you did for the List1 ListBox.

The AddItem method uses the same syntax as in the ListBox example, only the object is Combo1 instead of List1.

```
Combo1.AddItem "Betty"
```

Use this example to enter the names to match the List1 list. When you do this, the list will be populated with the names at runtime. If you wish, you can enter additional names in the Properties window in the List property pane.

There are still controls to be added to the frmcontrol form. Add five more command buttons. These buttons should be named Command1 through Command5. Give the buttons Captions ZERO through FOUR. That is, Command1 has a Caption "ZERO," Command2 has a Caption "ONE," and so on.

Next, each CommandButton (Command1 through Command5) is used to display an item in the ListBox based upon the ListIndex value. For Command1, the ListIndex is set at zero. Because array elements begin at zero, rather than one, the ListIndex value of zero will correspond to Command1. You set the Caption of Command1 to ZERO, so a click of ZERO will cause the string value of the ListIndex value zero for List1 to be displayed as the Label Caption.

TAKE NOTE

LISTBOXES, LABELS, AND COMBOBOXES

The Label Caption can contain only one value, whereas the ListBox and the ComboBox can contain numerous data values. These controls have a number of features built in to add, delete, and access items from a set of values entered at design time or runtime.

CROSS-REFERENCE

Chapter 6 also deals with **ComboBoxes** and Lists.

FIND IT ONLINE

The site **http://web2.airmail.net/gbeene/ tut-ctrl.html** has an overview of controls.

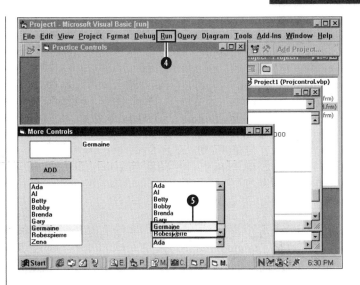

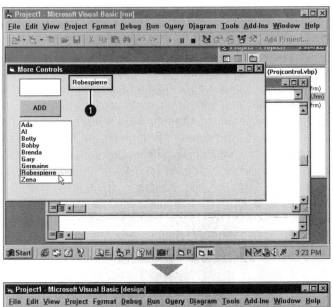

① Set the Label1 AutoSize property to True. Run the program and note the size change in Label1.

② Select the ComboBox.

③ Click the Style property and select Dropdown Combo.

④ Run the program.

⑤ Select a name on the Combo1 list.

Listing 8-3: The AddItem Method for Combo1

```
Private Sub Form_Load()
    List1.AddItem "Betty"
    List1.AddItem "Bobby"
    List1.AddItem "Gary"
    List1.AddItem "Brenda"
    List1.AddItem "Germaine"
    List1.AddItem "Ada"
    List1.AddItem "Al"
    List1.AddItem "Robespierre"
    List1.AddItem "Zena"
    Combo1.AddItem "Betty"
    Combo1.AddItem "Bobby"
    Combo1.AddItem "Gary"
    Combo1.AddItem "Brenda"
    Combo1.AddItem "Germaine"
    Combo1.AddItem "Robespierre"
    Combo1.AddItem "Al"
    Combo1.AddItem "Ada"
    Combo1.AddItem "Zena"
End Sub
```

▶ Add the code in Listing 8-3 to the Form_Load procedure following the List1 statements.

Changing Objects with ScrollBars

Having made the five `CommandButtons` Command1 through Command5, you will need to add the code to make the specific name appear on the `Label Caption` when each button is clicked. For `List1`, the index will be from zero to the last number added minus one. So if there are six names in `List1`, the first will be zero and the last five. This does not seem so strange when you remember that all arrays begin with the element zero. Thus, the code for the `Click` procedure for Command1 will be:

```
List1.ListIndex = 0
```

And the procedure for Command2:

```
List1.ListIndex = 1
```

Go ahead add the procedure code for all five `CommandButtons`. Double-click the `CommandButton`, select each `CommandButton` object and the `Click` procedure, then add the code.

In addition to the buttons that change the caption in the label box, you are going to try something new. Just as you have seen the background colors change as the mouse cursor moved, you will find that other procedures affect runtime events.

You will use the same principle you used in Chapter 5 to make the background color of the `frmevents` form change as the scrollbar was moved. Similarly, you will arrange to change the size of a command button with the `ScrollBar`'s horizontal movement. Just as colors can be transformed by mouse events, other properties of objects can also be manipulated.

Add a new `CommandButton` named "Cmdsize" and give it the caption "Change Size." Place it on the right side of the form about midway between top and bottom (about 1400 twips from the top). You are going to make this button expand and contract depending upon the movement in a scrollbar.

Add a `Horizontal ScrollBar` control, placing it on the right side of the form about 5000 twips from the left and about 600 twips above Cmdsize. Follow this up by adding a `Vertical Scrollbar` control about 2000 twips to the right of Cmdsize at the same distance from the top of the form. The width of the `Horizontal Scrollbar` and the height of the `Vertical Scrollbar` should be no more than 1000 twips. Make sure these three objects are as pictured. Position the button below the `HScroll1` control and to the left of the `VScroll1` control.

The point here is that if the button is too close to other controls, there will not be room enough for it to grow. Of course, if it gets too big, you can always reverse the direction of the scrollbars and make it shrink.

The code should be attached to the `HScroll1` object, because it is the `Change` event of the scrollbars that manipulates the size of the button. This can be handled with only one statement placed in the `HScroll1_Change` procedure.

```
Private Sub HScroll1_Change()
    Cmdsize.Width = HScroll1.Value
End Sub
```

`Width` is a property of `HScroll1`, and the size is going to change relative to the `Value` of the scrollbar's position.

TAKE NOTE

Scrollbars are displayed at runtime only if the object's text flows past its borders. If part of a child form is hidden behind the border of the parent MDI form, a horizontal scroll bar will be shown. The `TextBox` control is an exception to this because it will always display scroll bars. Setting `ScrollBars` to `False` will prevent an object from having scroll bars, regardless of its contents.

CROSS-REFERENCE

Chapter 9 continues providing more examples of controls.

FIND IT ONLINE

Find info on scrollbars property at **http://msdn.microsoft.com/library/devprods/vs6/vbasic/vb98/vbproscrollbars.htm.**

Listing 8-4: The Index CommandButtons

```
Private Sub Command1_Click()
    List1.ListIndex = 0
End Sub
Private Sub Command2_Click()
    List1.ListIndex = 1
End Sub
Private Sub Command3_Click()
    List1.ListIndex = 2
End Sub
Private Sub Command4_Click()
    List1.ListIndex = 3
End Sub
Private Sub Command5_Click()
    List1.ListIndex = 4
End Sub
```

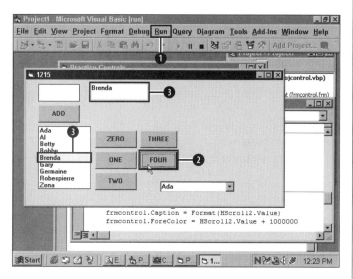

❶ Enter the code in Listing 8-4 for the Command1–Command5 Click procedures and run the program.

❷ Click one of the buttons.

❸ The name's position should match the label display.

Listing 8-5: The Hscroll1 Change Event Procedure

```
Private Sub HScroll1_Change()
    Cmdsize.Width = HScroll1.Value
End Sub
```

▶ Attach the code to the HScroll1 Scrollbar.

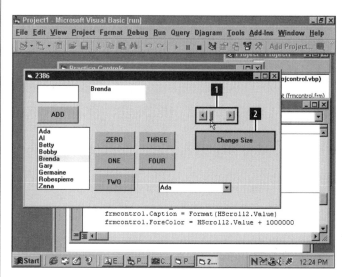

1 Add the code shown for the Change event procedure. Run the program and move the horizontal scrollbar.

2 See the Change Size button get wider.

Modifying Controls at Runtime

Now that you know how to engineer the change in button width based upon the position value of the ScrollBar, you can add another feature that you used previously. Because the position of the scrollbar changes, you can see for yourself what is occurring, but you don't know how much change is taking place. You can measure that change in twips (1440^{ths} of an inch).

Just as you did in Chapter 5, you can add a statement to the HScroll1_Change procedure.

```
frmcontrol.Caption = Format(HScroll1.Value)
```

Remember that the form caption can display the value of any object as long as the object has a Value property. This will not work for the size of the Command button, because it does not have a Value property.

Coding the Change event for the Horizontal ScrollBar resulted in making the Change Size (Cmdsize) button grow horizontally. Now you need to make the button grow vertically as well.

The Vscroll control is the same as the HScroll control, except that its position moves up and down instead of back and forth. You need to program the height of the Cmdsize button instead of the width. Double-click the Vertical ScrollBar and change the code you used for the Horizontal ScrollBar to use the ScrollBar Value to change the height property of the button.

In a previous chapter, you were able to move a scrollbar and see the background color continually change as the mouse moved around the form. Now, you will try your hand at clicking and dragging a scrollbar and see the background and foreground colors of a label box shift as the bar moves forward or backward.

At this point you have done some significant things with the label box on the frmcontrol form. Yet there are still new events you can program. Because you have done the background color shift on the form, you can try your hand at manipulating the color in the label box. Check the Label1 AutoSize Property to make sure it is set to False. The goal for this exercise is to change the foreground and background colors of the Label1 box when a scrollbar is moved.

Add a new Horizontal ScrollBar control near the top of the form above the HScroll1 bar. As the bar is moved from right to left and back, the colors will change. Because both foreground and background colors will change, at some intervals, the colors may be the same, so the foreground will blend in and not be noticeable.

Double-click and enter the Code window. Select the HScroll2 object and the Change procedure. This time you will be changing the Label1 object's background and foreground properties, so you will need a separate statement for each. You can use the Value of HScroll2, or you can add an integer number to that value to get a larger range of color values.

The BackColor property will take effect for the Label control only if the BackStyle property is Opaque. At runtime, remember that the label will only have a foreground value if you click a name in the ListBox to display it in the label box.

TAKE NOTE

Be wary of writing a Change event procedure for a control that changes the contents of the control. You can set a flag to prevent more changes from occuring until the current change has been completed.

CROSS-REFERENCE

Chapters 2 and 9 discuss using controls as well.

FIND IT ONLINE

You can download controls from this site. **http://msdn. microsoft.com/vbasic/downloads/controls.asp**

▶ *Add the statement to the* HScroll1 Change *procedure:*

```
Label1.Caption = Format(HScroll1.Value)
```

❶ *Run the program, move the scrollbar, and observe the number in the label box.*

Listing 8-6: Changing Button Size with the Vertical ScrollBar

```
Private Sub VScroll1_Change()
    Cmdsize.Height = VScroll1.Value
End Sub
```

1 *Add the code in Listing 8-6 and run the program.*

2 *Move the vertical scrollbar.*

3 *See the button change size.*

Listing 8-7: Changing Background and Foreground Colors

```
Private Sub HScroll2_Change()
    Label1.BackColor = HScroll2.Value + 1600000
    Label1.ForeColor = HScroll2.Value
End Sub
```

▶ *Enter the code in Listing 8-7 to see the label colors change.*

Using the Image Control

The Image control is often referred to as a "Lightweight" control because it uses fewer system resources than the PictureBox. Besides the great advantage of saving system resources, the Image control offers options not available with the PictureBox. Image repaints the screen (if loading successive pictures), and it stretches pictures.

There are other functions and properties you have with the PictureBox you do not have with the Image control. Generally, you should use the Image control when you have limited system resources (slow computers and little memory are two examples), need greater speed, and don't need features not offered by the PictureBox.

The Image control supports bitmaps (meaning .bmp Windows bitmap files), Graphics Image Format (.gif), Joint Photographic Experts Group (.jpg), Windows Metafiles (.wmf), cursors (.cur) and icons (.ico).

You can add images at design time by changing the Picture property on the Image object. This you do from the Properties window, clicking in the space to the right of the property listed. Where (None) is currently written, the series of dots will appear and you get a dialog box enabling you to select a path and filename to display. This is the easiest method of getting a picture on a form. This would be the preferred way to simply illustrate your form or button with a picture.

The design-time strategy is fine if you want to use the same picture on your form always. If you want the user to select a picture or want to the picture to appear at runtime, then you may wish to code the loading of the picture.

If you can find a space on your frmcontrol form, place an Image control. You may want to tell people they can select a picture, so place a Label control above the Image control. Select the Label (Label2) and change the caption property to "Click for Pic" or something equally easy for users to identify. If you are in a fanciful mood, you might change the background of the Label to a bright color by changing the BackColor property.

Double-click the Image1 control to open the Code window. You should know where you have an appropriate picture file. If not, you can use the Windows directory as you did with the Draggin project. The simplest way to bring a picture into the Image control is to name the picture and path in the code. You need to use the Picture property (as you can in the Properties window) and the LoadPicture function.

Because the Label2 control sits on top of the Image control, you may wish to allow the user to click the label to get the picture as well as on the image. You will not be able to see the outline of the Image control at runtime.

TAKE NOTE

▶ **USING PICTURES AT RUNTIME**

You can add a picture from the clipboard at runtime, as well as loading it from a file. You can also copy pictures from one control to another. You can just as easily remove the picture at runtime or in response to a user's request. Image controls automatically size to fit the picture loaded into them event though they do not have the AutoSize property.

CROSS-REFERENCE

Chapter 9 continues with examples of controls.

FIND IT ONLINE

The site http://msdn.microsoft.com/library/tools/vbce/html/usectrls_22.htm has lots of info on the Image control.

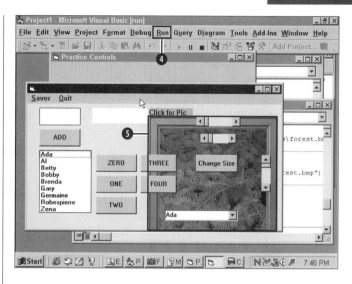

Listing 8-8: The Label1_Click Procedure

```
Private Sub label2_Click()
    Image1.Picture =_
LoadPicture("c:\windows\forest.bmp")
End Sub
```

Listing 8-9: Image1_Click Procedure

```
Private Sub Image1_Click()
 Image1.Picture = _
LoadPicture("c:\windows\forest.bmp")
End Sub
```

① *Place an* Image *control on the* frmcontrol *form.*

② *Place a* Label *control above the* Image *control.*

③ *Make a caption for the* Label.

▶ *Notice the* LoadPicture *function is added in the* Label's Click *procedure.*

▶ *Enter the code in Listing 8-8.*

▶ *Enter the code in Listing 8-9 in the* Image *object* click *procedure.*

④ *Run the program. Notice that you cannot see the outline for the image.*

⑤ *Click the* Image *or the* Label.

Utilizing the Timer Control

The Timer control enables you to control time events independent of the user. Timer events can be firing in the background even though other commands are being executed.

There is no specific duration of a timer interval that can be controlled. Rather you can control the Timer's interval property, which specifies the number of milliseconds between timer events. In a sense, the Timer works like the Pause loop used in Chapter 3. There, the length of time it takes for each pass through the loop is dependent upon the processor speed. Also, Timer events are dependent upon other demands on system resources. If the application or others running concurrently are making demands on the system, the Timer control may not be able to generate events as often as you expect.

The timer interval can be as long as about one minute. For greater accuracy, the Timer can check the system clock.

The Timer must be placed on a form where it will only be visible at design time. Therefore, the placement of the Timer on a form is not important as long as it is somewhere on the form.

If you want the user to initiate some Timer event in runtime, you should set the Enabled property to False. The procedure should set the Enabled property to True in order to begin the function. If, on the other hand, you want the intervals to start immediately upon launching the application, and no user intervention is necessary, you can set the Enabled property to False.

Select your frmcontrol form once again and place the Timer control anywhere on the form. You are going to make the Label1 box do more work. In addition to the other values you have displayed on it, you will now commandeer it to show the system time.

Select the Timer control and right-click for the Properties window. You will notice that the Timer has very few properties compared with the other controls you have used. The key properties to set are Enabled and Interval.

If the Timer's Enabled property is set to False, nothing will happen in the time function you are about to set up. This is because setting the Enabled property to False means the timer is turned off when the project is launched. Set the Enabled property to True if you want the Timer working in the background without user intervention.

The Interval property will control how often the system time is displayed. A rule of thumb is to set it at 1000 for each second. You can play around with the interval once you see how the control works. To begin, set the property at 2000. This should make the time display on the label change about every two seconds.

In the ScrollBar exercise, you used the Label1.Caption to display the Horizontal ScrollBar's position value. In this case, the Timer control will display the system time in intervals of two seconds (if the Interval property is set to 2000). You will use the system function "Time" and the Str function to format the time value.

TAKE NOTE

▶ TIMER INTERVALS

An important factor to keep in mind is that the interval you set is more a case of frequency than duration. When you set the value of the interval property, remember that the interval is not really accurate to the millisecond. Because the closest degree of accuracy is the clock tick (1/18) of a second, you should allow for the error margin. It is recommended that you set the interval for about one-half the precision you need. Also, when you set a short interval so that the event occurs very often, it taxes the processor, making more demands upon the system, which slows down the response.

CROSS-REFERENCE

Chapter 9 uses the Timer function also.

FIND IT ONLINE

The site **http://msdn.microsoft.com/library/tools/vbce/html/ controls_28.htm** has even more info if you search for similar topics at other locations.

Listing 8-10: Timer Display Using the Str Function

```
Private Sub Timer1_Timer()
    If Label1.Caption <> Str(Time) Then
        Label1.Caption = Time
    End If
End Sub
```

▶ The Label1 *caption is used to display the system time.*

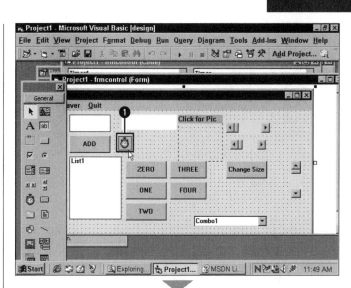

Listing 8-11: Timer Display Using the Format Function

```
Private Sub Timer1_Timer()  1
    If Label1.Caption <> Format(Time)_
Then
        Label1.Caption = Time
    End If
End Sub
```

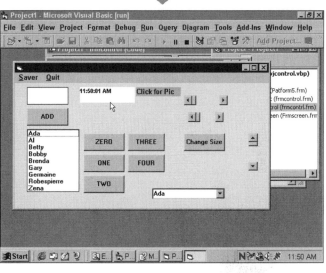

1 *Remove the* Str *function and use the* Format *function instead.*

1 *Place the* Timer *control anywhere on the form. Double-click the* Timer *and enter the code in Listing 8-10.*

▶ *Run the program after entering the code in Listing 8-10. Enter the code in Listing 8-11 and restart.*

▶ *Is there a difference in time format using each function?*

Using Drive, Directory, and File Controls

The `DriveListBox` enables a user to select a valid drive at runtime. The `DriveListBox` identifies the drives available to users on a particular system. The box will show all mapped drives. Basically, everything that shows in My Computer will be accessible to the user for selection.

The `DirListBox` displays all the available directories (folders) on a selected drive. As soon as the user makes a selection of the drive, the directories (folders) on that drive are displayed in tree fashion. The display style is like that in the Windows Explorer.

The `FileListBox` further enables you to select files from a selected drive and directory, provided those files exist. If the `Pattern` property has been changed to a particular file extension, then only those files will appear in the `FileListBox`. For example, if you wanted the user to select only certain types of graphic files to place in a `PictureBox` or `Image` control, you could add `*.jpg` or `*.bmp` to the `Pattern` property pane in the Properties window. This is similar to using a Filter with the `CommonDialog` control. In fact, you can alternatively use the `CommonDialog` control for this project. This works like the example in Chapter 7, when you used the `CommonDialog` control in conjunction with the `RichTextBox` control to open files. The `List`, `ListCount`, and `ListIndex` properties are set to enable users to select a particular file.

The `ListCount` property furnishes information about the count of items for each object. For the `DriveListBox`, the `ListCount` property contains the number of drives on the system. The `ListCount` property holds information on the number of directories also. But for the `FileListBox`, the `ListCount` reflects the number of files that match the `Pattern` property value.

The `ListIndex` property has a value of –1 before the user has selected any file. The first file in the list has a value of zero, and the last file a value of one less than the value of `ListCount`. `ListCount` and `ListIndex` are used in the application you will add to the Projcontrol project.

Add a new form to your project. Name it Frmscreen and give it a caption "Screen Saver." You will also need to add a menu item to your `frmcontrol` form as well. From the Menu Editor, add the new item. Call it mnusaver with a caption "Saver" and insert the code in the `mnusaver` click procedure to `Show` the form. This will enable to you to get to the new form. Of course, you can also use the knowledge you gained in the previous chapter on menus and set up a form to drive the application.

In this part of your project, you are going to make yourself a screen saver. You will use the PictureBox, Timer, Drive, Dir, and File list boxes.

In advance, you should identify a directory having a list of files of one graphic type you would wish to be displayed in a screen saver. You can use pictures from a photo CD, files from the Windows directory, or whatever you choose. You cannot display TIFF files. It is probably best if you hand-pick several files (JPG is a good file type because the file sizes are small due to compression. They also make good-looking screen savers.) Try to select files that are about the same size when displayed on the screen.

Place the `DriveListBox` very near the top of the form and place the `FileListBox` immediately under it. Place the `DirListBox` to the right and parallel with the `FileListBox`. Right-click the `FileListBox` and set the `Pattern` property to your preferred type of graphic files.

Continued

TAKE NOTE

THE CHANGE EVENT AND THE PATH

When you set up your application for use, you want the user to be able to select the drive, directory, and files. To do this, you use the `Change` procedure associated with the `Drive`, `Dir`, and `File` objects. To allow the procedures to store the pathname, you make the directory path equal to the drive and the file path equal to the directory. In this way, you associate all three components of the file path.

CROSS-REFERENCE

Chapter 9 contains the continuation of the Saver application.

FIND IT ONLINE

The site **http://msdn.microsoft.com/library/devprods/vs6/vb/html/vbconusingfilesystemcontrolstogether.htm** offers extensive info on the file system controls.

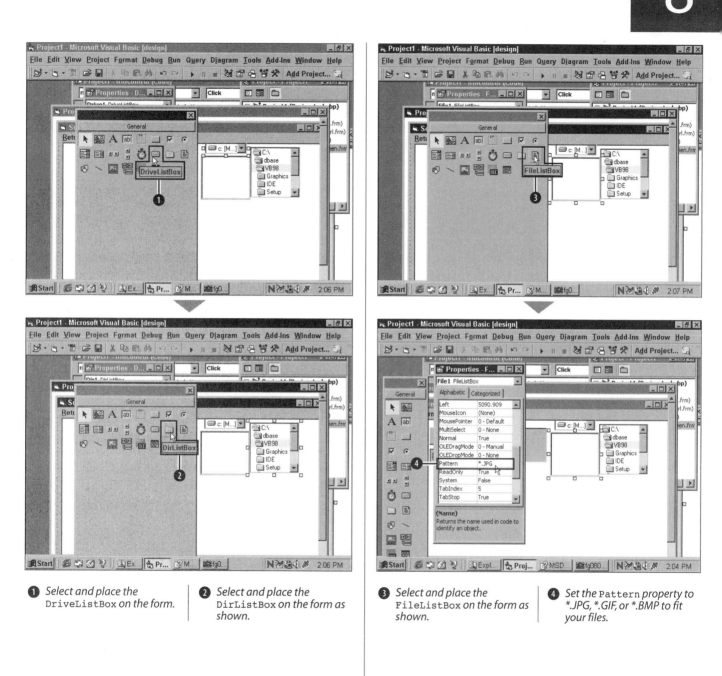

① Select and place the DriveListBox on the form.

② Select and place the DirListBox on the form as shown.

③ Select and place the FileListBox on the form as shown.

④ Set the Pattern property to *.JPG, *.GIF, or *.BMP to fit your files.

Using Drive, Directory, and File
Controls *Continued*

There must be a way to associate the drive, directory, and file to form a path. Double-click the `Drive` control. In the Code window, select `Drive1` from the object list, then `Change` as the procedure. You are doing this because you want to allow the users to change the drive, based on where their files are. You also want to associate the drive with the directory, so you add the statement:

```
Dir1.Path = Drive1.Drive
```

This ensures that the directory path is the same as the drive. Next, you want to act similarly for the path of the file. So you again enter the Code window, select `Dir1` from the object list, and then again select the `Change` procedure. This time, you enter the statement:

```
File1.Path = Dir1.Path
```

If the file path is the same as the directory path, then you will be able to select files that belong in that specific directory, which was selected from the `DirListBox`. This all means that at runtime, the drive and directory are set to default from where the application was launched. The `Change` procedure is to allow the user to make different selections.

In order to capture the filename to use in loading the picture, you need to refer to the path names in the `Drive1` and `Dir1` `Change` procedures, because they store the pathname.

Double-click the `File1` object. Once in the Code window, you can load the picture with just one statement:

```
Picture1.Picture = LoadPicture(File1.Path +
"\" + File1.FileName)
```

Here you are using the `LoadPicture` function, setting the path to the `File1` path that you (the user) select.

There is another, more professional way of accomplishing the same feat. The application would look better and be more informative if you displayed the file path on the form. Then the whole file path would be easier to see than what is scrunched into the `FileListBox`. You can do this by changing the caption on the form with this statement:

```
Frmscreen.Caption = File1.Path + "\" +
File1.FileName
```

This allows you to set the form caption to the full path of the file. Now you can load the picture by using the caption.

```
Picture1.Picture =
LoadPicture(Frmscreen.Caption)
```

The first statement you wrote combined both of the following statements to display the picture, but by rewriting the code you were able to give the project a little more finesse. Run the program using the first code example, and then rerun it to see the change in the form caption.

In the next chapter, you continue your construction of the screen saver. This time, you will add the `PictureBox` and `Timer` controls.

TAKE NOTE

▶ UNDERSTANDING THE INDEX

The index number sequences are based on current directories and subdirectories for `Drive`, `Directory`, and `File` controls at runtime. The directory that is currently displayed is represented using the index – 1. To display the current value of the Index, add the following statement to the `Click` procedure in Listing 8-13: `Print File1.ListIndex`. Then run the program, select several files in succession, and observe the index value. You should see the numbers appear on the left of the form.

CROSS-REFERENCE
Chapter 10 deals further with arrays and indices.

FIND IT ONLINE
The site **http://msdn.microsoft.com/library/devprods/vs6/vb/ html/vbconfilesystemcontrolsscenarioafileseekerapplication .htm** has a sample application.

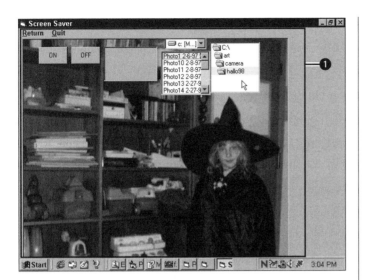

Listing 8-13: The File1_Click Procedure

```
Private Sub File1_Click()
    Frmscreen.Caption = File1.Path + "\"_
+ File1.FileName
    Picture1.Picture =_
LoadPicture(Frmscreen.Caption)
 End Sub
```

Listing 8-12: Drive and Directory Change Procedures

```
Private Sub Dir1_Change()
    File1.Path = Dir1.Path
End Sub
Private Sub Drive1_Change()
    Dir1.Path = Drive1.Drive
End Sub
```

❶ Enter the code to execute loading the picture selected. Run the program.

▶ Add the code in Listing 8-13 to enhance the usability of the application by displaying the file path on the form caption.

▶ Run the program after adding the code.

❷ Note the path is shown on the form caption.

Personal Workbook

Q&A

1 What other controls are combined in the `ComboBox` control?

_____

_____

_____

2 How can you increase the size of a label as the text increases in size?

_____

_____

_____

3 With what control is the `AddItem` method commonly used?

_____

_____

_____

4 How many values can the label caption contain?

_____

_____

_____

5 Which objects' properties can be changed with the movement of scrollbars?

_____

_____

_____

6 What is an example of a lightweight control?

_____

_____

_____

7 Which is a more efficient use of system resources, the `Image` control or the `PictureBox`?

_____

_____

_____

8 What is the function of the `Timer` control?

_____

_____

_____

ANSWERS: PAGE 523

EXTRA PRACTICE

1 Create a form and place a `DriveListBox`, `DirListBox`, and `FileListBox` on it.

2 Create an application using both an `Image` control and a `PictureBox` control.

3 Add a new form to the Projcontrol project. Plan to have a `Timer` function and a `PictureBox` on it.

4 Plan a new project with several controls on a form. Practice naming and giving captions for each control.

5 Practice changing the `Timer` interval property and observing its results.

REAL-WORLD APPLICATIONS

✔ Your boss wants you to create an application that utilizes a screen saver. He wants his staff to see photos of employees working very hard as a motivational tool. He wants each photo to stay on the screen about 10 seconds before changing. Design the project.

✔ Your aunt would like to have an application that would enable her to view all the photos she took at the family reunion, then selecting the ones she wants to print on her new inkjet printer. Design a scenario for this project.

✔ Your friend, Joe S., needs an input form that would let his staff select items from a list, then fill in the items if they do not appear on the list. What control is ideal for this task?

Visual Quiz

Which control is ideal for opening a file?

_____

_____

_____

_____

_____

CHAPTER **9**

MASTER
THESE
SKILLS

Using Dialog Controls

In this chapter, you will continue with the Projcontrol project, completing the functionality of the screen saver. Also in store for you is a greater involvement with ActiveX controls. You will learn that there is a set of Standard ActiveX controls as well as those you create yourself.

You have been introduced to ActiveX controls by adding them from component libraries to the toolbox. You did this when you added the CommonDialog, ToolBar, and Coolbar controls. In this chapter you will continue to learn about the Visual Basic Standard Controls, but you will develop more understanding and skills with ActiveX controls.

As you know, controls are used to obtain user input, help users make selections among options, access databases (locally and remotely), modify other applications' data, and generally assist users in carrying out their work.

Each control has a set of properties, methods, and events that is peculiar to itself. There are many situations in which you could use any one of several controls to accomplish the same goal. Which control you choose and how you choose to implement it depends upon your knowledge of how a specific control functions. The Image and the PictureBox are controls that have similarities, but your decision of which one to use depends on the demands of your application. The File System controls provide similar functions to the CommonDialog control, at least in terms of accessing files.

After you have explored the examples in this book, you will be able to evaluate an application design and determine the best approach to its realization.

Using the PictureBox

By this time, the `PictureBox` will seem to be an old friend. You used it in the Projevents project on the `frmdraggin` form, to contain a picture in the drag-and-drop procedure. Now you will use it to create your screen saver application.

A `PictureBox` can contain pictures. It displays bitmaps, icons, and metafiles. A *bitmap* is a picture made up of bits turned on or off. A photo is a bitmap. However, not all bitmaps have the same file format and extension. The most common format under Windows is the Windows bitmap (`.bmp`). The two different bitmap formats that compress files, JPEG and GIF, have different compression schemes. You would use each depending upon what type of graphic you have. JPEGs are best for photos with 24-bit color, and GIFs are best for spot color illustrations.

The popular TIFF (Tagged Image Format File) bitmap format is not supported. This format is the usual file format in the publishing industry and also works cross-platform with most operating systems, such as Macintosh OS.

The Windows Metafile format (`.wmf`) stores vector, rather than bitmap, data. It is a draw, rather than a paint, format. Icon files (`.ico`) and cursor files (`.cur`) are also supported by the `PictureBox` control.

`PictureBoxes` are important because they do much more than contain photos or illustrations. They can be used to hold other objects such as option buttons. One good reason to use the `PictureBox` to hold option buttons or other controls is that controls placed directly on an MDI form must have an `Align` property. Because the `PictureBox` has this property, you can place it on the MDI form and then place other controls inside it.

The `PictureBox` also can be a destination in Dynamic Data Exchange (DDE). Here, the `PictureBox` will accept the picture coming from a DDE source.

You should prepare a directory with graphic files in the correct format for the saver project as outlined in Chapter 8. Using the preceding graphic file information,

decide on a format. If you have few picture files, you can use the `.bmp` files in the `Windows` directory. There should be a few anyway. Other sources are the Internet, scanning family photos, downloading pictures from a digital camera, or purchasing CDs with catalogs of photos or illustrations in the Windows Metafile format. Beware of software packages that store photos in a proprietary format. You can use only the formats already discussed.

Continuing with the Screen Saver (`frmscreen`) form, select and place a `PictureBox` control on it. Enlarge the `PictureBox` to encompass the other controls (`FileListBox`, `DriveListBox`, and `DirListBox`). Stretch it so that it fills nearly all the form. If you have not yet done so, select Tools ➪ Menu Editor and make two menu items, "Return" and "Quit." Give the menus the names (mnurtn and mnuquit). Code the routines for these menu options.

Run the program. Select a drive, a directory, and an appropriate graphic file from the list boxes. You need to have a succession of pictures to display in order for the screen saver to work. If you have a list of files in one directory, click each file in turn and watch the screen change.

TAKE NOTE

OTHER PICTUREBOX FEATURES

You can "paint" a bitmap using the `PaintPicture` method on the `PictureBox` control as well as loading pictures into it. In addition to pictures, you can add custom graphics and text with the `DrawPoint`, `DrawLine`, and `DrawCircle` methods. Output of these graphic methods is determined by the `DrawWidth`, `DrawStyle`, `FillColor`, `FillStyle`, and `ScaleMode` properties.

CROSS-REFERENCE

Chapter 16 delves further into this topic.

FIND IT ONLINE

Check out Mabry's site for commercial controls and some trial downloads: **http://www.mabry.com/proplist/index.htm**.

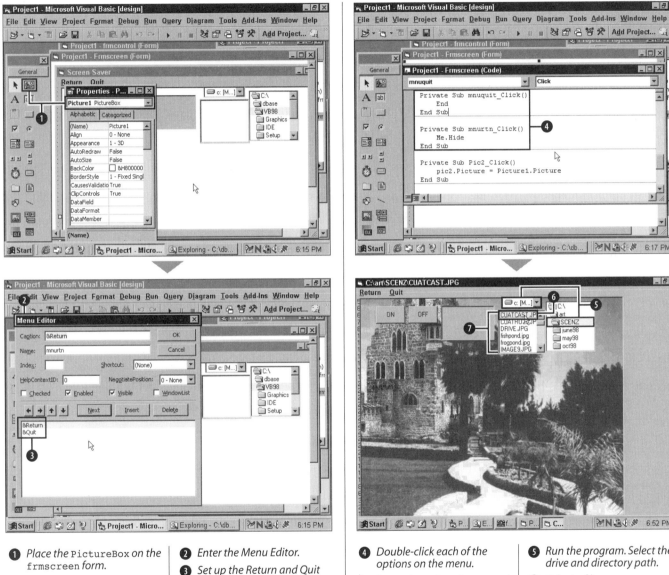

① *Place the* `PictureBox` *on the* `frmscreen` *form.*

② *Enter the Menu Editor.*

③ *Set up the Return and Quit menu options.*

④ *Double-click each of the options on the menu.*

▶ *Insert the code to Return and Quit.*

⑤ *Run the program. Select the drive and directory path.*

⑥ *Select a file.*

⑦ *Click successive files to see them displayed.*

Timing the Screen Saver

As you learned in the last chapter, the `Timer` control can control events firing at equal intervals, with or without the user's participation.

Without further ado, place the `Timer` control anywhere on the `frmscreen` form. You will remember that the placement is not significant, because the `Timer` control is not displayed at runtime.

Now, you need to set the time `Interval` property, so right-click the `Timer` control to get the Properties window. Set the `Timer Interval` property to 3000 (about three seconds). `Enabled` is the other property to set.

If you want the timer to begin immediately at runtime, you should set `Enabled` to True. That is, the `Enabled` property should be True if you want the `Timer` control to work in the background outside user intervention. If you want the user to have control of when the `Timer` event begins, you should set `Enabled` to False, then allow the user to make the decision of when the cycle should start.

At this time, your big question should be "how does the screen saver cycle through a series of pictures automatically?" You will be able to answer this question as soon as you understand how the `ListIndex` and `ListCount` properties work.

When you added the Command1 to Command5 buttons to the `frmcontrol` form in the last chapter, you used the `ListIndex` control to select the names in the `List1` `ListBox`. The first name on the list has a value of 0, the second name, a value of 1, and so one, with the fifth name having a value of 4. For this reason, the captions on the buttons (ZERO, ONE, TWO, THREE, and FOUR) refer to the `ListIndex` value rather than the numeric position of names on the list. If you want to display the first name, the `ListIndex` value is always zero.

`ListCount` expresses the value for the number of items in a list for the controls that use lists. This includes the `ComboBox`, `DirListBox`, `DriveListBox`, `FileListBox`, and `ListBox` controls. Because the `ListIndex` value is −1 when no item is selected, and the first item is 0, the `ListCount` value is always one integer higher than the highest `ListIndex` value.

You already added the code to load the picture in the last exercise. In fact, you can click the filename in the `FileListBox` and cause the file to be displayed. What you need to do now is to arrange for the `Timer` control to display the pictures in succession at the intervals you set.

Keep in mind that an `Interval` of 1000 is about one second. That means your screen saver must cycle at least once per minute. This is no problem, as most screen savers change much more frequently than that. You set the `Timer Interval` property in the Properties window, but you also can write code to set the interval to begin at runtime.

You will need to set up some conditional statements for your `Timer` procedure. In the Code window select the `Timer1` object, then the `Timer` procedure. Notice that is the only procedure available for the `Timer` control. You need to write the procedure to reset the `ListIndex` to 0 when the end of the list of files in the selected directory is reached. If files are left in the directory, then the index should be incremented by 1 so that the next picture can be loaded.

Continued

TAKE NOTE

THE TIMER INTERVAL

The `Timer` control is built on the concept of frequency of occurrences. The time interval is set to milliseconds, but due to the machine cycles, the closest tolerance you can set time is to 1/18 second. In any case, if you set the `Interval` property of the `Timer` control to 1000, that will equal about one second. Accordingly, each 1000 increment is about one second. Thus, if you want your screen saver to cycle every five seconds, then set the interval to 5000. The maximum interval you can set is 32535, which is about one minute.

CROSS-REFERENCE

Chapter 8 discusses the **Timer** control.

FIND IT ONLINE

The site **http://www.allexperts.com/software/visual.shtml** has a volunteer staff of VB experts.

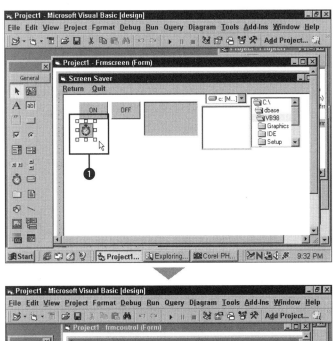

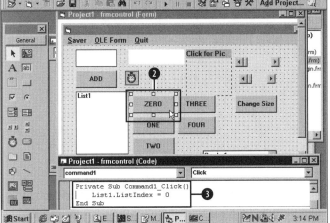

Listing 9-1: The Timer Event Procedure

```
Private Sub Timer1_Timer()
    If File1.ListIndex = File1.ListCount
- 1 Then
        File1.ListIndex = 0 ⬅❹
    Else
        File1.ListIndex = File1.ListIndex + 1


    End If
End Sub
```

❺

❹ *Reset the index to 0 when it is at the end of the list, because ListIndex is 1 minus the value of ListCount.*

❺ *If the last file has not been encountered, advance the index by 1 to go to the next file.*

❶ *Place the* Timer *control on the* frmscreen *form.*

❷ *Select the ZERO button on the* frmcontrol *form.*

❸ *Viewing the code in Listing 9-1 shows ListIndex = 0.*

Timing the Screen Saver

Continued

The `Timer` will control the timing of the `LoadPicture` event so that the picture changes at every interval, as execution continues moving down the list with the incrementing of the index.

There is one problem. There is no way to start the ball rolling, or start showing the pictures. If you need to have the user select a directory containing correct graphics files for display, then you need to have a way to initialize the `Timer`. Because you set the `Timer`'s `Enabled` property to True from the Properties window, then the program will attempt to start in the default directory. This is not so good if there are no files. What you need now is a command button to start the process, so that you can make a directory selection and then start it by pressing the button.

Place a command button at the top left of the `frmscreen` form. Name it "Cmdon" and give it the caption "ON." Because you can turn the saver on, maybe you should be able to turn it off as well, so make another button named "Cmdoff" with the caption "OFF" and place it next to the ON button. For the Cmdon button, in the Code window, select the `Cmdon` object and the `Click` procedure. This part is simple. You are going to set the properties in the code. Enable the `Timer`:

```
Private Sub Cmdon_Click()
    Timer1.Enabled = True
End Sub
```

And disable it for the Cmdoff button:

```
Private Sub Cmdoff_Click()
    Timer1.Enabled = False
End Sub
```

There is another feature you have to add to the project. If you are going to have the `Enabled` property set at runtime by the user, set the interval at the time the process is initialized when you press the ON button.

```
Private Sub Cmdon_Click()
    Timer1.Enabled = True
    Timer1.Interval = 3000
End Sub
```

So add this statement to the Cmdon button code below the `Enabled` property statement. You already set the preceding properties in the Properties window, so you need to view the Properties window again and change them back to the defaults, `Enabled = False` and `Interval = 0`.

Enter the code and run the program. Select a drive, a directory, and an initial file from the File System list boxes. Next, you should press the ON button to start the process. If all goes well, the pictures in the selected directory should be displayed in succession about each three seconds.

Now you can make a picture in picture — like a small picture you'd see superimposed upon the larger TV screen — in your screen saver. Add another, smaller `PictureBox` (about one inch square) to the `frmscreen` form. Place it inside the large `PictureBox` named "Pic2." Double-click the Pic2 `PictureBox` and select the `Pic2` object in the Code window's object list and the `Click` procedure. Then enter this code:

```
Private Sub Pic2_Click()
    pic2.Picture = Picture1.Picture
End Sub
```

In this statement, you copy the same picture that is currently being viewed in your screen saver. When you click the small `PictureBox` at runtime, you will get a snapshot of the current big picture inside the little box.

TAKE NOTE

CONTROLLING THE TIMER CROSS

You can use the `Timer` control, and other controls, in Internet development. To do this, search the Microsoft site for the document "Creating a Slide Show using the ActiveX Timer Control."

CROSS-REFERENCE

Chapter 20 has more information on additional controls.

FIND IT ONLINE

The site **http://msdn.microsoft.com/library/techart/msdn_ nctmr.htm#timerref** has source code for developing a slide show.

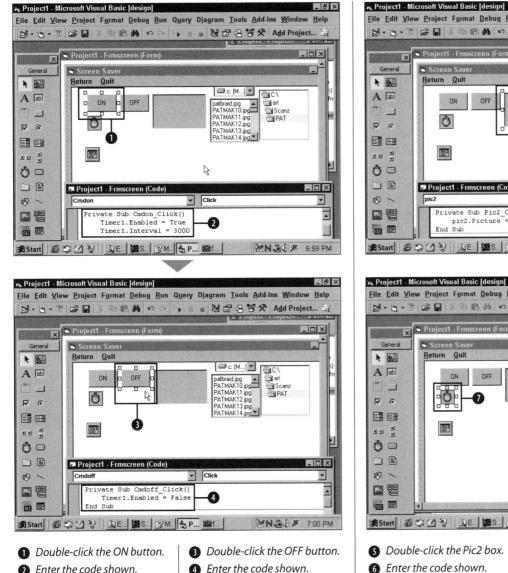

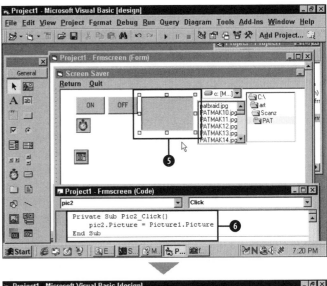

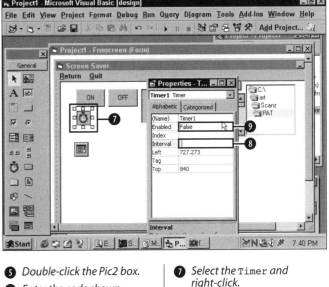

① *Double-click the ON button.*

② *Enter the code shown.*

③ *Double-click the OFF button.*

④ *Enter the code shown.*

⑤ *Double-click the Pic2 box.*

⑥ *Enter the code shown.*

⑦ *Select the* Timer *and right-click.*

⑧ *Change* Enabled *to False.*

⑨ *Remove the value from* Interval.

Creating Help Dialog Boxes

The CommonDialog control is obtained by selecting Components from the View menu and selecting Microsoft Common Dialog Controls 6.0. This will place the control in your toolbox. Select the tool and place it anywhere on the frmscreen form. Name it dlgpixhelp. You can enter the name in the property pages by right-clicking the Commondialog control.

The CommonDialog control is not visible at runtime and cannot be sized. In order to access it, you must use it in conjunction with another control. You have had some experience with the CommonDialog control when you used it with the RichTextBox to open a file and display it in the text box. One of the interesting features of the CommonDialog control is the Help feature. The Windows Help Engine is accessed through the CommonDialog control. You can display a Help file for your project by using the Help dialog box.

You use the Help dialog feature of the CommonDialog control through the ShowHelp method. You then use the constants to specify how you want your users to access the help files. You need to set the HelpFile and HelpCommand properties of the CommonDialog control to one of their appropriate constants or values before using the ShowHelp method. If you do not, Winhlp32.exe will fail to display the Help file. There are ways to have the CommonDialog control display specific contextual help, providing you know the HelpContextId property of the help document.

In this exercise, you will have help operate from a menu option. With the frmscreen form selected, select the Menu Editor from the Tools menu. Insert a menu bar option between Return and Quit. "Help" should be the caption and mnuhelp the filename. If you have plans for specific types of help, you will need to explore the various help files existing on your system. If you are running Windows 95/98, you should be able to find the help files in the Windows, Windows\System, or Windows\Help directories. You can search for files with an .hlp extension.

For the purposes of the exercise, you need not find an entirely appropriate help file. If you were creating the frmscreen application for end users, you might create a special help file for that application. Or you might have a Windows Help file in mind for some aspect of the application. Again, if you are going to provide context-sensitive help, you will need to use the HelpContextId property for that purpose. Here, you are mainly concerned with learning how to tap the Windows Help Engine.

You will use the ShowHelp method and the HelpFile and HelpCommand properties. HelpFile and HelpCommand must be set before ShowHelp can display the Help file. Because you have added the Help option to your menu bar, you must add the method to the Click procedure for mnuhelp. Double-click the new Help option on the frmscreen form.

In the Code window, select the mnuhelp object. Use the name of the dialog box you placed on the form, then set the HelpCommand property to the constant cdlHelpContents. Next, specify the name of the actual file you will use. For an easy example, you can use the Windows.hlp file. If it is in a different directory than that shown, it must be changed to the correct directory on your system. Finally, use the ShowHelp command to show the help file.

TAKE NOTE

▶ THE COMMDLG.DLL FILE

The CommonDialog control furnishes you with a collection of dialog boxes to open and save files; select fonts, colors, and print options; and access Windows Help. One thing to keep in mind is that the CommonDialog control will not function without the dynamic link library file, Commdlg.dll. This file must be in your Windows\System directory or the CommonDialog control will not work.

CROSS-REFERENCE

Chapter 8 also uses the **CommonDialog** control.

FIND IT ONLINE

The site **http://msdn.microsoft.com/library/devprods/vs6/vb/html/vbidxcommondialogcontrolconstants.htm** has the constants for the **CommonDialog** control.

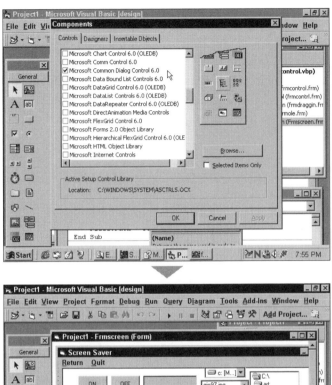

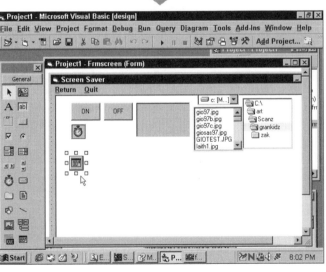

▶ This is the Components Controls dialog.

▶ This is the commondialog control icon.

Listing 9-2: Displaying a Help File

```
Private Sub mnuhelp_Click()

    ' Set the HelpCommand Property
    dlgpixhelp.HelpCommand =
cdlHelpContents ← ❶
    ' Specify the Help file.
    dlgpixhelp.HelpFile =
"c:\Windows\help\windows.hlp" ← ❷
    ' Display the Windows Help engine.
    dlgpixhelp.ShowHelp ← ❸
    Exit Sub
```

❶ Set the `HelpCommand` property to the constant `cdlHelpContents`.

❷ Specify the name of the actual file (`Windows.hlp`).

❸ Use the `ShowHelp` command to show the help file.

Creating Font Dialog Boxes

Continuing our work with the `CommonDialog` control, create a project named Projdialog with a form named `frmdialog`. If you want, you can use the projmenus project and the `frmmenu1` form from Chapter 7. If you do use the existing project and form, rename them accordingly and use Save As to save each of them in the same directory with your work for this chapter. Otherwise, you will overwrite the work you have done and will not be able to recover it.

In this exercise, you will use some other functions of the `CommonDialog` control. You have had some experience with the Open and Help options. We have at our disposal the Font, Save As, Color, and Printer functions, as well as more work with the Open option.

If you have not done so, place a `RichTextBox` control on the form. Select the Microsoft `RichTextBox` Control 6.0 from the Components option on the Project menu. Name the `RichTextBox` control `rchTestText`. Place a `CommonDialog` box on the `frmdialog` form as well. Name the `CommonDialog` control `dlgTestFont`.

You will need specific menus for this form. If you are reusing the older form, the menus will need revision. With the form selected, select the Menu Editor from the Tools menu. The first menu should be the File menu (mnufile) with Open, Save, Print, and Exit options. Also, make an Edit menu with a Select Font option. Refer to the instructions in Chapter 7 to construct menus using the Menu Editor.

Prior to displaying the Font Dialog box, you must set the `Flags` property of `dlgTest` to accommodate screen fonts, printer fonts, or both. If this is not done, you will get an error message that no fonts exist. This is because sometimes a system is set up without both screen and printer fonts matching. The `Flags` property makes sure the correct font exists before presenting the font selection dialog box. You have the option of setting the `Flags` property to both screen and printer fonts.

Select the Edit menu option on your form, and then select the Select Font option to access the Code window. Select the `mnufont` object and the `Click` procedure. Add

the statement to set the `Flags` property of `dlgTest` to `cdlCFBoth` (both screen and printer fonts).

```
dlgTest.Flags = cdlCFBoth
```

Once the `Flags` property is set, you can use the `ShowFont` method to display the font you select. Once again, you use the `CommonDialog` control to display the Font Dialog box.

```
DlgTest.ShowFont
```

So far, you have created a procedure connected to mnufont that will present a user with a dialog box displaying fonts installed on the system. The user can select one of these fonts (including point size and style), but nothing much will happen as a result. Try running the program. The dialog box looks fine, but when you type some text in the `rchTestText` box, the default font doesn't change.

In order to have the controls take action when you select a new font, you must set additional properties of the `RichTextBox` and `CommonDialog` controls. The font selection is taking place under the auspices of the `dlgTest`, but no values are being passed to the `rchTestText` control. You need to connect the properties of the `RichTextBox` and the `CommonDialog` control. Do this by setting the font properties of `rchTestText` equal to `dlgTest`.

TAKE NOTE

USING FLAGS TO CONTROL FONTS

Through flags, you can control allowable font sizes and types as well as to list only the supported screen fonts or the fonts supported by the default printer. You also can restrict loading certain types such as true type fonts and vector (outline) fonts and also limit font sizes to a specific range. There are also flags to present error messages when a wrong selection or no selection is made.

CROSS-REFERENCE

Chapter 8 and Chapter 11 address similar issues related to the **CommonDialog** control.

FIND IT ONLINE

The site **http://msdn.microsoft.com/library/devprods/vs6/ vb/html/vbctlcommondialogcontrolfontdialogexamplex.htm** has an example of the Font dialog box.

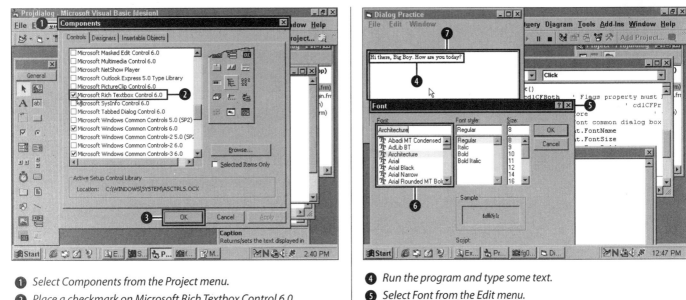

① Select Components from the Project menu.

② Place a checkmark on Microsoft Rich Textbox Control 6.0.

③ Click OK.

④ Run the program and type some text.

⑤ Select Font from the Edit menu.

⑥ Pick a font from the dialog box.

⑦ Observe the font in the text box.

Listing 9-3: The mnufont Procedure

```
Private Sub mnufont_Click()
    dlgTest.Flags = cdlCFBoth    ←①
            ' Set Flags property to cdlCFBoth, cdlCFPrinterFonts,
        ②┐  ' or cdlCFScreenFonts before ShowFont method.
    dlgTest.ShowFont    ' Display Font common dialog box.
    rchTestText.Font.Name = dlgTest.FontName
    rchTestText.Font.Size = dlgTest.FontSize        ←③
    rchTestText.Font.Bold = dlgTest.FontBold
    rchTestText.Font.Italic = dlgTest.FontItalic

End Sub
```

① Set the Flags property to screen and printer fonts.

② Display the dialog box.

③ Set the text box font properties to the equivalent properties of the CommonDialog control.

Creating Open Dialog Boxes

In a previous chapter, you learned about the `RichTextBox` control. You used it with the proj-menus project. There, you created a `RichTextBox` and used the `Open` option to open a rich text file.

`RichTextBox`es also can open vanilla text (ASCII or ANSI) files. These files can be viewed with the TYPE command in DOS. They are files that contain no formatting and use only the ASCII or ANSI character set. Examples would be your system's `Autoexec.bat` or `Config.sys` files, or any file viewed and edited in Notepad. You can use your `frmdialog` form as a kind of Notepad.

In order to use the `RichTextBox` Open dialog to select a text file, you need to make some changes from the previous code you wrote for the `Open` procedure for the `RichTextBox` control. The former procedure was used to load rich text files, so the code must be changed. However, the logic is the same. You need only change the portion that refers to the file filter.

Design time, run time and break mode are the three modes available in Visual Basic. Design time is the mode in which you design and create an application. Run time is the mode in which the program is executing. Break mode suspends program execution in order to examine and change data. While in design time, select the Open option from your `frmdialog`'s File menu. From the Code window, select the `mnuopen` object and the `Click` procedure. Set the filter for text files only.

```
dlgTest.Filter ="Text Formatfiles|*.txt"
```

Now you will not be able to view files of any other type. Remember, the previous exercise used the filter `*.rtf` to restrict potential file selection to rich text format files. At this point, you are ready to display the dialog box.

```
dlgTest.ShowOpen
```

Use the ShowOpen command to fetch the dialog box. Once that statement has been completed, the file can be loaded into the text box. The `LoadFile` method is set to the `FileName` property of the dialog control with the `rtfText` specification.

```
rchTestText.LoadFile dlgTest.FileName, rtfText
```

If a file has the correct extension but is not really of that type (perhaps someone renamed it incorrectly), you will get a weird-looking display.

Once you complete the `mnuopen_Click` procedure, run the program, click the Open option on the File menu, and open a text file on your system. Now, you shouldn't have to look far, as there are many text files on anyone's hard drive. For example, all readme files are text. If you aren't sure where to find them, look to your old standby, the `Windows` directory. Lots of applications place readme files there. Just about any file with a `.txt` extension is text. If you try to load a file that has been misnamed, either you will get garbage or it will look weird. You won't be able to load a program file, because it will be filtered out from the display.

Here is another chance to test the Select Font option on the Edit menu. Load a text file, then use your dialog box to change the font.

TAKE NOTE

▶ LIMITING FILE TYPES BY EXTENSION

File filters function to restrict the display (and loading) of files not allowed in a specific application. Using the file extension as a filter restricts the files. One example would be the limitation of graphic files to one or two formats (`.jpg`) or (`.gif`). The `RichTextBox` can be used for files of the `.rtf` or `.txt` formats. When the wildcard asterisk precedes the file extension, this means any filename is allowed as long as it has the stated extension.

CROSS-REFERENCE

Chapter 7 used a similar example with a different file type.

FIND IT ONLINE

The site **http://msdn.microsoft.com/library/devprods/vs6/vbasic/ cmdlg98/vbctlcommondialogcontrolopensaveasdialogs examplex.htm** includes examples of Open and Save As boxes.

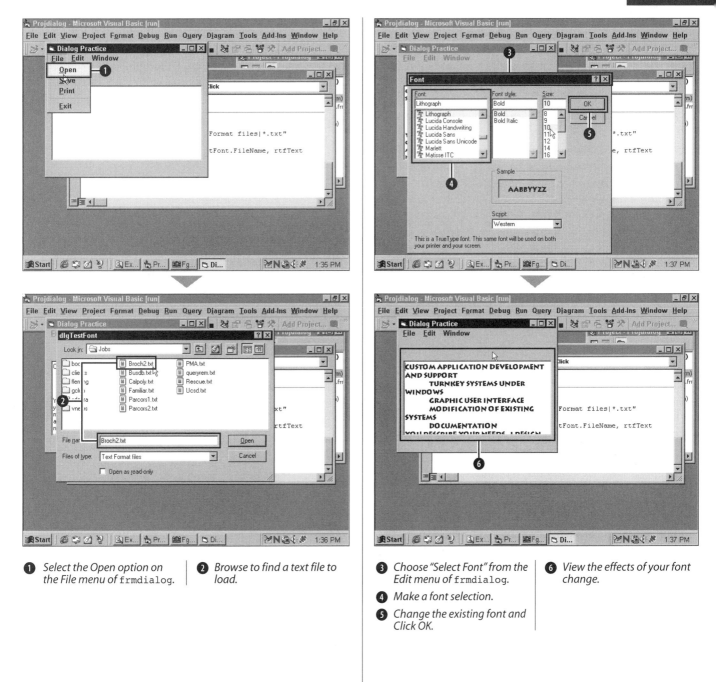

① Select the Open option on the File menu of frmdialog.

② Browse to find a text file to load.

③ Choose "Select Font" from the Edit menu of frmdialog.

④ Make a font selection.

⑤ Change the existing font and Click OK.

⑥ View the effects of your font change.

Creating Save As Dialog Boxes

The Save As dialog is the complement to the Open dialog box. The Open dialog method is ShowOpen, and the Save As dialog method is ShowSave. The dialog boxes are similar in that they both display an explorer view of the drive, directory, and files. Using both dialog boxes, you also can select the full path including a specific file.

The Save As dialog appears a duplicate of the Open dialog, except for the caption of the boxes. Also, as with the Open dialog box, you can use the Filter property to restrict the display to certain types of files, such as text files as we used for the Open dialog exercise.

The Flags property can be used to change various elements on the dialog as well as prompt the user when certain actions may occur, such as overwriting a file. The flag property cdlOFNOverwritePrompt will present a dialog box inquiring whether you want to overwrite the file if that filename already exists.

The cdlOFNAllowMultiselect flag property will allow multiple file selections by holding down the Shift key while pressing down an arrow key, so the files are highlighted. However, Windows 95 and NT 4.0 do not support long filenames for this option.

There is another flag property, cdlOFNNoLongNames, which will prevent loading long filenames. Using the cdlOFNReadOnly property will cause the Read Only box to be checked by default.

You can find the flags constants in the Microsoft CommonDialog Control object library (MSComDlg) in the Object Browser. Select the FileOpenConstants Class and view the flags in the Members pane.

In design time, click the Save option on the File menu, on the frmdialog form. In the Code window make sure the mnusave object is selected, along with the Click procedure (although Click is the only procedure available for this object).

You set flags for Save just as you did for the Font dialog box. It is not necessary to set flags properties for this dialog, but you will set the overwrite prompt flag, because it is a good safety measure to avoid overwriting a file that you mean to keep.

```
dlgTest.Flags = cdlOFNOverwritePrompt
```

You can have multiple flags properties by using the Or keyword between the two flags constants.

To display the Save As dialog box, you add the following statement:

```
dlgTest.ShowSave
```

Add the statement to the Click procedure, below the Flags property constant. The ShowSave method displays the Save As dialog box just as the ShowOpen method caused the Open dialog box to be presented in the mnuopen procedure. Finally, the SaveFile method of the RichTextBox control is the counterpart of the LoadFile method used in the mnuopen procedure.

TAKE NOTE

SETTING SCROLLBARS FOR THE TEXT BOX

Perhaps you've noticed that the file you loaded into the RichTextBox did not completely display. That is because the default doesn't include scrollbars. Because the text wraps, you may want to set the Scrollbar property to Vertical. If you want the user to be able to see the text normally, you should set the scrollbars property to Both. If you don't set this property at design time, there will be no scrollbars at runtime.

CROSS-REFERENCE

There are similar examples in Chapter 7, Chapter 8, and Chapter 11.

FIND IT ONLINE

The site **http://msdn.microsoft.com/library/wcedoc/vbce/ methods_86.htm** has information on the **ShowSave** method.

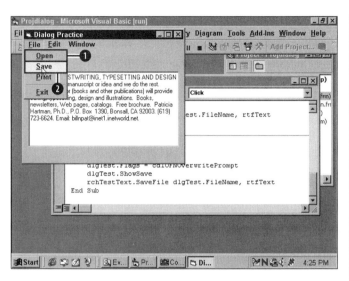

❶ *Run the program and select Open from the File menu.*

❷ *Open a file, then select Save to save it.*

▶ *Add the code to set the* Flags *property to show an overwrite prompt.*

❸ *Run the program and load a file.*

❹ *Save the file with the same name.*

Listing 9-4: The Save As Dialog Procedure

```
Private Sub mnusave_Click()
    dlgTest.Flags = cdlOFNOverwritePrompt ←❶
    dlgTest.ShowSave ←❷
    rchTestText.SaveFile dlgTest.FileName, rtfText ←❸
End Sub
```

❶ *Set the* Flags *property of the* CommonDialog *control to prompt for overwriting the existing file.*

❷ *Add the statement to display the Save As dialog box.*

❸ *Associate the* FileName *property of the* CommonDialog *with the* SaveFile *method for* rchTestText.

Creating Color Dialog Boxes

The Color Dialog aspect of the `CommonDialog` control follows the logic of the other dialog boxes available with this control. This time, the selection of color is available for various objects. In the dialog boxes previously covered in this chapter, the boxes displayed the typical boxes you see every day in Windows applications.

The color dialog box is a color palette with swatches of colors you can choose. The full palette includes mixing colors to define a new shade. The default is the full palette. You can prevent users from mixing new shades to define colors by setting the `Flags` property. For this property to return a color in a Color dialog box, the `cdlCCRGBInit` flag must be set.

To begin, you will create a new menu item on the Edit menu bar of your `frmdialog` form. With the form selected, select the Menu Editor from the Tools menu. Add the new option on the Edit menu after Select Font. Name the item Select Color. Name the menu mnucolor. Be sure to indent the item by pressing the right arrow in the Menu Editor dialog. Returning to the form, access the Code window and select the `mnucolor` object and the `Click` procedure. You will initialize the RGB color component, so you enter the statement:

```
dlgTest.Flags = cdlCCRGBInit
```

This statement causes the color dialog to return the selected color. Next you need to cause the dialog to display the color, just as you used the `ShowFont` and `ShowOpen` in the other examples. The `Showxxxx` syntax refers to the display of the dialog box. Thus, you use the `ShowColor` method.

```
dlgTest.ShowColor
```

This statement uses the method of the `dlgTest` `CommonDialog` control. Finally, you must decide what color property you will set. You can set the `BackColor` property to change the color of the form itself, rather than objects on the form. To do this, use the statement:

```
frmdialog.BackColor = dlgTest.Color
```

This statement sets the background color of the `frmdialog` object to the color of the `CommonDialog` control you have named `dlgTest`. The procedure looks like this:

```
Private Sub mnucolor_Click()
    dlgTest.Flags = cdlCCRGBInit
    dlgTest.ShowColor
    frmdialog.BackColor = dlgTest.Color
End Sub
```

What if you want to change the text color as well? You can do this easily, but first, use the Menu Editor to add an option to the Edit menu. Take this chance to make your existing color option specific. Rename the Color option to Background Color. Add the option (indented under Edit) "Text Color," and name it `mnutcolor`. Back in the Code window, select the `mnutcolor` object's `Click` procedure and add the `ShowColor` method once again. Now, you will need to refer to the `RichTextBox`, because the text really belongs to that object. You add a statement similar to the `rchTestText SaveFile` method:

```
rchTestText.SelColor = dlgTest.Color
```

This time, you set the Selected Color of the text box to the dialog control's Color property. This will change the color of the selected text in the text box. It will also change the color of the text you type immediately after choosing a text color. The color dialog box works just like the box for selecting the background color. Here is the `mnutcolor` `Click` procedure:

```
Private Sub mnutcolor_Click()
    dlgTest.ShowColor
    rchTestText.SelColor = dlgTest.Color
End Sub
```

CROSS-REFERENCE

Chapter 14 also uses the **CommonDialog** control.

FIND IT ONLINE

The site **http://msdn.microsoft.com/library/devprods/vs6/vbasic/cmdlg98/vbctlcommondialogcontrolcolordialog examplex.htm** has sample code for the Color Dialog box.

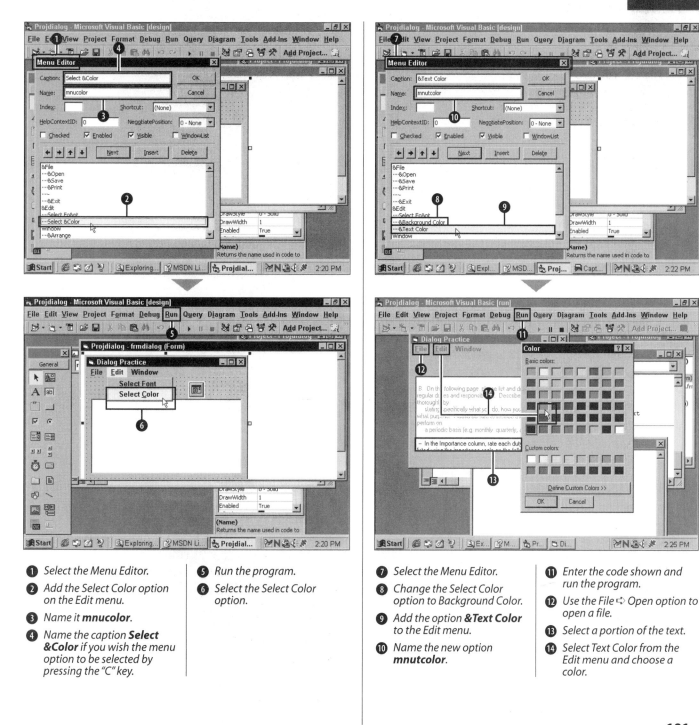

① Select the Menu Editor.

② Add the Select Color option on the Edit menu.

③ Name it **mnucolor**.

④ Name the caption **Select &Color** if you wish the menu option to be selected by pressing the "C" key.

⑤ Run the program.

⑥ Select the Select Color option.

⑦ Select the Menu Editor.

⑧ Change the Select Color option to Background Color.

⑨ Add the option **&Text Color** to the Edit menu.

⑩ Name the new option **mnutcolor**.

⑪ Enter the code shown and run the program.

⑫ Use the File ➪ Open option to open a file.

⑬ Select a portion of the text.

⑭ Select Text Color from the Edit menu and choose a color.

Creating Print Dialog Boxes

The Print dialog box is used to specify the method of printing output. It does not actually send output to the printer. It does provide the user with information about the default printer and enables the user to choose another printer installed on the system.

The printing process is a great deal more complicated than the other functions associated with the dialog box control. Because the printing process is so complex, the portion covered here is only that necessary to understanding the Print dialog box. This exercise will give an example of printing using the default printer only. A complete discussion of the document printing process is covered in Chapters 13 and 14, dealing with file input and output.

The user's selections in the Print dialog box are stored in the properties, Number of `Copies` `FromPage` (beginning page), `ToPage` (ending page), .`hDC` (device context), `Orientation` (portrait or landscape).

Once again, flags constants related to printer control can be set for the `dlgTest` dialog control. Which flag must be set depends upon what you need to do. If you merely want to print the contents of the `RichTextBox`, you must be concerned about the device context constant, `cdlPDReturnDC`. That is because the device context for the printer is necessary for the system to print. The device context is returned in the `dlgTest` control's `hDC` property. The `hDC` property identifies the specific printer. In this exercise, the only printer to which you will be printing is your default printer. This statement sets the `Flags` property for the printer device context:

```
dlgTest.Flags = cdlPDReturnDC
```

The `ShowPrinter` method is required to display the Print dialog box. This is the counterpart of the `ShowColor` and `ShowOpen` methods of the Color and Open dialog boxes.

```
dlgTest.ShowPrinter
```

The next statement is the counterpart of the `RichTextBox` `SelColor` method used in the Color

Dialog section earlier in this chapter. This is the `SelPrint` method, which also uses the `hDC` property of the `CommonDialog` box, `dlgTest`.

```
rchTestText.SelPrint dlgTest.hDC
```

It is interesting that the printing is not independent of the text box object. It really works in conjunction with the object that contains the text to be printed. Enter the code so that the procedure contains the following:

```
Private Sub mnuprint_Click()
    dlgTest.Flags = cdlPDReturnDC
    dlgTest.ShowPrinter
    Printer.Print ""
    rchTestText.SelPrint dlgTest.hDC
End Sub
```

TAKE NOTE

PRINTING

Using the dialog box to print is not as easy as it was to use the Color, Open and Save As, and Font dialog boxes. This is because the act of printing involves device control. Controlling any peripheral device through a communications port involves input/output issues. Printing from a device has several parts: 1) You have to write code to start the printing process. 2) There are printer drivers installed on your system and those of users. 3) The printers each will have different capabilities and features. The code you write can determine the quality of the output if it is within the printers' capability, but the actual drivers installed on any system will limit what you can do in your application.

CROSS-REFERENCE

Chapter 14 deals more intensively with printing.

FIND IT ONLINE

The site **http://msdn.microsoft.com/library/devprods/vs6/ vbasic/cmdlg98/vbctlcommondialogcontrolprintdialog examplex.htm** has examples of the Print dialog.

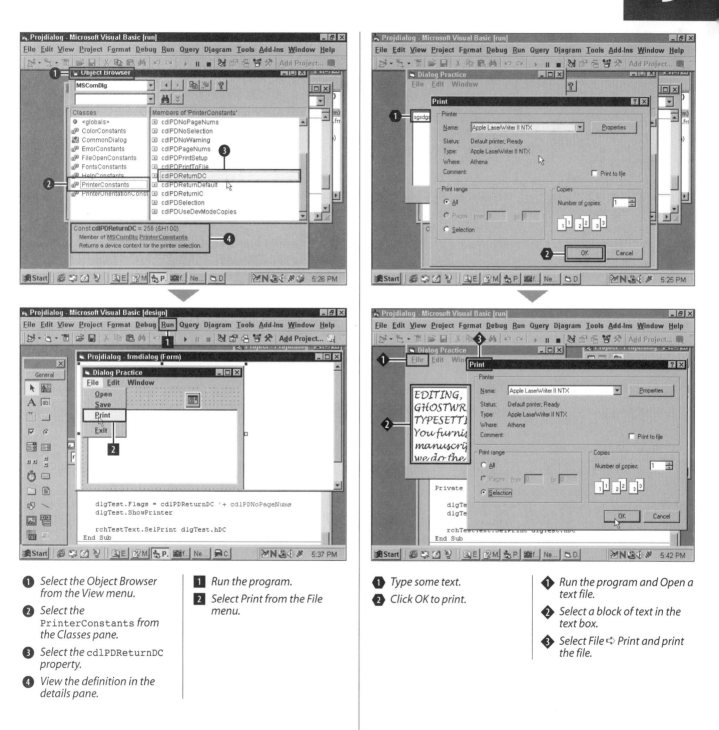

① *Select the Object Browser from the View menu.*

② *Select the* PrinterConstants *from the Classes pane.*

③ *Select the* cdlPDReturnDC *property.*

④ *View the definition in the details pane.*

1 *Run the program.*

2 *Select Print from the File menu.*

① *Type some text.*

② *Click OK to print.*

④ *Run the program and Open a text file.*

② *Select a block of text in the text box.*

③ *Select File ⇨ Print and print the file.*

193

Using Libraries of Controls

You have become familiar with several of the many libraries of control available from the Project menu's Components menu. The `RichTextBox` is available in the Microsoft Rich Textbox Control 6.0 library. The `CommonDialog` control is found in the Microsoft Common Dialog Control 6.0 library. A number of controls are found in the three Microsoft Windows Common Controls 6.0 libraries.

The Components dialog box includes all registered ActiveX controls, insertable objects, and ActiveX designers. Each library is contained in a filename with the `.ocx` extension. To add any controls that are included in a library, you identify the library where the control(s) exist and place a checkmark in the box next to the library name.

Insertable objects include applications such as spreadsheets, draw and paint programs, editors, and documents from other applications. When you make your selection, click OK and you will find the toolbox has been enhanced by the addition of the ActiveX controls from the library you selected.

Removing a control from the toolbox is done by selecting Components from the Project menu and then unchecking the check box next to the library containing the control you want to remove. You can reference an object in your code without having the control in your toolbox by setting a reference to the library in your code.

You can reference the object library of another application by selecting References from the Project menu. You place a checkmark next to the reference you wish to add, just as you did for adding the Components libraries. If you wish to add a reference not listed, you use the Browse button to look for the application on your system. If you search for an application on your hard drive and identify it, but it can't be added, you will get a message to that effect.

When you have selected a reference library, you will be able to view it in the Object Browser. Once you make the selection and confirm that it appears in the Object Browser, you can reference it in code.

If you make references to an application such as an Excel spreadsheet, you can have your applications extract the data from the spreadsheet and make calculations based upon the spreadsheet values. You can use objects from any application that supports ActiveX. Microsoft products do this, as do many draw and paint (photo editing) programs. In fact, many of those applications are listed in the available references from the Project menu.

Applications that support ActiveX technology, such as Microsoft Excel, Microsoft Word, and Microsoft Access, provide objects that you can manipulate programmatically from within your Visual Basic application. For example, you can use the properties, methods, and events of a Microsoft Excel spreadsheet, Microsoft Word document, or Microsoft Access database in your application.

In addition to using Component libraries and adding references to libraries, you also can create your own components, including code libraries and ActiveX controls. You can even include licensing when you distribute your package. You also can design ActiveX documents to display in Internet browsers.

TAKE NOTE

▶ USING DLLS

You can make calls directly to DLLs (dynamic link libraries). When you call these procedures, you may use procedures developed in a different language or from the Windows operating system. The DLLs contain procedures that your applications can link to and use at runtime. If a Windows DLL is in the `Windows\System` directory, all applications are able to share it. This is why during installations, you may get messages to the effect that a certain file with a `.dll` extension is being copied to your system. These Windows DLLs are referred to as the Windows API (application programming interface).

CROSS-REFERENCE
Chapter 10 has further information on this topic.

FIND IT ONLINE
The site **http://msdn.microsoft.com/library/periodic/period98/html/Object-Oriented_Reuse.htm#sidebar1** has an interesting discussion regarding reuse of components.

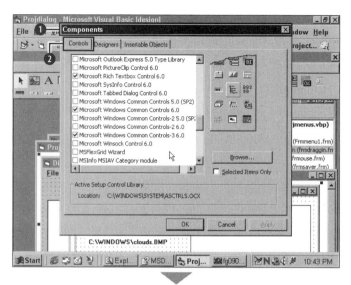

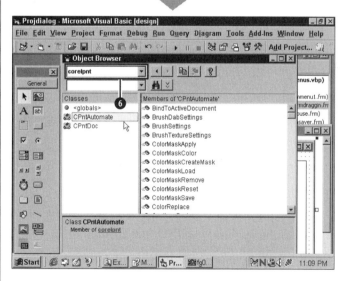

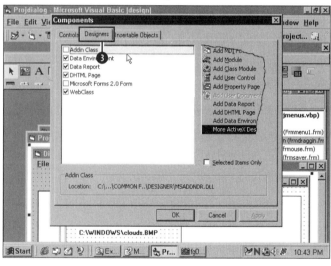

1. Select Components from the Project menu.

2. Select Controls.

3. Select Designers from the Components menu.

4. Select Insertable Objects from the Components menu.

5. Select an application on your system, such as Corel Photo Paint.

6. View the library in the Object Browser.

Personal Workbook

Q&A

1 What are some uses of the `PictureBox` control?

_____

_____

_____

2 What does the `Enabled` property of the `Timer` affect?

_____

_____

_____

3 Why is the `CommonDialog` control such an important addition to the toolbox?

_____

_____

_____

4 What does the Font Dialog box let you do?

_____

_____

_____

5 Which is the default option on the Color Dialog box, full palette or limited, and what does it consist of?

_____

_____

_____

6 What are some reasons the Printing process is more complicated than the other dialog box functions?

_____

_____

_____

7 How do filters work to allow viewing of only certain file types?

_____

_____

_____

8 How do you add components to your application from libraries?

_____

_____

_____

ANSWERS: PAGE 524

EXTRA PRACTICE

1. Create a form and place a `PictureBox` on it. Set the `PictureBox` `Picture` property to a path and filename of a graphic file.

2. Create an application that will enable you to create shapes within the `PictureBox`.

3. Add a `PictureBox` and a `Timer` to a form. Write a procedure to load a picture in the `PictureBox` at regular intervals.

4. Set up an application with a form and a menu bar providing options to Open, Save, and Print a file.

5. Practice setting `Enable` to True and False, then running your application.

REAL-WORLD APPLICATIONS

✔ Your little brother (cousin, child) is fascinated by the slide show application you wrote. Design a show for him in mind that will display pictures of things he particularly likes, for example, his favorite sports stars, games, toys, and so on.

✔ Your boss once again is plaguing you to write an application for entering financial data on a form. This time, you need to include menu options to let the users save their work to a file and print what's on the form. Design the form.

✔ You are dissatisfied with the accounting program you use to do your monthly bills. You really need a custom program that would take spreadsheet data and save it in a text format. Design the application as you would like it to work.

Visual Quiz

Where should the `CommonDialog` control properly be placed?

_____

_____

_____

_____

_____

_____

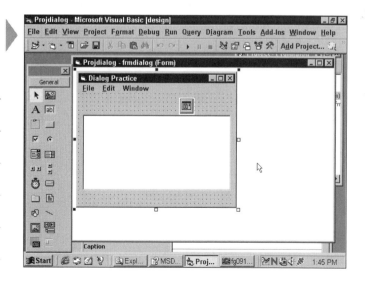

PART

III

Contents of 'Desktop'

Name

My Computer

Network Neigh

Internet Explore

Microsoft Outloo

Recycle Bin

My Briefcase

3252-9

3259-6

3261-8

3262-6

3281-2

3286-3

DE Phone List

Device Manager

In

Iomega Tools

Increasing Programming Skills

This Part focuses on developing more advanced working skills with programming techniques, as well as learning about more Visual Basic features.

The focus in the previous parts was to develop basic skills, and become familiar with most features in the Integrated Development Environment. Now we turn toward polishing your work. You will learn how to find errors in programs (debug), anticipate potential errors, and head them off before they cause problems.

A new topic introduced in this Part is file input and output. Input/Output involves opening and writing to records and files, but it affects much more. For example, Input/Output includes actions such as writing to devices like printers and peripherals connected to communication ports. In addition, Input includes data entry and obtaining data from peripheral devices (mice, keyboard, bar code reader, modem, and so on).

The purpose of debugging is to find out how an error occurred and to prevent it from happening again. You may have omitted a property, forgotten to define a variable or made any one of a number of mistakes. The tools offered by Visual Basic are a full complement of those available in any programming language. In addition to debugging tools, the interface itself provides ongoing error correction by invoking the Debug engine when a problem is detected.

You also begin to work with database projects in this Part. You learn to connect to a database through OLE DB or through Data Source Names. When you access a database through Visual Basic, the Microsoft Jet database engine and its connection management routines are accessed. The Jet engine makes every attempt to open as few connections as possible and share connections whenever possible.

CHAPTER 10

Learning to Use Advanced Data Features

In this chapter, you learn about the use of arrays and functions. *Arrays* are usually used to store groups of variables used in a procedure for the same purpose. Arrays can be assigned to other arrays. *Functions* perform specific tasks and can return values. Functions also can return arrays.

In the process of assigning array variables remember the variable types and whether the values of each type are compatible.

A big question is: "What is advanced Visual Basic programming?" The answer is found in these next pages. The language elements user-defined types, arrays, control arrays, string manipulation, conversion functions, and function procedures make up the more advanced programming techniques.

You can work with multiple projects in one programming session. You can set up a project just for testing purposes. In the Professional or Enterprise edition, you create and debug applications with multiple components. You can create and debug project groups containing standard executable projects, `ActiveX` executable projects, `ActiveX` dynamic-link library projects, or `ActiveX` control projects.

In earlier versions of Windows, the system settings were stored in files with the `.ini` extension. In Windows 95 and later, settings are stored in the Registry. You can manipulate Registry settings in Visual Basic. You can retrieve and save Registry settings. The System Info option included on the `About` Form enables you to retrieve and review your system's settings.

Another advanced concept is selective compilation. That is, you can compile different parts of your code, thereby controlling the application's functioning. This may enable you to create different but parallel versions of your application. You also can create and add resources to your projects through resource files (`.res`). You can write functions that can be called from procedures.

Conserving Resources with Arrays

You have had a small amount of exposure to arrays in this book and you may have programmed using arrays in other languages or in previous versions of Basic. Arrays enable you to have ranges of variables in numeric order, all of which carry out some function in the same way. Array variables have the same general name, but each element in an array is numbered consecutively.

Arrays are ways of using a number of variables with the same name to carry out some task. Creating array variables is sort of like cloning a variable into multiples of itself. Each of these multiple variables is identified by an index. The numeric position in the index identifies the element in the array. For example, if you had three age categories, you might have three simple variables: Age1, Age2, and Age3. If you used these variables in an array, you would have three array variables: Age(1), Age(2), and Age(3).

The advantage in setting up an array is that referring to these variables in code is much easier. You can do calculations in loops, instead of requiring a line of code for each occurrence. If X is the element in the array, you can increment X repeatedly and make reference to Age(X), instead of Age1, Age2, and Age3. Obviously, this feature is increasingly important, as your number of variables becomes progressively higher.

If you have a loop in which you want to increment a series of variables on each pass through the loop, then you can declare an array and take care of the entire process with the same general code. The following example could be a real chore if you had hundreds of Mysal variables.

```
Mysal1 = I+1
Mysal2 = I+1
Mysal3 = I+1
    . . .
```

If you made these items array variables instead of simple variables, you could change the code to something like this.

```
For I = 1 to 100
      Mysal(I) = Mysal(I)+1
Next I
```

Can you see the economy in code? Arrays usually use fewer system resources as well. At any rate, they use less code space in the program.

Suppose you have to produce a report showing subtotals for each of six geographic regions, each providing six modes (types) of service. You need to accumulate a subtotal value for each mode in each region. You respond to this need by declaring six regional variables called Costsub1 to Costsub6.

Because you need subtotals for six modes of service in each of the six regions, you decide to create 36 additional variables called Colm1a to Colm6f. The variables (Colm1a through Colm1f) represent subtotals for six modes in region 1. They will hold the values and accumulate new values as they are read in from a database. The beginning statement would look like this:

```
Costsub1 = Costsub1 + Colm1a
```

To translate this into simple variables without using any arrays, you would have 36 separate statements. Because there are six Costsub variables and six Colm variables, there would be 36 lines of code for this routine. If there were 100 instances of Modes, you would have 600 separate statements.

Imagine trying to code simple variables where you had hundreds of these calculations to make. The module size would be impressive, to say the least.

On the other hand, not all economies are worthwhile. If you are concerned about the size of a module, you needn't worry about restricting some items. Comment lines and blank lines are not compiled by Visual Basic, so no reason exists to exclude them.

CROSS-REFERENCE

Chapter 16 covers some of the information here.

FIND IT ONLINE

You will find a lot of info on arrays here:
http://web2.airmail.net/gbeene/tut-samp.html#add.

> **TAKE NOTE**
>
> ▶ **CONTROL ARRAYS VERSUS VARIABLE ARRAYS**
>
> Control arrays are not the same as the variable arrays discussed here. The *variable arrays* are declared in code and are different from the control arrays specified in the Properties Window at design time when you set the index property of a control. One big difference is *control arrays* allow replacement of segments of the array, while variable array elements are always continuous. That is, some elements in between the lower and upper bounds of a variable array cannot be removed.

Listing 10-1: The Cost Subtotal Debacle

```
Costsub1 = Costsub1 + Colm1a 'Accumulate Region 1 subtotal for mode1
Costsub1 = Costsub1 + Colm1b 'Accumulate Region 1 subtotal for mode2
Costsub1 = Costsub1 + Colm1c 'Accumulate Region 1 subtotal for mode3
Costsub1 = Costsub1 + Colm1d 'Accumulate Region 1 subtotal for mode4
Costsub1 = Costsub1 + Colm1e 'Accumulate Region 1 subtotal for mode5
Costsub1 = Costsub1 + Colm1f 'Accumulate Region 1 subtotal for mode6
Costsub2 = Costsub2 + Colm2a 'Accumulate Region 2 subtotal for mode1
. . .
Costsub6 = Costsub2 + Colm6f 'Accumulate Region 6 subtotal for mode6
```

▶ *Here you have the outline for the 6 Costsub variables and the 36 Colm variables.*

Listing 10-2: Using the Array as a Solution

```
For Reg = 1 To 6 'Counter for each region.
    For Modes = 1 To 6 'counter for each mode.
  Costsub(Reg) = Costsub(Reg)+ Colm(Reg,Modes)'accumulates subtotal
    Next
Next
```

▶ *The previous code summarizes subtotals for a cost report.*

▶ *Costsub(1) to Costsub(6) is a one-dimensional array with six elements. The Colm array is a two-dimensional array having 36 elements, with Reg and Modes as simple variables representing elements in the array.*

Working with Arrays

Arrays that are data typed as numeric cannot be mixed with string variables. However, if the declaration doesn't specify variable type (which makes it Variant by default) or declares it as a Variant type, the array can have both numeric and string types. Normally, you would not mix variable types in arrays because the array variables usually are designed to perform the same function and, therefore, are of the same type. The example using Age categories would obviously not need to mix types. The categories would either all be string (Under 18, 18-55. Over 55) or they would all be integer (1, 2, 3).

Sometimes an array is built to hold numeric values, but another array is read in and the old array values are replaced with new ones. In this case, the Variant type should be used.

Different types of arrays exist: Fixed and Dynamic. *Fixed arrays* have declarations that specify the upper bounds of the array. *Dynamic arrays* can grow as new elements are added. You declare an array as dynamic by giving it an empty dimension list, for example, Dim MyDynAray().

```
Dim Modes (6) As Integer
```

This is how you might declare the array used in the example. If the array is outside the module in which it is declared, the statement would be:

```
Public Modes (6) As Integer
```

Both of the previous statements declare the upper bound for arrays with six elements. You also can specify the lower bound for the array by giving a range.

```
Dim Modes (2 To 6) As Integer
```

This specifies the array will not begin with zero as it would by default. Instead, it will begin with 2. Memory limitations and considerations must avoid declaring higher boundaries than needed, as the space is reserved whether or not the array uses the elements.

Just as you can assign the value of one variable to another

```
A = B
```

You can assign the values in one array to another. This is a powerful feature unavailable in the pre Visual versions of Basic. Instead of reading in an entire array and then replacing the old values with new ones from the other array, you can just make the reassignment.

Problems in reassignment might occur if the array types aren't compatible and if the arrays don't have the same number of elements (regardless of how they are dimensioned). You should make the determination of whether the arrays will be compatible before making the reassignment.

Errors occur when you are not careful in writing procedures to read each element in an array. The upper bound of an array should be one less than the total number of elements in the array. This is true because the first element is zero. Thus, if you have ten array variable elements, you will receive a subscript out of range error if you set the parameters of the loop from 1 to 10. If you want to avoid the error, you must make the loop iterate nine times.

For this exercise, you are going to create a new project called "`projarray`." Name the form "`Frmarray`" with the caption of "Array Practice."

TAKE NOTE

▶ MIXING TYPES IN ARRAYS

Generally, you can mix defined types of numeric variables in an array as long as you remember some rules. Although it works to assign an integer to a Long integer, it will not work in reverse. Assigning a Long to an integer would cause an overflow error if the actual values exceeded the limit of integer values.

CROSS-REFERENCE

Chapter 13 deals with array variables.

FIND IT ONLINE

Here is information on searching arrays:
http://web2.airmail.net/gbeene/tut-samp.html#search

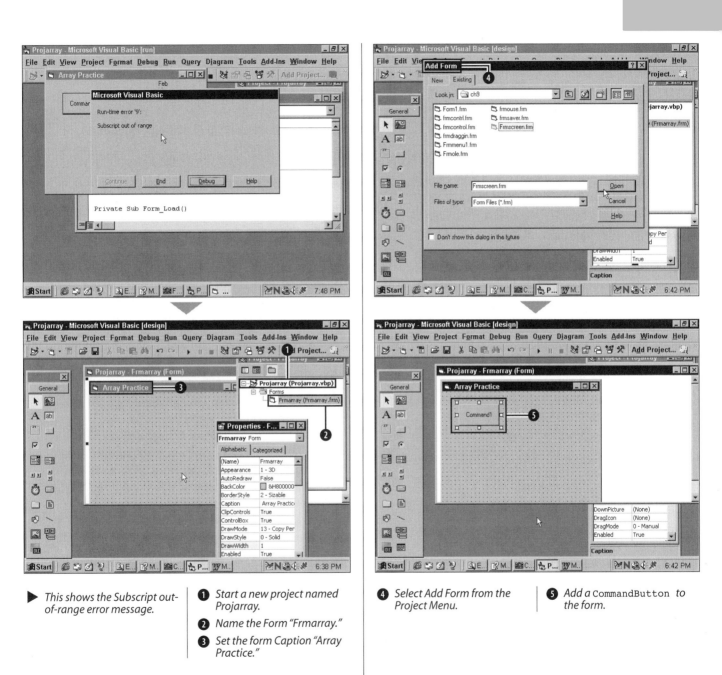

▶ *This shows the Subscript out-of-range error message.*

❶ *Start a new project named Projarray.*

❷ *Name the Form "Frmarray."*

❸ *Set the form Caption "Array Practice."*

❹ *Select Add Form from the Project Menu.*

❺ *Add a* CommandButton *to the form.*

Using Array Functions

The *array function* can return variable values for each element in the array. Normally, the array notation consists of a variable name with the element's index number enclosed in parentheses, as in the following example.

```
Dim X As Variant
```

You also can assign an array to the previous variable *X*,

```
X = Array ("one", "Two", "Three")
```

And, you can assign one element in the previous array to a different variable.

```
I = X(2)
```

A variant variable can contain arrays of any data type, except fixed length strings.

To create an array function, you assign an array to a variable and then have the value of one of the elements returned by assigning it to a simple variable. You are going to declare two variables, named `Mymonth` and `ThisY2k`. If you use the Dim statement with no data type mentioned, they will both become Variant data types.

Double click your `Frmarray` form to view the code window. Select the Form object and the Load procedure. This procedure is carried out when you launch the application and the form loads. Assign the Array to the `ThisY2k` variable.

```
Thisy2k = Array("Jan", "Feb", "Mar", "Apr"..)
```

Place each month in quotes, so each element in the `ThisY2k` array is an abbreviation for a month. Because no lower bound is stated, the assumption is it is one. Next, you use the `Mymonth` variable you declared and set it equal to an element in the `ThisY2k` array.

Double-click the `Command1` button you just placed on the `Frmarray` form. In the code window, select the `Command1` object and the Click procedure. Now arrange for the display of the array elements. The wonderful feature of arrays is you can use `For..Next` loops (or other loop types) to generate many statements without writing much code. In other words, the array is powerful.

Set up your array to print each element (each month abbreviation) as if on a list.

```
For I = 0 to 11
```

Because you have a command button on the form, you don't want to display the data under it, so use the Tab function to indent the display. You can experiment with different tab settings to print the months where you prefer, if you wish.

```
Print Tab(45); Thisy2k(i)
```

This causes the printing of the array elements on the form in the desired place (you hope!). Of course, you follow the For with a Next to make another pass through the loop until the limit is reached.

In this exercise, you have seen how easy it is to declare an array in a Variant data type variable and then reassign values to additional variables. Many ways exist to apply this knowledge, which you will soon learn.

TAKE NOTE

▶ **USING OPTION BASE**

Remember, you count the first element in an array as 0, so the months would range from 0 to 11, not 1 to 12. If you prefer to deal with array elements beginning with 1, you can use the `Option Base` statement to set the base to 1 rather than 0. The `Option Base` statement (Option Base 1) should be placed at the top of your module, above the Dim statements. Optionally, the `Lbound` and `Ubound` functions would enable you to specify the lower and upper bounds of the array. If you change the base of the array, the `For..Next` loop can be changed to begin with 1 as well.

CROSS-REFERENCE

Chapter 13 also covers arrays.

FIND IT ONLINE

This URL tells how to tell when an array is dimensioned:
http://www.mvps.org/vbnet/code/helpers/isbounded.htm.

Listing 10-3: Returning Values from Array Elements

```
Dim Mymonth, ThisY2k  ←❶

Private Sub Form_Load()
      ┌─❷
  ThisY2k = Array("Jan", "Feb", "Mar", "Apr", "May", "Jun", "Jul", "Aug", _
  "Sep", "Oct", "Nov", "Dec")
  ' Return values assume lower bound = 1.
  Mymonth = ThisY2k(2)    ' Mymonth contains "Feb".
               ❸
End Sub
```

❶ Declare the variables.
❷ Set the array to the value of the variable, ThisY2k.
❸ Set Mymonth equal to the second element in ThisY2k.

Listing 10-4: Displaying the Array Contents

```
Private Sub Command1_Click()
    For i = 0 To 11 ←❺
❹ ┌ Print Tab(45); ThisY2k(i)
    Next ←❹            ❻
End Sub
```

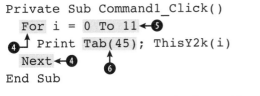

❹ Set up a For..Next loop to display the variable values.
❺ Note the array elements range from 0 to 11.
❻ Use the Tab to control where on the form the display occurs.

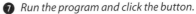

❼ Run the program and click the button.

Creating Control Arrays

So far, the arrays created have been at run time. Control arrays are created at design time. To construct an array of controls, the elements in the array must be of the same data type and they must share event procedures. The minimum array size is one element, but the array can be as large as your system resources can support. The index is of the Integer type and the maximum index value of your control array is 32767.

If your project meets the previous specifications, you can examine the options to see if you can improve your project by conserving code and creating a better interface.

Do you remember the Controls form you used in Chapter 8? This form (Frmcontrol) was used to provide examples of many different controls. On it you had a ListBox, a Label, a TextBox, and among other objects, five command buttons. These buttons were named Command1 through Command5 and had captions, ZERO, ONE, TWO, THREE, and FOUR.

When you click each button, the corresponding name listed in the ListBox is displayed on the Label. That is, the button number matches the List1.ListIndex value. You coded statements in click procedures for each button setting the List1.ListIndex value to correspond to names in the order they appear in the ListBox. The ZERO button has the code attached to display the first name, the ONE button has code for the second name, and so on, to the fifth button and the fourth name.

The buttons require five separate procedures in your form module. If they could be array controls, then they could share the same procedure. The criteria, "Are the elements of the same type?" and "Do they all call the same procedure?" can be met, as you soon see.

Add the frmcontrol form to your Projarray project by selecting Add Form, Existing from the Project Menu. Locate the form from where you saved the Chapter 8 project and add it to the new project for this chapter. Before you make changes to the old form, use Save frmcontrol As.. to save the form in your current directory. Also, add a menu to the form in the Menu Editor and name it

mnucontrol with the caption "Control Form." Add the Click procedure to display the frmcontrol form, so you have a way of accessing the form at run time.

Now, you are going to remove all those buttons, ZERO to FOUR. Select and place a new button on the form. It will be named Command1 by default. Select Copy from the Menu Bar or the ToolBar, (also you can right click) to Copy the button. When you do this, you will be asked if you want to create a control array. This is because you cannot have two controls with exactly the same name unless they are different elements in an array.

Go ahead and respond affirmatively. You can copy command1 or simply paste it over and over until you have all five buttons as you did originally. Name each of the button captions as they were named before (ZERO through FOUR). Remember, the captions can be different because these are not the same variables, but different variables in an array.

Now, double click each of the buttons. Do you see you enter the same procedure each time? Instead of going into the five separate button click procedures, you enter the same procedure over and over. This means the one procedure must work for all five buttons. You may wonder how this can be, when the label must display different names when each button is pressed.

TAKE NOTE

▶ **REDIMENSIONING ARRAYS**

The ReDim statement is used to resize a previously declared array. You can use the ReDim statement any number of times in a procedure, but you cannot use ReDim to change the data type — with the exception of the Variant type, for which you can change the type using the As Type keyword. If you resize an array to be smaller than the original, the eliminated elements are not recoverable.

CROSS-REFERENCE

Chapter 15 deals with the use of arrays.

FIND IT ONLINE

This site has code to use an array to make an alarm:
http://www.mvps.org/vbnet/code/helpers/randomarray.htm.

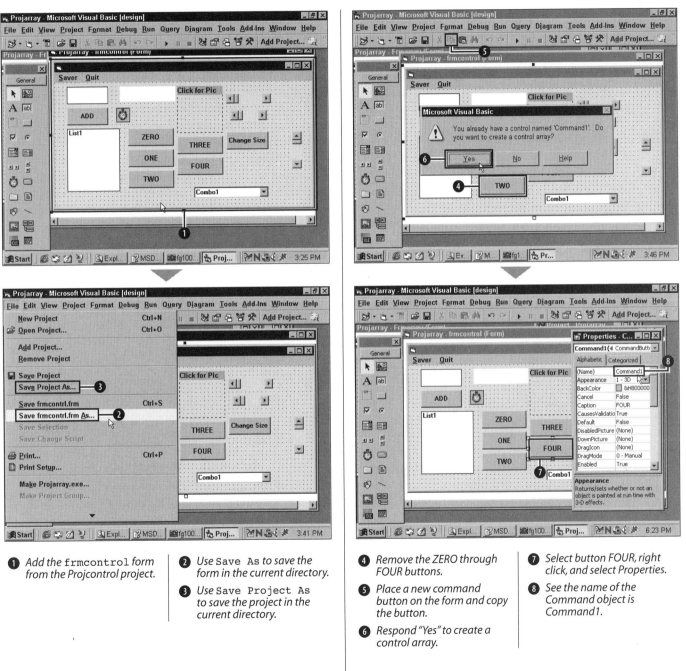

① Add the frmcontrol form from the Projcontrol project.

② Use Save As to save the form in the current directory.

③ Use Save Project As to save the project in the current directory.

④ Remove the ZERO through FOUR buttons.

⑤ Place a new command button on the form and copy the button.

⑥ Respond "Yes" to create a control array.

⑦ Select button FOUR, right click, and select Properties.

⑧ See the name of the Command object is Command1.

Creating Menu Control Arrays

Remember how you set up the same procedures in the `Projcontrol` project? You set the `ListIndex` property of the List1 object to the value of the index.

Each click procedure set `ListIndex` at the required value. A much easier way exists to do the same thing without writing as much code. When you enter the code window and select the `Command1` object and the `Click` procedure, you will see something new. The built-in procedure adds the clause "Index As Integer" in the parentheses. This indicates the object is an array. Instead of hard coding the `ListIndex` value as you did previously, all you need to do is use the `Index` property of each array element. If you check the `Properties Window` with each of the buttons selected in turn, you will see the index value of each button is different.

Notice, also, the `Index` property value for each button matches the value you formerly assigned to the `List1.ListIndex`. Now you needn't go to that trouble. All you need is one statement using the Index to provide the `ListIndex` value.

`List1.ListIndex = Index`

This is only one example of how much more efficient arrays are than using simple variables or single controls.

Another example of ways you can use control arrays is the Menu Control Array. Just like the control array you just completed, the Menu Control Array elements must share the same name and event procedures. If you needed more than one menu option with the same procedure, then an array would work. This example doesn't take any coding, except the click procedure you would need in any case.

Select your `Frmarray` form. Select `Menu Editor` from the `Tools` Menu. Above the `Control Form` option you added, insert a new menu named *mnustuff* with the caption *Stuff*. You add four options under this Menu option, but they are different from those you added in the past. These will be elements in a Menu Control Array.

Insert the first menu option under `Stuff` and indented (so it becomes part of the lower-level menu). Name this *mnuitems* with the caption *Open File 1.* Now you are going to assign this control to an array. Type a zero in the space to the right of the Index box. Add a second option below, also indented and parallel with the option you just added. Give this option the same name *mnuitems* with a caption *Open File 2.* This time, set the Index value to one. Add a separator bar at the same level below the last option.

Remember to give it the same name and set the index at two, even though the separator bar does nothing. Make the separator bar by placing a hyphen in the caption space. Finally, add a fourth option with an index value of three and again, the same name (*mnuitems*). You can give this option the caption *Other files.*

Add a `RichTextBox` named `RchTest2` and a `CommonDialog` box named `dlgTest2` to the `frmarray` form, so it looks like the `frmdialog` form from the `Projdialog` project in the last chapter. Double click one of the `Stuff` menu options (it doesn't matter which) and enter the code to display the Open dialog box. The code can be copied from the last project, but remember to change the `RichTextBox` and the `CommonDialog` object names to match the names in this project.

TAKE NOTE

▶ CONTROL ARRAY PROPERTIES

Each element of the control array has its own set of properties. This means the captions of each can be different. It would be a big handicap if this were not true because you would then have command buttons all looking exactly alike. The advantage in making a control array is that of saving code and resources. Also your project will be more elegant and easier to debug. Again, you must have only one procedure for each event for the entire array.

FIND IT ONLINE

Here is a routine for radio button markers on menus:
http://www.mvps.org/vbnet/code/menu/radiobutton.htm.

Listing 10-5: Old Button Procedures compared with Control Array

```
Private Sub Command1_Click()
    List1.ListIndex = 0
End Sub
Private Sub Command1_Click()
    List1.ListIndex = 1
End Sub
Private Sub Command1_Click()
    List1.ListIndex = 2
End Sub
Private Sub Command1_Click()
    List1.ListIndex = 3
End Sub
Private Sub Command1_Click()
    List1.ListIndex = 4
End Sub
```

▶ *This is the lengthy procedure before using a Control Array.*

```
Private Sub Command1_Click(Index As Integer)
    List1.ListIndex = Index
End Sub
```

▶ *This is the efficient code for the Control Array.*

Listing 10-6: The Menu Control Array Procedure

```
Private Sub mnuitems_Click(Index As Integer)
    dlgTest2.Filter = "Text Format files|*.txt"
    dlgTest2.ShowOpen
    RchTest2.LoadFile dlgTest2.FileName,
rtfText
End Sub
```

▶ *The procedure is identical to the old procedure because the event is exactly the same in each case, but it can be used for all options under* Stuff.

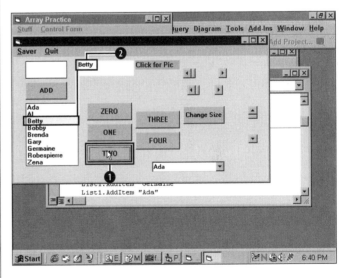

❶ *Run the program and click on a numbered button.*

❷ *The name shows on the label.*

Writing a Function Procedure

You have already used functions in several projects. For example, in Chapter 5 you used the CHR and ASC conversion functions. But many types of functions exist: String, Mathematical, Date, System and Conversion functions. In addition, you can write your own functions and then call them in a procedure.

The syntax of the Function statement is as follows:

```
[Private|Public][Static]Function procedurename
(arguments) [As type]
statements
End Function
```

Using the Frmarray form, you will create a function to use the month elements from the This y2k array you set up in your Form_Load procedure. You also use a string function to parse the month abbreviation you have been using.

Place a TextBox (Text1) and a ListBox (List1) control on your frmarray form. Your goal here is to display the first month in the TextBox and then display all the months in ThisY2k in the scrolling ListBox. Offhand, this doesn't seem difficult because you have experience displaying the ThisY2k array. This time, you will create a function and then have a procedure call it. This time, you are going to create a function to perform some of the tasks. This function will be a simple one and not all the possible arguments will be used.

In the code window, type a function statement in keeping with the previous format. Name your function ListMonth. Declare strName as a string type.

```
Function ListMonth(strMonth As String)
```

Next, you will set the TextBox text equal to the variable, strMonth. Use the AddItem method of the ListBox to add the TextBox text, which you will give an initial value of "Jan" because this is the first month in your array. Finally, use End Function to end the function.

So far, you have a function, but you don't have any way of using it. Create a menu option on the form called Tasks.

Make an option under that called Function example. Double click and in the code window for that procedure (mnufunction_Click), call the ListMonth function and set the strMonth variable equal to "Mar."

```
ListMonth strMonth:="Mar"
```

Now you can run the program. Click function example on the Tasks menu. You should see "Jan" in the TextBox and "Mar" in the ListBox. This may not seem exciting, but it is evidence you called a function in your procedure.

You can use your array with a loop to display all the months in the scrolling TextBox. The beauty of the function is you needn't do anything more to the function except call it. Remove your statement that assigns the "Mar" value to the strMonth variable. Replace it with the values in the ThisY2k array. In addition, add the string function, Left. The Left function enables you to look at the leftmost (*n*) characters in a string variable. Companion functions are Mid (characters in the middle of a string) and Right (rightmost characters of a string).

```
ListMonth strMonth:=Left(ThisY2k(i), 2)
```

Because the variable is contained in an array, you must enclose the array element in parentheses, as well as the number of leftmost characters you are selecting. If strMonth were a simple variable, the statement would look like this:

```
ListMonth strMonth:=Left(ThisY2k, 2)
```

This would leave out the array element, which is unnecessary for a simple variable. You are now going to use a For-Next loop to display each one of the array elements in the ListBox. Because the option base has been set at 1, you can have a For statement that makes 12 passes through the loop, with 1 as the first pass. Add these statements and run the program.

CROSS-REFERENCE

Chapter 12 and Chapter 15 use functions also.

FIND IT ONLINE

This tells how to call procedures:
http://msdn.microsoft.com/library/devprods/vs6/vbasic/vbcon98/vbconfunctionprocedures.htm.

TAKE NOTE

► INITIALIZING VARIABLES

After defining a variable and before using it in a procedure, a good practice is to initialize it. If you are reusing variables and inserting new values, you must reinitialize them to remove the old values. For numeric variables, this means setting values to zero. For strings, it means giving it a null string as a value, expressed as " " (two quotation marks with no spaces between). A fixed-length string is zero filled. You initialize `Variant` types to `Empty`. Each element in a user-defined type variable is initialized separately. You use the `Set` statement to initialize an object variable and then initialize the object variable to `Nothing`.

Listing 10-7: The ListMonth Function

```
Function ListMonth(strMonth As String)
    Text1.Text = strMonth
    List1.AddItem Text1.Text
    Text1.Text = "Jan"
End Function
```

❶

❶ Enter the previous function in the frmarray module.

Listing 10-8: The Menu Click Procedure

```
Private Sub mnufunction_Click()
    For i = 1 To 12
        listmonth strMonth:=Left(ThisY2k(i), 2)
    Next
End Sub
```

❷

❷ Add the previous procedure to the Function Example option on your Task Menu.

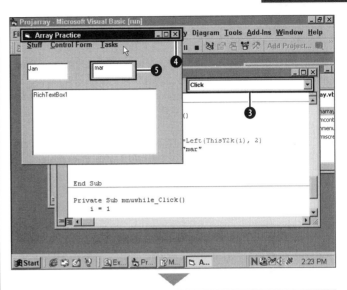

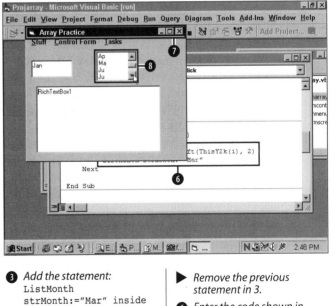

❸ Add the statement:
`ListMonth strMonth:="Mar"` inside the Menu click procedure.

❹ Run the Program.

❺ Note that "Mar" appears in the `ListBox`.

► Remove the previous statement in 3.

❻ Enter the code shown in Listing 10-8.

❼ Run the program.

❽ Note the months displayed are abbreviated to two letters.

213

Using Intrinsic Functions

Just as you used the Intrinsic Functions in the last topic and in several other projects, you can use them to manipulate strings, carry out mathematical calculations, do date calculations, and accomplish system and other functions as well. You are already familiar with the ASC and the CHR functions, which you explored in Chapter 5.

String functions manipulate strings. They enable you to change characters to ASCII codes and vice versa. They enable you to parse strings, looking at just parts of each string of characters. The Left function selects only the leftmost *n* characters. If you specify:

```
Print Left(myvar, 1)
```

It means the first character beginning from the left will be printed. If myvar has the value "Hi There," then the "H" will be printed. A corresponding Right function deals with the rightmost characters in a string. The Mid function enables you to choose, not only where the string begins, but where it ends. So, the Mid function has two parameters, the beginning part of the string and the ending part. Suppose you wanted to select the third and fourth characters in a string. You would code

```
Print Mid(myvar,3,2)
```

This says you want to print the string, beginning with the third character and you want to see two characters (the third character and the next one).

Another interesting string function is the InStr function. InStr searches for a string within a string. If you are checking to see if a certain phrase or a few letters in some text exists, this is the way to go. If you have a string named instpractice with the text, "I am Weird." The syntax is

```
Print InStr(1, instpractice, "Weird")
```

This function returns a value (number), which is the place in the entire string where the search string was first encountered.

Create a new form named Frmfunctions. You need to add a menu option on the Main form — Frmarray — to access this new form. Access the Menu Editor with Frmarray selected. Move the Control Form menu down one level and create an Other Forms menu. Add the Functions menu parallel to the Control Form menu and one level down from the Other Forms menu.

Create the procedures to Show the Frmcontrol and Frmfunctions forms in the mnucontrol and mnufunctions procedures, as you did for previous menus in the Menu Editor.

```
Private Sub mnucontrol_Click()
    frmcontrol.Show
End Sub
Private Sub mnufunctions_Click()
    Frmfunctions.Show
End Sub
```

Add TextBox and Label controls to the form. Enter the Menu Editor with the Frmfunctions form selected and add four menus: Strings, Math, Date and Exit. Don't worry about making options under any except the Strings Menu. Create Left, Right, Mid, and InString options under Strings. Name them mnuleft, mnuright, mnumid, and mnuinstr.

TAKE NOTE

▶ **NEW FUNCTIONS**

A number of new functions are in Visual Basic. A few of them are MonthName, (returns a string for name of month), FormatCurrency (returns an expression formatted as currency using the currency symbol, FormatDateTime (returns an expression formatted as date and time), FormatNumber (returns an expression formatted as a number, and FormatPercent (returns an expression multiplied by 100 and with a trailing percentage character).

CROSS-REFERENCE

Chapter 13 uses string conversions.

FIND IT ONLINE

Here is info on String functions: **http://msdn.microsoft.com/ library/sdkdoc/dasdk/odap75yr.htm**.

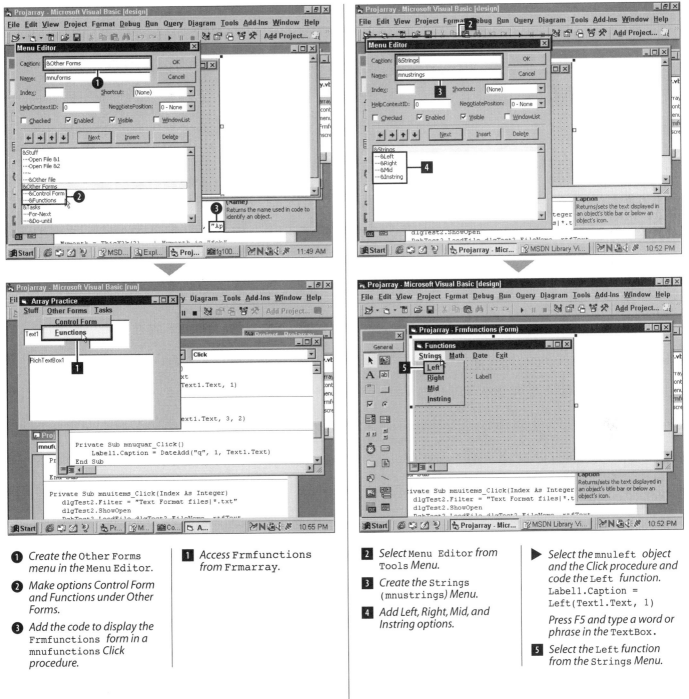

① *Create the* Other Forms *menu in the* Menu Editor.

② *Make options* Control Form *and* Functions *under Other Forms.*

③ *Add the code to display the* Frmfunctions *form in a* mnufunctions *Click procedure.*

1 *Access* Frmfunctions *from* Frmarray.

2 *Select* Menu Editor *from* Tools *Menu.*

3 *Create the* Strings (mnustrings) *Menu.*

4 *Add Left, Right, Mid, and Instring options.*

▶ *Select the* mnuleft *object and the Click procedure and code the* Left *function.*
Label1.Caption = Left(Text1.Text, 1)

Press F5 and type a word or phrase in the TextBox.

5 *Select the* Left *function from the* Strings *Menu.*

Using String Functions

The goal here is to learn how to use the string functions, so you will use the `TextBox` to enter a string of your own choosing. The `Label` serves to display the results of the string calculations. Click the `Left` option on the `Strings` Menu in the design mode. In the code window, enter the code for the `mnuleft` procedure that will print the leftmost character you type in the `TextBox`.

```
Label1.Caption = Left(Text1.Text, 1)
```

What you are doing here is setting the Label caption to the value of the result of the string calculations. To make the Left string function easier to understand, you could create variables to store the values, such as:

```
A = Label1.caption
B = Text1.Text
```

Then the statement would be A = Left(B,1). After you enter the statement for the procedure, run the program. Select the new form (`Frmfunctions`) from the old form's (`Frmarray`) menu option and type some letters in the textbox. Click the `Strings` Menu Left option and observe the results on the `Label`.

Continuing with the `Frmfunctions` exercise, you need to add the code for the other string functions, `Right`, `Mid` and `InString`. The Right function uses the same logic as the `Left` function, except using the same statement you used in the previous `Left` statement will display the rightmost instead of the leftmost character. The argument is `Right(string, length)`. This means if you want the `Right` function to return the letter *u* from "Hey You," you would use a statement such as:

```
MyRight = Right("Hey You", 1)
Label1.Caption = Right(Text1.Text, 1)
```

If you prefer to set a variable to the value of Text1.Text, you would reference the variable in the previous statement instead of Text1.Text.

The process for examining the middle of a string (the `Mid` function) is a little different. In this exercise, you use two arguments separated by commas. The `Mid` function has the named arguments `Mid(string, start[, length])`. Thus, if you wanted to return the third and fourth characters in a string, ABCDEF, you would use the statement:

```
MyMid = Mid("ABCDEF", 3, 2) : Print MyMid
```

The `start` argument is 3 and the `length` argument is 2.

The `InStr` function is used to search for a string within a string. You might do this if you were looking for a name in a block of text, or searching for a particular item of data. The syntax is: `InStr([start, ]string1, string2[, compare])`

If you wanted to find the string "Violets" in the larger string "Roses are Red, Violets are Blue" the syntax would be:

```
MyInstr = InStr(1, "Roses are Red, Violets _
are Blue", "Violets")
```

The value returned is the starting position of the word "Violets," which is 16. If you change the search to look for "Roses" instead, then the value returned is 1. For your practice, suppose you want to pick out any particular word. When you run the program, type a phrase containing that word. Click on `InString` on the `Strings` Menu.

TAKE NOTE

MORE NEW STRING FUNCTIONS

Some of the new string functions are: `WeekdayName` (returns the name of the week for an integer value. Sunday =1), `Join` (returns a string created by joining a number of substrings contained in an array), `Replace` (replaces a substring within a string a specified number of times), `StrReverse` (returns a string with the characters reversed). `Round` (returns a number rounded to the number of decimal places specified in the argument).

CROSS-REFERENCE

Chapter 15 and Chapter 13 use string manipulation.

FIND IT ONLINE

This is code for a number to text conversion.
http://www.mvps.org/vbnet/code/helpers/numbertotext.htm

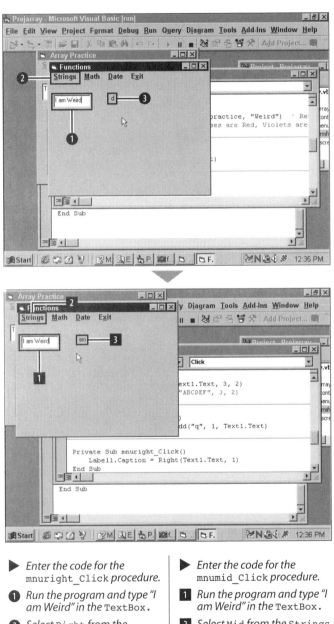

Listing 10-9: The Right, Mid and InStr Function Code

```
Private Sub mnuright_Click()
  Label1.Caption = Right(Text1.Text, 1)
End Sub
```

▶ *The* Right *Function Procedure.*

```
Private Sub mnumid_Click()
  Label1.Caption = Mid(Text1.Text, 3, 2)
End Sub
```

▶ *The* Mid *Function Procedure.*

```
Private Sub mnuinstr_Click()
 Label1.Caption = InStr(1, Text1.Text,Weird")
End Sub
```

▶ *The* InStr *Function Procedure.*

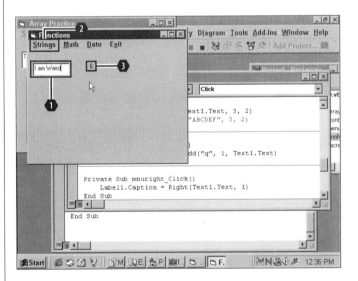

▶ *Enter the code for the*
mnuright_Click *procedure.*

1 *Run the program and type "I am Weird" in the* TextBox.

2 *Select* Right *from the* Strings *menu.*

3 *View the letter d.*

▶ *Enter the code for the*
mnumid_Click *procedure.*

1 *Run the program and type "I am Weird" in the* TextBox.

2 *Select* Mid *from the* Strings *menu.*

3 *View the letters "am."*

▶ *Enter the code for the* mnuinstr_Click *procedure.*

1 *Run the program and type "I am Weird" in the* TextBox.

2 *Select* InString *from the* Strings *menu.*

3 *View the number 6.*

217

Using Date Functions

The Date Functions you use in this exercise are the `DateAdd` and the `DateDiff` functions. `DateAdd` enables you to add and subtract time intervals from dates. You can ask the question "What Date will it be two months from now?" or "what date will it be three days from now?" The interval arguments are `Year` (yyyy), `Quarter` (q), `Month` (m), `Day of Year` (y), `Day` (d), `Weekday` (w), `Week` (ww), `Hour` (h), `Minute` (n), `Second` (s).

Once again, you need to prepare your form with the appropriate menus. With the `Frmfunctions` form selected, open the `Menu Editor` and create the following menu options under Date: `DateAdd (,mnudadd)`, `Dateadd quarter (mnuquar)`, `Dateadd day (mnuday)`, `Dateadd Weekday (mnuweek)`, `DateDiff (mnudiff)`. Give these menu options names beginning with the letters, "mnu" as before.

Create the procedures for these functions. You use the `Label Caption` as before to display the results of your menu selections. The syntax for the `DateAdd` functions is `DateAdd` (interval, number, date). If you want to check the future date one month hence, use the syntax:

```
Print DateAdd("m", 1, "12-12-1998")
```

Try this using the `Immediate Window`. The correct value of 01/12/1999 should be returned. Because you are going to use the Label Caption, change the statement to substitute Text1.Text for the string date you entered in the `Immediate Window`. Be sure you type the date in the box before selecting the menu option because you didn't yet set up any error handling. An empty `TextBox` will generate an error.

```
Label1.Caption = DateAdd("m", 1, Text1.Text)
```

The next menu option is supposed to display the quarter post the date you enter in the `TextBox`. Here the argument is *q* for quarter. Formulate the statement and enter it as you did for the previous option, changing the argument to *q* instead of *m*.

```
Label1.Caption = DateAdd("q", 1, Text1.Text)
```

Next, you make the option for the `Day` addition. This option should return a value one day in advance of the date you type in the `TextBox`. To add days to a date, you can use `Day of Year ("y")`, `Day ("d")`, or `Weekday ("w")`.

Again, be sure to enter the date in the box before selecting the menu option. Remember, a nonexistent value will generate an error.

```
Label1.Caption = DateAdd("d", 1, Text1.Text)
```

Finally, the procedure for the addition of a number of days is *w*, so this time, add two days to the entered date.

```
Label1.Caption = DateAdd("w", 2, Text1.Text)
```

When you have entered the code into the four procedures, you can test them by running the program. Enter a date in the box, select each menu option in turn, and view the captions in the `Label` box.

The `DateDiff` function returns a number that represents the difference between two dates. The argument is `DateDiff(interval, date1, date2[, firstdayofweek[, firstweekofyear]])`.

In this example, you use the `Now` function (the current date and time). The first date is subtracted from the second date, so if you want to subtract today from tomorrow, you get a positive number. If you subtract today from yesterday, you get a negative number. In this exercise you subtract whatever is your current system time from the date you enter in the box, using the following statement.

```
Label1.Caption = DateDiff("d", Now, Text1.Text)
```

Enter the code run the program, and then select the `DateDiff` menu option after you type in a date.

CROSS-REFERENCE

Chapter 12 provides some error handling routines for these procedures.

FIND IT ONLINE

Here is a discussion of y2k issues:
http://www.microsoft.com/technet/year2k/?RLD=53.

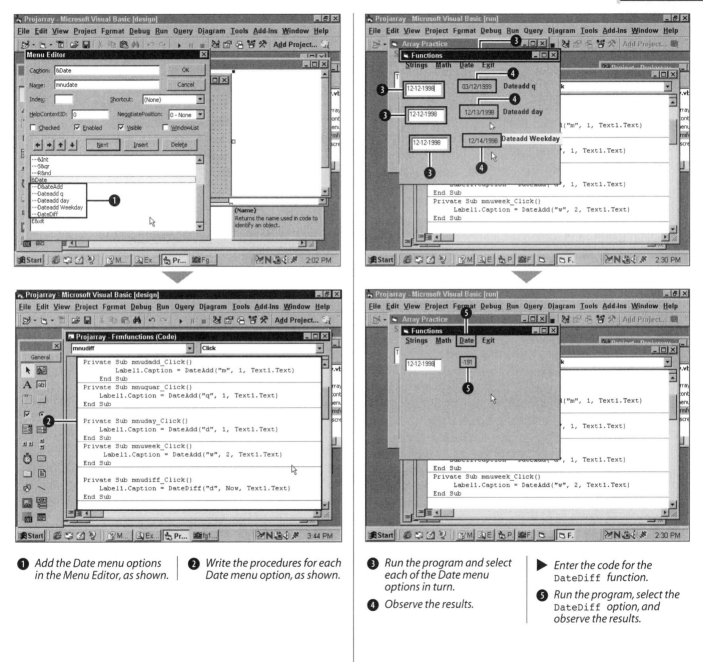

① Add the Date menu options in the Menu Editor, as shown.

② Write the procedures for each Date menu option, as shown.

③ Run the program and select each of the Date menu options in turn.

④ Observe the results.

▶ Enter the code for the `DateDiff` function.

⑤ Run the program, select the `DateDiff` option, and observe the results.

Using Math Functions

Just as with the String and Date functions, Mathematical functions use arguments and expressions in procedures. In a sense, arguments and expressions may seem more familiar with mathematical than with strings and dates. You probably have used formulae to calculate math problems. If you're not in a technical or science field, you probably have not used expressions with nonmathematical problems.

In this exercise, you need to add the `Math` menu to `Frmfunctions`. In the `Menu Editor`, create three options under the Math menu. Caption them `Int` (`mnuint`), `Sqr` (`mnusqr`), and `Rnd` (`mnurnd`). Give them the names listed and make sure they begin with "mnu" as the first three characters.

After setting up the menu options for these math functions, you must set up the function procedures, just as you did with the string and date functions.

The `Int` function converts a real number to an Integer. The syntax is `Int(Number)`. If A = 99.999, then the Integer of A would be 99. Because you are using the `Label` `Caption` to display the result, the procedure to convert a number from the `TextBox` to an integer is:

```
Private Sub mnuint_Click()
    Label1.Caption = Int(Text1.Text)
End Sub
```

You write this procedure as you did before by selecting the `mnuint` object and the Click procedure. When you run your application and type a decimal figure in the `TextBox`, you see the integer conversion displayed in the Label box.

The next math function you use is the `Sqr` function. This procedure finds the square root of a number. The argument here is any double or numeric expression greater than or equal to zero. For example:

```
Yursqr = Sqr(4) 'This will return 2.
```

For whatever number you type into the `TextBox`, the procedure will find the square root. Double click the `Sqr` menu option on your `Frmfunctions` form. In the code window, set up the procedure to return the square root of any number entered in the `TextBox`.

```
Private Sub mnusqr_Click()
    Label1.Caption = Sqr(Text1.Text)
End Sub
```

The procedure is for the `mnusqr` option. Enter the code and press F5 to run the program. Type a number in the `TextBox` before selecting the `Sqr` option on the menu. The square root of whatever number you enter is displayed in the `Label` box.

The `Rnd` function is a random number generator, as used in Chapter 5 on the `frmouse` form to change the background colors when the mouse moved. The argument is a single, any valid numeric expression. Seed is the value used to begin the generation of random number sequences.

For any beginning seed, the same number sequence is generated because each successive call to the `Rnd` function uses the previous number as a seed for the next number in the sequence.

You want to type a number and arrange to have a random number generated each time you click the `Rnd` menu option. This means you have a start number so the number you type is the seed for the random number generated. This formula produces random numbers in a given range.

```
Int((Hinumber-Lownumber1)*Rnd +Lownumber)
```

For your purposes, you need to write the procedure so the random number generated displays in the `Label` box in response to the number typed in the `TextBox`.

```
Private Sub mnurnd_Click()
    Label1.Caption = Int((Text1.Text * Rnd) + 1
End Sub
```

Here, the `Label` displays the Integer of the value entered in the `TextBox`, multiplied by the `Rnd` function + 1. The number 1 is added to avoid generating zeros.

CROSS-REFERENCE

Chapter 13 uses functions in manipulating data.

FIND IT ONLINE

This is documentation on Math functions: **http://msdn. microsoft.com/library/devprods/vs6/vbasic/vbenlr98/ vaidxmathfunctions.htm.**

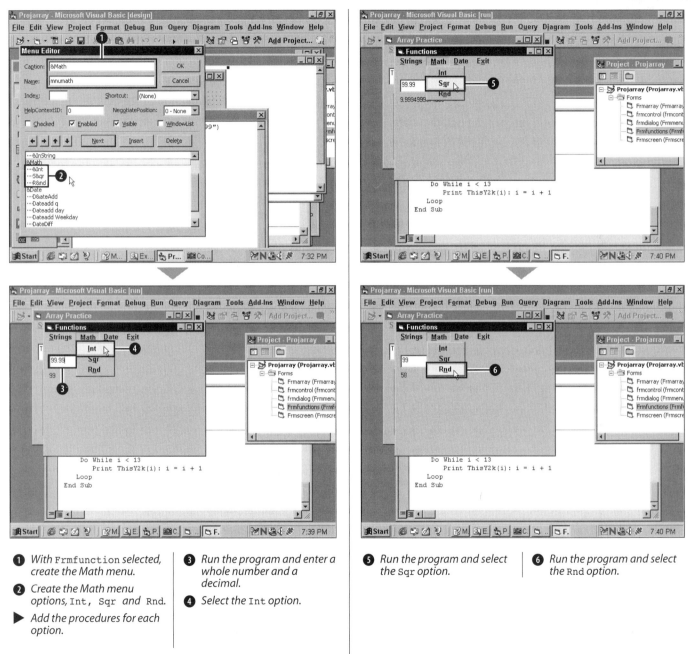

① *With* Frmfunction *selected, create the Math menu.*

② *Create the Math menu options,* Int, Sqr *and* Rnd.

▶ *Add the procedures for each option.*

③ *Run the program and enter a whole number and a decimal.*

④ *Select the* Int *option.*

⑤ *Run the program and select the* Sqr *option.*

⑥ *Run the program and select the* Rnd *option.*

Personal Workbook

Q&A

1 What type of data does a string function deal with?

_____

_____

_____

2 How many elements are in an array?

_____

_____

_____

3 What is the difference between a Control array and other arrays?

_____

_____

_____

4 What types can't you mix in an array?

_____

_____

_____

5 Name three new functions in Visual Basic.

_____

_____

_____

6 What value will the Right function return?

_____

_____

_____

7 What is the function for date subtraction?

_____

_____

_____

8 What is the seed in the random function?

_____

_____

_____

ANSWERS: PAGE 524

EXTRA PRACTICE

1. Create a form and menus with options for date functions. See how many different calculations you can make.

2. Make a menu and options for string functions. Try some not covered in the exercises.

3. Use the Now function on a menu option. Write a function procedure to print the date and time in a label box.

4. Set up an application using an array to print a series of names and addresses.

5. Practice naming menu procedures and options. Set up an option to calculate the square of a number entered in a TextBox.

REAL WORLD APPLICATIONS

✔ Your neighbor has a problem dealing with figures. Write an application that enables him to do some simple calculations by selecting options on a menu or pressing command buttons.

✔ An employee at your company is buying a home and is interested in finding a program to calculate mortgage interest. Write an application for her to do the math.

✔ Your friend has a rival in another company. This guy constantly brags that he is a genius with dates. He says this because he can add and subtract dates without a calendar. Your friend would be thrilled if you could write an application to do all kinds of date arithmetic to show him he doesn't need to strain his brain. Write him a little program to impress his rival.

Visual Quiz

What is the interval argument in this function?

_____

_____

_____

_____

_____

_____

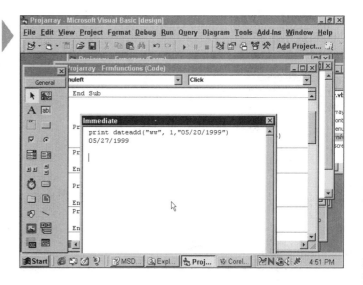

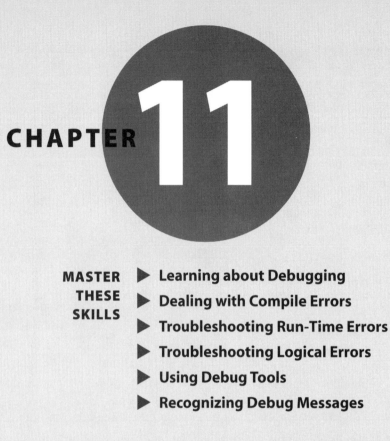

CHAPTER **11**

MASTER
THESE
SKILLS

▶ **Learning about Debugging**

▶ **Dealing with Compile Errors**

▶ **Troubleshooting Run-Time Errors**

▶ **Troubleshooting Logical Errors**

▶ **Using Debug Tools**

▶ **Recognizing Debug Messages**

Debugging

The debugging process was touched on in Chapter 2, but that discussion was confined to debugging only as it relates to the IDE. The information in Chapter 2 included the `Immediate` Window, the `Watch` window, and the `Locals` window. These windows enable you to observe the changes in variable values while a procedure is executing.

In addition to the windowing environment, Visual Basic provides a number of tools. The system tools include breakpoints, break expressions, displaying variables and properties values, stepping through code by single statements or single procedures at a time, and watch expressions. Special features are the capability to Continue after changing code, going to the next statement in execution, and testing procedures while in Break mode.

Generally, the errors you need to fix fall into three categories: compile errors, run-time errors, and logical errors.

Compile errors may actually not occur until the program is run, but they result from mistakes like spelling errors or missing objects.

Run-time errors are not triggered until you select some option that has a procedural error. When a calculation is supposed to take place and one of the values is invalid a run-time error occurs. A common error of this type occurs when one of the variables in an division calculation has a zero value.

Logical errors occur when the syntax and the values are correct, but the logic that went into developing the expressions is faulty. If results are not as expected, perhaps variables were not reset to zero.

Learning about Debugging

Debugging is greatly aided by the large complement of debugging tools Visual Basic provides. These tools are specifically designed to spot run-time and logical errors. But debugging is not legerdemain. In the final analysis, you must ferret out the errors yourself. You can use the tools on the `Debug ToolBar` to analyze the program's execution. Part of the process is simply trying to determine what factors could cause the problem, and then testing to disprove or verify your hypothesis.

The `Debug ToolBar` provides the same options as on the `Debug Menu` on the Menu Bar.

The Start option begins program execution, the Break option halts program execution and the End option terminates program execution. The debugging tools are `Toggle Breakpoint, Step Into, Step Over, Step Out, Locals Window, Immediate Window, Watch window, Quick Watch` and `Call Stack`.

The `Toggle Breakpoint` option enables you to set a point in the code where the program will halt execution. You can then `Step Into` or over each line of code.

`Step Into` executes the next executable line of code, stepping into each procedure following the normal process of execution. If an error is in the line you are stepping into, you get the same error message you got when the program was begun normally.

`Step Over` executes the next executable line of code without stepping into procedures. This means the program execution still will not run if a run-time error exists.

`Step Out` continues execution through the current procedure, breaking at the next line of code in the calling procedure. Again, if a run time error exists, Stepping Out will not continue the program's execution.

The `Locals Window` displays the current value of local variables at the point where the program halted execution. If the problem can be detected by the value of a variable at any point in execution, the Locals Window will display the value of the problem variable, as well as those of all other variables.

The `Immediate Window` is one in which you have a command line interface. For all of you pre-Windows programmers, this is where you can execute statements immediately by using the Print command in Break mode. If you need to know the value of a particular variable, you can execute the statement `Print Z` and then press `Enter` to see the result.

The `Watch Window` displays the values of specific variables you select and watch the value change as the program executes.

The `Quick Watch` displays the current values of expressions while in Break mode.

The `Call Stack` displays a dialog box with all procedures that have been called, but have not completed execution. It typically shows the current procedure where a break occurred.

For the exercises in this chapter, load the `projarray` project from the last chapter, use Save As.. to rename the project as `projbug` in a new directory, save the forms in the new directory as well, using `Save Formname As..` for each form.

TAKE NOTE

AUTO SYNTAX CHECK

Visual Basic comes complete with an `Auto Syntax` checking feature. When a syntactically incorrect character is typed, an error dialog box pops up with the compile error message. The kind of errors the Auto Syntax checker catches are omitted parentheses or a character out of sequence. The Auto Syntax checker is poor at picking up on the selection of an incorrect property or misspelling a variable name. It is worthwhile turning on the checker anyway, though, because catching some errors is better than catching none. Select `Editor` from the `Tools, Options Menu`. Then check the box next to `Auto Syntax Check`.

CROSS-REFERENCE

Chapter 12 shows how to prevent error messages.

FIND IT ONLINE

Information regarding bug fix is in the service pack for Visual Studio: 6.0.http://www.mvps.org/vbnet/dev/updates/vs6sp1.htm.

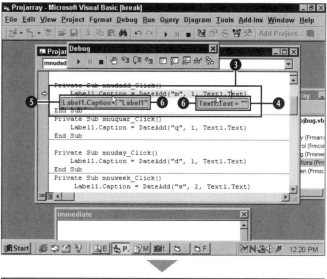

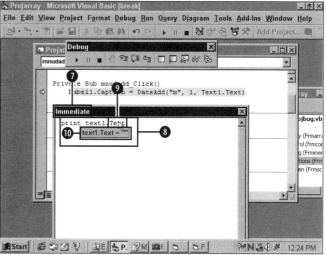

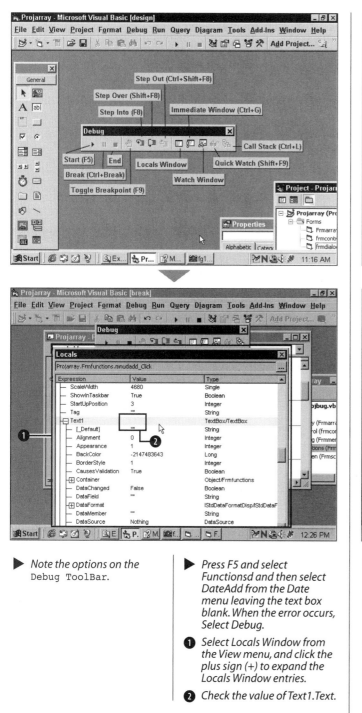

▶ Note the options on the Debug ToolBar.

▶ Press F5 and select Functionsd and then select DateAdd from the Date menu leaving the text box blank. When the error occurs, Select Debug.

① Select Locals Window from the View menu, and click the plus sign (+) to expand the Locals Window entries.

② Check the value of Text1.Text.

③ Find the `mnudadd_Click` procedure in the code window.

④ Place your cursor over the Text property in the Text1.Text statement.

⑤ Place the cursor on the Label1.Caption clause.

⑥ Observe the values of both.

⑦ Open the Immediate Window.

⑧ Type the statement shown and press Enter.

⑨ Place your cursor over the Text property.

⑩ See the values in both 10 and 11.

Dealing with Compile Errors

Compile errors are simply incorrect code. These include syntax errors, such as unbalanced parentheses, quotes in the wrong place, and spelling errors. The spelling error is a common one for most programmers, but in Visual Basic, it does not need to happen. By now, you have seen the context pop-up menu when you are typing in the code.

When you type in an object's name and then type the period prior to entering the property name, the context menu will offer you suggestions of possible properties. If you accept the help by double-clicking the chosen property, it will be placed correctly in your procedure and you needn't worry about typos. At times, though, the menu seems to slow you down and you want to keep on typing.

To avoid the possibility that some compile errors will be missed until a procedure is encountered at run time, use the `Start With Full Compile` option on the `Run Menu`. Some types of compile errors you may run into are `For-Next`, `While-Wend`, and `Sub-End Sub`. These beginning and ending statements are matched at , whereas `GoSub` and `Return` are matched at run time.

You can practice deliberately creating syntax errors and then running the application to see how the compiler responds to the errors. Select the `Frmfunctions` form and locate the `mnudadd_Click` procedure. Make a change in the syntax. Did the system catch it? Make sure you set the `Auto Syntax` checker on by selecting the Editor from the `Tools, Options` Menu. Place a checkmark in the `Auto Syntax Check` box.

Run the program, select the Functions option, and select the `DateAdd` option on the Functions menu. The compile error message box will pop up.

Another compile error you can simulate is the missing character syntax error. This time, select the same procedure as in the previous example, but this time leave off the ending parenthesis. Run the program. Select the `Functions` form and then the `DateAdd` option on the Date Menu. This is a different Compile error message.

Select the `Frmarray` form and add a Tasks menu named `mnutasks` and with a For-Next option named mnufor. In the code window, create a For-Next loop to display each array element in the ThisY2k array.

```
Private Sub mnufor_Click()
    For i = 1 To 12
        Print Tab(55); ThisY2k(i)
    Next
```

Run the program and select the For-Next option on the Tasks menu. If the program runs successfully, then you must create a compile error. End the program and add a comment character in front of the Next in the procedure.

```
'Next
```

Run the program once again. Select the `For-Next` option from the `Tasks` menu. You should get a compile error. If you press F5 to Start, you won't get the error until you select the `mnufor` procedure. If you use `Start With Full Compile`, you immediately get the compile error.

TAKE NOTE

COMPILER LIMITATION ERRORS

A code limitation of 64K exists for procedures. If you exceed this limit, you get the error message that the Code for this procedure exceeds 64K when compiled. The fix is to break the procedure into smaller procedures.

Having too many local, nonstatic variables causes another compiler error. Local, nonstatic variables are defined within a procedure and reinitialized each time the procedure is called. A 32K limitation is on Local, nonstatic variables in a procedure. The solution for this error is to declare some of the variables in the procedure using the Static statement. Static variables are allocated memory from different resources than nonstatic variables.

CROSS-REFERENCE

Chapter 12 provides some solutions to these common bugs.

FIND IT ONLINE

This is a great place to start looking for resources:
http://www.vb-web-directory.com/.

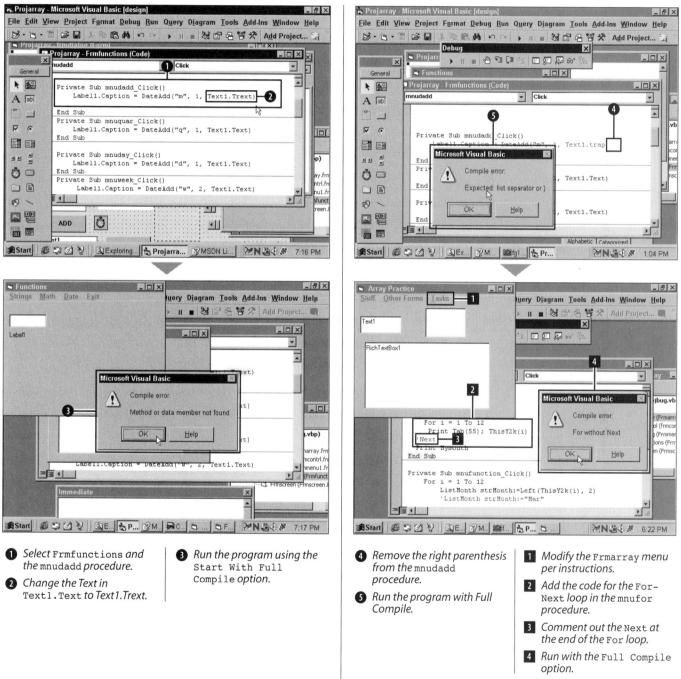

❶ Select Frmfunctions and the mnudadd procedure.

❷ Change the Text in Text1.Text to Text1.Trext.

❸ Run the program using the Start With Full Compile option.

❹ Remove the right parenthesis from the mnudadd procedure.

❺ Run the program with Full Compile.

1 Modify the Frmarray menu per instructions.

2 Add the code for the For-Next loop in the mnufor procedure.

3 Comment out the Next at the end of the For loop.

4 Run with the Full Compile option.

Troubleshooting Run-Time Errors

When a run-time error is encountered, the program's execution is halted, you receive an error message, and you can choose to End execution or to enter Debug mode. If you choose the End the program, you learn nothing in terms of identifying the error, so you shouldn't do that unless you are sure you know the nature of the error.

When you choose Debug mode, you are suddenly back in the code window with the offending line highlighted. You can pause the cursor over each object in the selected statement to see the variable values or you can use the various debug tools.

In the last chapter, you may have gotten a run-time error message when you selected the Date functions from the Date Menu on `Frmfunctions`. If this happened, you may have determined this was because you failed to enter anything in the text box prior to selecting the Date menu options. Of course, the date functions also failed to work when you did not enter text in the text box. If you had followed the instructions to type text before selecting menu options, you would not have seen the error message.

Run the program, select `Functions` from the `Other Forms` menu, and then select `Dateadd q` from the `Date` menu. Do not enter any date or text in the text box. When the program execution breaks, click the `Debug` box on the Run-time error dialog box.

In the Immediate window, you can use Print Debug to execute a statement immediately. If the program was halted in the `mnuquar` procedure, the line that you wrote in order to produce a date addition of one quarter to the entered date will be shown highlighted (selected). To debug, you should enter a statement that will display the values of variables in the window.

```
Print label1.Caption
```

The response will be `Label1` if `Label1` is the caption property. This means nothing (such as a date calculation) has replaced the default caption for the label box. You can easily check by restoring the Properties Window for Label1. Next, type the statement:

```
Print Text1.Text
```

You will likely see nothing because no value exists for `Text1.Text`. The Immediate window displays variable values at the break point. Your clue here is no date value exists for either `Label1.Caption` or `Text1.Text`.

Now ask yourself why no value exists for either the label or the text. The answer is no value exists for the text because you forgot to enter it. No value exists for the label caption because that only results from the value in the text box. If you had entered the date "12-21-1998," you would be able to display the date with the Print Text1.Text statement. The label caption would be the result of whichever function you selected from the Date or other menu.

If you Select `Label1` as a Watch, you see the default value is "Label1." You can't step through the code in this instance because you trigger the error each time you press `F8`. If you view the `Locals Window`, you see the same. However, the `Locals Window` is somewhat more confusing to view because it contains all variables and properties available at the break point. You must find the `Label1` object and then look on the list for the `Caption` property. You also can check to see what is the default property.

CROSS-REFERENCE

Chapter 2 tells about the role of the interface in debugging.

FIND IT ONLINE

This site tells how to raise errors: **http://www.citilink.com/ ~jgarrick/vbasic/beginners/errors.html#Raise**.

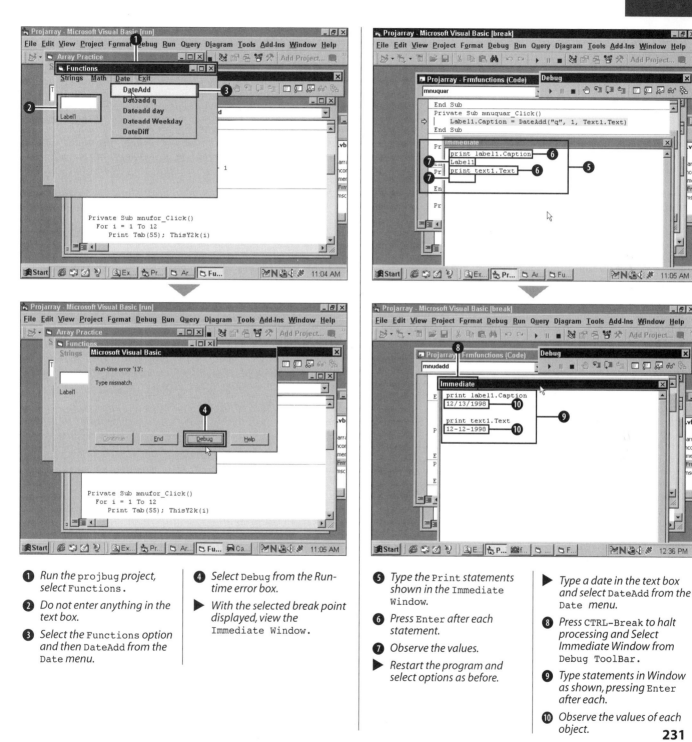

① *Run the* projbug *project, select* Functions.

② *Do not enter anything in the text box.*

③ *Select the* Functions *option and then* DateAdd *from the* Date *menu.*

④ *Select* Debug *from the Run-time error box.*

▶ *With the selected break point displayed, view the* Immediate Window.

⑤ *Type the* Print *statements shown in the* Immediate Window.

⑥ *Press* Enter *after each statement.*

⑦ *Observe the values.*

▶ *Restart the program and select options as before.*

▶ *Type a date in the text box and select* DateAdd *from the* Date *menu.*

⑧ *Press* CTRL-Break *to halt processing and Select Immediate Window from* Debug ToolBar.

⑨ *Type statements in Window as shown, pressing* Enter *after each.*

⑩ *Observe the values of each object.*

Troubleshooting Logical Errors

Logical errors are often the most difficult to detect. This is because logical errors do not always halt program execution. They may not be found for months, or even years, in production applications. If you had written an application that performed extensive calculations, calling many procedures and with multidimensional arrays, used defined classes and structures, it could be some time before errors were identified.

If the errors were subtle, the detection of any problem might require months or even years. For example, errors could be intermittent, depending upon values entered into a database. If the problem values were entered only once per year, then nothing would be amiss until that time rolled around. Once the problem is detected, though, the fix could be easy. Here, the big difficulty is in knowing a problem exists.

You will, hopefully, identify logical errors in testing your program. As the developer, you must be informed of all parameters for the project. If the users do not inform you of everything you need to know, it's unlikely you will identify problems during the testing process.

Another type of logical error is the endless loop. You can try this. Set up a Do-Until loop, which continually resets the counter so it never reaches the Until value. Obviously, deliberately making a logic error is different from inadvertently making one.

Select the Frmarray form and select the Menu Editor from the Tools menu. Add another option to the Tasks menu. Name the option mnudo with the caption "Do-until." Double-click the option and, in the code window, create a procedure for Do-until. Select the mnudo object and the Click procedure.

Making a logic error actually requires some logical reasoning. What is the easiest way to create an endless loop? The Do-Until statement is used to continue looping until some condition is met. You first set up a condition and then make sure the condition is never met. This means you are forced to use CTRL+Break to terminate processing.

First create a counter variable. This can be declared up front if you are using Option Explicit. If not, you can create the variable on the fly, by giving it a beginning value "i = 1." You can use the value 10 to increment the counter variable, "i." You also want to have some action carried out within the loop, so you can print the elements in the ThisY2k array once again. Use the Tab function so you can see the array elements displayed on the form where a free space occurs. You have

```
Private Sub mnudo_Click()
    i = 1
    Do Until i = 10
        Print Tab(50); ThisY2k(i): i = i + 1
    Loop
End Sub
```

If you use the previous statements, you have a loop that continues until "i" reaches the value of 10. Each pass through the loop, the value of "i" is incremented by one. The Do-Until clause determines that processing will stop once the value of 10 is reached. You need a way to keep the process looping. You can add another condition to prevent the counter from ever reaching 10.

TAKE NOTE

STATEMENTS IN IMMEDIATE WINDOW

If you tried to use certain statements in the Immediate Window, you may have received an "Invalid in Immediate Pane" error message. Dim, Function, Option Base, Option Explicit, Private, Public, Declare, Const, ReDim, and Static are some of these statements. All statements must be on one line. If you have several statements such as a For-Next loop, they must be on one line separated by colons.

CROSS-REFERENCE
Chapter 2 briefly introduces the Debug Windows.

FIND IT ONLINE

Debugging Tips: **http://msdn.microsoft.com/isapi/ msdnlib.idc?theURL=/library/officedev/office/html/ debuggingvisualbasiccode.htm.**

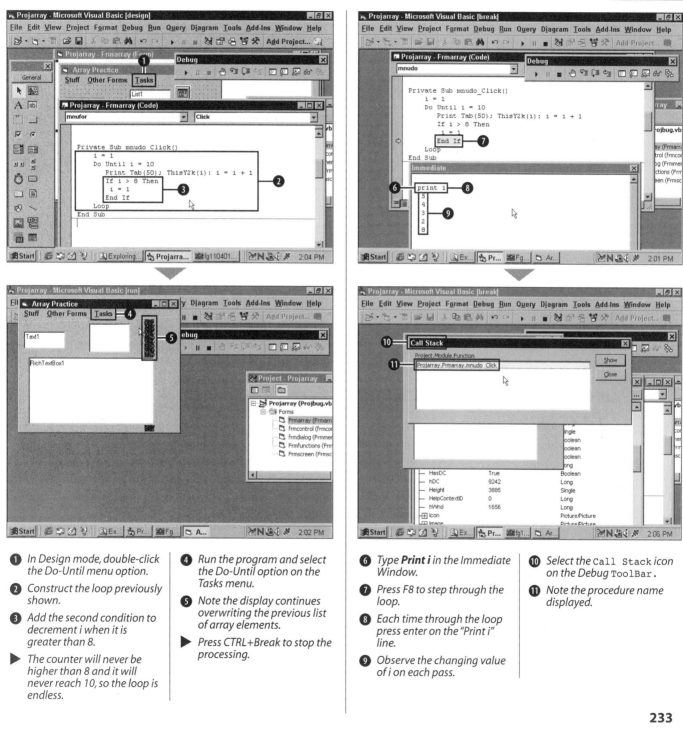

① *In Design mode, double-click the Do-Until menu option.*

② *Construct the loop previously shown.*

③ *Add the second condition to decrement i when it is greater than 8.*

▶ *The counter will never be higher than 8 and it will never reach 10, so the loop is endless.*

④ *Run the program and select the Do-Until option on the Tasks menu.*

⑤ *Note the display continues overwriting the previous list of array elements.*

▶ *Press CTRL+Break to stop the processing.*

⑥ *Type **Print i** in the Immediate Window.*

⑦ *Press F8 to step through the loop.*

⑧ *Each time through the loop press enter on the "Print i" line.*

⑨ *Observe the changing value of i on each pass.*

⑩ *Select the* `Call Stack` *icon on the Debug* `ToolBar`.

⑪ *Note the procedure name displayed.*

Using Debug Tools

The tools available to debug your applications are found on the Debug ToolBar and the Debug Menu. Some of these tools have already been discussed in terms of the various types of errors returned.

The importance of Break mode cannot be overrated. Break mode is important in debugging procedures and in helping to discover compile, run-time and logic errors. Breaking during program execution stops the operation of the program, freezes it in time, and preserves variable values and property settings. You can check values and make adjustments to the code, see which procedures have been run and which procedure was currently in process, change and display variable values, execute statements on the fly, and manually execute statements.

The error handling in Visual Basic is determined by the Options set on the General tab on the Tools, Options menu. If Break on All Errors is selected, the error handlers you placed in your code will be disabled. When the error is encountered, you enter Break mode. Once this option is set, it is in effect on start up. However, you can change the option by right clicking while in the code window. This brings up the context menu where you can select Toggle to Toggle a Breakpoint, Break on All Errors, and Break on Unhandled Errors.

You can use Break mode by pressing CTRL+Break, selecting Break from the Run Menu, selecting the Break button on the Debug ToolBar, or setting a Breakpoint.

Step Into enables you to move through procedures one statement at a time. Step Into is not available at run time, but it must be used in Break mode. You step through procedures by pressing F8, clicking Step Into from the Debug ToolBar or the Debug menu. There are times when stepping into a statement brings up the Run-time error dialog box.

Step Over ignores calls to other procedures when the procedure call is in a statement stepped into. In this case, the next statement executed by Step Over will be the next statement in the same procedure. It is available in Break mode.

Step Out skips over the rest of the statements in the procedure currently being executed. It is invoked from the Debug menu, the Debug toolbar, and the Keyboard shortcut is CTRL+Shift-8. Step Out is available only in Break mode.

Run to Cursor enables you to skip large blocks of code in which you know no errors exist. It is available in Break mode. To use Run to Cursor, place your cursor where you want to halt execution, then click the Run to Cursor icon on the Debug Menu or the icon on the Debug ToolBar. You also can use the shortcut CTRL+F8.

Add Watch enables you to set an expression (usually a variable value) that halts program execution when the value is true, when the value changes or when you manually Break the program. This is helpful when you have a loop in which a value changes each time through the loop, but the program does not execute the way you expect. One example is the logic error in the Do-Until loop previously discussed.

Continued

TAKE NOTE

BREAKING IN MOUSE AND TIMER EVENTS

Sometimes unanticipated problems occur in setting breakpoints in programs using MouseMove or in procedures with Timer events. When you execute a procedure with a Breakpoint, the program execution halts just before that line is executed. When the program Breaks, the normal program execution is interrupted, sometimes causing strange occurrences.

CROSS-REFERENCE

Chapter 5 is a place to test some of the Debugging tools.

FIND IT ONLINE

How to use the Immediate pane: **http://msdn.microsoft.com/ isapi/msdnlib.idc?theURL=/library/officedev/office/html/ debuggingvisualbasiccode.htm**.

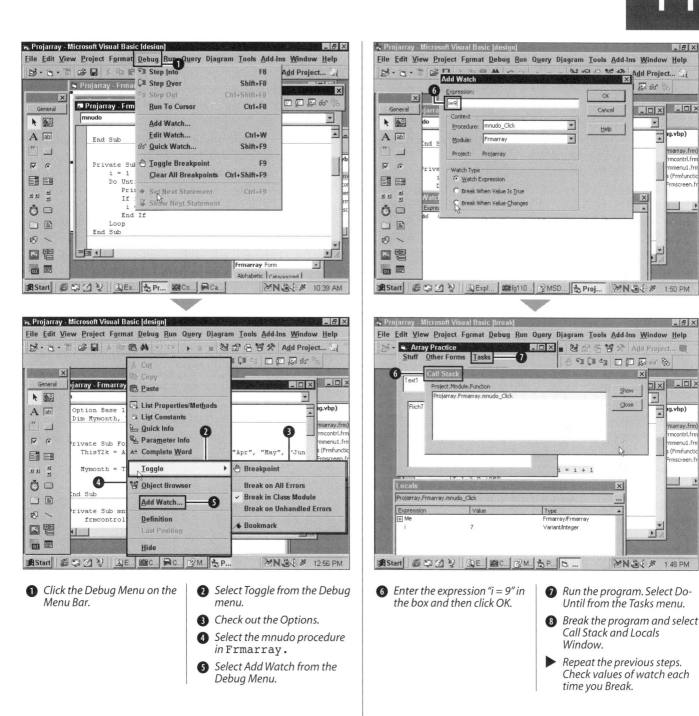

① Click the Debug Menu on the Menu Bar.

② Select Toggle from the Debug menu.

③ Check out the Options.

④ Select the mnudo procedure in `Frmarray`.

⑤ Select Add Watch from the Debug Menu.

⑥ Enter the expression "i = 9" in the box and then click OK.

⑦ Run the program. Select Do-Until from the Tasks menu.

⑧ Break the program and select Call Stack and Locals Window.

▶ Repeat the previous steps. Check values of watch each time you Break.

Using Debug Tools

Continued

In the debugging exercise for the mnudo procedure, the counter "i" was reset to 1 when the counter was greater than 8. Because resetting the counter prevented it from ever reaching the value of 10, the loop would never end. This situation is not good if you expect the loop to end in due course, but it is a good exercise in the Watch debugging option.

You can break the procedure at a different point and use the statement:

```
Print i
```

This displays the value of the counter in the Immediate Window. You also can use the Call Stack, Show option. You can also display the value in the Locals Window.

The Watch exercise in the previous topic shows you can actually observe the variable values changing as the program executes. You can step through the procedure line by line, watching the counter variable change value, in keeping with the program's execution.

`Edit Watch` enables you to modify the watch expression already entered. `Quick Watch` enables you instantly to see the value of a selected expression. To do this, you must select the expression in a line of code in the code window. Otherwise, you get the message no selection exists. `Quick Watch` enables you to check if the current value of a variable is the same as that value shown in the code. You can use `Quick Watch` from the `Debug` menu, Debug `ToolBar,` or press Shift+F9.

`Toggle Breakpoint` enables you to set a point at which the program execution will enter Break mode. The Breakpoint cannot be set on lines with only comments or any other nonexecutable statement. You can toggle using F9, the `Debug ToolBar,` or the `Debug` Menu. `Clear All Breakpoints` clears all the breakpoints you set throughout the project and uses the shortcut CTRL+Shift+F9.

`Set Next Statement` enables you to select the next statement to be executed provided it is in the same procedure. While in break mode, choose `Set Next Statement` from the `Debug` menu and then place your cursor on the next statement you want executed.

`Show Next Statement` will highlight the next statement to be executed, provided you `select Step Into, Step Over, Step Out, or Run to Cursor` after you select `Show Next Statement.`

At the same time you are using the `Debug` menu options to debug your project, you can view the same values from the current procedure in the Locals Window. You will see the Locals Window is updated each time you change from Run to Break mode.

The first column in the Locals Window shows the variable currently being accessed. — the system variable, `Me` — expands to show all the objects in a class module. In this project, the variable "i" is shown in the Expression column and will be displayed with a potentially different value each time you `Break`. The second column displays the Value of the expression and the last column displays the `Data Type` of the variable. You can resize the columns by clicking and dragging.

When you add a Watch statement, you can observe the value change each time you execute the code to increment or decrement the counter variable. The Watch window displays the value of a variable as you step through the code. For example, set the value of *i* using the Add Watch option, and then step through the loop, using the F8 key. In turn, select Run to Cursor, and Set Next Statement from the Debug menu. As you press the F8 key to step through each of the options (Run to Cursor and Set Next Statement), the Watch window will show if the value of *i* matches the value you entered. If it does not, the value is displayed as "False."

CROSS-REFERENCE

Chapter 2 discusses the Watch window with respect to the interface.

FIND IT ONLINE

Debug Tools: **http://msdn.microsoft.com/isapi/ msdnlib.idc?theURL=/library/officedev/office/html/ debuggingvisualbasiccode.htm.**

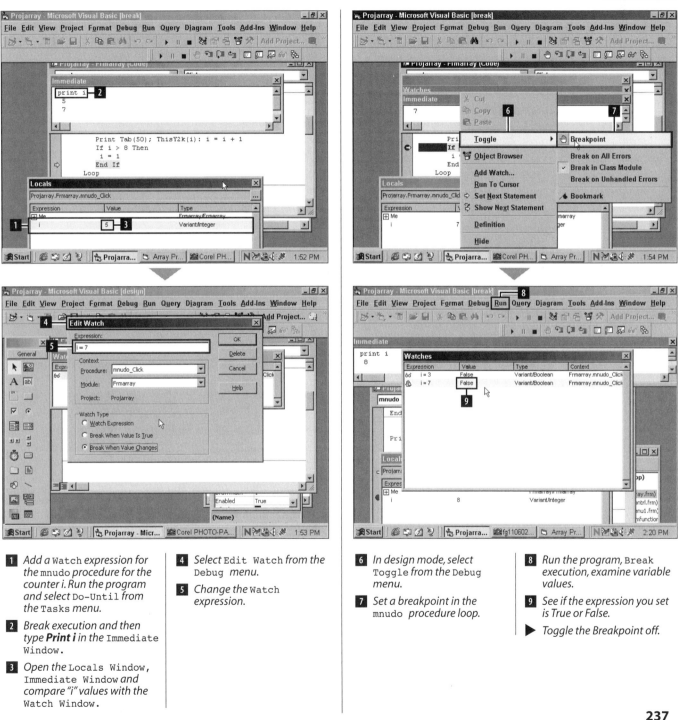

1 *Add a* Watch *expression for the* mnudo *procedure for the counter i. Run the program and select* Do-Until *from the* Tasks *menu.*

2 *Break execution and then type* **Print i** *in the* Immediate Window.

3 *Open the* Locals Window, Immediate Window *and compare "i" values with the* Watch Window.

4 *Select* Edit Watch *from the* Debug *menu.*

5 *Change the* Watch *expression.*

6 *In design mode, select* Toggle *from the* Debug *menu.*

7 *Set a breakpoint in the* mnudo *procedure loop.*

8 *Run the program,* Break *execution, examine variable values.*

9 *See if the expression you set is True or False.*

▶ *Toggle the Breakpoint off.*

Recognizing Debug Messages

During the course of the exercises you just completed, you no doubt encountered a number of error or dialog box messages. As you know by now, times occur when an error message comes in response to an inadvertent omission as often as it does to an actual error. The Watch option is no exception.

If you fail to Add a `Watch` and then click the `Quick Watch`, you may get a "No watch expression selected" message. Also, if you entered a watch expression in the Add Watch dialog box, you may get the "Selected Watch Expression Invalid" message. This usually results from not having selected the Watch expression by highlighting a portion of the procedure being tested.

This means selecting $i = 1$ or the $i = 10$ in the current `mnudo` procedure. This occurs because an expression must exist to compare with the watch you entered in the `Add Watch` or `Edit Watch` dialog box. At the point where you use the Quick Watch, you can then add to the watches from that dialog box.

An error is returned when you exceed the maximum number of watch expressions. If you have many projects and procedures loaded, you could get a message that `Watches` may have been deleted. This occurs to recover from an out-of-memory situation. If you want to keep working, you should close any unnecessary projects or applications.

If you are having difficulty with syntax checking, dragging-and-dropping text, and so forth check your options in the `Editor.` Select `Options` from the `Tools` menu and then the `Editor` tab. The `Auto Syntax Check` option should be selected if you intend to have the system identify and correct syntax errors before running the project. If you check the box next to `Require Variable Declaration`, the `Option Explicit` statement will be added to general declarations in all new modules.

Check `Auto List Members` if you want the context dialog box to help complete your statements in the code window as you enter them. If this item is selected, you get this help when you type an object and then a period. The `Auto List Members` dialog box offers possible properties to complete the statement.

`Auto Quick Info` shows values of information about functions and their parameters. You are familiar with the `Auto Data Tips,` which display pop-up variable values in Break mode when you pause the cursor over the variable names in the code window or the Immediate Window.

If you check the `Auto Indent` box, you can indent your code by pressing the `Tab Key`. The `Tab Width` parameter sets the number of spaces each `Tab` press moves the code indentation. The default is four spaces.

Under the `Window Settings` group, checking the `Drag-and-Drop Text Editing` enables you to drag-and-drop code from the code window to the Immediate and Watch Windows. The Default to Full Module View makes the code window default to viewing the entire module, rather than only the procedure on which you are working. If you check the Procedure Separator box, you can hide or show the separator bars that show below each procedure. These do not show if you are in Procedure View.

TAKE NOTE

▶ SETTING WATCH EXPRESSIONS

A *watch expression* must be about an object that can be watched. For example, you can't watch a comment line or a sub procedure. In this exercise, the only value it makes sense to watch is the value of the counter variable as it changes value through the loop. Although `ThisY2k` is a variable, it cannot itself, have values. Because it is an array variable, only its elements can have values. Thus, if you enter "ThisY2k = 2," you get a type mismatch message in the Value column of the `Watches Window`.

CROSS-REFERENCE

Chapter 12 has more information regarding debug messages.

FIND IT ONLINE

Examining code: **http://msdn.microsoft.com/isapi/ msdnlib.idc?theURL=/library/books/techlang/hcvb/html/ examiningcode.htm**.

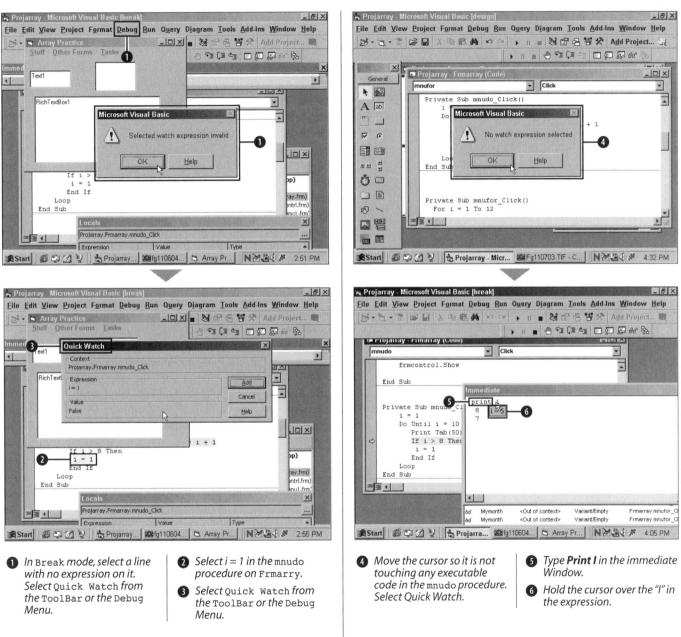

① *In* Break *mode, select a line with no expression on it. Select* Quick Watch *from the* ToolBar *or the* Debug *Menu.*

② *Select i = 1 in the* mnudo *procedure on* Frmarry.

③ *Select* Quick Watch *from the* ToolBar *or the* Debug *Menu.*

④ *Move the cursor so it is not touching any executable code in the* mnudo *procedure. Select Quick Watch.*

⑤ *Type* **Print I** *in the immediate Window.*

⑥ *Hold the cursor over the "I" in the expression.*

239

Personal Workbook

Q&A

1 What mode is most often used in debugging?

_____

_____

_____

2 How is the Locals Window used in debugging?

_____

_____

_____

3 A typo in a variable name is an example of what type of error?

_____

_____

_____

4 What type of error stops program execution and presents a dialog message?

_____

_____

_____

5 What Debug tool gives you a command line interface in `Break` mode?

_____

_____

_____

6 What Debug tool enables you to execute program statements one line at a time?

_____

_____

_____

7 How does `Step Into` differ from `Step Over`?

_____

_____

_____

8 What is the most difficult type of error to detect?

_____

_____

_____

ANSWERS: PAGE 525

EXTRA PRACTICE

① Develop a project that uses For-Next loops. Practice breaking at different points in execution. Add Watches and observe changes in values.

② Add some new menu options to the Tasks menu. Set up Do-While and For-Next loops. Create endless loops. Observe the changes in counter values.

③ Use the Immediate Window to test your previously developed project. See how many statements you can execute in the immediate mode.

④ Use the project you previously developed or create a new project to test for errors. Create command buttons labeled For-Next and Do-While. Set up procedures for these buttons, including looping structures. Halt processing and examine the counter variable values.

REAL WORLD APPLICATIONS

✔ How could you test for date format problems in the previous application? What would be a good place to start?

✔ Your client, Joe Z., has a complex application developed by another consultant with many modules containing arrays and nested loop structures. The program has been in use for several months and all has gone well until the last week. Now, totals for one category of accounts are nearly double the amounts they should be. You told Joe you would look at the problem and design a method to test for the bug(s).

Visual Quiz

Which watch expression is invalid?

_____

_____

_____

_____

_____

_____

_____

CHAPTER **12**

MASTER
THESE
SKILLS

▶ Accessing Data
▶ Using the Visual Data Manager
▶ Using the Data Control
▶ Using the Data Aware Controls
▶ Using the Query Designer
▶ Using More Data Aware Controls
▶ Using the Data Link

Accessing Databases

Databases are methods of storing data with the purpose of eventually retrieving the data kept in mind. A database is distinguished by its ease of accessing data and the security of its storage. A database is a collection of facts. Those facts may be production figures or they may be names and addresses, batting averages, or stress characteristics of guided missiles.

Many kinds of databases have nothing to do with computers. File cabinets, card files, diaries, even cookbooks can be databases. Bank records, sales figures, census data, and supply inventories were recorded and stored long before there were computers. In short, facts in a database may be just about anything. The precise nature of the data in a database is profuse and never ending.

Again, a notable attribute of a database, which must be present if the database is to be of any value to the user, is its efficient organization. Any particular data element in the database must be accessible when needed. Having a body of information is not enough. The user must be able to view, change, add, or delete material in the database.

Also, in a computer database, data are stored on disk instead of on paper and in manila folders. Data are input by typing on the computer's keyboard, by using a bar code reader, or by using an electronic sensing device, instead of handwriting. The data are then organized in specific ways, according to the instructions created by the programmer. Those instructions are, of course, the computer program.

Databases' capability to retrieve the stored data depends upon knowing the location of the data. Data should be stored in a format so the whereabouts of any item or any part of any item is instantly available to the user. If Part Number is a data element you need to store and retrieve, then Part Number must be accumulated, sought, and found by the system.

Databases are organized in files and records. The terms file and record predate computers. The computer has improved immensely on the idea of the old metal cabinet with its many manila folders containing sheets of paper and goes far beyond what could be done with those means. Both in speed and capacity, the computerized database has far outstripped precomputer databases.

The first computer databases were really data files. They were often not relational, meaning they were comprised of one file per database. Contemporary databases have replaced the terms file and record with table and row. Database tables are organized into rows and columns, much like spreadsheets. The column in a database is the analog of the field in a data file.

Most databases now are relational. *Relational databases* are made up of multiple files or tables. Common fields link the various tables to one another.

Accessing Data

Data from all sources are increasingly in demand today. In the days of the mainframe, databases of various types existed. CICS (Customer Information Control System), ISAM (Indexed Sequential Access Method) and VSAM (Virtual Sequential Access Method) are some types of databases. On personal computers have been the dBase, Paradox, other proprietary file formats, as well as spreadsheets and text files. Increasingly, SQL databases are being used. These databases (like Oracle and Microsoft SQL Server) are capable of handling huge amounts of data enabling fast searching.

Because all data are clearly not going to exist in one format, an important challenge has been to develop engines that would make all kinds of formats available and easily accessible. Visual Basic has three basic approaches to data access: DAO *(Data Access Objects)*, RDO *(Remote Data Objects)* and *ADO (ActiveX Data Objects* and OLE DB*)*. DAO is the oldest of the trio and uses the Microsoft Jet Engine. ADO is the newest interface and simplifies access by using OLE. This allows ADO to make common forms of data, such as e-mail, text, graphics, relational and nonrelational databases, (virtually any data source) usable and accessible.

DAO uses the Microsoft Jet Engine as is used by Microsoft Access. You can use DAO to connect to Access tables and several other database formats (.DBF, .DB), but this is not the speediest or the most flexible interface.

RDO is also an interface to ODBC *(Open DataBase Connectivity)*. This is an older interface and it is not efficient with ISAM databases or the Microsoft Jet Engine. To use RDO, you must access it through existing ODBC drivers installed on your system. Although it may be replaced by ADO, currently RDO is used as an interface to SQL Server, Oracle and other relational database products.

ADO is most interesting in the development of Internet applications. It provides some of the functionality of DAO and RDO, but not all the functions of either. Which you use depends upon the application. The Remote Data control is not shipped with the Learning or Professional Edition of Visual Basic, so it is not an option to use the control unless you have the Enterprise Edition. In terms of learning, the most reasonable interface to use is the DAO model.

The ADO data access technology works with OLE DB as the data provider to access both large scale Internet databases and small databases on personal computers.

OLE DB provides uniform access to diverse data and is part of the Component Object Model (COM) interfaces. OLE DB works for multiple environments and types of data storage. OLE DB is a replacement for the ODBC technology that uses specific drivers for each database type. You can examine the ODBC icon in the Windows Control Panel and see the drivers installed on your system. These drivers must be used if you access data through the DAO control. The OLE DB-ODBC data provider accesses data similarly to the older ODBC, but it allows access to a broader range of data sources.

TAKE NOTE

CONNECTING TO A DATABASE

Opening a database involves opening or creating a database object. The database object can symbolize a Microsoft Jet database (.mdb file), an ISAM database (for example, Paradox), or ODBC database connected through the Microsoft Jet database engine. To connect to an ODBC database, you use the OpenConnection method. The connection holds information such as the server name, the datasource name, the RecordsetType. RecordSource, and so forth.

CROSS-REFERENCE

Chapter 3 accessed sample databases.

FIND IT ONLINE

You can find info on DAO here: **http://msdn.microsoft.com/isapi/ msdnlib.idc?theURL=/library/sdkdoc/daosdk/dagl2mnj.htm.**

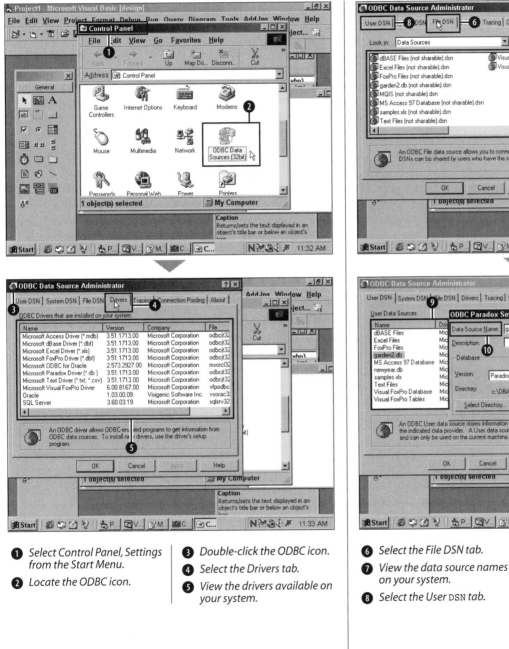

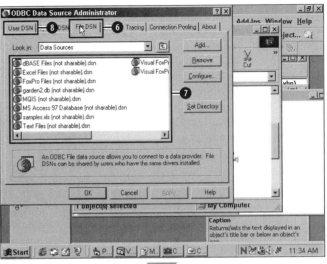

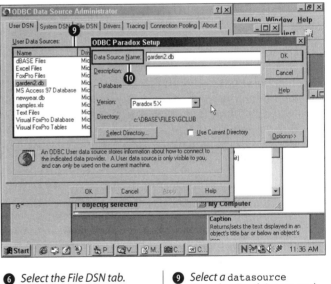

1 Select Control Panel, Settings from the Start Menu.

2 Locate the ODBC icon.

3 Double-click the ODBC icon.

4 Select the Drivers tab.

5 View the drivers available on your system.

6 Select the File DSN tab.

7 View the data source names on your system.

8 Select the User DSN tab.

9 Select a datasource (Paradox, Excel, Access, and so forth).

10 Select Configure and view the Data Source Name.

► Select Add to see what data sources you can add and add an available driver to your system.

Using the Visual Data Manager

The list of Visual database tools seems almost endless. One of these helpful devices is the *Visual Data Manager*, which is an application written in Visual Basic and is an aid to database access via DAO. This is available in the Professional Edition.

The Visual Data Manager is a utility to enable you to create and access database tables. You can modify tables (add records and change field characteristics). You can view data using the Recordset types Table, Dynaset, and Snapshot. You also can use the three types of forms available (Single record, Data control, and Data grid) in the Visual Data Manager.

You can Import and Export all databases currently supported by the ODBC drivers installed on your system. You can execute SQL commands on the databases. You can build queries with the SQL commands, as long as the databases are indexed.

You can copy table structures within the database or to different databases and do transaction processing, depending upon whether the database driver supports those features. If you are accessing an Access database, you generally can use all features.

The databases supported are Jet MDB, Dbase III and IV, FoxPro 2.x, Paradox 3.x and 4.x, Btrieve, Text, Excel, and SQL Server, both DDL and DML. The support only extends to databases other than Jet engine (Access) if you have installed the ODBC drivers in the Control Panel. When you install your database product (such as Paradox, dBase, and so forth), the program typically installs those drivers in your ODBC setup. You still have to make the database selection as outlined previously.

The Visual Data Manager supports QueryDef creation, modification, execution as well as JET security creation and modification. Relational and referential integrity is provided in table management.

The Visual Data Manager is a project you can open, just as any other Visual Basic project. Click the Open Project icon on the ToolBar and open the Visdata project that is in a subdirectory of the Samples directory. Samples are usually installed under the MSDN98 directory, several levels down. You can use Visdata this way or you can use it as an Add-Ins application from the Add-Ins Menu. If you open it as a project, you are free to modify it, study it, or do whatever suits you.

Select the Visual Data Manager from the Add-Ins Menu. Select Open Database and then select a database type to which you have provided connectivity (Microsoft Access) from the File menu. Then select the specific database (biblio.mdb) from the Open dialog box. You can then use the various views and create a form with the Data Form Designer on the Utility Menu. When you create a form this way, it appears in the Visual Basic Window, not in the Visual Data Manager. You need to go back into Visual Basic to see the form.

TAKE NOTE

VISDATA AS A CODE SOURCE

A number of useful routines are in the VisData.BAS module that you can use in another project. Some of the routines are called from a form and need to be rewritten to make the form operate correctly. Also, if you do not add the VisData module to your project, you need to declare the global variables used in that module. You can add any of the forms you see in the Project Explorer to your own project.

CROSS-REFERENCE

Chapter 13 gives further material on the construction of databases.

FIND IT ONLINE

Info on the Visual Data Manager is here: **http://msdn.microsoft. com/library/devprods/vs6/vb/html/vdidxcontents.htm.**

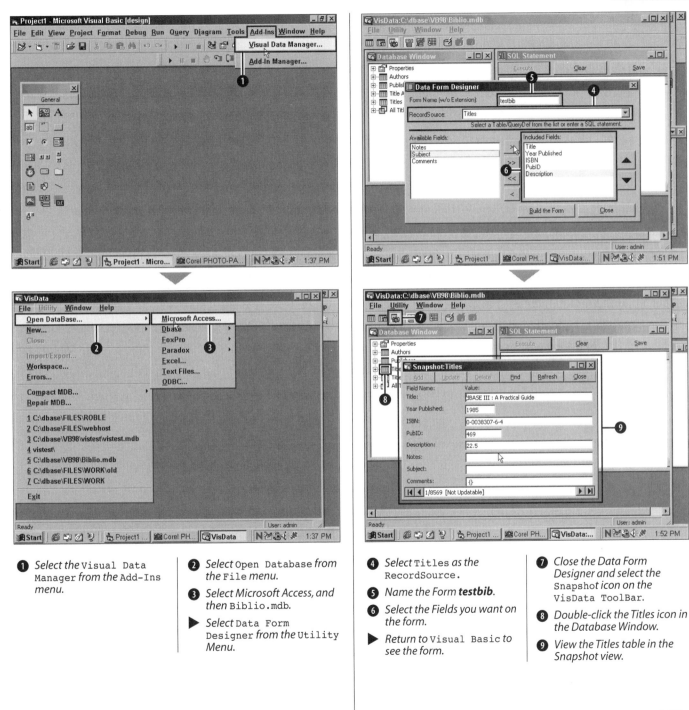

1 *Select the* Visual Data Manager *from the* Add-Ins *menu.*

2 *Select* Open Database *from the* File *menu.*

3 *Select Microsoft Access, and then* Biblio.mdb.

▶ *Select* Data Form Designer *from the* Utility *Menu.*

4 *Select* Titles *as the* RecordSource.

5 *Name the Form* **testbib**.

6 *Select the Fields you want on the form.*

▶ *Return to* Visual Basic *to see the form.*

7 *Close the Data Form Designer and select the* Snapshot *icon on the* VisData ToolBar.

8 *Double-click the Titles icon in the Database Window.*

9 *View the Titles table in the Snapshot view.*

Using the Data Environment Designer

You can use the Data Environment designer to create a database connection, set data and command object relationships, and create data reports.

Before using the Data Environment designer, you must reference it by selecting References from the Project menu. From the References dialog box, select Data Environment 1.0, and then click OK.

The Data Environment designer is added to your Visual Basic project, the Data Environment designer window appears, and a Connection object is added to your Data Environment. Access the Data Environment designer from the Project Menu where you select Add Data Environment from the options. The Data Environment designer enables you to set connection properties and drag commands onto forms.

Create a new project named DataProject. Name the form frmDataEnv with the caption *Data Env*. Select "Add Data Environment" from the Project menu. Name the Data Environment object DataEnvBiblio1. Right-click for the Connection properties dialog box. Select the database name by clicking the file box to the right.

Select the Microsoft Jet engine from the list of OLE DB providers. Click next and select Biblio.mdb database from the VB98 directory. Click OK. Right-click the DataEnvironment1 object below the Designers folder in the Project Explorer window. Name the connection Biblio from the Properties Window. The ConnectionSource from the Properties Window should be the same as that selected from the Properties dialog box.

You have established a connection to the Access database, Biblio. You could use a Data control to view and edit the data, and you can use the Data Report to create a report format. Now, select the connection Biblio and right-click to select Add Command or select it from the toolbar. Name the Command1 object *BibTitle*. Right-click the object to select Properties. In the General tab, select the Connection as Biblio, the Database Object as Table, and the Object Name as Titles. Click OK. If you expand the BibTitle icon, you will see the fields in the Titles table.

Select Add Data Report from the Project menu. Change the Name property to DataRprtBib and the caption to Biblio report. Click each of the report bands (headers and detail), positioning the Properties Window so you can see each has different properties. With a header band selected, right-click and select Retrieve Structure. This transfers the structure from the Data Environment (DataEnvBiblio1) to the report.

Now, with the Biblio Report open, position the Data Environment object (DataEnvBiblio1) so you can drag the Title field into the detail area of the report. Place the field immediately under the Detail (Titles-Detail) band on the report. This creates a report to display a list of all the book titles.

Return to the Data Env form (frmDataEnv) and place a command button on it, named cmdatarpt, with a caption, Bib Report. Enter the code in the cmdatarpt Click procedure to Show the DataRprtbib report. Once this is done, you can run the program, click the Bib Report button, and display the report. You can create more complex reports by selecting two or more tables and relating them on a common field, so you display titles within another category, such as Publishers.

TAKE NOTE

▶ FINE TUNING IN THE REPORT WINDOW

If you place the Titles field in the detail area, the field box will be too small to display the full title. You can stretch it horizontally or vertically if you prefer the titles to wrap to the next line. You may delete the Label because it adds nothing to this report. If you run the report this way, you will notice extra space between each title listed. You can move the report bands closer together by selecting each and dragging.

CROSS-REFERENCE

Chapter 14 provides more data handling instruction.

FIND IT ONLINE

The Data Environment designer is discussed in: http://msdn.microsoft.com/mastering/free/mvb6_ie4/mvb9800427.htm.

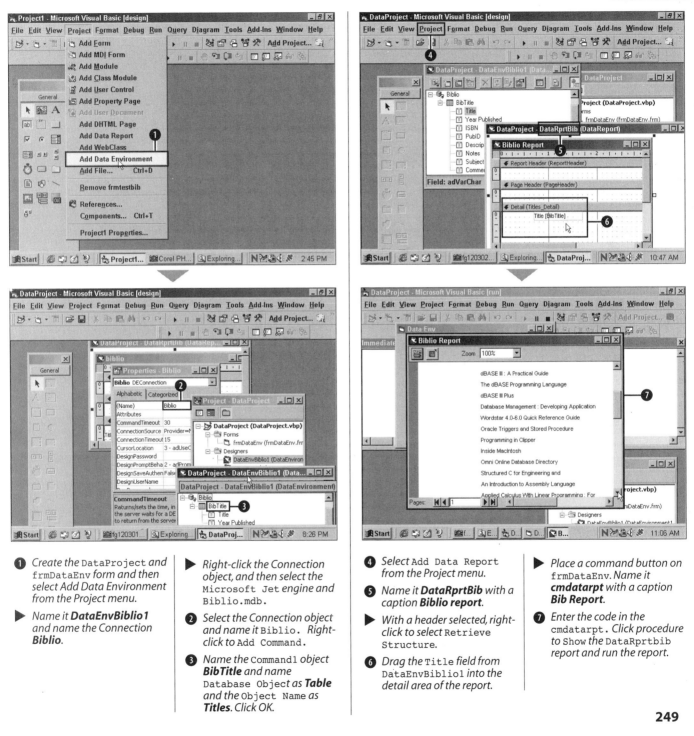

① Create the DataProject and frmDataEnv form and then select Add Data Environment from the Project menu.

▶ Name it **DataEnvBiblio1** and name the Connection **Biblio**.

▶ Right-click the Connection object, and then select the Microsoft Jet engine and Biblio.mdb.

② Select the Connection object and name it Biblio. Right-click to Add Command.

③ Name the Command1 object **BibTitle** and name Database Object as **Table** and the Object Name as **Titles**. Click OK.

④ Select Add Data Report from the Project menu.

⑤ Name it **DataRprtBib** with a caption **Biblio report**.

▶ With a header selected, right-click to select Retrieve Structure.

⑥ Drag the Title field from DataEnvBiblio1 into the detail area of the report.

▶ Place a command button on frmDataEnv. Name it **cmdatarpt** with a caption **Bib Report**.

⑦ Enter the code in the cmdatarpt. Click procedure to Show the DataRprtbib report and run the report.

249

Using the Data Control

The DAO Data control can be added to any form. When Connect and DatabaseName properties are set, you can access databases and do most functions without writing code. The Data control carries out its actions on one specific record on which it is currently set. When Data control moves to a different record, data are passed to any bound controls on the form.

Most actions of the Data control are done automatically. It can take care of adding records, editing, and so forth. If you develop a production application, you need to develop some error-handling procedures to deal with errors not handled by the Data control.

The DataList, DataCombo, DataGrid, and MSHFlexGrid are known as Bound controls. Bound controls are able to manage multiple records when bound to a Data control. These controls allow the display and use of several records at once.

Several intrinsic controls (Picture, Label, TextBox, CheckBox, Image, OLE, ListBox and ComboBox controls) are referred to as data-aware because they can be bound to a field of a Recordset controlled by the Data control. The MaskedEdit and RichTextBox controls are also included in the Professional and Enterprise Editions.

The Microsoft Jet database engine is always activated when you use a Data control to create a Recordset object. Recordsets are automatically filled when you use the Data control, but when you create Recordsets through code, you must include the Recordset building in the code statements.

The Recordset and Database Data Access Objects can be included in your procedures. The Data control can access any of the Jet engine (Version 3.0) Recordset objects. The dynaset Recordset type is created by default.

In the next exercise, you create a new project, named Projdata1, which uses the Data control and the TextBox to access and display data in a Microsoft Jet engine database (Biblio).

Name the form frmdata. Place a Data control on it. Enter the Menu Editor and make a menu option captioned "Quit" and named mnuquit. In the code window, create the mnuquit_Click procedure to End the program.

With the Data1 object selected, change the Connect property to Access and the DatabaseName property to the Biblio database. To do this, click the dots next to the Connect property and then select Access. Next, click the down arrow to the right of the DatabaseName property, and find Biblio on your system.

The RecordsetType property should be set to Table and the RecordSource property set to the Authors table. Now, you must bind the TextBox to the Data1 control. Select the TextBox, change the DataSource property to Data1, and change the DataField to Author. Run the program. You can change the record displayed in the TextBox by clicking the arrows on the Data1 control.

To see how the Data control works, you can try writing a procedure to change the function of the Data control arrows. Double click the Data control, and then select Data1 and the Validate procedure. Add the statement Data1.Recordset.MoveLast. When you run the program, you will get only the first and last record in the Authors table.

TAKE NOTE

▶ JET ENGINE OPERATIONS

During the Jet engine's process of creating a Recordset from a database (like Biblio.mdb), all other Visual Basic events are suspended but you can still access other Window applications. Pressing CTRL+Break during the Recordset building process generates an error and displays the Debug window.

CROSS-REFERENCE

Database error handling routines are discussed in Chapter 13.

FIND IT ONLINE

Here is what's new in DAO: **http://msdn.microsoft.com/isapi/ msdnlib.idc?theURL=/library/devprods/vs6/vb/html/ dadefdao.htm.**

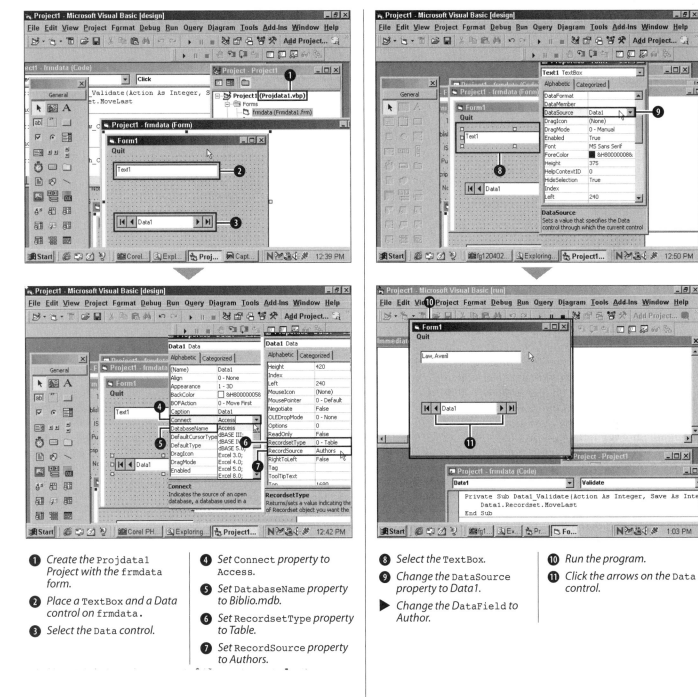

① *Create the* Projdata1 *Project with the* frmdata *form.*

② *Place a* TextBox *and a Data control on* frmdata.

③ *Select the* Data *control.*

④ *Set* Connect *property to Access.*

⑤ *Set* DatabaseName *property to Biblio.mdb.*

⑥ *Set* RecordsetType *property to Table.*

⑦ *Set* RecordSource *property to Authors.*

⑧ *Select the* TextBox.

⑨ *Change the* DataSource *property to Data1.*

▶ *Change the* DataField *to Author.*

⑩ *Run the program.*

⑪ *Click the arrows on the* Data *control.*

Using the Data Aware Controls

In addition to the previously existing data aware controls (`CheckBox`, `ComboBox`, `DBCombo`, `DBList`, `FlexGrid`, `Image`, `Label`, `ListBox`, `Masked Edit`, `MSChart`, `PictureBox`, `RichTextBox`, and `TextBox`), several new ActiveX controls with greater specificity are now in database function. Data Binding capability has been added to existing data bound controls.

The new controls include the `DataGrid`, `DataList`, `DataCombo`, `HierarchicalFlexGrid`, `Data Repeater`, `MonthView`, and `DateTimePicker` Controls. Each of these controls is better tailored to the use of OLE DB. These new controls add the `DataSource`, `DataMember`, and `DataField` properties.

The new controls you will use are the `DataGrid` control works with the `ADO Data` Control or `ADO Recordset` objects. The `DataCombo` can use `OLE DB` data sources. The third control is the `Hierarchical FlexGrid`, which will display hierarchical cursors created with the `Data Environment`.

The previously created `DataEnvironment` will serve you in the next exercise. You may create a new project named `DataProject` and an accompanying `DataEnvironment` named `DataEnvBiblio1` (as in the next to last exercise). Or, you may use the current project and rename it using "Save Project As.." on the File menu. If you save the current project under the new name, you should add two new forms and remove the old forms.

In either case, name one form (this should be the first form) `FrmDataCont`, with the caption **Data Aware Controls**. Name the second form `FrmDataQ` with the caption **Query Form**.

On the `FrmDataCont` form, place a `DataCombo`, a `DataGrid`, and an `MSHFlexGrid` control. Enlarge the form as needed. If these controls are not displayed on your `ToolBox`, load the libraries from `Components` on the `Project` menu. You need the Microsoft DataGrid Control 6.0 (OLE DB), Microsoft DataList Controls 6.0 (OLE DB), and Microsoft FlexGrid Control 6.0.

Set the `DataCombo` properties in the `Property Window`. The `DataSource` will be the `DataEnvironment` you created in the previous work. If you skipped this, you can refer to the instructions under the Data Environment Designer Topic. The `DataMember` is the `DataEnvBiblio1` command object, `BibTitle`. The `DataField` property is Title.

For the `MSHFlexGrid`, the `DataSource` and the `DataMember` properties are the same as for the `DataCombo`. No field property exists for this control because it displays all fields in the table (or those defined in `DataEnvBiblio1`). Repeat the properties you set for the `MSHFlexGrid` for the DataGrid.

In the `Menu Editor`, create a menu option captioned *Query form* and named mnuq. Create a "Quit" option as well. In the code window, write the two procedures (`mnuq_Click` and `mnuquit_Click`). Place a command button on the form, naming it `CmdNext` and the caption *Next Record*. Write the click procedure for the `CmdNext` button. When you enter the code **DataEnvBiblio1** and type the period, you are prompted with the options available. Now you're all set. Run the program and view the data.

TAKE NOTE

▶ NEW PROPERTIES

The `DataSource` property enables you to set the source database to any valid database, an ADO source or the Data Environment. The `DataMember` would be a set of records in the `DataSource`. In the `DataEnvironment`, this would be the table referenced under the Connection. The `DataField` property typically refers to a field in a database table, (the Title field from the Titles table in the `Biblio` database).

CROSS-REFERENCE

Chapter 13 has further information on Data Aware Controls.

FIND IT ONLINE

This site has info on ActiveX data controls: **http://msdn.microsoft.com/mastering/free/mmd68/mmd9801032.htm**.

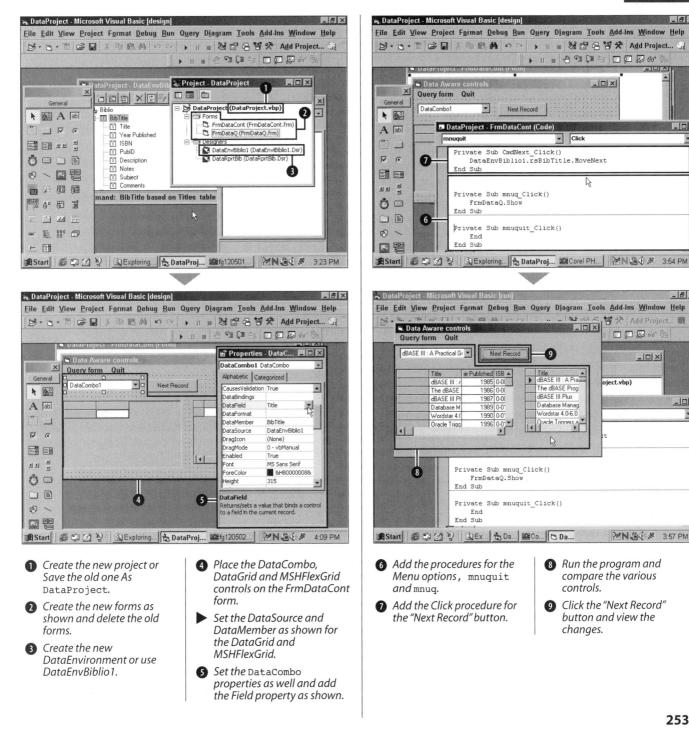

① *Create the new project or Save the old one As* `DataProject`.

② *Create the new forms as shown and delete the old forms.*

③ *Create the new DataEnvironment or use DataEnvBiblio1.*

④ *Place the DataCombo, DataGrid and MSHFlexGrid controls on the FrmDataCont form.*

▶ *Set the DataSource and DataMember as shown for the DataGrid and MSHFlexGrid.*

⑤ *Set the* `DataCombo` *properties as well and add the Field property as shown.*

⑥ *Add the procedures for the Menu options,* `mnuquit` *and* `mnuq`.

⑦ *Add the Click procedure for the "Next Record" button.*

⑧ *Run the program and compare the various controls.*

⑨ *Click the "Next Record" button and view the changes.*

Using the Query Designer

When you wrote the "Next Record" button procedure, you may have wondered what the rationale is for the statement:

`DataEnvBiblio1.rsBibTitle.MoveNext`

The `DataEnvBiblio` object is your `DataEnvironment`. Its members can be seen in the `Object Browser`. The `rsBibTitle` object is shown as a member of `DataEnvBiblio1`. The methods available for this member are shown in the pop-up menu. You can select `MoveNext`, `MovePrevious`, `MoveFirst`, or `MoveLast` if you wish but, remember, the button may not work as you expect. The option to `MoveLast` displays only the first and the last record in the `recordset`. These methods move the record pointer through the `recordset`, depending upon the method used.

You may have been wondering what the purpose is of the `FrmDataQ` form. You are going to enhance your data display project by creating a database query and displaying it on the second form.

You can use your `DataEnvironment` object to create and save a query. The query results can then be used in a report displayed on a form.

You create the new `Command` object as you did before by clicking the `Add Command` button on the `DataEnvBiblio1` toolbar or by right-clicking the connection in the `Data Environment` designer and selecting `Add Command` from the menu. This enables you to specify the `Command` object's name, which connection it uses, and its `DataSource`. To display this dialog box, right-click the `Command` object in your data environment and then choose `Properties` from the shortcut menu.

In the `Properties` dialog box, set the `Connection` to `Biblio` and then click the `SQL Statement` option button. Click the `SQL Builder` to get the `Query Designer`. You need to select the `Column`, `Table` and `Criteria` for the query. In this exercise, you develop a query to display the `Title` and `Year Published`, containing only those titles published in 1985.

Click the down arrow adjacent to the Column header. Select `Title`. Select `Titles` under the column headed "Table." Move down one line and select `Year Published` as the Column and `Titles` again as the Table. Under `Criteria`, type an equal sign and "1985." While in the `Query Designer`, you can right-click and select Run from the Shortcut menu. You see the query results at the bottom of the `Query Designer` window.

Check to make sure you see only titles with the publication year as "1985." The `SQL` statements are a little tricky to get straight at first. Any time you want to select more than one field, you must put the extra fields on subsequent rows.

When you close the designer, you are prompted to save your work. When you have saved and exited, you see the new objects under the `SQL Command1` object. These objects are labeled "Title" and "Year Published."

Drag each of the `Title` and `Year Published` objects onto the `FrmDataQ` form. Notice they bring labels along with them. You can keep the labels or delete them, depending upon how you want the form to look. You may want to widen the Title `TextBox` to have room to display the entire title.

TAKE NOTE

IDENTIFYING DATABASE OBJECTS

When you use the `Diagram` and `Grid` panes to identify with tables and fields in your database, the `Query Designer` automatically adds the correct syntax. If you are working with multiple tables, the table name qualifiers are added to column names. If you type your own commands in the `SQL` pane of the `Query Designer`, however, you must provide required information for the `SQL Server` to recognize the object you want.

CROSS-REFERENCE

The discussion of databases continues in Chapter 13.

FIND IT ONLINE

This site has information on Query Designer dialog boxes: **http:// msdn.microsoft.com/library/devprods/vs6/davinci/html/dvovr dialogboxesq.htm.**

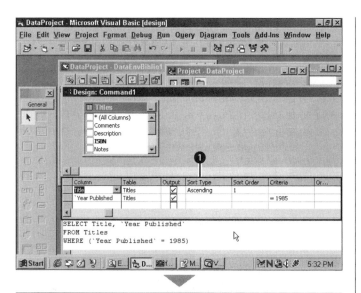

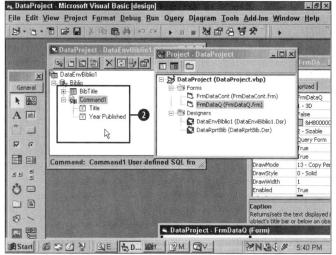

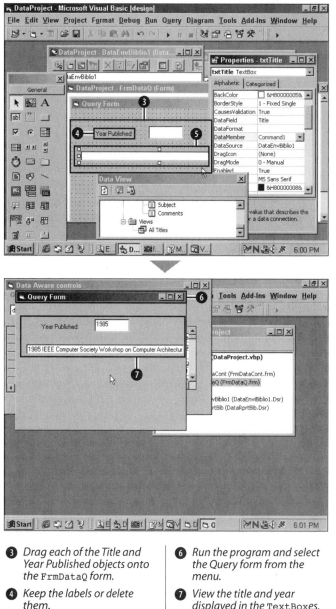

▶ Click Add Command DataEnvBiblio1 *toolbar, right-click, and select* Properties. *Set the Connection to* Biblio *and then click the* SQL Statement *option button.*

▶ Click the SQL Builder *box.*

❶ *Select the Column, Table, and Criteria for the query.*

▶ *Choose* Run *from the Shortcut menu. The query results are at the bottom of the* Query Designer *window.*

❷ *Select the* DataEnvBiblio *object and view the new* Command1 *objects.*

❸ *Drag each of the Title and Year Published objects onto the* FrmDataQ *form.*

❹ *Keep the labels or delete them.*

❺ *Widen the Title* TextBox.

❻ *Run the program and select the Query form from the menu.*

❼ *View the title and year displayed in the* TextBoxes.

Using More Data Aware Controls

B e sure you have the Data controls in your ToolBox. Select Components from the Project menu and then place checkmarks next to the Microsoft DataGrid Control, Microsoft DataList Controls, and Microsoft ADO Control.

The query report on the Query form is correct except the Title TextBox can only display one title. This assumes more than one book in the database was published in 1985. If you looked at the database in the Visual Data Manager or in the Query Designer, you know several titles fall into this category. The question is how to display them.

The DataGrid is one good way to do it. Place a DataGrid on the Query form below the Year Published TextBox. Now, set the properties in the Properties Window. This time, you are going to select Command1 instead of BibTitle as the DataMember. This is because Command1 is the second command you added to the Biblio connection. The first command was BibTitle and contained data from the entire Titles table, rather than a sample of the Titles table that resulted from a query. The Command1 object is the object you selected as an SQL statement created in the Query Designer.

The DataSource will be the DataEnvironment (the same as for the TextBox). After adding the properties, you can run the program again, selecting the Query form from the FrmDataCont form. Now when you observe the 1985 book titles, you will see a list with a scrollbar, enabling you to scroll up and down the list.

You can set the DataSource property of a data control to a data source. This capability enables you to create applications that can use data from many sources. Many new ways exist to present data to end-users. OLE DB versions of all the data bound controls now exist. The DataList and DataCombo controls are the ADO/OLE DB equivalents of DBList and DBCombo controls.

The linking capability of data sources is perhaps the most amazing feature of the new data access technology. In the previous example, you have used the DataEnvironment object to attach a database to data aware controls. In addition, you can set the DataSource property of controls at run time to bind to data sources dynamically. You can create user controls that are data sources, similar to the ADO Data Control.

The OLE DB features are included in all Editions. OLE DB is a set of COM (*Component Object Model*) interfaces that provide applications with uniform data access from varied sources. These interfaces support the amount of DBMS functionality appropriate to the data source, enabling it to share data. ADO is the way programmers access OLE DB.

In the next exercise, you use the Data Link technology that employs the ADO control to access a link file you create on your system (or a remote system). This capability to set up linkage to local and remote data sets is increasingly important as developing Internet applications becomes more significant.

CROSS-REFERENCE
More data controls can be found in Chapter 13.

FIND IT ONLINE
This deals with Customized user interfaces in OLE DB providers:
http://msdn.microsoft.com/library/sdkdoc/dasdk/oled8qsp.htm

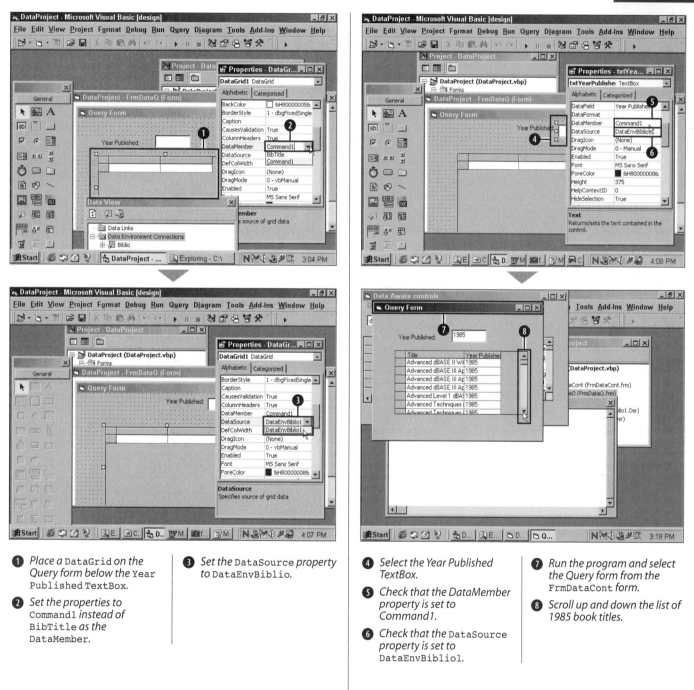

① *Place a* DataGrid *on the Query form below the* Year Published TextBox.

② *Set the properties to* Command1 *instead of* BibTitle *as the* DataMember.

③ *Set the* DataSource *property to* DataEnvBiblio.

④ *Select the Year Published TextBox.*

⑤ *Check that the DataMember property is set to* Command1.

⑥ *Check that the* DataSource *property is set to* DataEnvBiblio1.

⑦ *Run the program and select the Query form from the* FrmDataCont *form.*

⑧ *Scroll up and down the list of 1985 book titles.*

Using the Data Link

The ADO Data control provides a quick, easy way to link data source providers to data bound controls. All data bound controls include a DataSource property. A data source written to OLE DB specifications constitutes a data provider. You can, of course, create your own data provider with the class module.

The ADO Data control has the advantage of enabling you to create applications that access data without writing code. This advantage makes it worthwhile to add the ADO control to your project, even though you can use the Data controls on forms directly without the ADO control.

In the next exercise, you use the ADO control with the DataGrid to show data relationships between tables in a database. The Biblio database you have been using in previous database exercises is used here. This time, you use two different tables from Biblio.mdb. Biblio contains a Publishers table and the familiar Titles table. Because many more titles than publishers are likely to be in the database, suppose the application you are creating is designed to show all the titles published by any given publisher.

You use the DataList control to show the Company Name field from the Publishers table. When the user clicks any company name, the DataList control furnishes the PubID for the company. Using this ID, your query can be built to retrieve all records in the Titles table that have a matching PubID. When the user clicks a publisher's Company Name field on the DataList control, all the titles published by that publisher are displayed in the DataGrid control.

Create a new project, ProjDataLink. Name the form FrmDataLink with the caption Data Links. Prior to doing anything more with the project, you need to set up a Data Link. This is similar to the process of setting up a data source when you created the Data Environment. In this case, you set up the link from Windows.

Select Windows Explorer from the Start menu. Place your cursor in the right pane of the Explorer in a directory where you want the link to be placed. This could be the VB98 directory or any directory of your choice. You create the OLE DB data source by right-clicking and selecting New from the pop-up menu. Select Microsoft Data Link from the New options. Name the file **Biblio**.

Again, right-click and select Properties on the pop-up menu. Click the Connection tab. Select Provider and then click Microsoft Jet 3.51 OLE DB Provider. Click Next and then click the ellipsis button on the Connection tab. Choose the Select Access Database box to locate the Biblio.mdb database, which is usually in the VB98 directory. Test the connection by selecting that option in the dialog box.

Place two ADO Data controls on the Data Links form, both at the bottom of the form and on either side of the form. Name the first ADO control ADOPubs and the second ADOTitles. Next, place a DataList control above the first ADO control and a DataGrid control above the second ADO control.

Continued

TAKE NOTE

DATAGRID FEATURES

The DataGrid control is similar to a spreadsheet because it displays rows and columns that represent fields and records from a Recordset object. The DataGrid is used to create an application that enables reading and writing to many types of databases. One important feature of the DataGrid control is it can be rapidly set up at with little code. Setting the DataSource property of the DataGrid control results in the control being filled with data from the Provider source. The DataGrid's columns can be edited and resized.

CROSS-REFERENCE

Many data aware controls are used in Chapter 21.

FIND IT ONLINE

Here is an example of a Data Link: **http://msdn.microsoft.com/ library/devprods/vs6/vb/html/vbconcreatingnorthwindodbcd atasource.htm**.

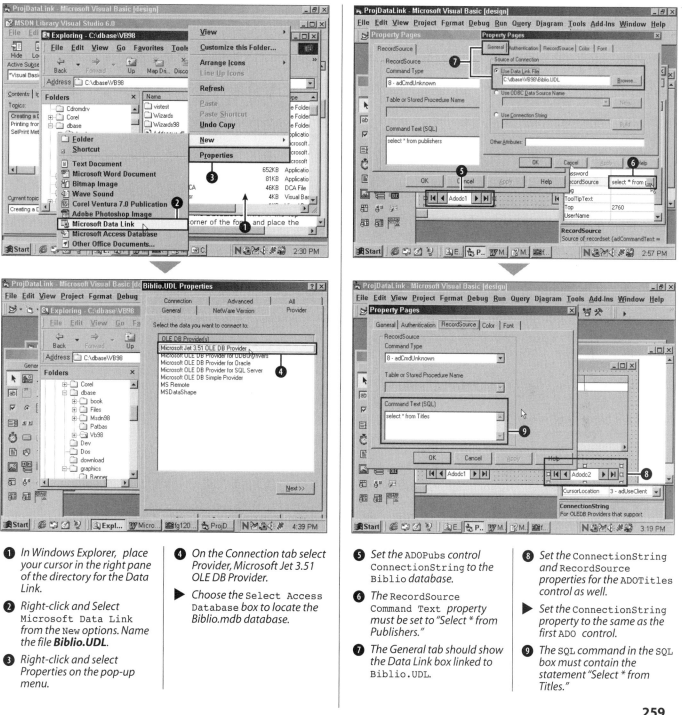

① In Windows Explorer, place your cursor in the right pane of the directory for the Data Link.

② Right-click and Select Microsoft Data Link from the New options. Name the file **Biblio.UDL**.

③ Right-click and select Properties on the pop-up menu.

④ On the Connection tab select Provider, Microsoft Jet 3.51 OLE DB Provider.

▶ Choose the Select Access Database box to locate the Biblio.mdb database.

⑤ Set the ADOPubs control ConnectionString to the Biblio database.

⑥ The RecordSource Command Text property must be set to "Select * from Publishers."

⑦ The General tab should show the Data Link box linked to Biblio.UDL.

⑧ Set the ConnectionString and RecordSource properties for the ADOTitles control as well.

▶ Set the ConnectionString property to the same as the first ADO control.

⑨ The SQL command in the SQL box must contain the statement "Select * from Titles."

Using the Data Link

Continued

What is happening here is you are setting the properties of the respective `ADO` controls each to a different table in `Biblio`, which relate to the `DataList` for `ADOPubs` and the `DataGrid` for `ADOTitles`.

Set the properties for the `DataList` control to `ADOPubs` for the `DataSource`, Company Name for `ListField`, and `PubID` for `BoundColumn`. Once the `DataSource` is set, the fields from the Publishers table are displayed on the drop-down list when you click the properties pane `Listfield` and `BoundColumn`. The `ListField` property is set because the Company Name is the only field that must be displayed because you are choosing from that field to view the records in the Titles table.

Only the `DataSource` property must be set for the `DataGrid` because it will display the data from querying that source. To be able to click publishers' `Company Name` in the `DataList` and to have this event bring about the display of a list of titles for that publisher in the `DataGrid`, you must write a `Click` procedure for `DataList1`.

You must declare a string variable for a new query.

```
Dim strQuery As String
strQuery = "Select * FROM Titles WHERE PubID =
" & DataList1.BoundText
```

This query uses the `BoundText` property of the `DataList` control to supply a value for `PubID`. The query requests all titles having the same `PubID`. This query is assigned to the `RecordSource` property of the `ADO` Data control named `ADOTitles`.

```
With AdoTitles
     .RecordSource = strQuery
.Refresh
End With
```

After refreshing this control, the `DataGrid` is updated with the new `recordset` of all the titles that have been published by the publisher.

```
With DataGrid1
```

```
.ClearFields
.ReBind
End With
```

You can now run the program and select a publisher's name on the `DataList` to view the titles displayed on the `DataGrid`.

A run-time error may be intermittent. That is, you may be able to select a publisher's name and see the associated titles displayed in the `DataGrid` a few times but, eventually, you will get a run-time error. You can choose to go into the debug window or to End. Although a complete discussion of error handling comes in a subsequent chapter, you can "fix" the problem to run your application by adding the statement above the `.Refresh` command:

```
On Error Resume Next
```

When you run the program now, you can select any of the publishers' Company names in the `DataList` box and, in turn, view the titles attributed to them in the displayed in the `DataGrid`.

TAKE NOTE

▶ LINKING TABLES

Relational databases use ID fields to link tables. The ID field is contained in two or more tables in the database. As long as the ID number is unique, these tables can be connected using this field. The Biblio database stores the names of publishing companies in a table named "Publishers." The table contains several fields, such as address, city, ZIP code, and phone number. The Name and PubID fields are the most significant fields in the table. The Name field stores the name of a publisher, whereas the PubID field stores a code. This value is important because it exclusively identifies the publisher and provides a link to the table.

CROSS-REFERENCE

Some of the same issues relinking database tables are discussed in Chapter 21.

FIND IT ONLINE

How to connect to a database: **http://msdn.microsoft.com/ library/officedev/odeopg/deovrconnectingtodatabasebyusing datalinkfile.htm.**

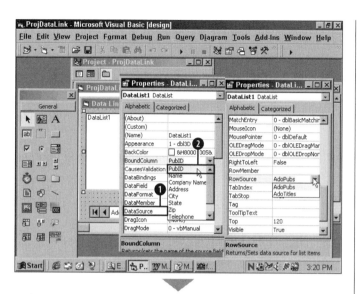

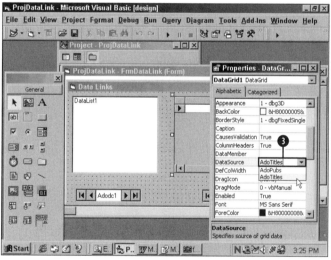

① *Set the properties for the* `DataList` *control to* `ADOPubs` *for the* `DataSource`.

② *Set* `ListField` *properties to Company Name and* `BoundColumn` *properties to* `PubID`.

③ *Set only the* `DataSource` *property for the* `DataGrid.` *to* `ADOTitles`.

Listing 12-1: The DataList Procedure

```
Private Sub Datalist1_Click()
    Dim strQuery As String
    strQuery = "Select * FROM Titles WHERE PubID _
= " & DataList1.BoundText
        With AdoTitles
        .RecordSource = strQuery
        On Error Resume Next
        .Refresh
    End With
    With DataGrid1
        .ClearFields
        .ReBind
    End With
End Sub
```

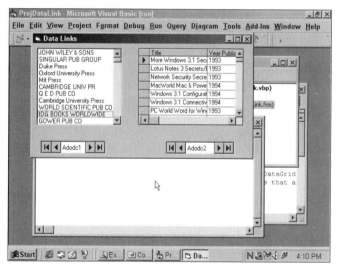

▶ *Enter the code in Listing 12-1 to show a list of titles in the* `DataGrid` *for the selected publisher in the* `DataList`.

▶ *Run the program.*

Personal Workbook

Q&A

1 What is currently the favored data access interface?

_____

_____

_____

2 How do you install the Visual Data Manager?

_____

_____

_____

_____

3 How do you access the Data Environment Designer?

_____

_____

_____

4 How do you add a connection to the Data Environment?

_____

_____

_____

5 To which type of database interface is the Data Control applied?

_____

_____

_____

6 Which control is ActiveX? (DataGrid, Data control, or ListBox)

_____

_____

_____

7 What tool can you use in the Data Environment to query a database?

_____

_____

_____

8 What property provides the Data Link when using the ADO Data control?

_____

_____

_____

ANSWERS: PAGE 525

EXTRA PRACTICE

1. Plan a project that accesses two different tables from a database. Create a form to use ADO Data controls to display a list of products when the supplier name is selected from a list.

2. Create a project and a form that use the `DataCombo` in conjunction with the `DataList` control to display-linked data.

3. Practice using the example from the Data Link topic with a different database. You can use the other (Nwind.mdb) database shipped with Visual Basic or another database.

4. Using the ODBC icon in the Control Panel, select a database driver listed and then select a database on your hard drive to create a connection available through ODBC.

REAL WORLD APPLICATIONS

✔ Your company has a Paradox database (Ourdata.db) that contains data critical to the company. Because the programmer who set it up has already left, the data have not been accessed. The Paradox program is unavailable because your company has no license and is not budgeted. Figure out the best way to use the data in the database without having to buy Paradox.

✔ Your client has decided he wants you to develop a new order entry database (and application) for his tool company in which he can store and enter data on customers, products, and orders. He wants a state-of-the-art database using the most efficient interface. What would you recommend to him? Why? How would you convince him of your recommendation?

Visual Quiz

Which control does not belong?

_____

_____

_____

_____

_____

_____

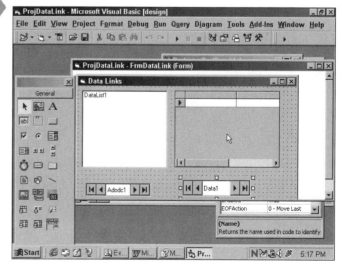

CHAPTER **13**

MASTER
THESE
SKILLS

▶ **Planning for Errors**

▶ **Trapping Errors with On Error GoTo**

▶ **Managing Errors on the Function Form**

▶ **Handling Invalid Array Index Errors**

▶ **Handling Device Errors**

▶ **Building an Error Handling Function**

▶ **Using the Err Object**

▶ **Raising Errors**

Handling Errors

A thorough discussion of the debugging process was presented in Chapter 11. In an ideal world, no need for error handling would exist. All errors would be automatically intercepted by the system. Even Visual Basic is not encapsulated in an ideal dimension, though, and you must anticipate actions will occur to cause run-time errors.

As previously mentioned, tools are provided in Visual Basic to detect both compile and run-time errors in the debugging process. These tools include breakpoints, break expressions, displaying variables and properties values, stepping through code by single statements or single procedures at a time, and watch expressions. Generally, the errors you need to fix fall into three categories: Compile errors, run-time errors, and logical errors.

The focus in error handling is the run-time error. Run-time errors are triggered when you select some option that has a procedural error. Perhaps the most common error of this type is the division by zero error. This occurs when one of the variables in an equation has a zero value. Because dividing by zero is impossible, a run-time error will be generated. Of course, a way to deal with this is simply to anticipate this type of error and use code to take care of it.

Other familiar causes of errors are hardware problems, absence of a disk in the currently logged drive, missing files, and incorrect drive letter and path designations. In addition, you experienced some errors in the projects you created. For example, a missing date value in a text box generated an error in a date calculation routine. Other problems have been missing data, overflow errors, and incorrect file types.

All these errors and more can be dealt with through error-handling techniques designed to deal with just such problems. The crucial factor is to anticipate the possibility of errors. Thinking about what could possibly go wrong when you design a project can help. Sometimes, if you are in a hurry, assuming the user will figure out what not to do when faced with run-time errors is tempting. This is a bad policy because your users may be of many varieties and backgrounds. Also, quality applications are incredibly forgiving and intuitive.

Planning for Errors

Regardless of how careful you are in planning your application and in writing code, errors can occur. Files are deleted by mistake, disk drives become full, 3or network drives change drive designation. These problems cause run-time errors, which can be handled using code.

Debugging is the course of action you take to locate and fix bugs in your applications. After creating a number of projects, you discover you repeatedly encounter the same type of error. By planning your project, you can take care of errors using centralized error handling. By building the error handling into the design of the application, you will have reduced code and efficiently handled continually recurring errors.

Remembering error handling occurs in a hierarchical fashion can help. Visual Basic will search for the closest error handler. For example, if an error occurs in a procedure where no error handler exists, but the calling procedure has error handling, the program uses the error trap in the calling procedure. This feature can be helpful or not so helpful. If the error handler is appropriate to the second procedure (not just the one in which it appears), all is well. But if the error handler is appropriate only in its own procedure, unexpected results can occur.

In a new directory, create a new project named **ProjError** and a form named **FrmError** with a caption **Error Practice**. Place three command buttons on the form. Give them the captions of **Divide by 0**, **Overflow Error**, and **Type Mismatch**. You are going to use the On Error statement, which has three forms: `On Error GoTo Line or Label`, `On Error Resume Next`, or `On Error GoTo 0`.

The `On Error GoTo` routine processes errors by branching to the specified line or label to carry out the error handling instructions. `On Error resume Next` routine specifies that encountered errors will transfer control to the statement immediately following the statement where the error occurred. This is the preferred method when dealing with objects. The `On Error Goto 0` routine disables error handling in the procedure where it is placed. You should place an Exit Sub just before the error handling routine to prevent the error code from running when no error has occurred.

For your project, you need to create three procedures to generate errors and then set up the handlers for the errors. Generally, making programs fail is much easier than making them work successfully, so you probably will find errors easy to create.

Attempting a calculation that is outside the scope of the variable or type causes "Overflow Error." You can do this easily by writing a `Click` procedure for `Command1`, where a value is set higher than allowed for the type. For example, an Integer variable may be only as high as 32767. If your routine tries to set the value higher, an error is returned. If you declare your variable (*X* for example) as Integer and then set up a `For-Next` loop in which the value of *X* can go as high as 32768, an error is generated.

First, set the value of *X* to 30000 and then run the program.

```
For X = 1 To 30000
FrmError.Caption = Format$(X)
    Next X
```

Click the `Overflow` button and watch the counter on the Form's Caption. No error is returned because the value of *X* does not exceed the limit for this type. Change the value to 32768 and rerun the program. Now you get the prompt to Debug or End.

TAKE NOTE

▶ DIVIDE BY ZERO

Although the divide by zero error is used here as an example, dealing with it like this may not be the best way to handle such an error when developing end user applications. A user will not know what "divide by zero" means. A user would not know why the error was generated, especially when the calculation is probably do to internal inconsistencies in the application.

CROSS-REFERENCE

Chapter 11 has a good discussion on the problem of discovering why programs don't work.

FIND IT ONLINE

This provides a tutorial on error handling:
http://web2.airmail.net/gbeene/tut-err.html.

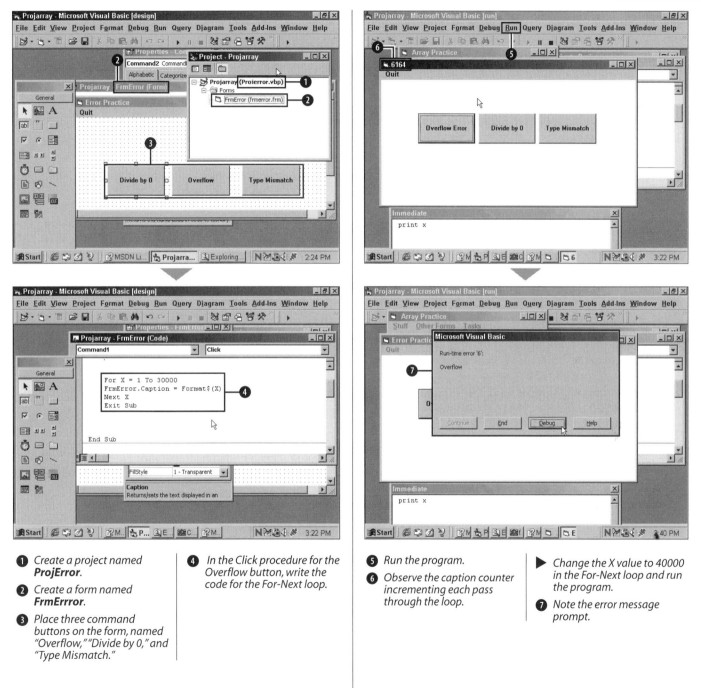

① Create a project named **ProjError**.

② Create a form named **FrmErrror**.

③ Place three command buttons on the form, named "Overflow," "Divide by 0," and "Type Mismatch."

④ In the Click procedure for the Overflow button, write the code for the For-Next loop.

⑤ Run the program.

⑥ Observe the caption counter incrementing each pass through the loop.

▶ Change the X value to 40000 in the For-Next loop and run the program.

⑦ Note the error message prompt.

Trapping Errors with On Error GoTo

The question now is how to keep the program running even though a definite problem exists because the range in *X* is too high. As long as this problem exists, an error will be generated, unless you intervene and set up an error handler. In this project, you will use the `On Error GoTo` statement. You can set up a line label called "Shucks" to take care of the problem. "Shucks" will be the line containing the error handler. You set up the condition for error handling with the statement:

`On Error GoTo Shucks`

This statement causes the execution to branch to the line labeled "Shucks," thereby carry out the instructions so labeled. Be sure to place the Exit Sub statement just before the `Shucks` error routine.

```
Exit Sub
Shucks:
    MsgBox "Overflow Error"
    Resume Next
```

The `On Error Resume Next` error handler tells the system to go to the next line in program execution after encountering an error. The Message box message tells the user about the error. After the user acknowledges the message (by clicking OK), the program moves to the next line.

Now that you have some experience with error handling, you can venture to write error handling for the other two buttons. The "divide by 0" routine is also pretty easy to construct. All you need to do is set up an equation using variables and a statement dividing a number by zero. Because you have already declared *X* and *Y* as Integer variables, use them in an equation in which one variable is divided by the other. One of the variables' values is zero. You can use expressions such as the following:

$$X = 7: Y = 0: X = X / 0: Y = X / Y$$

Run the program after setting up this Click procedure for Command2. The program ends with the dialog prompt to End or Debug. You can deal with this error the same way you handled the Overflow error. Use the statement:

`On Error GoTo Shucks2`

This statement sends the routine to the Shucks2 line label, where the error handler is set up to deal with the divide by zero error. Use the `Msgbox` to field the error exactly as you did previously. This time, the message is "Divide by Zero Error." You may think the error handling doesn't have much to it because with and without the error handler, the dialog box informs you of the error. The big difference is, without the error routine, the program crashes and, with the error handling, you get a message, but the program continues.

The third example of this error handling method works the same way. In this example, you make the mistake of assigning a string value to a `Variant` type and then use it in a mathematical calculation. The variable *a* is used in an equation after it has been assigned the value of "2000k." Clearly, 2000k is not a numeric variable. Remember, the Variant type will accommodate numbers and strings, depending on the values assigned to the variables. You need to assign the variables' values like the following:

$$X = 8: \quad a = "\ 2000k": \quad X = a * X$$

The multiplication of 8 by "2000k" will surely generate an error. Make the appropriate additions to the procedure similarly to those just discussed. You can now run the program, acknowledge the `Type Mismatch Error` Dialog box and then resume.

TAKE NOTE

▶ ERROR HANDLING HIERARCHY

At the time an error is detected, Visual Basic reviews the calls to determine where the error handling routines are located. The calls list is shown in the Call Stack dialog box and contains information regarding all the procedures called before the current one. You can view the list in Break mode. If the current procedure lacks error handling, the nearest error routine on the calls list is executed.

CROSS-REFERENCE

Chapter 11 explored various methods of finding errors.

FIND IT ONLINE

If you want to take Prof. Smiley's exams, you can take a sample free: **http://www.johnsmiley.com/tester/ login.asp**.

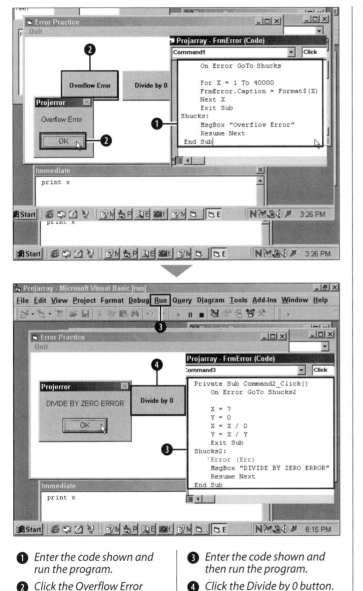

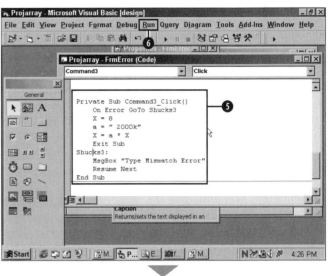

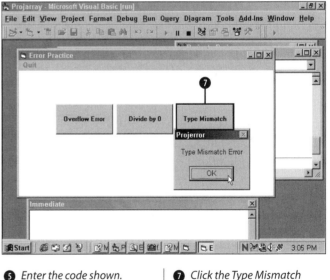

① Enter the code shown and run the program.

② Click the Overflow Error button.

③ Enter the code shown and then run the program.

④ Click the Divide by 0 button.

⑤ Enter the code shown.

⑥ Execute the program.

⑦ Click the Type Mismatch button.

Managing Errors on the Function Form

You learned about the On Error statement and its variations. Now's the time to apply what you learned to some of the problems you encountered while progressing in your self-teaching venture. In Chapter 10 you used a number of controls and functions. Among the projects created is Projarray. The Functions form was used to develop String, Mathematical, and Date functions.

A bug you probably worked around is the run-time error, caused by leaving the text box empty. Program execution was halted because no data existed on which to do the Date calculations. The Date function you used did not have any error trapping. You undoubtedly figured out a date (or at least some number) must exist to prevent the error.

Also, instructions in Chapter 10 instructed you to enter a date. A user might easily make the mistake of selecting the function from the menu before writing in a date, however. If the program execution is halted, the user has no choice except to relaunch the program.

Use the Add Form option on the Project menu to add the Frmfunctions form from Projarray. Remember, the Date function created an error if you selected any of the Date functions from the menu without first entering a date in the text box. You now have a way to correct the problem.

Go ahead and bring the Frmfunctions into your current (Projerror) project. Use Save Frmfunction.frm As.. from the File menu to save the form in your working directory/folder. Use the Menu Editor to create an Other Forms menu named "mnuother." Add the Functions option to the Other Forms menu. Do this as you did with the other projects. Name the menu option "mnufunctions" with a caption "Functions." Add the Click procedure for mnufunctions to Show the Frmfunctions form. Now you need to select the project in the Project Explorer and use Save Project As to save the project in the current directory.

Now that you have a way to access the Functions form, run the program, select the Functions option on the Other Forms menu, and select a date function. Do not enter any date value in the text box. Again, the program executed is halted and you are prompted to End or Debug.

Here is the chance you have been waiting for. End the program and click the mnudadd (Date Add) option to enter the code window. Add the On Error code to this procedure. This time, call the Error line BooBoo.

```
On Error GoTo BooBoo
```

Place the statement at the top of the procedure. After the statement using the DateAdd function, place the Exit Sub statement, then the line with the error routine label, BooBoo and a colon.

TAKE NOTE

▶ REUSING THE ERROR ROUTINE CODE

The other functions on the Functions form have similar difficulty, with the exception of the String functions. This is because a string type has no expectations or constraints for the type of data it contains. Number and date functions rely on numbers to use in the calculations. When the numbers are not there, an error is generated. You can deal with the remaining errors just as you did with the DateAdd option. You can copy the BooBoo error handler code and place it in the other procedures on the Frmfunctions form. Of course, you will want to change the message to the users appropriately to the situation.

CROSS-REFERENCE

The possibility of generating errors was discussed in Chapter 11.

FIND IT ONLINE

The VB Resource Center has tutorials on error handling: **http:// dialspace.dial.pipex.com/town/place/ggy11/vbbeg/beg6. htm#BM1.**

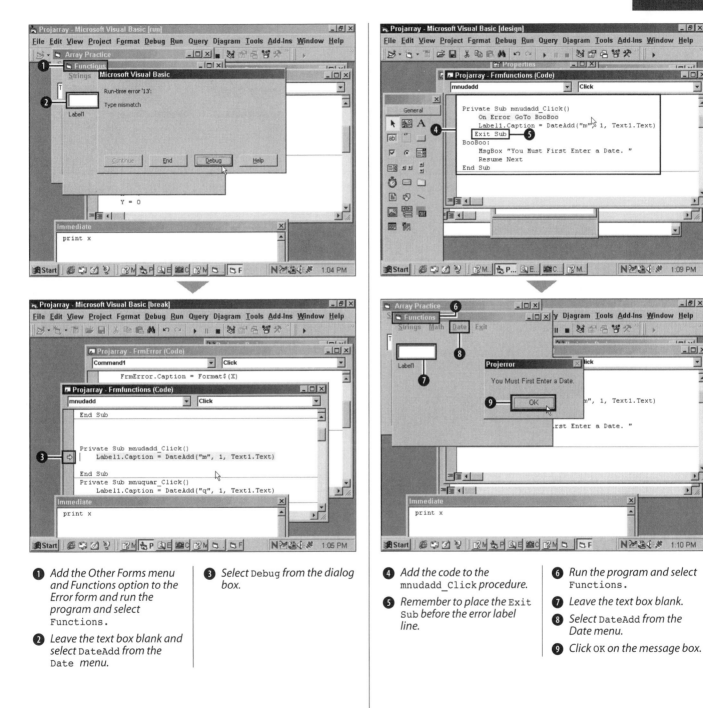

① Add the Other Forms menu and Functions option to the Error form and run the program and select Functions.

② Leave the text box blank and select DateAdd from the Date menu.

③ Select Debug from the dialog box.

④ Add the code to the mnudadd_Click procedure.

⑤ Remember to place the Exit Sub before the error label line.

⑥ Run the program and select Functions.

⑦ Leave the text box blank.

⑧ Select DateAdd from the Date menu.

⑨ Click OK on the message box.

Handling Invalid Array Index Errors

Another error you undoubtedly encountered is the file error on the `Screen Saver` form. Select `Add Form` from the `Project` menu and add the `Frmscreen` form from Chapter 9. Use "Save Frmscreen As.." to save the `Screen form` in the current project.

This project uses the `File system` controls to enable user selection of a drive and directory. The project then uses the Timer control to change the display continually by scrolling down the list of files in the selected directory, displaying each file in the `PictureBox` in turn. When you worked with this project, you may have pressed the On button before selecting a directory of graphic files. If so, you got an "Invalid property array index" error message.

In the `Menu Editor`, add the `Screen Form` option to the `Other forms` menu on the `FrmError` form. Also, write the `mnuscreen_Click` procedure to `Show` the `Frmscreen` form.

```
Private Sub mnuscreen_Click()
    Frmscreen.Show
End Sub
```

Run the program, selecting the `Screen` form option from the `Other forms` menu and then click the On button. The program execution halts with the invalid array index message. Try fixing the error using the technique you just used in the previous exercises in this chapter. The error is occurring in the `Cmdon_Click` procedure, so add the On Error statements there. Name the error routine "ErrNofile."

```
Private Sub Cmdon_Click()
On Error GoTo ErrNofile
    Timer1.Enabled = True
    Timer1.Interval = 3000

ErrNofile:
MsgBox "You must select a directory"
Resume Next
Exit Sub
End Sub
```

Here you are placing the `On Error GoTo` statement as the first line of the click procedure. The `Timer` control statements were there originally and are necessary to cause the change in display. The subsequent statements are the same as those used in the previous exercises. You are getting the message to select a directory but, before you can do anything about it, you get the `Invalid Array Index` message and the program breaks.

Two things are happening here. First, you have done nothing to correct the original problem: the `File1.ListIndex` is invalid because it has a negative value. The second problem is the `Timer` is turned on (Enabled is set to True) when you get the message to select a directory. Both problems must be solved to create a smooth functioning application. This problem is perplexing because it deals with two issues, both of which contribute to the confusion.

The `Timer` enabling could be an easy fix, if it works. You can try setting `Enabled` to `False` for the `Timer`, and then rerunning the program and examining the results.

This causes a new problem: clicking OK on the message box doesn't `Enable` the `Timer` control and clicking the On button again does not help either. You can turn the `Timer` off with the `Off` button, but you keep getting the same dialog box (reminding you to select a directory) when you turn it back on with the On button.

Continued

Continued

TAKE NOTE

GENERATING AND TRAPPING YOUR OWN ERRORS

Testing for errors by generating your own is often helpful. You also can trap your own errors. You can add your error numbers to the `vbObjectError` constant. You do this by adding constants to the Declarations section of the module.

CROSS-REFERENCE

Chapter 9 provides instruction in the Screen Saver form.

FIND IT ONLINE

This is Chuck Easttom's Error Handling information:
http://www.geocities.com/~chuckeasttom/vb/Error.htm.

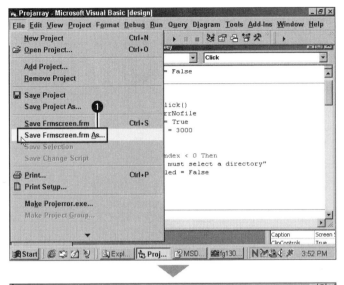

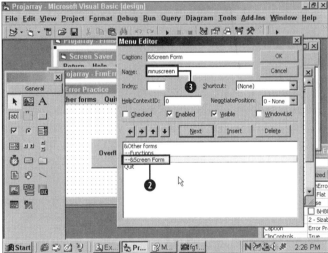

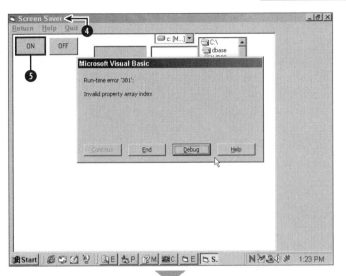

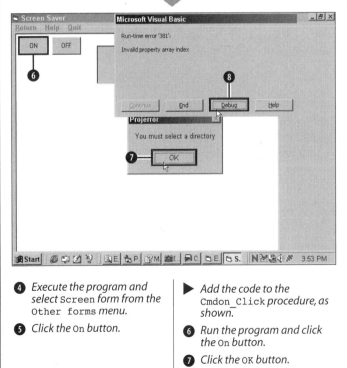

① *Select Add Form from the Project menu and Save* `Frmscreen.frm` *As.. from the File menu.*

▶ *Save the form in your current directory for the* `Projerror` *project.*

② *Use* `Menu Editor` *to add the* `Screen` *form option to the Other forms menu.*

③ *Name the option* `mnuscreen`.

④ *Execute the program and select* `Screen` *form from the* `Other forms` *menu.*

⑤ *Click the* `On` *button.*

▶ *Add the code to the* `Cmdon_Click` *procedure, as shown.*

⑥ *Run the program and click the* `On` *button.*

⑦ *Click the* `OK` *button.*

⑧ *Click the* `Debug` *button.*

Add this statement to the procedure.

```
Timer1.Enabled = False
```

Run the program. Click On. Double click a directory containing graphic (*.JPG or *.GIF files). Click On. Now each time you click the On button, you get the message to "Select A Directory." This occurs even though you have a picture displayed on the screen. And, on top of this, your pictures don't change. However, you no longer get the Invalid Array Index message.

You can see what is happening if you set a Breakpoint on the line with the message box statement. Just right-click the line and then select Toggle, Breakpoint. Now, execute the program and step through the procedure a line at a time (Step Into) by pressing F8. You can see you are turning off the Timer each time you respond to the dialog box, which you get each time you click the On button to turn the Timer on.

Clearly, at this point you know you must do more than change the Timer settings. Perhaps you should return to the initial Invalid Array Index problem.

A file must be selected by the Timer control to provide an index value. Again, no file is selected because you haven't selected a directory. Scroll down the module to the Timer1 procedure. Note the conditions you set up to increment the File1 index counter.

```
If File1.ListIndex = File1.ListCount - 1 Then
     File1.ListIndex = 0
  Else
     File1.ListIndex = File1.ListIndex + 1
End If
```

You have set up conditions to take care of resetting the value of the index to zero, but if the value of File1.ListIndex is less than zero, the array has an invalid value. You must necessarily correct the array problem to build an error handler.

The first error (Invalid Array Index) can be dealt with by using conditional statements to ensure the index is valid. You used conditions to set up the Timer Interval in this procedure, so can you use yet another condition to correct the problem.

Create an If-End If command block to trap and change the index when it is less than zero. Place both the MsgBox and the Timer statement in this command block.

```
If File1.ListIndex <= 0 Then
     MsgBox "You must select a directory"
     Timer1.Enabled = False
End If
```

Now, if the value of File1.ListIndex is a negative number, (meaning no file is, in fact, being indexed) you can prompt the user to select a directory. At the same time, you can disable the Timer control. Note, these statements are only executed if the condition is being met, whereas before, you were executing those statements regardless of the index value.

You may have an error situation, but you may also have a directory and file selected, in which case the prompt to select the directory makes no sense. This way, the situation is much cleaner. Now you can click the On button (by mistake) at the beginning and acknowledge the message, and then click On to restart the slides. You may have dealt with the error message by making sure you selected a directory before clicking the On button. That is a sort of work around, but you must allow users to make mistakes and to recover from them.

TAKE NOTE

▶ USING THE INDEX PROPERTY

The Invalid property array index error (381) means you tried to set a property array index to a value outside its allowable range. The Index property must be an integer or a numeric expression evaluating to an integer. The index value of the List property for a ListBox must be from 0 to 32,766.

CROSS-REFERENCE

You can find the Projcontrol project in Chapter 9.

FIND IT ONLINE

This VB site tells how to design an error handler: **http://msdn. microsoft.com/library/officedev/office/web/014. htm#CH014H102.**

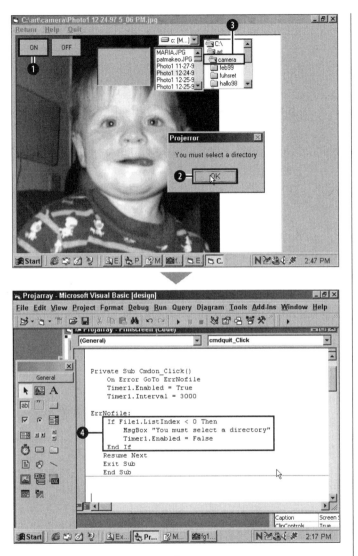

Listing 13-1: The Original Cmdon_Click Procedure

```
Private Sub Cmdon_Click()
    Timer1.Enabled = True
    Timer1.Interval = 3000
End Sub
```

▶ *This is the contents of the original procedure for the* ON *button on the* Screen form.

▶ *Add the code to set* Enable *to* False *in the* Cmdon *procedure.*

❶ *Run the program and click the* On *button.*

❷ *Click the* OK *button on the dialog box.*

❸ *Select a directory containing appropriate graphic files.*

❹ *Add the If-End If command block shown.*

❺ *Run the program and select Screen form. Click* ON.

❻ *Select a directory containing graphic files.*

❼ *Click* ON *again. Watch the screen saver work.*

275

Handling Device Errors

What other errors can be generated by your screen saver application? What if you were to select Drive A: as the drive in the graphic file path? Perhaps you already tried this and got the familiar End or Debug dialog box this time with the `Device Unavailable` message. That is, you would get this error if there were not a floppy in the drive.

If you have a floppy disk in the drive, but it contains no graphic files of the allowed types — *.gif, *.jpg, *.bmp, *.wmf, *.ico, or *.cur — files on the disk will not be displayed. If you attempt to load a graphic file that is not of the allowed type, usually a TIFF (*.`tif`), you will get an error message. So, the graphic file filter is built into the interface.

In any case, you need to take care of the `Device Unavailable` error. This error routine belongs in the `Drive1_Change` procedure because this is where the error will be triggered. You can set a breakpoint in that procedure, run the program, select the `Screen form,` and select `Drive A:` from the Drive drop-down list. Be sure no disk is in the drive to cause the error. When the program execution halts, press `F8` to step through the procedure. If you get an error dialog box before the Breakpoint, you must move the Breakpoint so it is on the first line of the procedure.

Nothing is wrong with getting an error message because it provides information to the user. What you don't want is for program execution to stop because this leaves the user with nothing to do but try to determine how to run the program without causing an error. This usually results in the user abandoning the application. If part of the user's job description is to use the application, then the information regarding the error will be imparted to the developer.

You can start by defining constants to represent the errors and to represent the intrinsic error codes in Visual Basic. The `Device Unavailable` error number is 68, so give your constant the value of 68.

```
Const myErrDevUnavail = 68
```

Name the constant as in the previous. This declaration must be the first line in the `Drive1_Change` procedure. This statement comes before the `On Error` statement:

```
On Error GoTo DiskErr
```

`DiskErr` is the name you give the line label for the error routine. It could just as well have been "Shucks" or "Oops." These two previous lines are placed before the original line setting the Dir1 object's path equal to the Drive1 object's drive property. The `DiskErr` error routine follows:

```
DiskErr:
    If (Err.Number = myErrDevUnavail) Then
      Msg = "Put a floppy in drive A:"
      If MsgBox(Msg) = vbOK Then
        Resume
      Else
        Resume Next
        End If
    End If
    Exit Sub
```

When the `Device Unavailable` error occurs, this code shows a message explaining the problem. The `Resume Next` statement then causes the procedure to continue execution at the statement, following the one at which the error occurred.

TAKE NOTE

▶ ERROR TRAPPING STYLES

Two basic styles exist of trapping errors and providing the user with information regarding the errors. The `Basic-Style` uses a method to raise an error. A client application might use an error handler to trap errors generated by the method. The `Windows API-Style` returns a value for an error code. The application uses the value to determine if an error has occurred. The Basic style uses `On Error Resume Next` and `On Error GoTo`, which is the more familiar style.

CROSS-REFERENCE
The information presented here ties in with the information in Chapter 11, Chapter 9, and Chapter 10.

FIND IT ONLINE
This reference is for device unavailable errors:
http://msdn.microsoft.com/library/devprods/vs6/vb/html/vamsgdevunavailable.htm.

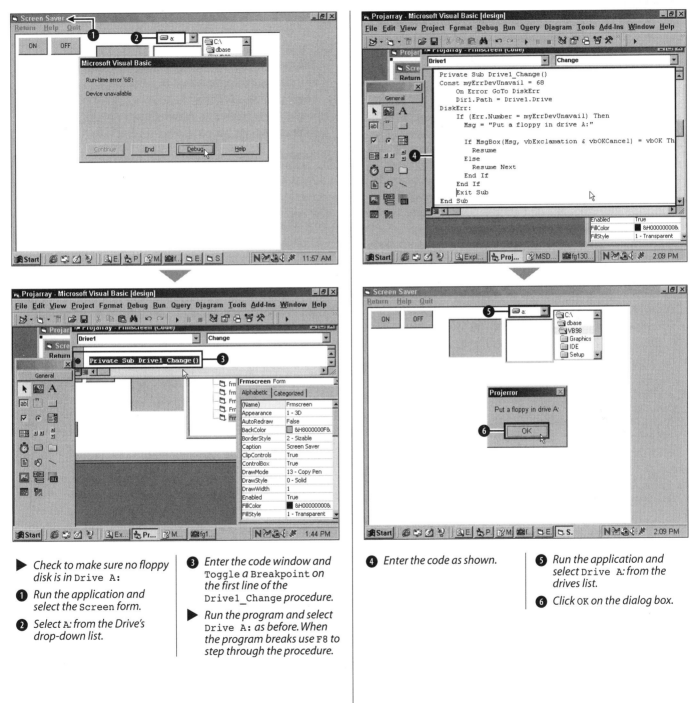

▶ Check to make sure no floppy disk is in `Drive A:`

① Run the application and select the `Screen` form.

② Select `A:` from the Drive's drop-down list.

③ Enter the code window and *Toggle a Breakpoint on* the first line of the `Drive1_Change` *procedure.*

▶ Run the program and select `Drive A:` *as before. When the program breaks use* `F8` *to step through the procedure.*

④ Enter the code as shown.

⑤ Run the application and select `Drive A:` *from the drives list.*

⑥ Click `OK` on the dialog box.

277

Building an Error Handling Function

Up to this point, you have dealt with errors in an individual manner. Instead, you can write centralized functions to deal with errors by calling a function. The `Error Practice` form was used in examples of inline error processing. Your form has instances of three types of errors: The `Overflow error`, the `Division by zero error`, and the `Type Mismatch` error. The `On Error GoTo` Line method was used to intercept errors of specific types in each procedure.

Instead of building an error routine in each of the button click procedures, you could have declared a function to deal with the errors. As in the previous example in Chapter 10, a function procedure is called by another procedure to perform a specific action, depending upon encountering certain conditions.

In this error function, you include the `On Error GoTo Line` in the function procedure, whereas it is now included in the Click procedure. Create the function, named "Division," and declare the variables for the numerator and denominator.

```
Function Division(xnum, yden) As Variant
```

Next, create a constant to contain the error number of the `Division by Zero` error. Use the `On Error GoTo` in this routine, rather than in the `Command2_Click` procedure.

```
Const myDivByZero = 11
     On Error GoTo MathFix
```

No significance is in the spelling of the constant. What is important is that a constant is set to the value (11) of the error message. You are naming the error routine **MathFix** in your function. Because the name of the function is Division, you set up the variables declared in this `function (xnum and yden)` as equal to the function with xnum representing the numerator and `yden` as the denominator. Thus, when the variables are passed to the function, this action will be carried out on the variables from the `Click` procedure.

```
Division = xnum / yden
     Exit Function
```

The `Err` object has a `Number` property, which is a numeric code evaluating to an error. You set the `Err` object's `Number` property equal to the constant you created to represent the error you are trapping. Continue writing the code for the `MathFix` routine.

```
MathFix:
  If Err.Number = myDivByZero Then
       MsgBox "DIVIDE BY ZERO ERROR"
       Resume Next
  End If
```

If the error number is the same as the constant, a message box is displayed to the user. In some cases, such a message would mean nothing to the user who will be unlikely to know the why or whereabouts of the zero. Here, though, the user is responsible for entering the zero in the text box.

Continued

TAKE NOTE

ENABLING AND DISABLING AN ERROR TRAP

The `On Error` statement specifies an error handler that enables the error trap. The error trap is enabled as soon as the `On error` statement is executed. The trap is disabled only when an `Exit (Function, Sub, Property)` or `End (Function, Sub or Property)` statement is encountered. The error trap can also be disabled by using the `On Error GoTo 0` statement.

CROSS-REFERENCE

An example of a function procedure is included in Chapter 10.

FIND IT ONLINE

This is a reference for error functions: **http://msdn. microsoft.com/library/officedev/excel/D11/ SEA2C.HTM**.

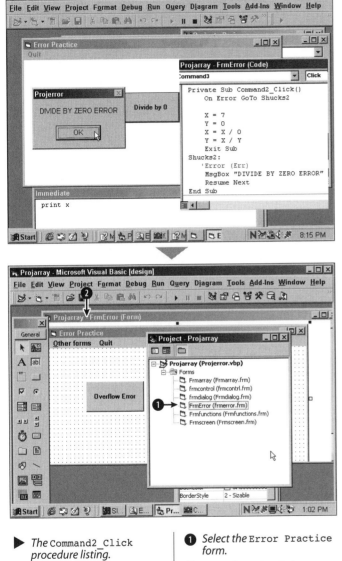

Listing 13-2: The Division Function

```
Function Division(xnum, yden) As Variant
     Const myDivByZero = 11
     On Error GoTo MathFix
     Division = xnum / yden
     Exit Function
MathFix:
   If Err.Number = myDivByZero Then

       MsgBox "DIVIDE BY ZERO ERROR"
     Resume Next

     End If

End Function
```

▶ *Build the preceding Function Procedure.*

▶ *The* `Command2_Click` *procedure listing.*

❶ *Select the* `Error Practice` *form.*

❷ *Enter the code window.*

Building an Error Handling Function *Continued*

Prior to making changes in the `Divide by Zero` routine, you must make some changes on the `Error Practice` form. Place one `TextBox` above the `Divide by 0` button and another below the button. The first text box will collect data from the user. The second box will display the dividend. Place a Label control above the first text box. Give the Label the caption "Type a Number."

Next, you must revamp the `Command2_Click` procedure. The exercise in the topic "Trapping Errors Using On Error GoTo," carried out the zero division mathematics without benefit of user intervention. In fact, the user would have no idea what was going on without looking at the code. In a compiled program, looking at the code is not an option and you would not want it to be one.

Instead of burying the errors in the code, you will give the users a chance to make their own errors. By doing so, you enhance the user's understanding of why the division error occurs and also give them control over the error.

To accommodate the new function, you need to declare new variables. In the declaration section of the module, declare `Y` and `b` `As Variant` types. Remove the `Y As Integer` declaration. You see the reason for this change in the Division function just created. The variable, `Y`, will take on the value of the user entry in the text box, so it is no longer what was essentially a `Constant` in the procedure.

Here you are using the Val function to convert the string in the text box to a number. You must do this because you want to perform calculations on the value entered by the user as text.

```
Y = Val(Text1.Text)
X = 5
```

You can leave *X* as is or give it any positive value you like.

```
b = Division(X, Y)
Text2.Text = Str(b)
Exit Sub
```

The variable *b* is used to pass the *X* and *Y* values to the `Division` function is contained in the Division function. The `String` conversion of *b* is necessary to display the figure in a text box. The procedure is then exited and ended. Notice your original `On Error GoTo` routine is absent. Those lines have been removed because they are not needed. This is because the error trapping routine is now in the function, rather than in the `Click` procedure for the command button.

By using the statement

```
b = Division(X, Y)
```

you are calling the `Division` function. Once the variables *X* and *Y* are passed to the `Division` function, they will represent `xnum` and `yden`. The division is done using the *X* value for `xnum` and the *Y* value for `yden`. If the *Y* (`yden`) value is zero, the error is trapped and the dialog box displays the Division by Zero message and execution resumes.

TAKE NOTE

USING `resume` AND `resume next`

Resume Next is used when you want execution to continue, beginning on the line subsequent to where the error occurred. Resume will begin where the program left off. When you believe the error routine will be unable to correct the error (merely announce it), you should use Resume Next. When you have a series of conditional statements that "fix" the error so it no longer exists, you can use *Resume*.

CROSS-REFERENCE

Error handlers are used in Chapter 15 and Chapter 20.

FIND IT ONLINE

This gives info on trappable errors: **http://msdn .microsoft.com/library/officedev/excel/D10/ SE6F1.HTM.**

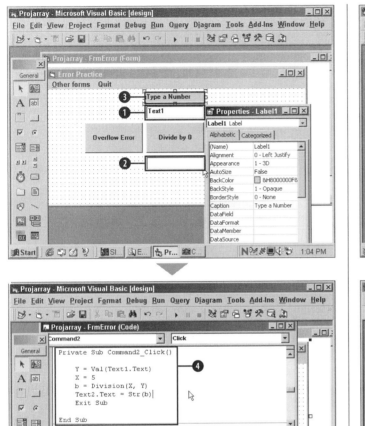

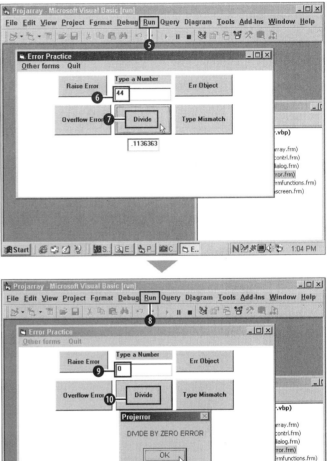

1 Place a TextBox control above the Command2 (Division by 0) button on the Error Practice form.

2 Place another TextBox control beneath the Command2 button.

3 Place a Label control above the Text1 text box with the caption, "Type a Number."

4 Modify the Command2_Click procedure as shown.

5 Run the program.

6 Type a positive number in the top text box.

7 Click the Divide button.

8 Run the program.

9 Type a zero in the top text box.

10 Click the Divide button.

Using the Err Object

The Err object's Number property contains a numeric code that identifies the error. Err.Number contains information regarding the most recent run-time error. You supply an error number and a text string describing the error. When using Err.Number you are using the Err object's number property. In fact, the default property of the Err object is Number.

Using this method, the occurrence of a run-time error fills the properties of the Err object with information that exclusively determines the error and information that can be used to handle it.

Place a fourth command button on the Error Practice form. Give it the caption "Err Object." The purpose of this exercise is to have a routine that will anticipate a type of error using Err.Number and also deal with an unanticipated error that occurs. The On error GoTo Line statement will anticipate the Type Mismatch error (13) because you may assume a calculation could not take place if the user typed letters in the text box.

This time, double click the Err Object button to enter the code window. Name the On Error statement "Gosh."

```
On Error GoTo Gosh
```

Set the variables and values as you did for the Command3 (Type Mismatch) button. You need to set a variable equal to the Text1.Text box data, assign a value to *X* and use an equation to generate values (and potentially to make errors).

```
X = 8
a = Text1.Text
X = X / a
```

The Gosh routine uses If-Then-Else-End If conditions to trap errors and display messages. Because the Type Mismatch error is Err.Number 13, you use this statement as you did in the previous examples.

```
Gosh:
    If Err.Number = 13 Then
        MsgBox "Type Mismatch Error"
        Resume Next
```

Even though you anticipate a type mismatch error, you may miss additional potential errors and wish to cover them with a statement referring to their specific descriptions. The Description property contains the text of the error message that will be displayed on the screen.

```
Else:
  Msg = "Unexpected error #" & _
Str(Err.Number) & Chr(13) & Err.Description
  MsgBox Msg, vbCritical
  Resume Next
```

The Err.Description is responsible for supplying the text for the error message. You could, of course, do without the extended error message. You needn't display the error number and text on separate lines, which is taken care of by the Chr(13) ASCII functions. You can now run the program and test your procedure.

TAKE NOTE

▶ RESETTING THE ERR OBJECT

After an Exit Sub, Exit Function, Exit Property, or Resume Next statement in an error routine, the properties of the Err object are reset to zero values or zero length strings. Err must be reset using the Clear method. The Err object's properties cannot be reset using the Resume statement outside the error routine.

CROSS-REFERENCE

Refer to Chapter 11 for the discussion regarding solving run-time errors.

FIND IT ONLINE

Here is info on VBA's Err Object: **http://msdn. microsoft.com/ library/officedev/odeopg/ deconthevbaerrobject.htm**.

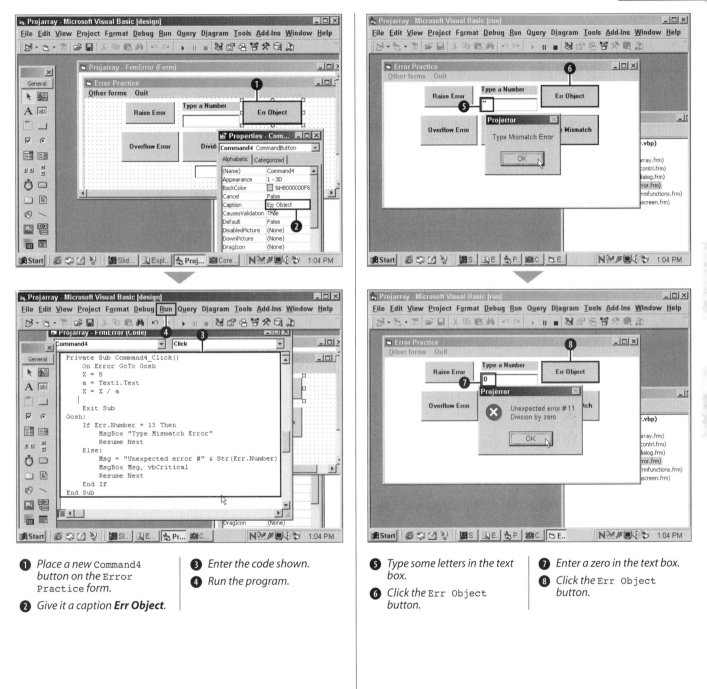

① *Place a new* `Command4` *button on the* `Error Practice` *form.*

② *Give it a caption* **Err Object**.

③ *Enter the code shown.*

④ *Run the program.*

⑤ *Type some letters in the text box.*

⑥ *Click the* `Err Object` *button.*

⑦ *Enter a zero in the text box.*

⑧ *Click the* `Err Object` *button.*

Raising Errors

Raising an error means to generate a run-time error in your code. If you wonder why anyone would want to do this, more than one answer exists to your question. The general answer is you can return more information than you can with the Error statement. You can also pass error information from your component to an application written in another language. Client applications can receive the errors your component raises.

Another good reason to use the Raise method is, in a multi-component application, the error message will surface to the portion of the application where an invalid value was entered. This is important when you collect input from one module and then process the input in a different module.

Raise is used to cause run-time errors instead of using the Error statement. Raise allows the source generating the error to be identified in the Source property. Because of the HelpFile and HelpContext arguments, online Help for the error can be referenced. Using Raise enables you to set a custom error message for such situations as when users encounter conditions from which the application cannot recover.

Place a fifth command button on the Error Practice form. Give it a caption, "Raise Error." The purpose of this exercise is to Raise a certain type of error and also deal with an unanticipated error that occurs. This time, the On Error Resume Next statement will be used. This differs from the On Error GoTo Line routine you have been using in most of the exercises. Place the On Error statement at the beginning of the Command5_Click procedure.

```
On Error Resume Next
```

The variable *b* must be set to the value of the contents of the Text1.Text box. This is to obtain user input to be used as the error number to raise.

```
b = (Text1.Text)
```

The Err.Clear must first be used to clear the most recent error message to avoid presenting an error already in memory. The Err.Raise statement is the Err object's Raise method and will be used here to display a message related to that selected by the user.

```
Err.Clear
Err.Raise b
```

The variable *b* contains the value entered in the Text1.Text box, so you are raising the error number that corresponds to the number the user entered. If the user enters 6, the message will relate to the Overflow error, if 13 is entered, the message will refer to the Type Mismatch, and so forth. Next, the condition must be set to evaluate error numbers only if they are valid error numbers.

```
If b > 0 and b > 65535 Then
   Msg = "Error # " & Str(Err.Number) & " you_
tried a "& Chr(13) & Err.Description
   MsgBox Msg, , "Error", Err.HelpFile,
_Err.HelpContext
```

Because *b* contains the user-entered value, you want to evaluate only positive numbers that are valid errors. These are positive numbers in the 0–65535 range.

The variable, Msg, is set equal to the text, "Error #" and the string value of the Err object's Number property and is concatenated with the phrase "You tried a." The character 13 code is the value of the Enter key and the description follows on the second line of the dialog box. To handle invalid codes, you need to add an Else statement.

```
Else
   MsgBox "Not a valid error number"
```

That concludes the Error Raising exercise. Run the program and test the procedure.

TAKE NOTE

ERROR NUMBER RANGE

The Err.Number property is a positive number in the 0–65,535 range. The Err object's Description property portrays the error related to the entered error number. The number and the Description are associated to produce a specific error message.

CROSS-REFERENCE

Chapter 16 uses some error procedures.

FIND IT ONLINE

This reference is for Raising Errors in class modules:
http://msdn.microsoft.com/library/officedev/
odeopg/deconerrorhandlinginclassmodules.htm.

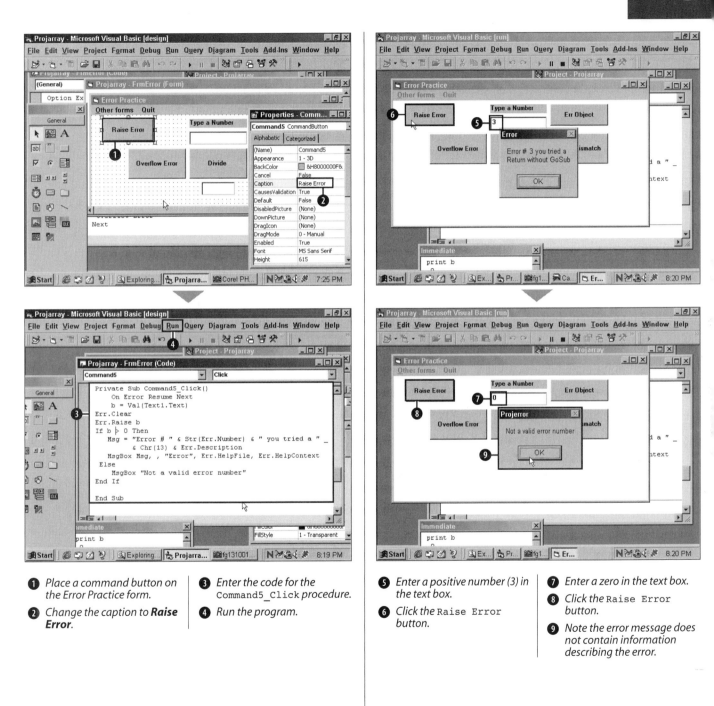

① Place a command button on the Error Practice form.

② Change the caption to **Raise Error**.

③ Enter the code for the Command5_Click procedure.

④ Run the program.

⑤ Enter a positive number (3) in the text box.

⑥ Click the Raise Error button.

⑦ Enter a zero in the text box.

⑧ Click the Raise Error button.

⑨ Note the error message does not contain information describing the error.

Personal Workbook

ANSWERS: PAGE 526

Q&A

1 What does it mean to plan for errors?

_____

_____

_____

_____

2 Performing calculations outside the scope of the application causes what error?

_____

_____

_____

_____

3 Give an example of inline error processing?

_____

_____

_____

4 Error handling mostly deals with what type of errors?

_____

_____

_____

5 `On Error GoTo Bozo` exemplifies what type of `On Error` routine?

_____

_____

_____

_____

6 What is the default property of the `Err Object`?

_____

_____

_____

7 What is an example of an unrecoverable error?

_____

_____

_____

8 How do you refer to a program-generated or a user-defined error?

_____

_____

_____

EXTRA PRACTICE

1. If you want to develop a routine in which input errors are returned to a calling application, rather than in the portion of the application doing the calculations, how would you begin?

2. Add a new command button and a text box to the Error Practice form to collect input from a user. Build an error routine that will check to see if the input falls within a specific range. Display an appropriate error message if the input is incorrect.

3. Use the Immediate Window to determine the values of the variable *b* used to retain values from the text box.

4. Implement an On Error routine using Resume and Resume Next. What difference does it make to use different routines?

5. Write an error function to carry out multiplication on integers. Return an error if the numbers entered in a text box or the numbers returned in a second text box are not integers.

Visual Quiz

Which of these command buttons' procedures call a function procedure?

_____

_____

_____

_____

REAL WORLD APPLICATIONS

✔ Your cousin Moe is a beginning programmer in Visual Basic. He wants you to help him design an error handler to trap division by zero, and type mismatch and illegal function call errors. How would you advise him?

✔ If you could not use inline error handling, how would you design an error trapping function to prevent program execution from halting with input causing a division by zero error?

✔ A firm interested in an accounts receivable application had a former programmer who never set up any error handling and their users constantly crash the application. They heard that you are good with error handling technique. They have a problem screening typos in numeric input. How would you approach the assignment?

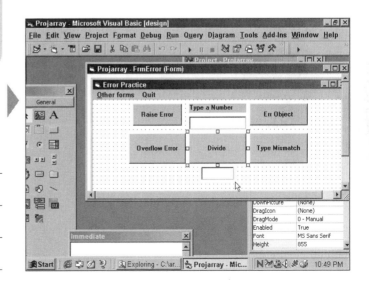

CHAPTER **14**

MASTER
THESE
SKILLS

▶ **Understanding File Types**
▶ **Using Sequential Files**
▶ **Creating Random Access Files**
▶ **Writing Random Access Files**
▶ **Reading from Random Access Files**
▶ **Trapping File Errors**
▶ **Using Binary Files**
▶ **Printing from Files**

Managing Data File Input and Output

Most of what goes on with computers involves input and output. *Input* includes any way data get into the computer. Examples are the keyboard, mouse, graphic pencil and pen, touch screen, bar code reader, microphone or other audio input, video capture board, telephone line and modem or router and cable, and magnetic media (hard drives, floppy drives, tape, and CD).

Output includes nearly as much versatility. *Output* types are printer, plotter, monitor or other display, teletype, sound card and speakers, recording device, telephone line and modem or router and cable, and magnetic media (hard drives, floppy drives, tape, and CD).

Notice some items are used for both input and output, while others only go one way. The sound card can accept input from a microphone or audio input, as well as output sound to speakers or another device. The telephone line and the modem can accept input or provide output, as is the case with the cable and another computer or router. A disk or tape drive can either be read from or written to.

Imagining a printer or a monitor providing input to a computer is difficult. In fact, bidirectional communication is between the computer and a printer when the computer sends a signal to the printer and the printer acknowledges the signal. You see evidence of this when you turn on your computer and printer simultaneously and hear the printer initializing as the system boots up. In common parlance, communication is a two-way street.

In Chapter 12 you learned about accessing, displaying, and using data. In this chapter, you learn more about what's behind the scene in data access. File input and output deal with concepts more basic to the operating system than simply providing access to existing databases.

Understanding File Types

Visual Basic 6 offers easier ways of working with files than existed in the previous versions. The new File System Objects (FSO) furnish these newer options.

In the computing world, a number of file types exist. The basic file types available in Visual Basic are Sequential, Random Access, and Binary. These file types have been around for a long time and, fortunately, the older ways of working with them are still available. The use of the FSO currently provides direct file access in those situations where you need it. If you are using database format files, you do not need the File System Objects because, as you saw in Chapter 12 you can use the data controls to access databases.

In other words, the File System Objects supply direct access to the data files themselves. In using the data controls, you are using an interface that transparently provides you with the use of the data without enabling you to have the same kind of control that direct access offers.

All files consist of bytes arranged on magnetic media. How the bytes are patterned is what determines the file type. The Sequential file is also referred to as `textstream` because the data consist of text stored in blocks. The text is ASCII or ANSI text, the same kind of text you can view from the `DOS` prompt when you type the word **TYPE**, succeeded by a filename. If the file you view with the `Type` command is not text, you will view strange characters and perhaps hear strange beeps. Sometimes viewing a Binary file using the Type command can even hang your system.

Random Access files are files with a fixed record length and a fixed field length. That is, if you decide every record is 100 bytes, then all records in the file are that length. Each field also is a specified length. If the `Last Name` field is 20 characters in one record, it is the same in all records for that file.

This means you decide the maximum length for each field. The system will fill in the remainder of each field with blanks if the name is shorter than the number of spaces allocated. This enables you instantly to find a record based upon record length specifications. If you know the positions of each field in a record and each record in a file, you can access specific fields and records without reading through the entire file. This is comparable to accessing a specific sound track on a CD, whereas on a tape, you would have to read through the entire tape to find a specific song.

Binary files are any combination of bytes. These files can be structured arbitrarily. The data could be from a signal, byte stream, or any binary level data. Binary access is perhaps the most flexible format. The only caveat is you must know how the data were originally stored to retrieve data from the Binary file.

TAKE NOTE

CREATING FILES

You cannot yet create Random or Binary files with the File System Object model. You must use the `Open` command to create either Random or Binary files. The FSO is primarily used to create Sequential files. The commands you can use are the new object-oriented File System objects, such as `Copy`, `Delete`, `Move`, and `OpenAsTextStream`, among others, or by using the older existing functions, such as `Open`, `Close`, `FileCopy`, `GetAttr`, and so forth.

CROSS-REFERENCE

Chapter 12 deals with the other side of the coin in terms of data access.

FIND IT ONLINE

Carl and Gary have file resources at:
http://www.cgvb.com/persistence.boa

Table 14-1: FILE COMMANDS AND FUNCTION COMPARISONS

	Sequential	Random	Binary
Close	X	X	
Get		X	X
Input( )	X		X
Line Input #	X		
Open	X	X	X
Print #	X		
Put		X	X
Type...End Type		X	
Write #	X		

▶ This is a delimited text file viewed using the Type command in DOS.

▶ If you have a spreadsheet file, export it as ASCII delimited.

❶ Use the Type command to view it at the DOS prompt.

▶ This is a Random Access file viewed using the Type command.

▶ If you have a Random Access file on disk, you can view it with the Type command. The file can be created using a Basic or Visual Basic program that creates such files.

Using Sequential Files

In Chapters 7, 9, and 10, you used the RichTextBox to retrieve both ASCII text and Rich Text files. In these previous exercises, you also used the CommonDialog controls' Open dialog box to retrieve the file. You can read the text data from a database the same way. That is, you can create a mailing database from any word processor or database program (Access, Paradox, Fox Pro, and so forth), export it, and read it back using file commands.

You can go about this task in two ways. First, because Sequential files are simply a string of characters written to disk, such as the text you are reading now, you can use the method you already experienced. Use the CommonDialog control and select a text file by browsing the drives. You can use Microsoft Word or any other word processor to type a phrase or paragraph. Use "Save As" to save the file as DOS text, ASCII or ANSI text, or text only. This is all there is to it.

For some situations today (and in the past), reading from and writing to Sequential files means you work with sequential databases. You read in data in the form of text (fields) delimited with commas and assign them to variables. The text fields are assigned to variables again and written back to disk when the time comes to save the information. Using the text box, you can edit the data read in from a file and then write it back to the same or a different file name.

Try this technique. In a word processor, type the following information and then save it as Text Only.

```
"Fruita","Hogmeyer","Hogmeyer's Hog Farm","San
Sloppe","CA","92222","222-222-2222","12/12/46"
[Enter]
```

The previous data represent a mailing database. The quotation marks surrounding the fields are there because this is the traditional way of delimiting string variables. Type the data for three records, giving each record a first name, last name, address, city, state, ZIP code, phone, and birth date, separated by commas and delimited by quotation marks. Press the Enter key at the end of each record and CTRL+Z to mark the end of the file.

Create a new project named Projfiles. Name the form FrmSeqFile with the caption **Sequential**. Use the Menu Editor to create Open, Save, and Quit menu items. Under the Open and Save options, create Delimited options. Add the procedure for the Quit option. Place a TextBox control on the form. Set the MultiLine property to true and the Text property to blank.

Use the Open command initially to open the file.

```
Open "h:\book\test.txt" For Input As #1
```

The path is set in quotes, depending on where your file resides. When you Open a file using File System commands, you must specify a number for the file. Typically, you would use different file numbers to read and to write. You then use the Input statement and the file number again to assign the delimited text to variables. The variable names may be any names (other than reserved words) you like. The variables are then attributed to the TextBox object. If you have created multiple records, you need to loop through the records until the end of the file is reached. If you are using Option Explicit, you must declare the variables up front.

TAKE NOTE

WORKING WITH EXPORTED DATA FILES

The chief reason to use File System commands is data have been exported from a database to text and must somehow be accessed. If you have a database management or spreadsheet program (dBase, Paradox, Access or Excel), you can create the data in that program and export it as delimited text. In this event, you will be asked to choose the separator (usually commas) and delimiter (usually quotes). The file is then created for you. You can read it as pure text in Notepad, Wordpad, a word processor, or using the DOS Type command. Here you will read it and write it back using file input and output commands.

CROSS-REFERENCE

Chapter 7 used the **RichTextBox** to read text files.

FIND IT ONLINE

Information on files is on the VB Explorer:
http://www.vbexplorer.com/vbtips.asp.

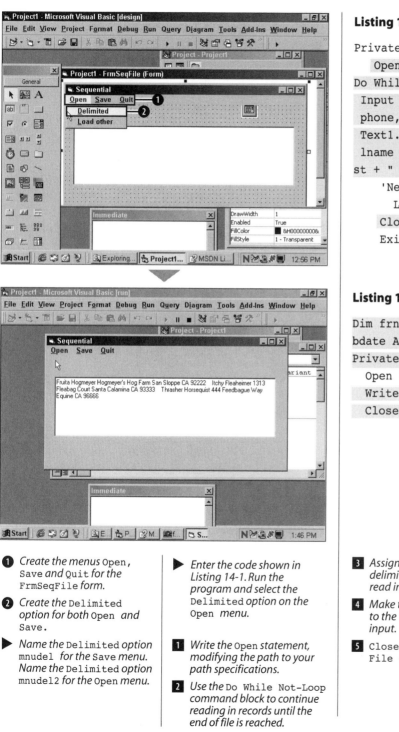

Listing 14-1: The Open Sequential File Menu Option

```
Private Sub mnudel2_Click()
    Open "h:\book\test.txt" For Input As #1    ◄①
Do While Not EOF(1)    ◄②
  Input #1, frname, lname, sa, ci, st, zip, Ł
  phone, bdate    ◄③
  Text1.Text = Text1.Text + frname + " " + Ł
  lname + " " + sa + " " + ci + " " + _  Ł    ◄④
st + " " + zip + "        "
      'Next rec
      Loop
      Close #1    ◄⑤
      Exit Sub
```

Listing 14-2: The Save Sequential File Menu Option

```
Dim frname, lname, sa, ci, st, zip, phone, ◄⑥
bdate As Variant
Private Sub mnudel_Click()    ◄⑦
  Open "c:\temp\textout.txt" For Output As #2
  Write #2, Text1.Text    ◄⑧
  Close #2    ◄⑨
```

❶ Create the menus Open, Save and Quit for the FrmSeqFile form.

❷ Create the Delimited option for both Open and Save.

▶ Name the Delimited option mnudel for the Save menu. Name the Delimited option mnudel2 for the Open menu.

▶ Enter the code shown in Listing 14-1. Run the program and select the Delimited option on the Open menu.

① Write the Open statement, modifying the path to your path specifications.

② Use the Do While Not-Loop command block to continue reading in records until the end of file is reached.

③ Assign variables to the delimited fields as they are read in.

④ Make the text box text equal to the values of the variables input.

⑤ Close the file to prevent a File Open error.

⑥ Declare the variables at the beginning of the module.

⑦ Use the Open statement and the path customized for your system, outputting the file as previously.

⑧ Use the Write command to write the contents of the text box text to the specified file name.

⑨ Close the file.

Creating Random Access Files

You can use the same data for the Random Access file exercise that you used in the Sequential file exercise. Although the Random Access file may contain exactly the same data, the approach to storage is completely different.

Whereas the Sequential file is simply a bunch of text characters (which may be delimited), the *Random Access* file contains data ordered in files and records. In the Sequential file, you have to search to the end of the file to find a specific field and record. For example, Thrasher Horsequist's home state would be near the end of the file. Your application would be unable to determine where in the file his state was located until it read through the entire file.

Random Access files, on the other hand, store the numbers of each record in the file and can instantly retrieve any data field in a record. This feature may be unimportant in your file with only three records, but in a file with 100,000 records, it is critical. Databases, which you worked with in Chapter 12, have provisions for managing fields and records similar to Random Access files. But, in the early computing world, Random Access files were one of the first techniques devised to make data readily accessible and manageable.

Creating a Random Access file is quite different from creating a Sequential file. The Sequential file you used in the previous exercise could be gotten from a number of other applications. You could have created the file in Notepad, Wordpad, or even in the DOS Text Editor. The point is the Sequential file is text, whether the text is a document or a file containing mailing label data.

A Random Access file is only used to maintain database type records. Here each record (row) is the same length and each field (column) is the same width. Maintaining the requirements is important because this is how you are able to find the location of a specific record instantly. If the record length and the lengths of all the fields are known, then the exact position of any data item can be computed. You may be wondering why anyone would use Sequential files. Because Sequential files have been around for a long time, the answer is partly because they have a history and partly because they are easy to create and maintain. If the files are small, then the process of obtaining records is not a difficult one.

You are going to create a new form for this project. Name it `FrmRandm` and give it a caption property of "Random Files." Place four `TextBox` controls on the form in a single column on the left side. Make three of them large enough to type in names and make the fourth one the size to input a state code. Set the Text properties of each box to a blank. Check the `TabIndex` property to make sure the top text box property is zero and each successive box from top to bottom is incremented by one. This is so when you are entering data, you can press Tab to move down the form. The `TabIndex` property determines their order.

TAKE NOTE

ACCURACY IN RECORD LENGTH

The Put statement writes subsequent data at the end of one record and at the start of the next if the length of the data being written is shorter than that specified in the Len clause of the Open statement. The area at the end of a record and the beginning of the next record contains the contents of the file buffer. For this reason, the record length must be accurate in the Len statement. If the record length is too long, the records' fields won't match up. If the record length is too short, an error is generated.

CROSS-REFERENCE
References to files are contained In Chapter 12.

FIND IT ONLINE
Sequential file information can be found at:
http://msdn.microsoft.com/library/devprods/vs6/vb/html/vbconusingsequentialfileaccess.htm.

Table 14-2: DETERMINING FIELD LENGTH

First Name (20)	Last Name (25)	Address (35)	City (20)	State (2)	ZIP (10)
Fruita	Hogmeyer	Hogmeyer's Hog Farm	San Sloppe	CA	92222
Itchy	Fleaheimer	1313 Fleabag Court	Santa Calamina	CA	93333
Thrasher	Horsequist	444 Feedbague Way	Equine	CA	96666

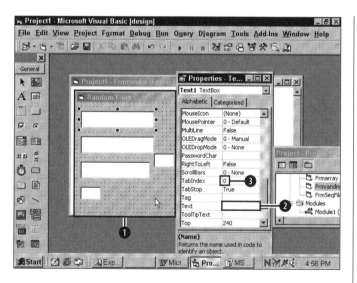

▶ *Here are your familiar three records with fixed field and record length.*

❶ *Place four* TextBox *controls on the* Frmrandm *form.*

❷ *Select each and delete the Text caption property.*

❸ *Check the* TabIndex *property to make sure the boxes have consecutive Tab Stops.*

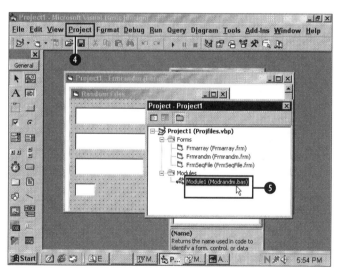

❹ *Select* Add Module *from the* Project *menu.*

❺ *Name the Module* Modrandm.

Writing Random Access Files

Now double-click the `Modrandm` module to enter the code window. You are now going to declare a Type that relates to the records you plan to have the file contain. You will define an `AddressBook` data type to represent the records containing data like that in an address book.

Because all Random Access file records must have the same length, you can make that determination when you make the Type declaration. `Firstname` and `LastName` have a fixed lengths of 20 and 25 characters, respectively. When the actual data field has fewer characters than the designated length, the remainder of the field is filled with blanks. Fields too long for the specification will be truncated. In addition to the type declaration, you will declare a Public variable "Rec" as of type `AddressBook`. The `Rec` variable will be used to identify the record.

Next, place four command buttons on the form to the right of the text boxes. Give these buttons the following captions from the top down: **Initialize, Add Record, Edit Record, Done**. Now, you are going to code each one of these click procedures with the information to do just what the button says. To the left of the Edit Record button, place a fifth `TextBox` control.

The Initialize button will create the file. Your Random Access file is called **Myadd**. Use the Open statement in the `Command1_Click` procedure to open the file as a random file and specify the length.

```
Open "myadd" For Random As #1 Len = 67
    rc = 1
```

You also want to begin the record counting with the number one, so add that statement. If you don't specify the path, the file will be created in your logged directory, which is usually the VB98 directory when you are running Visual Basic.

The `Command2` procedure says it will let you `Add Records` to the file, so this procedure must contain the information to take the text entered in the text boxes and write it to disk. In Random Access file I/O, you use the `Put`

`#`(file number) command to do this. You can make this exercise easy to do if you remember the exercises using the `RichTextBox`, `ListBox` and `TextBox` controls. There you set variables to the value of the text in the text boxes. You do the same here. The only difference is the `Rec` variable is used to identify that the field belongs to the record.

```
rec.Firstname = Text1.Text
```

Of course, you will first busy yourself entering data in the text boxes so you have something to write to file. Next, you use the `Put #`(file number) command with the records number and the `rec` variable to write to the file. Also, you must increment the record counter to avoid overwriting the same record again and again.

```
Put #1, rc, rec
    rc = rc + 1
```

The counter takes care of advancing the record, so each time you press the `Add Record` button, you add another record to the file. Continue entering records by overwriting the info in each text box and press the `Add Record` button after each addition.

CROSS-REFERENCE

Files, such as sound files, are discussed in Chapter 15.

FIND IT ONLINE

Random Access files are described at:
http://msdn.microsoft.com/library/devprods/vs6/vbasic/vbcon98/vbconusingrandomfileaccess.htm.

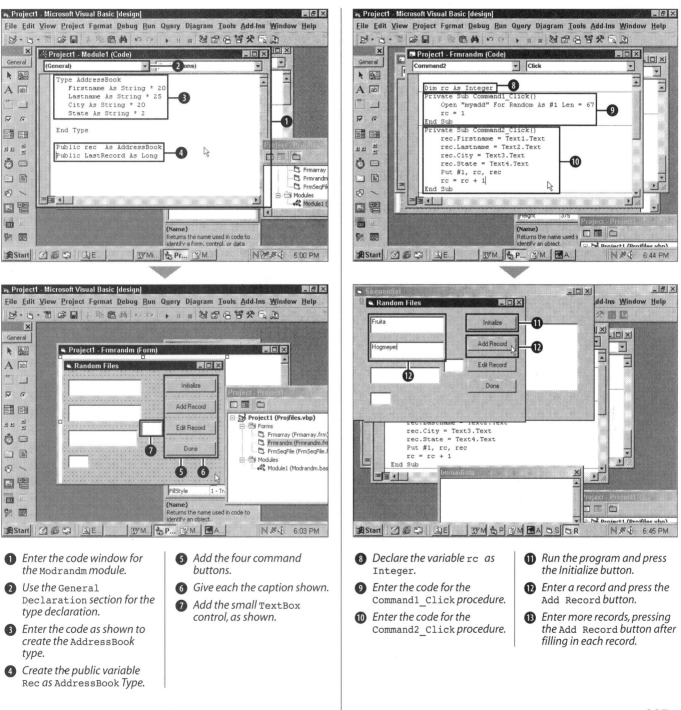

① Enter the code window for the Modrandm module.

② Use the General Declaration section for the type declaration.

③ Enter the code as shown to create the AddressBook type.

④ Create the public variable Rec as AddressBook Type.

⑤ Add the four command buttons.

⑥ Give each the caption shown.

⑦ Add the small TextBox control, as shown.

⑧ Declare the variable rc as Integer.

⑨ Enter the code for the Command1_Click procedure.

⑩ Enter the code for the Command2_Click procedure.

⑪ Run the program and press the Initialize button.

⑫ Enter a record and press the Add Record button.

⑬ Enter more records, pressing the Add Record button after filling in each record.

Reading from Random Access Files

Having created the Random Access file and saving some records, the next step is to arrange to locate and read the records you saved. As promised, you will be able to access any record in the file as quickly as you can access the first record. The records can be retrieved randomly because the records lengths are stored, which allows their exact locations in the file to be known.

To avoid confusion about which button does what, this is a good time to give each button a name, rather than Command1, Command2, and so forth. Name the Initialize button **Cmdinitialize**, the Add button **Cmdadd**, the Done button **Cmdone**, and the Edit button **Cmdedit**. Giving the buttons names associated with their functions helps to distinguish them, particularly when you didn't create the buttons in the order described here.

Just as you opened the file using the Initialize button, you must close it when you finish. Use the Done button to finalize your data entry. This is simpler than using the Open command.

```
Close #1
End
```

This closes the file manually (because the user is required to use the button to close the file). The Open file process is also user controlled. A sophisticated application probably would not require the user to click buttons to open and close the file. This would likely be built into the code, closing a file when the user completes one process, and opening a file prior to an attempt to read or write records.

The End statement here is used to quit the program, as well as signifying the session is finished. In this exercise, the buttons on the form are helpful because they bring attention to the events taking place during the file access.

The Edit Record function is built into the Cmdedit_Click procedure because it is initiated when you click the Edit button. In this procedure, you use the variable rec from the Type declaration you made in the module. The process in the previous Add Record routine is reversed for the Edit record task. That is, instead of writing a record, you are retrieving a record. The rc (record number) variable is assigned the value entered in the fifth text box (the last one you created).

```
rc = Val(Text5.Text)
```

Because the text entered constitutes a string, it must be converted to a number to become a record number. You use Get #(file number) to retrieve a record from a Random Access file, so the statement is similar to that used in the Put # statement.

```
Get #1, rc, rec
```

The record number variable (rc) and the variable (rec) from the AddressBook Type declaration, follow the Get statement. The variable assignments to the text box text used in the Add Record routine are switched around for the Edit Record task.

```
Text1.Text = rec.Firstname
```

In the Add routine, the variable takes on the value of the text, but for retrieving the record, the text must adopt the value of the variable read from the file. This completes the exercise for retrieving the Random Access file.

TAKE NOTE

▶ THE GET STATEMENT'S OPERATION

The record length specified by the Len clause in the Open statement must be at least two bytes greater than the actual length of the string. This is because Get reads a two-byte descriptor that contains the length of the string. Get then reads the data to be identified with the variable.

CROSS-REFERENCE
Substantial information regarding working with files is in Chapter 21.

FIND IT ONLINE
Check out **http://msdn.microsoft.com/library/devprods/vs6/ vbasic/vbcon98/vbconmanipulatingfiles.htm** for help on how to work with files.

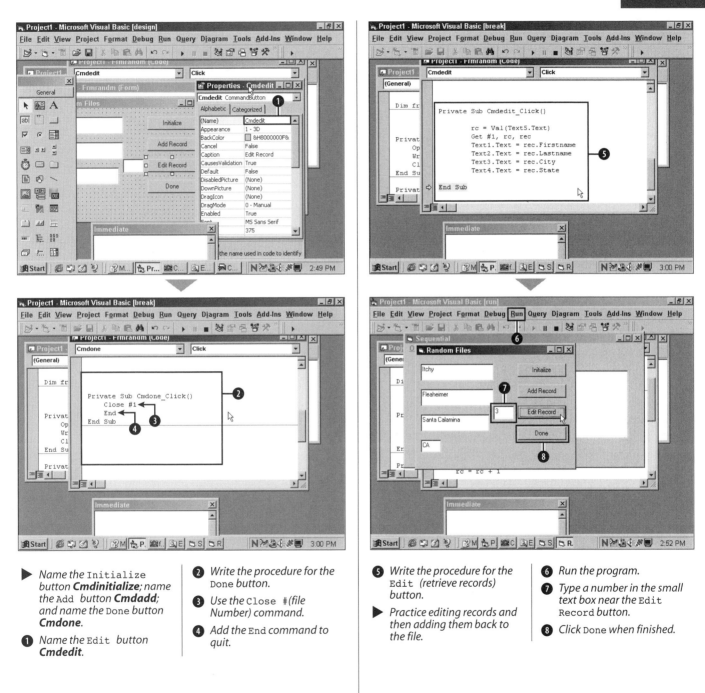

► *Name the* Initialize *button* **Cmdinitialize**; *name the* Add *button* **Cmdadd**; *and name the* Done *button* **Cmdone**.

❶ *Name the* Edit *button* **Cmdedit**.

❷ *Write the procedure for the* Done *button.*

❸ *Use the* Close #*(file Number) command.*

❹ *Add the* End *command to quit.*

❺ *Write the procedure for the* Edit *(retrieve records) button.*

► *Practice editing records and then adding them back to the file.*

❻ *Run the program.*

❼ *Type a number in the small text box near the* Edit Record *button.*

❽ *Click* Done *when finished.*

Trapping File Errors

When you run this program, you will find a few bugs exist, meaning your project will benefit from some error trapping.

For example, you must enter a value in the record number text box before pressing the Edit button. If you tried to Get a record (Edit Record button) without first entering a number in `Text5.Text`, the program would stop execution and you would receive a `Bad Record Number` error (63) message and the prompt to End or Debug. If you compounded the problem by failing to click the Initialize button to open the file, you got the `Bad file Name or Number` error (52) message.

If you played around with the program, pressing the buttons, you may have clicked the `Initialize` button more than once. If so, you got a `File Already Open` error (55). Most likely, you clicked `Add Record` prior to opening the file. Again, you got an error 52, `Bad File Name or Number` error. This is because until you open the file, it has no name, so the program cannot access it. This gives you three different errors to trap.

Sometimes you can intercept errors without using the On Error function. Often, you can write code setting up conditions in the procedure under which the error is prevented or trapped. An example of this is in the Edit Record (`Cmdedit_Click` procedure). The first error you are likely to encounter in the process of using the `Random Access` file form is failing to enter a record number prior to clicking the Edit Record button.

A way of dealing with this type of error is to check for a null character in the text box. Insert this If clause above the code you wrote in the `Cmdedit` procedure.

```
If Text5.Text <> "" Then
```

This way, a test will exist to see if the box is empty. The condition is set up so your statements are only carried out if the text exists.

```
rc = Val(Text5.Text)
        Get #1, rc, rec
```

Follow with the rest of the statements you placed in the procedure.

```
Text1.Text = rec.Firstname
        Text2.Text = rec.Lastname
        Text3.Text = rec.City
        Text4.Text = rec.State
```

You need to send the user a message, so you add the Else clause to present the user with a message box and then you can end the procedure.

```
    Else
    MsgBox "You must enter record number!"
 End If
End Sub
```

This takes care of the null error, but the Bad File (error 52) caused by failing to click the Initialize button still exists. The additional problem with this procedure is, even if you enter a record number in the text box, you will get an error (52) if you fail to click the Initialize button. So you must add an error routine.

Continued

TAKE NOTE

▶ **ADDING RECORDS TO RANDOM ACCESS FILES**

When you want to add new records to a `Random Access` file, use the Put #(file number) statement. Set the record number variable value equal to the number of records in the file plus one. To add a record to the myadd file that contains three records, set the record number equal to 4. You can write a series of records to the file by using a counter to increment the record number as each record is saved.

CROSS-REFERENCE

You'll gain more exposure to files in Chapter 22.

FIND IT ONLINE

This site deals with centralized error handling: **http://msdn. microsoft.com/library/devprods/vs6/vbasic/vbcon98/ vbconcentralizederrorhandling.htm.**

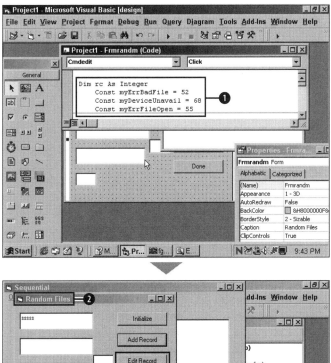

Listing 14-3: The Null Text Checker

```
Private Sub Cmdedit_Click()
    If Text5.Text <> "" Then
        rc = Val(Text5.Text)
        Get #1, rc, rec
        Text1.Text = rec.Firstname
        Text2.Text = rec.Lastname
        Text3.Text = rec.City
        Text4.Text = rec.State
    Else
    MsgBox "You must enter record number!"
    End If

End Sub
```

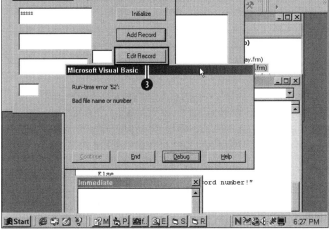

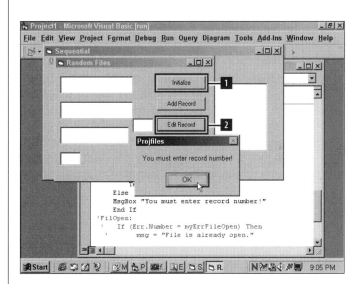

❶ In the declarations section of the code window, create the constants for the error numbers as shown.

❷ Run the Random *File* application.

❸ Click the Edit Record button leaving the adjacent text box blank.

1 Add the code shown in the Listing 14-3 and run the program and click the Initialize button.

2 Click the Edit Record button, leaving the text box blank.

Trapping File Errors

Continued

You can draw on your experience in the last chapter to build an error routine for the `Bad File Name` or `Number` error. Create an error label **BadFile** to use with `On Error GoTo`.

```
On Error GoTo BadFile
```

Make a line label **BadFile** below the `If-Else-End If` block you wrote to select and trap the null text in `Text5.Text`. Draw on your previous error-trapping exercises to trap this error. Remember, you want to identify the `Err.Number` with the `myErrBadFile` constant. Also, present the user with a message box and then have the execution resume when the user clicks "OK."

Because you fixed the Edit button problems, the user now knows to click the Initialize button to open the file. But what if the user forget the file has already been opened and continue to click the Initialize button? The answer is one you can find out for yourself and you should experience when testing the procedure. A `File Already Open` (error 55) message occurs and execution stops. The trap for this error is similar to the `Bad File Name or Number` error.

You want to prevent the program from crashing and notify the user to stop trying to open the file and to go ahead with another command. Call the error line label `FilOpen` and build a routine as you did for `BadFile`.

At least two errors can bring the program to a halt in the Add Record procedure. One is the `Bad File` error and the other is the `Device Unavailable` error. You are familiar with the `Device Unavailable` error because you used trapping for that error in Chapter 13. This is an error not yet discussed in this chapter, but it could cause the program execution to halt if your file was defined as being on drive A:. Taking care of any errors you can anticipate, rather than waiting for them to occur, is prudent.

Because at least two potential errors exist that you can imagine happening in the Add Record procedure, you may as well use the `Select Case` statement. As you may recall, `Select Case` offers a set of conditions in which to test the value of an expression. This is an alternative to the `If` block statements. For the `On Error` routine, you can use the `BadFile` label already used for the `Edit Record` button. Use the constants you have declared (`myErrBadFile` and `myDeviceUnavail`). They will be tested for in each case.

```
Select Case Err.Number
    Case myErrBadFile
```

When the error number equals that set up in your constant declaration, the code following the `Case myErrBadFile` will be executed.

```
msg = "Initialize the file first."
    If MsgBox(msg) = vbOK Then
        Resume Next
        End If
```

After this block of code is executed, the next case will be considered. Use similar statements for the `myDeviceUnavail` condition, substituting the appropriate **message Place floppy in Drive** or any message you choose to display. The point is, when the user clicks OK to acknowledge the receipt of the message, the program resumes execution. Remember to `End` the `If` blocks and the `End Select` after both conditions have been set. Also, you should place an `Exit Sub` near the end of the `Select Case` block. You can use `Select Else` prior to `End Select` as a blanket clause to catch any other conditions.

Listing 14-5: The Add Record Error Trap

```
Private Sub Cmdadd_Click()
 On Error GoTo BadFile
    rec.Firstname = Text1.Text
    rec.Lastname = Text2.Text
    rec.City = Text3.Text
    rec.State = Text4.Text
    Put #1, rc, rec
    rc = rc + 1
BadFile:
    Select Case Err.Number
```

CROSS-REFERENCE

Chapter 13 used many of these error routines.

FIND IT ONLINE

Here is information on On Error GoTo: **http://msdn.microsoft.com/library/officedev/office97/web/014.htm#CH014H105.**

```
Case myErrBadFile
    msg = "Initialize the file first."
    If MsgBox(msg) = vbOK Then
        Resume Next
    End If
Case myDeviceUnavail
    msg = "Place floppy in drive."
    If MsgBox(msg) = vbOK Then
        Resume Next
    End If
Case Else
    Exit Sub
End Select
End Sub
```

▶ *Enter this code to trap errors in the* Add Record *procedure.*

Listing 14-4: The Edit Record Error Trap

```
Private Sub Cmdedit_Click()
    On Error GoTo BadFile
    If Text5.Text <> "" Then
        rc = Val(Text5.Text)
        Get #1, rc, rec
        Text1.Text = rec.Firstname
        Text2.Text = rec.Lastname
        Text3.Text = rec.City
        Text4.Text = rec.State
    Else
    MsgBox "You must enter record number!"
    End If
BadFile:
    If (Err.Number = myErrBadFile) Then
        msg = "Click the Initialize button."
            If MsgBox(msg) = vbOK Then
                Resume Next
            End If
    End If
        Exit Sub
End Sub
```

▶ *Add this error-trapping code to the null-checking routine for the* Edit Record *procedure.*

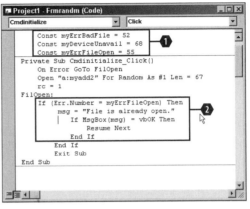

① *Enter the code shown in the* Declarations *section if you have not done so.*

② *Add the error-trapping code for the* Cmdinitialize_Click *procedure.*

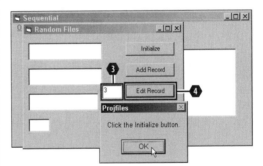

③ *Enter the error-trapping code for the* Edit Record *procedure and run the program and enter a record number in the* Text5 *box.*

④ *Click* Edit Record.

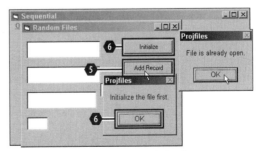

▶ *Enter the error-trapping code for the* Add Record *procedure.*

⑤ *Enter a value in the* Text5 *box and click the* Add Record *button.*

⑥ *Click Initialize and then click Initialize again.*

303

Using Binary Files

The important thing to remember when using Binary File Access is Binary files must contain numbers only. You can read and write only numbers to Binary files. You can create arrays of the Byte data type or declare any variables you use to store your data as a double. If you declare the variable used to contain your data as an integer, your program will crash when you enter a number with a value greater than integer.

As with the Random Access Files, the File System Object model does not offer Binary file creation or use. Binary files are created and accessed much like Random Access files. An advantage of using Binary files is data storage is more efficient than with Random Access and Sequential files. This is because no padding is in shorter fields, as is in Random Access. Data are stored in bytes, rather than characters, as in Sequential files.

The retrieval is not as easy as with either Sequential or Random Access files. You probably would use Binary files only when you have extremely limited disk space. Such files may be ideal for scientific projects in which workers collected data out in the field using laptop computers with limited storage. They might also be used for such applications as reading and writing bar codes. In fact, any type of application that uses a lot of numerical data would be a good use of Binary files.

You can draw on your experience with Random Access files in setting up a little exercise using Binary files. Place two new command buttons on your Random Files form. Place them near the bottom of the form, away from the other buttons. These buttons' procedures will be used to write to and read from a Binary file.

Start by declaring `mynumber` as a `Double` type in the declarations section of the module. You will use this variable in both the `Command1` and `Command2` procedures. Begin with the `Command1_Click` procedure. In Binary file access you use the `Open` statement, as with the other file types.

```
Open "myadd2" For Binary As #1
```

As with Random Access, you state the type of access you intend. The Len clause is ignored with Binary files because the data are not in stored fixed record lengths. You also use the `Put #(file number)` statement, with the variable identifying the file contents. Set your `mynumber` variable equal to the value entered in the Text1.Text box.

```
mynumber = Val(Text1.Text)
```

Because this file type can only contain numerical data, you must convert the text to a number value using the `Val` function. Finally, you use the Put statement. Remember to use the two-comma delimiters if you do not specify a record number. This is always required in the Put statement. The syntax is: Put [#]file number, [record number], variable name.

```
Put #1, , mynumber
```

Because `mynumber` is the variable you are using to store your data, you use this when writing the file and in reading it back in as well.

The `Command2` procedure will be used to read the file contents into the `Text1.Text` box. The `Open` statement is used, again similarly to that in Random Access. This time, assign the file number as #2. This is so you can open and read from the file in one session. Follow the guidelines you used with Random Access to complete the `Command2_Click` procedure.

TAKE NOTE

▶ PUT STATEMENT BINARY EXCEPTIONS

Similarities exist between Random Access and Binary files' use of the `Put` statement, with a few exceptions. For example, `Put` saves variable-length strings that are not elements of user-defined types without the two-byte descriptor. The number of bytes written is equal to the number of characters in the string. The Len clause in the `Open` statement is ignored and no descriptors are written for arrays, unless they are user defined.

CROSS-REFERENCE

Graphic Binary files are used in Chapter 21.

FIND IT ONLINE

This site tells how to open a Binary file: http://msdn.microsoft.com/library/devprods/vs6/vbasic/vbcon98/vbconusingbinaryfileaccess.htm.

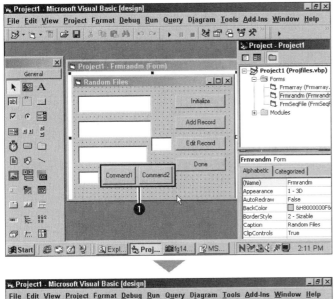

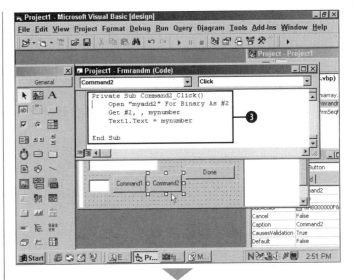

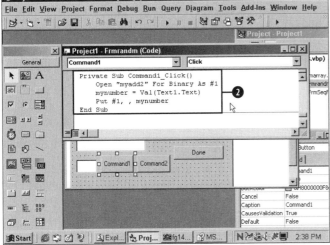

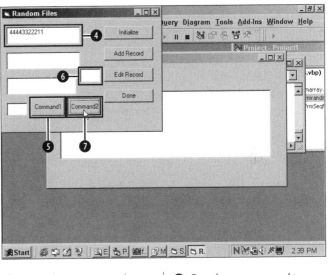

① *Place two Command button controls on the Random Files form.*

② *Enter the code shown for the* Command1 *procedure.*

③ *Enter the statements shown for the* Command2 *procedure.*

④ *Run the program and type some numbers in the* Text1.Text *box.*

⑤ *Click the* Command1 *button.*

⑥ *Select the numbers in the text box and delete them.*

⑦ *Click the* Command2 *button.*

305

Printing from Files

In Chapter 9 you used the `CommonDialog` control to display a Print Dialog box for printing from the `RichTextBox`. You used the `ShowPrinter` method to display the Print Dialog box. With the `SelPrint` method, you used the `hDC` property of the `CommonDialog` control to carry out the printing function from the default printer.

This method worked quite well to display the dialog box allowing the selection of a printer. These methods work only with the `RichTextBox` and not with the text in the `TextBox`. To print from the text boxes containing your information from the `myadd Random Access` file, you need to use another approach.

As with the Forms and other object collections, the *Printers collection* is an object that contains all the printers installed on the system. You can see all the printers installed on your system by checking the Settings, Printers options on the `Windows Start Menu`. Also, they are the available from the `Windows Control Panel`. Each printer in the collection has a unique index for identification. Starting with 0, each printer in the collection can be referenced by its number. When you used the `CommonDialog` control to print previously, you referenced the default printer by using the hexadecimal code `hDC`. You can create an array of available printers and allow the selection of any in the collection.

The simplest way to get data in the `myadd` file printed is to use the `Printer` object. The Printer object has a number of properties you can select. The properties of the Printer object initially match those of the default printer set in the `Windows Control Panel`. At run time, you can set any of these properties, which include: `PaperSize, Height, Width, Orientation, ColorMode, Duplex, TrackDefault, Zoom, DriverName, DeviceName, Port, Copies, PaperBin,` and `PrintQuality`.

Place a command button named `Cmdprint` with the caption **Print** on the bottom of the form. Create a `Cmdprint` procedure for the Print button. In this project, you have several text boxes that contain information you want to print, so you use the Printer object's Print property, along with the text box objects' text properties.

`Printer.Print Text1.Text`

Make statements for each text box for which you want to print the contents. To print the `myadd` Random Access file, execute the program, `Initialize` the file, enter a record number, and click the `Edit Record` button. Print by clicking the `Print` button. What could be simpler? If you have problems getting the job to print, this is because you need to add a command — `EndDoc` — to advance the page and send all pending output to the spooler. If you click the `Done` button, the output will be sent to the printer anyway because Visual Basic calls `EndDoc` if you end the program without calling it.

You can also set many other properties. You might try typing the word **Printer**, followed by a period to bring up the context menu of properties you can set. You also can view properties in the `Object Browser`. For a little fun, try changing the `FontSize` property.

TAKE NOTE

▶ KILLING A PRINT JOB

The `KillDoc` Method is used to stop the current print job. You could set up an error-trapping routine and give the user a chance to cancel the print job if a problem occurs. If the system's Print Manager is in effect, `KillDoc` deletes the entire job. If the Print Manager is not set up, part of the job may already have reached the printer. `KillDoc` can stop only the portion of a job that has not yet been sent to the printer. Printer drivers affect the amount of data sent to the printer.

CROSS-REFERENCE

Chapter 16 discusses printing graphics.

FIND IT ONLINE

A summary of Printer properties is included at: http://msdn.microsoft.com/library/partbook/egvb6/html/printingtext.htm.

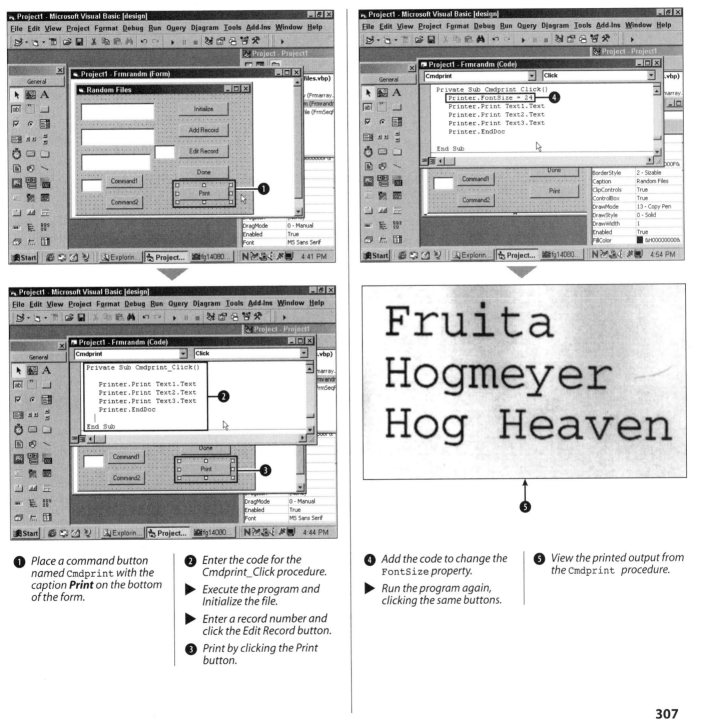

① Place a command button named Cmdprint with the caption **Print** on the bottom of the form.

② Enter the code for the Cmdprint_Click procedure.

► Execute the program and Initialize the file.

► Enter a record number and click the Edit Record button.

③ Print by clicking the Print button.

④ Add the code to change the FontSize property.

► Run the program again, clicking the same buttons.

⑤ View the printed output from the Cmdprint procedure.

Personal Workbook

Q&A

1 What type of file has a specified record length?

_____

_____

_____

2 What file stores all data as text?

_____

_____

_____

3 What statement is used by all file types?

_____

_____

_____

4 What file commands are used by Binary and Random Access, but not Sequential files?

_____

_____

_____

5 How do you declare a record type variable?

_____

_____

_____

6 Besides the record length, what other object may have a specified length?

_____

_____

_____

7 What do you need to retrieve a record from a Random Access file?

_____

_____

_____

8 What object is easiest to use to print data you stored in a data file?

_____

_____

_____

ANSWERS: PAGE 526

EXTRA PRACTICE

1. Add error-trapping routines to the `Cmdprint` procedure. Use `On Error`.

2. Use the Immediate Window to determine the values of the variable `mynumber` used to accept input and display values in the text box.

3. Create a form with at least four text boxes to collect input for a Random Access file. Add several records to the file. Write a routine to Read all the records in order, displaying each record in turn.

4. Design a project using Random Access files for a mailing list. Collect name, address, and telephone number data. Write the code to print each record. How would you print a report summarizing the records?

REAL WORLD APPLICATIONS

✔ Your client, Zachary, wants you to write a program for him to store personnel data in files not accessible by currently popular database management programs. What would you advise him to use?

✔ Your are being consulted by an experimental laboratory that has a need for storing millions of records of purely numeric data, captured from a signal device attached to a serial port. Develop a proposal to present to the company.

✔ Design a word processor using text box controls. Devise ways to write, read, and print the data without using the `CommonDialog` control.

Visual Quiz

What is the number that should be displayed in the Immediate Window, based upon what you see in the executing program?

_____

_____

_____

_____

_____

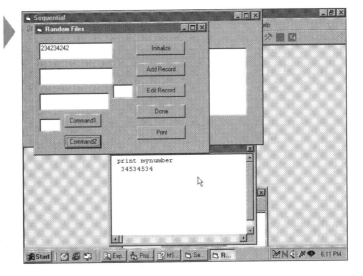

PART

IV

Contents of 'Desktop'

Name

My Computer

Network Neigh

Internet Explore

Microsoft Outloo

Recycle Bin

My Briefcase

3252-9

3259-6

3261-8

3262-6

3281-2

3286-3

OE Phone List

Device Manager

In

Iomega Tools

Using Graphics and Multimedia Features

This Part centers on increasing skills in graphic methods and use of images, as well using the Visual Basic multimedia features.

The focus in the previous Part was on developing more advanced working skills with programming techniques. You have now acquired skills in data file and database access, debugging, and error trapping. You can combine what you have learned to advance yourself further in the areas touched on in the beginning chapters.

This Part gives you the opportunity to become acquainted with the hot new features used on the Internet and in today's media. New topics that are discussed in this Part include using animation, playing music and other sound files, drawing, and using images in applications.

We have explored the graphic controls, but did not probe as deeply into their uses as we do in this section. You will learn about the Multimedia control that allows you to manage Media Control Interface (MCI) devices. You will also learn to create shapes, use drawing tools, paint, use images on forms, resize images, and change images. In addition, you will become familiar with the wonders of OLE, learning about the fantastic features that allow you to interface with other applications.

In short, besides learning a lot, I expect you to have fun with this Part! Multimedia and graphics are the cool areas of Visual Basic.

CHAPTER **15**

Developing Multimedia Applications

One of the factors responsible for influencing multimedia development is the Internet. Because the Internet has become so important recently, the shift is toward the audio and visual side of computer applications. The combination of the Graphic User Interface (GUI) and the popularity of the Internet has resulted in the World Wide Web, with all its accouterments. Almost no one can help being excited by the prospects for the future of online communication. Sound, graphics, and animation are constants that are in demand in the ever-changing Internet environment.

Specifically, multimedia refers to sound, graphics, and animation. You can use several controls to produce these features, but the control you will work with most is the Multimedia Control that manages Media Control Interface (MCI) devices.

Almost any applications you develop can benefit from sound and graphics. You can use icons to indicate selection options and pictures as labels. A typical use of animation is to display progress. For example, when you copy files, you see the pages moving from the source to the destination. Also, trash flies from the computer to the trash bin and disk drives open and close. Most of these examples of animation are done by playing Audio Video Interleaved (AVI) files.

In this chapter, you learn to use media, such as the Media Control Interface (MCI). The MCI is the source of much of the multimedia access in Visual Basic.

In addition to the host of multimedia features provided by the `MCI` control, animation tools are available. The animation control plays `AVI` animation files without sound. If you wish to play movies with sound, you can use the `MCI` multimedia control. Much of the interest in animation today centers around the Internet.

`DirectAnimation` is one type of `Multimedia` controls and scripting methods used to animate Web sites and provide integration with Dynamic HTML (DHTML). `DirectAnimation` has complete support for media types, such as 2D vector graphics, images and sprites, 3-D geometry, video, and sound.

The `DirectAnimation` controls provide access to many of the DirectAnimation scripting functions. The controls enable you to present exciting vector graphics, image, and animation over the Internet with a modest amount of code and minimal download times.

For this chapter, you will find samples of sound and video files at the Hitek Designs Web site. The URL is: `www.hi-tekmall.com`.

A link is on the Home page to the program and sample files, which you can save and use.

Learning about the Multimedia Control

The MCI control manages the recording and playback of multimedia files on MCI devices. The control looks like a set of VCR controls containing a set of buttons that supplies MCI commands to devices such as sound cards, MIDI sequencers, CD-ROM drives, audio CD players, videodisc players, and videotape recorders and players. The `MCI` control also supports the playback of `Video for Windows` using `AVI` files.

The Multimedia control uses a set of sophisticated commands, known as *MCI commands,* which control a range of multimedia devices. Many of these commands correspond directly to a button on the Multimedia control. The Play command carries out the same instructions as the Play button on the VCR panel.

Before beginning the exercises in this chapter, you need to load the following `Component` controls from the Project Menu: the `CommonDialog` control, the `DirectAnimation Media` controls, the `Multimedia control 6.0`, `Microsoft Windows Common Controls (6.0 and 2 6.0)`. You can use the `Multimedia` control either by using the control directly on the form or from code. If you choose to use the control's buttons, the user can click the button of choice to play, stop, go back, go forward, and so forth. If you want to use the MCI functions, but you don't want the control to be visible, set the `Visible` and `Enabled` properties to `False.`

The `Multimedia` control has all the functionality to support the devices previously listed, but a limit of one device per control exists. That's right, if you want to play a CD and a WAV file from one form, using menu options or buttons, you must place two MCI controls on the form.

For this chapter, create a new project named **ProjMedia** and save it in a new folder. Name the form **FrmMedia** with the caption, **MultiMedia Form**.

As you can see, you can do a lot of things with the `Multimedia` control. To start, you can play a sound CD from your system's CD-ROM drive. Place a `Multimedia` Control (`MMControl`) on the `MultiMedia` Form. Next, use the Menu Editor to create a menu called **Device Types** named, **mnudevice.** Add the menu option CD Audio, named **mnucd** under the `Device Types` menu.

Double-click the form to enter the code window, select `Form` as the object, and `Load` as the Procedure. Enter the property values for `Notify, Wait,` and `Sharable` necessary to open the operation. This initializes the control when the form is loaded.

```
MMControl1.Notify = False
MMControl1.Wait = True
MMControl1.Shareable = False
```

When the Notify property is set to True, it generates a Done event after the next command is concluded. The Done event furnishes a response, indicating the outcome of the command. The Wait property decides if the Multimedia control will wait for the next command to finish before giving control back to the program (True = will wait, False = will not wait. The `Shareable` property determines the restriction status of media devices by other procedures or programs (True = Shareable, False = Not Shareable). The `DeviceType` property is used to specify the type of MCI device (CDAudio, Sequencer, and so forth).

CROSS-REFERENCE

Refer to the multimedia information in Chapter 22.

FIND IT ONLINE

This site is the home for Windows media technologies. **http://www. microsoft.com/windows/windowsmedia/default.asp.**

TAKE NOTE

▶ ### MULTIMEDIA CONTROL FEATURES

The Multimedia control is, in essence, a Visual Basic interface to a collection of MCI commands. The Multimedia control consists of buttons that issue MCI commands

These commands are available with the Command property: `Play`, `Open`, `Close`, `Pause`, `Stop`, `Back`, `Step`, `Prev`, `Next`, `Seek`, `Record`, `Eject`, `Sound`, and `Save`. The `Command` property enables you to give commands to the device via the `Cmdstring$` argument and the command is executed immediately.

Table 15-1: THE MCI COMMANDS

Command Property	Function
Back	Moves backward through existing tracks.
Close	Closes an MCI device.
Eject	Ejects an Audio CD from the drive.
Next	Goes to the beginning of the next track. Uses the Seek command.
Open MCI	Opens an MCI device.
Pause	Pauses playing or recording. When already paused, it resumes playing.
Play	Plays an MCI device.
Prev	Uses the Seek command to go to the beginning of the current track. Goes to the beginning of the previous track or to the beginning of the first track, if at the first track.
Record	Records MCI device input.
Save	Saves an open file.
Seek	Seeks track forward or backward.
Step	Steps forward through available tracks.
Stop	Stops an MCI device.

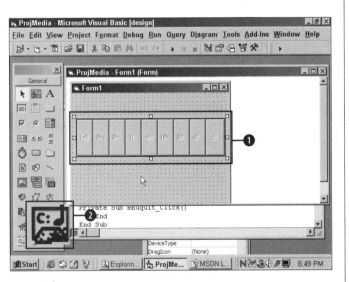

① *Place a Multimedia control on the form in your new project, ProjMedia.*

② *Note the icon representing the MCI control.*

Playing a CD with the Multimedia Control

Double-click the CD Audio option on the Device Types menu to enter the code window. In the `mnucd_Click` procedure, set the `MMControl1` property, `DeviceType` as "CDAudio." Then set the `Command` property to "Open."

In addition to opening the device and playing your CD, you must also think about closing it. Making provisions for closing open devices before exiting an application to release system resources is important.

```
MMControl1.Command = "Close"
```

Place this statement in the `Form Unload` procedure, selecting `Form` as the object and `Unload` as the procedure. This will take care of closing the control when the form is unloaded.

You can now test the program by running it and selecting CD Audio from the Device Types menu. Be sure to place a sound CD in your CD-ROM drive first. When that is completed, you can add some features to your multimedia application.

When you add a new device type to your Multimedia application, you must also add a new `Multimedia` Control. Again, you needn't display each control, but you must have it present on the form. You can make the control invisible by setting the `Visible` property to False. Of course, you may wish the control to stay visible so the user can interact with it. In this exercise, you are going to allow the control to remain visible.

Suppose you decide to add controls for playing several types of sound and animation files on the same form to be accessed from the same menu. This means a lot of code, doesn't it? For example, if you have four Multimedia controls on the `FrmMedia` form, you must write four blocks of the same code to initialize each control. Right? Wrong. You can create an array of the Multimedia controls. This way, you can address the duplicate processes in a `For-Next` loop. This not only makes the code better looking, it is also easier on you. This is better programming.

When you place the next Multimedia control on the form, give it the same name as the first, **MMControl1**. You will be prompted "You already have a control named MMControl1. Do you want to create a control array?" Because no two objects can have exactly the same name, the alternative is to create an array of different elements. This is what you want to do, so you click "Yes." Now, the second Multimedia control on the form will be `MMControl1(1)`, because the first one (CD Audio) is now `MMControl1(0)`.

You now need to change the code in the `mnucd_Click` procedure to reflect the control array variable's name, `MMControl1(0)`. You do not have to change the substance of the `DeviceType` and `Command` property statements. Just add the array element number to the name of the control.

CROSS-REFERENCE

You also can refer to the information in Chapter 9 to refresh your knowledge of the `CommonDialog` control.

FIND IT ONLINE

This is from VB Explorer:
http://www.vbexplorer.com/vbs_ms.asp#tip1.

▶ **OPENING THE MULTIMEDIA CONTROL**

When you open the Multimedia control at the time the form loads, the Multimedia control identifies what actions are applicable for the device's current state. Therefore, the proper buttons are enabled when supported MCI devices are opened.

Listing 15-1: The CD Audio Open Procedure

```
Private Sub Form_Load()
 MMControl1.Notify = False
   MMControl1.Wait = True
   MMControl1.Shareable = False
 End Sub
Private Sub mnucd_Click()
    MMControl1.DeviceType = "CDAudio"
    MMControl1.Command = "Open"
End Sub
Private Sub Form_Unload(Cancel As Integer)
       MMControl1.Command = "Close"
 End Sub
```

▶ *Create the CD Audio menu option in the Menu Editor.*
▶ *Enter the code for the* mnucd_Click *procedure.*

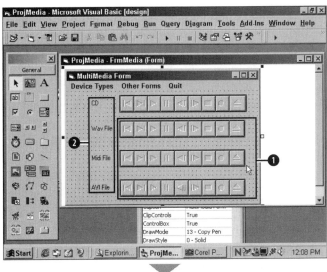

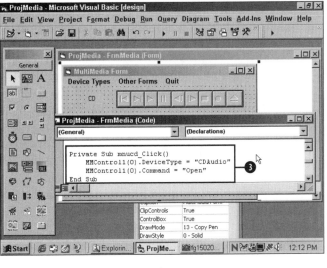

❶ *Place the additional* Multimedia *controls on the* FrmMedia *form.*

▶ *Add each* Multimedia *control to the* MMControl1 *control array.*

❷ *Place the* Label *controls shown on the form as well.*

❸ *Correct the code for the* mnucd_Click *procedure.*

Playing Sound Files with the Multimedia Control

Continue to develop of your project by expanding the Device Types menu options in the Menu Editor. Add options for playing `Wave audio` (digitized Waveform files) and the Sequencer, Musical Instrument Digital Interface (MIDI) sequencer files. The file extensions for these files are `.Wav` and `.Mid`, respectively.

Name the `Waveform` File option, `mnuwav` and the `Midi` file option, `mnumidi`. Add a fourth option for the Video you will play in the next exercise. Name the Video menu option `mnuvideo`. Give these options appropriate captions. Remember to indent your options one level under the Device Types menu by clicking the right arrow above the menu options window.

The next task is to modify the code for the `Form_Load` and `Form_Unload` procedures to account for the MMControl1 array variables. The neatest way to do this is to set up a `For-Next` loop for each procedure.

```
For X = 0 To 3
   MMControl1(X).Notify = False
   MMControl1(X).Wait = True
   MMControl1(X).Shareable = False
  Next X
End Sub
```

This way, you take care of each control's `Notify`, `Wait`, and `Shareable` properties at once. You can follow the same tactic for the `Form_Unload` procedure you use to `Close` the media devices.

When you refer to a `Multimedia` control's `DeviceType` property, you use a string to identify it. For example, you used the string, "CDAudio " to refer to the CD-ROM device in the `mnucd` procedure. To play the Wave audio files, you use the string, "WaveAudio," and to play the MIDI files, you use "Sequencer" as the string, following the `DeviceType` property.

```
MMControl1(1).DeviceType = "WaveAudio"
```

The control array variable here is element one because it is the second control in the array. The following statement tells the system where to find your Waveform file.

```
MMControl1(1).FileName = "C:\Windows\media\ _
tada.wav"
```

The `Windows\Media` directory typically contains an assortment of `Waveform` and `MIDI` files. You are free to use whichever you want. Take your choice, but make sure you have stated the path correctly. Finally, you need to add the Open statement for the `Command` property.

```
MMControl1(1).Command = "Open"
```

The `mnumidi` procedure is quite similar. You simply substitute "Sequencer" for "WaveAudio" as the `DeviceType` string.

```
MMControl1(2).DeviceType = "Sequencer"
```

And of course, you adjust the path statement to reflect the location of the MIDI file. Remember, these files have the `.Mid` extension. The example uses `Canyon.Mid` because that is usually placed in the Windows\Media directory during the installation of `Windows`.

```
MMControl1(2) .FileName = "C:\Windows\media\ _
canyon.mid"
```

Once again add the `Open` statement to the `Command` property as the last line in the procedure.

CROSS-REFERENCE

Chapter 14 helps to manage files.

FIND IT ONLINE

Carl and Gary's link to games uses a lot of multimedia stuff: http://www.cgvb.com/links/lpage.boa/GAMES.

Table 15-2: STRINGS USED TO IDENTIFY DEVICE TYPE

Device type	String used	File Extention
CD Audio	CDAudio	
Digital Audio Tape	DAT	
Digital video in a window	DigitalVideo	
Other MCI device	Other	
Overlay device	Overlay	
Image Scanner	Scanner	
Musical Instrument Digital Interface (MIDI) sequencer	Sequencer	.mid
Video cassette recorder or player	VCR	
Audio Visual Interleaved video	AVIVideo	.avi
Videodisc	Videodisc	
Digitized waveform files	Waveaudio	.wav

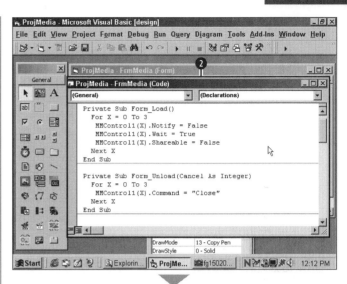

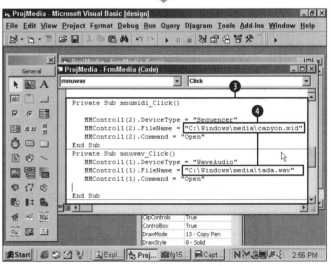

❷ Write the code for the Form_Load and Form_Unload procedures.

❸ Enter the code for the mnumidi and the mnuwav Click procedures.

❹ Check the file paths to be certain where the files exist on your system and modify accordingly.

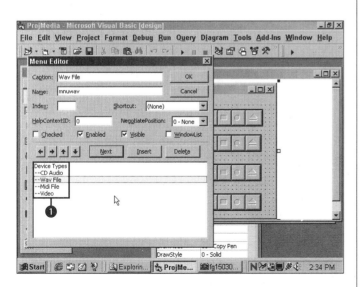

❶ Create the options for the Device Types menu.

Playing Animation Files on the Multimedia Control

When you finish experimenting with your sound files, you can turn your attention to the next topic, which is animation.

Animation is one of the coolest features you can use in an application. Of course, you don't want to overdo it. Too much animation can be distracting and even annoying. Some Web sites are positively littered with animated objects. The key is to make your animation tasteful, useful, and to the point.

The nice thing about using animation in Visual Basic applications is many ways exist to approach the same goal. What is animation? *Animation* means changing media over time or in reaction to user input. Media includes sound, two-dimensional (2D) images, and three-dimensional (3D) objects, along with their corresponding camera and lights, colors, textures, and other visual or audio properties.

You can begin your experience with animation by using the now familiar `Multimedia` control in much the same way you used it to play CDs and sound files. Because you already added the Video option to your `MultiMedia` Form Device Types menu, you have much of the job completed. Check the `MMControl1(3)` label to see that you have identified the file as `AVI`.

Double-click the `mnuvideo_Click` procedure to enter the code window. You can use the other menu procedure statements with modifications. Again, the Video option addresses the fourth variable (`MMControl1(3)` in the control array. You must change the device type string from that in any previous menu procedure to the correct one for the type of animated file you intend to use. In this exercise, you use a file called `AudioVisual Interleaved video` (`AVI`). This is also sometimes called the `Microsoft Video` file.

```
MMControl1(3).DeviceType = "AVIVideo"
```

This indicates you must have available a file with a .avi extension. Quite of few AVI files are in a Videos subdirectory in the default VB98 directory. The path is typically: `C:\VB98\Graphics\Videos`. You should be able to find plenty of the files there, but they are files that will look familiar to you as a Windows user, such as `FileCopy.avi, Search.avi,` and so forth. These are the animations you see when you copy files in Windows Explorer, search, or try to find a file. If you prefer, you can play files from the `www.hi-tekmall.com` Web site or from your favorite graphic file source.

The next lines are similar to the procedures to play sound files and CDs. You set the `FileName` property to match the location of the file you wish to play. The `Command` property is set to `Open.` That's it. You can go ahead and play the video. A dialog box will pop up to display it. Click the Play button on the control and then click the reverse button to replay the video.

TAKE NOTE

▶ THE HWND PROPERTY

The *hWnd property* is used with Windows API calls and it represents a handle (or placeholder) that all controls are assigned in Windows. It is often used as an argument to associate two controls and specifies the output window for MCI devices that use a window to display output.

CROSS-REFERENCE

Chapters 16 and 17 discuss graphics uses.

FIND IT ONLINE

This site explains how animation works:
http://www.catalystpics.co.uk/book.htm.

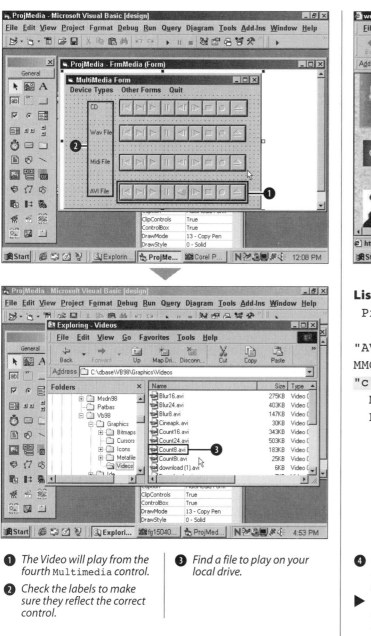

Listing 15-2: The Video Play (Menu) Procedure

```
Private Sub mnuvideo_Click()
        MMControl1(3).DeviceType =
"AVIVideo"
MMControl1(3).FileName =
"c:\art\3d\wsites.avi" ◄─⑤
    MMControl1(3).Command = "Open"
    End Sub
```

① The Video will play from the fourth Multimedia control.

② Check the labels to make sure they reflect the correct control.

③ Find a file to play on your local drive.

④ Copy a file from the Hitek Designs web site, if you prefer.

▶ You can obtain code for all chapters and topics at this site.

▶ Enter the code shown.

⑤ Modify the file name and path according to your system.

Adding Animation to Your Application

As discussed at the beginning of this chapter, many options exist for playing sounds and animation in Visual Basic. In addition, you still have not explored some features in the `Multimedia` control. When you played your video, a dialog box displayed the animated file. A better way exists to display it. You can use a `PictureBox` to show the animated file. This has the advantage of enabling you to control where the display occurs, instead of being at the mercy of the dialog box.

You can make the change quite easily. Simply add a `PictureBox` control to your `FrmMedia` form, placing it to the right of the `Multimedia` controls. You may need to enlarge the form to make room for all the controls. To link the Multimedia control to the `PictureBox` control, you need to use the hWnd handle Windows assigns to all forms and controls. The `Multimedia` control's handle property (`hWndDisplay`) must be set to the value of the `PictureBox1` hWnd property.

```
MMControl1(3).hWndDisplay = Picture1.hWnd
```

The references to the handle associates the `Multimedia` control and the `PictureBox` control, so the animated clip is played in the `PictureBox` area instead of a dialog box.

This is exactly what animation is in reality: the appearance of animation. When you use software to create an `AVI` file or an animated `GIF` file, the software is simply making lots of pictures to display in succession.

Add a new form to your `ProjMedia` project. Name it **FrmAnim** with the caption **Animation Form**. Don't forget to add a menu on the `FrmMedia` form for "Other Forms." Also add an option under `Other Forms` captioned **Animation** and named **mnuanim.** You also need menus on your `Animation Form`. In the Menu Editor, make a `Return` and a `Quit` option, name `mnureturn` and `mnuquit,` respectively. Write the code for these options, using `mnureturn_Click` and `mnuquit_Click` procedures to `Show` the previous form and to `End` the program. By now you are familiar with these menu procedures.

You can make your own graphics in a photo editor for this exercise or copy them from the `www.hi-tekmall.com` Web site. The files you need from the Web site are Butterfly1.bmp and Butterfly2.bmp. If you make your own graphics, you may find you need to toggle more than two. You also can use icons (found in the VB98\graphics\icons directory) that are slightly different, toggling them back and forth to create the illusion of movement.

Use two pictures for this exercise. Declare an array named `ButrPics As` type `Picture`. This array has only two elements, one for each picture you are toggling between.

```
Dim ButrPics(1) As Picture
```

Create a `Form_Load` procedure by double-clicking the form. Select the `Form` object and the `Load` procedure. Use the `Set` statement to assign an object reference to the array variables. The `LoadPicture` function specifies the filename and assigns the picture to the `Picture` property of the form.

TAKE NOTE

SIMPLE ANIMATION TECHNIQUES

In addition to playing animation files with the `Multimedia` control, you can include simple animation merely by rotating still pictures. You may remember having a deck of cards that produced simple animation when you were a child. Each card in the deck had a picture slightly different from the other. When you shuffled the cards, the picture seemed to move. You can employ this same technique by using several graphics that are displayed in succession, creating the appearance of animation. You also can use two graphics — toggling them back and forth — to simulate movement.

CROSS-REFERENCE

Refer to the use of the Timer control in Chapter 8.

FIND IT ONLINE

Here is an example of how to play a `.wav` file:
http://www.vbexplorer.com/tips/src22.htm.

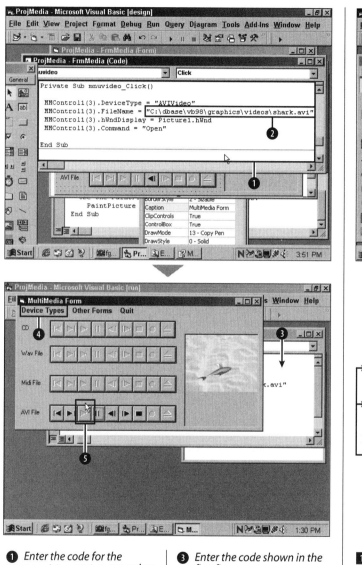

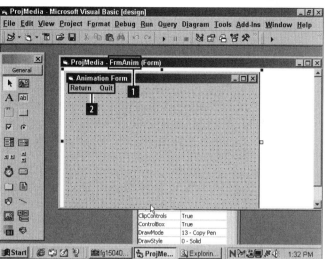

Listing 15-4: The `Form_Load` **procedure to Load the Bitmaps.**

```
Dim ButrPics(1) As Picture
Private Sub Form_Load()
Set ButrPics(0) = LoadPicture
("c:\vb98\graphics\bitmaps\Butterfly1.bmp")
Set ButrPics(1) = LoadPicture
("c:\vb98\graphics\bitmaps\Butterfly2.bmp")
End Sub
```

❶ *Enter the code for the* `mnuvideo_Click` *procedure.*

❷ *Modify the path to fit your system's path for the* `AVI` *file you intend to use.*

❸ *Enter the code shown in the first figure.*

❹ *Run the program and select Video from the Device Types menu.*

❺ *Click the Play button on the AVI file control.*

1 *Add an* `Animation Form` *named* `FrmAnim` *to the* `FrmMedia` *project.*

2 *Use the Menu Editor to add* `Return` *and* `Quit` *options, named* `mnureturn` *and* `mnuquit`.

3 *Use the* `Set` *statement to assign an object reference to the array variables.*

4 *Use the* `LoadPicture` *function to specify the filename and assign the picture to the* `Picture` *property of the form.*

Using the Timer Control in Animation

So far, you have added the code to load the butterfly pictures, but if you try to run the program and select the animation option from the menu, nothing happens. The form stays blank. This is because you load the pictures when the form is loaded, but you made no provision for showing them. You need to have the `Timer` control manage the picture display. The pictures must be toggled back and forth with perfect timing, so they look like one butterfly flapping its wings and flying. One picture has wings up and the other has wings pulled back.

Place a `Timer` control on the `Animation` Form. Set the `Enabled` property to True and the `Interval` property to 100. You can experiment with the interval because that controls the speed of the butterfly's wings flapping.

Double-click to add a `Timer` procedure. In the code window, create a static variable, `intCount` As Integer) to retain the variable's value until the form is closed.

```
Static intCount As Integer
```

Use a conditional command block to continue switching between the two pictures.

```
If intCount = 0 Then
    intCount = 1
Else
    intCount = 0
End If
```

If the integer variable counter equals zero, then it is switched to one. If the integer variable counter doesn't equal zero, then the statement sets it to zero. The zero represents one butterfly picture and the one represents the other butterfly picture. This way, whatever value the counter has, the conditional statements change it. The counter is associated with the elements in the `butrPics` array by using the `intCount` variable to represent the array element.

```
PaintPicture ButrPics(intCount), 0, 0
```

Use the `PaintPicture` method to display the two bitmaps in the `ButrPics` array. The `PaintPicture` method draws the contents of a graphic file (bmp, .wmf, .emf, .cur, .ico, or .dib) on a `Form` or a `PictureBox` control. Because you are using the `Form_Load` procedure, the picture is displayed on the form. If you had placed one on the form, you could also display it in a `PictureBox` control.

The zeros following the comma are the coordinates `x1` and `y1` given to display the picture. You can manipulate these values and move the picture to a different location on the form.

When you run the program, the butterfly animation will begin as soon as the form is loaded. Now that you have the `Timer` control set up to control the timing of the animation, you may want to arrange to stop it. Place a Command button approximately in the middle of the form. Give it the caption "Stop Butterfly." Double-click the button, and then select the `Command1` object and the `Click` procedure to disable the `Timer` control.

```
Timer1.Enabled = False
```

Setting the `Timer`'s `Enabled` property to `False` will stop the animation. The next topic will examine the `Animation` control as it is used for a similar purpose.

TAKE NOTE

THE TIMER'S ENABLED PROPERTY

The `Enabled` property of the `Timer` control allows it to be enabled or disabled at run time. This means you can disable the `Timer` event if it doesn't apply to what's going on in the application. You can disable an animation or sound by setting the Timer Enable property to `False`. Setting the `Timer` control by setting `Enabled` to `False` cancels the countdown set up by the control's Interval property.

CROSS-REFERENCE

Refer to Chapter 8 for Timer control applications.

FIND IT ONLINE

This is about Multimedia Timers: http://msdn.microsoft.com/library/sdkdoc/multimed/mmtime_5h83.htm.

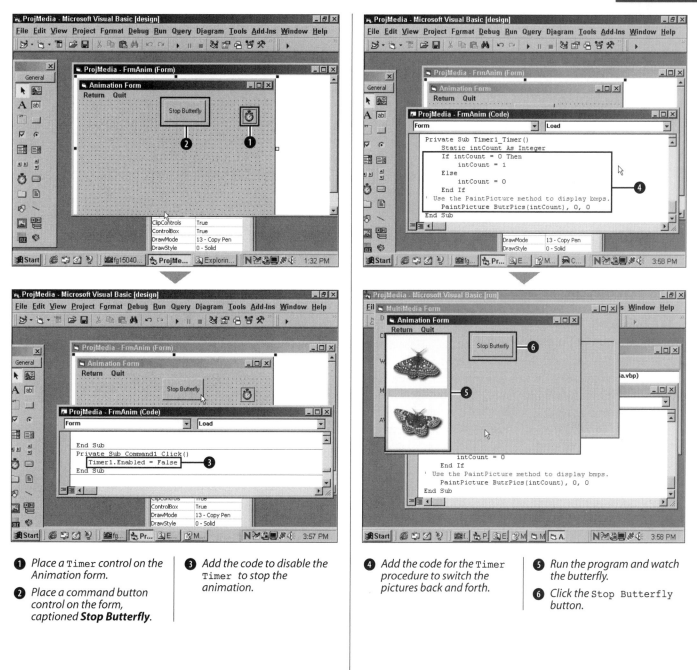

① Place a Timer control on the Animation form.

② Place a command button control on the form, captioned **Stop Butterfly**.

③ Add the code to disable the Timer to stop the animation.

④ Add the code for the Timer procedure to switch the pictures back and forth.

⑤ Run the program and watch the butterfly.

⑥ Click the Stop Butterfly button.

Using the Animation Control

The `Animation` control is an alternative to the `Multimedia` control. It cannot play sound video clips. The control also is particular about the specific AVI files it will play. The `Animation` control often will not load compressed files. If sound is on the clip or if it doesn't recognize the `AVI` format, an error 35752 will be generated.

To begin, add a `CommonDialog` control to the `Animation Form`. Name it `CdlgA`. This control will be used to enable user selection of a path and file, so you configure the `CommonDialog` control to enable the user to find files with the `.avi` extension.

Add the `Animation` control to the `Animation Form`. The icon in the `ToolBox` looks like a tiny filmstrip. If it doesn't appear in the `ToolBox`, check to make sure you loaded the Component controls for `Microsoft Common Controls-2 6.0`, which are found in the `MSCOMCT2.OCX` file. The `Animation` control will resize itself smaller, if necessary, so don't worry about sizing it to fit your file. Do place the `Animation` control away from the area where you are displaying the butterfly. You can use the default name for the control as Animation1.

Place two command button controls on the `Animation Form`, positioning them both above the `Animation` control. Name one command button **CmdPlay** and the other **CmdStop**. Their captions can be **Play AVI File and Stop Playing**, respectively.

The animation is going to be controlled from these buttons, rather than playing immediately when the form is loaded, as with the butterfly animation. Double-click the CmdPlay button to get into the code window. Select the Click procedure from the list. Refer to the `CommonDialog` control to filter the file list for `.avi` files.

```
CdlgA.Filter = "avi files (*.avi)|*.avi"
```

Use the `ShowOpen` method to display the `CommonDialog`'s Open dialog box.

```
CdlgA.ShowOpen
Animation1.Open CdlgA.FileName
```

The `Play` method of the `Animation` control has the arguments, `repeat`, `start`, and `stop`. These arguments determine how many times a file is played, the frame at which to begin playing, and where to stop.

```
Animation1.Play
```

If the `Repeat` argument is not used, the file will continue to play until the user ends the program or makes some provision to stop playing. Enter the code window by double-clicking the Stop Playing button. Select the `CmdStop` object and the `Click` procedure. Use the `Stop` argument to control the animation.

```
Animation1.Stop
```

You also can use the `Play` method's arguments to play specific frames a specific number of times.

```
Animation1.Play 5, 1, 20
```

Changing the `Play` method to that previously shown will result in the animation frames 1 through 20 being repeated five times.

TAKE NOTE

THE BACKSTYLE PROPERTY

You can use the `BackStyle` property to display the background color of the `Animation` control. The BackStyle property has the options "opaque" and "transparent." The animation graphic can be displayed on either type of background. This works by setting a value for the `BackStyle` property that establishes whether the `Animation` control draws the Animation on a transparent background or on the background color specified in the animation clip.

CROSS-REFERENCE

Common features are in Chapter 16.

FIND IT ONLINE

Vbnet tells how to select multiple files with the common dialog:
http://www.mvps.org/vbnet/faq/cdlgmultiselect.htm.

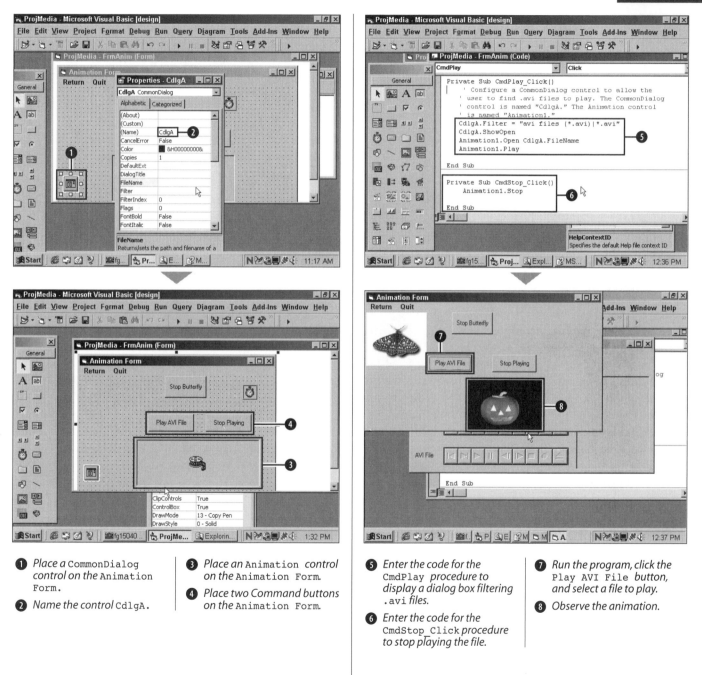

① *Place a* CommonDialog *control on the* Animation Form.

② *Name the control* CdlgA.

③ *Place an* Animation *control on the* Animation Form.

④ *Place two Command buttons on the* Animation Form.

⑤ *Enter the code for the* CmdPlay *procedure to display a dialog box filtering* .avi *files.*

⑥ *Enter the code for the* CmdStop_Click *procedure to stop playing the file.*

⑦ *Run the program, click the* Play AVI File *button, and select a file to play.*

⑧ *Observe the animation.*

Using the Windows Media Player Control

The Windows `MediaPlayer` control may be the best kept multimedia secret in Visual Basic. The `MediaPlayer` control can be selected from Component Controls on the Project menu. The file that must be present in the Windows\system directory on your system is MXDSM.OCX. This control does everything the Multimedia control does and usually does it better. You can play all the sound files and some animation files that are problematic on the `Multimedia` control.

Other cool features of the `MediaPlayer` are its capability of being embedded on HTML pages for Internet use and its use as an OLE object. One of the reasons not much information is available about the `MediaPlayer` is it is not typically discussed in the Visual Basic documentation and it is not included in many publications.

The `MediaPlayer` control is an `ActiveX` control and furnishes multimedia playback resources to Visual Basic applications, as well as Web pages and OLE applications. It offers a programming interface for various network multimedia formats. The `MediaPlayer` control incorporates many of the features of the `ActiveMovie` control and other controls, such as `NetShow`. The *Windows Software Development Kit (SDK)*, a tool for Windows developers, furnishes the documentation for this exciting control.

You can try this control for yourself and compare it with those you have already used. Place the `MediaPlayer` control on the `Animation Form`. You will undoubtedly need to move your other controls around a bit and enlarge the form. Allow plenty of space for the `MediaPlayer`. Place two command buttons above the `MediaPlayer` control. Name one button `CmdMedia` with the caption **Media Player WAV**. Name the other button `CmdMedia2` with a label **Media Player MPG**. You will need to locate some `Mpeg` (`.mpg`) files to play. You can find sample files to play in various formats at the Web site: `www.hi-tekmall.com`.

In the code window, select the `CmdMedia` object and the Click procedure to enter the code for the `MediaPlayer MPG` button. Borrow the code you used for the `Play AVI File` button and modify it to reflect the `MediaPlayer1` object.

```
MediaPlayer1.Open CdlgA.FileName
MediaPlayer1.Play
```

You want to play Waveform files, so change the file type for the `CommonDialog` filter.

```
CdlgA.Filter = "wav files (*.wav)|*.wav"
```

In addition, you must add the `On Error Resume Next` statement, otherwise the program will terminate with the well-known `End-Debug` message.

Create the procedure for the `Media Player MPG` button. Modify the code you previously used to accommodate the differences in the filter needed for the file extension. The `MediaPlayer` and `CommonDialog` controls are the same. Again, be sure you know where the `Mpeg` files are located before running the program.

TAKE NOTE

▶ THE MEDIAPLAYER CONTROL

The `MediaPlayer` control is based on Microsoft DirectShow(tm) technology. *DirectShow* is a Component Object Model (COM) established architecture that uses plug in components called *filters* to process multimedia data. The filters are set up to accept digital input, manage the data, and pass the results on to the next filter.

CROSS-REFERENCE

Chapter 22 also uses `Multimedia` controls.

FIND IT ONLINE

Here is information on the `MediaPlayer`: **http://msdn. microsoft.com/downloads/samples/Internet/imedia/netshow/s media/NS3/player/demo.htm**.

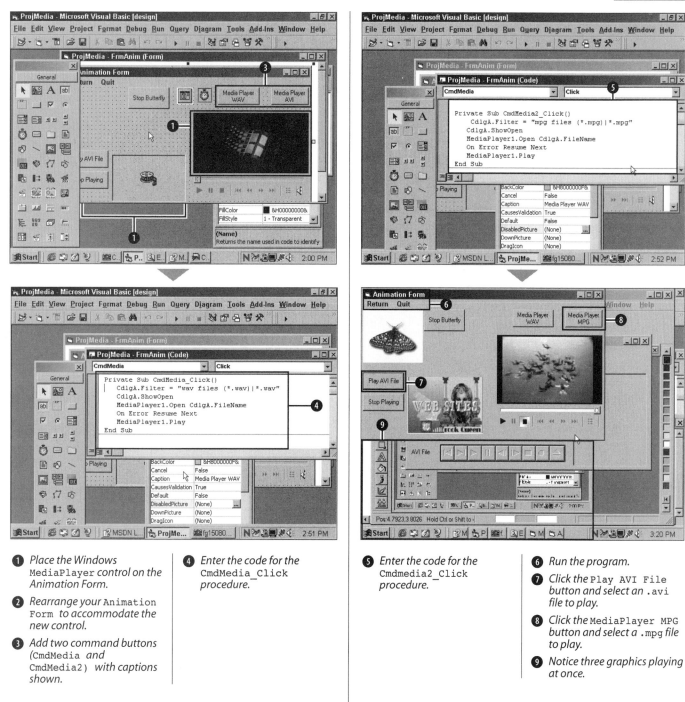

① Place the Windows
MediaPlayer *control on the*
Animation Form.

② Rearrange your Animation
Form *to accommodate the*
new control.

③ Add two command buttons
(CmdMedia *and*
CmdMedia2) *with captions*
shown.

④ Enter the code for the
CmdMedia_Click
procedure.

⑤ Enter the code for the
Cmdmedia2_Click
procedure.

⑥ Run the program.

⑦ Click the Play AVI File
button and select an .avi
file to play.

⑧ Click the MediaPlayer MPG
button and select a .mpg *file*
to play.

⑨ Notice three graphics playing
at once.

Personal Workbook

Q&A

1 What `Multimedia` control property values must be set to initialize the control?

_____

_____

_____

2 How many multimedia devices can you play per `Multimedia` control?

_____

_____

_____

3 Name two animation file types?

_____

_____

_____

4 Name two different controls you can use to display animation?

_____

_____

_____

5 How can you play animation without using a control?

_____

_____

_____

6 How do you get the `Animation` and `Multimedia` controls in the ToolBox?

_____

_____

_____

7 What does the `Multimedia` control do that the `Animation` control can't do?

_____

_____

_____

8 Name some features of the Windows `MediaPlayer` control?

_____

_____

_____

ANSWERS: PAGE 527

Developing Multimedia Applications

EXTRA PRACTICE

1 Add error-trapping routines to the `mnuwav`, `mnumidi`, and `mnucd` procedures.

2 Add sound to the `Frmscreen` form in the `Projcontrol` project from Chapter 10. Set it up to synchronize with the slide show.

3 Create a new form in the `ProjMedia` project. Experiment with the `Multimedia` controls in your `ToolBox`. Can you use some of the same commands with different controls?

4 Can you play different animation files with the `Animation` control? Try playing `.MOV` (Quicktime for Windows). Try the same with the `Multimedia` control.

5 Plan a project to combine sound and graphics files in a children's game.

REAL WORLD APPLICATIONS

✔ Your company is implementing a new employee training program. It is dispensing with the old orientation videos. You are asked to help design a new Visual Basic application incorporating music and film files to be shown on the company's intranet. Design the application.

✔ Your favorite game developer is holding a contest to see who can design the most innovative multimedia role-playing game. You are intrigued by the prospect. You only have to set up a 20-second segment to enter. Go for it.

✔ Your aunt has a Web site to advertise her editing and publishing company. She could use your assistance in developing some cool sound and graphics.

Visual Quiz

Which of these controls shown on the Animation Form at design time are not visible at run time?

_____

_____

_____

_____

_____

_____

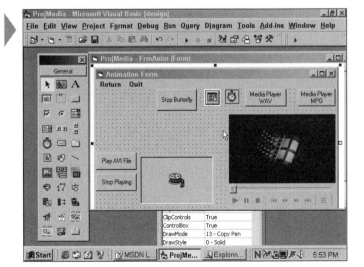

CHAPTER **16**

Working with Graphics Methods and Controls

Graphics methods and controls are the keystone of the World Wide Web. This is similar to the statements made in the last chapter on Multimedia applications, but the Internet is far from the only use of graphics in applications. The old look of text with keyboard character graphics is now one from the dark past. Thank goodness, no more smiling faces are created with punctuation keys! Virtually all applications using a Graphic User Interface (GUI) are imbued with graphics and sound (where pertinent).

You already have some experience with graphics methods. Basically, a *Graphics method* is one that works on `Form`, `PictureBox`, or `Printer` objects. Or, as you saw in the last chapter, draws and paints at run time. The graphics methods are `Circle`, `Cls`, `Line`, `PaintPicture`, `Point`, `Print`, and `PSet`.

Now that you are primed to love graphics, accepting any limitations on what you can do is difficult. Graphic files do have a considerable amount of overhead, but you can watch for some things without having to forego the fun of using graphics. Following are some tips to help avoid a drain from graphics on system resources.

Use the image control to display bitmaps. The `Image` control uses fewer resources than the `PictureBox` control. You can usually have several times the `Image` controls as PictureBoxes using the same amount of memory.

Load bitmaps from files as needed and share pictures. You can store pictures in resource files and use the LoadResPicture function to load them at run time.

Use the PaintPicture method. You can load a picture once and use the PaintPicture method to display it over and over or only when needed.

Free the memory used by graphics. You can set the `Picture` property to `Nothing` to remove it from memory when not needed.

Use rle-format bitmaps or metafiles. Instead of using `.bmp` files, which are large, you can use compressed formats. CompuServe `GIF` and `JPG` files are both compressed and make smaller files to work with. `GIF` files do not use loss compression, so don't compromise quality, but `JPG` compression results in lower quality of images. In the case of the Internet, no advantage exists in displaying high-resolution files because the display is under 100 dots per inch. Extremely large pictures often have been scanned at 300 or more dots per inch.

Learning to Use Graphics Controls

One of the delights of using Graphics methods in Visual Basic applications is that you can do so many different things and perform so many different feats, the possibilities are almost infinite. Some of the methods are not as cool as others, but one application that is hard to beat is the manipulation of graphics' placement on a form. You could use this technique to make a background or just for the effect, as you do in the following exercise.

Create a new project for this chapter. Name the project ProjGraphic and the form FrmGraphic. Give the form a simple caption such as **Graphics**. Remember to save your project and form in a new or separate directory. Create a menu in the Menu Editor. Give the menu two items: Pictures (named mnupix) and Quit (named mnuquit). Make two options on the Pictures menu, Tile Pix (named mnutile) and Make Wallpaper (mnuwall).

The PaintPicture method enables you to paint pictures wherever you wish on a form, in a picture box, or to a printer. The syntax is

```
object.PaintPicture picture, x1, y1, width1,
height1, x2, y2, width2, height2, opcode
```

In this exercise, the object is the form and the place where the picture is rendered. The pic argument is a Picture object from the Picture property of the form. You can obtain some simple graphic files from the www.hi-tekmall.com Web site if you do not have appropriate files on your system or on CD. You can also purchase clip art and photos for a nominal cost at computer fairs, online, by mail order, and at retail stores.

The process will be familiar to you because the last chapter has a similar example. Declare your picture as a variable type Picture. In this exercise, our graphic is Flowa, name of the bitmap.

```
Dim flowa As Picture
```

Next, select the Form object and the Click procedure from the code window drop down lists. Use the Set statement to assign an object reference to the Flowa variable.

```
Set flowa = LoadPicture("c:\art\flowa2.jpg")
```

When you add graphics to the Form_Load event, you should set the AutoRedraw property of the Form to True. This is because you want the graphic drawn after the form is displayed. Forms are invisible during the loading process.

If you plan to add controls on your form, this allows the controls to be visible after you finish tiling your graphic. On the other hand, if you want any added controls to be invisible, then the AutoRedraw property should remain False. Remember these factors when you design your applications with graphics.

Double-click the Tile Pix menu option. In the code window, select the mnutile object and the Click procedure. You need two For-Next loops to engineer the tiling of the graphic over the entire form. To get the full effect of the tiling, make sure the graphic is either the Flowa.jpg from the hi-tekmall Web site or make your graphic about 50 pixels square.

TAKE NOTE

GRAPHICS METHODS CHARACTERISTICS

Graphics methods draw on forms or picture boxes, or send output to a printer. You show where you want the drawing to start by stating the name of a form or picture box control and then the method you are using. The default place to start drawing is the form. Every form or picture box has a set of requirements used by its system of coordinates and it has a set of properties.

CROSS-REFERENCE

References can be found in Chapter 5 and Chapter 15.

FIND IT ONLINE

You can find he basics of Graphics methods here:
http://msdn.microsoft.com/library/partbook/egvb6/html/
generatingsimplegraphics.htm.

Working with Graphics Methods and Controls

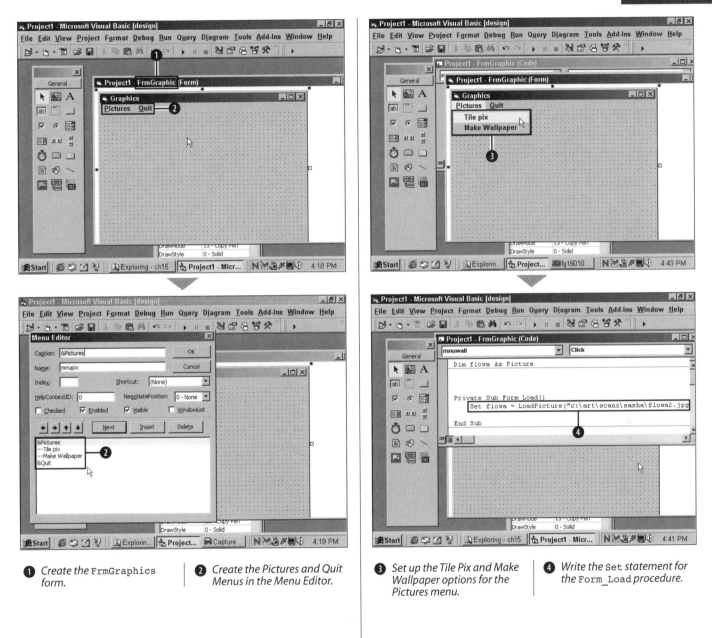

① Create the FrmGraphics form.

② Create the Pictures and Quit Menus in the Menu Editor.

③ Set up the Tile Pix and Make Wallpaper options for the Pictures menu.

④ Write the Set statement for the Form_Load procedure.

Using the PaintPicture Method

The PaintPicture method is an alternative to the Windows `BitBlt` function. The `BitBlt` function uses API calls to paint an image from a source object to a destination object. The Visual Basic PaintPicture method is a much easier way to create multiple copies of images. Also, no optional arguments exist in `BitBlt`.

In the PaintPicture method, the `destX, destY` values stand for the beginning position where the graphic is drawn. The `ScaleMode` property of the form (in this case) determines the unit of measure. The `Height1` and `Width1` are optional arguments and, if the single precision values are entered, they represent the destination height and width of the picture.

The `x2` and `y2` values also are optional and stand for the coordinates of a clipping region within a picture. The second `Height` and `Width` optional values indicate the sizes of the clipping region within a picture. The `Opcode` argument can only be used with bitmaps and determines the placement of bits in the bitmap as the object is drawn.

For this exercise, you omit the `x2y2, Width2, Height2` and `Opcode` arguments (because they are optional). Leave the `ScaleMode` property at `Twip` for the time being.

```
FrmGraphic.PaintPicture flowa, j * flowa.Width,
_    i * flowa.Height, flowa.Width, flowa.Height
```

In this code, the line is wrapped with a space followed by the underscore character. Here, the object `flowa` is the name of the bitmap used. The letters (*i* and *j*) are loop variables and should be declared as integers.

```
For i = 0 To 10
   For j = 0 To 10
      FrmGraphic.PaintPicture flowa, j *
flowa.Width, _
      i * flowa.Height, flowa.Width,
flowa.Height
   Next j, i
```

The parameter `j * flowa.Width` is the x position where the picture will be drawn, which increments on each pass through the *j* loop. The `i * flowa.Height` is the *y* position where the picture will be drawn and increments on each pass through the *i* loop. The last two parameters (`flowa.Width` and `flowa.Height`) determine the size of the picture, which stays the same throughout.

You can run the program, click the Tile Pix menu option and observe the tiling effect on the form. This same technique is also used on the Web to make a background or wallpaper for Web sites. You need to use a picture that has blended edges to make this effective. The example file `Clouds` works well to produce a sky effect to use as a backdrop for an application or Web page.

Identify a file that suits the purpose of a background or obtain one from the `hi-tekmall` Web site. Declare the new variable Clouds in the declarations area of the form. Use the Set statement to identify the path and file name of the picture in the `Form_Load` procedure.

TAKE NOTE

▶ USING DIFFERENT CONTAINERS

If you do not want to use the form as your picture container, you can use an `Image` control as the picture container instead of a `PictureBox`. This is because the picture container has lower overhead than a `PictureBox`. You can change the `Visible` property to False if you don't want to show the source. You can pass the Image control's `Picture` property to `PaintPicture` or to any of your procedures that take Picture parameters.

CROSS-SREFERENCE

References to this topic are found in Chapter 8.

FIND IT ONLINE

Here is information about clipping lines: **http://magic.hurrah.com/~sabre/graphpro/line6.html#Why.**

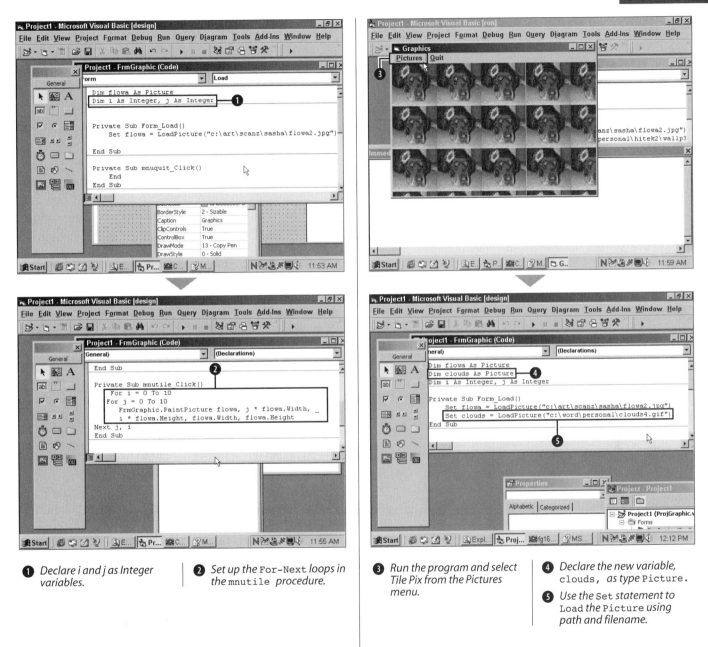

① *Declare i and j as Integer variables.*

② *Set up the For-Next loops in the* mnutile *procedure.*

③ *Run the program and select Tile Pix from the Pictures menu.*

④ *Declare the new variable,* clouds, *as type* Picture.

⑤ *Use the* Set *statement to* Load *the* Picture *using path and filename.*

Changing Parameters in the PaintPicture Method

Enter the code window mnuwall Click procedure by double-clicking the Make Wallpaper menu option and copying the code from the mnutile procedure. Modify the arguments to accommodate the new filename (clouds instead of flowa).

Run the program and click the Make Wallpaper option. If you used the clouds GIF file, you will see a blue sky with scattered clouds. If you used a graphic of your own making, do the edges blend in properly? If not, you should edit the picture or find another.

You can change the display of the flowa (or any other) picture in a number of ways. You can use some of the optional arguments or change the required ones. Changing the x1 and y1 required arguments results in the picture start coordinates being moved.

```
FrmGraphic.PaintPicture flowa, (j + 1) * _
flowa.Width,
        (i + 1) * flowa.Height, flowa.Width, _
flowa.Height
```

For example, changing both the x1 and y1 coordinates by adding (i + 1) to the parameter simply offsets the beginning x and y points of the tiling effect. Changing the x1 coordinate to (j + 1) results in painting one row of pictures in the middle of the form. A different kind of change you can make is to add the x2 and y2 optional arguments to change the clipping region within the picture.

```
FrmGraphic.PaintPicture flowa, j * _
flowa.Width, i * flowa.Height, _
flowa.Width,flowa.Height, 60 * j, 60 * i
```

The previous statement adds the x2 value of 60 times *j* and the y2 value of 60 times *i*. This results in stretching the picture as the pictures are painted across the form. Observing from the upper left-hand corner to the lower right-hand corner, you see the picture become larger. To really stretch the bits in the picture, remove the x2 and y2 values. Add the values shown in the following.

```
FrmGraphic.PaintPicture flowa,
j * flowa.Width, i * flowa.Height, _
 (j + 1) * flowa.Width, _
(i + 1) *  flowa.Height
  Next j, i
```

Run the program and select Tile Pix. Do you see the radical change in the shapes of the tiled picture? You have changed the size of the picture in this example. Because the original size of the picture was small, the only way it could be made larger is to stretch the bits in the bitmap. When the bitmap is enlarged, its resolution decreases.

Bitmaps are made up of bits, each of which is turned off or on. As you enlarge a bitmap, the resolution of the picture decreases. A way you can make this apparent is to change the ScaleMode property of the form to Point or Pixel (rather than the default Twip). Try this and rerun the program. The bits are so big, you may have trouble determining what the graphic is.

TAKE NOTE

GRAPHICS METHODS VERSUS. GRAPHICS CONTROLS

Graphics methods are always carried out by writing code. You need to run the program to see what effect your method has. Graphics controls, on the other hand, are more effective if you only need to make simple designs constructed at design time. For this reason, Graphics controls are easier to use than Graphics methods.

CROSS-REFERENCE

Find references for Graphics controls in Chapter 9.

FIND IT ONLINE

Here is a simple tutorial on graphics: **http://www.perplexed.com/GPMega/index.htm.**

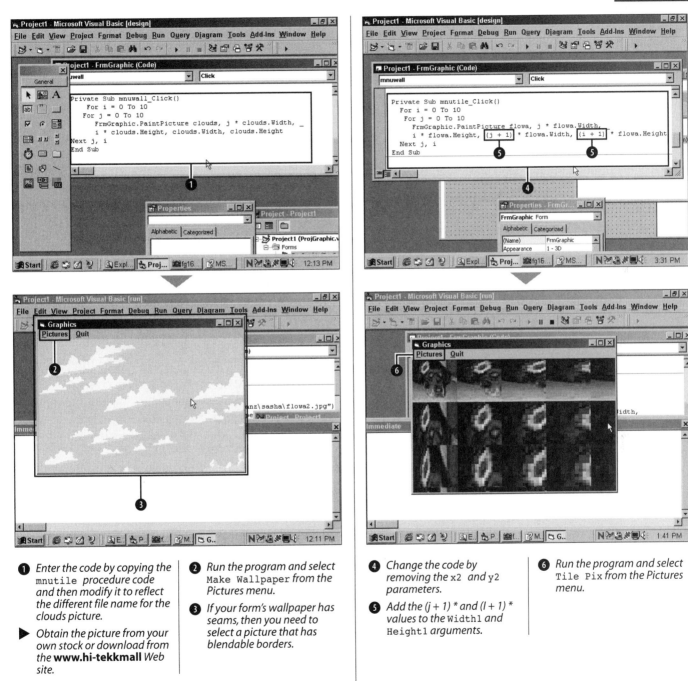

❶ *Enter the code by copying the* `mnutile` *procedure code and then modify it to reflect the different file name for the clouds picture.*

▶ *Obtain the picture from your own stock or download from the* **www.hi-tekkmall** *Web site.*

❷ *Run the program and select* `Make Wallpaper` *from the Pictures menu.*

❸ *If your form's wallpaper has seams, then you need to select a picture that has blendable borders.*

❹ *Change the code by removing the* x2 *and* y2 *parameters.*

❺ *Add the (j + 1) * and (l + 1) * values to the* Width1 *and* Height1 *arguments.*

❻ *Run the program and select* `Tile Pix` *from the Pictures menu.*

Using Vector Graphics with PaintPicture

A *vector graphic* does not degrade as it is enlarged beyond its original size. This is because a vector graphic is not composed of bits, but rather it is based on a formula of coordinates. Thus, you can enlarge a vector graphic to be virtually any size without compromising its display. You can confirm this by enlarging a vector graphic and viewing the result. The vector graphic supported by Visual Basic is a Windows Metafile with a .WMF file extension.

You can create your own Windows Metafile in a draw program, such as CorelDraw or Adobe Illustrator. Draw the image freehand or use clip art, and then use the Save As.. or Export options to save in the Windows Metafile or .WMF format. You also can find graphics in various formats on the Internet.

Use the Rose.wmf file or a similar Windows Metafile in a new procedure called mnustretch. You must first add the Stretch Pic to the Pictures menu. In addition, in the declarations section of the form, declare the "rose" file as Picture.

```
Dim rose As Picture
```

Add the Set statements to identify and load the picture file.

```
Set rose = LoadPicture("c:\art\ged\rose.wmf")
```

Modify the code in the mnutile procedure as follows. Here, the parameters are the same as in the Make Wallpaper procedure. Add the mnustretch procedure and the following code.

```
FrmGraphic.PaintPicture rose, j * rose.Width, _
i * rose.Height, rose.Width, rose.Height
```

Add the code and run the program. You should see rows of tiled roses, similar to the flowa tiling. Now you are going to expand the size of the roses in the mnustretch procedure. Modify the code by multiplying the rose width and height by the variable $i + 1$. Run the program again. What you should see is that the rose becomes larger as the tiling progresses, but does not lose resolution.

```
FrmGraphic.PaintPicture rose, _
j * rose.Width,i * rose.Height, _
   (i + 1) * rose.Width, (i + 1) * rose.Height
```

What you have done is to increase the size of the rose with each row due to the incremented values of i in the loop. Do you see the rose is as clear in the larger pictures as in the smallest? This is an example of what you can do with the PaintPicture method by manipulating the coordinates and the dimensions of the original. You also see the raw material, in terms of what picture format you begin with, is important.

In the next topic, you begin using controls to manipulate graphics files.

TAKE NOTE

▶ PAINTPICTURE COMPARED TO OTHER METHODS

The utility of the PaintPicture method results from its capability to merge the functionality of BitBlt and StretchBlt. To copy both, PaintPicture uses many optional arguments. Most of the PaintPicture arguments (except for the first two coordinates) are optional. Following the source picture, the arguments are the beginning point of the destination, the destination size, the source starting point, the source size, and, finally, the raster operations.

CROSS-REFERENCE

References to Graphics methods are in Chapter 17.

FIND IT ONLINE

You can find a graphics tutorial at the following site: http://dialspace.dial.pipex.com/town/place/ggy11/vbadv/adv53.htm.

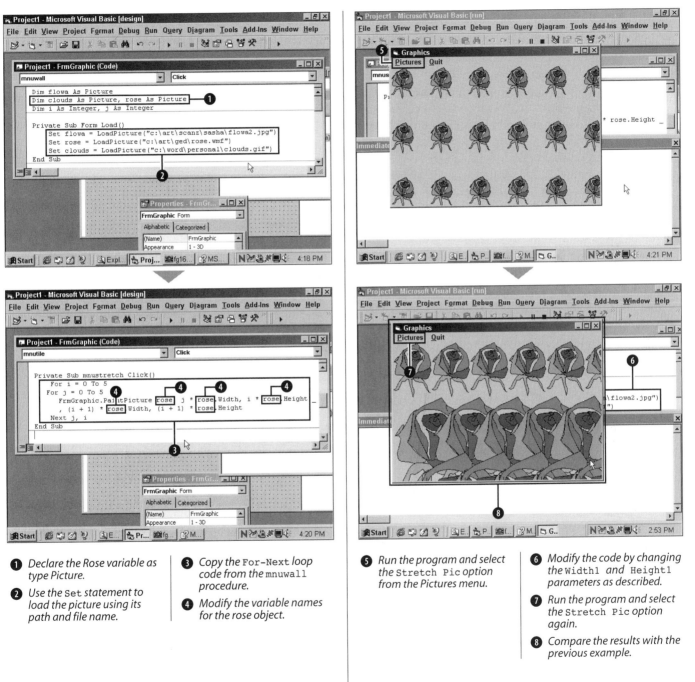

1. Declare the Rose variable as type Picture.

2. Use the `Set` statement to load the picture using its path and file name.

3. Copy the `For-Next` loop code from the `mnuwall` procedure.

4. Modify the variable names for the rose object.

5. Run the program and select the `Stretch Pic` option from the Pictures menu.

6. Modify the code by changing the `Width1` and `Height1` parameters as described.

7. Run the program and select the `Stretch Pic` option again.

8. Compare the results with the previous example.

Using the Line and Shape Controls

You just explored Graphics methods. Graphics methods are different from Graphics controls. Graphics methods are often used because they offer some shortcuts to using controls. Methods also enable you to use less code to create effects at run time. Placing the controls at design time may be an easier solution, however, if you are creating simple designs for the user interface.

In this exercise, you are going to use the Line and Shape controls to create a somewhat whimsical user interface for an ice cream company. Add a form using `Add Form` from the Project menu. Name the form `FrmShapes` and give it the caption **Lines and Shapes**.

Drawing `Line` and `Shape` controls on a form is easy. Place a Label control centered near the top of the `FrmShapes` form. Make the title, **Tutti Frutti Cones**. Right-click and select properties. In the `Properties Window`, change the `Font` properties by clicking in the second column of the `Properties Window`. Choose `Kids` or `Comic Sans` font, whatever font on your system presents a whimsical image. Also, change the point size of the font to 16, so it looks like a title should look.

Change the `BackColor` property of the `Label` to bright pink. Do this by clicking the right column of the `BackColor` property. When the dialog box opens, select the Palette tab and then pick a bright color. Make sure you set the `BackStyle` property to `Opaque`, rather than `Transparent`. Also, change the `Alignment` property to `Center`.

Now you get to have some fun creating shapes for your ice cream company form. Think of this as a splash screen type of form, as it is a promotional kind of form. Make an ice cream cone by using the `Line` control to draw the cone shape and then place a filled circle on top of the cone. To make the colors look correct, you manipulate the `BorderStyle`, `BorderColor`, `FillColor`, and `FillStyle` properties. The ice cream portion of the cone should be pink `FillColor` and solid FillStyle. The `BorderColor` should be about the same color. The `BorderStyle` must be solid.

You can make the cake shape from two ovals and a rounded square shape. The rounded square is the body of the cake and is a lighter color than the oval, which is the top of the cake. Another oval shape is placed at the bottom of the cake; it has the same `FillColor` as the body of the cake. This is to create the illusion of a rounded bottom. The `BorderColor` of the cake's bottom shapes should blend with the `FillColor`. The soda is made using the `Line` control for the soda glass, two ovals for the top and bottom of the glass, and two lines for the straws. Here's a trick to getting the soda straws parallel to one another: Set the properties of the X1, X2, Y1, and Y2 coordinates in the Properties Window, rather than trying to adjust them by clicking and dragging.

You also can use the `Frame` control as a container for the shapes. First, place the `Frame` control and then add the shapes to make the soda glass. You can right-click to send objects to the back or bring them to the front, if some objects get behind others. You also can use the format menu to `Align` and `Order` objects. When you place the shape objects on the `Frame` control, you can move the whole group of objects by moving the `Frame`. This is important when you have many objects that would be difficult to move one by one. Thus, the `Frame` is a container for a collection of objects.

TAKE NOTE

GRAPHICS CONTROLS SAVE RESOURCES

Graphics controls (Line and Shape) can be used effectively at design time. Used instead of Graphics methods, they require fewer system resources and less code. If you want to place a rectangle on a form, you could use the Line method to draw the rectangle at run time. You could save memory and code by using the shape control at design time.

CROSS-REFERENCE

Chapter 17 also uses Graphics controls.

FIND IT ONLINE

This site gives source code for generating axial lines: **http://magic.hurrah.com/~sabre/graphpro/line1.html#Example**.

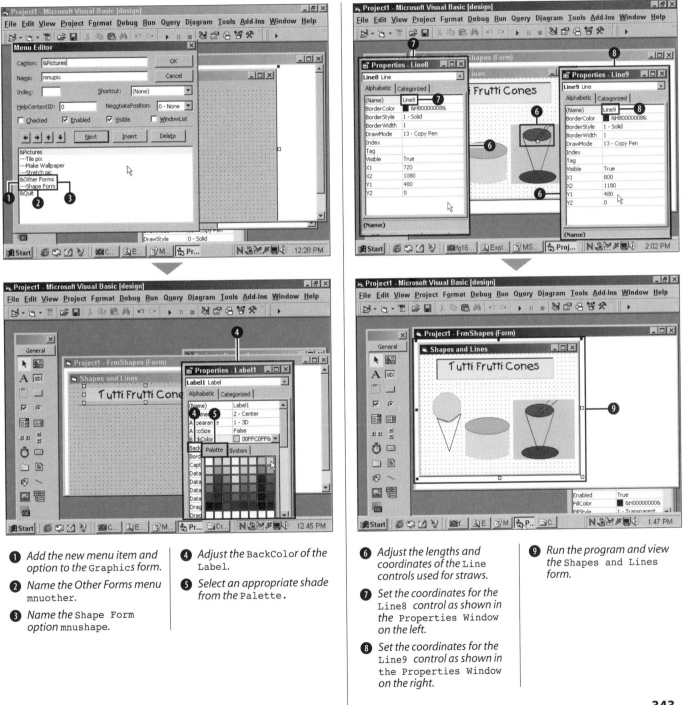

1. Add the new menu item and option to the Graphics form.

2. Name the Other Forms menu mnuother.

3. Name the Shape Form option mnushape.

4. Adjust the BackColor of the Label.

5. Select an appropriate shade from the Palette.

6. Adjust the lengths and coordinates of the Line controls used for straws.

7. Set the coordinates for the Line8 control as shown in the Properties Window on the left.

8. Set the coordinates for the Line9 control as shown in the Properties Window on the right.

9. Run the program and view the Shapes and Lines form.

Drawing Lines and Shapes Randomly

You have seen that you can make illustrations from the simple Line and Shape controls, just by placing them on a form. The exciting applications you can create by using graphic methods to draw lines and shapes are much more interesting and have more uses than placing controls on a form.

The process is a lot of fun because you can accomplish some astonishing displays by using random-number generation. Graphic methods (`Circle, Cls, Line, PaintPicture, Point, Print,` and `Pset`) can be combined with controls to produce many different effects. Animation can be simulated without using animated graphic files.

One of the simplest examples of this technique is that of the original screen savers. Unlike the screen saver project you worked on earlier, which was really a slide show effect, the first screen savers usually produced moving lines and shapes. Sometimes there were patterns to the movement. Fractals were sometimes used and they have long been available in shareware and freeware. The idea is to use mathematical algorithms to draw or paint objects on the screen in some pattern or in some random manner, so constant movement occurs.

At first, the idea can be a little intimidating, particularly if math was not your strong suit. Most developers, or those who aspire to be developers, find it in their best interests to learn a little about the mathematics used in graphics programming. Again, this is fun and not difficult to learn so you can do some interesting applications.

In the previous exercise in this chapter, you used the PaintPicture method to tile pictures on the form. In this exercise, you expand your skills by combining skills you developed in previous chapters. You used the random number generator in Chapter 5. You have had a number of experiences in placing Graphics controls, such as `PictureBoxes` on Forms. For this material, you draw on your experience with the Timer control, the Line and Shape controls, and the Menu Editor. In addition, you get more practice using arrays and coordinates.

To begin, add a new form to your project using Add Form from the Project menu. Name the form **`FrmAutoShapes`** and give it a caption **AutoShapes and Lines**. Name the form this way because you are going to automate the drawing. In the `Menu Editor`, give your form a menu called **`mnuChoice.`** Give it an appropriate caption, such as **Pick a Design**.

Add four options to the menu: `mnuGal (Galaxy), mnuMagic (Magic), mnuColli (Collisions),` and `mnuRings (Rings)`. You can name these objects anything you wish, but if you change the menu names (not captions), you must modify the code to reflect the different nomenclature. You have much more freedom with the captions because they are not addressed in code.

Add a Command button and a Timer control to your form. Name the Command button **`cmdPlay`** with the caption **Play**. Set the `Timer Interval` property at 50. You can experiment with this interval once you get the program written. The interval may depend somewhat on the speed of your processor. If you have a not-so-new system, you should set it at 1.

TAKE NOTE

LIMITATIONS OF GRAPHICS CONTROLS

Although Graphics controls are wonderful if you can use them at design time, they have some limitations. Graphics controls cannot be layered, unless they are inside another container that can be placed on other controls. They cannot receive focus at run time. Graphics controls cannot be used as containers and they do not have a Windows handle (hWnd property).

CROSS-REFERENCE

Learn more about Graphics methods in Chapter 17.

FIND IT ONLINE

Dimitry K's site has lots of information about game programs: **http://www.yucc.yorku.ca/~dmkhodor/Ftp/vb/.**

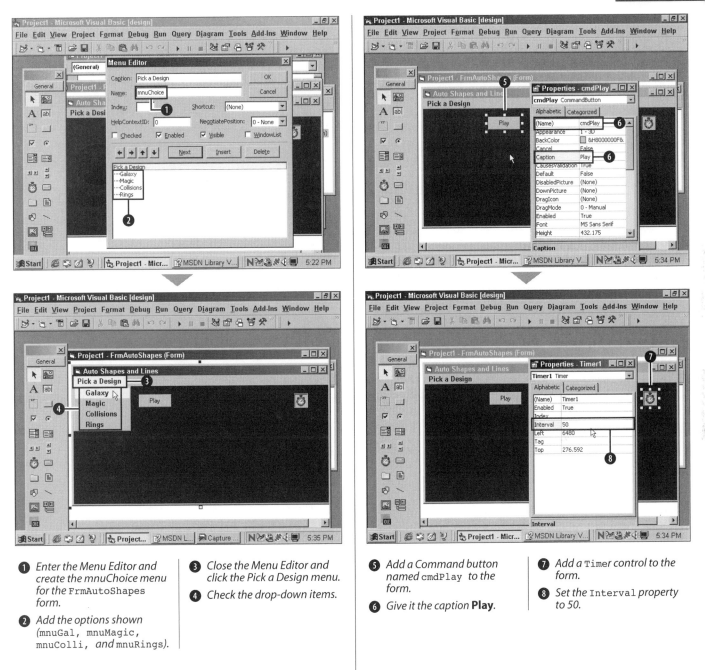

① *Enter the Menu Editor and create the mnuChoice menu for the* FrmAutoShapes *form.*

② *Add the options shown (*mnuGal, mnuMagic, mnuColli, *and* mnuRings*).*

③ *Close the Menu Editor and click the Pick a Design menu.*

④ *Check the drop-down items.*

⑤ *Add a Command button named* cmdPlay *to the form.*

⑥ *Give it the caption* **Play**.

⑦ *Add a* Timer *control to the form.*

⑧ *Set the* Interval *property to 50.*

Writing the Play Button Procedure

You are going to do something in this project that is new to you. You are not only going to code the menu option procedures, but also make procedures for objects not shown in the Object pane.

As a first step, declare the variables, `Xspot, Yspot, GameFlag, R,G, B`. The variables — `Xspot` and `Yspot` — are the *X* and *Y* coordinates and track positions of objects. A good idea is also to place the `Option Explicit` statement at the beginning of the `Declaration` section of your module. `GameFlag` controls the off and on status of the game, based on the `cmdPlay` button. `GameFlag` also clears the screen of colors when the `Stop` button is pressed. The `R, G,` and `B` variables control the color of the graphics, based on the random generation of colors.

Before building the specific game design procedures, you are going to construct the command button options to `Play` and `Stop` playing the design animations. Double-click the `cmdPlay` button, select the `cmdPlay` object, and the `Click` procedure. First, declare the local variables, `X1` and `Y1`, which set the initial `X` and `Y` coordinates for the `Magic` subroutine.

Use Select Case to test for the status of the `cmdPlay` button (True or False). `GameFlag` is the variable you are using as a flag to detect the status of the button.

```
Select Case GameFlag
```

The two cases will be True and False. Here, you also set the caption on the `cmdPlay` button, depending on the last click (`Play` or `Stop`).

```
Case True
        cmdPlay.Caption = "Play"
        GameFlag = False
        mnuChoice.Enabled = True
```

The button's caption property is changed to `Play`, `GameFlag` is changed to False, and `mnuChoice.Enabled`

will be true when the game has been stopped. At the point where the design is playing, the value of `Gameflag` will be False and the value of `mnuChoice.Enabled` will be True. Suppose you selected the `Magic` menu option.

```
If mnuMagic.Checked = True Then
Cls
```

In the previous code , the Checked status of `mnuMagic` is true, so the statement (`Cls`) is executed.

When the execution reaches the `Case False` command block, the caption will be changed to "Stop," the `GameFlag` set to True, and the `mnuChoice.Enabled` will become False. Next, a series of conditional statements regarding the menu option Checked status:

```
Case False
        cmdPlay.Caption = "Stop"
        GameFlag = True
        mnuChoice.Enabled = False
```

If the case were False, the following statements would be executed.

```
If mnuMagic.Checked = True Then
Randomize
DrawWidth = Int(4 * Rnd + 1)
X1 = Int(FrmAutoShapes.Width - 2000 * Rnd + 1)
Y1 = Int(FrmAutoShapes.Height - 1000 * Rnd + 1)
```

The Randomize statement initializes the random-number generator. The seed used here is the system timer. The line width is set using the `DrawWidth` property and again using the Rnd function to create different width lines. Initial width and height of the X- and Y-coordinates are set to a random location on the form using the Rnd function.

CROSS-REFERENCE

Refer to Chapter 8 for Graphics controls information.

FIND IT ONLINE

This site has good explanations of graphics and animation: **http://www.catalystpics.co.uk/book.htm**.

TAKE NOTE

▶ **DRAWSTYLE, DRAWMODE, AND DRAWWIDTH PROPERTIES**

The *DrawWidth* accounts for the width in pixels of the lines being drawn. There are 16 *DrawModes*, which determine the color of the display, with the effect dependent upon the color of a line drawn at run time. Using a random number between 1 and 16 changes the mode each time the design is played. *DrawStyles* determines the type of line drawn. The styles range from solid lines to dots and dash combinations. This property has no effect when the width of the line is more than 1 pixel.

Listing 16-1: The cmdPlay **Procedure**

```
Select Case GameFlag
    Case True
        cmdPlay.Caption = "Play"
        GameFlag = False              ◀━❶
        mnuChoice.Enabled = True
                                        ❷
        If mnuMagic.Checked = True Then
            Cls
        ElseIf mnuGal.Checked = True Then
            Cls
        ElseIf mnuRings.Checked = True Then
            Cls
        ElseIf mnuColli.Checked = True Then
            Cls
```

❶ If the Play has been stopped: Reset the caption, GameFlag, and mnuChoice.Enabled options.

❷ Remove the display from the form depending upon the menu selection. (If mnuMagic is the selection, remove lines from the form; if mnuGal is selected, remove stars from the form; and so forth.)

```
        End If
    Case False
        cmdPlay.Caption = "Stop"
        GameFlag = True
        mnuChoice.Enabled = False
    If mnuMagic.Checked = True Then
            Randomize ◀━❶
                                    ❷
    DrawWidth = Int(4 * Rnd + 1)   ┃
    X1 = Int(FrmAutoShapes.Width - 2000 * Rnd + 1)
    Y1 = Int(FrmAutoShapes.Height - 1000 * Rnd + 1)
ElseIf mnuGal.Checked = True Then
            DrawWidth = 10 ◀━❸
ElseIf mnuColli.Checked = True Then
            DrawWidth = 30 ◀━❹
ElseIf mnuRings.Checked = True Then
            DrawWidth = Int(5 * Rnd + 1)◀━
            DrawStyle = vbDot ◀━❻          ❺
            DrawMode = Int(16 * Rnd + 1)◀━
    End If
    End Select
End Sub
```

❶ If the Play has been started: Initialize the random-number generator.

❷ Set the initial X, Y coordinates to random points on the form.

❸ For mnuGal, set the size of the stars.

❹ For mnuColli, make big circles.

❺ For mnuRings, use the Randomize function to set the DrawWidth property and the DrawStyle as dots and draw lines using random DrawModes.

❻ Note, the DrawStyle (vbDot) will not be in effect when the line width is greater than 1 pixel.

Creating the Galaxy Option

The next action to take is to write Form procedures. In the code window, select the Form object and the Load procedure.

```
GameFlag = False
```

Setting GameFlag to False gives the correct status to the flag when the program is run. Because no opportunity has occurred to select a design, the game is not running.

Next, select the Form object and then select the Unload procedure. Type only the statement End to close the form.

```
End
```

You can also add an Exit option to your menu. Use the End statement to end, as you did in the Form_Unload procedure.

To carry out the work of this application, you need to write several procedures for each design option on the menu. The first is the Galaxy menu option. Test for the Checked status of each of the options. The only Checked property that should be True in this procedure is the Galaxy Checked property. When a menu option is Checked, a checkmark is displayed next to it on the menu. Double-click the mnuGal option and select the mnuGal object and the Click procedure in the code window.

```
mnuGal.Checked = True
```

Write statements for each of the other options (mnuColli, mnuRings, mnuMagic) and set their Checked status to False.

While still in the code window, create a Private Sub named **galaxy**.

```
Private Sub galaxy()
End Sub
```

Set the values of the RGB variables to 255 times the Rnd function.

```
R = 255 * Rnd
G = 255 * Rnd
B = 255 * Rnd
```

These color variables can have values from 0 to 255, so each will stand for the Red, Green, or Blue values. The resulting mix will create the colors of the stars in the galaxy. The Xspot and Yspot variables you declared set the horizontal and vertical positions of the stars on the form.

```
Xspot = Rnd * ScaleWidth
Yspot = Rnd * ScaleHeight
```

Use the PSet method to set a color for the stars wherever they are drawn.

```
PSet (Xspot, Yspot), RGB(R, G, B)
```

The Xspot and Yspot coordinates determine the position of the stars. The RGB function uses an argument for each color (Red, Green, and Blue). Each argument must be in the range of 0–255. Depending upon the values of each color, the mix will result in one color. Zero for each color would result in black and 255 for each color would create white. In this exercise, you are using a random generator to produce different colors on the fly.

Double-click the Timer control and write a Timer procedure to call the galaxy procedure.

```
If mnuGal.Checked And GameFlag = True Then
        galaxy
```

You are testing for the Checked property value of mnuGal, to see if it is Checked and GameFlag is True. If both conditions are met (the game is on), then the galaxy procedure is called. You can play the game at this point by remarking out the variable declarations and other code that refers to the other procedures.

CROSS-REFERENCE

Check Chapter 17 for more information on Graphics methods.

FIND IT ONLINE

This site has graphics tools that are free and for $$:
http://www.burdicksoft.com/Tools.html.

TAKE NOTE

▶ **PSET METHOD**

The *PSet method* gives a point on an object a specified color. The color can be specified by using the QBColor function (colors 0-15) or by using the Randomize function. If no color is specified, the current ForeColor is used. When the DrawWidth is greater than one, the point affected by PSet is centered on the object.

Listing 16-2: The mnuGal **Menu Option Procedure**

```
Private Sub mnuGal_Click() ← ❶
    Cls
    mnuMagic.Checked = False
    mnuColli.Checked = False
    mnuGal.Checked = True        ← ❷
    mnuRings.Checked = False
End Sub
```

Listing 16-3: The Galaxy **procedure**

```
Private Sub galaxy() ← ❸
    R = 255 * Rnd
    G = 255 * Rnd
    B = 255 * Rnd
Xspot = Rnd * ScaleWidth          ← ❹
Yspot = Rnd * ScaleHeight
PSet (Xspot, Yspot), RGB(R, G, B)
End Sub
```

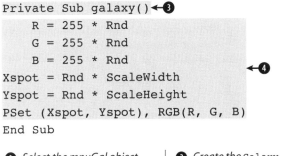

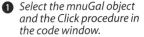

❶ *Select the mnuGal object and the Click procedure in the code window.*

❷ *Enter the code for the menu option procedure.*

❸ *Create the Galaxy procedure.*

❹ *Enter the code for the Galaxy procedure.*

Listing 16-4: The Timer **Procedure**

```
Private Sub Timer1_Timer()
    If mnuGal.Checked And GameFlag = True Then
        Galaxy
    End If
End Sub
```
↑
❺

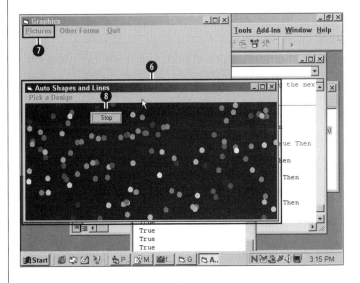

❺ *Select the Timer object in the code window and enter the code shown.*

❻ *Remark all statements and variable declarations that would prevent your program from running.*

❼ *Run the program and select the Galaxy option.*

❽ *Click Play.*

349

Creating the Magic Option

If you try out the Galaxy option, you should expect to see many round dots of different colors popping up all over the form.

The magic option is going to draw a series of randomly placed lines on the form. The lines take different directions and are of different lengths and widths, and they are continually changing. To carry out these functions, you need the same procedures you set up for the `Galaxy` option.

Set up the menu `Magic` procedure by double-clicking the `mnuMagic` option on the Pick a Design menu. Create the `Click` procedure by setting the `Checked` property of `mnuMagic` to True.

```
mnuMagic.Checked = True
```

Once again, you set the Checked status for the other menu options to False. This is so the currently selected option is going to be the one playing and its status will be correctly observed by the `cmdPlay` procedure when you click the `Play` or `Stop` button.

The `Timer` procedure will call the `Magic` procedure to begin the display. Add this statement to the `If` command block in your `Timer` procedure.

```
ElseIf mnuMagic.Checked And GameFlag = True _
Then
        Magic
```

The conditional statement here is `ElseIf` because it follows the `If` statement in the previous exercise. The `If-End If` command block uses `ElseIf` to set up procedure calls for each of the subsequent menu options.

When the Magic procedure is called, the process of drawing the lines on the form is begun. You must declare X2 and Y2 as local variables here and then assign values to the RBG variables.

```
R = 255 * Rnd
G = 255 * Rnd
B = 255 * Rnd
```

The values for the RGB variables are assigned from the Rnd function, based on the generation of random numbers between 0 and 255. Depending upon the draw for each variable, the resulting colors will be a mix of the RGB values.

The ending points (`X2` and `Y2`) of the lines are randomly generated using the `Rnd` function. Because you don't want to have lines with zero ending points, you should add 1 to the `Rnd` generated number.

```
X2 = Int(FrmAutoShapes.Width * Rnd + 1)
Y2 = Int(FrmAutoShapes.Height * Rnd + 1)
Line -(X2, Y2), RGB(R, G, B)
```

The RGB function has three arguments: one for each color (Red, Green, Blue). Each has a value in the range 0–255. This takes care of the Magic menu option.

TAKE NOTE

THE RND FUNCTION

The generation of a number is determined upon the value of a number. For any seed (the starting number for the Rnd function), the previous number generated functions as the seed for the next number. You use the Randomize statement with no argument to initialize number generator based on the system timer. When you do not want a zero value generated, you should add the number 1 to your formula.

CROSS-REFERENCE

Refer to Chapter 5 for an example of a Draw program.

FIND IT ONLINE

This site offers Active Server Paint (ActiveX DlI):
http://www.coherentdata.com/cvisual/aspaint/.

Listing 16-5: The `mnuMagic` **Menu Option Procedure**

```
Private Sub mnuMagic_Click()  ①
    Cls
    mnuMagic.Checked = True
    mnuColli.Checked = False  ②
    mnuGal.Checked = False
    mnuRings.Checked = False
End Sub
```

Listing 16-7: The `Timer` **procedure for Magic**

```
ElseIf mnuMagic.Checked And GameFlag = True Then
⑤         Magic
```

Listing 16-6: The `Magic` **Procedure**

```
Private Sub Magic()  ③                    ④
    Dim X2, Y2
    R = 255 * Rnd
    G = 255 * Rnd
    B = 255 * Rnd
    X2 = Int(FrmAutoShapes.Width * Rnd + 1)
    Y2 = Int(FrmAutoShapes.Height * Rnd + 1)
    Line -(X2, Y2), RGB(R, G, B)
End Sub
```

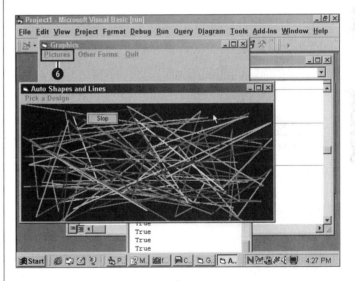

① *Select the* mnuMagic *object and the Click procedure in the code window.*

② *Enter the code for the menu option procedure.*

③ *Create the* Magic *procedure.*

④ *Enter the code for the* Magic *procedure.*

⑤ *Add this statement to the If command block in the* Timer *procedure.*

▶ *Remove remark symbols from the statements you remarked to run the previous option. Remark statements and variable declarations that pertain to the options not yet done.*

⑥ *Run the program and select the* Rings *option and click Play.*

Creating the Collisions Menu Option

The Magic menu option is quite different from the Galaxy option. Creating new patterns for each option could be difficult, but with a good imagination and the Visual Basic tools, it is easy. The most difficult part of the process is stopping the experimentation. Continuing to change the random number setup, the `DrawStyle`, `DrawMode`, or `DrawWidth` options, or tweaking this or that is easy. You finally have to stop changing your design option. Of course, changing the code around is a great way to learn.

In this exercise, you are going to make a display that uses some features of the Galaxy option and adds changes to the background color to simulate explosions or collisions.

Set up the menu `Collisions` procedure by double-clicking the `mnuColli` option on the Pick a Design menu. Create the `Click` procedure by setting the Checked property of `mnucolli` to True.

```
mnuColli.Checked = True
```

Once again, you set the Checked status for the other menu options to False. This is so the currently selected option is going to be the one playing and its status will be correctly observed by the `cmdPlay` procedure when you click the `Play` or `Stop` button.

The `Timer` procedure will call the `Magic` procedure to begin the display. Add this statement to the `If` command block in your `Timer` procedure.

```
ElseIf mnuColli.Checked And GameFlag = True _
Then
    Collide
```

The conditional statement here is `ElseIf` because it follows the `If` statement used previously. The `If-End If` command block uses `ElseIf` to set up procedure calls for each of the subsequent menu options.

```
R = 255 * Rnd
G = 255 * Rnd
B = 255 * Rnd
```

The values for the RGB variables are assigned from the `Rnd` function based on the generation of random numbers between 0 and 255. Depending upon the draw for each variable, the resulting colors will be a mix of the RGB values.

The Xspot and Yspot variables you declared set the horizontal and vertical positions of the colliding blobs on the form.

```
Xspot = Rnd * ScaleWidth
Yspot = Rnd * ScaleHeight
```

Use the `PSet` method to set a color for the blobs wherever they are drawn.

```
PSet (Xspot, Yspot), RGB(R, G, B)
```

The Xspot and Yspot coordinates determine the position of the stars. The RGB function uses an argument for each color (Red, Green, and Blue). Each argument must be in the range of 0–255. Depending upon the color, the mix will produce one color. A zero value for each color would produce black and 255 for each color would create white. Just as in the `Galaxy` exercise, you are using a random generator to produce continually different colors.

The key factor that makes this option differ from the `Galaxy` option is you vary the background color to simulate collisions between the careening objects. The `BackColor` flashing makes the scene turbulent.

```
FrmAutoShapes.BackColor = QBColor(Int(2 * Rnd))
```

Here, the `BackColor` is set to a random number between 0 and 2. If the random number multiplier is greater, the blobs are not easily differentiated from the background.

CROSS-REFERENCE

References to this topic can be found in Chapter 17.

FIND IT ONLINE

Here are VB games to play, source code included:
http://hem1.passagen.se/fylke/.

Listing 16-8: The `mnuColli` **Menu Option**

```
Private Sub mnuColli_Click()  ←❶
    Cls
    mnuMagic.Checked = False
    mnuGal.Checked = False  ←❷
    mnuRings.Checked = False
    mnuColli.Checked = True
End Sub
```

Listing 16-9: The `Collide` **Procedure**

```
Private Sub Collide()  ←❸          ❹
    R = 255 * Rnd                  ↓
    G = 255 * Rnd
    B = 255 * Rnd
Xspot = Rnd * ScaleWidth
Yspot = Rnd * ScaleHeight
Assign the confetti bit a random color.
PSet (Xspot, Yspot), RGB(R, G, B)
FrmAutoShapes.BackColor = QBColor(Int(2 * Rnd))
```

Listing 16-10: The `Timer` **procedure for Collide**

```
ElseIf mnuColli.Checked And GameFlag = True Then
        Collide           ↑
                          ❺
```

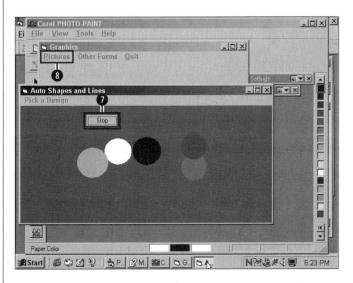

❶ *Select the* `mnuColli` *object and the* `Click` *procedure in the code window.*

❷ *Enter the code for the* `menu option` *procedure.*

❸ *Create the* `Collide` *procedure.*

❹ *Enter the code for the* `Collide` *procedure.*

❺ *Add this statement to the* `If` *command block in the* `Timer` *procedure*

▶ *Remove remark symbols from the statements you remarked to run the previous option. Remark statements and variable declarations that pertain to the options not yet done.*

❻ *Run the program and select the* `Rings` *option.*

❼ *Click Stop.*

Creating the Rings Menu Option

After drawing lots of objects on the form in random positions, the Rings option offers a little more variety. Notice the familiar Rnd function is still making its contributions to the exercise, however. Set up the menu `Collisions` procedure by double-clicking the `mnuRings` option on the Pick a Design menu. Create the `Click` procedure by setting the `Checked` property of `mnuRings` to `True`.

```
mnuRings.Checked = True
```

Set the `Checked` status for the other menu options to `False`. This is so the currently selected option will be the one playing and its status will be correctly observed by the `cmdPlay` procedure when you click the `Play` or `Stop` button.

The `Timer` procedure will call the `Rings` procedure to begin the display. Add this statement to the `If` command block in your `Timer` procedure.

```
ElseIf mnuRings.Checked And GameFlag = True
Then
    Rings
```

Again, the conditional statement is `ElseIf` because it follows the `If` statement used previously. The `If-End If` command block uses `ElseIf` to set up procedure calls for the Rings option.

```
Dim Radius
```

Declare a new local variable that will be used to determine the size of the rings.

```
R = 255 * Rnd
G = 255 * Rnd
B = 255 * Rnd
```

These variables are the same as in other options. Again, the values for the RGB variables are assigned from the Rnd function, based on the generation of random numbers between 0 and 255. Depending upon the draw for each variable, the resulting colors will be a mix of the RGB values.

```
Xspot = ScaleWidth / 2
Yspot = ScaleHeight / 2
```

Because the `ScaleWidth` and `ScaleHeight` are divided by two, the Xspot and Yspot variables you declared earlier will set the position of the rings in the center of the form. Next, you need to determine the size of the rings.

```
Radius = ((Yspot * 0.9) + 1) * Rnd
```

The height of the rings is determined by multiplying the `ScaleHeight` of the form by .9 and then adding 1. The random number generator will produce a number between zero and approximately half the form's height.

```
Circle (Xspot, Yspot), Radius, RGB(R, G, B)
```

The rings are drawn on the form, depending upon the randomly generated `Radius`, `Xspot`, and `Yspot` coordinates. The colors have been randomly generated using the function already discussed.

Clearly you have many options for changing the parameters used to produce the displays. You can also manipulate the random number range, the *X* and *Y* positions, the colors, and the concepts.

TAKE NOTE

▶ USING COLOR FUNCTIONS

The RGB or QBColor functions can be used to set BackColor, ForeColor, or the colors of lines and shapes used in Graphics methods. The valid range for a normal RGB color is 0 to 16,777,215 (&HFFFFFF). The QBColor function uses numbers from 0–15.

CROSS-REFERENCE
Refer to Chapter 15 for information on displaying graphics.

FIND IT ONLINE
Play the game and see What VB can do: **http://www. abstractworlds.com/closeapproach/**.

Listing 16-11: The mnuRings **Menu Procedure**

```
Private Sub mnuRings_Click()
    Cls
    mnuMagic.Checked = False
    mnuColli.Checked = False
    mnuGal.Checked = False
    mnuRings.Checked = True
End Sub
```

Listing 16-13: The Timer **Procedure for Rings**

```
ElseIf mnuRings.Checked And GameFlag = True Then
        Rings
```
❸

Listing 16-12: The Rings **Procedure**

```
Private Sub Rings()  ❶
Dim Radius          ❷
    R = 255 * Rnd
    G = 255 * Rnd
    B = 255 * Rnd
    Xspot = ScaleWidth / 2
    Yspot = ScaleHeight / 2
    Radius = ((Yspot * 0.9) + 1) * Rnd
    Circle (Xspot, Yspot), Radius, RGB(R,G,B)
End Sub
```

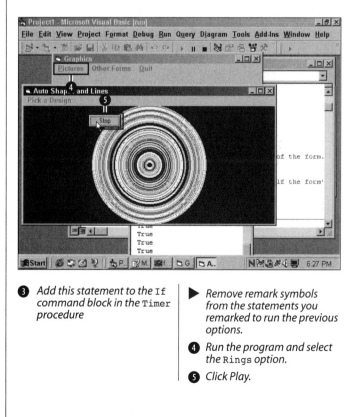

❶ Create the Rings *procedure.*

❷ Enter the code for the Rings *procedure.*

❸ *Add this statement to the* If *command block in the* Timer *procedure*

▶ *Remove remark symbols from the statements you remarked to run the previous options.*

❹ *Run the program and select the* Rings *option.*

❺ *Click Play.*

Personal Workbook

Q&A

1 What is the difference between Graphics methods and Graphics controls?

_____

_____

_____

2 Where can you use the PaintPicture method?

_____

_____

_____

3 Where can you draw using Graphics methods?

_____

_____

_____

4 What property determines the unit of measure in the PaintPicture method?

_____

_____

_____

5 How can you create a background or wallpaper effect?

_____

_____

_____

6 Name some Graphics methods.

_____

_____

_____

7 Name some Graphics properties used to Draw on Forms or `PictureBox` controls.

_____

_____

_____

8 What do the X1 and Y1 arguments in the Line method represent?

_____

_____

_____

ANSWERS: PAGE 527

Working with Graphics Methods and Controls

EXTRA PRACTICE

1. Add a new option to the Pick a Design menu. Define the nature of the display. How can you vary it?

2. Add sound to one of the Pick a Design menu options. What is the best way to get sound to play while the picture is being drawn?

3. Write a new option for the Pick a Design menu — this time, using rectangles. What method will you use to draw the shapes?

4. Use the skills you have developed in this chapter to enhance the children's game you developed in the last chapter.

REAL WORLD APPLICATIONS

✔ You have been given the assignment of writing a design-drawing, screensaver program for the employees at your company. Expand the exercises in this chapter to make a full-blown application complete with user interface.

✔ Combine what you have learned in this chapter with that in the Multimedia chapter to enter the game developer's contest. Combine the Graphics methods in both chapters to enhance your game to complete a 30-second segment.

✔ Your Aunt Hannah's Web site needs more splashy animation, including some for free programs visitors can download. Create a simple program with line and shape animation methods.

Visual Quiz

Where on this form should the Graphics controls used in the Magic and Rings options be placed?

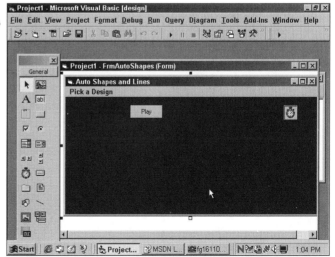

_____

_____

_____

_____

_____

_____

CHAPTER **17**

MASTER THESE SKILLS

▶ Drawing and Copying Images

▶ Working with Bitmaps

▶ Displaying Images

▶ Working with the PictureClip Control

▶ Selecting a Region with the PictureClip Control

▶ Using Control Arrays with Image Controls

▶ Creating the Puzzle Procedure

▶ Moving Cards with the Move Method

▶ Creating the Deal Procedure

Using Images

You have been using graphics methods and controls in several chapters so far. You may now feel as though you have learned nearly everything about the subject. You can always learn something more about Visual Basic. In fact, you can always learn more in nearly any programming language. The graphics methods and controls you have used include animation, bitmaps, vector graphics, draw and paint methods.

In the last two chapters, a strong case was made for the importance of the World Wide Web in promoting an interest in graphics and multimedia in general. But the Web isn't the only showcase for graphics. All GUI applications now use graphic techniques and use images.

You may have heard that the `Image` control has far less overhead than the `PictureBox` control. You will explore just how you can put this knowledge to use. You also learn which are appropriate uses of the `Image` control and which are not.

In this chapter, you focus on images, including the `Image` control and methods. Like the `PictureBox`, the `Image` control is used to display graphics. `Image` controls can display graphics in a number of formats (`bitmap`, `icon`, `metafile`, `enhanced metafile`, `JPEG` or `GIF files`).

Usually, the `image` control is preferable for displaying bitmaps because it uses fewer resources than the `PictureBox` control. You can generally have several times the Image controls as `PictureBoxes` making the same demands on memory.

The `Image`, `shape`, and `line` controls are considered useful because they are "lightweight" controls. This is because they include a few of the properties, methods, and events found in the `PictureBox` control. And that is why they normally demand fewer system resources and perform faster than the `PictureBox` control.

You have practiced using the `Circle`, `Line`, `Point` and `Pset` methods with the `PictureBox` control. These methods work well with the `PictureBox` control because, in many ways, it is an ideal choice to display pictures.

Drawing and Copying Images

In this exercise, you construct a random-line drawing application that fills a picture box with lines and then enables you to click in another box to copy the contents of the first box.

Create a new project, named **ProjImages,** with a form named **FrmImages** and captioned **Image Practice**. Create a menu in the Menu editor for the Image Practice form. Title the menu Other Forms (mnuOther) and give the menu one option, "Exit." Later, you add forms to the Other Forms menu and place a separator bar above the Exit option. Double-click the Exit option and write the procedure to End the application.

Place two `PictureBoxes` on the form. Place a Label control below the boxes. Type in a caption directing the user to Draw lines by clicking in the box on the left, then click in the box on the right to copy the picture. Declare two variables in the form's declaration section.

```
Dim x1, y1
```

Double-click the form, select the `Load` procedure, and set AutoRedraw to True for `Picture1`. This creates a persistent graphic.

```
Picture1.AutoRedraw = True
```

Next, select the Picture1 object and the `Click` procedure. Declare the variables R, G, and B (these are the same as those in the previous exercise and they will generate random numbers for each color function). In addition, declare two local variables to represent the picture box's `ScaleWidth` and `ScaleHeight`.

```
Dim PW, PH
```

Because you are going to draw bunches of thick lines in the first box, you should set the `FillStyle` property to solid. `VbFSSolid` is a `FillStyle` constant.

```
Picture1.FillStyle = vbFSSolid
```

Next, set the x1 and y1 variables equal to the scale height and width of the `Picture1` box. Use the Random function with this value. Remember to add one to the Rnd function.

```
x1 = Int(Picture1.ScaleWidth * Rnd + 1)
```

Set the `FillColor` property to `QBColor` using a random integer between 0 and 15. This produces colors ranging from black (0) to white(15) as the drawing progresses.

```
Picture1.FillColor = QBColor(Int(Rnd * 15))
```

Set PW and PH to the scale height and width of the `Picture1` box. Also, give `Picture1` a DrawWidth property value of 4. This makes a fairly thick line.

```
Picture1.DrawWidth = 4
```

Next, draw the line in a random location using the x1 and y1 coordinates. Add the RGB function to draw with randomly selected colors.

```
Picture1.Line -(x1, y1), RGB(R, G, B)
```

Finally, select the Picture2 object and the `Click` procedure to do the copying.

```
Picture2.Picture = Picture1.Image
```

When you execute the program, keep clicking in the leftmost box until you have sufficient lines and then click in the rightmost box to copy the picture.

TAKE NOTE

▶ **USING AUTOREDRAW**

When the `PictureBox` is used with the `Image` and `AutoRedraw` properties, you can create persistent graphics. Persistent graphics are those stored in memory and will be in effect when the `AutoRedraw` property is set to True. Setting the `AutoRedraw` property value to False disables automatic repainting and the Paint event is summoned when it is necessary to repaint a display. Also, the screen won't clear with the `Cls` command.

CROSS-REFERENCE
The PictureBox is introduced in Chapter 9.

FIND IT ONLINE
This site offers animated GIFs: **http://www. codewriters.net/html/graphx.cgi**.

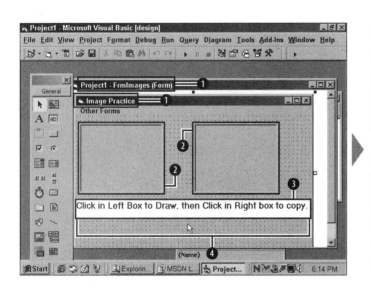

Listing 17-1: The Image Copying Routine

```
Dim x1, y1
Private Sub Form_Load()          ← 5
    Picture1.AutoRedraw = True
End Sub
Private Sub mnuExit_Click()
    End
End Sub
Private Sub Picture1_Click()
Dim PW, PH
    R = 255 * Rnd
    G = 255 * Rnd               ← 6
    B = 255 * Rnd
 Picture1.FillStyle = vbFSSolid
 x1 = Int(Picture1.ScaleWidth * Rnd + 1)   ← 7
 y1 = Int(Picture1.ScaleHeight * Rnd + 1)
 Picture1.FillColor = QBColor(Int(Rnd * 15))
    PW = Picture1.ScaleWidth                ← 8
    PH = Picture1.ScaleHeight
    Picture1.DrawWidth = 4 ← 9
    Picture1.Line -(x1, y1), RGB(R, G, B) ← 10
End Sub
Private Sub Picture2_Click()
    Picture2.Picture = Picture1.Image ← 11
End Sub
```

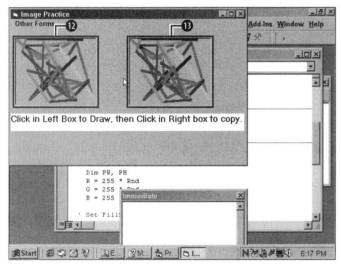

5 Declare the x1, y1 variables and set AutoRedraw to True.

6 In the Picture1_Click procedure, declare local variables, set FillStyle to Solid.

7 Set the coordinate variables to the ScaleWidth and ScaleHeight property of the PictureBox control.

8 Randomize the FillColor of the box.

9 Set the DrawWidth of the box.

10 Set the line method to draw the line and use the randomly generated colors.

11 Create the Picture2_Click procedure to copy the left picture into the right box.

1 Create the FrmImages form and make an Other Forms menu in the Menu Editor.

2 Place two PictureBox controls on the form.

3 Place a Label control on the FrmImages form below the picture boxes.

4 Type in a Text property value like the one shown for the Label control.

12 Run the program and make a number of mouse clicks in the left picture box.

13 Click once in the right picture box to copy the lines in the left box.

Working with Bitmaps

You already have seen you can use bitmap images in different ways in several different chapters. Shape and line controls can be used for drawing graphics objects on a form. These controls don't include any events, but they can be used handily in designing user interfaces.

The Image control is incredibly versatile. You can even use it to design buttons for your forms. The Image control recognizes the Click event, so you can use this control anywhere you might use a command button. This is an expedient way to create a graphic button instead of one with a caption. Grouping some image controls together across the top or bottom of the form also serves as a toolbar.

One thing to remember when using an Image control as a command button is, while you can click it, it does not appear to be depressed. When released, it does not appear to pop back. The state of the image button does not change when it is clicked.

This exercise is included to gain experience with the Image control. Although the Image control has less overhead than the PictureBox control, they are often used together. The Shape control also is often used with the Image control. Here, you use a Shape control to highlight the selected images located in four Image controls. You also manipulate the background and a text display to draw attention to the selected items. You combine the PictureBox, Shape, and Image controls in this project.

Use the Add Form option on the Project menu to add a new form to the project. Name the form, FrmTarot with a caption **Tarot Cards**. This exercise could be a first step in creating a Tarot Card game. At any rate, you could use these techniques in such a game.

Place a Shape control on the left margin of the Tarot form. The shape and the images must be the same dimensions. The Width property should be 1,500 twips and the Height property should be 2,685 twips. Place four Image controls, making sure the Height and Width property values match. You can place the Image controls in a row

across the top of the form, level with the shape. Name the Shape control ShpTarot and name the four Image controls ImgCups, ImgPent, ImgWands, and ImgSwords.

As you undoubtedly have guessed, the shapes will be filled with Tarot card images. You need to obtain some appropriate pictures to use. You also can copy images from the www.hi-tekmall.com Web site, as already mentioned. A number of bitmaps, as well as project code, are used in various topics in this book. Of course, you can use any images, including those you create yourself. Make sure the pictures are the correct size. You can resize images in photo editing or paint programs, such as Windows Paint, Adobe Photoshop, or Corel Photopaint.

In addition to these controls, place a Label control (named LblTarot) with the caption **Click on Image to Select**. Set the Font property to Arial Black 12-point size (or a common font in at least 12-point size).

Finally, place a PictureBox control named PicTarot and set the Align property to Align Bottom.

TAKE NOTE

USE SMALL BITMAPS

Windows bitmap (.bmp files), are big. You can use files with compressed formats. CompuServe GIF and JPG files are both compressed and make smaller files to work with. GIF files do not use loss compression, so they don't compromise quality, but JPG compression results in lower quality images. If you are using bitmaps on the Internet, no advantage exists in displaying high-resolution files because the display is under 100 dots per inch.

CROSS-REFERENCE

Refer to Chapter 16 for using the PictureBox.

FIND IT ONLINE

Here is a list of programming newsgroups:
http://www.codewriters.net/.

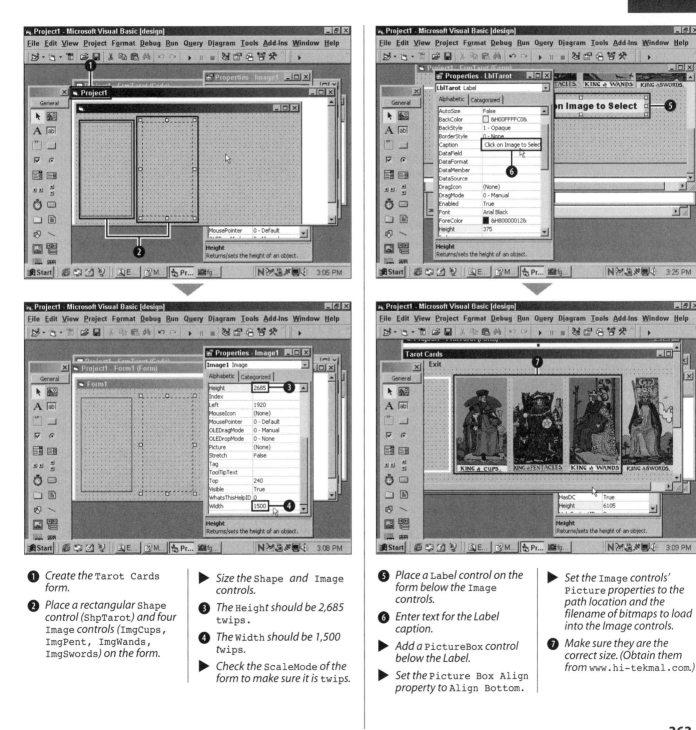

① Create the `Tarot Cards` form.

② Place a rectangular `Shape` control (`ShpTarot`) and four `Image` controls (`ImgCups`, `ImgPent`, `ImgWands`, `ImgSwords`) on the form.

▶ Size the `Shape` and `Image` controls.

③ The `Height` should be 2,685 twips.

④ The `Width` should be 1,500 twips.

▶ Check the `ScaleMode` of the form to make sure it is twips.

⑤ Place a `Label` control on the form below the `Image` controls.

⑥ Enter text for the `Label` caption.

▶ Add a `PictureBox` control below the `Label`.

▶ Set the `Picture Box Align` property to `Align Bottom`.

▶ Set the `Image` controls' `Picture` properties to the path location and the filename of bitmaps to load into the `Image` controls.

⑦ Make sure they are the correct size. (Obtain them from www.hi-tekmal.com.)

Displaying Images

When you finish adding all the controls, your form should closely resemble the one in the illustrations. Remember to add a Tarot Cards option named `mnuTarot` to the Other Forms menu on the `FrmImages` form. In the code window, select the mnuTarot object and the `Click` procedure, and then use the Show command to display the form from the menu.

The object in this exercise is to move the Shape over each of the cards as it is clicked to show it is selected. At the same time, you add a change in the background color as each card is selected. You could expand this concept to include a full Tarot deck and "deal" the cards, if you wished.

In the code window, select the Form object and the `Load` procedure to set the `ShpTarot Left` property to 100. This simply positions the `Shape` control to the left of the `Image` controls.

```
ShpTarot.Left = 100
```

Next, double-click the `ImgCups` image and select the `Click` procedure in the code window. You want to move the shape like a frame over the King of Cups graphic, so you align the left properties of each.

```
ShpTarot.Left = ImgCups.Left
    PicTarot.Cls
    FrmTarot.BackColor = QBColor(5)
    ShpTarot.BorderColor = QBColor(14)
    PicTarot.Print "King of Cups: Still waters
run deep."
```

The Cls command clears the screen of the text in the `PictureBox` control. You set the `BackColor` property of the form to magenta and the `BorderColor` of the Shape to yellow. The text explaining the card's meaning displays in the `PictureBox` control. Now you see the point of aligning the `PictureBox` to the bottom of the form.

Next, do the procedure for the `ImgPent Image` control. Click the ImgPent object and select the `Click` procedure. Again, align the left edges of the shape and image.

Clear the `PictureBox` control and assign colors to the shape border and the form background. A good idea is to pick contrasting colors so the shape, which is like a frame, will stand out from the background. Finally, the text for the King of Pentacles is entered.

Go ahead and complete the procedures for the `ImgWands` and `ImgSwords` controls. The `ImgWands` procedure is similar to the previous two. The background color for the Kind of Wands is dark cyan and the `BorderColor` is light red. The slogan "Love AND money AND fun" is an interpretation of the traditional meaning of the Tarot card.

The procedure for `ImgSwords` uses a bright yellow background and a deep magenta border for the `Shape` control. Basically, this routine can be copied and pasted, and then the colors changed. Keeping the `BorderColor` contrasting to the `BackColor` works best. When you finish the procedures, run the program select the Tarot Cards menu option and click each card picture to see the `Shape` control pop onto the selected picture.

TAKE NOTE

ROWS AND COLUMNS

Any composite picture can be divided into rows and columns. The height of a row is determined by dividing the height of the source bitmap by the number of rows. The width of each column is determined by dividing the width of the source image by the number of columns. The number of rows and columns in each source bitmap is based on how they are defined in the procedure.

CROSS-REFERENCE
Working with ActiveX controls is discussed in Chapter 20.

FIND IT ONLINE
This site offers icon utilities, such as converting BMPs into icons: **http://www.cyberus.ca/~ldorais/mycat.htm#icon**.

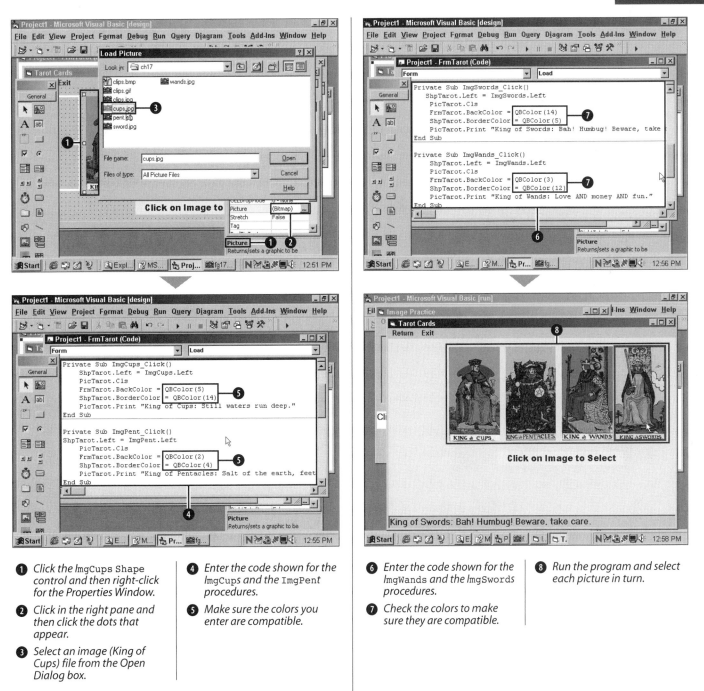

① Click the *ImgCups* Shape control and then right-click for the Properties Window.

② Click in the right pane and then click the dots that appear.

③ Select an image (King of Cups) file from the Open Dialog box.

④ Enter the code shown for the *ImgCups* and the *ImgPent* procedures.

⑤ Make sure the colors you enter are compatible.

⑥ Enter the code shown for the *ImgWands* and the *ImgSwords* procedures.

⑦ Check the colors to make sure they are compatible.

⑧ Run the program and select each picture in turn.

Working with the PictureClip Control

The next exercise also can use the Tarot pictures, but in a unique way. In the previous exercise, the pictures were discrete entities, each loaded separately. In this example, you display only portions of a picture.

Here you learn about a new control, the `PictureClip`. This control must be in your ToolBox, so select the Microsoft `PictureClip` Control 6.0 from Components, Controls on the Project menu.

You must begin with a composite picture or at least a picture with several viewable portions. You can combine several pictures into one in any photo-editing application. You create a new blank image, paste several smaller images into it, and then save it as a new file. When using bitmaps, use `GIF` or `JPG` files, as they are compressed.

Windows `Bitmap` (`BMP`) files are huge and not practical to use in most applications. Internet, especially requires small graphic files because each graphic viewed must first be downloaded. At the Baud rate of 56kb, a 500K file will take a while before it can be viewed. If many graphics are on one page — including animation — visitors will avoid the site or turn off the graphics.

The same graphics files used in the exercises are available from the `www.hi-tekmall.com` Web site. Source code for all the projects is also at that site.

The `PictureClip` control enables you to select and display parts of a source bitmap or icon. Instead of loading many pictures, where each picture consumes memory, you can load one large picture and use the `PictureClip` to display any region of the picture needed by your application at a particular moment. The `PictureClip` enables you to specify regions based upon the *X* and *Y* coordinates of the upper left area you want to display.

The `PictureClip` gives you a more efficient device for storing multiple picture resources. Basically, you use a source bitmap containing all the individual images you intend to use in your application. You could use this control to store all the images needed in a tool bar, and then refer to specific images when they are needed.

Properties you use with the `PictureClip` control include the `ClipX` and `ClipY` properties. With these properties, you specify the upper-left corner of the clipping region. You use the `ClipHeight` and `ClipWidth` properties to specify the area of the clipping region to be displayed. This works in two ways. You can identify the upper-left corner of the clipping region or specify the clipping region using the `ClipHeight and ClipWidth` properties. The second way is to divide the source bitmap into numbered rows and columns. The `GraphicCell` property is used to display individual cells.

Create a new form using the Add Form option on the Project menu. Name the form **FrmPix** and give it the caption **Picture Clips**.

Set up Return and Quit menus in the Menu Editor. Place a `PictureBox` control in the top-left corner of the form. Also place two `TextBox` controls underneath the `PictureBox`.

TAKE NOTE

▶ **BOUNDARY ERROR**

If you type values in the text boxes that are outside the area of the bitmap, you get an error 32015 returned. This is because the user-specified values for the ClipX and ClipY properties specify coordinates outside the boundary of the bitmap loaded in the `PictureClip` control.

CROSS-REFERENCE

References for the `PictureBox` are found in Chapter 9.

FIND IT ONLINE

This site contains information on the `PictureClip` control:
http://msdn.microsoft.com/library/devprods/vs6/vbasic/picclp98/vbprocliphgt_pclip.htm.

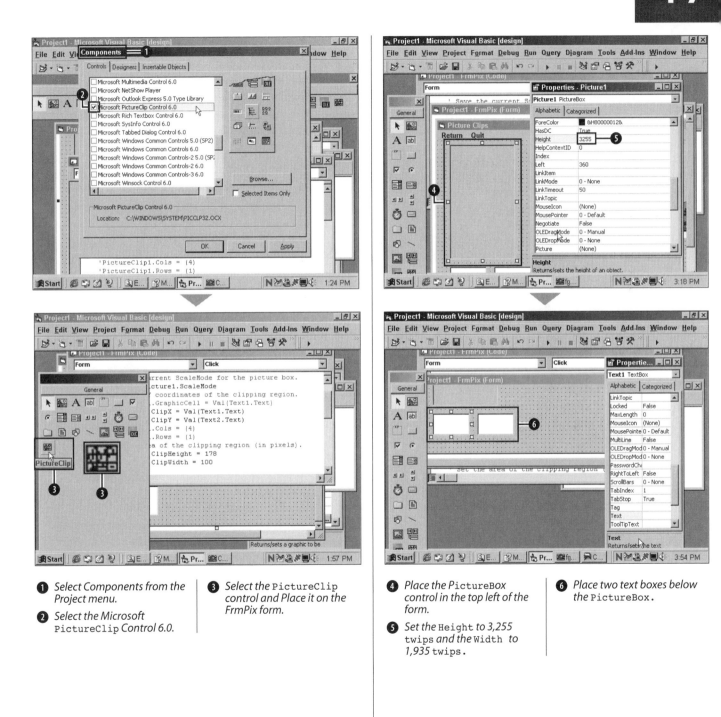

① Select Components from the Project menu.

② Select the Microsoft PictureClip Control 6.0.

③ Select the PictureClip control and Place it on the FrmPix form.

④ Place the PictureBox control in the top left of the form.

⑤ Set the Height to 3,255 twips and the Width to 1,935 twips.

⑥ Place two text boxes below the PictureBox.

Selecting a Region with the PictureClip Control

The scenario in this exercise is to provide the user with two text boxes in which to enter data for the *X* and *Y* coordinates for the upper-left portion of the bitmap to be displayed. The action is triggered by a mouse click on the form.

Select the `PictureClip` control from the ToolBox and place it on the right-hand side of the FrmPix form. Right-click the `PictureClip` control and select Properties for the `Property Pages`. Click the Picture tab and browse to find the `image` file. Select the file containing the composite picture (`Clips.JPG`, in this case). Click OK. The image used here is a composite of the four card pictures used in the last topic. The four cards (Cups, Pentacles, Wands. and Swords) are placed in one row with Cups on the left and Swords on the right.

The `ScaleMode`, `ScaleHeight`, `ScaleWidth`, `ScaleLeft`, and `ScaleTop`, `ClipX`, `ClipY`, `ClipWidth`, and `ClipHeight` properties are used with the `PictureClip` control. The `ScaleMode` property is used to set a value related to the unit of measure when using graphics methods. You must set a variable to equal to the `ScaleMode` property.

```
Dim SaveScale As Integer
SaveScale = Picture1.ScaleMode
```

The `SaveScale` variable is set equal to the `ScaleMode` property of `Picture1` to retain that value so it can be reset later.

```
PictureClip1.ClipX = Val(Text1.Text)
PictureClip1.ClipY = Val(Text2.Text)
```

The `ClipX` and `ClipY` properties are used to specify the upper-left corner of the clipping region, meaning the upper-left corner of the part of the composite picture in the `PictureClip`, which you (or the users) want displayed in the `PictureBox`. Here the ClipX value is that of the first text box. The value entered by the user determines the clipping region.

```
PictureClip1.ClipHeight = 178
PictureClip1.ClipWidth = 100
```

You use the `ClipHeight` and `ClipWidth` properties to specify the area of the clipping region to be displayed. Of course, the portion of the composite that will be displayed depends upon the coordinates entered by the user. The area shown will be 178 by 100, but that area could contain part of one card and part of another — again, depending upon the values entered.

```
PictureClip1.StretchX = Picture1.ScaleWidth
PictureClip1.StretchY = Picture1.ScaleHeight
```

Here, the `StretchX` and `StretchY` properties of the PictureClip object are set equal to the `ScaleWidth` and `ScaleHeight` of the `PictureBox`. This works to make the graphic fit the box. The `StretchX` and `StretchY` properties define the shape of the graphic to be copied. Depending upon the relative sizes of the `PictureBox` and the clip region, the graphic is either shrunk or stretched.

Using the related `ScaleHeight`, `ScaleWidth`, `ScaleLeft`, and `ScaleTop` properties, you can create a custom coordinate system with both positive and negative coordinates. These four Scale properties interact with the ScaleMode property.

```
Picture1.Picture = PictureClip1.Clip
Picture1.ScaleMode = SaveScale
```

In the previous code, the contents of the `PictureBox` is the same as the clipped region of the `PictureClip`. The ScaleMode is returned to its saved value from the beginning of the procedure.

TAKE NOTE

▶ **CHOOSING BITMAPS**

Make sure each image is the same size so that individual parts fill the space evenly. The `scale mode` of the `PictureBox` must be 3 pixels.

CROSS-REFERENCE

Find references in Chapter 16.

FIND IT ONLINE

Contains information on the ClipX and ClipY properties: **http:// msdn.microsoft.com/library/devprods/vs6/vbasic/picclp98/ vbproclipx_pclip.htm.**

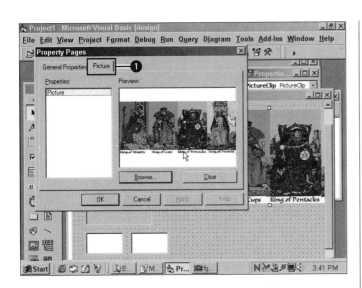

① *Identify a bitmap to load and add in the* PictureClip *Properties Picture tab.*

Listing 17-2: Procedure for Clipping a Region
Private

```
Sub Form_Click()
  Dim SaveScale As Integer
    SaveScale = Picture1.ScaleMode
    PictureClip1.ClipX =Val(Text1.Text)
    PictureClip1.ClipY = Val(Text2.Text)

    PictureClip1.ClipHeight = 178
    PictureClip1.ClipWidth = 100

    Picture1.ScaleMode = 3
    PictureClip1.StretchX = Picture1.ScaleWidth
    PictureClip1.StretchY = Picture1.ScaleHeight
  Picture1.Picture = PictureClip1.Clip
  Picture1.ScaleMode = SaveScale
End Sub
```

▶ *Enter the previous code.*
▶ *Be sure you have the correct clipping region defined for your specific graphic.*

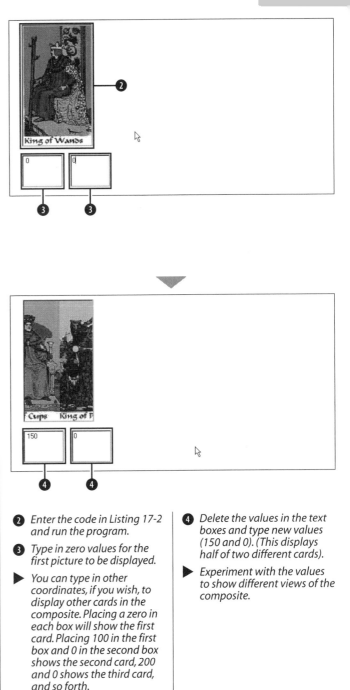

② *Enter the code in Listing 17-2 and run the program.*

③ *Type in zero values for the first picture to be displayed.*

▶ *You can type in other coordinates, if you wish, to display other cards in the composite. Placing a zero in each box will show the first card. Placing 100 in the first box and 0 in the second box shows the second card, 200 and 0 shows the third card, and so forth.*

④ *Delete the values in the text boxes and type new values (150 and 0). (This displays half of two different cards).*

▶ *Experiment with the values to show different views of the composite.*

Using Control Arrays with Image Controls

You can construct an interesting game by making a few adjustments to the PictureClip Clipping Region exercise. In fact, the experimentation with the Tarot cards may have given you some ideas. What if the row of cards were a single picture, such as a family photo? Instead of a composite of several discrete pictures, try using an ordinary bitmap image.

You can use your own scanned or any digital photo. You also can get the picture used in this exercise by downloading it from www.hi-tekmall.com. You must first crop or resize the photo as 300 by 300 pixels. Remember, too, you must set the `PictureBox ScaleMode` to 3 (unit of measure is pixels).

The picture is 300×300, so if you divide it into two rows and two columns, you will have four quadrants each of 150 pixels $\times0$ 150 pixels. This is a round figure, so this is why you are advised to obtain or make a square bitmap. The PictureClip control uses rows and columns moving from right to left, down to the lower left, and left to right again.

If you divide your photo into these four quadrants, you can offer users a puzzle in which they try to guess the correct coordinates to reconstruct the picture. This is much like working a jigsaw puzzle where you search for the correct piece to fit a space. Instead of physical puzzle pieces, though, you have electronic ones, represented by coordinates of the source bitmap. You still search for the correct piece of the puzzle, but the X and Y coordinates of each left corner are the sources of the "pieces."

First, use the Add Form option on the Project menu to add the new form, **FrmPuzzle**. Give the form a caption **Puzzles**. On the form, place a `PictureClip` control on the left side of the form. Place a `PictureBox` control on the right side of the form. You need four equal-sized boxes of approximately 150 pixels high and wide. This means you set the `ScaleHeight` and `ScaleWidth` each at 150. Check the `ScaleMode` property to make sure it is set to pixels.

When you place the second `PictureBox` control, name it `Picture1`. Respond Yes to the prompt as to whether you want to create an array. You see the name of the object change to reflect the different elements in the array. The first `PictureBox` will be named `Picture1(0)` and the second, `Picture1(1)`. Create two more picture boxes, naming each one `Picture1`. Each of them is then added to the array and named `Picture1(2)` and `Picture1(3)`.

Now, create two text boxes for each of the four picture boxes. These will each be used to enter the X and Y coordinates for the picture boxes. The first text box is, by default, named Text1. Add a second `TextBox` and give it the same name. Once again, you are prompted to create an array of text1 boxes. Now, when you add the other two, they become part of the array of Text1. The Picture1(0) box is associated with the Text1(0) text box and the Text2(0) text boxes. Create a second array of text boxes 1 through 4. Place the Text2 array boxes below the row of Text1 array boxes.

Use the `Label` control to label the boxes A, B, C, and D. The Text1(0) and Text2(0) boxes are under A, and the Text1(3) and Text2(3) boxes are under D.

CROSS-REFERENCE

Find references for control arrays in Chapters 8 and 9.

FIND IT ONLINE

Here is documentation on Rows and Cols properties:
http://msdn.microsoft.com/library/devprods/vs6/
vbasic/picclp98/vbproclipx_pclip.htm.

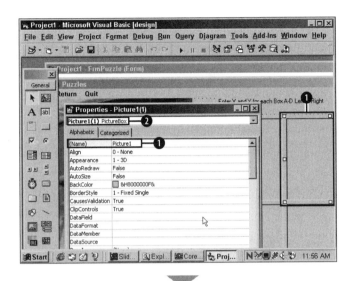

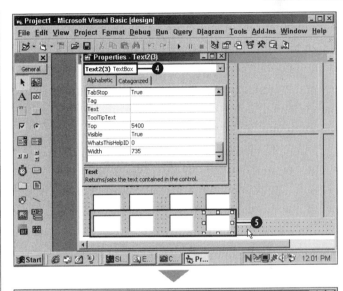

① *Add a* `PictureBox` *control to the FrmPuzzle form and then add a second* `PictureBox` *control, naming it* `Picture1`.

② *Respond Yes to Create an Array and note that the second box will be* `Picture1(1)`.

③ *Create a control array of four* `Text1` *text boxes.*

④ *Create a second control array of* `Text2` *textboxes.*

⑤ *Place them below the* `Text1` *control array.*

⑥ *Place a label control above the text boxes.*

⑦ *Label them A, B, C, and D.*

▶ *Right-click the* `PictureClip` *control and select* `Properties`.

⑧ *On the* `Property` *pages, select* `Picture` *and browse to find the* `Poolkids.jpg` *or other bitmap.*

Creating the Puzzle Procedure

You can modify the code you used in the last (Pictures) exercise. After copying the code from the FrmPix form, You need to modify it to take into account the three control arrays you set up when you placed the controls on the Puzzles form. Because you also changed the shape of the bitmap from one row with four columns to two rows and two columns, you must change the `ClipHeight` and `ClipWidth` to accommodate the difference. Because the variable you declared to retain the value of the `ScaleMode` was a simple variable, you must declare an array to replace it.

```
Dim SaveScale(4) As Integer, Z As Integer
```

`SaveScale` was not an array in the previous exercise, but it must be here because four picture boxes are in the control array. Declare Z to use in the For-Next loops to increment the counter for the array elements.

The `PictureClip` control is not an array, so the code here does not need to be changed except to reflect the pixel dimensions of the bitmap. The bitmap is 300 pixels square, so each quadrant (A, B, C, D) is 150 pixels.

Begin the For loop by setting the `SaveScale` control array elements to the value of the `PictureBox` control array elements.

```
For Z = 0 To 3
    SaveScale(Z) = Picture1(Z).ScaleMode
```

As each pass is made through the loop, a different control in the arrays is manipulated.

```
PictureClip1.ClipX = Val(Text1(Z).Text)
PictureClip1.ClipY = Val(Text2(Z).Text)
Picture1(Z).ScaleMode = 3
```

In the previous, the `PictureClip` control takes on the value of the upper-left corner of the clipping region specified in the `Text1` and `Text2` control arrays. Remember, the clipping region means the upper-left corner of the part of the composite picture in the `PictureClip` you want displayed in each `PictureBox`. Here, the `ClipX` value is that of the first text box. The value entered by the user determines the clipping region for each of the picture boxes.

```
PictureClip1.StretchX = _
Picture1(Z).ScaleWidth
PictureClip1.StretchY = _
Picture1(Z).ScaleHeight
Picture1(Z).Picture = PictureClip1.Clip
```

The `StretchX` and `StretchY` properties of the PictureClip object are set equal to the `ScaleWidth` and `ScaleHeight` of each `PictureBox`. This makes each clipped portion of the graphic fit each box. The `StretchX` and `StretchY` properties define the shape of the graphic to be copied. Depending upon the relative sizes of the `PictureBoxes` and the clip region, each portion of the graphic is shrunk or stretched.

When each set of X and Y coordinates is changed in the A, B, C and D textboxes, the portions of each shift to show different portions of the picture. You needn't restart the program to reenter the X and Y values.

End the loop with the Next statement. Run the program and practice typing different values for each of the text box pairs. If you want to construct the picture to be as closely matched up as possible, enter the values for A: X=0 Y=0, B: X=150 Y=0, C: X=0 Y=150, D: X=150 Y=150. Change the values and see the change in the composite picture.

TAKE NOTE

Scalemode PROPERTY

Setting the value of any other `Scale` property to any value sets `ScaleMode` to 0. Setting the `ScaleMode` property to a number higher than 0 changes `ScaleHeight` and `ScaleWidth` to the new unit of measurement and sets `ScaleLeft` and `ScaleTop` to 0. The `CurrentX` and `CurrentY` property settings change to reflect the new coordinates of the current point.

CROSS-REFERENCE

More information is available on graphics in Chapter 16.

FIND IT ONLINE

This has a code example of the `PictureClip` control:
http://msdn.microsoft.com/library/devprods/vs6/vbasic/picclp98/vbproclippclipx.htm.

Listing 17-3: The `Puzzle` **Procedure** ❶

```
Private Sub Form_Click()
   Dim SaveScale(4) As Integer, Z As Integer
   PictureClip1.ClipHeight = 150
   PictureClip1.ClipWidth = 150
  For Z = 0 To 3
    SaveScale(Z) = Picture1(Z).ScaleMode
   PictureClip1.ClipX = Val(Text1(Z).Text)
   PictureClip1.ClipY = Val(Text2(Z).Text)
Picture1(Z).ScaleMode = 3
picture box.
PictureClip1.StretchX = Picture1(Z).ScaleWidth
PictureClip1.StretchY =
Picture1(Z).ScaleHeight
Picture1(Z).Picture = PictureClip1.Clip
Picture1(Z).ScaleMode = SaveScale(Z)
  Next Z
 End Sub
```

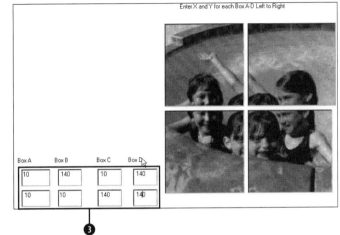

❸ *Change the XY values in the text boxes and observe the change in puzzle pictures.*

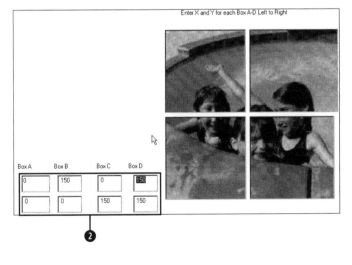

❶ *Enter the code previously shown and execute the program.*

❷ *Enter the XY values shown for the four pairs of text boxes.*

Moving Cards with the Move Method

In the last exercise, you used the `PictureClip` control to display portions of a bitmap. You then positioned the regions of the bitmap based upon user-entered coordinates. In this exercise, you return to the Tarot cards. Dealing the cards gives you a chance to practice using the Move method.

The Move method enables you to change the position of a form or control, and uses the syntax:

```
object.Move left, top, width, height
```

The argument is mandatory, but the subsequent arguments are not. If you specify any arguments to the right, you must also specify those between the Move keyword and the argument you use. In other words, you may not skip any arguments.

Use the Add Form option on the Project menu to add the FrmMove form. You may give it the caption "Moving Cards." You use the Move method to simulate the movement of cards when they are being dealt. Add four picture boxes to the form. As you add each one, use the same name (`Picture1`) so you create a control array, like the one in the Puzzle exercise. Your `PictureBox` controls should be staggered on the left side of the form, so the last box `Picture1(3)` is below and to the right of the others. The first box should be on top.

In the Properties Window, select the `Picture` property and load each of the four Tarot card bitmaps for each `PictureBox` in the control array. Size the picture boxes so the cards fit exactly as you did in the FrmPix example.

In the Menu Editor, add an Options menu with options to Deal Cards, Return and Quit. Name the Deal Cards option mnuDeal. Add the procedures for the Return and Quit options, using Show and End for each.

Add a `Timer` control and a Command button to the form. Caption the Command button "Reset Cards." This exercise is somewhat like the Auto Shapes and Lines portion of the ProjGraphic project in the last chapter. This project includes many methods and controls you already used, but it applies new uses to them.

The goal is to move the cards you placed on the form as if they were being dealt out to someone. To do this, you need to create a different movement of the cards each time they are dealt. The cards begin on the left and move downward and to the right, or upward and to the right. To create the random effect. you can use the `Rnd` function, which is used here several times in the procedures. Declare Z, J, L, and Directn. These variables are used as counters and to hold the values of random numbers.

Begin with the `mnuDeal_Click` procedure. You need a way to tell if the Deal Cards option has been selected, so set the `Checked` property to True when the menu item is selected.

```
mnuDeal.Checked = True
Directn = Int(100 * Rnd + 20)
L = Int(10 * Rnd)
```

Also create the random-number generation for Directn and L. You are adding 20 to the equation, so numbers under 20 are not generated.

TAKE NOTE

▶ MOVING AND SCALING PROPERTIES

The `Left`, `Top`, `Height`, and `Width` properties are used for operations founded on the external dimensions of an object. This includes moving or resizing an object. You can use the `ScaleLeft`, `ScaleTop`, `ScaleHeight`, and `ScaleWidth` properties for maneuvers using internal dimensions of an object. Only the `PictureBox` control, Form, and Printer objects use the scale-related properties.

CROSS-REFERENCE

Chapter 16 contains parallels with the `Deal` procedure.

FIND IT ONLINE

Here is documentation on the Move method: **http://msdn.microsoft.com/library/devprods/vs6/vbasic/vb98/vbmthmove.htm**.

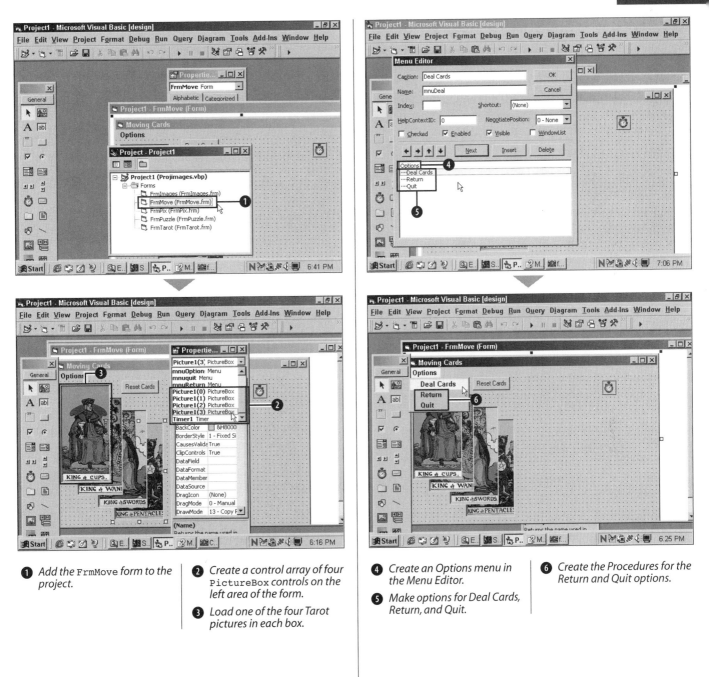

① *Add the* FrmMove *form to the project.*

② *Create a control array of four* PictureBox *controls on the left area of the form.*

③ *Load one of the four Tarot pictures in each box.*

④ *Create an Options menu in the Menu Editor.*

⑤ *Make options for Deal Cards, Return, and Quit.*

⑥ *Create the Procedures for the Return and Quit options.*

Creating the Deal Procedure

Before setting up the `Deal` procedure, you need to add a `Timer_Timer` procedure. The `Timer` control is going to be responsible for controlling the speed of the movement of the cards being dealt. Use the `Checked` property of the menu option to call the `Deal` procedure.

```
If mnuDeal.Checked Then
    Deal
```

This sends the execution to the `Deal` procedure only if the user has selected the Deal Cards option on the menu.

Now you are ready for the `Deal` procedure. This is what you design to happen when the Deal option is selected. Create the `Private Sub Deal()`. Remember, when the Deal option is selected, the Directn and *L* random numbers ware selected. There are two parts to the procedure. These two options create variation in the direction and movement of the cards. Within each part, the random numbers also cause variation.

First, because *L* can have a value of 0 to 10, you set up options based upon values over and under the number 4. If *L* is less than 4, then execution moves to the Bigdeal line; if *L* is equal to or over 4, execution goes to the Smalldeal line.

Once at the `Bigdeal` and `Smalldeal` lines, For-Next loops are executed to increment the elements in the `PictureBox` control array. This reduces the amount of code necessary to carry out the tasks and do the calculations. The Move method is used to move the Left and Top of each picture.

```
J = Z + 2: K = Directn * 0.25
Picture1(Z).Move Picture1(Z).Left + (J *
Directn), Picture1(Z).Top + (J * K)
```

In the previous, *Z* is the loop variable that determines which box is being moved. The Move method is operating on the Left using the current value of the Left position plus *J* multiplied by the value of Directn. The Top is being moved by the amount of the current value of the Top position plus *J* (*K*. Using the value of `Directn` makes the position and speed change randomly. The range of numbers selected is between 20 and 100. The amount of each movement varies, simulating differences in speed.

Changing the `Timer Interval` property also can control the speed. In fact, you must give the `Timer Interval` a value or nothing will happen. You can set it to 50 as a starting point. If this is too slow or too fast, you can change it. The two factors — random numbers used in the Left and Top position calculations — and the Timer Interval determine the cards speed as they are dealt.

The `Smalldeal` line also varies the movement.

```
J = Z + 4: K = Directn * 0.1
```

Here, the values of *J* and Directn are further changed from those in the Bigdeal line. The movements are greater simulating greater speed.

Finally, you must reset the pictures to their original placing. Use the Command button `Click` procedure to do this.

```
mnuDeal.Checked = False
Picture1(0).Top = 120
Picture1(0).Left = 120
```

The `Checked` property value is set to False so the process can begin again when the Deal option is selected.

TAKE NOTE

THE COORDINATE SYSTEM

The default coordinate system is always in twips. When you move a control on a Form or in a container such as a `PictureBox`, the coordinate system of the container object is used. The coordinate system or unit of measure is set with the `ScaleMode` property at design time. You can use the Scale change to change the coordinate system at run time.

CROSS-REFERENCE

Chapter 16 offers some parallels with the procedures in this exercise.

FIND IT ONLINE

Here is an example using the Move method: http://msdn.microsoft.com/library/devprods/vs6/vbasic/rdo98/rdpromovefirstx.htm.

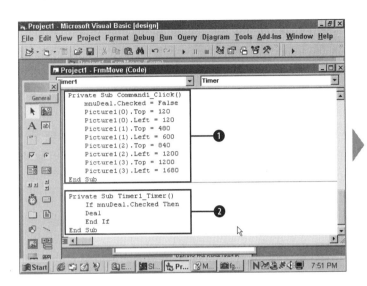

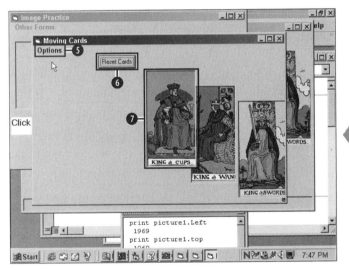

① Enter the Code for the Command1_Click *procedure.*

② Enter the code for the Timer *procedure.*

⑤ Run the program and select the Deal Cards option.

⑥ Press the Reset button and Deal again.

⑦ Do the previous so you can see differences in the cards' movements.

Listing 17-4: The mnuDeal_Click **and** Deal **procedures**

```
Private Sub mnuDeal_Click()
    mnuDeal.Checked = True
    Directn = Int(100 * Rnd + 20)  ←❸
    L = Int(10 * Rnd)
End Sub                                      ❹
Private Sub Deal()
    If L < 4 Then
        GoTo Bigdeal
    End If
    If L >= 4 Then
        GoTo Smalldeal
    End If
Bigdeal:
 For Z = 0 To 3
    J = Z + 2: K = Directn * 0.25
    Picture1(Z).Move Picture1(Z).Left + (J *
Directn), Picture1(Z).Top + (J * K)
Next Z
Smalldeal:
    For Z = 0 To 3
    J = Z + 4: K = Directn * 0.1
    Picture1(Z).Move Picture1(Z).Left + (J *
Directn), Picture1(Z).Top + (J * K)
  Next Z
End Sub
```

❸ *Enter the code for the* mnuDeal *procedure.*

❹ *Enter the code for the* Deal *procedure.*

Personal Workbook

Q&A

1 Setting what property enables you to create persistent graphics?

_____

_____

_____

2 What properties determine the positions of the clipping region?

_____

_____

_____

3 What properties determine the area of the clipping region for the `PictureClip` control?

_____

_____

_____

4 What does the `ScaleMode` property value of 3 stand for?

_____

_____

_____

5 What color function has arguments based on colors 0–15?

_____

_____

_____

_____

6 What does the Print command do when used in code?

_____

_____

_____

7 What do the `StretchX` and `StretchY` properties do?

_____

_____

_____

8 What properties must be set for the `Timer` control to function?

_____

_____

_____

ANSWERS: PAGE 528

EXTRA PRACTICE

1 Add a new option to the Options menu on the Moving Cards form. Define the nature of the display. How can you vary it?

2 Write a new procedure for the Moving Cards form. Create an option to shuffle the cards and stack them in a deck.

3 Write a new option for the Image Practice form that will draw circles instead of lines.

4 Use a family photo in an application similar to the Puzzles application. Copy regions of the photo into a series of boxes.

REAL WORLD APPLICATIONS

✔ You entered a contest to write a fortune-telling game. Use what you have learned in this chapter to create a game using a deck of cards, dice, or other objects that can be thrown, dealt, or tossed to predict the future.

✔ You have been assigned the task of designing an application and outlining the procedures for an application that will display photos of employees associated with their names and ID numbers.

✔ Aunt Hannah is having more trouble with her Web site. She needs to display photos of her Sunday School class and move them around on the screen. She wants you to help her.

Visual Quiz

Is the selected control part of a control array?

_____

_____

_____

_____

_____

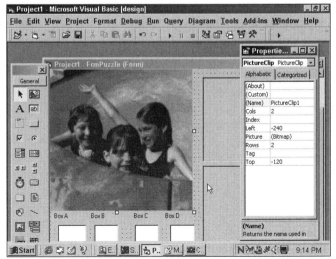

CHAPTER 18

Understanding OLE

The last three chapters focused on many graphics types. The multimedia chapter (Chapter 15) introduced animated graphics. Chapters 16 and 17 explored the use of draw and paint operations, as well as the use of bitmaps. This chapter concludes the discussion begun in Part IV.

The subject of Object Linking and Embedding is tied in with graphics. This is primarily because graphics applications are often those that promote the interest and need to incorporate in Visual Basic applications. For example, you can embed a paint program so your users have all the tools in that application available.

The existence of the image editing applications in the Insertable Objects tab on the Components menu demonstrates that these types of applications most often employ the automation necessary for Object Linking and Embedding.

Object Linking and Embedding (OLE) is the facility that enables you to incorporate components from different programs within an application. Stated in the simplest terms, *Linking* is the act of attaching the objects in an external application. *Embedding* occurs when you place these objects in a container, such as the OLE container.

Using the `OLE container` control, you can link or embed objects from any application that supports automation. This includes Microsoft products, such as Word and Excel. It also includes Corel products, such as Draw and PhotoPaint, MicroGrafx, and many others. You can see what products are listed under Insertable Objects under the Components option on the Project menu. Any products installed on your system are shown there and you can select them to be inserted in your applications.

The resulting application using OLE is known as *document centered* because you can import documents from various applications to be combined and to function together in your new application.

Linking and Embedding Objects

The following are a few of the things you can do with OLE:

▶ Create an object at run time from one embedded in the `OLE container` control.
▶ Bring objects from the Clipboard as new objects.
▶ Use icons to represent objects.
▶ Create a linked object for your application.
▶ Bind the `OLE` control to data in a database.
▶ Enable the user to update any changes to data in the `OLE container`.

You can add the `OLE container` control to your application by placing it on your form. You can then use the container to hold an object.

Or, you can create a class of an object by selecting from the products listed under Insertable Objects, under the Components option on the Project menu. Any products you installed on your system will be shown there. You can select an application from those listed. When you select the application from the Insertable Objects tab, it appears in your ToolBox as a control.

For the first topic exercise, create a new project named ProjOLE with a form, FrmOLE. Create a menu in the Menu Editor. Create a menu called Other Applications, named mnuOther and one to Exit the project, called mnuExit.

Select Components from the Project menu and then click the Insertable Objects tab. The applications listed show you all the products that support OLE. This means you can insert objects created in these applications into the `OLE container` and you can also insert an object's class into the ToolBox. Select a Paint Program.

Place an `OLE container` control on the form. Right-click and then check the Create from File box. Find the file on your system. You can select graphic files from the

VB98\Graphics\Bitmaps directory. When you make your selection, the file is inserted in the `OLE container`. You needn't select an application for this operation. If you select a `.BMP` graphic file, it will be inserted. If you select a `WAV` or `MIDI` file, you must have the means to play them on your system.

You can select the MIDI Sequencer from the Insertable Objects tab. Then you can play a `MIDI` file at run time. If the Sequencer is not listed with the Insertable Objects, you probably will be unable to use objects requiring that application.

Draw another OLE container control on the form. Right-click and check to see if you have the MIDI Sequencer on the list of objects. If so, check the Create from File box. Select one of the MIDI files in the Windows\Media directory. If you prefer to play a WAV or other sound file, load another file from the Windows\Media (or other) directory.

Launch the program and right-click to get the pop-up menu. For the sound files, you can `Play, Edit` and `Open`. If you choose `Open`, the VCR graphic will be displayed and you can click the File menu to open a new file. The Edit option for the sound files enables you to select the Edit menu on the VCR.

TAKE NOTE

▶ OLEDRAG

The OLEDrag method is called by the MouseMove event after data is selected, the button is pressed, and the mouse is moved. No arguments exist for this method. The major principle here is to use manual dragging to begin. This sets the course for the OLEStartDrag event to provide settings for the dragging.

CROSS-REFERENCE

Refer to Chapter 5 for information regarding mouse events.

FIND IT ONLINE

Check out this site, which has OLE-related downloads: http://www.vbexplorer.com/download.asp.

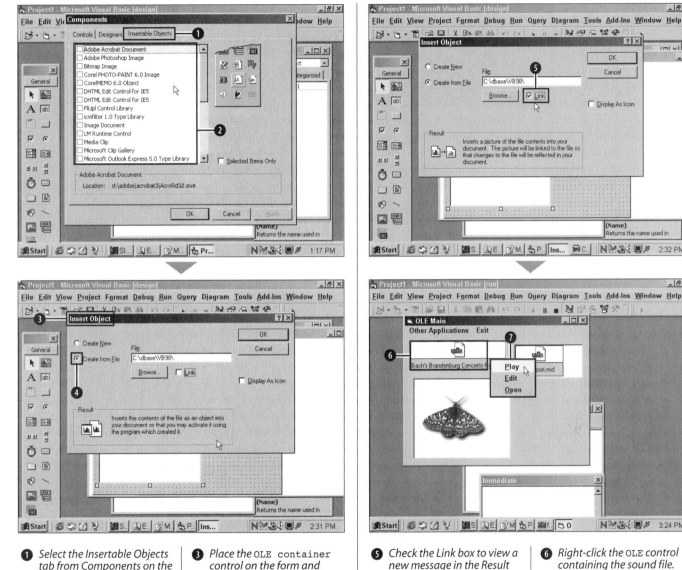

① Select the Insertable Objects tab from Components on the Project menu.

② Check the applications you can use for Linking and Embedding.

③ Place the OLE container control on the form and right-click and then select Insert Object from the pop-up menu.

④ Check the Create from File box.

⑤ Check the Link box to view a new message in the Result pane.

▶ Select a Sound file from the Windows\Media directory.

⑥ Right-click the OLE control containing the sound file. Note the pop-up menu.

⑦ Select Play, Edit, and Open, in turn.

Using OLE Objects

Selecting the pop-up menu options by right-clicking the `OLE Container` Object gives you many tools. For one thing, the menu bar you created in the Menu Editor has been replaced with the Microsoft Paint menu.

When you right-click the Bitmap container, the Edit option for the bitmap sets up a box with scrollbars and a pencil tool. You can draw on the picture with the pencil or select a new color from the Colors menu. The Image menu enables you to Rotate, Stretch, and so on just as the Microsoft Paint program does. In fact, any object you embed incorporates the menu of the default application used with that object, as stored on your system.

When you insert an object into the `OLE` control, `the Class`, `SourceDoc`, and `SourceItem` properties are set for you. Setting these properties identifies the source application, the file name, and data in the file.

The key difference in Linking and Embedding an object at design time is, when you embed data from a file, a copy of the specified file's data is displayed in the `OLE container` control. When you insert a linked object, the data continue to reside in the source file. The container contains only the link information. This means inserting a Linked object can be a problem when you are on a network because all users must have access to the path and file that is linked. To save changes to the source file, you must use the Update method.

Further, the embedded (not linked) object does not run the parent application, but substitutes its menu for the form, including the `OLE container` control. To stop the execution here, you need to close the form. This means clicking the icon in the upper-left corner of your form and then selecting Close. No exit option is on the superimposed menu.

The linked object furnishes users with a facsimile of the external application, while the embedded object superimposes the external program's menu on the Visual Basic form's menu bar. Because these are quite different interfaces to present to users, the intent of the application should be carefully considered.

Another option besides embedding or linking an object at design time is to embed an empty object to be filled at run time. To do this, you select Insert Object as before, but do not check the `Create from` File. Instead, select `Create New` and then select the Paintbrush Picture application. At run time, the user can right-click the `OLE` control and select Open. From the Paintbrush menu, select "Edit, Paste From..." Select the file from the file dialog box. To exit, select "Exit & Return to."

You also can use the Paste Special at design time to insert the contents of the Clipboard into the `OLE container` control.

TAKE NOTE

▶ OLE DRAG-AND-DROP PROCESSES

Although drag-and-drop events are generated in both manual and automatic processes, these events are only generated for the source and the target of the drag-and-drop when the process is manual. The automatic drag-and-drop generates no events for the target side of the process.

CROSS-REFERENCE

Chapter 9 provides insight into controls that provide drag-and-drop capability.

FIND IT ONLINE

This file uses drag-and-drop methods: **http://www. vbexplorer.com/files/dragdrop.zip**.

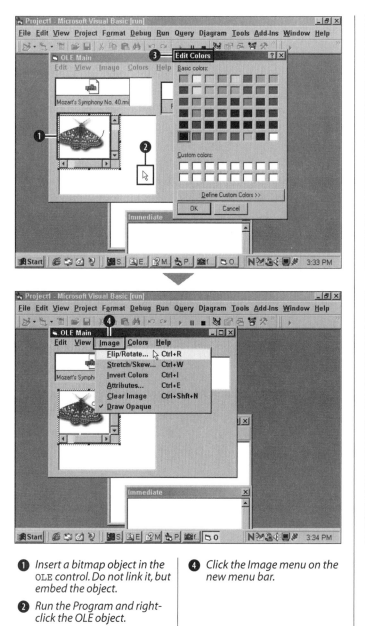

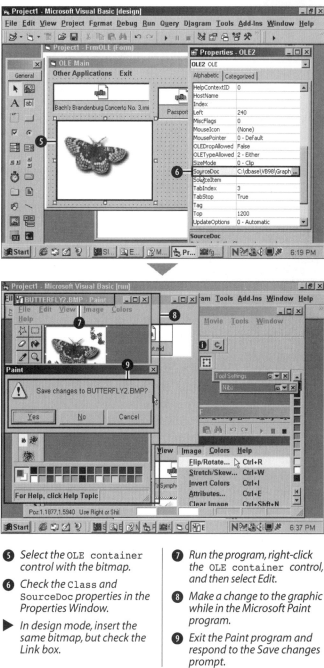

① *Insert a bitmap object in the OLE control. Do not link it, but embed the object.*

② *Run the Program and right-click the OLE object.*

③ *Select Edit Colors from the new menu on the menu bar.*

④ *Click the Image menu on the new menu bar.*

⑤ *Select the OLE container control with the bitmap.*

⑥ *Check the Class and SourceDoc properties in the Properties Window.*

▶ *In design mode, insert the same bitmap, but check the Link box.*

⑦ *Run the program, right-click the OLE container control, and then select Edit.*

⑧ *Make a change to the graphic while in the Microsoft Paint program.*

⑨ *Exit the Paint program and respond to the Save changes prompt.*

Adding OLE Objects from Applications

Add a new `OLE container` control to the FrmOLE form. Right-click and select Insert Object from the pop-up menu. Check Create from File. Browse to select a Microsoft Word document. Now, the document will appear in the `OLE container` control, just as the sound file and the bitmap did.

Execute your application, right-click the `OLE3` control, and then select Edit from the pop-up menu. Now you can edit the document. Notice the Word menu has replaced the form's menu bar. You have access to all the controls on the Word menu except no File menu exists. There is no Exit option, but you can close the application by selecting the `Form` control on the form's title bar above the menu bar on the left. You also can click one of the other OLE objects to release the Word menu and return to the form's original menu. Practice changing fonts in the document. Select Word Count from the Tools menu and check other menu options.

Next, create a link for the same document. In the design mode, right-click the `OLE container` control, select Create from File as before, select the same file, and then check the Link box. Now the document looks as it did in the preceding example.

Execute the application. Right-click the `OLE3 container` control and select Edit. Now the screen changes to the Microsoft Word window, as if you had launched the Word program itself. Make some changes in the document and then select Exit from the File menu. Notice you are prompted to save changes, which did not happen in the previous example.

It is clear you cannot save edited items by selecting the menu option to save when the object is embedded. If you select Open instead of Edit from the pop-up menu, however, you are suddenly in the Word window, just as you were when you linked the document. You do not have a Save option on the File menu, but you can use the Update or Save copy option to save your changes. Try both the Edit and Open options with the OLE bitmap as well. Practice with various files and embedding and linking.

Paste and Paste Special can be used in Design mode to insert objects into the `OLE container` control. These commands paste the contents of the Clipboard, so be sure the Clipboard document is the correct format or you will receive an error message.

Practice also with the OLE sound file. You can use the same options to Edit and Open, but you also have a Play option. When you use the Play option, you see the object with the VCR controls, but you have no menu bar. If you choose to Edit or Open, you have the controls with a menu bar.

Again, you must consider carefully how you will handle linked and embedded documents in users' terms before creating these options. The user viewpoint is important because you must anticipate how the user will want to employ the OLE features.

CROSS-REFERENCE

Refer to Chapter 15 for information on combining sound and graphics.

FIND IT ONLINE

Drag-and-drop is explained here: **http://msdn.microsoft.com /library/devprods/vs6/vbasic/vbcon98/vbcondroppingoledrag sourceontooledroptarget.htm.**

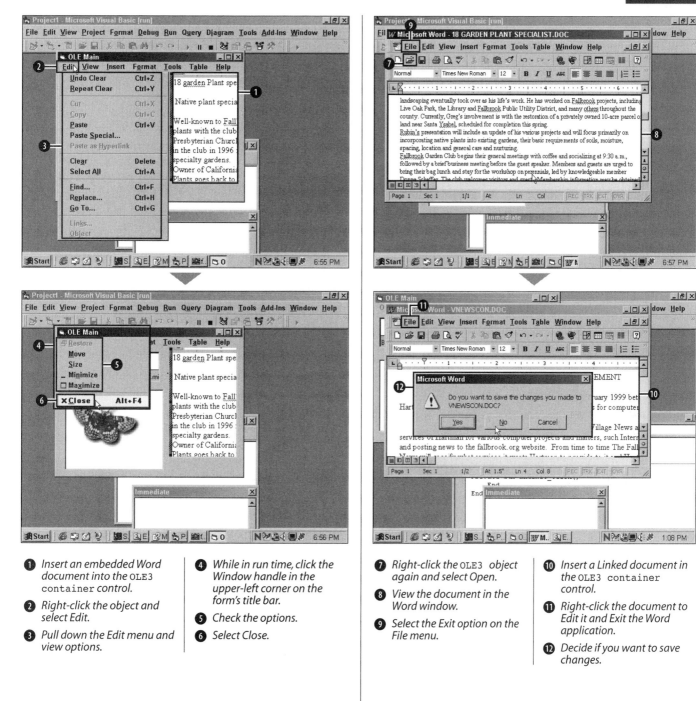

① Insert an embedded Word document into the OLE3 container control.

② Right-click the object and select Edit.

③ Pull down the Edit menu and view options.

④ While in run time, click the Window handle in the upper-left corner on the form's title bar.

⑤ Check the options.

⑥ Select Close.

⑦ Right-click the OLE3 object again and select Open.

⑧ View the document in the Word window.

⑨ Select the Exit option on the File menu.

⑩ Insert a Linked document in the OLE3 container control.

⑪ Right-click the document to Edit it and Exit the Word application.

⑫ Decide if you want to save changes.

Inserting OLE Objects at Run Time

So far, you have been inserting objects into the OLE container controls at Design time. You made the decisions as to the type of documents and the actual files that would be inserted. You also decided whether they would be embedded or linked. But what would happen if you turned over that decision making power to the user? In fact, most applications you can imagine would probably give that discretion to the user. Can you imagine the developers of Microsoft Word deciding what document you should open?

The application you are creating may not be a good comparison to Word, but how would you know what the user's needs are? True, you can load a sample document into an OLE container control and the user can then open a new document by selecting Open on the pop-up menu. But does a need exist to make any selection in Design mode?

Add a new form to the project called FrmRunTime. Give the form a caption, such as OLE at Run Time. Draw two OLE container controls on the form. Make the one on the left (OLE1) a little larger than OLE2.

Make Labels for the controls by drawing Label controls on the form. The first OLE control is going to enable the user to make a selection from the Insert Object dialog box, so ask the user to double-click the container. The second OLE control will be coded to load the butterfly picture when clicked, so make that label appropriate for that function.

Instead of loading the objects at design time, you can enable the users to select them at run time. First, create empty OLE containers, by responding to the Insert Object dialog box with Create New and then by selecting the Class of object you expect to be inserted in the container, that is, Microsoft Word. The container will then be empty at run time, enabling the user to make a selection.

The Class of the object is important, as you can see in the Properties Window. Your system will have a list of object classes for the applications installed on your system. You can view a list of valid class names available on your system, select a control, such as the OLE container control, and select the Class property in the Properties window. The

Class for OLE1 should be Word.Document and the Class for OLE2 should be Paint.Picture.

Because you want the user to make the selection of file, you want the user presented with a dialog box.

```
OLE1.InsertObjDlg
```

This simple statement is all that is needed to invoke the Insert Object dialog box.

Next, the other OLE container control will be coded to load a specific file at run time because, in this case, the user will not be allowed to make a choice.

```
OLE2.CreateEmbed "C:\ _vb98\graphics\
bitmaps\butterfly2.bmp"
```

The CreateEmbed method is used to create an embedded object. The CreateLink method is used to create a Link. These are two ways you can load a graphic at run time. You also can use the CreateEmbed method to enable the user to make a file selection, but specify the Class of file to be created. This statement will ensure the user selects an appropriate file Class, which happens to be a bitmap here.

```
OLE2.CreateEmbed "", "Paint.Picture"
OLE2.CreateEmbed "", "Word.Document"
```

The second statement shows the syntax for inserting a Word file.

TAKE NOTE

▶ OLE PROPERTIES

You needn't set the Class and SourceDoc properties when using the CreateEmbed method to create an embedded object. When you set up a new object, the application associated with the class name must be in the Windows Registry. This should take place when you go through each application's Install program.

CROSS-REFERENCE
Check Chapter 9 to review the controls that support OLE linking and embedding.

FIND IT ONLINE
Linking and Embedding is discussed here: **http://msdn. microsoft.com/isapi/msdnlib.idc?theURL=/library/books/ winguide/platfrm2/d5/s1167e.htm**.

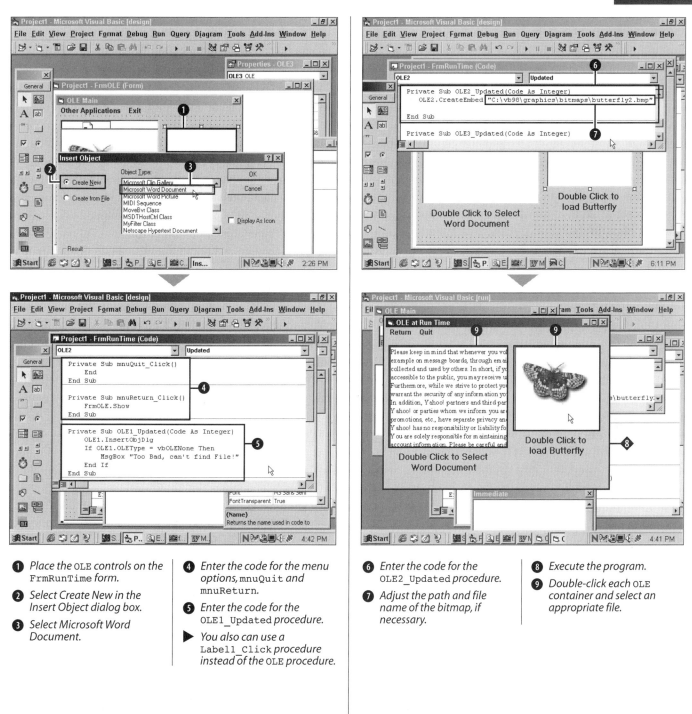

① *Place the* OLE *controls on the* FrmRunTime *form.*

② *Select Create New in the Insert Object dialog box.*

③ *Select Microsoft Word Document.*

④ *Enter the code for the menu options,* mnuQuit *and* mnuReturn.

⑤ *Enter the code for the* OLE1_Updated *procedure.*

▶ *You also can use a* Label1_Click *procedure instead of the* OLE *procedure.*

⑥ *Enter the code for the* OLE2_Updated *procedure.*

⑦ *Adjust the path and file name of the bitmap, if necessary.*

⑧ *Execute the program.*

⑨ *Double-click each* OLE *container and select an appropriate file.*

Dragging-and-Dropping OLE Objects

OLE drag and drop is a powerful tool. You are not merely moving objects from one container to another; you are moving the actual data contained in the source.

In carrying out an OLE drag-and-drop operation, specific events are brought about on the source and target sides. Whether the drag-and-drop operation is automatic or manual, the events associated with the source object are always accomplished. But, the target events are only generated in a manual-drop operation.

Most Visual Basic controls support automatic OLE drag-and-drop features, for which no code is required. If you use manual dragging and/or dropping, code will be required. You can easily check to see if controls support OLE drag-and-drop by viewing the Properties in the Properties Window. Look to see if there are OLEDropMode and OLEDragMode properties.

The OLEDragMode property provides automatic or manual dragging of controls, as long as the control supports it. The OLEDropMode property specifies how a control will react when an object is dropped. The OLEDragDrop event distinguishes when an object is dropped onto a control. The OLEStartDrag event denotes the data formats and drop effects the source control supports when the dragging begins. The OLEDrag method begins the manual dragging and is available for controls that do not have automatic drag-and-drop.

Manual dragging-and-dropping is often used to have better control over the events. It must be used if automatic drag-and-drop is not supported by the control.

You used the DragDrop procedure in Chapters 8 and 9. In those projects, you dragged the filename over the PictureBox control and, as a result, a bitmap appeared in the PictureBox. In this case, a drag-and-drop operation did not involve an OLE container control. In that project, the OLEDragMode is set to Manual because the user is expected to do the dragging. The OLEDropMode is set to None.

How you determine the events and the ways you will react to them depends upon how you decide to execute the drag-and-drop capability. As in the FrmDraggin example, if you want to be able to let the user choose which file to drag-and-drop, then the OLEDragMode property can be set to Manual. In this case, the DragMode property is also set to Manual.

If it is important to check the data before you drop it into a control, you need to use Manual drag-and-drop settings. Because so many possibilities exist, drag-and-drop can range from simple to quite complex. The easiest plan is to drag-and-drop automatically between controls. However, other ways exist to carry out OLE drag-and-drop without writing much (or even any) code.

TAKE NOTE

OLE AUTOMATION

Automation used to be called *OLE automation*. You can Link and Embed with any control that supports automation. The OLE container control differs from other controls that support automation in its capability to make document-centered applications. Using the OLE container control, you can display and copy data as if you were actually running an external application.

CROSS-REFERENCE

Check Chapters 8 and 9 to review the controls supporting automation.

FIND IT ONLINE

This site has information on dragging the source over the target.
http://msdn.microsoft.com/library/devprods/vs6/vbasic/vbcon98/vbcondraggingoledragsourceoveroledroptarget.htm

Table 18-1: DRAG-AND-DROP SCHEMATIC

Events From Source	Events To Target
OLE Start Drag	OLEDragDrop
OLESetData	OLEDragOver
OLEGiveFeedBack	
OLECompleteDrag	

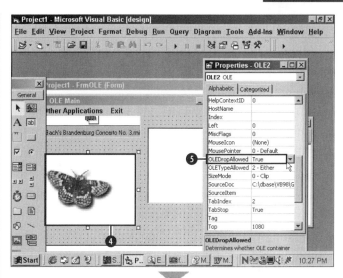

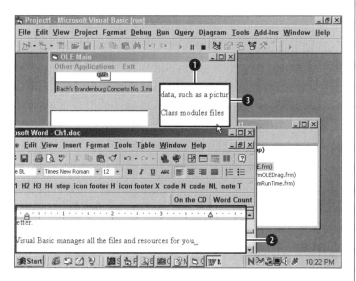

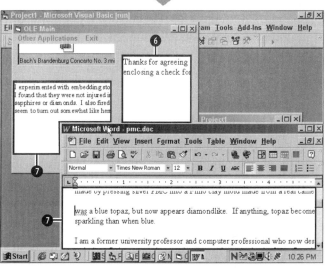

① *Run the application and right-click the* OLE3 *container on the OLE Main form.*

② *Open a document in the Word window.*

③ *Select a portion and drag it into the* OLE3 *container.*

▶ *If this action did not work, check the* OLEDropAllowed *property. It should be set to True.*

④ *In Design mode, select the* OLE2 *container.*

⑤ *Set the* OLEDropAllowed *property to True.*

⑥ *Open a Word document from the* OLE3 *control.*

⑦ *Click-and-drag a selected portion of the document into the* OLE2 *container control.*

▶ *Practice changing the* OLEDragAllowed *and* DragMode *properties. What effects do the changes make?*

Dragging from External Applications

You have practiced dragging-and-dropping from various OLE containers and applications. In each case, you selected portions of a file or browsed to find a file in the Insert Object dialog box. Some other possibilities still exist. In addition to these other achievements, you can bring files into a control directly from the Windows Explorer.

Add a new form named FrmOLEDrag to the project. Create a Menu Options menu in the Menu Editor. Give it Return and Exit options. Write the mnuReturn and mnuExit procedures. Place a TextBox on the form. Set the OLEDragMode, OLEDropMode and DragMode properties to Manual. Set the MultiLine property to True.

You need to create a function to bring the files from the Explorer into the TextBox. In fact, you can call the function BringFilz. The process you use in this exercise is similar to the exercises in Chapter 14. You need to declare filename, text line, and text string variables. You open the files and obtain input from the file contents. Finally, the file will be closed.

```
Sub BringFilz(ByVal Words As TextBox, ByVal _
WordFx$)
```

Use ByVal in the argument list to specify the argument is passed by value. Words is the variable that represents the argument and it is of the TextBox type. WordFx is the filename variable. Next, the file is opened.

```
Open WordFx For Input Access Read Lock Read _
Write As #1
```

Use the Open command, as you did with the binary and sequential files in Chapter 14. Remember the Open statement syntax:

```
Open pathname For mode [Access access] [lock]
As [#]filenumber [Len=reclength]
```

Declare the variables WordStr and WordLine. Because you are not selecting and dragging in this exercise, You must read and copy the entire file. To do this, you must test for the End of File and also impose a limit on the text.

```
While Not EOF(1) And Len(WordStr) <= 30000
  Line Input #1, WordLine
  If WordStr <> "" Then WordStr = WordStr & _
vbCrLf
  WordStr = WordStr & WordLine
Wend
```

You can also input each line using Line Input. When you do this, you must test for empty text, and then add a carriage return and linefeed to format the text. You can use the constant vbCrLf in place of the Chr(13) + Chr(10) ASCII codes. Next, you set the WordStr variable equal to itself and the line input. Finally, close the file.

Continued

TAKE NOTE

CREATING EMPTY EMBEDDED OBJECTS

If you use the CreateEmbed method without specifying an object, you create an empty embedded object. You can further specify the type of object (Excel spreadsheet or Word document) the user will select.

CROSS-REFERENCE
Review the TextBox control in Chapter 9 and Chapter 10.

FIND IT ONLINE
Here information on Linked and Embedded objects:
http://msdn.microsoft.com/library/books/winguide/Platfrm2/D5/S1167C.HTM.

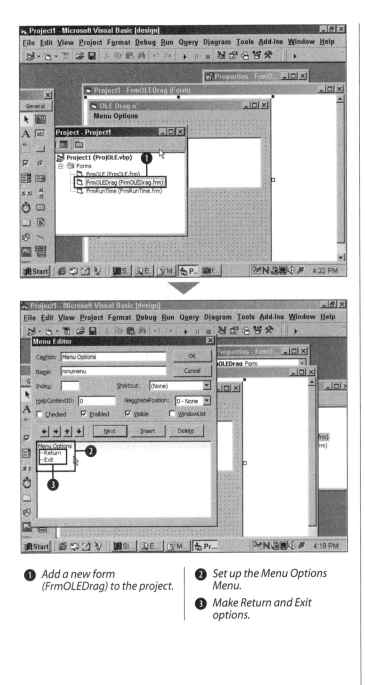

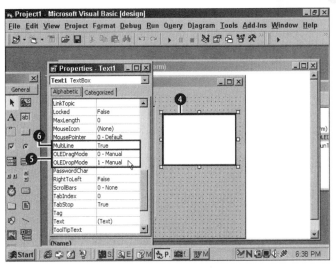

❹ *Place a TextBox on the form.*

❺ *Set the DragMode,* OLEDragMode, *and* OLEDropMode *properties to Manual.*

❻ *Set the* MultiLine *property to True.*

Listing 18-1: The BringFilz Function

```
Sub BringFilz(ByVal Words As TextBox, ByVal _
WordFx)
Open WordFx For Input Access Read Lock Read _
Write As #1
Dim WordStr, WordLine
While Not EOF(1) And Len(WordStr) <= 30000
    Line Input #1, WordLine
    If WordStr <> "" Then WordStr = WordStr & _
vbCrLf
    WordStr = WordStr & WordLine
Wend
Close #1
Words.SelStart = Len(Words)
Words.SelLength = 0
Words.SelText = WordStr
End Sub
```

❶ *Add a new form (FrmOLEDrag) to the project.*

❷ *Set up the Menu Options Menu.*

❸ *Make Return and Exit options.*

Dragging from External Applications *Continued*

Bringing the `BringFilz` function to a conclusion, the `SelStart`, `SelLength`, and `SelText` properties are needed to set the insertion point of text (SelStart), set the number of characters (SelLength), and return the string containing the text (SelText).

```
Words.SelStart = Len(Words)
Words.SelLength = 0
Words.SelText = WordStr
```

These properties are usually used in conjunction with the Clipboard. Now that the `BringFilz` function is complete, you must turn to writing the `OLEDragDrop` procedure for Text1.

Double-click the TextBox to enter code in the code window. Select the Text1 object and the `OLEDragDrop` procedure. You are interested in dragging-and-dropping text files (hence, the TextBox), so you use the GetFormat method and the vbCFFiles constant to test for the specified format.

```
If Data.GetFormat(vbCFFiles) Then
Dim vRC
```

When the determination is made that the data consist of a list of files (vbCFFiles), the new variable is declared.

The `GetFormat` format property has settings constants for file formats. The vbCFFiles constant specifies the format of a list of files. In addition, seven other constants exist.

The `vbCFText` constant specifies `Text` (.txt files), vbCFBitmap (Bitmap files), vbCFMetafile (metafile files),

vbCFEMetafile (Enhanced metafile files), vbCFDIB (Device-independent bitmaps), vbCFPalette (Color palette), vbCFFiles (List of files) and vbCFRTF (Rich text format files).

```
For Each vRC In Data.Files
BringFilz Text1, vRC
Next vRC
End If
```

This command block is similar to a For-Next loop and is responsible for bringing each one of the files selected into the TextBox. The `BringFilz` function is called to index the files. The For Each-Next loop is used to pass through a series of elements in a collection or array. The routine exits when no more elements are in the group. The vRC *variable* is a counter for the file elements in the array.

TAKE NOTE

CODE COMPONENTS

Code components used to be called OLE servers. These include libraries of objects that offer options to organize your code to be recycled. You can save and reuse your great procedures for use with other applications.

CROSS-REFERENCE

Check Chapter 10 to review the use of arrays.

FIND IT ONLINE

Here is information on OLE objects: **http://msdn. microsoft.com/library/books/inole/S10B6.HTM.**

Listing 18-2: The `OLEDragDrop` **procedure**

```
Private Sub Text1_OLEDragDrop(Data As _DataObject, Effect As Long, Button As Integer, _
Shift As Integer, X As Single, Y As Single)

If Data.GetFormat(vbCFFiles) Then
Dim vRC
For Each vRC In Data.Files
BringFilz Text1, vRC
Next vRC
End If

End Sub
```

▶ *Enter the text for the* `Text1_OLEDragDrop` *procedure.*

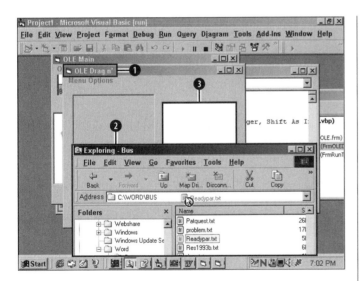

❶ *Run the program and select the OLE Drag n' form.*
❷ *Launch the Windows Explorer and select a file.*
❸ *Drag the file over the TextBox.*

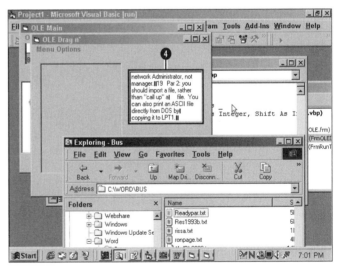

❹ *Drop the file on the TextBox.*

Copying from the Clipboard

Thus far, you have dragged-and-dropped objects from one control to another and between applications. In this exercise, you copy to the Clipboard and Paste into a `PictureBox` control. You also can paste directly onto the form.

Once you write the code, you can run Windows Paint from Accessories on the Start menu, open a bitmap on your system, and then copy it to the Clipboard. Once on the Clipboard, you can click anywhere on the OLE Drag n' form. Dialog boxes prompt you to paste the picture and then clear it from the Clipboard.

Draw a PictureBox on the left side of the FrmOLEDrag form. Check to see the `OLEDragMode` and `OLEDropMode` properties are set to Manual. Instead of dragging the picture into the PictureBox, copy it to the Clipboard and then paste it when prompted. You can open the bitmap before or after you launch your application.

Create a `Click` procedure for the Form1 object. Declare a variable (Msg) to hold the string message.

```
Dim Msg
Msg = "Choose OK to copy the picture from _
the Clipboard."
```

```
Dim Msg
Msg = "Choose OK to copy _
   the picture from the Clipboard."
```

The `Click` procedure is triggered when the user clicks anywhere on the form. The prompt is to let the user know there must be a bitmap to copy from the Clipboard to the PictureBox. The prompt must be acknowledged before the bitmap will be copied.

```
Picture1.Picture = Clipboard.GetData()
```

When the bitmap has been copied to the PictureBox, another message dialog box appears to clear the Clipboard.

```
MsgBox "Clear Clipboard!"
Picture1.Picture = LoadPicture()
```

The LoadPicture method is used with no picture specified to clear the PictureBox.

Suppose you have not loaded a picture onto the Clipboard. What then? You can easily add code to copy a picture to the Clipboard. Just add a message box message to load the bitmap.

```
Msg = "Choose OK to load a bitmap onto the _
Clipboard."
 MsgBox Msg
```

First clear the Clipboard of any data and copy the picture with the SetData method. Clipboard.Clear ' Clear Clipboard.

```
Clipboard.SetData LoadPicture("GRAD.jpg"), _
vbCFDIB
```

Use `LoadPicture` and specify the .JPG file type. Use the constant `vbCFDIB`, instead of `vbCFBitmap` because this is not a .BMP file. The `vbCFDIB` stands for Data Independent Bitmap and is used for all bitmaps other than Windows Bitmaps.

```
If Err Then
      Msg = "Can't find the .jpg file."
      MsgBox Msg    ' Display error message.
      Exit Sub
 End If
```

In case no file is present on the path, add an error routine.

TAKE NOTE

CONTROLS SUPPORTING OLE

The objects providing support for manual dragging-and-dropping only are: Forms, MDI forms, Document Objects, User Controls, and Property Pages. These objects contain the `OLEDropMode` property. The OLE container control has the `OLEDropAllowed` property, which can be set to True or False.

CROSS-REFERENCE

Review the discussion on Mouse Events in Chapter 5.

FIND IT ONLINE

Editing OLE objects is this site's topic: **http://msdn.microsoft. com/library/books/winguide/platfrm2/d5/s11688.htm.**

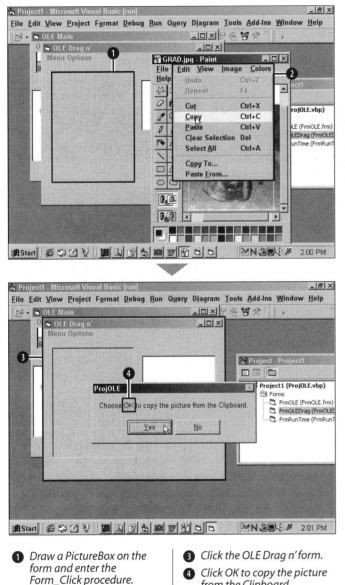

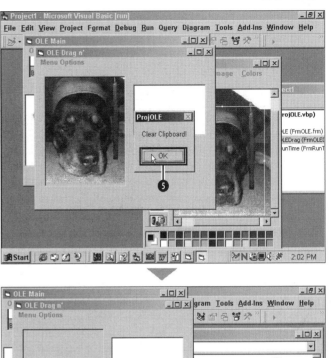

1. *Draw a PictureBox on the form and enter the Form_Click procedure.*

2. *Copy a picture to the Clipboard using Windows Paint or another bitmap editor.*

3. *Click the OLE Drag n' form.*

4. *Click OK to copy the picture from the Clipboard.*

5. *Click OK to clear the Clipboard of the image.*

6. *Add the new code to the Form_Click procedure that loads a bitmap from a designated path and then run the program.*

7. *Click the form and click OK to load the bitmap.*

397

Personal Workbook

Q&A

1 Name some controls that feature OLE drag-and-drop.

_____

_____

_____

2 How do you access the menu options for the `OLE container control`?

_____

_____

_____

3 What is the difference between Linking and Embedding?

_____

_____

_____

4 Which events are not generated for the target side of the drag-and-drop process?

_____

_____

_____

5 In which mode(s) can you use Paste and Paste Special to copy data to an `OLE container` control?

_____

_____

_____

6 Which drag-and-drop property value is most likely to require code: Manual or Automatic?

_____

_____

_____

7 What is the chief difference between `the OLE container` control and the other controls that support automation?

_____

_____

_____

8 What methods are used to copy data to and from the Clipboard?

_____

_____

_____

ANSWERS: PAGE 528

EXTRA PRACTICE

1 Add a new form to the ProjOLE project. Create a new drag-and-drop operation between two different controls.

2 Change the OLE at run time form module, so the OLE operations are initiated from the Label controls, rather than the OLE container controls.

3 Create a project that incorporates a Word processor with a form dedicated to that function.

4 Create a family photo album application with `OLE container` controls positioned to display the photos, complete with labels and captions.

REAL WORLD APPLICATIONS

✔ Your employer just called a meeting and asked you to add a Word processing feature to one of the applications you recently developed. How can you add this feature to an existing application?

✔ Your old pal, Joe Smooka, desperately needs help with his personnel database. He contracted with a developer to set it up five years ago. Now, Joe has switched everything to Windows and the old data are running under an old DOS application. Joe needs a database developed using the old data, but he now needs to add the capability to display employees' photos as part of the records in the database. The old developer is gone but, before he left town, he converted the data to ASCII text. How can you help your old pal?

Visual Quiz

What properties should be set for the TextBox on the OLE Drag n' form? How should they be set?

_____

_____

_____

_____

_____

_____

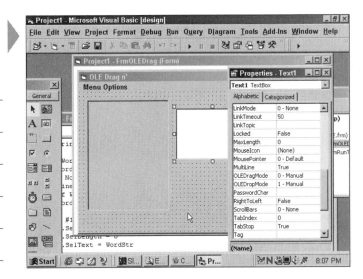

PART

V

Contents of 'Desktop'

Name

My Computer

Network Neigh

Internet Explore

Microsoft Outloo

Recycle Bin

My Briefcase

3252-9

3259-6

3261-8

3262-6

3281-2

3286-3

DE Phone List

Device Manager

In

Iomega Tools

Using Advanced Features

This Part centers on increasing your understanding of the Extensibility model, learning to use ActiveX Controls, and developing applications with a Web orientation.

The focus in the previous Part was centered on increasing skills in graphic methods and use of images as well using the Visual Basic multimedia features.

You have now acquired skills to work with the cool new features used on the Internet as you continue to work with multimedia. New topics you will become familiar with now include how to extend the Visual Basic environment using Wizards and Add-Ins and building new ActiveX Controls. Internet development skills include using HTML and DHTML; constructing and customizing a Web browser; using VBScript and Active Server Pages; and packaging and distributing your applications.

By this point in the Teach Yourself process, you have developed a firm grasp on programming fundamentals and even such advanced features as array handling. You have been introduced to topics on databases and files, as well as debugging and error handling. You have delved into a number of topics on the uses of methods, events, and controls. You also have a basic foundation in the newer areas of multimedia and graphics.

This last Part covers what can be considered the newest features in Visual Basic development — ActiveX and the Internet. We begin with an exploration of the VB Extensibility model in the form of Add-Ins and Wizards. Then, we move on to using and developing your own ActiveX controls. Next, you will be introduced to Internet programming, including HTML, DHTML, browser and e-mail application creation, and Internet client- and server-side scripting.

Finally, you will compile your programs and put an application together in one package for distribution to users. How this is done is dependent upon how the package is to be deployed and installed at the end user's site. All this is covered in the practical and concise exercises of each lesson.

By the end of this Part, you will have mastered the basic tools and concepts to send you well on the way to developing the complex Visual Basic applications demanded in today's world. May all your ventures be successful!

CHAPTER **19**

MASTER
THESE
SKILLS

▶ **Exploring the Add-Ins**
▶ **Creating Your Own Add-In Manually**
▶ **Connecting the Add-In project**
▶ **Creating an Add-In via the Addin Project**
▶ **Compiling an Add-In via the Addin Project**

Using the Add-Ins

Add-Ins are extensions to the Visual Basic model. They enable you to add features to the product. Add-Ins can be set up to run only within the Visual Basic environment or they can run standalone. The type of project you choose will determine whether the Add-In can run as a standalone Application (Out-Of-Process) or must be run within the Visual Basic environment (In-Process). If you choose to have your Add-In run outside Visual Basic (as VisData does), then you should select the `ActiveX.EXE` new project option. Selecting the `ActiveX.DLL` project will result in an Add-In that must be run within Visual Basic.

You have used several of the Add-Ins in the course of the book. Now it's time to review those that haven't been discussed.

Add-Ins are tools that can be made to function differently in different situations. You can develop your own Add-In and place it on the Add-In list. Add-Ins are — first and foremost — extensible. This means they extend the Visual Basic environment beyond the essentials with which it started. The Visual Basic Add-Ins provide a modular system for adding and even broadening the normal base of operations.

The Add-In Manager

The *Add-In Manager* is the facility that enables you to install these enhancements. To install the new Add-In, the developer must correctly install it so it can be accessed by the Add-In Manager. The Add-In Manager is available on the Add-Ins menu. To use an Add-In, you click the Add-In Manager and highlight the selection you want to add. You place a check mark in the Loaded/Unloaded box. You also can check the Load on the Startup box, so you always launch Visual Basic with the selected Add-In loaded. Adding the Add-In application usually results in the addition appearing as an option on the Add-Ins menu.

Wizards

Wizards, as you know, assist you in development. They make your work much easier by automating many of the development tasks. For example, you have used the Data Form Wizard and the Application Wizard. You use the Package and Deployment Wizard in a subsequent chapter. Many other Add-Ins and several Wizards are available in the Visual Basic 6 package.

All editions of Visual Basic include the Application Wizard and the Professional and Enterprise editions include the Data Form Wizard and an ActiveX Document Wizard, for example. The Application Wizard and the Wizard Manager both appear in the New Project dialog box.

Exploring the Add-Ins

Because you already have some knowledge and experience with the available Add-Ins, those already covered and those subsequently to be discussed, will be touched on briefly here.

The Application Wizard

In Chapter 3, you explored the basic uses of the Application Wizard. In addition, for starters, you can create a Web browser, automate the creation of Data forms, and create an About form.

One of the cool things you can do is to create a Splash screen. The *Splash screen* enables you to get as creative as you want. You can cause the Splash screen to stay visible for a specified time period (using the `Timer` control) and you can display graphics, movies, and produce sound. Just about anything you have learned to do in this book can be used on your application's Splash screen.

Possibly the most useful facet of the Application Wizard is the database interface it can generate. You can build an interface to a Microsoft Access database or to any Remote ODBC database for which you have a driver.

In any case, the Application Wizard creates a sophisticated application with MDI forms, Data forms, and so forth. The Application Wizard generates code, saving you the need to learn to write code at all. Of course, even if you are (by now) a veteran Visual Basic developer, you can benefit by using the Application Wizard and then modifying the code to customize your application.

Data Form Wizard

The Data Form Wizard is included with the Professional and Enterprise Editions, and is accessible from the New Projects window and the Application Wizard. The *Data Form Wizard* gives you the ability to build forms that can be bound to local and remote data sources. It also enables you to use ADO code.

You can choose between various types of form layouts. The Single record form is limited to showing database information with one record per window. The Grid form looks like a spreadsheet, displaying records one per row.

The *Master/Detail* form requires a one-to-many relationship between tables in the database. One master record usually exists for several detail records. A typical application might have one customer record (Master) to many order records (Detail).

The *MS Chart* displays data in chart format. You can select between several styles such as Pie, line, and bar. Aggregate functions are also available with the MS Chart. Examples of aggregate functions are average, count, sum, and so forth.

The *MS Hflex Grid* shows data in a table format with many options. The Data Form Wizard offers several options for style (Classic, Professional, Contemporary, and Win32 application). You also have a choice in managing column width and sorting. Finally, you can add captions for your column headers, instead of displaying the field names.

Continued

TAKE NOTE

▶ INSTALLING WIZARDS

You can install and remove Wizards using the Add-In Manager. After installation, most Wizards appear as options on the Add-Ins menu. The Application Wizard, Data Form Wizard, and the Wizard Manager also appear on the New Project window.

CROSS-REFERENCE

The Application Wizard is discussed in Chapter 3.

FIND IT ONLINE

Here are some API programming tips: **http://pages. hotbot.com/edu/tincani.andrea/my_vb_tips.html.**

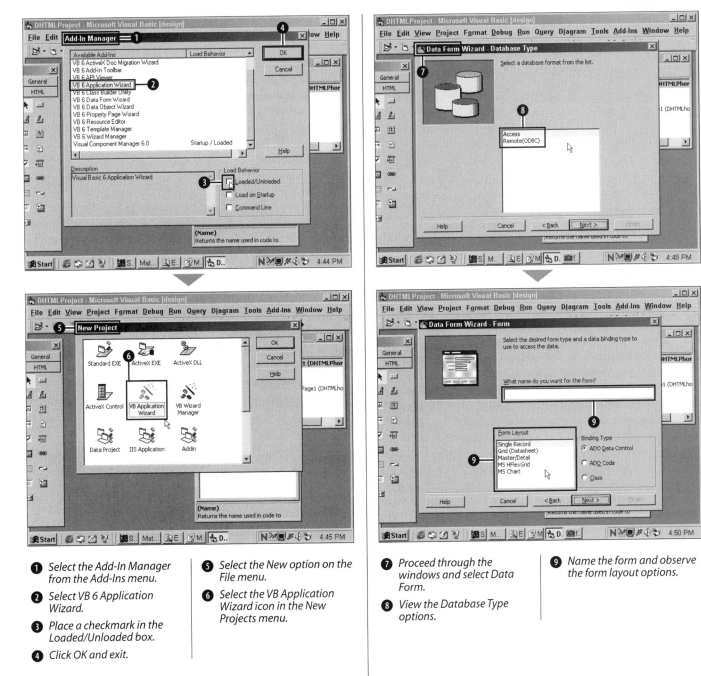

1. *Select the Add-In Manager from the Add-Ins menu.*

2. *Select VB 6 Application Wizard.*

3. *Place a checkmark in the Loaded/Unloaded box.*

4. *Click OK and exit.*

5. *Select the New option on the File menu.*

6. *Select the VB Application Wizard icon in the New Projects menu.*

7. *Proceed through the windows and select Data Form.*

8. *View the Database Type options.*

9. *Name the form and observe the form layout options.*

The examination of several Add-Ins available through the Add-In Manager continues with the Data Object Wizard.

Data Object Wizard

The *Data Object Wizard* offers assistance in code generation for creating custom data sources and user controls. This process works only if you have set up a data environment for obtaining and updating data. There is a required command (Select) and optional commands (Insert, Update, and Delete).

Using this Add-In would be indicated if you plan to create and update records from stored procedures, create user controls, write code regarding data relationships, or use verbose text descriptions for lookup values.

The Windows (API) Viewer

The API text Viewer Add-In can be accessed from the Microsoft Visual Basic 6.0 Tools option on the Windows 95/98 Start menu (found separately from Visual Basic) as well as being included in the Add-Ins list.

You can call API functions from Windows using code. The *Windows API Viewer* includes thousands of procedures, functions, subs, constants, and types you can declare and use from Visual Basic. The `Win32api.txt` file contains the declarations for many Windows API procedures used in Visual Basic. You can copy the code and paste it into your module.

The Property Page Wizard

The *Property Page Wizard* helps you make property pages selections to use with your user control. The Available Properties List gives you a list of properties from which to choose for your user control. To make use of the Property Page Wizard, you must have properties on the user control

that can be placed on a property page. If your user control has no properties that can be placed on a property page, you receive a warning from the Property Page Wizard to that effect. You are then advised to use the ActiveX Control Interface Wizard first.

The ActiveX Control Interface Wizard

The *ActiveX Control Interface Wizard* assists you to create primary code for the control's interface. It does not have anything to do with creating the user interface. If you want to be in a position to use the ActiveX control Interface Wizard, you must first create the interface elements for the ActiveX control.

The ActiveX Control Interface Wizard enables you to set properties, methods, and events for the ActiveX control interface. When you open a project that includes a user control, you can use the Interface Wizard to create and customize the interface. You make a selection of object properties and, after making the selections, you view the report that can be saved. The code is changed to reflect selections made from the menus.

Continued

> **TAKE NOTE**
>
> ▶ **RESOURCE FILES**
>
> You can store strings, bitmaps, data, and icons in resource files, to be loaded when needed. The resource file can be referenced in code to load the information. To edit resource files, you must use the Add-In Manager to load the Resource Editor, checking the Loaded/Unloaded box.

CROSS-REFERENCE
The Windows API Viewer is discussed in Chapter 2.

FIND IT ONLINE
This is a guide to Add-In resources: **http://msdn.microsoft.com/ vbasic/downloads/resguide/default.asp.**

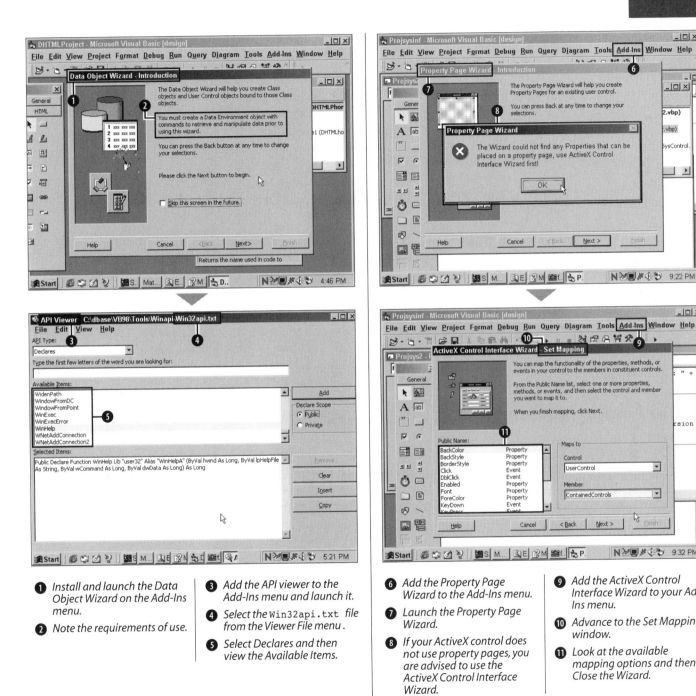

① Install and launch the Data Object Wizard on the Add-Ins menu.

② Note the requirements of use.

③ Add the API viewer to the Add-Ins menu and launch it.

④ Select the Win32api.txt file from the Viewer File menu.

⑤ Select Declares and then view the Available Items.

⑥ Add the Property Page Wizard to the Add-Ins menu.

⑦ Launch the Property Page Wizard.

⑧ If your ActiveX control does not use property pages, you are advised to use the ActiveX Control Interface Wizard.

⑨ Add the ActiveX Control Interface Wizard to your Add-Ins menu.

⑩ Advance to the Set Mapping window.

⑪ Look at the available mapping options and then Close the Wizard.

Exploring the Add-Ins

Continued

The Visual Data Manager

The *Visual Data Manager,* an application written in Visual Basic, is an aid to database access via Data Access Object (DAO). The Visual Data Manager is available in the Professional and Enterprise Editions.

With the Visual Data Manager, you can create and use database tables. You can change the tables and view data using the Recordset types Table, Dynaset, and Snapshot. You also can use available form types (Single record, Data control, and Data grid) in the Visual Data Manager.

Also, you can Import and Export all databases currently supported by the ODBC drivers installed on your system. You can execute SQL commands on these and you can build queries with the SQL commands.

The Visual Data Manager is a project you can open by clicking the Open Project icon on the Toolbar and opening the Visdata project, which is in a subdirectory of the Samples directory. The Samples are usually installed under the MSDN98 directory, several folder-levels down. You can use Visdata as an Add-Ins application from the Add-Ins menu.

The Add-In Toolbar

The *Add-In Toolbar* provides you with immediate access to your Add-Ins without going to the Add-Ins menu, selecting the Add-In Manager, and Loading or Unloading each of the options you want. Even though your Add-In appears on the Add-In Toolbar, it is not loaded until you click the icon.

You can add and remove items from the Toolbar by clicking the icon bearing a plus (+) sign and a minus (-) sign separated by a slash. This is the first icon on the Toolbar. If you are working with a number of Add-Ins, which you must alternately load and unload, the Toolbar is quicker than going through the several steps necessary to load and unload items from the menu.

You start the Toolbar initially by loading it from the Add-In Manager on the Add-Ins menu, just as you load any of the Add-Ins on the list. Once loaded, you can add and remove items.

The Add-In Toolbar is handy if you are using several different Add-Ins in your development project. Clicking the Toolbar to make changes in the Add-Ins you are working with is a time saver. The Add-In Toolbar also is an enhancement to your project to enable users to select the custom Add-In you distributed with your application.

For this reason, the Add-In Toolbar object model's object has two different methods available. These methods are the `AddToAddInToolbar` method and the `RemoveAddInFromToolbar` method. This enables you to produce the Add-In Toolbar via code. Using these methods, you can offer your application's users the option of removing and adding Add-Ins to the Toolbar.

TAKE NOTE

USING CODE TO ADD ITEMS TO THE ADD-IN TOOLBAR

You can write a procedure to add Add-Ins to the Add-In Toolbar. The code must make reference to the .DLL file produced when the Add-In is compiled. Also, the code must connect the Add-In.

CROSS-REFERENCE

Chapter 12 fully explains the uses of the Visual Data Manager.

FIND IT ONLINE

This is an update for the Application Wizard: **http://msdn. microsoft.com/vbasic/downloads/download.asp?ID=034**.

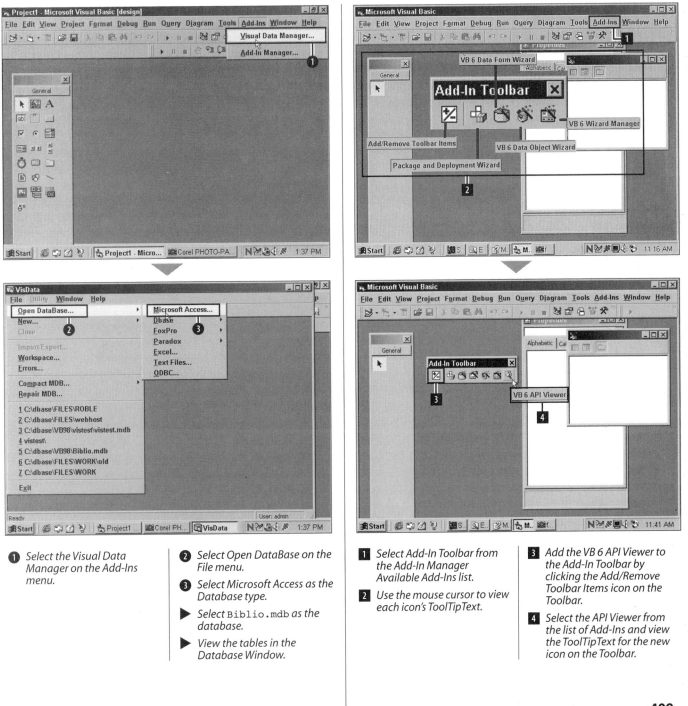

① Select the Visual Data Manager on the Add-Ins menu.

② Select Open DataBase on the File menu.

③ Select Microsoft Access as the Database type.

▶ Select Biblio.mdb as the database.

▶ View the tables in the Database Window.

1 Select Add-In Toolbar from the Add-In Manager Available Add-Ins list.

2 Use the mouse cursor to view each icon's ToolTipText.

3 Add the VB 6 API Viewer to the Add-In Toolbar by clicking the Add/Remove Toolbar Items icon on the Toolbar.

4 Select the API Viewer from the list of Add-Ins and view the ToolTipText for the new icon on the Toolbar.

Creating Your Own Add-In Manually

You can create your own Add-In to appear on the Add-Ins menu and on the list of Add-Ins under the Add-In Manager. The first step in creating an Add-In is to create a new project with a class module. Then, you must add a reference to the Add-In and compile it as an executable (.EXE) or dynamic linked library (.DLL) file.

You can create our own Add-In in two different ways. One way is to add the reference to the VBADDIN.INI file via code and the other way is to use the Addin icon on the New Project menu. Creating the Addin project is simpler because all the structure code is generated for you. Look at how to create an Add-In using the manual method.

To begin, select New Project from the File menu. Select the ActiveX.DLL icon to create an in-process new project. Add references to the Microsoft Visual Basic 6.0 Extensibility and Microsoft Office 8.0 Object Library. Do this by selecting References from the Project menu, and then placing check-marks next to the specific references above. You need these references to create Add-Ins, regardless of the method you use to do it. Name your project **AddInSProj**.

Select Add Module from the Project menu. Name the module ModAddin.Bas. Then enter the code (in the module) that will be responsible for registering the new Add-In entry to the Vbaddin.INI file. Visual Basic recognizes the Add-In only if the vbaddin.INI file has been updated with the entry for the new Add-In. Declare the following function to call the Windows API WritePrivateProfileString function. Note that the parameters are passed ByVal, not ByReference.

```
Declare Function _
WritePrivateProfileString& Lib _
"kernel32" Alias "WritePrivateProfileStringA" _
(ByVal AppName$, ByVal KeyName$, ByVal _
keydefault$, ByVal FileName$)
```

This and the EnterINI procedure make the entry in the Vbaddin.INI file.

The Class module should be named AddInSampl. Add a reference to the IDTExtensibility object in the general declarations area.

```
Implements IDTExtensibility
```

Select the IDTExtensibility object in the Object box, and then click each of the events showing in the Procedure list for this object. The four procedures (OnConnection, OnDisconnection, OnStartupComplete and OnAddInsUpdate), should each be added to the Class module, AddInSampl. Only two of these procedures are actually used in this exercise, although you must place comments in the other two to persist through the compilation process. All four procedures must be present so the Add-In will work.

TAKE NOTE

THE EVENT PROCEDURE PARAMETERS

The VBInst parameter refers to the current instance of Visual Basic. This is how you access the extensibility object model to create the Add-In. The ConnectMode parameter's three settings (AfterStartup, Startup, and ExternalStartup) tell Visual Basic how the Add-In was loaded. The RemoveMode parameter expresses how the Add-In was disconnected.

CROSS-REFERENCE

Instructions in creating an ActiveX control in Chapter 20 fit in with the extensibility model.

FIND IT ONLINE

This site describes how to roll your own add-in: **http://msdn. microsoft.com/library/periodic/period97/periodic/vbpj/ Balena.htm.**

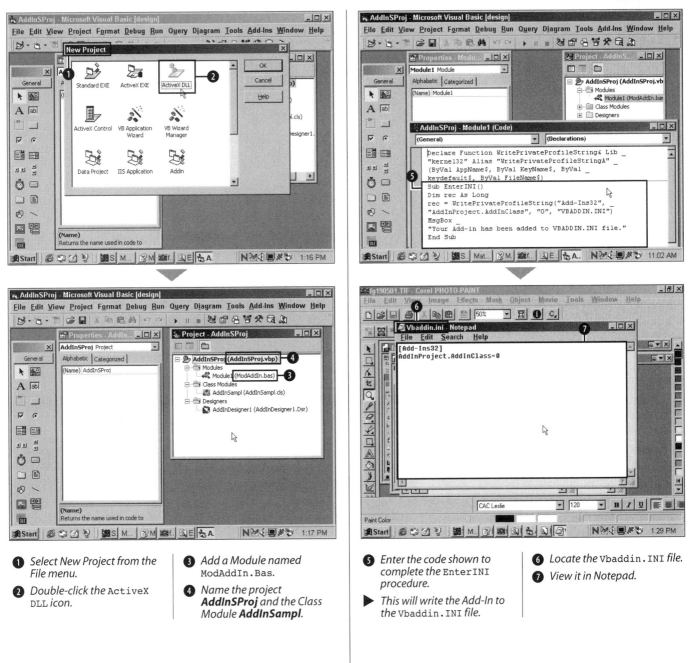

① Select New Project from the File menu.

② Double-click the **ActiveX DLL** icon.

③ Add a Module named **ModAddIn.Bas**.

④ Name the project **AddInSProj** and the Class Module **AddInSampl**.

⑤ Enter the code shown to complete the **EnterINI** procedure.

▶ This will write the Add-In to the Vbaddin.INI file.

⑥ Locate the Vbaddin.INI file.

⑦ View it in Notepad.

Connecting the Add-In Project

```
private Sub IDTExtensibility_OnConnection(ByVal VBInst As Object, _
ByVal ConnectMode As VBIDE.vbext_ConnectMode, ByVal AddInInst As VBIDE.AddIn, _
custom() As Variant)
    MsgBox " You have just connected your own Add-In"
End Sub
Private Sub IDTExtensibility_OnDisconnection(ByVal RemoveMode As _
VBIDE.vbext_DisconnectMode, custom() As Variant)
    MsgBox "Your Add-In has just been disconnected"
End Sub
```

The OnConnection and OnDisconnection procedures each have a MsgBox message, saying "Add-In is connected" or "Add-In is disconnected." The other procedures may have any comments you want to place there, as long as they are commented out. (See code shown above.)

The *state of connectivity* (connected or disconnected) occurs most simply when you click the Add-In Manager's OK button after loading it. When you unload the Add-In and click OK, the memory used by the Add-In is released. For this reason, if you close the Add-In's form, the memory is released because it is still connected. If you want to connect the Add-In programmatically, you can set the Add-Ins collection Connect property to True. You also can write a procedure to connect and disconnect the Add-Ins, and then perform an Update method. This will signify to Visual Basic that the Add-In should be connected. The Update action will set the flag to one, which will result in connection.

At this point, you are ready to compile. Select Make AddInSProj.dll... on the File menu. Compiling the project registers the Add-In for your system. Now you want to test your Add-In. select the Immediate Window from the View menu and type the name of the module EnterINI procedure in the window. Press Enter. The dialog box should pop up announcing "Your Add-In has been added to VBADDIN.INI file." To complete testing your Add-In, you can open a new project, select your Add-In from the Add-In Manager's list, check the Loaded box, and then select it from the Add-Ins menu.

Once an Add-In is registered in the Windows Registry and referenced in the Vbaddin.INI file, the new Add-In can respond to events and perform functions. You can then connect the Add-In manually (by selecting it from the Add-Ins) or do it by writing a procedure.

In the last exercise, you created a reference to the new Add-In by writing a procedure to add it to the Vbaddin.INI file. The other way is to use the Add-In Designer to make the reference. The *Add-In Designer* takes care of adding the reference to the INI file and also generates some essential code for your Add-In. Using the Add-In Designer, you can set properties to determine the Add-Ins load performance, its name, description, and version. The Add-In Designer also ensures the .DLL or .EXE file is registered correctly.

TAKE NOTE

▶ CHANGING ADD-IN NAMES

You can change the name appearing in the Add-In Manager. Select the Object browser from the View menu, and right-click the name of the class handling your Add-Ins OnConnection and OnDisconnection events. Select Properties from the menu. Enter your new name in the Description box, and then click OK. This text will be saved when you save the Add-In.

CROSS- REFERENCE

The Add-In Manager is discussed in Chapter 1.

FIND IT ONLINE

Here is a summary of API Basics: http://msdn.microsoft.com /library/officedev/odeopg/deovrapibasics.htm.

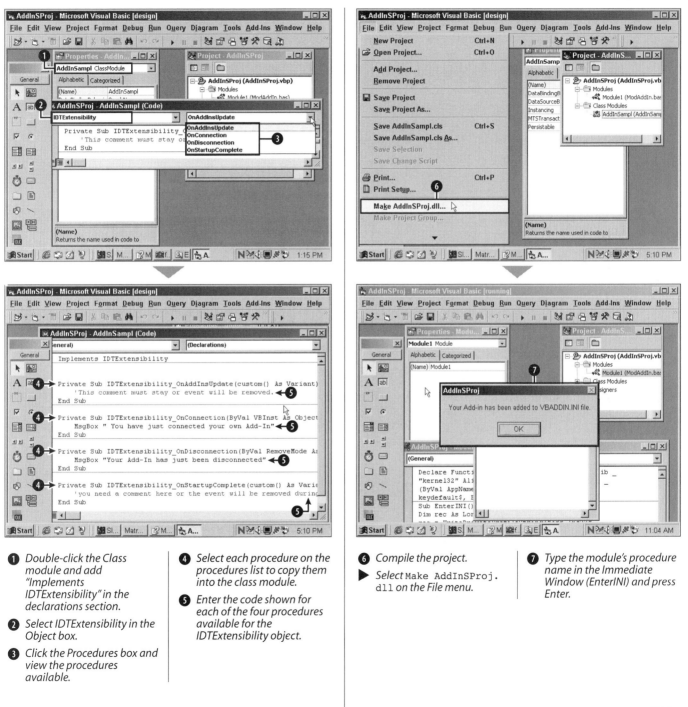

① *Double-click the Class module and add "Implements IDTExtensibility" in the declarations section.*

② *Select IDTExtensibility in the Object box.*

③ *Click the Procedures box and view the procedures available.*

④ *Select each procedure on the procedures list to copy them into the class module.*

⑤ *Enter the code shown for each of the four procedures available for the IDTExtensibility object.*

⑥ *Compile the project.*

▶ *Select* Make AddInSProj. dll *on the File menu.*

⑦ *Type the module's procedure name in the Immediate Window (EnterINI) and press Enter.*

Creating an Add-In via the Addin Project

The alternate way (from the last exercise) of creating an Add-In is to choose the `Addin` Project icon directly from the New Project window. When you do this, your project will consist of a form and a Designer (Connect.Dsr). Name the form `frmNewAddIn`. Right-click the project in the Project explorer window and select Project Properties. Name the project `NewAddin`.

Double-click the Designer object (Connect.Dsr) and select the General tab. Type a name in the `Addin` Display Name box. This name will be displayed in the Add-Ins list under the Add-In Manager option. Make the Display Name AddInSampl. Type a description of the function of the Add-In in the `Addin` Description box.

The Application should be Visual Basic and the version should be 6.0. Under initial load behavior, the options are Command line/Startup, Startup, Command line, and None. Select None because you don't want this Add-In to load initially when you launch Visual Basic. The "Addin is command line safe" option should be checked if you want the Add-In to run in the background with no visible interface. In this case, do not check the box.

Click the form, and then double-click to view the code generated. Two public variables have been created: VBInstance and Connect. VBInstance is declared as type VBIDE.VBE. All Add-Ins created with Visual Basic must have the Root Object in the extensibility model. This is the VBE object. The *VBE object* symbolizes the Visual Basic environment. The VBE holds all the extensibility objects and collections. These consequently have properties, methods, and events. When you connect an Add-In, you expose it to the Visual Basic IDE.

```
Public VBInstance As VBIDE.VBE
Public Connect As Connect
```

The Add-In Designer creates an Instance variable that stores and references the current instance (occurrence) of Visual Basic. If you have more than one instance of Visual Basic running, this variable can distinguish one from the other. The Add-In Designer is part of a template containing the basic code required to create the new Add-In project.

The template for designing Add-Ins includes a CommandBar event handler, some error-handling code, and the code to enable using the Add-In as a button on the Standard Toolbar. The Add-In Designer and template enable you to create a framework for your project. You can then change and attach code to extend Visual Basic. In this way, you can break the extensibility model into groups, each of which affects a different part of Visual Basic.

TAKE NOTE

▶ DISTRIBUTING YOUR ADD-IN

The act of installing the Add-In in the `.INI` file is something that must be taken care of if you distribute your application to end users. If you use this method of coding a procedure to do that, then you must make a provision for the end users to run the same, or a similar procedure, after they install the application. If you use the manual method of creating your Add-In, you should prepare a setup program to install the Add-In.

CROSS-REFERENCE

Creating an Add-In is much like creating a new control. See Chapter 20.

FIND IT ONLINE

This tells how to distribute a custom Add-In: **http://msdn. microsoft.com/library/officedev/odeopg/deovrdistributing comaddinscreatedwithvisualbasic60.htm.**

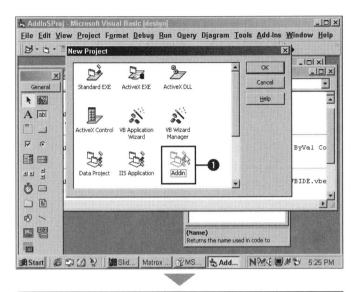

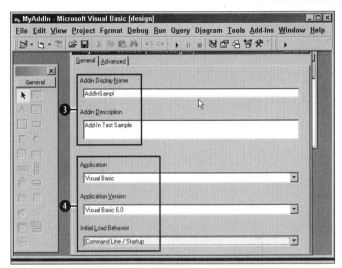

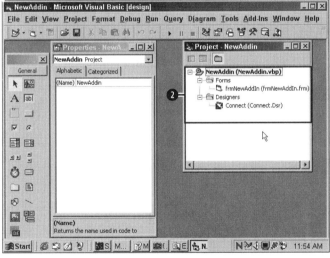

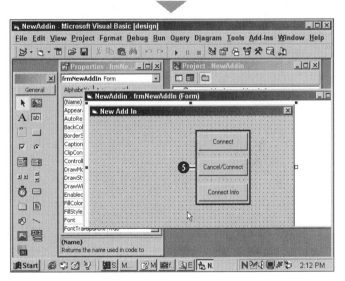

① Begin a new project by selecting the Addin icon in the New Project window.

② Name the new objects as shown.

③ Double-click the Connect.Dsr object and, in the Add-In Designer, give your Add-In a Display Name and description.

④ Complete the information for the General tab.

⑤ Create the buttons shown on the New Add-In form.

Compiling an Add-In via the Addin Project

Change the frmNewAddIn form caption to New Add-In. You want to cause something to happen when you connect your Add-In. Two buttons are built into the form created by the Add-In Designer. Remove these or modify them to resemble the buttons in the New Add-In form.

Add three new buttons. These should be Connect, Cancel/Connect, and Connect Info. The name of the button captioned Connect should be CmdConnect. The CmdCancel button should have a caption similar to Cancel/Connect. Finally, the CmdInfo button has a caption "Connect Info." These buttons each have a procedure to present a message or carry out a function to test the Add-In.

The CmdConnect button presents a message box with a message saying the Add-In is connected.

```
Private Sub CmdConnect_Click()

    MsgBox "The Addin is connected."
End Sub
```

The CmdInfo (Connect Info) button provides the information stored in the FullName property of VBInstance.

```
Private Sub CmdInfo_Click()
    MsgBox "AddIn operation on: " & _
VBInstance.FullName
End Sub
```

Create the Cancel/Connect button and a procedure using the Connect property.

```
Private Sub CmdCancel_Click()
    Connect.Hide
End Sub
```

The next step is to compile the project. Select Make NewAddin.dll on the File menu. When the project has finished compiling, you will find the new Add-In listed on the Add-In Manager's list of Available Add-Ins. Check the box under Load Behavior to Load the Add-In. Click OK. Clicking OK is important because your Add-In is not loaded until you do.

Now, click the Add-Ins menu. Next, you see the Add-In you just created displayed on the menu. Select the new Add-In. The Add-In will execute. Click the Connect button. A dialog box will pop up announcing the Add-In is connected. Now click the Connect Info button. The button results in a dialog box that provides the information regarding the application (Visual Basic) and the version (6).

When you click the Cancel/Connect button, the connection is hidden and the project appears to stop execution.

TAKE NOTE

▶ **MODIFYING THE ADD-INS TEMPLATE**

You can modify the template to create other Add-In projects. One type of project you can create is the changing, moving CommandBar. A *CommandBar* is a combination Toolbar and menu bar. The CommandBar collection and CommandBar object enable you to create, change, and delete CommandBars.

CROSS-REFERENCE

See Chapter 23 for remarks on adding support files to your application.

FIND IT ONLINE

This site has resources on the Add-In Manager: **http://msdn. microsoft.com/library/devprods/vs6/vbasic/vb98/ vbrgnaddinmanager.htm.**

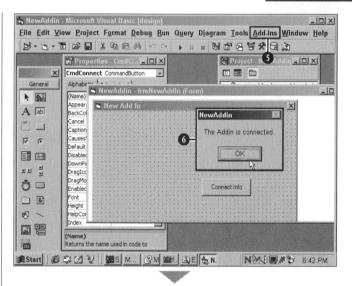

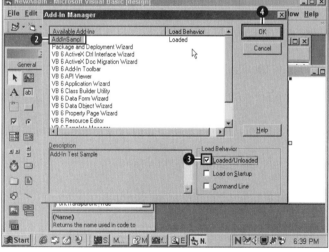

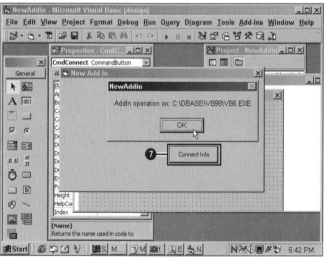

❶ Enter the code shown to complete the three button procedures.

▶ Compile the project by selecting Make NewAddin.dll.

❷ After compiling, check the Add-In Manager Available Add-Ins list to see your new Add-In.

❸ Check the Loaded box to Load the Ad-In.

❹ Click OK.

❺ Select your new Add-In from the Add-Ins menu.

❻ Click the Connect button.

❼ Click the Connect Info button.

▶ Click the Cancel/Connect button.

Personal Workbook

Q&A

1 Add-Ins are_____ to the Visual Basic model.

_____

_____

_____

2 The Data Form Wizard offers what types of forms?

_____

_____

_____

3 For what is the API Viewer used?

_____

_____

_____

4 How is the Visual Data Manager Accessed?

_____

_____

_____

5 How can you get quick access to all the Add-Ins you have loaded?

_____

_____

_____

6 How do you add a reference to a new Add-In that you create?

_____

_____

_____

7 How does a newly created Add-In get registered in your system?

_____

_____

_____

8 What is the VBE Object?

_____

_____

_____

ANSWERS: PAGE 529

EXTRA PRACTICE

1 Use the Data Form Wizard to create a custom form to display the Biblio database.

2 Use the Add-In Manager to load several different Add-Ins.

3 Add the Add-In Toolbar, and then practice adding and removing items.

REAL WORLD APPLICATIONS

✔ Your boss has selected you to spin off his new accounting and record-keeping product. Your job is to create a demo to advertise this new application. Use the Application Wizard to create a fancy Splash screen and demo application for the product.

✔ Use the Wizard manager to help your client, Aunt Fannie's, with the demo advertisement of the new Web site you created for the account.

✔ Your potential client, Racy's Department Store, has an old database in dBase III format that contains information regarding style trends over several decades. Racy's needs some drastic updating on the database. The IS Chief is interested in the Visual Basic extensibility model. What specific technology do you recommend to do the work?

Visual Quiz

How do you install this Toolbar?

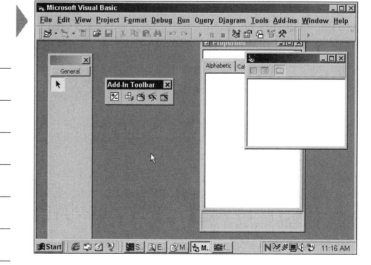

CHAPTER 20

Using ActiveX Controls

Thus far, several chapters have demonstrated the use of Controls. Previous chapters introduced many of the intrinsic controls and some `ActiveX` controls (`CommonDialog`, `DataGrid`, `MultiMedia`, `Media Player`, `Animation`, `PictureBox`, `PictureClip`, `Image`, `DataGrid`, `OLE`, and `ADO`) are a few of the `ActiveX` controls already used in the book.

In `ActiveX`, there are documents, code components, and controls. Which you use and how you use it depends upon the intended use and what you hope to accomplish.

Because you now have experience with `ActiveX` controls, you understand what they do. All controls are contained in forms or in other controls. Documents also are contained, but not in forms or other controls. Documents are almost always contained in browsers. This is because ActiveX documents are largely used on the Internet. Controls and documents share many events and properties. `ActiveX` controls are always displayed in the ToolBox and they are added from the Components option on the Project menu.

ActiveX components were formerly called *OLE Automation servers*. An *ActiveX component* is an application containing objects that can be applied to other applications. You have frequently accessed these component libraries to install components needed in your projects.

When you create an `ActiveX` control (or controls), it can be included in the Component Type Library along with the others listed. The new `ActiveX` control or component in which it is included will exist in a file having a .ocx extension. When you look in the Components Controls list, notice the filename is displayed in the status pane below the list.

In the chapter on OLE (Chapter 18), you learned to use the ActiveX technology when you used objects from other applications, such as Microsoft Word, Microsoft Paint, and so forth. *Code components* contain libraries of programmable objects. An object can be used in applications other than the one for which it was developed. When you use `ActiveX` controls, you are adding features to your application without having to create them yourself. You can purchase these controls from many vendors. The Internet is teeming with commercial Visual Basic sites to sell every kind of imaginable and unimaginable component.

Understanding ActiveX Components

There are `ActiveX` controls, code components, and documents. `ActiveX` controls are those you installed by adding them to your ToolBox in most of the projects you have undertaken. In fact, you have used more `ActiveX` controls so far than you have used the intrinsic controls (those initially contained in the ToolBox). `ActiveX` controls are compiled into files with the .OCX extension. If you develop several `ActiveX` controls and compile all the controls in a project, the .OCX file you build will include all the controls you developed.

ActiveX documents enable you to create interactive Internet applications. While ActiveX documents are not contained in forms, they can link to forms. These documents and forms can be displayed in the Internet Explorer. ActiveX documents can contain `ActiveX` controls. These documents can also act as code components. When you complete your document, it is compiled into a .VBD file.

ActiveX components include In-Process and Out-of-Process servers. The *In-Process servers* use files with a .DLL extension. Those that are .EXE files, are called *Out-of-Process servers*. To create these components, you must have the Professional or the Enterprise Edition of Basic 6.0.

The use of `ActiveX` controls and code components can add clout to your Web pages. You can use `ActiveX` controls to add menus, moving words, and animation to your Web site. So much is available for programming on the Internet (IIS, HTML, DHTML, `ActiveX` controls, ActiveX code components, ActiveX documents, Active Server Pages, and so forth), deciding what to use can be confusing.

The reasons you would decide on one technology over another would depend on what you have at your disposal and what would work best for your goal. If you want to use the Visual Basic language rather than DHTML or IIS, you may decide on developing ActiveX documents.

The ActiveX document model will give you better control over the entire browser window. When you write HTML code, only the contents of the page are under your control. The browser controls the browser window. You don't have control over the scroll bars or the menu, and so forth. When you use ActiveX documents, the browser downloads the associated files, just as your browser downloads the HTML code when you arrive at a Web site.

To author an ActiveX document, you must add a user document Object to an ActiveX EXE project. You can use the ActiveX Document Wizard to make the process easier.

CROSS-REFERENCE
Chapter 21 focuses on creating Internet applications.

FIND IT ONLINE
This is an ActiveX resource: **http://www.activex.org/**.

COMPILING, PACKAGING, AND SHIPPING ACTIVEX CONTROLS

If an ActiveX control is compiled as part of an Out-of-Process (.EXE) or In-Process .(DLL) file, it cannot be used in other applications. The control must be compiled into an .OCX file. The .OCX DLL file can contain more than one ActiveX control. This way, distribution is simplified. However, when you ship multiple controls in one DLL file, you must provide the vendor name in each control name included. You should preface the control name with the name of the company in the style: "MYCOMPANYControl1 Control." If the components are to be downloaded from the Internet, it is important to obtain digital signatures to correlate the vendor's name with a particular file. This provides responsibility for developers. A signature guarantees your users of the quality and safety of the components.

Table 20-1: TYPE OF ACTIVEX COMPONENT BY FILE TYPE GENERATED

ActiveX	EXE	DLL	OCX	VBD
Controls			X	
Documents				X
Code components In-Process		X		
Code components Out-of-Process	X			

Creating ActiveX Controls

ctiveX controls are just like any other controls in your ToolBox. In fact, when you create, compile, and register an ActiveX control, you will see it included in your ToolBox. If you create one or many ActiveX controls and then compile using Make Control name.ocx on the File menu, all the controls in the project are compiled into one `.OCX` file.

You probably have noticed by now that when you add controls from the Projects, Components menu, you sometimes get a family of controls and, other times, you only get one. The `Microsoft Common Controls` are examples of several controls residing in one .OCX file. The Media Player or CommonDialog are examples of only one control included in the .OCX file.

As you have found in your journey through this book, many `ActiveX` controls are supplied with Visual Basic. The Learning Edition contains only a few of these (referred to as the `Standard ActiveX` controls), but if you have the Professional or Enterprise Edition, you will reap a bonanza of `ActiveX` controls. The `ImageList`, `Multimedia MCI`, `PictureClip`, `ProgressBar`, `RichTextBox`, `StatusBar`, `SysInfo`, `TabStrip`, and `Toolbar` are a few of these.

A number of vendors sell `ActiveX` controls, but an interesting feature of Visual Basic is you can create your own `ActiveX` controls. Although many `ActiveX` controls are distributed with the Professional and Enterprise Editions, some specialized need always occurs, which only the development of a new control can address. You may also have found this to be true in your practice exercises. If so, you will enjoy the experience of making an entirely new control.

Once you decide on the functions and appearance of your control, you can begin building it. The process begins by selecting `ActiveX.EXE` or `ActiveX.DLL` from the New Project dialog box. You add properties, property procedures, and methods to your control.

When you finish, the resulting file is saved with a `.CTL` extension. At this point, you can make the .OCX file. The final step is registration. You must register the control with Windows to use it in a new project. The registration places the control on the list of controls in the Components option on the Project menu.

To begin the exercise, imagine the functions you want to see in a control but, as far as you know, those functions don't yet exist. Some ideas could be a calculator that adds two numbers together, a calculator that subtracts birth date from today's date to obtain age, a progress bar that performs specific functions, and so on. Most of the time when you make an `ActiveX` control, you are combining other controls with event and procedure code.

TAKE NOTE

USING THE HISTORY LIST

The capability to move backward and forward is contained in the `GoBack` and `GoForward` methods. These methods work by using the browser's history list. Versions of Internet Explorer 3.0 and later support the methods. You can check to see if a history list exists before moving back or forward.

CROSS-REFERENCE

Check Chapter 21 for information on Internet applications.

FIND IT ONLINE

This site shows you how to write COM programs: **http://www. microsoft.com/mind/defaulttop.asp?page=/mind/0999/vbcom/ vbcom.htm&nav=/mind/0999/inthisissuecolumns0999.htm.**

Table 20-2: STANDARD ACTIVEX CONTROLS

Control name	Class name	Description
ADO Data Control	ADODC	ActiveX Data Object allows connection to a database. Can be associated to other controls.
Common dialog	CommonDialog	Supplies dialog boxes opening and saving files, printing, and selecting colors and fonts.
DataCombo	DataCombo	Combines the features of the ComboBox and Data controls.
DataGrid	DataGrid	This control can be bound to the ADO Data control. Allows reading and editing of the recordset.
DataList	DataList	Combines data access and the standard ListBox.
Microsoft Hierarchical FlexGrid	MSHFlexGrid	Can display recordsets when bound to the Data Environment Designer. Cannot be edited.

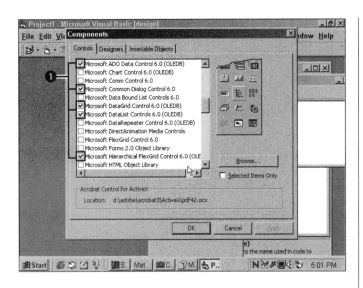

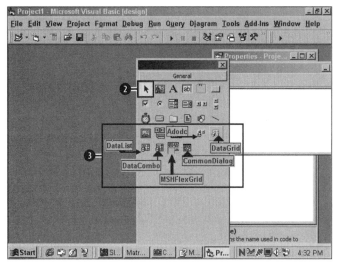

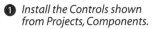

▶ *This table shows the* ActiveX *controls that are shipped with the Learning Edition.*

❶ *Install the Controls shown from Projects, Components.*

❷ *Pass your mouse over the Standard* ActiveX *controls in the ToolBox.*

❸ *View the ToolTipText for the Standard ActiveX controls in the* ToolBox.

Building an ActiveX Control

Wouldn't it be nice if a control enabled you to know what's going on with your system? Well, there is and it's called `SysInfo`. This ActiveX control responds to events regarding changes in the system, power status events and properties, plug and play events, desktop resizing, resolution changes, time changes, and operating system properties. `SysInfo` can do some cool things, such as return the AC power or battery status.

Unfortunately, `SysInfo` returns values about the state of these events and properties, and requires a fair amount of code to produce meaningful output. If you could combine the capability of the `SysInfo` control with some specific functions, you could design a new control. You are going to do just that in this exercise.

Create a new directory where you will store the files from this project. Open the New Project window and select `ActiveX` control. Visual Basic creates a `UserControl`, rather than the project and form with which you are now familiar. This is quite different from the exercises up to this point because there is no form at all in this project.

Right-click for Properties and name the control `SysControl`. Select the project in the Project Explorer and right-click for Properties or select `Project` Properties from the Project menu and name it **Projsysinf.** At this point, you have a `UserControl` that doesn't do anything. To make sure it does something, you need to add other controls from the ToolBox.

Add a text box, a command button, and the `SysInfo` control to your `UserControl` as if it were a form. Make a caption for the command button saying "Get OS Platform/Version." Set the `Text1 MultiLine` property to True. This new control is going to display the operating system platform and version in two places: a dialog box and the text box. When clicked, the command button will invoke a `msgBox`. When you click OK the `MsgBox`, the information will appear in the text box. So you will have created a specific function for the `SysInfo` control.

Your brave new `ActiveX` control will have only two procedures. One is for the Command button and one for the text box. Just as with every control in `Visual Basic`, specific syntax (properties) are associated with it. Here, you use the `SysInfo1` control's `OSVersion`, `OSBuild`, and `OSPlatform` properties to report the desired information. The OSPlatform consists of values from 0 to 2, `OSVersion` returns the actual operating system version number, and `OSBuild` provides addition OS info.

To build your control, you need to use some conditional statements to interpret and display the data returned by `SysInfo`. You can use `Select Case` here because three possible values could be returned by the `SysInfo.OSPlatform` property. In the `Command1_Click` procedure, declare `MsgEx` as String. Each Case (0-2) will use the `CStr` String conversion to display the information.

```
Case 1
MsgEx = "Windows 95/98, ver. " & _
CStr(SysInfo1.OSVersion) & "(" & _
CStr(SysInfo1.OSBuild) & ")"
```

If the value returned for `OSPlatform` is 1, then the previous code will be executed.

TAKE NOTE

▶ **THE VBD FILE**

Visual Basic always creates a temporary .vbd file for each ActiveX document in your project. The .vbd files can always be found in the same directory where Visual Basic is installed. But, if you are compiling an .EXE or a .DLL ActiveX document file, Visual Basic will create a .VBDfile in the same directory as the .EXE or .DLL file.

CROSS-REFERENCE

See how to build your own browser in Chapter 21.

FIND IT ONLINE

Check out Geek to Geek: **http://www.microsoft.com/mind/ defaulttop.asp?page=/mind/0999/vbcom/vbcom.htm&nav=/ mind/0999/inthisissuecolumns0999.htm.**

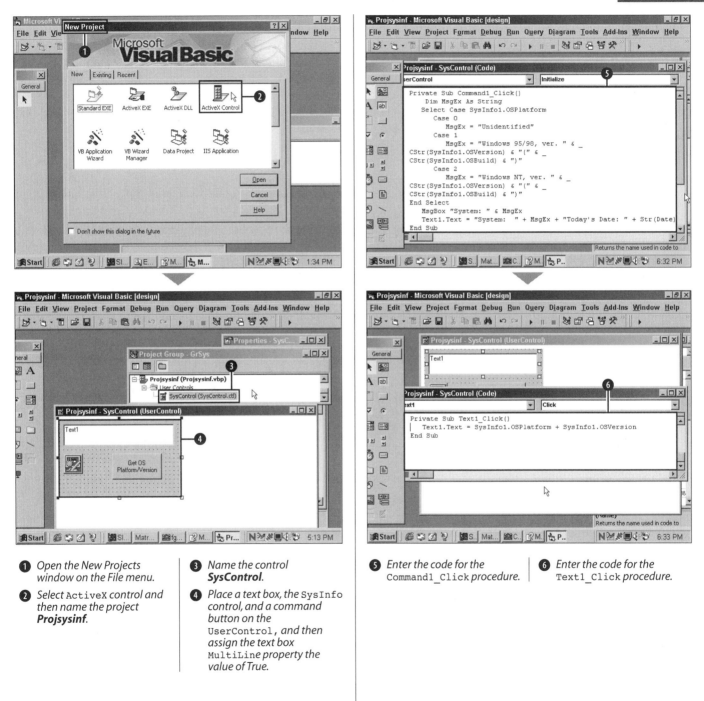

1. Open the New Projects window on the File menu.

2. Select ActiveX control and then name the project **Projsysinf**.

3. Name the control **SysControl**.

4. Place a text box, the SysInfo control, and a command button on the UserControl, and then assign the text box MultiLine property the value of True.

5. Enter the code for the Command1_Click procedure.

6. Enter the code for the Text1_Click procedure.

427

Testing the New ActiveX Control

Controls are not just code. They are objects you build in Visual Basic. Controls must be placed in containers. When compiled, registered, and packaged, they can be used and distributed by developers. Then, they reside in the ToolBox until selected and placed on forms by users.

Now you have a new `ActiveX` control, but what do you do with it? How can you test it? If you attempt to run the control as if it were a form-based project, you will find the control displayed in your Web browser. This is not necessarily bad, but it doesn't do you any good if you want to use the control in another project or if you want to compile and distribute your new control.

The next step toward completing the control is to create a new project and form for testing. Select Add Project on the file menu and add a Standard EXE project. This new project and its form exist only for the purpose of testing the control.

Name the new project **Projsys2** and the form, **FrmSysC.** Because you have created the project and form for testing the new `ActiveX` control, you have no other use for this project. To preserve this relationship, you should save both projects as a Project Group. Select Save Project Group As to save both projects as a group. When you want to test in the future, you can load the project group instead of individual projects. Name the Project group **GrSys.**

Now, click the close box in the upper-right corner of the `SysControl UserControl`. When you do this, notice a new control icon appears in the ToolBox. This icon represents your new control. Select the FrmSysC form and draw the new control icon on the form. That's it! Now you can run the project.

If you find the FrmSysC form's project is not running, even after placing the control on the form, check to make sure the Projsys2 project is selected as the Group Start up Object. To determine if this is the problem, you can select the Projsys project in the Project Explorer and right-click. Click the Set as Start Up option. This makes the project with the form the Start up project. If the project (Projsysinf) with the control is the startup, you will be back where you started before adding the new project and form.

At last you are ready to test your control. Press F5 or select Start from the Run menu. The form now displays the control you placed there. Click the "Get OS Platform/Version" button. A dialog box pops up to display the information about your OS and version. Click OK. Now the text box displays the same information and in addition, the system's date.

The next exercise explores other possibilities in the development of `ActiveX` controls.

TAKE NOTE

CONTROLS AND CONTROL CLASSES

When you create a new control you are creating a brand new control class. Controls all belong to control classes. When you select a control in the ToolBox and place it on a form, you are only creating an example of that control class.

CROSS-REFERENCE

Refer to Chapter 9 for a refresher in using controls in your projects.

FIND IT ONLINE

This is a list of ActiveX Web sites:
http://www.microsoft.com/com/tech/activex.asp.

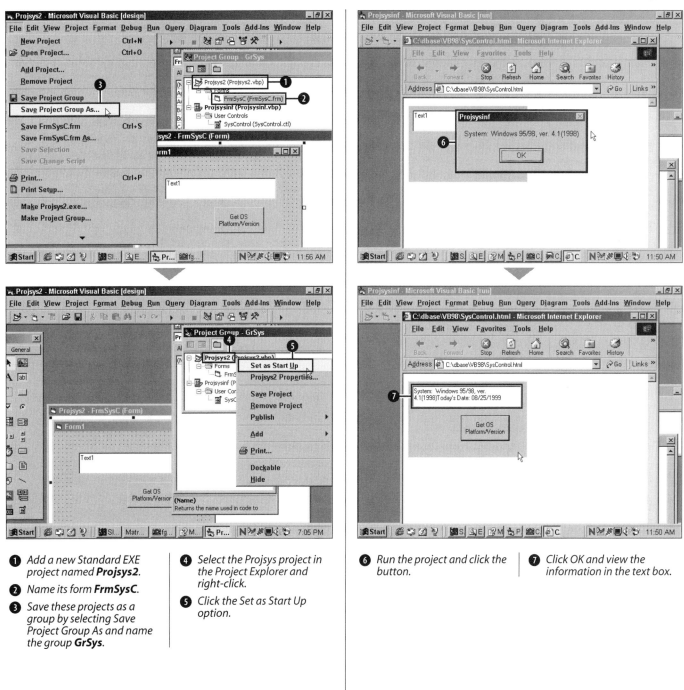

① Add a new Standard EXE project named **Projsys2**.

② Name its form **FrmSysC**.

③ Save these projects as a group by selecting Save Project Group As and name the group **GrSys**.

④ Select the Projsys project in the Project Explorer and right-click.

⑤ Click the Set as Start Up option.

⑥ Run the project and click the button.

⑦ Click OK and view the information in the text box.

429

Creating the ActiveX Drive List Control

The SysControl provides you with information about the system on which it's running. This is handy data to have, but you may also want to add other information about the system. Or, perhaps this is enough for your application and you see no point in adding features you won't use.

The next exercise offers a control with a different function to supplement your application. This time, you design a control to display all the drives on your system in a list.

Begin by selecting the ActiveX Control icon from the New Project window. Name the Project **ProjDrvControl** by selecting Project Properties from the Project menu or right-click the project name in the Project Explorer and select properties from the context menu. Name the User Control **DrvControl.**

Double-click the user control in the Project Explorer and draw a long, rather narrow text box on your control. Set the MultiLine property to True. Place two command buttons beneath the text box. Set the caption property on the top button to List Drives. Set the caption property on the lower button to Clear Window.

Declare the variables you plan to use for the FileSystemObject, the drive, DriveCollection, text string containing the drive letter and type of drive, the drive letter name, and a text message.

```
Dim fso, Drv, DrColl, Sname, DrName, Msg
```

The next task is to write a UserControl_Initialize procedure. This is analogous to the Form_Load procedure in a Standard EXE project. It runs when the program initially executes. The object of this exercise is to report all the system's drives along with the volume name. The syntax for the CreateObject function FileSystemObject is CreateObject(Class, Servername). In the following statement, the CreateObject function returns the FileSystemObject (fso).

```
Set fso = _
CreateObject("Scripting.FileSystemObject")
```

As you know, a number of collections exist in Windows and Visual Basic. The Drives Collection is one of these. The Drives Collection consists of all the drives listed in My Computer. The next command makes a variable equal to the drives in the collection.

```
Set DrColl = fso.Drives
```

The For-Each-Next loop enables you to examine each of the elements in a collection. Use this method to read each drive name and type to append a dash and the volume name to the drive letter.

```
For Each Drv In DrColl
        Sname = Sname & Drv.DriveLetter & " - "
        Sname = Sname & DrName & vbCrLf
        Text1.Text = Sname
Next
```

The variable, Sname, contains the text of the drive letter and adds each new drive letter on each pass through the loop. Each drive in the Drives Collection means the loop will execute as many times as necessary until all the system drives have been appended to the Sname variable.

TAKE NOTE

CONTROLS AND COMPONENTS

Control components produce .OCX files. These are also known as control components, as you know from obtaining control components from the Components option on the Project menu. One control component may contain more than one control. ActiveX control projects contain at least one .CTL file. When you build a project, the control component is given the .OCX file extension. Developers who obtain your control component and install it can use any of the controls you made available.

CROSS-REFERENCE

See Chapter 21 for a discussion on using ActiveX on the Internet.

FIND IT ONLINE

You can write ActiveX using ATL 3.0: **http://www.microsoft.com/ msj/0499/atl3activex3 /atl3activex3top.htm**.

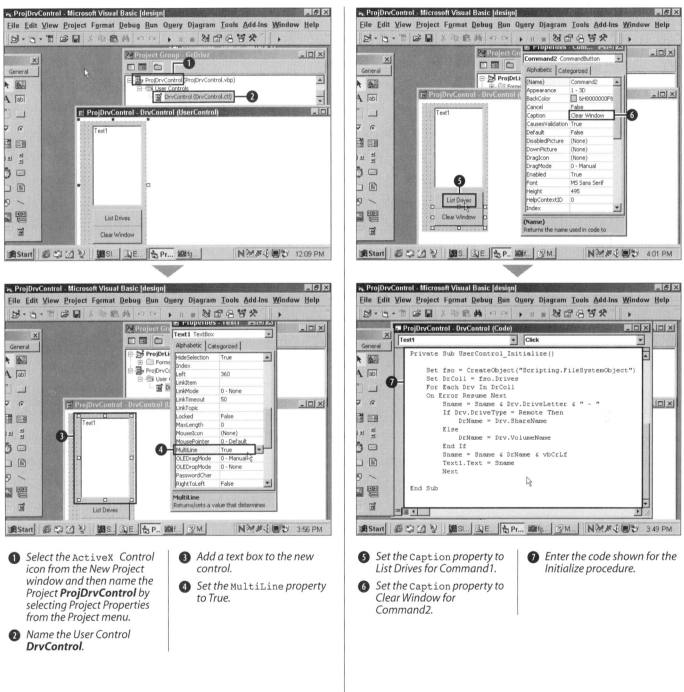

① Select the ActiveX Control icon from the New Project window and then name the Project **ProjDrvControl** by selecting Project Properties from the Project menu.

② Name the User Control **DrvControl**.

③ Add a text box to the new control.

④ Set the MultiLine property to True.

⑤ Set the Caption property to List Drives for Command1.

⑥ Set the Caption property to Clear Window for Command2.

⑦ Enter the code shown for the Initialize procedure.

Testing the Drive List Control

In addition to the previous procedure, you need procedures for the command buttons. Double-click the Command2 button (Clear Window) to enter the code window. Enter the statement:

```
Text1.Text = ""
```

This will have the effect of clearing the window of text. Because you are setting the value of the text box to null, no text will appear.

Select the `Command1` Object and the `Click` procedure to create the List Drives function. Set the text box text equal to the string of the Sname variable that contains the text of the drives obtained by iterating the For-Each loop.

```
Text1.Text = "System Drives:        " +
CStr(Sname)
```

The `Text1_Click` procedure reiterates the procedure for Command1.

To complete the control you need to create a new project and form for testing. Select Add Project on the file menu and add a Standard EXE project.

This new project and its form will exist only for the purpose of testing the control.

Name the new project ProDrList and name the form, FrmDrList. You are making the project and form for testing the new `ActiveX` control, just as you did for the previous control you developed. Again, save both projects as a Project Group. Select Save Project Group As to save both projects as a group. When you want to test in the future, you can load the project group instead of individual projects. Name the Project group **GrDrivz.**

Close the `DrvControl UserControl`. You must close the User control so the new control icon is visible in the ToolBox. This icon represents your new control. Select the FrmDrList form and place the DrvControl icon on the form. Notice the ToolTipText when the mouse is moved over the control in the ToolBox.

Remember to make certain the ProjDrList project is selected as the Group Start up Object. If it is not, your project will not execute displaying the control on the form. Select the ProjDrList project in the Project Explorer and right-click. Click the Set as Start Up option. This makes the project with the form the Start up project.

When you are ready to test your control, select Start from the Run menu. The form now displays the control you placed there. Click the "List Drives" button. The drives listed on your machine are displayed in the text box, along with the volume label. When you click the Clear Window button, the box is cleared of text. If you are on a network, the file server's mapped drives will be displayed as sys or vol1, depending upon the server's operating system. CD-ROM drives will have specific volume labels, as will SCSI or ZIP drives.

In the next exercise, you begin the creation of an ActiveX document.

CROSS-REFERENCE
Chapter 21 includes more advanced development techniques.

FIND IT ONLINE
This article tells how to write apps for Windows 98 and 2000: **http://www.microsoft.com/msj/0499/ multilangunicode/multilangunicodetop.htm.**

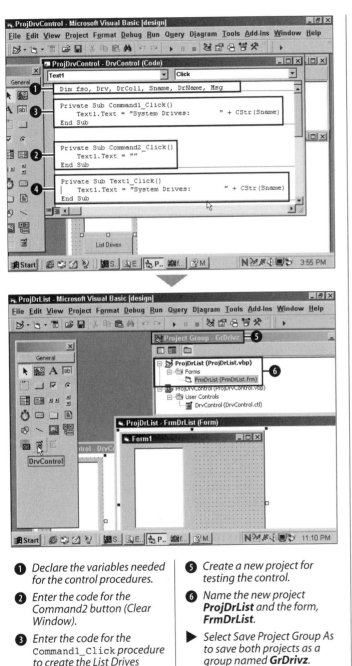

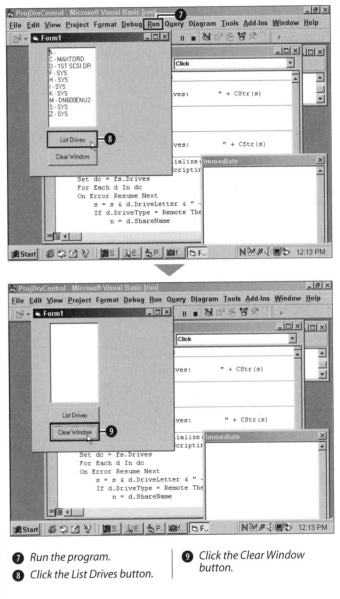

① Declare the variables needed for the control procedures.

② Enter the code for the Command2 button (Clear Window).

③ Enter the code for the Command1_Click procedure to create the List Drives function.

④ Enter the code for the Text1_Click procedure.

⑤ Create a new project for testing the control.

⑥ Name the new project **ProjDrList** and the form, **FrmDrList**.

▶ Select Save Project Group As to save both projects as a group named **GrDrivz**.

⑦ Run the program.

⑧ Click the List Drives button.

⑨ Click the Clear Window button.

Creating an ActiveX Document

While ActiveX documents and `ActiveX` controls share some features, they are quite different in other ways. Similarities with controls include the events `Initialize`, `InitProperties`, `WriteProperties`, `ReadProperties`, `Enterfocus`, `ExitFocus`, and `Terminate`. Also, ActiveX documents, like `ActiveX` controls must reside in a container object. Despite these similarities, the ActiveX document is more analogous to a form than it is to a control.

An ActiveX document is organized to include a UserDocument Object, code, code modules, and the controls you place on the UserDocument. UserDocument Objects are like forms in the sense that they are stored in `ASCII` text files, which include source code and the properties of the controls it contains.

UserDocuments have many of the events found on a form. `Activate`, `Deactivate`, `LinkClose`, `LinkError`, `LinkExecute`, `LinkOpen`, `Load`, `QueryUnload`, and `Unload` events are available on a form, but are not available on the `UserDocument`. `AsyncReadComplete`, `EnterFocus`, `ExitFocus`, `Hide`, `InitProperties`, `ReadProperties`, `Scroll`, `Show`, and `WriteProperties` events are those on the UserDocument, but they are not available for forms.

The `.DOB` file extension is used by Visual Basic for these files. Bitmaps and other graphX Xic files contained in the UserDocument are stored separately in a file with a `.DOX` extension.

The `.DOB` and `.DOX` files define the properties, events, and methods of the document. The ActiveX document can be compiled into either `ActiveX` `.exe` or `.dll`. ActiveX documents can be built into `.EXE` or `.DLL` files. The files with the `.EXE` extension are known as Out-of-Process components and the `.DLL` files are known as In-Process components. There also is a file with the `.VBD` extension and the browser must navigate to the path of that file.

The `.VBD` file must be placed in the same directory as the compiled component. Data in the `.VBD` file can be accessed and manipulated via standard OLE interfaces, such as using other Microsoft applications.

To help you develop an ActiveX UserDocument, Visual Basic offers the ActiveX Document Migration Wizard. This Wizard converts a Standard EXE project form and controls to an ActiveX UserDocument. This Add-In is accessed via the Add-In Manager.

Once loaded, this Wizard copies the form properties of an existing project to a new UserDocument. It comments out form code that does not work on the UserDocument. The ActiveX Document Migration Wizard also copies the controls from the form. You have the option of creating an ActiveX EXE (Out-of-Process) or DLL (In-Process) project. If a counterpart to events is between the old form and the new UserDocument, the event handlers is transferred.

TAKE NOTE

TRANSLATING FORMS EVENTS TO USERDOCUMENTS

If a form event has a UserDocument counterpart event, the ActiveX Document Migration Wizard replaces the word "form" with "UserDocument" in the code. If no counterpart exists for the event, it is copied to the general section of the code window and called as a procedure by the appropriate event for the UserDocument. For example, Form_Load has no exact counterpart, so it is copied to the General section and called from the correct procedure `UserDocument_Initialize`.

CROSS-REFERENCE

Chapter 22 discusses other uses for documents.

FIND IT ONLINE

Check this out for ActiveX components: **http://www2. crosswinds.net/~jba/VB/ActiveX/Index.htm**.

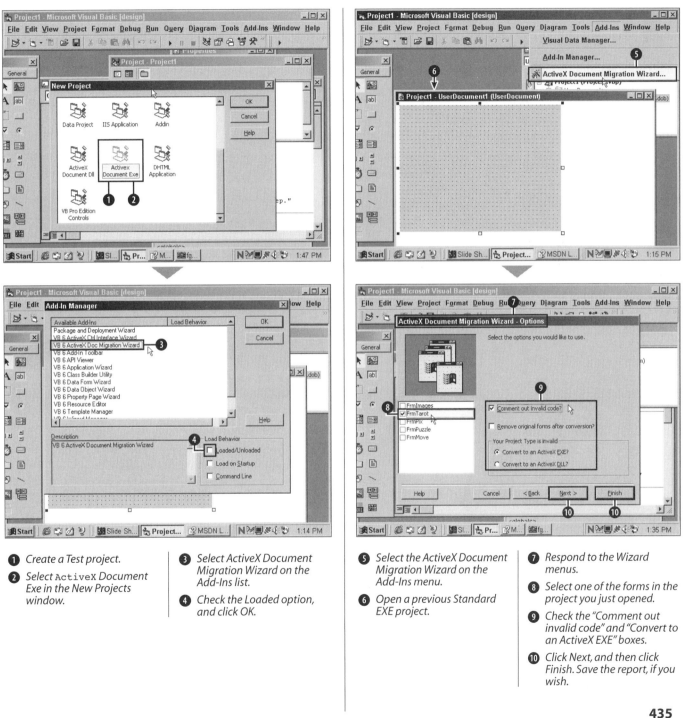

① *Create a Test project.*

② *Select* ActiveX *Document Exe in the New Projects window.*

③ *Select ActiveX Document Migration Wizard on the Add-Ins list.*

④ *Check the Loaded option, and click OK.*

⑤ *Select the ActiveX Document Migration Wizard on the Add-Ins menu.*

⑥ *Open a previous Standard EXE project.*

⑦ *Respond to the Wizard menus.*

⑧ *Select one of the forms in the project you just opened.*

⑨ *Check the "Comment out invalid code" and "Convert to an ActiveX EXE" boxes.*

⑩ *Click Next, and then click Finish. Save the report, if you wish.*

Using the ActiveX Document Migration Wizard

In the previous topic, you were able to practice using the ActiveX Document Migration Wizard. To do this, you can use nearly any of the previous projects' forms. Or, you can copy the code from a form and work out the differences in events and properties yourself. If you do so, you must draw replicas of all the controls on your new UserDocument because they will not have been copied over.

For example, the End command is most likely to be commented out because UserDocuments Terminate, rather than End. Form_Load is not used with UserDocuments because no form exists to load. UserDocuments Initialize instead. You can either change the procedure name to UserDocument_Initialize, or you can add that procedure and call the old `Form_Load` procedure.

When you practiced using the ActiveX Document Migration Wizard, you should have noticed the new user document was created in the old Standard EXE forms based project. This is not what you want to do. You can either copy the corrected code to the new UserDocument you created or Use "Save filename.dob As" to save the converted document in the same directory as your new UserDocument. To go over the steps exactly, begin your new project.

The new UserDocument you are going to build will be based on the FrmTarot form from the ProjImages project you worked on in Chapter 17.

Create a new ActiveX Document (EXE) project named ProjActxTarot. You can enter the ActiveX Document Designer, just as you did the Form Designer by double-clicking the UserDocument listed in the Project Explorer. The UserDocument you created is blank. You can translate the code from the old form to the new UserDocument yourself or use the ActiveX Document Migration Wizard.

Open the ProjImages project from the Chapter 17 directory where you saved it. Again, load the Wizard from the Add-Ins menu. When prompted, select the FrmTarot form to process. Check the "Comment out invalid code" and "Convert to an ActiveX EXE" boxes. Finish the conversion. You now have a new user document displayed in the Project Explorer under User Documents.

Select the `docFrmTarot.dob` icon in the Project Explorer and user Save document As to save the document in the same directory with your new UserDocument project. Now, open the document project you first created. When it loads, you can use Add User Document on the Project menu to add the converted form document to your new project. You can then eliminate the blank document you initially created when you created the new project.

Now you can rename your document **ActXTaro,** to be in keeping with the project name. In the next topic, you run your document in the browser.

TAKE NOTE

LOAD EVENT PROCEDURES IN USERDOCUMENTS

There is not an exact counterpart of the `Form Object's` `Load` event in the `UserDocument`. You can, instead, place `Load` event procedures in the Show event handler. The `Show` event is called each time the Web browser navigates to the ActiveX document, however. You can set a flag variable to prevent `Load` event procedures from running every time the `Show` event occurs.

CROSS-REFERENCE

Other references to user documents can be found in Chapter 22.

FIND IT ONLINE

This company sells an ActiveX component suite: http://www.protoview.com/press/9809acs3pr.asp.

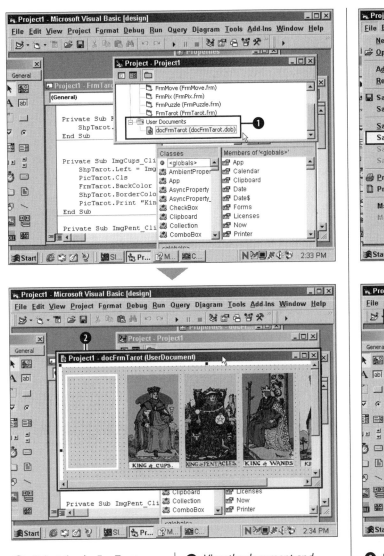

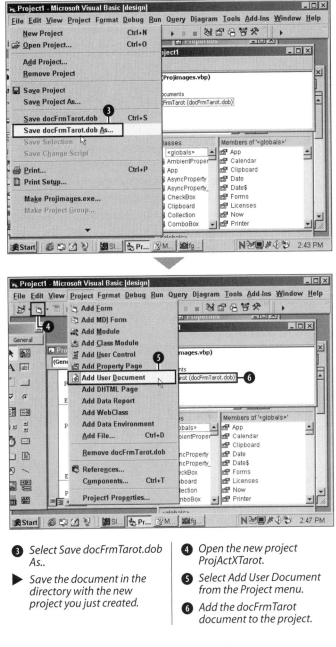

① Select the docFrmTarot UserDocument.

② View the document and compare it with the form from which it was made.

③ Select Save docFrmTarot.dob As..

▶ Save the document in the directory with the new project you just created.

④ Open the new project ProjActXTarot.

⑤ Select Add User Document from the Project menu.

⑥ Add the docFrmTarot document to the project.

Viewing the User Document in a Browser

One of the big advantages of using Visual Basic to program on the Internet is you needn't learn another language, as you would with HTML. Another asset is the Visual Basic programming environment. With your knowledge and the IDE, you have an entire development environment available, including the Visual Basic code window, debugger, and compiler.

Also, you have the capability of creating ActiveX documents that run in Internet Explorer. The ActiveX document is essentially a Visual Basic application that is accessible and usable in the Internet Explorer container. Your application will execute on the user's system. The code necessary to execute is contained within the ActiveX component.

In your User Document project, ProjActxTarot, you should note where the code has been changed. Double-click the document and find the `Form_Load` procedure.

```
Private Sub Form_Load()
    ShpTarot.Left = 100
End Sub
```

This procedure is supposed to be launched with the loading of the form. The ActiveX Document Migrations Wizard has left this code intact, but has called the procedure from the `UserDocument_Initalize` procedure.

```
Private Sub UserDocument_Initialize()
    Call Form_Load
End Sub
```

You could, of course, replace the `Form_Load` procedure with the `Initialize` procedure by copying the ShpTarot.Left statement into the `Initialize` procedure.

```
Private Sub UserDocument_Initialize()
    Shptarot.Left = 100
End Sub
```

This procedure will have the same effect as calling the `Form_Load` procedure.

Now you can test your UserDocument. Of course, to test it, you need to have Internet Explorer installed because it is the container from which the UserDocument will run.

Press F5 to run your project. You should see the familiar Tarot cards displayed in your Internet Explorer browser. If you do not see the cards, check the Internet Options on the Tools menu. Click the Security tab. If you selected Medium or Higher, you will be prompted before you can run your application. If this happens, you will be prompted in a File Download dialog box. When you see the File Download window, check the "Open this file from its current location" to access your document. You can also change your security settings in the `Internet Explorer`.

If Internet Explorer runs, but you do not see your document in the Explorer window, click Open on the File menu, type in the name of the temporary `.VBD` file created for your ActiveX document, and then click OK. You can check for the location of this file by using Windows Find. Typically, the file is placed in the VB98 directory, rather than the directory where you have saved your current projects.

Now, you can test your project in the same manner as any other ActiveX.DLL or .EXE project.

TAKE NOTE

▶ **USING VISUAL BASIC ON THE INTERNET**

You can create complex applications for the Internet using the controls with which you are familiar. Place PictureBoxes, CommandButtons, and so forth on your documents and they will be displayed in the Internet Explorer. If you were to write code in HTML, you would be faced with starting from scratch. You can add forms to your project by hyperlinking to them using filename or URL.

CROSS-REFERENCE

Chapter 22 contains more projects with UserDocuments.

FIND IT ONLINE

Here are patches for the Windows Common Controls regarding VB 5 projects: http://www.mvps.org/vbnet/dev/_acc/vb6/vb6upgradeutil.htm.

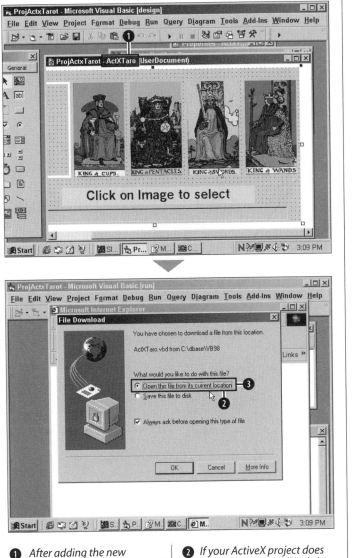

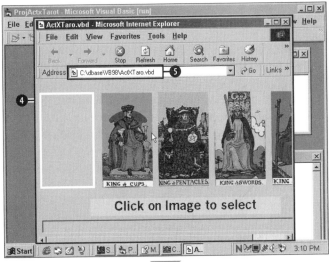

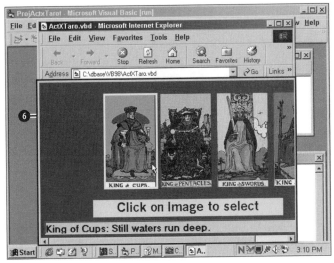

❶ After adding the new UserDocument to the ActiveX Document project, view the ActXTaro UserDocument to ensure it is the same as the original form.

❷ If your ActiveX project does not execute immediately in your browser ...

❸ Check the Open this file.. box in the File Download dialog window.

❹ View your ActiveX UserDocument in the Internet Explorer.

❺ If the Internet Explorer does not load your document, click Open on the File menu or type in the path and filename of your .VBD file in the Address box.

❻ Click the pictures to see the frame pop over each picture, as it did in the original application.

Adding a Second User Document to a Project

You can add new forms and user documents to an ActiveX project. If you add user documents to the ActiveX project, you need to prepare a means of navigating to that document. You cannot add menus directly to an ActiveX document, but you can add them to forms that are part of an ActiveX project.

For this exercise, you use the FrmMove form from the ProjGraphic project in Chapter 16. Use the ActiveX Document Migration Wizard to convert the FrmMove form into a user document as described in the previous topic.

Once you create and save the new docFrmMove document, add it to the ActXTarot project. Select Project, Add User Document to add the new document. Now you must add a means of connecting the two documents. Do this by using the Hyperlink Object and its NavigateTo method. Add a command button with the caption "Go to Deal Cards" to the docFrmTarot document. Add the following code to the Command1_Click procedure.

```
Hyperlink.NavigateTo "c:\vb98\docfrmmove.vbd"
```

You can modify this path to accommodate the actual location of the VBD file on your system.

When you need to navigate between UserDocuments in an ActiveX project, you have the choice of adding a form with a menu or another UserDocument with command buttons instead of menus. Command buttons, as you learned, use about the same code. The exception occurs when you are using a property on the menu that doesn't exist for the command button. This presents an interesting problem because most of the forms in previous projects use menus to make a selection.

Because your FrmMove form used a menu to cause the cards to move, you will need to change that function over to a command button. Add a command button. In the mnuDeal procedure, you used the Checked property to flag whether the Deal Cards option had been selected. If the menu and command button Click procedures both had Checked properties, you could copy the code in the menu procedure to the command button procedure.

Unfortunately, no Checked property exists for buttons. You need to create a variable to flag the status of the Deal Cards selection.

```
FlagX As Boolean
```

Add this variable declaration to the declaration list in the General Declarations section of the document. The rest is simply a matter of changing the mnuDeal.Checked property to a statement flagging the change in status for the FlagX variable in each occurrence of the status change.

TAKE NOTE

THE WRONG CONTAINER

Because you won't know in what type of container your ActiveX Document will be viewed, you must prepare your document. The TypeName function is used to get information about an object, such as determining the class of an object or the type of a variable. You can use the TypeName function to determine whether it is a completely wrong container. At this point, you should prepare a warning to the user about the lack of usability with this container. The correct container to use for viewing should also be mentioned.

CROSS-REFERENCE

Check Chapters 21 and 22 for more Internet programming ideas.

FIND IT ONLINE

This explains In-process and Out-of-Process ActiveX: **http://msdn.microsoft.com/library/devprods/vs6/vbasic/vbcon98/vbconinprocessoutofprocessdocumentobjects.htm**.

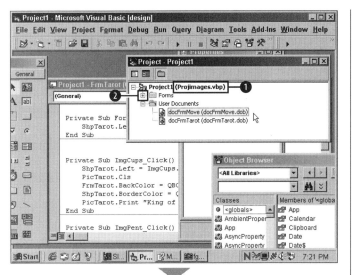

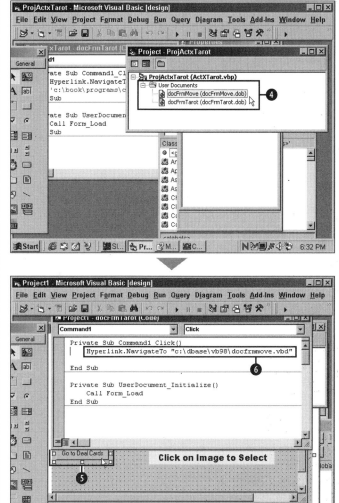

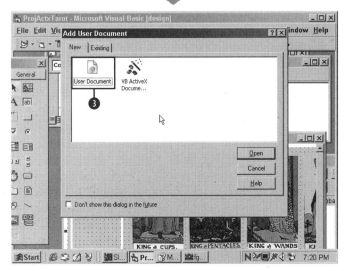

① Open the Projimages project.

② Use the ActiveX Document Migration Wizard to convert the FrmMove form to a UserDocument.

③ Open the ProjActxTarot project and select Add User Document on the Project menu to add the UserDocument you just created.

④ View the new UserDocument (docFrmMove) and open the UserDocument docFrmTarot.

⑤ Add a CommandButton (Command1) to docFrmTarot.

⑥ Add the code to NavigateTo a Hyperlink.

441

Finalizing the Second Document Addition

The variable — FlagX — is needed to carry out the movement of the cards, depending upon whether the Move Cards button was pressed.

For example, the `Command1 Click` procedure reset the Checked status to False, so the value of FlagX must also be False. The other place to add the statement for the FlagX variable is in the `Timer` procedure.

```
If mnuDeal.Checked = True Then
```

This statement should be changed to:

```
Private Sub Timer1_Timer()
    If FlagX = True Then
    Deal
    End If
End Sub
```

Luckily, you only need to make changes in a few places to add the function to a command button.

Now, you must add another button to the docFrmMove document to go back to the previous document. This is accomplished by using the hyperlink Object's `GoBack` method.

```
Private Sub Command3_Click()
    UserDocument.Hyperlink.GoBack
End Sub
```

The `GoBack` method is supported in Internet Explorer versions 3.0 and up. When clicked, the Go Back button reloads the first document.

If you try to view your document in an application that does not support the `NavigateTo` method (for example,

the Microsoft Binder), then the Windows Registry determines which application on your system does support hyperlinking and launches it. Depending upon your system, your browser may automatically launch your browser and display your documents.

You use the `NavigateTo` method to move from one ActiveX document to the other. This is the method you use to start another document in a browser, unlike running a program that starts with a form.

Once you add the code to return to the previous form, your project is nearly complete. Run the program. When the document is visible in the browser, click the Go to Deal Cards button. The other document will now load. In case you have not modified your browser security by selecting Internet Options from the Tools menu on Internet Explorer, you are prompted to save or open the document. Select Open to view it.

TAKE NOTE

DEBUGGING YOUR DOCUMENT

Visual Basic will notify you that stopping your project will cause an error in the application hosting the ActiveX document. This occurs if you return to Visual Basic and attempt to stop the project while your ActiveX document is shown in Internet Explorer. You can click NO to switch back to Internet Explorer and Quit the Internet Explorer or navigate to another URL.

CROSS-REFERENCE

Chapter 22 continues the groundwork laid in this chapter and in Chapter 21.

FIND IT ONLINE

Here's where to learn how to debug in Internet Explorer: **http://msdn.microsoft.com/library/devprods/vs6/vbasic/vbcon98/vbcondebuggingdocumentobjects.htm.**

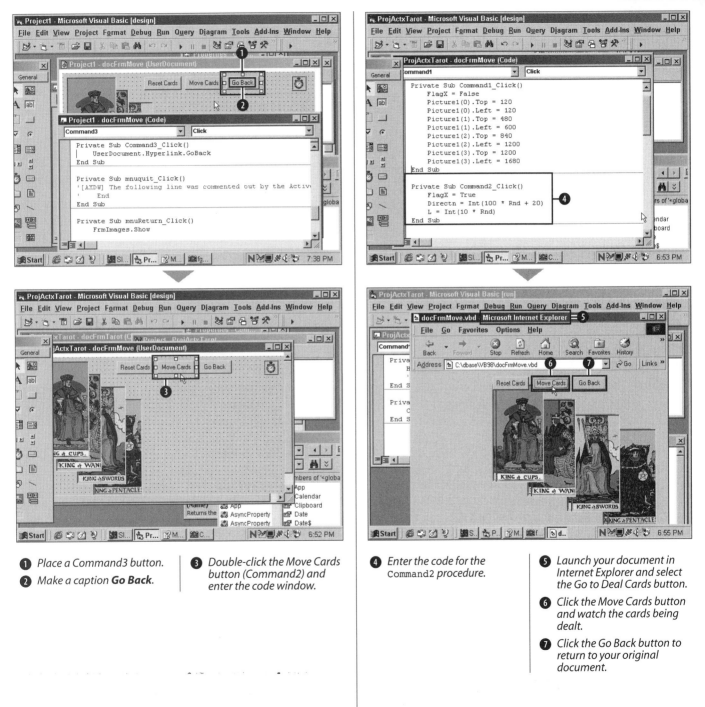

① *Place a Command3 button.*

② *Make a caption* **Go Back**.

③ *Double-click the Move Cards button (Command2) and enter the code window.*

④ *Enter the code for the* Command2 *procedure.*

⑤ *Launch your document in Internet Explorer and select the Go to Deal Cards button.*

⑥ *Click the Move Cards button and watch the cards being dealt.*

⑦ *Click the Go Back button to return to your original document.*

Personal Workbook

Q&A

1 What is the ActiveX counterpart of the form called?

_____

_____

_____

_____

2 What are some properties of UserDocuments?

_____

_____

_____

3 What kind of file stores the completed UserDocument?

_____

_____

_____

_____

4 What is the new ActiveX control called in the Project Explorer window?

_____

_____

_____

5 When you create a new ActiveX control, you are creating a __.

_____

_____

_____

6 What type of files (extension) are produced when you compile ActiveX components?

_____

_____

_____

7 What tool is available to convert existing forms into ActiveX documents?

_____

_____

_____

8 How are ActiveX documents displayed?

_____

_____

ANSWERS: PAGE 530

EXTRA PRACTICE

1 Develop a custom `ActiveX` control that reports information about the size of your desktop and video display.

2 Convert an existing form to an ActiveX document, replacing the menu procedures with command buttons.

3 Create a new ActiveX document that looks like an HTML page.

4 Design a Web site made up of ActiveX documents that you create.

REAL WORLD APPLICATIONS

✔ Your company has asked you to enhance its custom Web browser, which enables employees to access the company's database. The company would like to display a form in the browser showing version and system information.

✔ Your cousin, Robespierre, needs an enhancement to his company's Web site. He has heard a lot about ActiveX and he thinks it is magic. Now Robespierre wants you to revamp his home page. Create a UserDocument and a form to be executed at his Web site.

✔ Spuds Are Us, a company that manufactures potato products, has contracted with you to set up a Web site for them. They want a home page with lots of eye-catching animation and buttons to press. Go to it.

Visual Quiz

Which of these options in the ActiveX Document Migration Wizard should be checked?

_____

_____

_____

_____

_____

_____

CHAPTER **21**

Programming on the Internet

Internet applications consist of interactive applications that are accessed via the Internet or on a company's intranet. The applications can carry out sophisticated business processes, such as credit card processing and database searching. Server-based applications use the HTTP protocol. The processing takes place on a Web server and interacts with the user's Web browser.

In order to connect with the Internet, you will need to have an Internet service provider (ISP), a phone line or cable hookup, a modem, the Windows Dial-Up adapter, and a Web browser. You can find an ISP from an online service or from ads in the newspaper. Some cable companies offer cable modems and high-speed connectivity. Other technologies are currently available and more continually being developed. Most people use Internet Explorer or Netscape Navigator as browsers, but as you saw in Chapter 3, you can set up your own browser in Visual Basic.

Using Visual Basic, you can add content to Web pages easily. You can provide a user interface for all those who visit a Web site. The HTML page will perform various functions and can combine Visual Basic compiled code with HTML.

You can write IIS applications. These combine HTML (HyperText Markup Language) with compiled Visual Basic code. This is really the best of both worlds. Many Web sites on the Internet are written solely in HTML editors, but many sites also use combinations of DHTML (Dynamic HTML) and JavaScript, Java, and other languages and utilities.

The time has been so short since the beginning of the World Wide Web that it is somewhat surprising that developers are now spending a large percentage of development time in Internet applications. If you had worked with Visual Basic a couple of versions back, you would likely never have heard of using it to develop for the Internet. Now, the Visual Studio documentation is full of Internet programming information.

DHTML is a new technology in Internet Explorer that enables you to write Visual Basic code to respond to events and actions on HTML pages. You also can use the Web Publishing Wizard to publish your application to a Web site.

Another new Internet feature is asynchronous enhancements that provide more information about ongoing operations online. New language members have been added to Visual Basic to facilitate this new area.

Internet Explorer also provides new download support for ActiveX documents. Downloading ActiveX documents now functions the same as downloading ActiveX controls. Some things you can do using Visual Basic on the Internet are query databases upon user request, replace parts of Web pages with new content before they are accessed by the user's browser, create HTML elements, and simultaneously generate events at runtime.

These features provide an alternative to the various tools (CGI, Perl, and so on) that have been used piecemeal. In fact, Visual Basic is capable of performing these same functions.

Learning the Terminology

The Professional and Enterprise editions provide the capability to develop client-based and server-based applications for the Internet.

The precursor of the Network of all Networks **Internet** was created in 1957 and was known as Advanced Research Projects Agency network (ARPAnet). It allowed researchers, academics, and military personnel located at sites throughout the country to communicate with each other electronically. In the 1970s the classic applications used were e-mail, FTP (electronic transfer of entire files), Telnet (logging on remotely), and Usenet (electronic bulletin boards for interest groups).

The **World Wide Web** is an extension of the original Internet that added graphics capabilities. The essential features of the World Wide Web are Web sites that enable users to visit, view information, and interact in real time.

The acronym **URL** stands for Uniform Resource Locator, meaning the address (path and filename) of a domain on the World Wide Web. An example is `http://www. microsoft.com`.

If the filename is not specified, the browser will look for and launch a file named `default.htm` or `index.htm`. An alternative file extension is `.html`.

HyperText Transfer Protocol (HTTP) is an information transfer protocol used to transfer information over a TCP/IP (Transmission Control Protocol/Internet Protocol) backbone. When a user's Web browser makes a request of the HTTP server, the server responds to the request and the connection is then closed.

TCP/IP includes the suite of packet transmission protocols that provide communication on the Internet. There are a number of other network communication protocols outside the Internet (Novell's IPX/SPX for example). TCP/IP has a unique capability to route packets of data to any machine connected to the Internet.

File Transfer Protocol (FTP) is used to copy files to and from the Internet. This can be done using a command line interface that is usually in UNIX and looks like DOS. You enter commands at the command line, so you must know the commands to use.

More recently there have been Windows interfaces for FTP that allow you to click and drag files from the Internet to your system and vice versa. Of course, you must have permissions to the site in order to carry out transfers. To go to a FTP site, you use the characters FTP:// instead of HTTP:// on the command line in your browser.

The Common Gateway Interface (CGI) is a specification that lets developers use a variety of development tools. CGI programs (called scripts) process forms, page counters, and e-mail configuration. CGI scripts are stored on the Web server in a special directory (usually `CGI-BIN`) to be executed when called. CGI programs are written in C or Perl (other programming languages).

TAKE NOTE

▶ LEARNING ABOUT DHTML

DHTML applications allow you to create interactive applications that are based upon browsers. The HTML page is static and does not allow the user to interact with an application unless it is running on the server. DHTML uses a Document Object Model (DOM) to enable the programmer to create interactive applications. The DHTML application is located on the browser machine. There, it interprets and responds to actions initiated by users.

CROSS-REFERENCE

Chapter 1 contains references to the Visual Basic Interface that may be referred to here.

FIND IT ONLINE

This Q and A page is a valuable link: **http://members. aol.com/ymwymw/vbqa.htm**.

Java can refer to **JavaScript,** stand-alone Java programs, or **Java Applets.** Stand-alone Java programs do not require a Web page to be run. The key factor that favors Java is its platform independence.

JavaScript is an adaptation of the Netscape scripting language. It uses Java-type commands that are embedded into the HTML document. JavaScript is interpreted on the fly along with HTML. Java and JavaScript are two different entities.

Java applets are specialized programs designed to be used on Internet Web pages. A Java applet will run only if you have a Java-enabled Web browser.

An **IIS (Internet Information Server)** application is a Visual Basic application that uses a combination of HTML and compiled Visual Basic code in a dynamic, browser-based application. An IIS application resides on a Web server, where it receives requests from a browser, runs code associated with the requests, and returns responses to the browser.

In its simplest form, you can use an IIS application to intercept a user request and return an HTML page to the browser. A few of the things you can do with IIS applications includes querying databases, retrieving Web pages, and creating Web page input forms and graphics.

VBScript is a subset of Visual Basic that enables you to embed commands into HTML documents. VBScript is an interpreted language, executing along with the HTML commands. Currently, only Internet Explorer supports VBScript. Netscape is compatible only when a plug-in is added.

The original operating system on the Internet was **UNIX.** UNIX has traditionally provided great file services with low overhead, and the newer **Linux** operating system is not only low in overhead but is extremely inexpensive. The various versions of Linux (Redhat, Caldera, and Suse) can be purchased nearly anywhere software is sold and downloaded from the Internet. Linux servers are becoming

among the most popular because they do not have heavy hardware and memory requirements and the price allows almost anyone to become an Internet provider.

Windows NT is the more robust companion to Windows 95/98/2000. NT servers are far more demanding than UNIX/Linux of CPU performance and memory. NT servers' performance will degrade faster than Linux with a large number of hits (user visits to a site). Of course the performance will also depend upon the development language and tools of the developer.

The **socket** is the basic object that supports TCP/IP protocol. Sockets uses the client/server model to provide services. The server-side program provides services at a specific IP address and port. The server checks for service requests (Web pages) and then provides the service. Programs demanding services (a user with a Web browser) must know the IP address and port # in order to communicate. The socket model means that a client computer can be of any type. UNIX, Macintosh, DOS, or Windows platforms can all communicate on the Internet as long as they support TCP/IP.

Services on the Internet include FTP, Telnet, SMTP, and WWW. Each of these services requires a port address that will route service requests. Telnet is used for remote logging onto the Internet, and SMTP (Simple Mail Transfer Protocol) is the implementation of e-mail service.

TAKE NOTE

▶ WINDOWS SOCKETS CONTROL

Windows Sockets (WinSock control) allows Windows client machines to connect to a remote computer and exchange data using either the User Datagram Protocol (UDP) or the Transmission Control Protocol (TCP).

CROSS-REFERENCE

Chapter 22 moves forward from here.

FIND IT ONLINE

This site has HTML editors: **http://www.zdnet.com/ swlib/hotfiles/10html.html.**

Introducing HTML and DHTML

The Hypertext Markup Language (HTML) is the page description language on the Internet and intranets. It provides a facility for the design of Web pages. At first appearance, it looks much like many of the first word processors available under operating systems. HTML is reminiscent of the first versions of WordStar, a word processor that embedded formatting commands in the text to set up paragraphs, special fonts, underlining, italics, bold, and so on.

HTML uses formatting symbols to indicate what element is being formatted on a page. It is page centered, and each page constitutes a file with the `.htm` or `.html` extension. HTML is a markup language. The embedded commands provide instructions as to how the Web page will be organized. The HTML page is made up of elements or tags and is divided into the parts HTML, head, and body. The page is organized so that there are elements specific to each part of a page.

```
<HTML>
<HEAD>
<TITLE>     <TITLE>
</HEAD>
<BODY>
</BODY>
</HTML>
```

This code centers the page, with slashes indicating that a specific element has ended. The entire page is contained within the HTML tags, and the `TITLE` is contained within the `HEAD` tags. The main portion of the page is encapsulated in the `BODY` tags. Finally, HTML ends the page.

The `BODY` tags can contain many other tags as well. For example, there are tables, forms, alignment, font, and data commands. Images are indicated with the `<IMG>` tag. You can specify many attributes such as text and background color, style, and pattern. You can have background images, quotes, and hyperlinks to Web sites.

Dynamic Hypertext Markup Language (DHTML) applications use Internet Explorer (4.0 or later) in conjunction with Visual Basic. DHTML lets you create, modify, and enhance existing Web pages created in HTML editors.

One of the innovations introduced by DHTML is Cascading Style Sheets (CSS). Much like the style sheets used in page layout programs such as PageMaker and Ventura Publisher, these style sheets enable you to format Web pages. Advantages of style sheets include the ability to make a general change in a paragraph tag and have it reflected throughout the document. The key difference between DHTML and HTML is the dynamic aspect. DHTML enables you to change content of the page after the browser has loaded it.

TAKE NOTE

STYLE SHEETS

Style sheets contain definitions of various properties that maintain the appearance of the Web page. For example, font and font color and style, color of other elements, background, borders, and paragraph style are all elements that can be included in a style sheet or in multiple style sheets. DHTML pages can use inline (used to affect a single element), global (defined at the beginning of the document), and linked style sheets (that refer to a separate file where definitions are stored).

TAKE NOTE

NEW FEATURES WITH DHTML

Add exciting new features to your applications with DHTML. You can have text that flies off the page a word at a time, and rotating billboard-style transitions. Some browsers may not support DHTML, so plan your applications with this in mind.

CROSS-REFERENCE

Find further information on controls used here in Chapter 20.

FIND IT ONLINE

This site is ALIVE! deals with Web design: **http://members.xoom.com/charlysworld/**.

Listing 21-1: The Web Designs Page

```html
<html>
<head><!— CW_DATA     DOCROOT="/"
CWICON="mainwp35.ico"         MODIFIED="Monday,
October 13, 1997"     PUBLISHED="Monday, October
13, 1997"     STYLEFILE="an.htm" —>
<!— CW_DATAEND —>
<meta NAME="description" CONTENT="HiTek Designs
provides Free web page design with low cost,
reliable web hosting. ">
<meta NAME="keywords" CONTENT="hosting,
design,web page design, free web design, internet
pages">
<!— CW_BANNER CWCOMPONENT="Custom Banner"
CWICON="CBANNER.ICO" CWBANNERTEXT="Hi-Tek Web
Design"—>
<title>web page design and web hosting</title>
<meta name="Microsoft Border" content="tl,
default">
</head>
<body CWTYPE="BACKGROUNDS4" leftmargin="0"
bgcolor="#FFFFFF"
background="_borders/waves.jpg">
<h2 align="left"><font face="Arial"
size="4"><strong>Visit our clients'
sites:</strong></font>
</h2>
<table border="1" width="100%" cellpadding="3">
  <tr>
    <td width="400"><p ALIGN="left"><font
FACE="Arial" SIZE="2">Get your free web page
design and website now. You pay only $4.99 to
start. Each month pay only $4.99 to maintain your
website.
</font></p>
    <p ALIGN="left"><font FACE="Arial"
SIZE="2">Describe your needs, and give us your
ideas for a Web Page and we will translate them
into a finished product.
</font></td>
```

```html
  </tr>
</table>
<table BORDER="0" ALIGN="DEFAULT" WIDTH="100%">
  <tr>
    <td ALIGN="left" VALIGN="top"
width="400"><address>
      <strong><font face="Arial" size="3">The
Team</font></strong>
    </address>
    <p><font FACE="Arial" SIZE="2">Hi-Tek's Team
includes a systems analyst, a Novell Certified
Netware Engineer, a teacher and a
programmer.</font></td>
  </tr>
</table>
<h4 align="center"> <br>
</h4>
<p><img BORDER="0" </body>
</html>
```

▶ *View the example of HTML code.*

▶ *View the HiTek Designs Web page.*

CROSS-REFERENCE

Find additional exercises in Chapter 22.

FIND IT ONLINE

Here are browser plug-ins and add-ins: **http://www.
zdnet.com/swlib/topics/browsers.html.**

Creating a DHTML Project

Whereas IIS is server based, DHTML is client based. That is, IIS applications are executed on the Web server, and DHTML applications are executed in the browser.

DHTML enables you to create Web pages that dynamically change the content of the page at runtime without using server-side processing or scripts. DHTML lets you exercise greater control over page layout and table elements by offering greater precision than HTML editors offer. Also, some graphic formats not supported by HTML (.png files) can be used with DHTML.

To create a new HTML file in the DHTML editor, you can select DHTML Application from the New Project window. The Project Explorer window will show that the project has a Module and a Designer. The Designer will contain by default one DHTML page. When you click this page, instead of viewing a form, you will view the DHTML page. This is the DHTML Editor, where you can create a Web page from scratch.

You also can import an existing page that you have edited in FrontPage, Microsoft Word, or another Web page editor. You can add new pages to your project at any time, by selecting Add DHTML from the Project menu. This is similar to adding new forms to projects. If you have an existing page you created in a different editor, select Add DHTML Page from the Project menu. Check the "Save HTML in external file:" box and click Open. From the Open dialog box, browse until you find the file to load. When you make your selection, your file will appear on the new page you added. It will also be listed in the Project Explorer under DHTMLPage1.

The left pane of the DHTML Editor displays the tags for the different parts of your Web page. You can see the HTML tags by expanding the Document object. Expanding each object in turn will display all the tags on the page. The items on the toolbar include the Properties pages, Notepad editor, add Link, table operations, object order, and so on.

Add HTML elements to the page. When you are finished editing the page and are satisfied with the design and performance, you can select Make project DLL from the File menu to create the dynamic linked library (.dll) file. Visual Basic creates a DLL file that essentially is an ActiveX project. This DLL file must be placed in the server directory where your HTML files reside.

Click the toolbar icon on the far left. This is the Property page for the DHTML page. This is where you specify where the HTML file will be saved. If you have images, text, and such that make up the page, you will need to save them where those objects are located or copy the objects to the directory where your program files are located.

Once you have saved the file as an external HTML file (.htm extension), you can view it in the browser. When you are ready to preview your page in the browser, select Run to view the page in your browser. If you get an error message in the browser that the page is not found, select Open from the browser File menu and browse to find the HTML file. When you locate the file, it will be displayed in the browser.

Because the DHTML Editor is not as full featured as products like FrontPage, it may be more efficient to bring in a fully developed file to Visual Basic. You can copy sample HTML files from the **hi-tekmall.com** Web site if you wish.

TAKE NOTE

▶ EVENTS IN DHTML

Most events in DHTML are pretty much the same as in Visual Basic programming, but some event names are different for doing the same thing. Many DHTML events begin with the word "on." It helps to look these terms up in this fashion.

CROSS-REFERENCE
Find more DHTML programming in Chapter 22.

FIND IT ONLINE
CodeSmart is an add-on with a lot of functionality: **http://codesmart.hypermart.net/**.

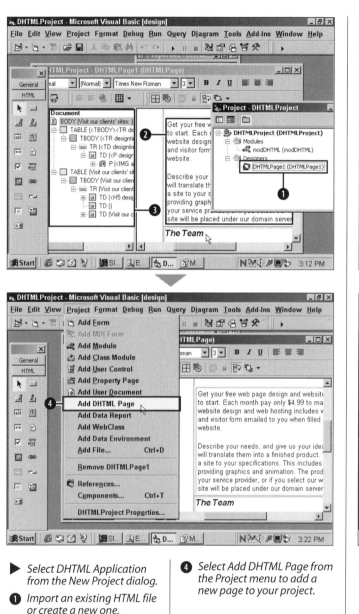

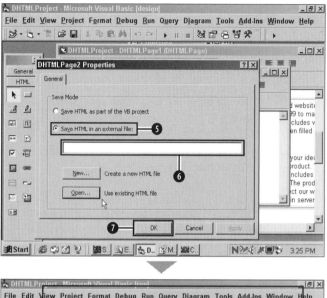

▶ Select DHTML Application from the New Project dialog.

① Import an existing HTML file or create a new one.

② Add elements to a new Web page, or Edit elements in an existing page.

③ View the tags in the left pane.

④ Select Add DHTML Page from the Project menu to add a new page to your project.

▶ Click the toolbar icon for the Property pages of your DHTML page.

⑤ Check the "Save in an external file" box.

⑥ Type in a path and filename to save your page as an HTML file.

⑦ Click OK.

⑧ Save your work, paying close attention to the path of your HTML file and then run the program to view in the browser.

⑨ Select Open from the browser File menu and browse to find it if your file can't be found.

Making Your Own Web Browser

In Chapter 3, you created an application that set up a Web browser by simply clicking that type of form. Also, you can select Web Browser as a form type in the Add Form dialog box. Either of these options will give you a nice-looking basic browser.

Of course, once you get started with programming, you begin to figure out how to improve almost any program. The browser is no exception. Further, it is not as sophisticated as most available browsers. You may want to have options other than Back, Forward, Stop, Refresh, and Home. At least, you will probably be able to think of many features to add.

In this exercise, you will create an original Web browser to start at a Home URL, then go to one specified. You will add new features and enhancements as you move toward developing a full-featured, custom-tailored browser.

Create a new project named **ProjBigBrowser.** Name the form **FrmBigBrowser**. The "Big" is to distinguish your project from someone else's "Little" browser. You could use the Browser form by adding a new form from the Project menu, but you don't need to do that. In fact, it is a lot more fun to set up your own toolbar with custom icons.

You first need to add controls from the Components option on the Project menu. Select Microsoft Internet Controls, Microsoft Internet MAPI Controls 6.0, as well as the Microsoft Windows Common Controls 3-6.0 and Microsoft Windows Common Controls 6.0.

Now, draw a `WebBrowser` control named `WeBrowserBig` on the form. Place the `WebBrowser` control across the bottom two-thirds of the form, filling all the space in that area. Add a `ComboBox` named `ComBrowse` above the `WebBrowser`. Next, add a `ToolBar` control. Add an `ImageList` control to the area of the `WebBrowser` control.

Create a menu in the Menu Editor with options of Mail (`mnuMail`) and Exit (`mnuExit`). Leave the Mail procedure blank for the moment, but add the `mnuExit` click procedure to `End`.

Now comes the fun of selecting icons for the toolbar. Select the toolbar and right-click to view the Property pages. Click the Images tab. Now you need to locate the appropriate icons to represent the options on the toolbar.

Click Insert Picture to add the first icon. In the Select Picture dialog, locate the `VB98\Graphics\Icons` directory on your system. There are subdirectories under the Icons directory by subject. Select an arrow pointing to the left from the `Arrows` subdirectory. Add a second icon (a forward-pointing arrow from the same directory).

You need to select three more icons from any Icon subdirectory you deem appropriate for the Refresh, Home, and Mail options.

Once you have selected the icons for the `ImageList`, click OK and select the `ToolBar`. On the General tab select `ImageList1` to the right of the `ImageList` drop-down menu. This binds the `ImageList` control to the `ToolBar` control.

CROSS-REFERENCE

There is a discussion using a Web browser in Chapter 3.

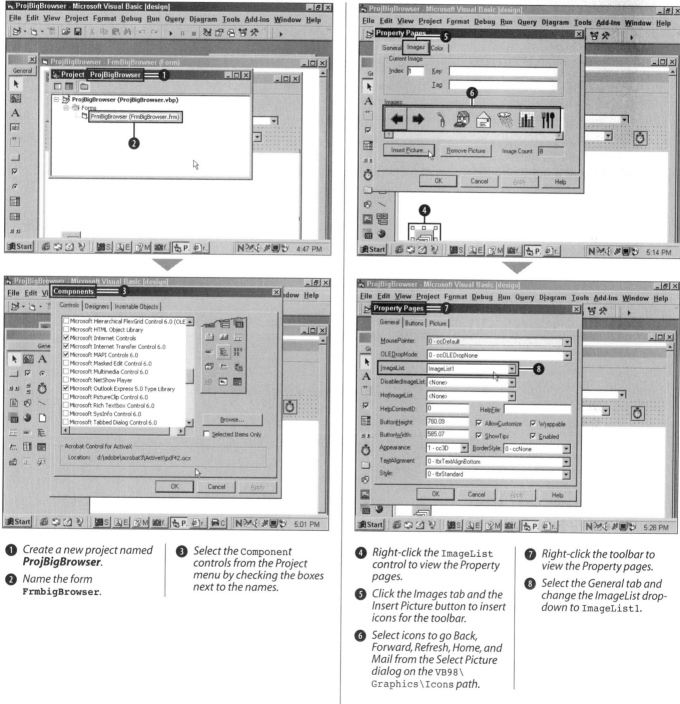

① Create a new project named **ProjBigBrowser**.

② Name the form **FrmbigBrowser**.

③ Select the Component controls from the Project menu by checking the boxes next to the names.

④ Right-click the ImageList control to view the Property pages.

⑤ Click the Images tab and the Insert Picture button to insert icons for the toolbar.

⑥ Select icons to go Back, Forward, Refresh, Home, and Mail from the Select Picture dialog on the VB98\Graphics\Icons path.

⑦ Right-click the toolbar to view the Property pages.

⑧ Select the General tab and change the ImageList drop-down to ImageList1.

455

Setting Up Web Browser Options

lick the Buttons tab. Click Insert Button. The Index counter shows 1. Type **Back** in the Key text box. Assuming that you inserted the icons in the `ImageList` in the order shown for the `ToolBar`, type a **1** in the Image box. You also can add ToolTipText if you wish. It will help users make selections in case your images are a little whimsical. The number two button needs the Key "Forward," the number three button Key should be "Refresh," the number four button should have the Key "Home," and the fifth button needs to have the Key "Mail."

The `Image` numbers can match the `Index` values as long as the images were inserted in order with the `ToolBar` options that they represent. For example, the number three button is the Refresh option, so the image displayed on that button should be the icon you selected to symbolize Refresh. If you inserted the icons at random, then you will need to change the image numbers for each index item.

When you are finished, check to make sure the options and images match. Click OK to return to the form. View the icons on the toolbar. If they don't look they way you expect, you can change them.

The plans for this Web browser are to carry out functions including going Back, going Forward, Refreshing the screen, returning to the Home URL, and displaying the Mail form. The means of performing these functions include a form load procedure, `Click` and `KeyPress` procedures for the `ComboBox` to navigate using a URL, menu option procedures, and a `ToolBar` procedure to respond to clicks on the toolbar buttons.

Most Web browsers have a button that enables you to customize a Home URL to which the browser will navigate upon launching. Suppose that you would like the Home Web site to be the IDG Books Worldwide home page. In that case, you would use the browser object's `Navigate` method to do the navigation.

```
Private Sub Form_Load()
    WeBrowserBig.Navigate "www.idgbooks.com"
    ComBrowse.Text = "www.idgbooks.com"
    ComBrowse.AddItem ComBrowse.Text
End Sub
```

The `Navigate` method is used to navigate to the resource identified in a string containing the Universal Resource Locator (URL). In this situation, the home page will be IDG Books Web site. The `ComboBox Text` property is set to the same. You do not necessarily need to do this. The `AddItem` method adds the text item to the `ComboBox` control.

The next topic will tackle the `ToolBar_ButtonClick` procedure and the navigation functions attached to the `ComBrowse ComboBox` control, and lay the groundwork for some future enhancements.

TAKE NOTE

▶ BOUND CONTROLS

If you decide to add new images to your image list after you have bound the `ImageList` control to the `ToolBar` control, you will have to unbind it before inserting or deleting images or changing the positions of the images in the list. To do this, you select Property Pages on the toolbar, select the General tab, and change the `ImageList` to `None`. After you have made your changes to the `ImageList`, you need to return to the `ToolBar` Property pages and reselect the `ImageList1` control as the `ImageList` on the General tab.

CROSS-REFERENCE

More information on using controls is in Chapter 9.

FIND IT ONLINE

This site has Web development tools: **http://www2.lario.com/ dna/subcat.asp?sct=22&catname=Web%20Development**.

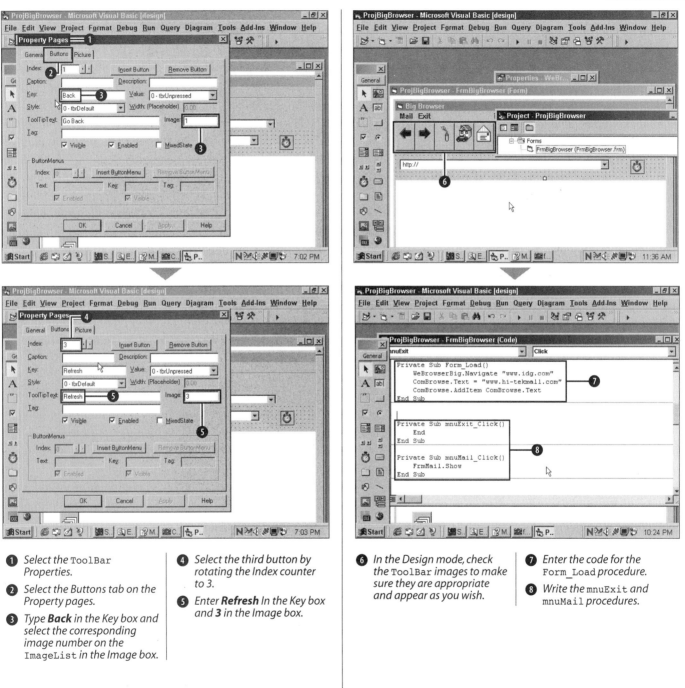

① Select the ToolBar Properties.

② Select the Buttons tab on the Property pages.

③ Type **Back** in the Key box and select the corresponding image number on the ImageList in the Image box.

④ Select the third button by rotating the Index counter to 3.

⑤ Enter **Refresh** In the Key box and **3** in the Image box.

⑥ In the Design mode, check the ToolBar images to make sure they are appropriate and appear as you wish.

⑦ Enter the code for the Form_Load procedure.

⑧ Write the mnuExit and mnuMail procedures.

Writing the ToolBar Buttons Procedure

For the `ToolBar_ButtonClick` procedure, you will use `Select Case` to cover the five options on the `ToolBar`. The object used in `Select Case` is Button, and the property is `Key`. `Button.Key` refers to the `Key` you set up on the `ToolBar Property Pages` when you selected the Button tab. The `Key` indicated there will determine the responses to these click events. The `GoBack` method executes a hyperlink jump back in the history list of sites that have been visited.

```
Case "Back"
          WeBrowserBig.GoBack
Case "Home"
          WeBrowserBig.GoHome
```

Each `Key` has a method associated with the `WeBrowserBig` object. The "Forward" `Key` uses the `GoForward` method, the "Refresh" `Key`, the `Refresh` method, and the "Home" `Key` uses the `GoHome` method. In the `Case` "Mail" option, the `FrmMail.Show` syntax is used to display the Mail form (which you have not yet created). Finally, you can add the `Exit` option to the `Case` statement to `End` the procedure and `Exit` execution.

```
Case "Exit"
                End
     End Select
```

The next feature needing your attention is the `ComboBox Click` procedure to initiate the navigation to the URL text typed in the `ComBrowse ComboBox`.

You will automatically start by navigating to the home address (URL) that you coded in the `Form_Load` procedure, `www.idgbooks.com`. But what if you want to enter a new URL and go to the other site? Your browser should be able to handle this. You would like to direct the browser to a new site, so you use the `Navigate` method as shown later.

```
WeBrowserBig.Navigate ComBrowse.Text
```

This is similar to the statement you placed in the `Form_Load` procedure, except that you substitute the `Text` property of the `ComboBox` for the string (`www.idgbooks.com`) you used before. This way, a click on the `ComboBox` will initiate the navigation to the specified URL.

That should work well, but you still have another need to address. What if the user just presses Enter? You can deal with that event by writing a `KeyPress` procedure just as you did in Chapter 5.

```
If KeyAscii = 13 Then
   ComBrowse_Click
End If
```

Now, a `KeyPress` of `Enter` (ASCII code 13) will call the `ComBrowse_Click` procedure and carry out those instructions.

Now that you have finished coding the procedures for `FrmBrowserBig`, you can launch the browser and try each option. You must of course have an Internet service provider in order to test the program. Make the connection and then launch your browser. Check the Back, Forward, Refresh, and Home options. This would be a good time to add the `FrmMail` form to the project, so that you can test the Mail option.

TAKE NOTE

OBJECT PROGRAMMING ON THE INTERNET

The basic concepts of object-oriented programming you have been using can be applied to Internet applications just as well as the applications based on forms. The object models and controls are the same or much the same.

CROSS-REFERENCE
Many development options are discussed in Chapter 22.

FIND IT ONLINE
This is a site with source code to download:
http://mars.spaceports.com/~malord/ie4.html.

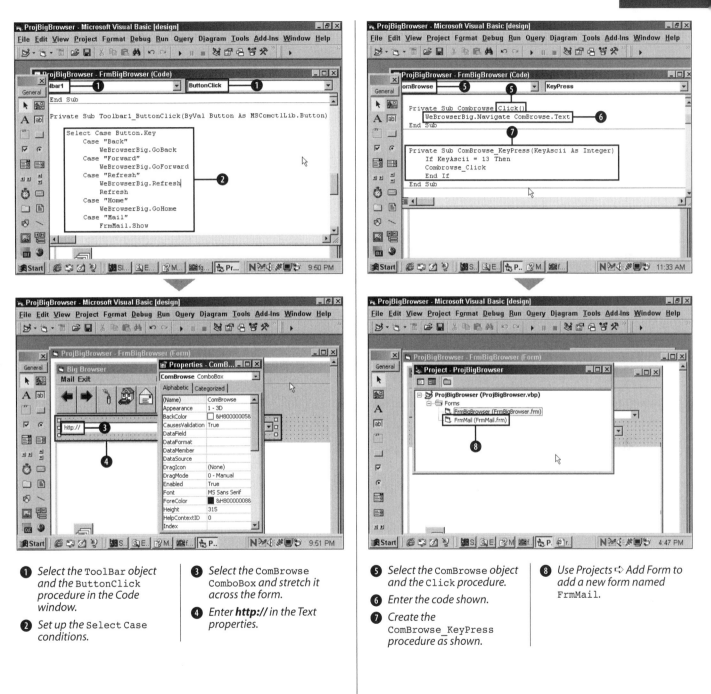

① *Select the* ToolBar *object and the* ButtonClick *procedure in the Code window.*

② *Set up the* Select Case *conditions.*

③ *Select the* ComBrowse ComboBox *and stretch it across the form.*

④ *Enter* **http://** *in the Text properties.*

⑤ *Select the* ComBrowse *object and the* Click *procedure.*

⑥ *Enter the code shown.*

⑦ *Create the* ComBrowse_KeyPress *procedure as shown.*

⑧ *Use Projects ➪ Add Form to add a new form named* FrmMail.

Adding Weather and Stock Quote Options

One of the best reasons for building your own Web browser is to customize it by adding features not always available in commercial browsers. It is true that you can add URLs to your Favorites list, but that is not truly customizing. How about making a browser that does exactly what you want? There are many ways you can apply the knowledge you will gain in this exercise to other areas. You will undoubtedly get ideas from the Weather and Stock Quotes menu and toolbar options used here.

In sum, the point of adding Stock and Weather information to this browser is that you enter the stock symbol and the zip code for weather in a combo box on your form, rather than on a form at the destination Web site. The idea here is that you are saved the time it takes to figure out how to navigate once you get to a site.

The thing that makes this exercise unique is that you pass the symbol or zip code parameters to the specific URL at the weather or stock quote site. This beats going to the Web site's home page and wandering around. Also, because you know your browser, you know exactly where to type the information.

Add two new buttons to the `ToolBar` (three if you did not yet add an Exit button). You will also need to add these images to the `ImageList`. When you try to add new images, you will receive a message that you can't modify a control that is bound to another control. Because you bound the `ToolBar` and the `ImageList` to each other in order to display the images on the `ToolBar`, you will need to remove `ImageList1` from the `ToolBar ImageList` drop-down.

Change `ImageList1` to None. After you do this, you can add the desired images at the end of the list and then bind `ImageList1` to the `ToolBar` again by changing the None to `ImageList` in the `ImageList` box on the Property pages General tab.

When you have bound the controls, click the Buttons tab, advance the Index counter to the last (Mail) option, and click the Insert button to add the new buttons to the `ToolBar`. Be sure to check the `ImageList1` image numbers so that they correspond to the buttons to which they will be attached. If you did not add the new icons to the end of `ImageList1`, then the numbers of the images will not correspond to the Index numbers of the buttons. This mistake is easy to notice, because the button images will look wrong.

Once you have selected new icons from the `VB98\Graphics\Icons` directory, you can create the `mnu Click` procedures and the `ToolBar Select Case` options for Stock Quotes and Weather.

TAKE NOTE

▶ **IIS AND DHTML**

The two major types of applications of Visual Basic to the Internet are Internet Information Server (IIS) and Dynamic Hypertext Markup Language (DHTML). IIS is used to create server-side applications that use processing on the server. DHTML is used to enhance HTML for browser-side processing.

CROSS-REFERENCE

Chapter 5 contains information regarding the `KeyPress` function.

FIND IT ONLINE

Great for an overview: **http://msdn.microsoft.com/library/ devprods/vs6/vbasic/vbcon98/vbmscwhatsnewininternet featuresvb98.htm.**

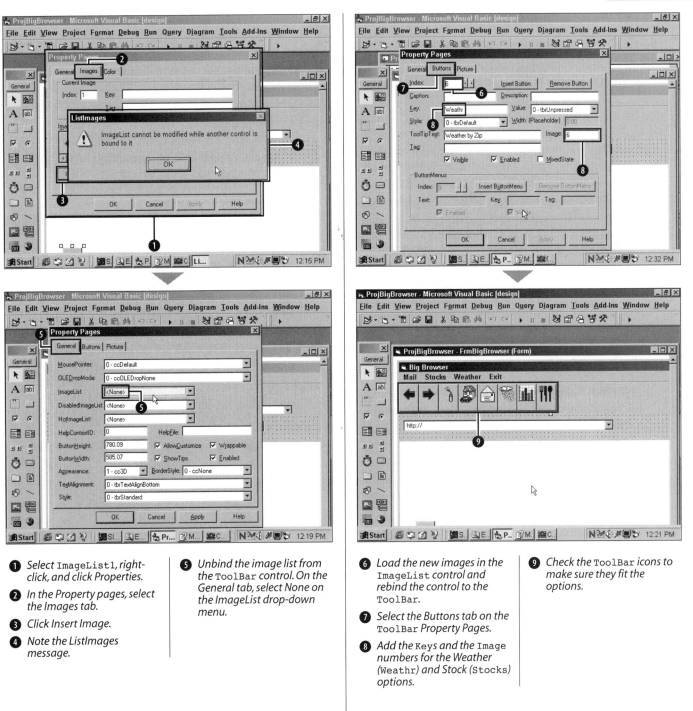

1. Select ImageList1, right-click, and click Properties.

2. In the Property pages, select the Images tab.

3. Click Insert Image.

4. Note the ListImages message.

5. Unbind the image list from the ToolBar control. On the General tab, select None on the ImageList drop-down menu.

6. Load the new images in the ImageList control and rebind the control to the ToolBar.

7. Select the Buttons tab on the ToolBar Property Pages.

8. Add the Keys and the Image numbers for the Weather (Weathr) and Stock (Stocks) options.

9. Check the ToolBar icons to make sure they fit the options.

Adding a Weather Option to the Browser

Before creating the new `ButtonClick Cases`, declare two new variables in the declaration section of the form.

```
Dim SeURL, WeathrURL
```

These will contain the Universal Resource Locator strings for the Weather and Stocks options. Also you need to modify the `Form_Load` procedure to take into account the additional home pages you are accessing. The two sites for the Weather and Stocks are Weather.com and Cnn.com. You could use the full path of the location for your lookups, but that is usually unnecessary information for users. You do, however, want to replace the Home URL (idgbooks.com) with the current site.

This part of the exercise harkens back to the chapters (8 and 9) dealing with controls. The `AddItem` method is used to add new items to the `ComboBox`. Using this method, you will be able to recall those URLs already accessed in a session. You will do this by using the `ListIndex` property.

```
ComBrowse.AddItem "http://www.idgbooks.com"
ComBrowse.AddItem "http://www.cnn.com"
ComBrowse.AddItem "http://www.weather.com"
ComBrowse.ListIndex = 0
```

By default, the first item added to a control will have a value of zero. Each item added will increment the index in the array by one. When you use the `AddItem` method to add cnn.com, the `ListIndex` value for that item is one. The weather Web page is two and so on.

You need to place another `ComboBox` on the form to the right of the `ToolBar` and above `Combrowse`. This will be used to enter the symbols for the Stocks and zip codes for the Weather report. Add the `ButtonClick Case` for the Weather button.

```
Case "Weathr"
WeathrURL = _
"http://www.weather.com/weather/ us/zips/"
```

`WeathrURL` contains a string for the URL where the search for zip codes' weather reports is handled. The tricky part of this exercise is to determine where this actually is done. If you merely enter the home page URL, you will arrive at that site and then have to search for the place on the form to enter the information.

In this exercise, you want to be able to enter the symbol in your `Combo1` box and then pass the parameter to the Web site. Some sites will require you to have access to a cgi-bin or Active Server Pages (ASP) directory for this function. If you want to add new menu options for different sites, you must experiment, because not all sites will let you into such server directories without a password.

```
WeathrURL = WeathrURL & Combo1.Text + ".html"
           WeBrowserBig.Navigate (WeathrURL)
             ComBrowse.ListIndex = 2
```

For this specific Web site, it has been determined (as of this writing) that the string ".html" must be appended to the zip code following the string contained in `WeathrURL` in order for the search parameter to be passed to this Web site. Obviously, this site has a separate HTML page for each zip code. The index for this option is two. Using the `ListIndex` property will display the URL in the ComBrowse box.

In the Code window select the `mnuWeathr` object and the `Click` procedure. The code you used for the `ToolBar` Weather button is essentially the same here.

TAKE NOTE

AUTOMATIC WEB BROWSER

You can use the Application Wizard to generate a Web browser form. This utility accesses the Form generator. Also, you can select a Web browser form in the Add Form window. The default browser includes a toolbar with icons and basic capabilities. You can use this to build on and create an enhanced browser this way.

CROSS-REFERENCE
You will find references to `AddItem` for the `ListBox` and `ComboBox` in Chapter 9.

FIND IT ONLINE
DHTML application info: **http://msdn.microsoft.com/library/ devprods/vs6/vbasic/vbcon98/vbcondevelopingclientinternet applications.htm.**

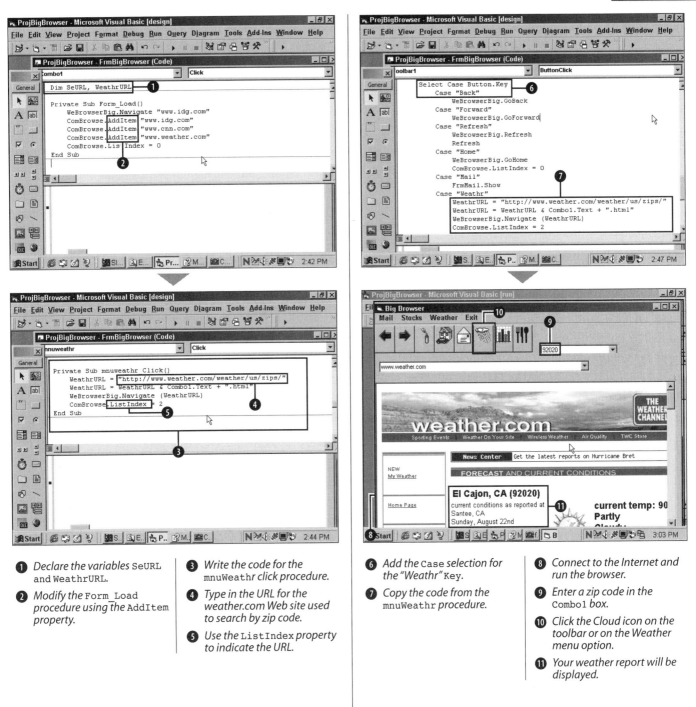

① *Declare the variables* SeURL *and* WeathrURL.

② *Modify the* Form_Load *procedure using the* AddItem *property.*

③ *Write the code for the* mnuWeathr *click procedure.*

④ *Type in the URL for the weather.com Web site used to search by zip code.*

⑤ *Use the* ListIndex *property to indicate the URL.*

⑥ *Add the* Case *selection for the "Weathr" Key.*

⑦ *Copy the code from the* mnuWeathr *procedure.*

⑧ *Connect to the Internet and run the browser.*

⑨ *Enter a zip code in the* Combo1 *box.*

⑩ *Click the Cloud icon on the toolbar or on the Weather menu option.*

⑪ *Your weather report will be displayed.*

Adding the Stock Quote Browser Option

The variable SeURL is set equal to the URL where the searching for stock symbols will be done.

```
SeURL = "http://qs.cnnfn.com/tq/stockquote?
symbols="
```

SeURL contains a string for the URL where the search for stock symbols is handled. Again, you need to determine where on the site this actually is done. If you merely enter the CNN home page URL, you will have to search for the location to enter the information.

You use the same ComboBox (Combo1) to enter the symbols as you did to enter the zip code for the weather report. Just as for the weather, you would like to be able to enter the symbol in your Combo1 box and then pass the parameter to the Web site. Web sites do not all manage the searching in the same way. So you must experiment, because not all sites will let you pass these parameters to their search engines.

```
SeURL = "http://qs.cnnfn.com/tq/stockquote?
symbols="
    SeURL = SeURL & Combo1.Text
    WeBrowserBig.Navigate (SeURL)
    ComBrowse.ListIndex = 1
```

For this specific Web site, it has been determined (as of this writing) that the stock symbol can be appended to the end of the URL shown in order for the search parameter to be passed to this Web site. The index for this option is 1. Using the ListIndex property will display the URL in the ComBrowse box.

In the Code window select the mnuStocks object and the Click procedure. The code you used for the ToolBar Stocks button can be copied to this procedure. When you finish with the code, inspect your work by launching your browser and selecting each menu item and ToolBar icon.

There are several ways you can work these menu and ToolBar procedures. For example, you could use the complete URL of the Stocks site to display on the combo box. You could do that by referencing the value of the Stock search variable (SeURL) with the AddItem method.

```
ComBrowse.AddItem (SeURL)
```

That code would cause the combo box line to display the full URL for the stock symbol search instead of only the home page URL (`http://qs.cnnfn.com/tq/stockquote?symbols=` instead of `http://www.cnn.com`). In addition, you also could use the syntax:

```
ComBrowse.Text = "http://www.cnn.com"
ComBrowse.AddItem ComBrowse.Text
```

This would have the effect of changing the text in the combo box to that of the string value in the first statement.

If you were developing a production Web browser, you would likely write a procedure that would maintain URL histories, so that a user could select any of the URLs on the list to return to the site. This way, you could create a Favorites list that the user could save and access permanently. The next topic continues our project with the development of an e-mail application.

TAKE NOTE

BROWSER APPLICATIONS

Many Internet applications have been completely based on the Web browser. For example, you could develop a database application accessed by employees in the field to maintain their account or order tracking online. This application could be run from the browser, giving these employees access only to the database.

CROSS-REFERENCE

Chapter 22 continues the discussion in this chapter.

FIND IT ONLINE

This discusses the Navigate method: **http://msdn.microsoft.com/workshop/author/dhtml/reference/methods/navigate.asp**.

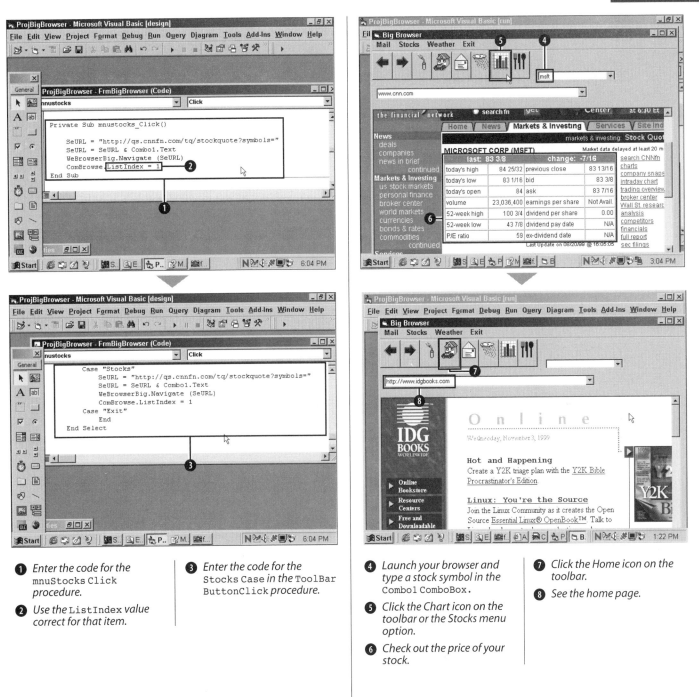

① *Enter the code for the* mnuStocks Click *procedure.*

② *Use the* ListIndex *value correct for that item.*

③ *Enter the code for the* Stocks Case *in the* ToolBar ButtonClick *procedure.*

④ *Launch your browser and type a stock symbol in the* Combo1 *ComboBox.*

⑤ *Click the Chart icon on the toolbar or the Stocks menu option.*

⑥ *Check out the price of your stock.*

⑦ *Click the Home icon on the toolbar.*

⑧ *See the home page.*

Setting up an E-mail Application

This exercise uses the Messaging Application Program Interface (MAPI). The two controls you will need for this application are the `MAPIMessages` and `MAPISession`. Load them (Microsoft MAPI controls 6.0) from the Components, Controls tab on the Project menu.

MAPI provides a set of system components that enable you to connect an e-mail application to MAPI-compliant information services. The MAPI controls are designed to interact with your basic message subsystem. This means that you must install a MAPI-conforming e-mail system such as Microsoft Exchange.

Your `Windows\System` directory must contain the MAPI DLL files installed in order to perform MAPI functions. The files installed on most Windows systems are MAPIstub.dll, `mapi32x.dll`, and `mapi32.dll`. You can check your system to locate these files. Without these files installed correctly, you will not be able to perform MAPI functions such as signing on and off. When you `SignOn`, the `SessionID` property returns a value that represents the session handle. This is associated with a messaging session.

The MAPI `Messages` control lets you receive, send, attach, and read messages from your inbox. The methods attached to these controls include `Compose`, `Copy`, `Delete`, `Fetch`, `Forward`, `Reply`, `ReplyAll`, `Save`, and `Send`. You use the `MAPISession` control to sign in and out of a session. This control will summon the underlying message subsystem on your system.

To begin, place the two MAPI controls (named `MmessBig` and `MsessBig`) on your new `FrmMail` form. They remain invisible at runtime, so they can be placed anywhere. Place a `TextBox` across the bottom half of the form, enlarging the form as desired. The messages will be viewed in the text box. Place an `ImageList` control and a `ToolBar` control on the form as well.

Now, you are going to set up your `ToolBar` with icons on each button as you did on the `FrmBrowserBig` form. You will need icons for Send, Read, and Exit. Follow the same method you used in the Web browser exercise to add the icons to your `ToolBar`, using the button Keys to represent `Send`, `Read`, and `Exit`. Bind the `ImageList` control to the `ToolBar` by selecting `ImageList1` on the `ImageList ImageList` drop-down on the Property pages General tab.

If you wish, you can add a menu bar option to Read Mail. Add the Return and Exit options on the menu bar. Write the mnuReturn procedure as usual (`FrmBrowserBig.Show`). The Exit option has a new statement:

```
MSessBig.SignOff
    End
```

Each time a session is begun, you must use the `SignOff` method.

TAKE NOTE

MAPI CONTROLS

MAPI controls are not only invisible at runtime, there are no events for these controls. You use them by setting their properties or using the `Send`, `Compose`, `Read`, `SignOn`, and `SignOff` methods.

CROSS-REFERENCE

There are more such applications in Chapter 22.

FIND IT ONLINE

WebBrowser control reference: **http://msdn.microsoft.com/ workshop/cframe.htm#/workshop/browser/webbrowser/ reference/reference.asp.**

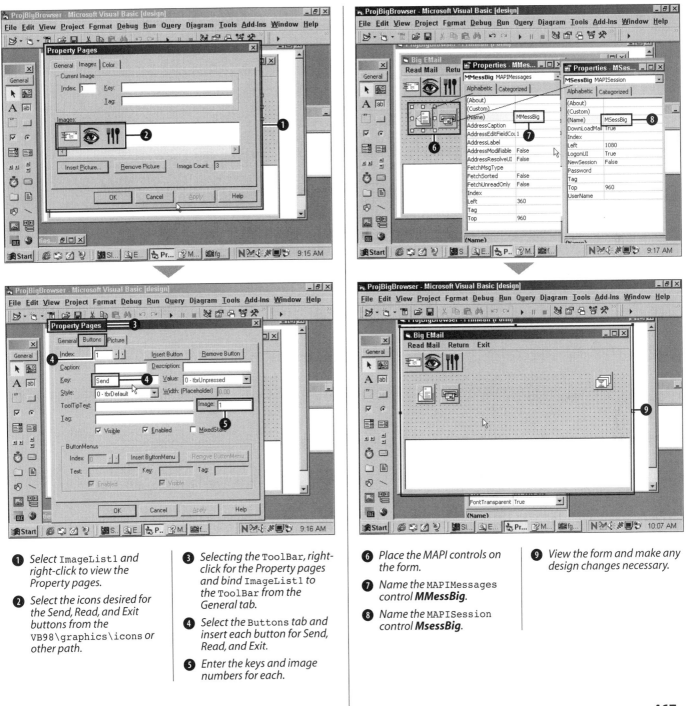

1 Select ImageList1 and right-click to view the Property pages.

2 Select the icons desired for the Send, Read, and Exit buttons from the VB98\graphics\icons or other path.

3 Selecting the ToolBar, right-click for the Property pages and bind ImageList1 to the ToolBar from the General tab.

4 Select the Buttons tab and insert each button for Send, Read, and Exit.

5 Enter the keys and image numbers for each.

6 Place the MAPI controls on the form.

7 Name the MAPIMessages control **MMessBig**.

8 Name the MAPISession control **MsessBig**.

9 View the form and make any design changes necessary.

Developing the E-mail Application

The `MAPISession` control performs the functions of signing on and off from sessions. The `MAPIMessages` control provides the functionality to carry out messaging functions within the session.

For the `mnuRead` procedure you will use the `MAPISession` `SessionID` and `DownLoadMail` properties and the `SignOn` method. You will be using the `MAPIMessages` `Fetch` method to obtain the messages from the mail subsystem.

```
MSessBig.DownLoadMail = True
MSessBig.SignOn
MMessBig.SessionID = MSessBig.SessionID
MMessBig.Fetch
MMessBig.MsgIndex = 0
Text1.Text = MMessBig.MsgNoteText
MSessBig.SignOff
```

The `DownLoadMail` property is set to true so that after the `SignOn` and `Fetch` methods are performed, the messages can be displayed. The `SessionID` of the messages control is set equal to the session control. The text box text is set equal to the `MsgNoteText` of the messages control. The `MsgNoteText` property contains the actual text of the e-mail.

Use the `Select Case` to select the appropriate functions for each of the `ToolBar` buttons. Use the Keys from the Property pages of the `ToolBar`'s Buttons tab to make each `Case`. The code for `Case` "Read" can be copied from the mnuRead procedure.

The `Send` function uses the `DownLoadMail`, `SessionID`, and `msgIndex` properties. Also, `Send` uses the `SignOn`, `Compose`, and `Send` methods to do the initial access, writing, and sending of messages.

In this application there is no Send on the menu bar, only on the toolbar, but you certainly can add that feature if you wish.

```
MSessBig.DownLoadMail = False
```

Here, the `DownLoadMail` property is set to False because you are not reading mail in this option.

```
MSessBig.SignOn
```

The session must be initiated again.

```
MMessBig.SessionID = MSessBig.SessionID
```

The `sessionID` again must be copied to the messages control.

```
MMessBig.MsgIndex = -1
```

The Compose buffer is activated when the `MsgIndex` property is set to minus one.

```
MMessBig.Compose
MMessBig.Send True
MSessBig.SignOff
```

The `Compose` method invokes the Compose dialog box. You can enter the e-mail address and message you want to send. The `Send` method will place the message in your mail system's outbox. Depending upon how your e-mail system is configured, the message will be queued to send the next time the inbox is opened or sent immediately. After the message goes into the outbox, you `SignOff` the system.

TAKE NOTE

WEB PAGES AND DESIGNERS

In the short tradition of the Internet, Web designers and graphic artists, rather than developers, have created most Web pages. However, artistic types are seldom programmers, while programmers can be artistic. As a developer, you have the option of using your skills on fully developed HTML pages, or creating Internet applications from scratch, employing all your skills in the entire process.

CROSS-REFERENCE

The information on ActiveX applications in Chapter 20 is highly appropriate to Internet applications.

FIND IT ONLINE

This has info on messages control: **http://msdn.microsoft.com/ library/devprods/vs6/vbasic/mapi98/vbobjmapim.htm**.

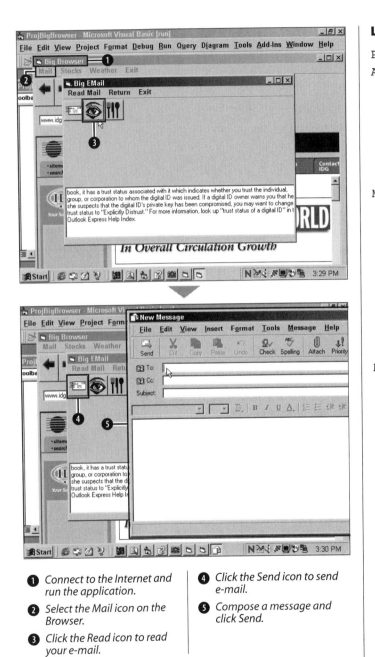

Listing 21-1: The Send and Read Mail Procedure

```
Private Sub Toolbar1_ButtonClick(ByVal Button
As MSComctlLib.Button)
    Select Case Button.Key

        Case "Send"
            MSessBig.DownLoadMail = False
            MSessBig.SignOn
            MMessBig.SessionID =
MSessBig.SessionID
            MMessBig.MsgIndex = -1
            MMessBig.Compose
            MMessBig.Send True
            MSessBig.SignOff

        Case "Read"
            MSessBig.DownLoadMail = True
            MSessBig.SignOn
            MMessBig.SessionID =
MSessBig.SessionID
            MMessBig.Fetch
            MMessBig.MsgIndex = 0
            'DataGrid1 = MMessBig.MsgNoteText
            Text1.Text = MMessBig.MsgNoteText
            MSessBig.SignOff
            FrmMail.Show
        Case "Exit"
            'MSessBig.SignOff
            End
    End Select
End Sub
```

▶ Enter the code for the ButtonClick *procedure.*
▶ Copy the code under the *"Read"* Case *for the* mnuRead_Click *procedure.*

❶ *Connect to the Internet and run the application.*

❷ *Select the Mail icon on the Browser.*

❸ *Click the Read icon to read your e-mail.*

❹ *Click the Send icon to send e-mail.*

❺ *Compose a message and click Send.*

Personal Workbook

Q&A

1 Who uses HTML?

_____

_____

_____

2 What do style sheets do?

_____

_____

_____

3 What is a URL?

_____

_____

_____

4 What is the difference between HTML and DHTML?

_____

_____

_____

5 What facilities exist in Visual Basic to develop Internet browsers?

_____

_____

_____

6 What does it mean to bind a control to another?

_____

_____

_____

7 What are some functions of the MAPI controls?

_____

_____

_____

8 What are the `GoBack` and `GoForward` methods used for?

_____

_____

_____

ANSWERS: PAGE 530

EXTRA PRACTICE

1 Add a new option to the `ToolBar` on the `WeBrowserBig` form to go to a Realtors' Web site that searches for houses by area or price.

2 Add a new menu procedure to the Mail application to include attachments in the mail sent.

3 Create an HTML page, including images.

4 Design an HTML page to be the home site for the Web browser application.

REAL-WORLD APPLICATIONS

✔ Your company would like to have a custom Web browser that would allow employees to access the company's database without providing them with access to other sites. You are asked to provide an initial design and to identify potential problems.

✔ Your Aunt Hannah is at it again. She needs help with her Web site. She wants you to create a new home page for her. Use HTML to write her a home page for the Interdenominational Sunday School Class.

✔ ACME Verticals, a small blinds company, has answered your ad for custom Web site development. They need to have an Internet site from which their employees can enter and retrieve data on order tracking. They also want a custom browser for the workers. Get busy.

Visual Quiz

Which of the forms in the Add Form dialog should be used for a Web browser?

_____

_____

_____

_____

_____

_____

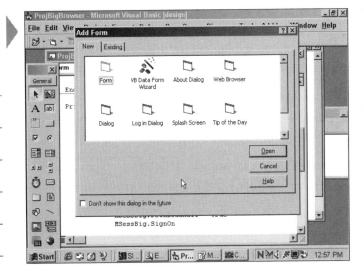

CHAPTER **22**

MASTER
THESE
SKILLS

▶ **Discovering VBScript**

▶ **Integrating VBScript into HTML Documents**

▶ **Completing the Horse News VBScript**

▶ **Validating Entries with VBScript**

▶ **Referencing the History List with VBScript**

▶ **Installing the Personal Web Server**

▶ **Introducing Server-Side Scripting**

▶ **Scripting Active Server Pages**

▶ **Requesting Server Information**

Developing Applications for the Internet

Chapters 20 and 21 have both discussed Internet programming. Chapter 20, "Using ActiveX Controls," dealt with ActiveX controls and documents, while Chapter 21, "Programming on the Internet," introduced DHTML programming and browser creation and customization. This chapter goes a step beyond those previous chapters to cover some more advanced techniques. Client- and server-side scripting will be introduced, as well as some topics not yet covered in the previous chapters.

In this chapter, you will build on the skills you developed in the last two chapters. You will learn more about HTML and DHTML and add the skills of using VBScript, using Active Server Pages, and developing Web applications.

ActiveX Scripting

VBScript communicates with host applications using ActiveX Scripting. ActiveX Scripting makes it unnecessary for browsers and other host applications to use special integration code for each scripting component. ActiveX Scripting lets the host manage the namespace available to the developer. Microsoft is working with other groups to define an ActiveX Scripting standard so that scripting engines can be interchangeable. ActiveX Scripting is used in Microsoft Internet Explorer and in Microsoft Internet Information Server.

Discovering VBScript

Microsoft Visual Basic Scripting Edition (VBScript), a recent addition to the Visual Basic programming languages, brings active scripting to a wide variety of milieux, including Web client scripting in Microsoft Internet Explorer and Web server scripting in Microsoft Internet Information Server. Not all browsers support it (Netscape, for example, does not).

VBScript will by now be very familiar to you, because it is so strongly related to Visual Basic. VBScript is a simplified form of Visual Basic that enables you to include VBScript commands with HTML documents. VBScript is interpreted and executes along with the HTML commands. Currently, only Internet Explorer supports VBScript. Netscape is compatible only when a plug-in is added.

VBScript provides ways for developers to link and automate many types of objects in Web sites. There are both many similarities and a few differences between VBScript and Visual Basic for Applications (VBA).

Differences between VBScript and VBA

VBScript has no support for classes as Visual Basic does. All development in VBScript is procedural. Neither is there any support for OLE. There is no support for control arrays, data access or file operations, debugging tools, MDI forms, built-in predefined constants. Further, there is no access to the Windows Help system.

There is support in VBScript for forms using the <FORM> </FORM> tag. Also modules are supported through the <SCRIPT> </SCRIPT> tag. VBScript also supports only the Variant variable type.

Using VBScript

Essentially, VBScript is used to develop applications on the Web. Internet applications can be developed in HTML, DHTML, Java, Jscript, or several other options, depending upon the kind of application you need to develop. You have been introduced to HTML in the last chapter. You can write applications in HTML using Microsoft Word or even Notepad. That is because HTML is made up of text. You can create a Web site using only HTML. However, you may not be able to create the kind of Web site you want using only HTML.

There are a number of editors using HTML. Some use HTML and other enhancements such as Java applets and DHTML. Microsoft FrontPage is one of the editors offering a full complement of enhancements.

VBScript is used with HTML to carry out functions that cannot be done using HTML. You can use the <SCRIPT> tag to begin using VBScript in your HTML document. First, create an HTML document similar to the example in the last chapter.

Table 22-1 shows a comparison between the features offered by Visual Basic and VBScript. It is apparent that VBScript offers a small subset of Visual Basic features, plus some of its own that VB does not share.

TAKE NOTE

WRITING OUTSIDE THE PROCEDURES

The VBScript code usually appears in sub or Function procedures. These procedures are called when your code initiates execution. You can write VBScript outside of the procedures as long as it is within a Script block.

```
<SCRIPT> </SCRIPT>
```

This code will be executed when the HTML page loads.

CROSS-REFERENCE
Many parallels exist in Chapter 21.

FIND IT ONLINE
This site contains the essentials in scripting: **http://msdn. microsoft.com/workshop/c-frame.htm#/workshop/ essentials/default.asp**.

Table 22-1: COMPARISON OF VBA AND VBSCRIPT FEATURES

Category	In VBScript and VBA	In VBScript Not in VBA
Array handling	Array, Dim, Private, Public, ReDim, IsArray, Erase, LBound, Ubound	
Assignments	Set	
Comments	Comments using ' or Rem	
Constants/Literals	Empty, Nothing, Null, True, False	
Control flow	Do...Loop, For...Next, For Each...Next, If...Then...Else Select Case, While...Wend	
Conversions	Abs, Asc, AscB, AscW, Chr, ChrB, ChrW, CBool, CByte, CCur, CDate, CDbl, CInt, CLng, CSng, CStr, DateSerial, DateValue, Hex, Oct, Fix, Int, Sgn, TimeSerial, TimeValue	
Dates/Times	Date, Time, DateAdd, DateDiff, DatePart, DateSerial, DateValue, Day, Month, MonthName, Weekday, WeekdayName, Year, Hour, Minute, Second, Now, TimeSerial, TimeValue	
Declarations	Const, Dim, Private, Public, ReDim, Function, Sub	
Error Handling	On Error, Err	
Formatting strings	FormatCurrency, FormatDateTime, FormatNumber, FormatPercent	FormatCurrency, FormatDateTime, Format Percent, MonthName, Weekday Name
Input/Output	InputBox, LoadPicture, MsgBox	
Intrinsic constants		vbLongTime, vbShortDate, vbLongDate, vbTristateFalse, vbTristateMixed, vbTristateTrue, vbTristateUseDefault
Literals	Empty, False, Nothing, Null, True	
Math	Atn, Cos, Sin, Tan, Exp, Log, Sqr, Randomize, Rnd	
Miscellaneous	RGB Function	
Objects	CreateObject, Err Object, GetObject	Dictionary, FileSystemObject, TextStream
Operators	Addition, Subtraction, Exponentiation, Modulus arithmetic, Multipication, Division, Integer Division, Negation, String concatenation, Equality, Inequality, Less Than, Less Than or Equal To, Greater Than, Greater Than or Equal To, Is, And, Or, Xor, Eqv, Imp	
Options	Option Explicit	
Procedures	Call Function, Sub	
Rounding	Abs, Int, Fix, Round, Sgn	Round
Strings	Strings, Asc, AscB, AscW, Chr, ChrB, ChrW, Filter, InStr, InStrB, InStrRev, Join, Len, LenB, LCase, UCase, Left, LeftB, Mid, MidB, Right, RightB, Replace, Space, Split, StrComp, String, StrReverse, LTrim, RTrim, Trim	Filter, InstrRev, Join, Replace, Split, StrReverse
Variants	IsArray, IsDate, IsEmpty, IsNull, IsNumeric, IsObject, TypeName, VarType	
Script Engine Identification	ScriptEngine, ScriptEngineBuildVersion, ScriptEngineMajorVersion, ScriptEngineMinorVersion	ScriptEngine, ScriptEngineBuildVersion ScriptEngineMajoVersion, ScriptEngineMinorVersion

Integrating VBScript into HTML Documents

You may have tried VBScript and find it compelling but intimidating because it is so hard to debug. While you get loads of help in Visual Basic, you don't get much in VBScript. Visual Basic provides you with the pop-up context menus, syntax checking, prompting, and the Immediate and other debug windows. VBScript, on the other hand, provides only an error message when the application runs.

The difficulty is that you do not use the Visual Basic IDE to create VBScript applications. You must use an HTML editor and use Internet Explorer to test them. This can involve a two-step process, unless you can use a product like Microsoft FrontPage or Corel Web Designer, which let you preview your work in the browser as a single step. If you test your work in Netscape or other browsers, you will find that some or all of the features don't work.

As frustrating as it can be, you can build some powerful Internet applications with VBScript. The most immediately handy are those that simply enhance an existing HTML document, or those in which a VBScript procedure will save steps and grief if attempted in HTML.

As you saw in the previous chapter, "Programming on the Internet," the HTML commands can be complex, but they are pretty simple when you are creating a simple page. For example, <HTML> begins each page, and </HTML> ends each page. The hierarchy of required commands falls in the order of:

```
<HTML>
<HEAD>
</HEAD>
<TITLE> </TITLE>
<BODY>
<FORM> </FORM>
</BODY>
</HTML>
```

You can see that the pattern is symmetrical, with most of the commands (not shown here) falling between the <BODY> and </BODY> tags. The <VBSCRIPT> and </VBSCRIPT> tags will go in between the <BODY> tags as well.

For this exercise, you will not use Visual Basic, unless you opt to create a DHTML project and use that editor (which is Notepad). If you use FrontPage, do not create a web, only a page. You can even use Microsoft Word or Notepad to create your file. You can then test it in Internet Explorer. You might want to refer to the previous chapter's discussion of HTML. Or if you have some experience with HTML or feel somewhat comfortable with it, proceed with the exercise.

TAKE NOTE

▶ USING DHTML PAGE DESIGNER

If you do decide to create a DHTML project in Visual Basic and use that editor, choose to save the page as an external file with an `.htm` extension. Do this by first selecting the DHTML Page Designer properties. Create the HTML file whichever way you wish.

CROSS-REFERENCE

Find additional information in Chapter 21.

FIND IT ONLINE

Here is a Welcome VBScript:
http://msdn.microsoft.com/scripting/maininfo.htm.

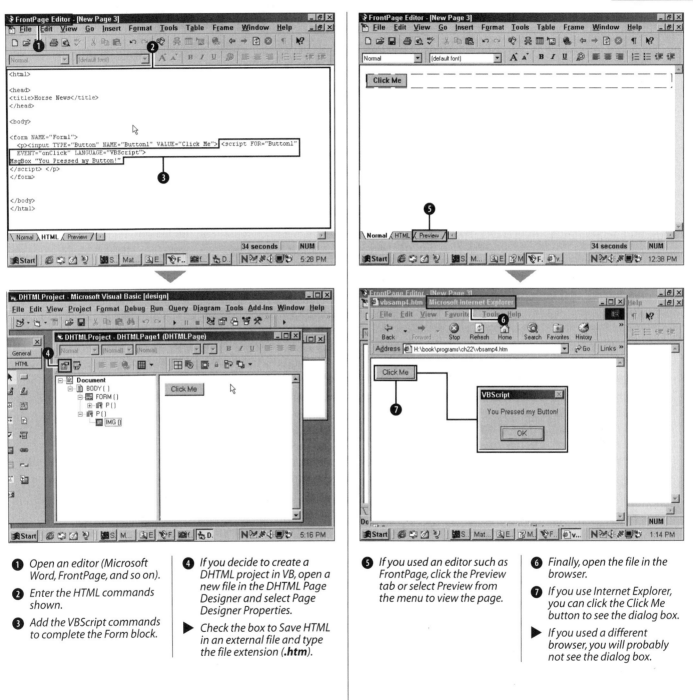

① *Open an editor (Microsoft Word, FrontPage, and so on).*

② *Enter the HTML commands shown.*

③ *Add the VBScript commands to complete the Form block.*

④ *If you decide to create a DHTML project in VB, open a new file in the DHTML Page Designer and select Page Designer Properties.*

▶ *Check the box to Save HTML in an external file and type the file extension (.htm).*

⑤ *If you used an editor such as FrontPage, click the Preview tab or select Preview from the menu to view the page.*

⑥ *Finally, open the file in the browser.*

⑦ *If you use Internet Explorer, you can click the Click Me button to see the dialog box.*

▶ *If you used a different browser, you will probably not see the dialog box.*

Completing the Horse News VBScript

Create the page named `vbsamp4.htm`. This exercise will have little going on, just a form with a button you can press and see a dialog box.

Write the HTML tags to begin, using `<HTML>`, `<HEAD>`, and `<TITLE>Horse News</TITLE></HEAD>`. Next begin the `<BODY>` block. Set up a Form block as well and name the form "Form1."

```
<form NAME="Form1">
  <p><input TYPE="button" NAME="Button1"
VALUE="Click Me">
<script FOR="Button1"    EVENT="onClick"
LANGUAGE="VBScript">
MsgBox "You Pressed my Button!"
</script> </p>
</form>
```

When you have finished writing the page, Save it as `vbsamp4.htm` and launch Internet Explorer and select Open from the File menu to open this file. Now you can test your work. For some additional interest, insert an image file (bitmap) using:

```
<p><IMG border="0" src="horsnews.jpg"
width=181 height=202 > </p>
```

Add this code to the end of the "Form" code. And view again. You should now see two horses reading a newspaper below the Click Me button.

Although most scripting code will be in the HEAD area, where the code can be organized, you can place SCRIPT blocks anywhere in the HTML page. SCRIPT blocks can be placed in both the BODY and HEAD sections if you wish. If your SCRIPTs will be called from the BODY section, you should keep your code in the HEAD section where it can be read before it will be called.

However, if you are embedding a SCRIPT in a form, you will need to keep the code there. In the Horse News example, this is exactly what you have done. Your script is placed within the form, because it is responding to the button click.

In this example, you are creating Form and Button objects and an event to which the VBScript will respond. Thus, the script FOR is a variation of the SCRIPT tag, due to the fact that it is written to respond to the onClick event. The code spells it out. The script is FOR Button1 in the onClick event, using the language VBScript. The message box fires upon the event. Finally, you ended the script block and the form block with the closing tags. You added the bitmap mainly as an afterthought, although a picture dresses up the plain page.

Here is something fun to try. In Visual Basic, open the Big Browser project from Chapter 21. View your Web page in your own browser by typing the local path for your page in the combo box (address space). For example, if the location of your HTML file is `C:\vb99\vbsamp4.htm`, then type in that path. Guess what? Your browser is fully functional. It displays the button and responds to the click.

TAKE NOTE

SCRIPT BLOCKS

You can write code without placing it inside procedures. However, most of the time, code is in procedures to be called only when it is called and executes. The code must always be in a SCRIPT block. When code is called from a SCRIPT block, it is executed only once, when the HTML page loads. This way, you can easily change the appearance of your page upon loading.

CROSS-REFERENCE

Use the Big Browser from Chapter 21.

FIND IT ONLINE

Here is the VBScript Page:
http://msdn.microsoft.com/scripting/maininfo.htm.

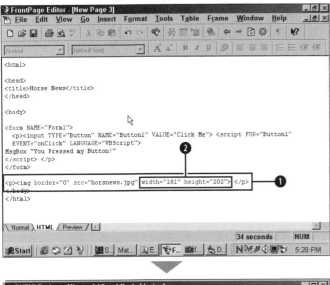

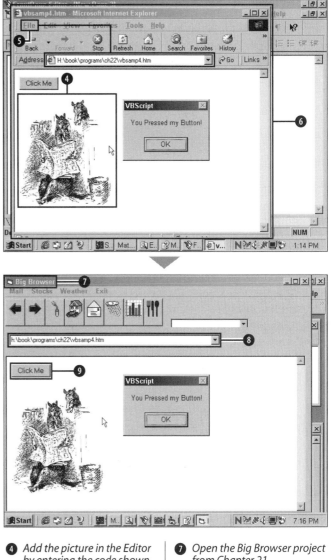

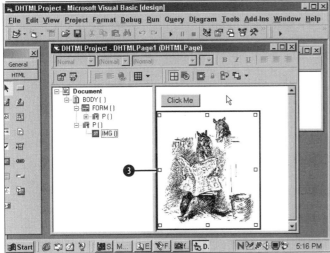

① Enter the additional code to load the picture.

② The width and height parameter functions much like those in VB projects object properties.

③ If you are using the Visual Basic Page Designer, add the image by right-clicking the outline of the picture and selecting Properties.

▶ Click the Image Source dots in the General section of the Property pages to select a picture on the correct path.

④ Add the picture in the Editor by entering the code shown and by placing an image in the same directory with the .htm file.

⑤ Open the file from the File menu on your browser.

⑥ View the completed page in the browser.

⑦ Open the Big Browser project from Chapter 21.

⑧ Run the program and type the path of your vbsamp4.htm file into the combo box.

⑨ View the page and click the button.

479

Validating Entries with VBScript

This exercise will do a little more than the last. Here, you will be prompted to enter a name. If the text box is empty, there is a different response than if something is typed in the box. The VBScript in this exercise will go a bit farther to demonstrate its uses.

In this example, there will also be a form. This time, the form will be used to capture the text input. The text box will be examined to determine if any text was entered, and a corresponding message will be displayed. If no text was entered, the message will be that the name must be entered. If any characters were entered in the form's text field, then a Thank You dialog box will appear.

Prepare to create a new page, using FrontPage, Notepad, Word, or your editor of choice. Begin the new page just as you did the previous one. Place the <HTML> tag at the top, and the <HEAD> tag next. If you wish, enter a <TITLE> beginning and ending </TITLE> as well. Add the </HEAD> ending tag. Begin the <BODY> block, then the <FORM NAME="YourForm">.

The form code is very much the same as for `vbsamp4.htm`. However, in this case, the VBScript is not contained in the form. The form is strictly an HTML form, with the Text Box, the Button, and the Submit value for the button.

```
<form NAME="YourForm">
  <p><input TYPE="TEXT"
NAME="txtNameText" SIZE="25">
<input TYPE="BUTTON" NAME="cmdSubmit"
  VALUE="Submit"> </p>
</form>
```

This produces a text box (form field) to the left of the command button. Below there is a prompt to "Enter Name." At that point, the SCRIPT block begins. Because the objective is not to respond to an event like the button click, the SCRIPT block can be placed outside the form.

The Button name is cmdSubmit, so the VBScript procedure is cmdSubmit_onClick. You will realize this is much like the Command1_Click procedure in Visual Basic. The difference is that the procedure name is onClick instead of Click. Here, just as in Visual Basic, you can declare variables. The difference with VBScript is that there is only the Variant type, so the type declaration need not contain the specific type.

Declare the MyForm variable to stand for the YourForm form. Then use the Set statement to set MyForm equal to the document in the YourForm form.

```
Sub cmdSubmit_OnClick
  Dim MyForm
  Set MyForm = Document.YourForm
```

You want to determine if the user entered some text, so you check to see if the text field is empty.

```
If Myform.txtNameText.Value = "" Then
      MsgBox "Please enter your name."
  Else
     MsgBox "Thank You."
  End If
End Sub
```

If the field is empty (signified by a null response), then a message box is displayed to "Please enter your name." If that is not the case (if there is something in the field), then the message box thanks you. The If-Then command block is ended, and the procedure is ended.

TAKE NOTE

▶ VBSCRIPT AND OUTLOOK

You can use VBScript with Outlook. Here, the VBScript is stored inside the Outlook items. These include mail messages, folders, appointments, and so on. VBScript provides security in this use, because it does not have commands that could result in damage.

CROSS-REFERENCE

Refresh your memory of form variables in Chapter 6.

FIND IT ONLINE

Here is a VBScript: **http://library.advanced.org/ 17131/scripting/vbscript/tut_ch4.html**.

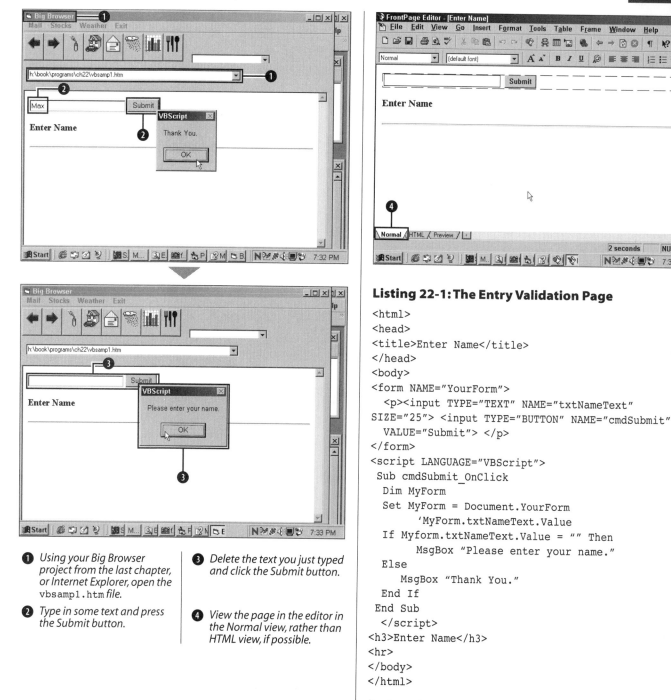

① *Using your Big Browser project from the last chapter, or Internet Explorer, open the* vbsamp1.htm *file.*

② *Type in some text and press the Submit button.*

③ *Delete the text you just typed and click the Submit button.*

④ *View the page in the editor in the Normal view, rather than HTML view, if possible.*

Listing 22-1: The Entry Validation Page

```html
<html>
<head>
<title>Enter Name</title>
</head>
<body>
<form NAME="YourForm">
  <p><input TYPE="TEXT" NAME="txtNameText"
SIZE="25"> <input TYPE="BUTTON" NAME="cmdSubmit"
  VALUE="Submit"> </p>
</form>
<script LANGUAGE="VBScript">
 Sub cmdSubmit_OnClick
  Dim MyForm
  Set MyForm = Document.YourForm
        'MyForm.txtNameText.Value
  If Myform.txtNameText.Value = "" Then
        MsgBox "Please enter your name."
  Else
        MsgBox "Thank You."
  End If
 End Sub
  </script>
<h3>Enter Name</h3>
<hr>
</body>
</html>
```

▶ *Enter the code and save it as **vbsamp2.htm**. Test it in a browser or browser preview mode.*

481

Referencing the History List with VBScript

The next exercise offers a different twist. In this VBScript application, you will create a Go Back button that will display the history list retained in the browser. By default, the history list is set to 50 URLs. That means that the last 50 URLs are stored in the browser's History list. If you press the back arrow, you will go back to the last URL you visited. Pressing the back arrow subsequent times returns to each URL maintained in the history list. Each URL is retained in the order in which it was accessed. So each time the back arrow is pressed, the next to last URL is displayed. This method performs the same action as a user choosing the Back button in the browser. The Go Back method is the same as `history.go(-1)`. Trying to go past the beginning of the history does not generate an error. Instead, you are left at the current page.

Write your HTML code beginning the same way you did in the previous two exercises. Make the title read "Using History List." After the `<BODY>` tag, make a `<FORM>` tag. Then set up your form with a button to move backward to the previous URL (or file in this case).

```
<input TYPE="button" NAME="Go Backward!"
VALUE="Back Button" LANGUAGE="VBScript"
  OnClick="call window.history.back(1)">
```

This will cause the browser to display the last item in the history list when the button is clicked.

Add another line to create another button containing a Go Forward caption.

```
<input TYPE="Button" NAME="Go Forward"
VALUE="Forward Button" LANGUAGE="VBScript"
onClick="Call window.history.forward(1)">
```

At this point, you can add the ending tags for Form, Body, and HTML. Now before you launch your browser, or Internet Explorer, to display your page, `vbsamp3.htm`, you should load another of the three files you created (`vbsamp1.htm`, for instance). Next, load the other file, so that you have a back and forward on your history list. Now press the Go Backward button and retreat to your previously loaded file. Press the Go Forward button and advance to the next file.

When you have loaded your HTML pages containing VBScript into the Big Browser you created in Chapter 21 and press the Go Backward button, you will then be at the previous file you accessed in the history list. You won't be able to press the Go Forward button, because `vbsamp3.htm` is no longer displayed in the browser window. You must press the forward arrow on your browser to return to `vbsamp3.htm`. Then you can press the forward arrow to move to the file you loaded after `vbsamp3.htm`.

This exercise completes the section on combining HTML and VBScript. The next section will move on to cover Active Server Pages using VBScript.

TAKE NOTE

BROWSER HISTORY

The Internet Explorer browser History folder contains recent links to pages you have visited in a specified number of days. You can reset the number of days set by clicking the up or down arrows. You can also press the button to clear all history. You access this from the Tools ⇨ Internet Options ⇨ General tab.

CROSS-REFERENCE

Refresh your memory regarding browser functions in Chapter 21.

FIND IT ONLINE

Here is a VBScript tutorial: **http://library.advanced. org/17131/scripting/vbscript/tutorialstart.html**.

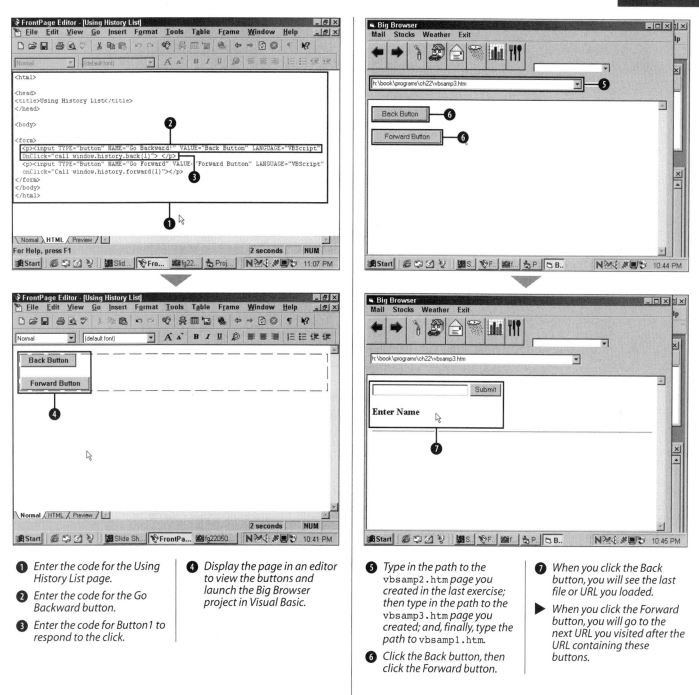

① Enter the code for the Using History List page.

② Enter the code for the Go Backward button.

③ Enter the code for Button1 to respond to the click.

④ Display the page in an editor to view the buttons and launch the Big Browser project in Visual Basic.

⑤ Type in the path to the vbsamp2.htm page you created in the last exercise; then type in the path to the vbsamp3.htm page you created; and, finally, type the path to vbsamp1.htm.

⑥ Click the Back button, then click the Forward button.

⑦ When you click the Back button, you will see the last file or URL you loaded.

▶ When you click the Forward button, you will go to the next URL you visited after the URL containing these buttons.

Installing the Personal Web Server

The last few topics discussed how to write VBScript to carry out client-side functions in Web pages. The client-side functions that were carried out (entering text, moving back and forth through the history list) were all performed in the browser. Largely, client-side applications are not completely effective because they do not work in all browsers. You will see the answer to this problem in the next topic, server-side scripting.

Either the IIS (Internet Information Server) or the Personal Web Server uses Active Server Pages. The IIS is available only with Windows NT 4.0 and up or with Windows 2000 Server. The Personal Web Server is for use with Windows 95/98. It is shipped on the installation CD but does not install with the typical installation.

First, you must have the Windows 95 or 98 installation CD. You will need to open the Control Panel and double-click the Add/Remove Programs icon. Click the Windows Setup tab. Select Internet Tools from the list of Windows programs. To view the options, you can click the Details button. In the next window, the Personal Web Server will be displayed. There must be a checkmark next to this item. When you click OK, the installation will begin. You also can download the Personal Web Server from the Microsoft site: `http://www.microsoft.com/ie`.

You also can install the Personal Web Server that ships with FrontPage 97 and FrontPage 98. In any case, you will be prompted to configure the location of files, including the home directory. Usually, the Personal Web Server creates a root directory at the location `C:\Webshare\WWWroot\` or `C:\Inetpub\WWWroot`. You also can usually use the address http://*localhost*/*directoryofchoice* to launch your scripts for browser preview.

When you install the Personal Web Server, it should be placed in your Startup folder, so that it loads and remains running in the background. If you click its icon in the Startup box, you can read its documentation in Internet Explorer.

The Personal Web Server uses your computer's name (the name entered when Windows was installed) after the http:// prefix. For example, if your computer's name is Max, then the home page would be located at http://max. This part of the installation is confusing because knowing operating system commands does not help much in figuring out where your files are. If the home directory that Personal Web Server uses is located at `C:\Webshare\wwwroot`, it may not be apparent when you open files to edit from http://max or http://localhost.

The Personal Web Server 4.0 has a new interface, and a Personal Web Manager. It also includes the Home Page Wizard. You can use it to create and edit your home page. It has automatic HTML scripting, so you need only answer questions to generate a Web page. It also has full support for Active Server Pages.

TAKE NOTE

REQUIREMENTS FOR ASP

In order to create Active Server Pages (server-side scripting), you must have Windows NT 4.0 or higher or the Windows 95/98 (4.0) Personal Web Server.

CROSS-REFERENCE

Find general information on online Help in Chapter 2.

FIND IT ONLINE

Find it here: **http://www.15seconds.com/issue/990902.htm.**

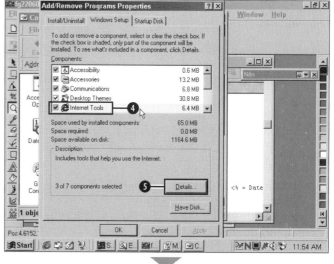

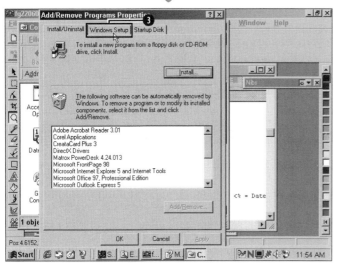

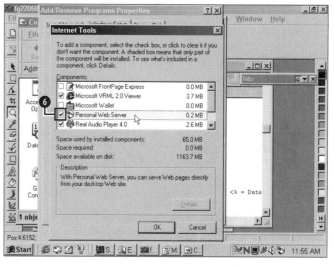

❶ Select Settings from the Start menu and select the Control Panel.

❷ Select Add/Remove Programs from the Control Panel.

❸ Click the Windows Setup tab.

❹ Select Internet Tools from the list of Windows programs.

❺ Click the Details button.

❻ Place a checkmark in the Personal Web Server box.

Introducing Server-Side Scripting

So far, you have been using VBScript to write client-side scripts. That is, client-side scripts execute on the client, rather than on the server. The page is downloaded into the user's (client's) browser and executes there. The problem with writing only client-side scripts is that they will not execute in many browsers. That is, if you try running the scripts in the previous topics using Netscape or AOL's browser, they are viewable in most cases, but they will not perform the functions for which you programmed them.

In order to use VBScript on the client side, you must test to see what browser is being used. Then, you can use different means depending upon the browser. Generally, Java script will work on Netscape, but without developing a test for each visitor you won't know which technique to apply.

On the other hand, if you use server-side scripting, you need not worry about the individual browsers accessing your site, because the scripts all execute on the server and not the client's browser.

Active Server Pages offers support for using existing scripting languages, such as Microsoft VBScript and Microsoft Jscript as well as third-party languages (Perl and so on), in HTML pages. Active Server Pages are also compatible with any ActiveX scripting language, and ActiveX components can be created in effectively any language.

Active Server Pages scripts run upon the request for a file with an `.asp` extension from a browser. The Web server calls Active Server Pages, which will read the entire file and execute commands. The page is then sent to the browser.

Because the scripts all run directly on the server, rather than individual browsers, the Web server serves the Web pages to the browser. Thus, it does not matter which browser a client has, because the browser receives the processed page from the server. Standard HTML is returned to the browser. Also, because only the results of the process are sent to the browser, users can't see the commands that generated the Web pages they view.

Active Server Pages use a command block syntax in which the commands are embedded within the less-than symbol and percent symbol (<%) and the reverse to end the block (%>).

If you would like to create an HTML page from which to link to the Active Server Pages, you can do that by entering the simple code:

```
<a href="http://max/aspsamp2.asp"> </a>
```

The example assumes that your machine's name is Max. Again, determine your machine's name from the Network icon on the Windows Control Panel. Click the Identification tab to see what your system was named. This was done either by you or by those who initially set it up. After coding the Web page, name it `default.htm` and save it in the location for your home page. Also, you can check the Personal Web Server to check the home page and home directory locations. Double-click the Personal Web Server icon on the area to the right of the Start menu. The Main button will display the information.

TAKE NOTE

WEB PUBLISHING ON A SMALLER SCALE

Personal Web Server is set up for Web publishing on a smaller scale. It provides many of the same services and features as Microsoft Internet Information Server (IIS), a strong Web server planned to carry out large-scale Web publishing services. You can use Personal Web Server to develop and test your Web applications, and then upload them to a Web server that is running Microsoft Internet Information Server.

CROSS-REFERENCE
Check the information on creating a browser in Chapter 3.

FIND IT ONLINE
Find help on ASP: http://support.microsoft.com/ support/default.asp.

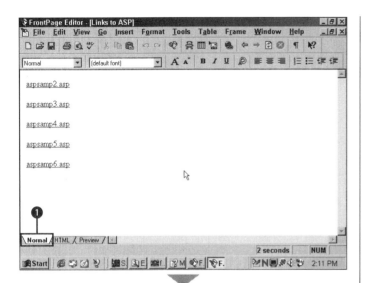

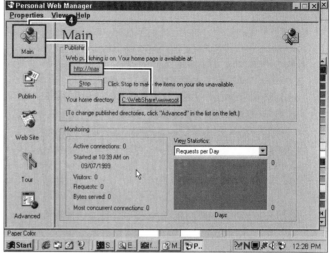

❹ Click the Main button to view the location of your home page and home directory.

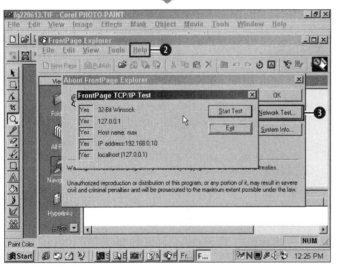

❶ In your editor, select the browser preview or normal view to view your Web page.

❷ If you have Microsoft FrontPage, select About from the Help menu in the FrontPage Explorer (not the Editor).

❸ Click the Network Test button to view your system name and settings.

▶ If you do not have Microsoft FrontPage, select the Network icon from the Windows Control Panel. Click the Identification tab to view the system name.

▶ Double-click the Personal Web Server icon in the Start Up area of your screen (usually the lower right-hand corner).

Listing 22-2: The Default Page

```
<HTML>
<HEAD>
<TITLE>Links to ASP</TITLE>
</HEAD>
<BODY
<p><a
href="http://www.hitekdesigns.com/aspsamp2.asp
">aspsamp2.asp</a></p>
<p><a
href="http://www.hitekdesigns.com/aspsamp3.asp
">aspsamp3.asp</a></p>
<p><a
href="http://www.hitekdesigns.com/aspsamp4.asp
">aspsamp4.asp</a></p>
<p><a
href="http://www.hitekdesigns.com/aspsamp5.asp
">aspsamp5.asp</a></p>
<p><a
href="http://www.hitekdesigns.com/aspsamp6.asp
">aspsamp6.asp</a></p>
</BODY>
</HTML>
```

▶ If you wish, you can create a Web page named default.htm to provide links to the Active Server Pages you will later create.

Scripting Active Server Pages

The advantage of Active Server Pages is that you can customize your Web pages for each user on the fly. You can arrange to have one type of page for one visitor type and another for a different type of visitor.

As you saw in the previous topic, Active Server Pages is part of the Windows NT package but can be implemented using the Personal Web Server. The chief benefit is using any one of a number of different scripting languages while targeting any browser. Because you have been using VBScript, you can continue to develop your Active Server Pages applications using it.

There are a number of quite sophisticated applications for Active Server Pages, but you will probably not want to tackle the most difficult applications at first. Some simple practice exercises include obtaining the date and time from the Web server.

When you create your Active Server Pages application, you begin with an ordinary HTML page and then embed the ASP command block within it.

```
<html>
<head>
<title>Pick a Number</title>
</head>
<body>
<center>
</center>
```

You will need to dredge up your experience with the random number generator from Chapters 16 and 17. Remember the syntax:

```
VarX = Int( 4 * Rnd +1)
```

Everything in the Active Server Pages command block must be placed within the characters `<%` and `%>`. Create a random number effect that operates each time you press the Refresh button. At first nothing shows on the screen in the browser window. When you click Refresh, a new number is displayed, and each time you Refresh the window, a new number will appear.

```
<% Dim Randumm
randomize
Randumm = int(Rnd* 10) + 1
%>
<% = Randumm %>
```

Notice that you do not need to use a command to print or display the result of the number generation on the screen. That occurs by default. Finally, finish up with the ending HTML tags:

```
</body>
</html>
```

The important part of this exercise is to name your ASP file with an `.asp` file extension. Active Server Pages files have the `.asp` file extension so that the server identifies the page and processes the code.

TAKE NOTE

COOKIES AND ASP

You may have wondered how Web servers track "cookies" (the information about sites that you have visited). Cookies are used to track SessionIDs by sending your browser a cookie with the creation of each new session. Usually this happens when the client machine requests an ASP page in a Web application. You can use this knowledge to prevent ASP from sending cookies.

CROSS-REFERENCE

Refresh your knowledge of the Randomize function in Chapter 16.

FIND IT ONLINE

Tutorial on ASP: **http://msdn.microsoft.com/ mastering/free/mwd64/mwd9800325.htm**.

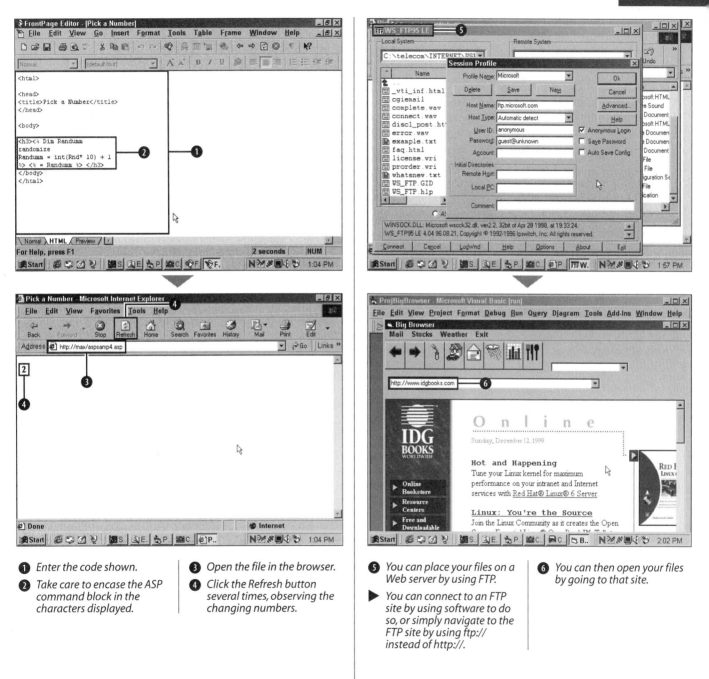

① Enter the code shown.

② Take care to encase the ASP command block in the characters displayed.

③ Open the file in the browser.

④ Click the Refresh button several times, observing the changing numbers.

⑤ You can place your files on a Web server by using FTP.

▶ You can connect to an FTP site by using software to do so, or simply navigate to the FTP site by using ftp:// instead of http://.

⑥ You can then open your files by going to that site.

489

Requesting Server Information

To make effective use of Active Server Pages technology, ideally you should put the Web server to work finding information to display in the user's browser. There are many different kinds of tasks. You can invoke other processes from Active Server Pages, such as Microsoft Transaction Server components. If you decide to do this, you will need to modify your system's Registry. Still another thing you can do with Active Server Pages is to set the values in "cookies."

The ASP objects Request information from the user, Respond by sending information to the user, control the Internet Information Server, maintain the user's current session, and share application information and settings.

The next exercise involves requesting and displaying the date and time from the server. Actually, one command can do both functions. You simply use the Now function, which requests both current date and time. Of course, that is the date and time on the server where the process is running. For example, if you place your file on a Web site, and then execute it, you will get the date and time on that server. This can be substantially different from your time zone if your Web site is far away.

Create your HTML code to start the page.

```
<html>
<head>
<title>AAAARRRRRGGGGH!</title>
</head>
<body>
<center>
<font size="6">Hello </font>
</center>
```

Next, set up the function using Active Server Pages.

```
<h3> The time is now <% = Now %>.
</font>
```

You can write the prompt in HTML, but the Now must be encased in the less than and percent sign symbols. Finish with the </BODY> and </HTML> tags. Save your file with the .asp extension. Open your file in the browser and check it out.

The next example also uses the date but adds the day of the week as well. Once again, set up your beginning and ending HTML code with <HTML>, <HEAD>, <TITLE>, and <BODY>. You also can set a font size if you wish. Next, write the prompt "It is..."

```
<h3>It is <% =WeekdayName(Weekday(Date)) _ %>,
<% = Date %>.
<% =WeekdayName(Weekday(Date)) %>, <% = Date
%>.
```

This part is the ASP code. The WeekdayName(Weekday(Date)) will request the name of the day as well as the date from the server. Finally, provide the ending HTML tags and save the file as ASPsamp2.ASP (or whatever pleases you). Open the file in your browser.

TAKE NOTE

▶ USING FRONTPAGE TO CREATE ASP

Save your ASP file in FrontPage by selecting Save As. In the Save As dialog box, enter the filename in the field that specifies URL. Make sure the filename has the .asp extension. You can give the title the same name as the file. Click OK.

CROSS-REFERENCE
Find help for HTML commands in Chapter 21.

FIND IT ONLINE
For information on Active Server Pages, see:
http://www.microsoft.com/transaction.

```
FrontPage Editor - [Hi there]
File  Edit  View  Go  Insert  Format  Tools  Table  Frame  Window  Help

<html>

<head>
<title>Hi there</title>
</head>

<body>
<font size="6">

<p>The time is now <% = now %>. </font></p>
</body>
</html>
```
①
②

```
AAAARRRRRGGGGH! - Microsoft Internet Explorer
File  Edit  View  Favorites  Tools  Help
Address  http://www.max/aspsamp5.asp

                    Hello

The time is now 12/12/99 4:28:06 PM.   ④
```
③

```
FrontPage Editor - [Hi There]
File  Edit  View  Go  Insert  Format  Tools  Table  Frame  Window  Help

<html>

<head>              ⑥
<title>Hi There</title>
</head>

<body>
<font size="4">

<p align="center">Hello </font></p>       ⑦

<h3>It is <% =WeekdayName(Weekday(Date)) %>, <% = Date %>. </h3>
</body>
</html>
```
⑤

```
Hi There - Microsoft Internet Explorer
File  Edit  View  Favorites  Tools  Help
Address  http://www.max/aspsamp2.asp
                         ⑧
                    Hello

It is Sunday, 12/12/99.
          ⑨
```

① Enter the code shown.

② Take care to place the <%
symbols outside the Now
function.

③ Access your file through your
local host machine or on
your Internet Web site.

④ The date and time of your
Web server should be
displayed.

⑤ Enter the code shown.

⑥ Enter a title if you wish.

⑦ Pay close attention to the
placement of the ASP code
symbols, <% and %>.

⑧ Open the ASP page in your
browser.

▶ You can use the Personal
Web Server by referencing
the local host path, or place
your file on your Web site.

⑨ The file should cause the
server to display its day of the
week and the date.

Personal Workbook

Q&A

1 What is the relationship between Active Server Pages and IIS?

_____

_____

_____

2 Can you use VBScript in Active Server Pages?

_____

_____

_____

3 What other kinds of scripts can be used in Active Server Pages?

_____

_____

_____

4 What are the symbols that set off the Active Server Pages command block?

_____

_____

_____

5 What is server-side scripting?

_____

_____

_____

6 Why can't VBScript be used in client-side scripts for all Internet applications?

_____

_____

_____

7 What is the best way to make sure all browsers can use the Web pages at a Web site?

_____

_____

_____

8 What the difference between server-side scripting and client-side scripting?

_____

_____

_____

ANSWERS: PAGE 531

EXTRA PRACTICE

1. Develop a custom VBScript to accept input from a form.

2. Create a VBScript that loads a graphic file, contains a button, and presents a dialog box when the button is clicked.

3. Make an Active Server Pages page that displays the time and presents a greeting depending upon the time of day.

4. Design a Web site using VBScript on one of the Web pages.

REAL-WORLD APPLICATIONS

✔ Your company has assigned you to create a new home page for their Web site. They specifically want the page to present users with the date, day of the week, and time, plus a greeting, "Good Morning " if they log on before noon or "Good Afternoon" if they log on after noon.

✔ A local bistro and dinner theatre, Aunt Fannie's, has hired you to create a cool Web site to promote their newest program "Fannie's Follies." Fannie wants lots of animation with moving and scrolling text and graphics. How would you approach the project in terms of the considerations of speed of access, security, and differences in users' browsers?

Visual Quiz

What is the URL being accessed?

_____

_____

_____

_____

_____

_____

_____

CHAPTER **23**

MASTER
THESE
SKILLS

▶ **Starting the Package and Deployment Wizard**

▶ **Using the Package and Deployment Wizard**

▶ **Packaging the Graphics Application**

▶ **Starting the Deployment Wizard**

▶ **Deploying to a Web Server**

▶ **Installing with the Setup Program**

▶ **Creating Setup Programs**

▶ **Using the Help Workshop**

▶ **Adding HTML Help with the HTML Help Workshop**

▶ **Adding Online Help to the VB Project**

Packaging Your Application

Throughout the book, you have been occupied with developing applications. You have mastered a number of technologies and learned about objects, properties, and methods. So far, you have covered a lot of material and traveled down many paths. Nevertheless, up to this point, you did not need to worry about how your potential users would be able to use these applications. You built projects in order to learn about the process. Now it is time to practice compiling, packaging, and deploying your work.

Once you complete and compile your applications, You can package and deploy them. Packaging enables you to combine all the necessary files in one package. Deployment is the process a developer goes through to correctly unpack all the files needed by an application and place them in appropriate locations where they can be used.

You have undoubtedly been through a number of installation programs and are familiar with the steps you went through in the process of copying files to a directory or directories from where the application could be launched.

If you were at least somewhat awed by the polished nature of the installation programs you have used, you may have wondered how they were developed. As you will see in the coming pages, there are programs available to assist you in the process of creating setup programs.

Perhaps the easiest way to perform these tasks is to use the Package and Deployment Wizard. The Package and Deployment Wizard walks you through the process, and you can select the defaults at each step to speed up the action. However, it is not often that going with the flow will address your entire package and deployment needs. In fact, there are quite a number of ways you can customize the package and deployment process.

Starting the Package and Deployment Wizard

There are two ways to package and deploy your products. You can manually create a setup program using the Setup Toolkit, or you can use the Package and Deployment Wizard.

The Setup Toolkit

The Package and Deployment Wizard uses the Setup Toolkit at the time your setup program is created. The Setup Toolkit project you create will include all the objects and code that the setup program needs in order to install the files onto your user's system. The `Setup1.exe` file, created by the Package and Deployment Wizard, is your application's major installation file.

The two programs used in the installation process are `Setup.exe` and `Setup1.exe`. The `Setup.exe` program is not modifiable. It carries out specific tasks that include copying the `Setup1.exe` program as well as the other files required by your application. You can modify the `Setup1.exe` program via the Setup Toolkit. It is important to back up the files in the `c:\VB98\Wizards\PDWizard\Setup1` directory, in the event that you make changes to any of the files. These are the files used by the Package and Deployment Wizard when you package your applications. Any changes to the `Setup1.exe` program will be reflected in the succeeding programs you package and deploy.

You can modify `Setup1.exe` by loading the `Setup1.vbp` project file into Visual Basic. You then make the changes in the way your project will look and function. This means that you will make the changes in the `Setup1.exe` file manually and then compile the `Setup1.vbp` project into the `Setup1.exe` file. Finally, you use the Package and Deployment Wizard to do the actual packaging and deploying of your application.

The Package and Deployment Wizard

Whether or not you modify the `Setup1.exe` program, you must first compile your project into an executable (`.exe`) file. Do this after you have fully debugged the project and are ready to ship it. It is possible to make modifications to the `.cab` files created by the Package and Deployment Wizard after they have been created, but it is better to wait until you are sure the project is completed before packaging and deploying it.

To compile your project, simply open your project, and then select the Make ProjName.exe... option on the File menu. Once you have created the `ProjName.exe` file, you use the Add-In Manager to load the Package and Deployment Wizard. Select Add-In Manager on the Add-Ins menu. Be sure to check the Loaded/Unloaded box under Load Behavior. Click OK. Next, when you select the Add-Ins menu, you will see the Package and Deployment Wizard listed as an option.

> ### TAKE NOTE
>
> #### THE WIZARD
>
> The Setup Toolkit and the Package and Deployment Wizard can be used to add features such as offering the user prompts about which files to install (online help) and other options. This way, you can add optional features to your applications.

CROSS-REFERENCE

Find the information about debugging your project in Chapters 11 and 13.

FIND IT ONLINE

For some humor, check this: **http://www.citilink. com/~jgarrick/vbasic/humor/drinternet.html**.

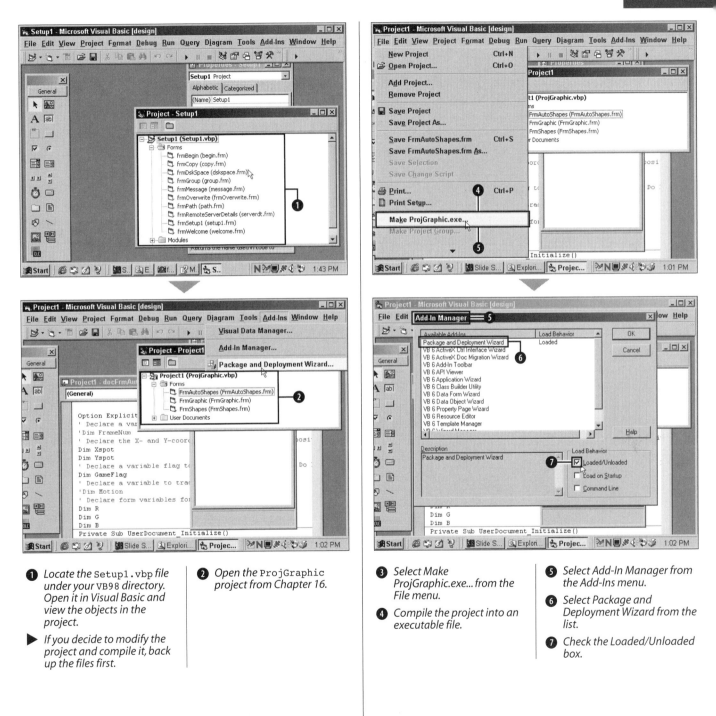

① Locate the Setup1.vbp file under your VB98 directory. Open it in Visual Basic and view the objects in the project.

▶ If you decide to modify the project and compile it, back up the files first.

② Open the ProjGraphic project from Chapter 16.

③ Select Make ProjGraphic.exe... from the File menu.

④ Compile the project into an executable file.

⑤ Select Add-In Manager from the Add-Ins menu.

⑥ Select Package and Deployment Wizard from the list.

⑦ Check the Loaded/Unloaded box.

Using the Package and Deployment Wizard

Once you compile the ProjGraphic project, you are ready to launch the Package and Deployment Wizard. Pull down the Add-Ins menu and select Package and Deployment Wizard from the options.

Notice that your options are to "Bundle this project into a distributable package," "Send one of this project's packages to a distribution site, such as an Internet server," or "Rename, duplicate, and delete your packaging and deployment scripts for this project."

Select the first option to produce a package with a CAB for the setup program. Next, you can choose a script if you have already created one. If you create a script, you can use it when packaging a later application and keep the same settings.

You can select the package type. Here you should select the Standard Setup Package. Next, choose a directory (folder) in which to assemble your package. If you select the directory where your `ProjGraphic.exe` file is located, the package will be placed in a subdirectory under that called `Package`.

At the next screen, you will be presented with a list of all the files and their source paths. You can then choose to add new files if you have written help or other files you wish to include. Notice that some files originate in the `Windows\System` directory. That is where the `.dll` files packaged with your application will be distributed when it is deployed using the setup program.

The Included Files list shows the names and locations of each of the files to be included in your package. The executable file you started with when you compiled the project is displayed at the top of the list and selected. If you wish, you can remove files from the list by removing the checkmark from the check box on the left. However, if you remove a file with dependencies, you will effectively remove all the files associated with it. You can recheck the box if you inadvertently removed the checkmark.

Placing your mouse over a given file will display a ToolTip describing the purpose of the file. This is a very handy feature. Run your mouse over each file to view its ToolTip.

You can add a file by clicking the Add button. The Add File dialog box will display, enabling you to find the file you want to add. The Wizard will search for dependencies (requirements of associated files) and add the dependent files. You must locate the graphic files needed by this application. Browse for them on your system and Add these to the package. Otherwise, your users will be notified that the program could not find `flowa2.jpg`, and so on.

At the next point, you have the option of creating only one `.cab` file or several. If you intend to ship your application on floppies, then you must select the Multiple CABs option. Otherwise, each file will be too large to fit on one floppy. If you plan to copy the package to a CD or to a Web site for downloading, then you can select the Single CAB option.

TAKE NOTE

▶ MODIFYING THE CAB FILES

The Package and Deployment Wizard can be used to first create `.cab` files and then used again to modify them if your have changed the setup. To do this, you use the `.ddf` file and a batch file created by the wizard and placed in the `Support` directory. Edit the `.ddf` file, then run the batch file provided. The batch file in turn will run a program, `Makecab.exe`, to recreate your `.cab` files.

CROSS-REFERENCE

Check Chapter 22 for similar applications.

FIND IT ONLINE

Here is the documentation for the P and D Wizard:
http://msdn.microsoft.com/library/officedev/odecore/derefpdwhiddplysubwiz.htm.

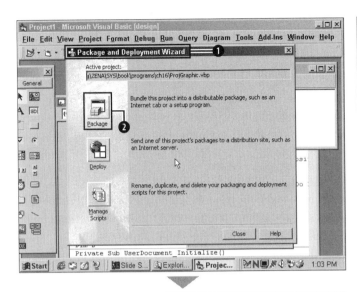

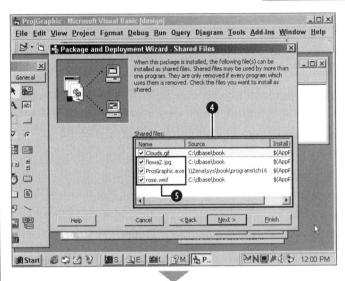

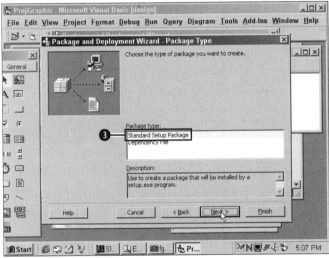

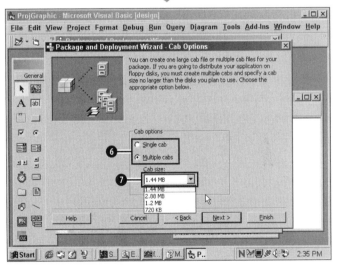

1 Open and compile the ProjGraphic project. Select the Package and Deployment Wizard from the Add-Ins menu.

2 Click the Package icon on the first screen.

3 Select the Standard Setup Package and then select the directory in which to prepare the package of files.

4 Check the list of files to be distributed with your application.

5 If prompted, click the Add button to add the graphic files (flowa2.jpg, Clouds.gif, and Rose.wmf).

6 Decide how you will distribute your application.

7 Select "Multiple cabs" and the 1.44MB size.

Packaging the Graphics Application

Now you are asked to decide on a title for your installation. This is the place where you can make up an impressive title for the installation. Remember how you were (at least somewhat) impressed by those installation programs you went through? Whatever you type here will be displayed in large letters on the user's screen during the installation. Go ahead and use the title **Graphic Project Lesson**.

You can create program groups for your applications either on the main level of the Start menu or within the Programs directory of the Start menu. You cannot create subgroups under the groups already created. If you try to do so, you will be prompted "You can only add groups to the Start Menu or the Programs Menu." If you add your program group to the Start menu (not under Programs), your group will appear above the list of applications under Programs.

Select Programs in the Start Menu Items window and then click the New Group button. Name your group **VBPractice**. If you click the new item button with VBPractice selected, you will add a shortcut to your application. Typically, this is used to reference a help file developed for your application.

The next window lets you choose where to install the application on the user's computer. The file list shows the names and current locations of all the files in the package. The locations of where is file is to be installed are shown in terms of the installation path or whatever location you specified on a previous screen in this process. The user will also be allowed to change the default location during the installation.

This option asks you to determine which files you would like to install as shared files. *Shared files* can be used by more than one application on the user's system. This type of file should not be removed unless there is no program installed that can use it. A shared file will not be removed by an uninstall program if there are currently installed programs that use the file. The ToolTip is available if you pass the mouse over the file(s) listed in the window. If only the executable (`.exe`) for your application is shown in the window, the file can be shared.

The last step, Finish, creates a deployment script containing your settings. You can deploy the project again and use the same settings. Also, you can use the Wizard in silent mode, which requires that you name a script to use for the processing. In order to remember the project with which the script is associated, you should try to give it a name that best describes the project. Finally, a report will be displayed and you will be prompted to save it if you wish. You can save it in a location where it will not be overwritten by subsequent uses of the Wizard.

At this point, the process is complete and you now have a package that will provide means of deploying your application to its intended users. To test the Wizard's product, you should move the files to a computer without Visual Basic installed and run the setup program to deploy it.

TAKE NOTE

THE PACKAGE AND DEPLOYMENT WIZARD FILES

There is a directory for support files and an input file (`.inf`) for the `.cab` in the same directory. The support files directory contains the `.ddf` file as well as other files necessary.

CROSS-REFERENCE

Chapter 21 discusses options in the same area.

FIND IT ONLINE

This is the Deployment script: **http://msdn.microsoft. com/library/devprods/vs6/vbasic/setpwz98/ vbwizpackagedeploymentwizarddeploymentscripts.htm.**

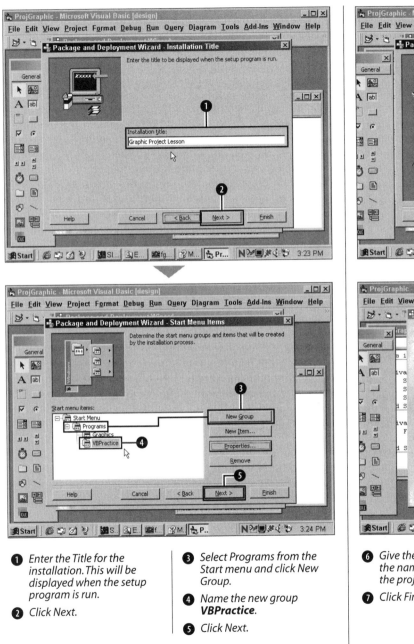

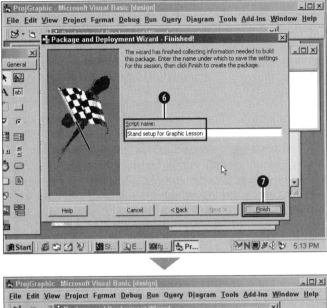

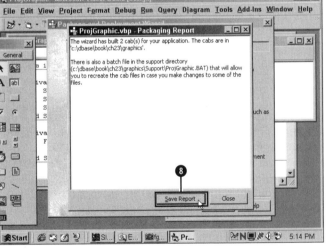

❶ Enter the Title for the installation. This will be displayed when the setup program is run.

❷ Click Next.

❸ Select Programs from the Start menu and click New Group.

❹ Name the new group **VBPractice**.

❺ Click Next.

❻ Give the script a name. Make the name as descriptive of the project as possible.

❼ Click Finish.

❽ Save the report where you will be able to locate it. You might save it in the same directory where your application was packaged, or in the original directory for the project.

Starting the Deployment Wizard

Once you have created the package, you are ready to deploy it. First, decide how to do this. Do you want to place it on floppy disks, a network, or a local folder (directory), or publish on the Web? If you decide to place your files on a floppy for distribution, select that option. For this exercise you can decide if you want the package deployed onto floppies or a directory on your hard drive.

Open the `ProjGraphic` project. Add the Package and Deployment Wizard on the Add-Ins menu, then launch it. This time, select the Deploy option on the first screen.

Next, select the Stand Setup for Graphic Lesson as the package to deploy. If you have created additional packages for practice, these will be shown on the list as well. The Deployment method is Floppy or Folder. If you plan to take the package to a different system without Visual Basic installed (as you should), you should select the Floppy Disks option.

If you select the Floppy Disks method, you must already have made that decision when you first packaged the application. If you did not, then the `.cab` files may be too large to fit on floppies. If you picked the One Cab File option, the file will be larger than the capacity of a floppy.

If you did not select this option in the packaging phase, you must go back and rebuild the package with smaller `.cab` files. If you will be able to test your setup program on a computer without Visual Basic, it may be easier to deploy onto floppies. Some alternatives would be to deploy onto a Zip cartridge or a CD if you have a CD writer.

If you gave a path for graphic files different from that for the project files, you will need to provide instructions to the user to copy them manually. For this reason, all files should be placed in the same folder or directory.

The key to success in deployment here is in the graphic files paths in the original project code. If you use a directory other than the project directory, then that directory structure must exist on all machines where the package is deployed.

```
Set flowa =
LoadPicture("c:\dbase\book\flowa2.jpg")
Set rose =
LoadPicture("c:\dbase\book\rose.wmf")
Set clouds =
LoadPicture("c:\dbase\book\clouds.gif")
```

Since the path is set to `\dbase\book\` on Drive C:, your users must copy the files to that same path or the graphics won't be found and an error will be generated. The setup program will not do this. You can add an error trap to the original code and explain to the user where the files should be. A better idea is to be very careful to place all the files used in your application in the same directory and specify that in the code. The files will all be deployed in the same directory specified by the user or under the program files directory by default. The code in the project should be changed as shown.

```
Set flowa = LoadPicture("flowa2.jpg")
Set rose = LoadPicture("rose.wmf")
Set clouds = LoadPicture("clouds.gif")
```

Of course, this means that the files in the original project must reside in the same directory as the project. It also means that you must now make the code changes to ProjGraphic and recompile, and then rerun the Package and Deployment Wizard.

TAKE NOTE

▶ **CAB FILE SIZE**

The Package and Deployment Wizard allows you to decide whether to create one large `.cab` file or several smaller `.cab` files. The smaller files split your package into a series of multiple `.cab` files. If you are going to deploy using floppies, you should use the multiple CABs.

CROSS-REFERENCE

Find the ProjGraphics project in Chapter 16.

FIND IT ONLINE

Info on CAB files is at **http://www.microsoft.com/ workshop/prog/cab/**.

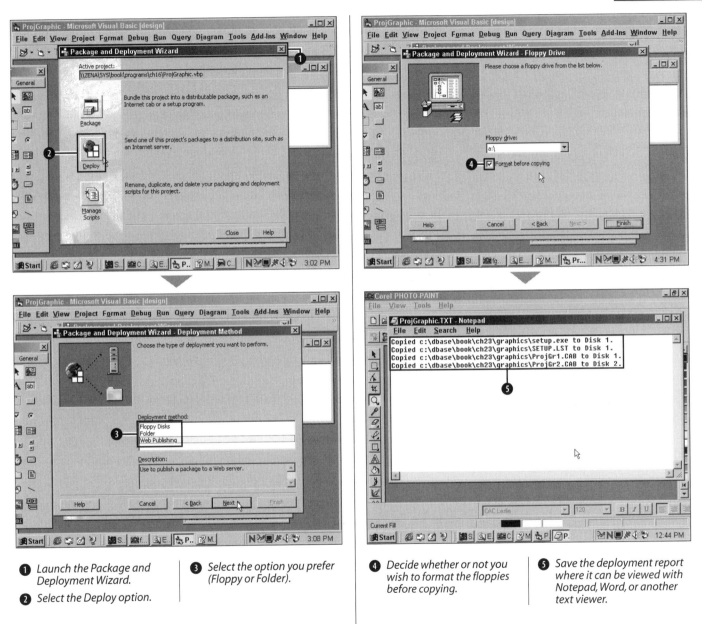

① Launch the Package and Deployment Wizard.

② Select the Deploy option.

③ Select the option you prefer (Floppy or Folder).

④ Decide whether or not you wish to format the floppies before copying.

⑤ Save the deployment report where it can be viewed with Notepad, Word, or another text viewer.

Deploying to a Web Server

The packaging and deployment process is a little different when you are planning to allow distribution of the application from the Internet. You probably would plan to place the file on an FTP (File Transfer Protocol) site for downloading by the purchasers or freeware users.

When you use the Package and Deployment Wizard to deploy your application for distribution over the Internet, an HTML file is generated. This file contains information (class ID, ID, and Codebase) about any controls included with the application. Internet Explorer checks the Registry to determine whether the control being distributed with the application exists on the target system. If not, it downloads it and installs the file in question.

The attributes checked by Internet Explorer are the Class ID (identification number of the control) generated by the control when you created it, the Codebase (the version number), and the ID (name property). If the control exists on the target system, but the version number there is lower than the one to be downloaded, the newer control will be installed.

For the next exercise, you will run through the process again, but this time sending the project's package to a Web site. Select the ProjGraphics project again. You can use the `.exe` file already compiled. Launch the Package and Deployment Wizard and select the middle button (Deploy).

Next, you will be shown a list of packages already assembled. If you have created additional packages besides the Graphic Lesson, you will see these on the list of packages to deploy.

Select the Stand Setup for Graphic Lesson. Next, pick Web Publishing as the Deployment method. Check the list of files to deploy. They should include at least two `.cab` files and the two setup files (`Setup.exe` and `Setup.lst`).

The next screen is shown only for the Web Publishing deployment option. It lists all possible files to deploy, including all your graphic files you may have forgotten about

(`clouds.gif`, `flowa2.jpg`, and `rose.wmf`). Be sure to place checkmarks in their check boxes; otherwise, these won't be deployed with your package.

When prompted for a Destination URL, give your FTP site's URL. You must have an FTP site from which your potential users can download this package. If you do not, check with your Internet service provider. Many times, the ISP offers a free home page and/or FTP access. If this is not an option for you, search the Web for free FTP sites. There are a number of sites offering free Web site hosting and possibly free FTP access as well.

If you give an actual FTP site, you will be prompted to enter your authentication information (user name and password). If you are not connected, you will likely get an error message saying the server name or address could not be resolved. You should be logged in when you attempt to do this.

When you use a Web site to publish on for the first time, you will need to save the URL as a Web Publishing site. At that time, the information you enter will be verified and can be reused in the future.

TAKE NOTE

▶ LOCATION OF GRAPHIC FILES

If you did not include your graphic files during the packaging phase, you will see a screen showing all the files potentially needed by the project. Examine this list and determine whether any additional files or folders should be included. If you look at this list, you will see that `Clouds.gif`, `flowa2.jpg`, and `Rose.wmf` are listed, but their boxes are not checked. If you expect users to be able to run these applications, you must include the pictures. Therefore, check those boxes.

CROSS-REFERENCE

Check the information in Chapter 21.

FIND IT ONLINE

Free Web hosting is available at **http//www.webjump.com.**

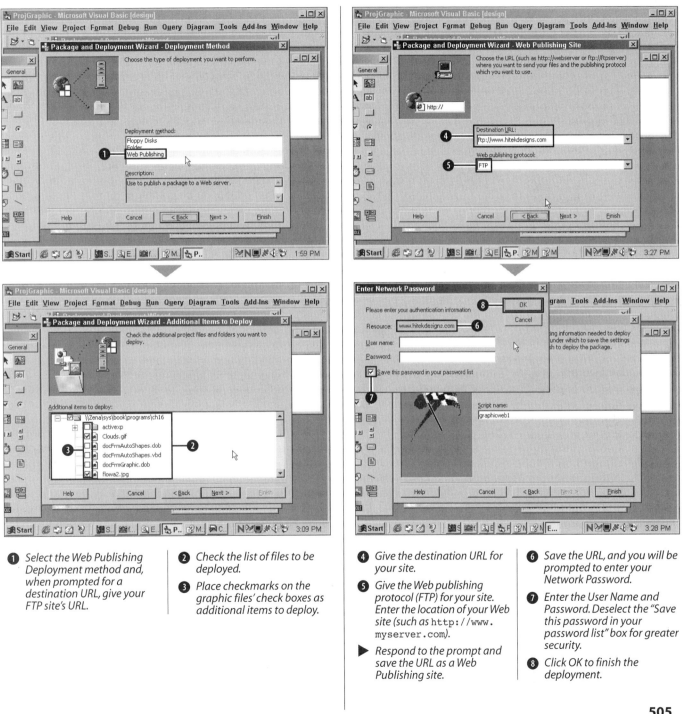

① Select the Web Publishing Deployment method and, when prompted for a destination URL, give your FTP site's URL.

② Check the list of files to be deployed.

③ Place checkmarks on the graphic files' check boxes as additional items to deploy.

④ Give the destination URL for your site.

⑤ Give the Web publishing protocol (FTP) for your site. Enter the location of your Web site (such as http://www.myserver.com).

▶ Respond to the prompt and save the URL as a Web Publishing site.

⑥ Save the URL, and you will be prompted to enter your Network Password.

⑦ Enter the User Name and Password. Deselect the "Save this password in your password list" box for greater security.

⑧ Click OK to finish the deployment.

Installing with the Setup Program

When you finish packaging and deploying your application, you will distribute it on floppies, CD, Zip cartridge, or the Internet. At that point, your anonymous user should not struggle with its installation but be at least as impressed as you have been using the standard installation programs distributed with your purchased software.

There is no better way to test your setup program than to do it yourself. If you deployed or copied the files onto floppies or some removable media, then you should install the application on a different machine. If you do not have another computer (perhaps a laptop), then you should try to have your friends or family members let you run through the installation on one of their systems.

To begin the installation program, place the first floppy disk containing the `Setup.exe` file in Drive A:. Click the Start menu and select Run. Type **A:\setup.exe** in the combo box. You will see a dialog box detailing the files that are being copied. You will be prompted for the next floppy. When the files are copied, the installation program will run.

In nice big letters, the name of the application being installed will be displayed, filling the entire screen. Depending upon what you named your application, "Graphic Project Lesson Setup" or the name you used will be displayed also on the title bar of a dialog box, welcoming you to the installation program. At the same time, you are asked to exit any programs you are currently running. This is typical of all installation programs. As you know, some programs share files and this would interfere with the process.

The default folder or directory in which the application is to be installed will be shown on the left. To the right is a Change Directory button that you may press if you wish to change it. This is an important option, because many users have a proprietary directory setup for specific kinds of applications. Forcing them to install everything in the Program Files directory is not good. At the bottom of the screen is a button to opt out of the installation. Clicking the icon picturing the computer will continue the installation.

The Choose Program Group dialog comes next. Here the user is prompted to select a Program Group for the application's items to be added. Because you created VBPractice for the group when you ran the Package and Deployment Wizard, the user can select that option, or another group that already exists.

Finally, the application was installed successfully. At any rate, you hope it will be when each user installs it. This is why you are installing it yourself in order to test your packaging and deployment skills.

The next topic will cover the steps involved in creating a custom setup program.

TAKE NOTE

► TESTING THE INSTALLATION PROGRAM

If you are not able to find another machine on which to test the installation program and you install it on your development system, you cannot be sure if it would run on a computer without Visual Basic or the required ActiveX controls installed. In addition, you should test the installation program on every applicable operating system.

CROSS-REFERENCE

Check Chapter 16 to determine the filenames and paths of all your images used in the ProjGraphic project.

FIND IT ONLINE

You can create a free Web site here: **http://www. spaceports.com/freesites/**.

Packaging Your Application

Graphic Project Lesson Setup

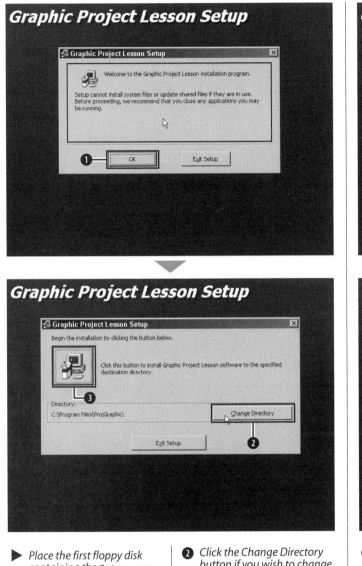

Graphic Project Lesson Setup

Graphic Project Lesson Setup

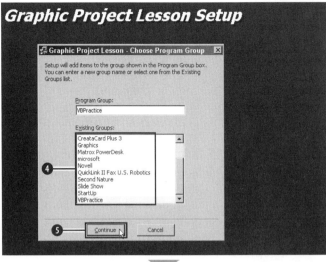

Graphic Project Lesson Setup

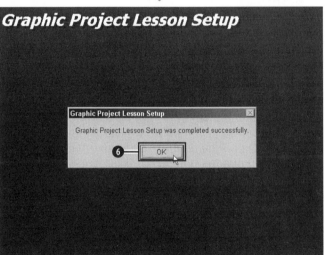

▶ *Place the first floppy disk containing the* Setup.exe *file in Drive A:. Click the Start menu and select Run.*

❶ *After you type A:\setup.exe in the combo box, you will see this Welcome screen. Click OK to continue.*

❷ *Click the Change Directory button if you wish to change the location in which the application will be installed.*

❸ *Click the icon picturing the computer to continue the installation.*

❹ *Accept one of the existing Program Groups or enter a new Group in which to add your application.*

❺ *Click Continue.*

❻ *Click OK to complete the installation.*

Creating Setup Programs

In addition to distributing files on floppies or CDs, you can place your package on the Internet for users to download and deploy. When you use the Package and Deployment Wizard this way, both distribution and support files are created.

As you noted in the previous exercise, the Wizard creates a separate directory for support files (`Support`) under the main directory you specified for the file location. The Wizard generates the following file types.

- ▶ The `.cab` file (stands for cabinet) contains the `.ocx` ActiveX component files and the `.inf` file.
- ▶ The `.htm` file is of course an HTML file used to display a Web page that includes a link to the `.cab` file.
- ▶ The `.ddf` (stands for Diamond Directives) file is used to create the `.cab` files. As you remember, you can recreate the `.cab` files by editing the `.ddf` file.
- ▶ The `.inf` file includes the information on installation.
- ▶ The .ocx files are ActiveX control component files that contain one or more ActiveX controls.

The `.dll` (dynamic link library) files are required by your application in order to run. These files generally belong in the `Windows\System` directory. The user's system may already contain the same `.dlls`, in which case, the user should be prompted to copy or not copy the files.

You can edit the code for the `Form_Load` event in the `Setup1.frm` form. You can add code after the code block calls the `ShowBeginForm` function. Basically, you modify the Setup Toolkit project to contain the prompts, windows, functions, code, or whatever information should be included.

You must decide which files you want to distribute. Where do you want to install the files on the users' computers? You can manually create your `Setup.lst` file to reflect the names and installation locations of all files that must be included for your project. Decide how to distribute files. You can create the `.cab` files for your project using the Makecab utility.

You can create a `Setup1.exe` for your project. Just compile the Setup Toolkit project with your changes. Then you can copy your files to the floppy disks, Zip cartridges, or CDs, or manually publish your files to the Web site using the Web Publishing Wizard, available in the ActiveX SDK.

If you want to add a task to the project, add code after the command block calls the `ShowBeginForm` function (`Sub ShowBeginForm`). When you change the code, close `Setup1.frm` and save the form and the Setup Toolkit project, and compile to create the `Setup1.exe` file.

In the example given, you should make sure that all possible files the user could choose to install in your custom dialog box were listed in the Add and Remove screen. When done, generate the distribution media.

TAKE NOTE

▶ THE SETUP TOOLKIT

The Setup toolkit can be used to create your own custom projects. You can use the Setup Toolkit in conjunction with the Package and Deployment Wizard. The Setup Toolkit enables you to customize the windows and other parts of the installation.

CROSS-REFERENCE

Chapter 3 equips you to make decisions about designing distribution options.

FIND IT ONLINE

This site has info on the Toolkit: **http://support. microsoft.com/support/kb/articles/Q122/7/37.asp.**

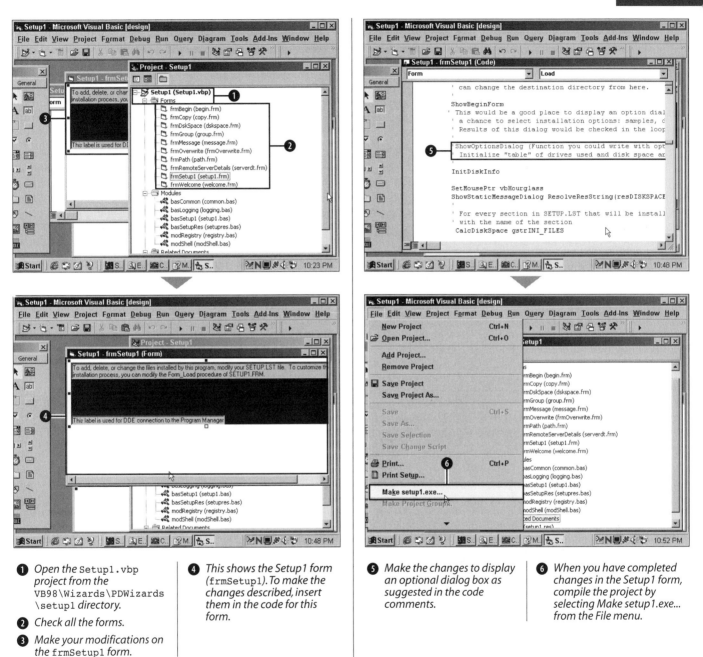

① *Open the* Setup1.vbp *project from the* VB98\Wizards\PDWizards \setup1 *directory.*

② *Check all the forms.*

③ *Make your modifications on the* frmSetup1 *form.*

④ *This shows the Setup1 form (*frmSetup1*). To make the changes described, insert them in the code for this form.*

⑤ *Make the changes to display an optional dialog box as suggested in the code comments.*

⑥ *When you have completed changes in the Setup1 form, compile the project by selecting Make setup1.exe... from the File menu.*

Using the Help Workshop

The Help Workshop is available to assist you in creating help text in response to the user's request from the menu or by pressing the F1 key. The handy program is not installed during the regular installation of Visual Basic. To install the Help Workshop, you must install it from the Visual Basic 6 CD. You will find the `hcw.exe` program in the `Common\Tools\` directory on the CD. You use this program to create files and compile them with the `.hlp` extension. These files, in turn, are added to the Visual Basic project by setting the `HelpFile` property of the project to the compiled help filename.

This process is carried out by first creating a rich text file in a word processor, or using one of the forms containing rich text boxes you created in previous projects. To create an acceptable help file in rich text format, you need to use specific tags that the Microsoft Help Workshop program can recognize. Unfortunately, you cannot use the Help Workshop as a rich text file editor. You must create the rich text file separately from the Help Workshop program and then add it to your project in the Workshop.

Fortunately, there is a very good help system for the Help Workshop, including a step-by-step outline of how to create the rich text file and how to compile it in the Help Workshop. Although the documentation is considerable for this program, the task of correctly writing the rich text file is so daunting that many references advise purchasing a third-party help authoring application.

The process begins with creating a new file in Word, or any rich text editor. List individual topics on which you wish to provide help. It helps to separate these topics with page breaks. Next, you add footnotes that function much like hyperlinks or bookmarks in HTML files. The process of debugging and correcting this text often renders the experience a lengthy one.

The idea is that you need to make a list of topics, then the topics named again, each on a separate page along with the help explanation. When you finish your help description, you save the file with the `.rtf` extension. In the event that you write the text in Notepad or an application that doesn't save RTF files, you can save the file with a `.txt` extension and later bring it into Word or WordPad and resave it. The difficulty with this scenario is that your formatting will not be preserved when you save in ASCII text format.

After saving your RTF file, launch the Microsoft Help Workshop and begin a new project by select New on the File menu. Add a topic file by clicking the Add button. Identify the rich text format file you just created.

Compile your work by choosing Compile on the File menu or Save and Compile in the Options window. After compiling, the results are displayed in a report showing the path, filename, and size of the resulting file.

The next step is to launch Visual Basic and open the project to which you are adding help. Select Project Properties and change the HelpFile name properties to that of the filename with the `.hlp` extension you just compiled.

TAKE NOTE

► GRAPHICS IN HELP FILES

You can add bitmaps (`.bmp`) and Windows metafiles (`.wmf`) to your Help system. You can give these graphic files hotspots to jump to as well. You also can use transparent bitmaps to these help files. If you add the letter "t" to the `bmx` statement, WinHelp will replace the white pixels in the bitmap with the background color of the currently active window.

CROSS-REFERENCE

The Projdialog project from Chapter 9 features a rich text box application.

FIND IT ONLINE

Help Workshop info is at **http://msdn.microsoft.com/subscriptions/index/Index/UniversalUS/U.S/4003.asp**.

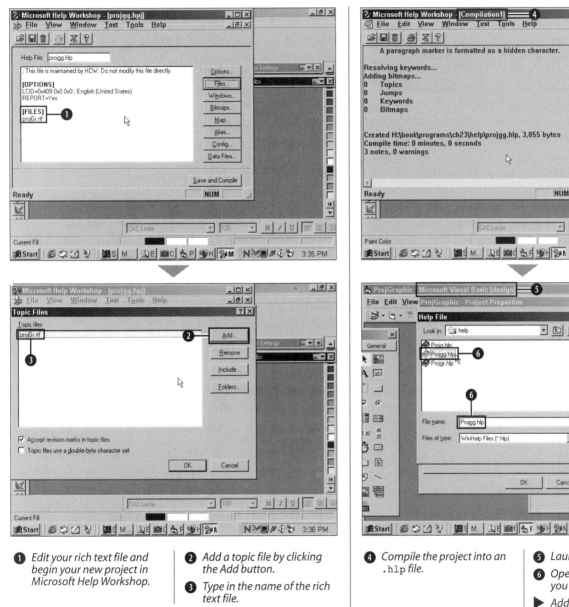

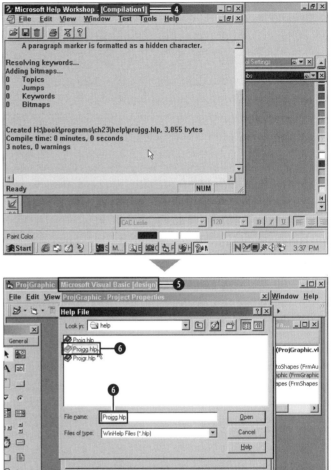

1 Edit your rich text file and begin your new project in Microsoft Help Workshop.

2 Add a topic file by clicking the Add button.

3 Type in the name of the rich text file.

4 Compile the project into an .hlp file.

5 Launch Visual Basic.

6 Open the project to which you are adding help.

▶ Add the HelpFile name property to the Project properties.

Adding HTML Help with the HTML Help Workshop

Recently, HTML Help was added to the Microsoft Web site, where it can be downloaded. It is a self-extracting and installing file, HTMLHelp.exe.

At the time Visual Basic 6 was first distributed, the predominant help system was the older WinHelp. As you found in the previous topic, this required tedious editing of rich text files and did not offer the functionality of HTML help. Some benefits of HTML help over the older help system are the capability of using a table of contents and index combined and the ability to hyperlink keywords.

The chief difference between the Microsoft Help Workshop and the HTML Help Workshop is the ability to incorporate HTML files in your help projects. Instead of struggling with text files, you can use your favorite HTML editor (FrontPage?) to design the help files, and then add them to the Workshop project.

You can compress HTML and graphic files into smaller (.chm) files. These can either be downloaded from the Web or distributed with applications. The HTML Help Workshop contains a help compiler and a WinHelp converter as well as other tools used to create and maintain help projects.

In addition to the preceding features, HTML Help Workshop itself uses HTML help files and, as a result, has a really showy interface in keeping with the Web look. There is even a tutorial for designing help for a Web site. Using this tool, you can create your own training cards. If you used the Help Workshop described in the last topic, you could have used the training cards to walk you through the creation of a help project.

Using the HTML Help Workshop, you not only add the latest look to your help system, you can add features not available with the older system. For example, you can create unique window designs, context-sensitive help, and shortcuts.

Once you access the Microsoft.com Web site and download the HTML Help system and install it, you are ready to set up your help files. If you have a favorite HTML editor, then you can set up the files in that first. You can use Microsoft Word or the Web Publisher distributed with Windows 95/98/2000 as well.

If you have no access to any other editor, you can use the editor provided in the HTML Help Workshop. In contrast to the older Help Workshop, HTML Help does offer the means to write HTML files. While it does not provide a complete interface, the HTML Help Workshop will let you preview your work in a browser and also provides an online HTML Tag Reference. These features make it well worth the download.

Edit your HTML file with the editor of your choice. Just as in the previous example, you will need to set up topics and then jump to the help for those topics. While the concept is simple, using the older system was not. If you use an editor like FrontPage, you will be able to type the topics and then insert a bookmark or hyperlink to the explanation of the topic.

CROSS-REFERENCE

Chapter 21 offers instruction coding a browser.

FIND IT ONLINE

This is the site where you can download the Workshop:
http://msdn.microsoft.com/workshop/author/htmlhelp.

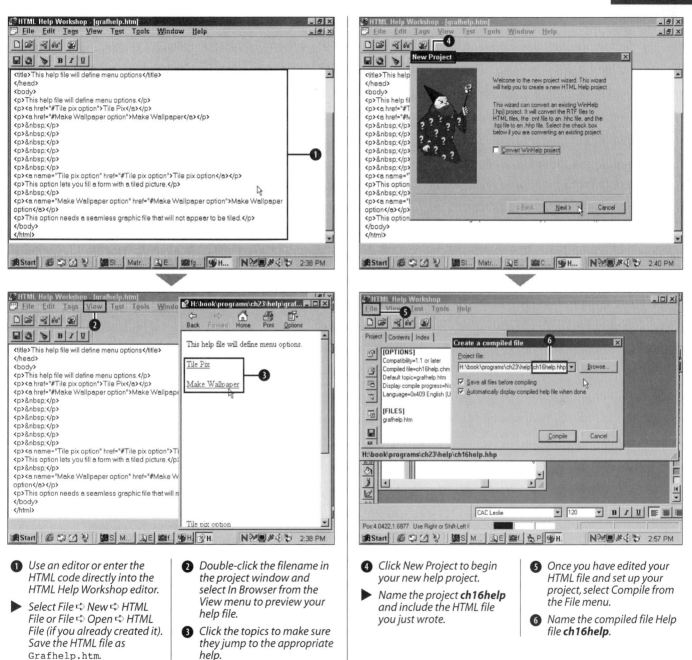

① Use an editor or enter the HTML code directly into the HTML Help Workshop editor.

▶ Select File ⇨ New ⇨ HTML File or File ⇨ Open ⇨ HTML File (if you already created it). Save the HTML file as Grafhelp.htm.

② Double-click the filename in the project window and select In Browser from the View menu to preview your help file.

③ Click the topics to make sure they jump to the appropriate help.

④ Click New Project to begin your new help project.

▶ Name the project **ch16help** and include the HTML file you just wrote.

⑤ Once you have edited your HTML file and set up your project, select Compile from the File menu.

⑥ Name the compiled file Help file **ch16help**.

Adding Online Help to the VB Project

Because you are going to use the ProjGraphic project from Chapter 16 in this exercise, you should make the topics in your HTML file fit the project. The Pictures menu on the **FrmGraphic** form has three options: Tile Pix, Make Wallpaper, and Stretch Pic. Your help topics should be one or more of these items. For example, topic one should be Tile Pix and topic two, Make Wallpaper. Below these topics should be a bookmark for each topic. Below the bookmarks, you will place the help text desired.

The Tile Pix option's bookmark will be placed lower down on the page and will be accompanied by a description, "This option lets you fill a form with a tiled picture." The help text and bookmark for the Wallpaper option convey to the end user what the option does.

When you finish composing and editing your HTML file, you should test it in your browser to make sure it works. It is possible to use the browser you created in prior chapters or the Internet Explorer, or use the View in Browser option in the HTML Help Workshop. If you used an editor such as FrontPage, you can use that application to view your file in a browser. In any case, once you are satisfied that the help file is complete, you can bring it into the HTML Help Workshop, create a new project, and then compile it into a **.chm** file. Then you can link this to your Visual Basic project by setting the **HelpFile** property.

You can create the HTML file first, open it in the HTML Help Workshop and then create the project, or create the file in the HTML Help Workshop. You can begin the project with the HTML file already opened, or create the project and add the HTML file. The project window is the key to what is happening in the HTML Help Workshop. However you create it, when you finish with your HTML file, name it **Grafhelp.htm**.

You will be asked to add an HTML file and specify the path where it is located if you begin the project before opening the HTML file. Next, you will be prompted to click Finish to create the new HTML help project. Once created, the uncompiled help project has a file extension of **.hhp**. Your project file will be named **ch16help.hhp**.

The information under [Options] shows the filename, topic HTML file, and language. Under [Files] is shown the HTML filename. The log file shows the name of the compiled help project, the file size, and the compressed file size. You also can save the log file for reference. Note the compiled filename for your project is **ch16help.chm**.

When you have completed compiling the Help project, you need to install it in your Visual Basic project. Launch Visual Basic and open the ProjGraphic project. Select Project Properties on the Project menu. Beside the Help File Name box, click the dots that indicate a possible file selection. Select the help project file (**ch16help.chm**) just compiled. The filename will now be added to these project properties.

Now run the application and press the F1 key. The Help window will pop up. Click Tile Pix and Make Wallpaper. If you coded the HTML file correctly, the cursor will jump to the help explanation you have provided.

TAKE NOTE

HELP AND ACCESSIBILITY

The Accessibility Word List helps identify common terms used regarding disabilities. The Help system also should include information on using online help. The Accessibility Word List can provide information about creating help topics.

CROSS-REFERENCE

Chapter 16 provides the basis for this exercise.

FIND IT ONLINE

This is the site for HTML help: **http://msdn.microsoft.com/workshop/Author/htmlhelp/?RLD=97**.

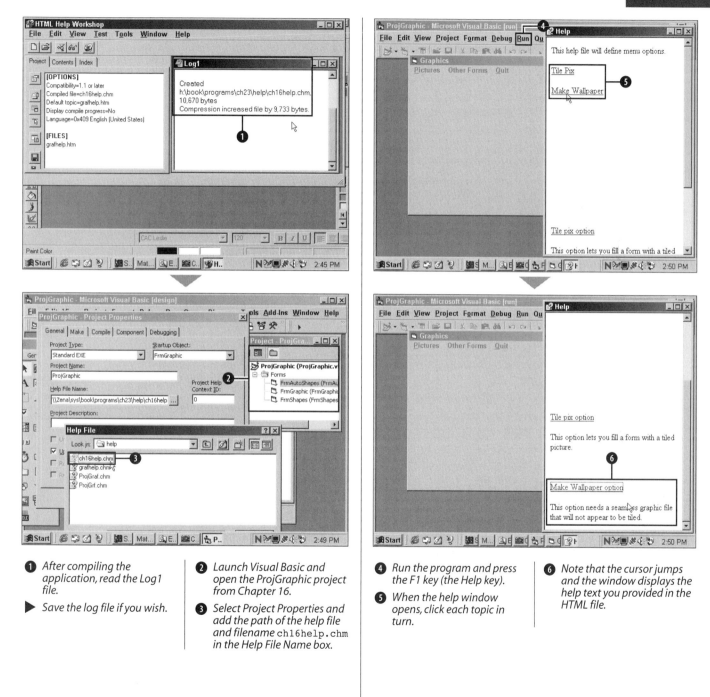

① After compiling the application, read the Log1 file.

▶ Save the log file if you wish.

② Launch Visual Basic and open the ProjGraphic project from Chapter 16.

③ Select Project Properties and add the path of the help file and filename ch16help.chm in the Help File Name box.

④ Run the program and press the F1 key (the Help key).

⑤ When the help window opens, click each topic in turn.

⑥ Note that the cursor jumps and the window displays the help text you provided in the HTML file.

Personal Workbook

Q&A

1 What is the Add-In that prepares Visual Basic programs for distribution?

_____

_____

_____

2 How can you customize the package and deployment of the applications you create?

_____

_____

_____

3 How can you use the same settings in subsequent deployments?

_____

_____

_____

4 What is a major difference in deploying an Internet application?

_____

_____

_____

5 What determines the CAB file size?

_____

_____

_____

6 What is the traditional way of creating help for a Visual Basic application?

_____

_____

_____

7 What is the help file extension for a rich text format help file?

_____

_____

_____

8 What is the newest help system allowing developers to provide help for their applications?

_____

_____

_____

ANSWERS: PAGE 531

EXTRA PRACTICE

1 Customize your project's Setup program to provide custom prompts for the installation of your application.

2 Package and deploy your application for downloading and installation from the Internet.

3 Package your application so that it can be installed from a network.

4 Design an HTML help package including graphics with hotspots.

REAL-WORLD APPLICATIONS

✔ A company in your consulting portfolio has developed an application plug-in to support a package they have discontinued. They would like to place the new product online at their Web site to be downloaded. The plug-in and the older application were both developed in Visual Basic. How would you address the company's needs?

✔ Aunt Fannie's was so happy with the cool site you designed for them that they want you to set up an FTP site so that they can offer their customers free graphics to download. How does one do this?

✔ Uncle Spud finally got his Visual Basic milk production calculation program going and is now stumped as to how to package it to sell to his fellow farmers. He wants you to orchestrate its packaging and deployment. How would you advise him to do that?

Visual Quiz

What kind of deployment is this dialog box used for?

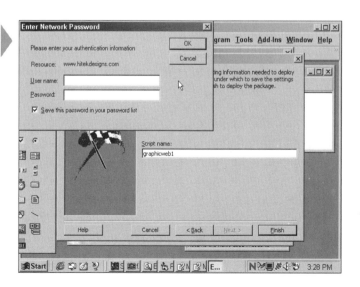

Personal Workbook
Answers

Chapter 1

1 **What has Windows got that DOS didn't have?**

A: A graphic user interface.

2 **What are the two options for a Windows interface type?**

A: SDI and MDI.

3 **What is the term used for the process of anchoring windows to a part of the application window?**

A: Docking.

4 **What are the development tools related to Visual Basic?**

A: VBA and VBScript.

5 **What is an event handler?**

A: Procedural code attached to an object.

6 **On which menu do you find the Project Explorer and the Properties Window?**

A: The View Menu.

7 **How do you change your environment to customize your Editor and Docking options?**

A: Tools, Options, Docking or Tools, Options, Editor.

8 **How can you add controls to the toolbox?**

A: Project Menu, Components, Controls.

Visual Quiz

Q: **The form shown at the right has a problem. How can you fix it?**

A: The problem is that the form is too small to show the command buttons. It can be made larger by changing the Height and Width properties in the Properties Window or by clicking and dragging it larger.

Chapter 2

1 **A Visual Basic object is unique in that it combines both_____ and _____.**

A: Data and Code.

2 **How can you add new controls to the toolbox?**

A: Select `Components` from the `Project Menu`, then select desired library from list.

3 **What value do you modify to change the tab order on the form?**

A: The `TabIndex` value

PERSONAL WORKBOOK ANSWERS

4 **What does the Windows Collection contain?**

A: Project Explorer, Properties Window, Object Browser, Code Windows, Designer Windows make up the Development Environment.

5 **How can you find the value of a variable as the program executes?**

A: Select Add Watch on the Debug Menu and enter an expression to break on. Also, halt processing by using CTRL Break, then use the Print statement to show the value of the variable.

6 **How can you add a new command to a menu on the Menu Bar?**

A: Select Customize from the View Menu, then select the Commands tab. Using click and drag, drag the appropriate command to the menu on the Menu Bar.

7 **Will Visual Basic 6 run on a Pentium 120MHz running Windows 98 with 16MB RAM?**

A: No. It will run on a Pentium 120MHz, but needs 24MB RAM.

8 **What is the best way to get online help?**

A: Use the Help Menu, selecting Microsoft on the Web. You can also connect to the Internet, then type in the `http://msdn.microsoft.com/vbasic/ technical/`.

Visual Quiz

Q: **Which of these options shown will give you online help?**

A: Virtually every one, except the About.. option.

Chapter 3

1 **What is a wizard?**

A: A utility that automates application development by generating code in response to selections you make from menus and prompts.

2 **What is the best use of the Application Wizard?**

A: To speed up application development and learn by examining generated code.

3 **What is the difference between the Standard forms and those created by the Data Forms Wizard?**

A: The Data Forms Wizard creates custom forms set up to access databases. The Standard Forms are used for various purposes.

4 **What is the purpose of icons on the toolbar?**

A: To graphically indicate the use of the button.

5 **How would you display a toolbar button's function in text?**

A: By setting the ToolTips text property for the object.

6 **How do you add new menu items to the default menus in the Application Wizard?**

A: By clicking on the plus sign in the Menus window, then adding the caption and name for the new item.

7 **What is a good reason to have a Splash screen?**

A: To display company, product, and version information about the application and to give the user something to look at while the application loads.

8 **What does the About form offer?**

A: An important feature is the System info, as well as the project name, description, and version number.

Personal Workbook Answers

Visual Quiz

Q: How and where does the form on the right display the URL?

A: By using the Navigate method and In the Combo1 ComboBox.

Chapter 4

1 What is an *object* in Visual Basic?

A: Objects are entities you can create and use in the process of developing a Windows application; virtually anything that becomes part of the application. Forms, Controls, Procedures, are all objects.

2 What is an *event*?

A: Events are actions taken by objects. They are what objects do.

3 How is a variable distinguished from a constant?

A: A variable has two or more subclasses. It can change in the course of a procedure. A constant does not change.

4 Would you use the default Variant type to define a variable that you intend to use as a counter, which gets incremented by 1 each time the execution loops? Why or why not?

A: No, because defining a counter as Integer is more efficient, since it allocates less memory up front. The Variant type must be converted when used in an expression.

5 How many "Hi's" will you get from the example in Listing 4-12?

A: 1200.

6 What data type would you select for a five-digit zip code?

A: Long integer.

7 Which would you choose to test for ten different age categories, with different events taking place for each possible category, the `If` command block or the `Select Case` structure?

A: Select Case.

8 What is the significant difference between the `Do-While` and the `For-Next` loops?

A: For Next is more efficient if you know the number of passes through the loop. Do While is better if you do not know how many passes must be made, but know the condition that must exist or continue to exist before dropping out of the loop.

Visual Quiz

Q: The code shown on the right has an obvious flaw. What is it?

A: Zip code is declared as Integer, but the values can go up to 9XXXX. Integer values can only go as high as 32767.

Chapter 5

1 What is the purpose of the `Sub Main` procedure?

A: It may be placed in a standard module and performs initialization tasks such as displaying a startup form.

2 What is the difference between `MouseUp` and `MouseDown`?

A: `MouseDown` is a click and `MouseUp` is the button release.

3 When would you use `MouseMove` rather than `MouseUp`?

A: When you want to have a value returned with cursor movement.

PERSONAL WORKBOOK ANSWERS

④ What is a good application for drag and drop?

A: Drag an object into a PictureBox or drag one control into another container.

⑤ How can you use the Immediate window?

A: To track variable values and to enter and execute commands at the command line.

⑥ How can you utilize the values generated by the `Change` event?

A: The values returned can be used to update values on forms or other objects. For example you can change the displays on controls from values generated by `Change` events.

⑦ What do `GotFocus` and `LostFocus` do?

A: They detect when the focus moves from one object to another.

⑧ What does it mean to lose the Focus?

A: The object has become deselected and the focus has moved to a new object. When a new object is selected, the previously selected object can be said to have lost the focus.

Visual Quiz

Q: What does this code do?

```
Private Sub Form_MouseMove(Button As Integer, _
Shift As Integer, X As Single, Y_ As Single)
    Form2.BackColor = Int(Rnd * 32000)
    Label1.Caption = Format(X) + ", " + Format(Y)
    Text1.Text = Format(X) + ", " + Format(Y)
End Sub
```

A: It causes the background color of the form to change depending upon the position of the mouse.

Chapter 6

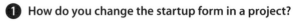

① How do you change the startup form in a project?

A: Select Project Properties from the Project Menu, then select the Startup Object.

② What name would you give `form1` in the project "Projmoney?"

A: `frmoney`, `frmmoney`, `frmbuck`, and so on, as long as the first three characters are `frm`.

③ What are the most important properties to set for a form?

A: Appearance, BorderStyle, BackStyle, Font, Name, Caption, BackColor, Height, Width, Enable are a few of the most important.

④ What is a forms collection?

A: The Forms Collection represents each loaded form in an application.

⑤ What is one thing you can do to reduce memory overhead?

A: Close forms when not in use, minimize the use of graphics, use Image instead of PictureBox, reset variable value to nothing after procedures.

⑥ What is an MDI form?

A: An MDI form contains other forms and manages multiple documents. Child forms are displayed within the window of the MDI form (parent). MDI forms are always loaded when a child form is loaded.

⑦ What control can you place directly on an MDI form?

A: You can place any controls that have Align properties on MDI forms.

8 What are ActiveX controls?

A: They are controls loaded from the Components libraries and modules and having .ocx file extension. ActiveX controls shipped with the Learning Edition are called Standard ActiveX controls. Examples are: ImageList, CommonDialog, DataCombo.

Visual Quiz

Q: What property is being set in the picture on the right? What object is the property set for?

A: BorderColor. The Shape control.

Chapter 7

1 What would be a good name for the main menu in an accounting application?

A: mnuacctng, or any name beginning with mnu.

2 Does the Menu Editor generate code for you?

A: No.

3 Which is the menu caption, "mnucaption" or "Tools"?

A: Tools.

4 How do you make sure a menu option indicates it is ready for selection?

A: Check the Enabled box.

5 For what type of interface is the WindowList property applicable?

A: An MDI application.

6 What actions do you take to make submenus in the Menu Editor?

A: Move the cursor to the line under the parent menu, and indent the submenu. Indent again on the next line for the first submenu option. Each subsequent option should be parallel under the first and so on.

7 If you wanted to view an ASCII text file, what control could you place on your form?

A: The RichTextBox control.

8 What control is commonly used to open and save files?

A: The CommonDialog control.

Visual Quiz

Q: Select the menu name that doesn't belong: mnulog, mnuopen1, menfile1, mnuup

A: menfile1, because it should begin with mnu

Chapter 8

1 What other controls are combined in the ComboBox control?

A: The ListBox and the TextBox.

2 How can you increase the size of a label as the text increases in size?

A: By changing the AutoSize property to True.

3 With what control is the AddItem method commonly used?

A: The ListBox ComboBox and the TextBox.

4 How many values can the label caption contain?

A: Only one value.

5 Which objects' properties can be changed with the movement of scrollbars?

A: Any object in the project in which a procedure is written controlling the events linked to the scrollbar.

6 What is an example of a lightweight control?

A: A lightweight control is one in which there is little memory overhead. Usually, this refers to the Image control versus the PictureBox control.

Personal Workbook Answers

7 Which is a more efficient use of system resources, the `Image` control or the `PictureBox`?

A: The `Image` Control provided it offers the features needed.

8 What is the function of the `Timer` control?

A: To initiate events at specified intervals.

Visual Quiz

Q: Which control is ideal for opening a file?

A: The FileListBox.

Chapter 9

1 What are some uses of the `PictureBox` control?

A: Loading bitmaps, drawing graphics, containing other controls.

2 What does the `Enabled` property of the `Timer` affect?

A: If it is Enabled at run time, events will be timed as soon as the program is launched.

3 Why is the `CommonDialog` control such an important addition to the toolbox?

A: Because it provides dialog boxes for Open, Save As, Fonts, Color, Print functions.

4 What does the Font Dialog box let you do?

A: It lets you choose a font (typeface, style and point size) from those available on your system.

5 Which is the default option on the Color Dialog box, full palette or limited, and what does it consist of?

A: The full palette, which includes mixing colors, is the default.

6 What are some reasons the Printing process is more complicated than the other dialog box functions?

A: Because it involves device control, not just allowing users to make selections.

7 How do filters work to allow viewing of only certain file types?

A: They restrict display to those with certain file extensions.

8 How do you add components to your application from libraries?

A: These libraries are listed under the Components option on the Project Menu and they consist of controls, designers, and insertable objects.

Visual Quiz

Q: Where should the `CommonDialog` control properly be placed?

A: Anywhere on the form.

Chapter 10

1 What type of data does a string function deal with?

A: Text.

2 How many elements are in an array?

A: A fixed array has the number of elements specified, but a dynamic array has no limits except certain system limitations (-2,147,483,648 to (2,147,483,648).

3 What is the difference between a Control array and other arrays?

A: A control array must be created at design time, while an array can be created at run time.

4 What types can't you mix in an array?

A: You can't mix types where you would violate logic and mathematical rules, such as changing to a number larger than the data type can handle (Long to an Integer or a Single or Double to a Long or Integer). Also, changing a String to a Number without using conversion functions would not work.

5 Name three new functions in Visual Basic.

A: WeekdayName, Replace, StrReverse, Round, Join, MonthName, FormatCurrency FormatDateTime, FormatNumber, FormatPercent.

6 What value will the Right function return?

A: The rightmost character(s) in the string, depending upon the argument.

7 What is the function for date subtraction?

A: DateDiff.

8 What is the seed in the random function?

A: It starts the random number generation sequence.

Visual Quiz

Q: What is the interval argument in this function?

A: Weekday.

Chapter 11

1 What mode is most often used in debugging?

A: Break mode.

2 How is the Locals Window used in debugging?

A: Viewing the current value of local variables where execution was halted.

3 A typo in a variable name is an example of what type of error?

A: Compile error.

4 What type of error stops program execution and presents a dialog message?

A: Run-time error.

5 What Debug tool gives you a command line interface in Break mode?

A: The Immediate Window.

6 What Debug tool enables you to execute program statements one line at a time?

A: Step Into/Step Over.

7 How does Step Into differ from Step Over?

A: Step Into executes each line of code no matter what it does. Step Over will not execute code that calls a different procedure.

8 What is the most difficult type of error to detect?

A: The logic error.

Visual Quiz

Q: Which watch expression is invalid?

A: thisy2k = 3, since it is a type mismatch.

Chapter 12

1 What is currently the favored data access interface?

A: ADO (ActiveX Data Objects).

2 How do you install the Visual Data Manager?

A: You can run it from the Add-Ins menu. Also you can open the Visdata project in the Samples directory.

Personal Workbook Answers

 How do you access the `Data Environment` Designer?

A: First make a reference to it by selecting Project, References, then choose `Add Data Environment` from the `Project` menu.

4 How do you add a connection to the `Data Environment`?

A: Select `Properties` with the `DataEnvironment` object selected. Select the `correct OLE DB` provider, then select the specific database from its pathname location.

5 To which type of database interface is the `Data Control` applied?

A: The `DAO` interface.

6 Which control is ActiveX? (`DataGrid`, `Data` control, or `ListBox`)

A: The `DataGrid`.

7 What tool can you use in the `Data Environment` to query a database?

A: The `Query Designer`.

8 What property provides the Data Link when using the `ADO Data` control?

A: The `DataSource` property.

Visual Quiz

Q: Which control does not belong?

A: The `Data Control` does not go with the ActiveX `DataGrid` and `DataList`.

Chapter 13

1 What does it mean to plan for errors?

A: Anticipate most errors.

2 Performing calculations outside the scope of the application causes what error?

A: Overflow error.

3 Give an example of inline error processing?

A: On Error.

4 Error handling mostly deals with what type of errors?

A: Run Time.

5 `On Error GoTo` Bozo exemplifies what type of `On Error` routine?

A: On Error GoTo Line label. (Going to a label).

6 What is the default property of the `Err` Object?

A: Err.Number.

7 What is an example of an unrecoverable error?

A: Division by zero, or an error in which the program cannot correct the error internally.

8 How do you refer to a program-generated or a user-defined error?

A: You are Raising an error.

Visual Quiz

Q: Which of these command buttons' procedures calls a function procedure?

A: The Command2 (Divide) button.

Chapter 14

1 What type of file has a specified record length?

A: Random Access file.

2 What file stores all data as text?

A: `Sequential` file.

3 What statement is used by all file types?

A: The Open statement.

4 What file commands are used by `Binary` and `Random Access`, but not `Sequential` files?

A: Put #(file number) and Get#(file number).

5 How do you declare a record type variable?

A: A Type declaration.

6 Besides the record length, what other object may have a specified length?

A: The Field length.

7 What do you need to retrieve a record from a `Random Access` file?

A: The record number.

8 What object is easiest to use to print data you stored in a data file?

A: The Printer object.

Visual Quiz

Q: What is the number that should be displayed in the Immediate Window, based upon what you see in the executing program?

A: The number shown in the text box (234234242).

Chapter 15

1 What `Multimedia` control property values must be set to initialize the control?

A: Notify, Wait, and Shareable.

2 How many multimedia devices can you play per `Multimedia` control?

A: Only one device per control.

3 Name two animation file types

A: AVI, MOV, Mpeg.

4 Name two different controls you can use to display animation?

A: `Multimedia` control, the `Animation` control, the Windows Media Player, Active Movie Control.

5 How can you play animation without allowing the user to select a control?

A: By using the `Timer` control to rotate pictures.

6 How do you get the `Animation` and `Multimedia` controls in the ToolBox?

A: You select them from Components on the Project Menu.

7 What does the `Multimedia` control do that the `Animation` control can't do?

A: It plays files with sound.

8 Name some features of the Windows MediaPlayer control?

A: You can embed it in HTML pages, use it as an OLE object, play sound and animation files with it.

Visual Quiz

Q: Which of these controls shown on the Animation Form at design time are not visible at run time?

A: The `Animation` control.

Chapter 16

1 What is the difference between Graphics methods and Graphics controls?

A: Controls are placed at design time. Methods are used at run time.

Personal Workbook Answers

2 Where can you use the PaintPicture method?

A: A form or picture box.

3 Where can you draw using Graphics methods?

A: Forms, Picture boxes and printer objects.

4 What property determines the unit of measure in the PaintPicture method?

A: The ScaleMode property.

5 How can you create a background or wallpaper effect?

A: The PaintPicture method.

6 Name some Graphics methods.

A: Circle, Line, Pset, Point, PaintPicture, Cls.

7 Name some Graphics properties used to Draw on Forms or `PictureBox` controls.

A: DrawMode, DrawStyle and DrawWidth.

8 What do the X1 and Y1 arguments in the Line method represent?

A: The initial width and height of the X and Y coordinates.

Visual Quiz

Q: Where on this form should the Graphics controls used in the Magic and Rings options be placed?

A: Controls aren't placed on the form, but the options are generated from code.

Chapter 17

1 Setting what property enables you to create persistent graphics?

A: AutoRedraw to True.

2 What properties determine the positions of the clipping region?

A: ClipX and ClipY.

3 What properties determine the area of the clipping region for the `PictureClip` control?

A: ClipHeight and ClipWidth.

4 What does the `ScaleMode` property value of 3 stand for?

A: Pixels.

5 What color function has arguments based on colors 0-15?

A: QBColor.

6 What does the Print command do when used in code?

A: Displays text or other values on the form.

7 What do the `StretchX` and `StretchY` properties do?

A: Define the area to which the Clip bitmap is copied.

8 What properties must be set for the Timer control to function?

A: The Interval and Enabled properties.

Visual Quiz

Q: Is the selected control part of a control array?

A: No, the `PictureClip` control is not in a control array.

Chapter 18

1 Name some controls that feature OLE drag-and-drop.

A: PictureBox, Label, and TextBox controls. You can check the Properties Window to see if the control supports OLEDragMode and OLEDropMode.

② How do you access the menu options for the `OLE container` control?

A: By right clicking on the `OLE container` control.

③ What is the difference between Linking and Embedding?

A: Linking leaves the data in the source file. Embedding copies the data from the source file.

④ Which events are not generated for the target side of the drag-and-drop process?

A: The Automatic mode.

⑤ In which mode(s) can you use Paste and Paste Special to copy data to an `OLE container` control?

A: The Design mode.

⑥ Which drag-and-drop property value is most likely to require code: Manual or Automatic?

A: Manual.

⑦ What is the chief difference between the `OLE container` control and the other controls that support automation?

A: The OLE control allows you create document centered applications.

⑧ What methods are used to copy data to and from the Clipboard?

A: `GetData` and `SetData`.

Visual Quiz

Q: What properties should be set for the TextBox on the OLE Drag n' form? How should they be set?

A: The OLEDragMode to Manual, OLEDropMode to Manual, and MultiLine to True.

Chapter 19

① Add-Ins are_____ to the Visual Basic model.

A: Extensions.

② The Data Form Wizard offers what types of forms?

A: MDI, SDI, Master/Detail, single record, multiple record, charts, grids.

③ For what is the API Viewer used?

A: To call API functions from Windows.

④ How is the Visual Data Manager Accessed?

A: It can be loaded from the Samples directory or selected from the Add-Ins menu.

⑤ How can you get quick access to all the Add-Ins you have loaded?

A: Use the Add-In Toolbar.

⑥ How do you add a reference to a new Add-In that you create?

A: By using code to add it to the VBAddin.INI file or creating an `Addin` project.

⑦ How does a newly created Add-In get registered in your system?

A: By compiling it.

⑧ What is the VBE Object?

A: `The Root Object` in the extensibility model, which symbolizes the Visual Basic environment.

Visual Quiz

Q: How do you install this Toolbar?

A: You install it from the Add-In Manager.

PERSONAL WORKBOOK ANSWERS

Chapter 20

1 What is the ActiveX counterpart of the form called?

A: UserDocument.

2 What are some properties of UserDocuments?

A: `AsyncReadComplete, EnterFocus, ExitFocus, Hide, InitProperties, ReadProperties, Scroll, Show,` and `WriteProperties.`

3 What kind of file stores the completed UserDocument?

A: When you complete your document, it is compiled into a .VBD file.

4 What is the new `ActiveX` control called in the Project Explorer window?

A: UserControl.

5 When you create a new `ActiveX` control, you are creating a _____ _____.

A: Control Class.

6 What type of files (extension) are produced when you compile `ActiveX` components?

A: Control components produce .OCX files.

7 What tool is available to convert existing forms into ActiveX documents?

A: The ActiveX Document Migration Wizard.

8 How are ActiveX documents displayed?

A: In the Internet Explorer.

Visual Quiz

Q: Which of these options in the ActiveX Document Migration Wizard should be checked?

A: "Comment out invalid code" and "Convert to activex.EXE."

Chapter 21

1 Who uses HTML?

A: Web page designers, lay persons and developers.

2 What do style sheets do?

A: They allow you to make global changes in particular objects.

3 What is a URL?

A: Universal Resource Locator. An Internet domain address.

4 What is the difference between HTML and DHTML?

A: DHTML adds functionality and enhancements to HTML. You can dynamically change the content of Web pages after loading with DHTML.

5 What facilities exist in Visual Basic to develop Internet browsers?

A: The Application Wizard, the Add Form window and creating your own from an ordinary form.

6 What does it mean to bind a control to another?

A: The properties on one control specify the second control.

7 What are some functions of the MAPI controls?

A: They are used to Send, Read, Compose Email and to SignOff and SignOn from the mail server.

8 What are the `GoBack` and `GoForward` methods used for?

A: To navigate the browser to and from a URL.

PERSONAL WORKBOOK ANSWERS

Visual Quiz

Q: Which of the forms in the Add Form dialog should be used for a Web browser?

A: The Web Browser form or the ordinary form. Others could be used but are not as appropriate.

Chapter 22

❶ What is the relationship between Active Server Pages and IIS?

A: IIS makes Active Server Pages possible, since it is the Internet Information Server.

❷ Can you use VBScript in Active Server Pages?

A: Yes.

❸ What other kinds of scripts can be used in Active Server Pages?

A: JScript, Java, and virtually any scripting language.

❹ What are the symbols that set off the Active Server Pages command block?

A: <% and %>.

❺ What is server-side scripting?

A: Code that executes on the Web server and not the client browser.

❻ Why can't VBScript be used in client-side scripts for all Internet applications?

A: Because different browsers will either execute or fail to execute the code.

❼ What is the best way to make sure all browsers can use the Web pages at a Web site?

A: Server side scripting, since the user's browser doesn't matter.

❽ What is the difference between server-side scripting and client-side scripting?

A: Server side executes on the Web server and Client side executes on individual browsers.

Visual Quiz

Q: What is the URL being accessed?

A: The browser is set to the home directory of the local Web server.

Chapter 23

❶ What is the add-in that prepares Visual Basic programs for distribution?

A: The Package and Deployment Wizard.

❷ How can you customize the package and deployment of the applications you create?

A: Use the Setup Toolkit.

❸ How can you use the same settings in subsequent deployments?

A: Save the Script.

❹ What is a major difference in deploying an Internet application?

A: An HTML file is created.

❺ What determines the CAB file size?

A: The location of deployment. For e.g., floppy disk deployment dictates smaller and more CAB files.

❻ What is the traditional way of creating help for a Visual Basic application?

A: The WinHelp system and the Microsoft Help Workshop.

Personal Workbook Answers

7 What is the help file extension for a rich text format help file?

A: RTF (Rich Text Format).

8 What is the newest help system allowing developers to provide help for their applications?

A: The HTML Help Workshop and HTML Help system.

Visual Quiz

Q: What kind of deployment is this dialog box used for?

A: It is used in the deployment of Web applications.

Glossary

A

Active Server Pages Active Server Pages is a server-based technology from Microsoft. ASP code can be embedded in a HTML document. The ASP code is processed by the Web server with the results passed to the client Web browser. ASP allows you to also build Web pages that are created on-the-fly by database content. ASP only runs on NT servers.

ActiveX ActiveX includes documents, code components, and controls. Which you use and how you use them depends upon the intended use and what you hope to accomplish.

ActiveX Components ActiveX Components are libraries of ActiveX controls, Designers, and Insertable Objects. You load component libraries to add the associated objects to your Project.

ActiveX Controls ActiveX controls are controls other than the Standard controls and have an `.ocx` file extension. They are often used to add functions to a Web page. Some components are available only in the Professional and Enterprise editions, and others are available from third parties.

ActiveX Data Objects (ADO) Control The `Data` control lets you create a relationship between controls with a `DataSource` property and data sources written to OLE DB specifications.

ActiveX Documents ActiveX documents enable you to create interactive Internet applications.

Add-In Manager When you want to use a wizard but do not want to access it from the Application Wizard, you can load it from the Add-In Manager on the Add-Ins menu.

Add-In Toolbar The Add-In toolbar provides you with immediate access to your Add-ins without going to the Add-Ins menu, selecting the Add-Ins Manager, and Loading or Unloading each of the options you want.

Add-Ins Add-ins are tools that can be made to function differently in different situations. You can develop your own add-in and place it on the Add-In list. Add-ins are first and foremost extensible.

Animation Control The `Animation` control is an alternative to the `Multimedia` control. It cannot play sound video clips, and it may not load compressed files.

Application Wizard The Application Wizard generates a full-blown interface without your writing code. You can use it with a Microsoft Access database or with any Remote ODBC database for which you have a driver.

Array An array is a group of variables with the same general name but with consecutive numbers for each element. Arrays allow you to have ranges of variables in numeric order that all carry out some function in the same way.

Glossary

B

Binary File Binary files can be any arbitrarily structured combination of bytes. You must know how the data were originally stored in order to retrieve data from the binary file.

Bitmap A bitmap is a picture made up of bits turned on or off. A photo is a bitmap.

Break Mode Break, on the Run menu, halts program execution. You can use the Break mode to edit and test your code as well. Select Break from the Run menu while your program is running, or press Ctrl+Break on the keyboard.

C

ComboBox Control The `ComboBox` control is so called because it is a combination of the `ListBox` and the `TextBox`. It is used to offer a selection and obtain input.

CommonDialog Control The `CommonDialog` control it used to present the user with dialog boxes to open, save, and select files; to choose colors and fonts, and to print. It is not visible at runtime and cannot be sized. You must use it in conjunction with another control.

Compile Errors Compile errors are simply incorrect code. These include syntax errors such as unbalanced parentheses, quotes in the wrong place, and spelling errors.

Component Object Model The Component Object Model (COM) interface is architecture for defining interfaces and interaction among objects used by divergent software applications. ActiveX, MAPI, and OLE are technologies built on the COM foundation.

Constant A constant is a value entered into an expression that cannot be manipulated by the program. Thus it is not changed in the course of the application.

Control Controls are essentially objects on a form that perform specific functions. The icons you see in the `ToolBox` represent the controls that you will build event procedures around.

Control Arrays Control arrays enable replacement of segments of the array, whereas variable array elements are always continuous. Control arrays are created at design time, rather than runtime.

Coolbar The Coolbar is found only in the Professional and Enterprise Editions. It can be used to create Internet Explorer type toolbars.

D

Data Access Objects The `DAO` data control can be added to any form, and when `Connect` and `DatabaseName` properties are set, you can access databases and do most functions without writing code. `DAO` uses the Microsoft Jet Engine as is used by Microsoft Access. You can use `DAO` to connect to Access tables and several other database formats (`.dbf`, `.db`).

Data Environment Designer You can use the `Data Environment` Designer to do such tasks as create a database connection, set data and command object relationships, and create data reports.

Data Form Wizard The Data Form Wizard helps customize your form. You can run the Data Form Wizard from within the Application Wizard, or by adding it via the Add-Ins menu.

Database Databases are structured methods of storing data. The purpose of data retrieval guides the development and design.

DataGrid Control This control works in conjunction with the ADO Data control and enables you to display data (including databases) in a spreadsheet or tabular format.

DataList and DataCombo These controls look like list boxes, but their lists can be filled in from a database source. They can function as lookups to different tables in the same application.

Debugging Debugging is the process of locating errors and solving problems that may interfere with program execution or produce incorrect results.

Divide by Zero The Divide by Zero error is generated when there are internal inconsistencies in an application. Variables and/or constants are assigned values, or incorrect values are generated that result in an equation where the divisor is 0.

Docking Windows can be anchored by clicking and dragging. This is called, DOCKING. You can also specify which windows can be docked by selecting Options from the Tools menu.

Drag and Drop At its simplest, drag and drop operations combine a number of features set up to allow an object to be dragged by holding down the mouse button and dropped onto another object by releasing the button.

Dynamic Data Exchange (DDE) The DDE protocol deals with linking and exchanging data between applications that run under Microsoft Windows.

Dynamic Hypertext Markup Language (DHTML) DHTML lets you create many spectacular visual effects by changing material on a Web page after the page has loaded in the browser. DHTML includes the Document Object Model (DOM) that lets you use all of the page objects and properties, including allowing the page to auto refresh. Using it, you can dynamically change page attributes transparent to the user. Programs can be speedy with little code, but it is not an object based language. It supports HTML 4.0, CSS, CSS-Positioning, and ECMAScript. The performance of DHTML under Netscape may not be predictable, since Netscape does not fully support HTML 4.0.

Error An error is a problem in code that either prevents execution (compile error), stops it (runtime-error), or causes mistakes in calculations long range (logical error).

Error Trapping and Error Handling These are techniques to intercept errors and redirect program execution or present the user with a specific message.

Event An event is something happening. An event can be a cause or an effect. The event may occur as a result of a prior action, or it may, itself, cause a different action. The usual event is a mouse click on a form button and is initiated by the user.

File All files consist of bytes arranged in some fashion on magnetic media. The arrangement of these bytes constitutes a structured series of records each made up of fields. The records are analogous to rows in a table, with the fields being comparable to the table's columns.

File System Controls The `Drive`, `Directory`, and `File` controls enable the selection of drives, directories (folders) and files at runtime. The `DriveListBox` identifies the drives available to users on a particular system. The `DirListBox` displays all the available directories (folders) on a selected drive. The `FileListBox` further enables you to select files from a selected drive and directory.

Focus When several controls are placed on a form, the user may interact only with the particular control that currently has the focus. Keyboard key presses or mouse movements and clicks control the focus.

GLOSSARY

Form When you select the Standard Exe project, the interface creates a form. The form is the basis for the events that will be taking place when the user interacts with the application. The form is there for you to build on, possibly setting up several forms in the process of developing your application.

Form Design Window When you first open a new project, Visual Basic creates a form, Form1, for you automatically. This form then becomes the default startup form for the project.

Forms Collection A forms collection is each loaded form in a project. This includes MDI forms, child forms, and all form objects.

Function A function is an expression that returns a value when executed. Functions can be called by procedures in order to carry out some calculation and then return to the calling procedure.

Graphics Controls Graphics controls are more effective if you need only to make simple designs constructed at design time. For this reason, graphics controls are easier to use than graphics methods.

Graphics Methods Graphics methods enable you to do such tasks as drawing and painting. They are always done by writing code. You then will need to run the program to see what effect your method has.

Help Workshop The Help Workshop is available to assist you in creating help text in response to the user's request from the menu or by pressing the F1 key.

HTML The Hypertext Markup Language (HTML) is the page description language on the Internet and intranets. It provides a facility for the design of Web pages.

I

Image Control The `Image` control is often referred to as a "lightweight" control because it uses fewer system resources than the `PictureBox`. Besides the great advantage of saving system resources, the `Image` control offers options not available with the `PictureBox`.

Microsoft Internet Information Server (IIS) Microsoft Internet Information Server (IIS) is a strong Web server planned to carry out large-scale Web publishing services.

L

Label The `Label` control is generally used to display labels adjacent to other objects they are describing. They may also be used to provide instructions to the user, but they cannot be edited at runtime.

Line Control The `Line` control enables you to draw lines on a form.

ListBox The `ListBox` control is used to enable users to select items from a list. If the list is longer that the number of items that will fit in the box, a scrollbar will be added to the box.

Logical Errors Logical errors are often the most difficult to detect. That is because they do not always halt program execution. They may not be found for months or even years in production applications.

M

Media Control Interface (MCI) The MCI control manages the recording and playback of multimedia files on Media Control Interface (MCI) devices.

Menu Menus guide the user through the application. They are a convenient way to give the user choices and options and they allow you to group the options into logical areas.

Menu Bar Right-click on the menu bar at the top of your screen and a dialog box will pop up with main menu bar options displayed in the left pane, while the options for each item on the menu bar are shown in the right pane.

Menu Editor The Menu Editor enables you to create custom menus for your application. Select the Menu Editor from the Tools Menu.

Module Because you have more than one form in your project, you must have a way of loading one of the forms first. The easiest way to do this is to have a module with a `Sub Main` procedure. A module is a file with a `.bas` extension containing code.

Multiple Document Interface (MDI) MDI programs allow more than one document to be open at once. For example, word processing and spreadsheet programs are MDI applications. All windows are enclosed in the MDI parent window.

O

Object An object is an entity you can create and use in the process of developing a Windows application. An object in Visual Basic can be virtually anything that becomes part of the application.

Object Browser The Object Browser enables you to view the class and members of an object. It is accessed from the View menu.

Object Linking and Embedding Object Linking and Embedding enables you to incorporate components from different programs within an application. Linking is attaching the objects in an external application. Embedding occurs when you place these objects in a container such as the OLE container.

Object Linking and Embedding Database (OLE DB) The ADO data access technology works for multiple environments and types of data storage. OLE DB is a replacement for the Open Database Connectivity (ODBC) technology that uses specific drivers for each database type.

P

Package and Deployment Wizard When your application is complete, you will need to package it, compiling and gathering all the files in the project. Then you can deploy it so that it can be distributed to end users for sharing or sale. The Wizard automates the entire process.

Personal Web Server The Personal Web Server is set up for Web publishing on a small scale. It provides many of the same services and features as Microsoft Internet Information Server (IIS), but it is for use with Windows 95/98. It is shipped on the installation CD but does not install with the typical installation.

PictureBox A `PictureBox` can contain pictures. It displays bitmaps, icons, and metafiles. It can act as a container for other controls and objects.

PictureClip Control The `PictureClip` control enables you to select and display parts of a source bitmap or icon. Instead of loading many pictures, each consuming memory, you can load one large picture and use the `PictureClip` to display any region of the picture needed by your application at a particular moment.

Pop-Up Menus Pop-up menus many times offer you help when you right-click on an object. Sometimes they pop up by themselves due to the context of what you are doing. They are also called context menus.

Glossary

Procedure A general procedure is written to tell the application how to carry out a task or function. It must be invoked by the application. An event procedure remains idle until called upon to respond to events caused by the user or by the system. A Sub procedure is a block of code that is executed in response to an event.

Project A project is the group of related and required files making up a complete software application or component.

Project Explorer The Project Explorer is the window that displays the parts of a project or project group. The View Code and View Object icons let you toggle between viewing the Form or other object and the viewing code attached to that object.

Properties Properties are attributes of objects. In Visual Basic, all objects have properties. For example, a form can have background and foreground colors, a caption, width, and height, as well as many other properties.

Properties Window The Properties window lists the properties for all objects in the design mode. The parts of the window are the Object box at the top of the window, the List tabs, and the Description pane. The Object box displays the object class and the name of the selected object. The List tabs list the currently selected object alphabetically and categorically.

Property Pages Property pages provide an additional way to view properties for ActiveX controls. Property pages have tabs for setting different properties.

R

Raising Errors When you raise an error, you generate a runtime-error in your code for the purpose of returning more information that you can get by using the Error statement.

Random Access Files Random Access files are files with a fixed record length and a fixed field length. Because you know the positions of each field in a record and each record in a file, you can find specific fields and records without reading sequentially through the entire file.

Remote Data Objects RDO is an interface to ODBC (Open Database Connectivity). It provides a layer of code over ODBC API and the driver manager that sets up connections and carries out intricate procedures. You use RDO similarly to DAO.

Rnd Function A new number in an application is determined by the value of a randomly selected number. For any seed (the starting number for the Rnd function), the previously generated number functions as the seed for the next number.

Runtime Runtime is the time that program execution is actually taking place. When you press F5 or select Start from the Run menu, runtime begins.

Runtime Errors Runtime-errors occur when the program is executing. When a runtime error is encountered, the program's execution is halted, you receive an error message, and you can choose to end execution or to enter Debug mode.

S

Sequential File Data are stored sequentially, delimited by some character (comma, quotes) so that the position of a record in a file cannot be determined without reading through the file unless the entire file is present in memory. The text consists of ASCII or ANSI "plain" text.

Setup ToolKit The Setup Toolkit enables you to customize the Setup program that will install your program on a user's machine.

Shape Control The Shape control enables you to draw shapes on a form. The shapes can be defined as rectangular or circular.

Single Document Interface (SDI) Only one document can be open at one time. An example is Notepad.

Splash Screen An introductory form that the user first sees when running an application. A splash screen may be used to show company logos, show version numbers, and even to occupy the user while the program loads. When you create your Application Wizard–generated project, you have the option of creating a splash screen.

T

TextBox The `TextBox` control is typically used to collect user input.

Timer Control The `Timer` control enables you to control timed events independent of the user. Timer events can be firing in the background even though other commands are being executed.

Toolbar A toolbar functions as a shortcut to the regular menu options. The IDE Standard toolbar is one that is by default directly under the menu at the top of the screen.

Toolbar Wizard If you have the Professional or Enterprise editions, you can use the Toolbar Wizard to create custom toolbars on forms.

Toolbox The Standard toolbox contains all the tools necessary to place controls on your forms. You can add components to the toolbox from the libraries by selecting Components from the Project menu.

U

URL This acronym stands for Uniform Resource Locator, meaning a string standing for the address of an Internet object. This often consists of a path and filename of a domain or subdomain on the World Wide Web.

User Document An ActiveX document is organized to include a `UserDocument` object, code, code modules, and the controls that you place on the `UserDocument`. `UserDocument` objects are like forms in the sense that they include source code and the properties of the controls that they contain.

V

Variable Variables are objects that vary in value. Their values change through some mechanism of a program. For example, the variable `name` can have different values, depending upon what is going on in the program.

Variable Array A variable array is declared in code and is different from a control array. Variable array elements are always continuous. That is, some elements in between the lower and upper bounds of a variable array cannot be removed.

VB Script VB Script is a less substantial programming tool than Visual Basic. It is used across platforms, probably most commonly on the Internet. You can write code in the Visual Basic Editor, but you cannot test or run it.

Vector Graphics A vector graphic does not degrade as it is enlarged beyond its original size. That is because it is not composed of bits, but rather it is based on a formula of coordinates.

Visual Data Manager This is an application written in Visual Basic that is an aid to database access via DAO (Data Access Object). This is available in the Professional Edition. It also is a utility to let you create and access database tables.

Glossary

W

Window Stated as simply as possible, a window is a rectangular area in which coding and form design take place, and in which properties and projects are selected. The Window environment is a place where you can design forms, implement controls, add properties, and write code.

Windows API The Windows Application Programming Interface (API) includes all the tools to which you have access under Microsoft Windows. Using code, you can call API functions from Windows. The Windows API includes thousands of procedures, functions, subs, constants, and types that you can declare.

Windows Collection The Windows Collection is made up of Windows objects. In Visual Basic these include the Project Explorer, the Properties window, the Object Browser window, Code windows, Designer windows, and the Development Environment.

Windows Media Player Control The Windows Media Player control can be selected from Component Controls on the Project menu. You can play all the sound files and some animation files that are problematic on the Multimedia control.

Wizards Wizards assist you in development. They make your work much easier by automating many of the development tasks.

Index

Index

Index

Index

Index

C

C++, 6
cab file, 498, 502, 508
cable hookup, 289, 447
calculations
  arrays, 202
  dates, 72
  errors, 270
  intrinsic functions, 214
  operators, 74–75
  order, 74
  string, 216–217
  strings, 71
Caldera Linux, 449
calendars, inserting, 153
Call Stack dialog box, 268
Call Stack option, 16
Call Stack tool, 226, 235, 236
calls, reviewing, 268
camera, digital, 176
captions
  buttons, 160
  form, 112, 162
  labels, 156–157
  menu, 54, 134
  storing, 48
cards, moving, 374–375
Cascade option, 144
Cascading Style Sheets (CSS), 450
CD-ROM, packaging, 498, 502
CD-ROM drive, 314
CDs
  ejecting, 315
  playing, 314, 316–317
CGI, 447, 448
cgi-bin, 462
Change Directory button, 506

Change events, 102–103, 162
characters
  controlling user entry, 154
  converting, 214
  files, dragging, 394
  reversing, 216
Chart control, 256
charts, 404
CheckBox, 18, 118, 119, 250, 256
Checked box, 134
Checked property, 144
checkmarks, 144
child menus
  MDI form, 140
Choose function, 80
Choose Program Group dialog, 506
CICS (Customer Information Control System), 244
Circle method, 333, 344, 359
circles, 353
Class Builder Utility, 45
class ID, 504
class modules files, 20
Class property
classes
  control, 428
  Data Object Wizard, 52
  defined, 28, 64
  OLE control, 384, 388
Click procedure, 228, 396
clients, 449
clipboard
  Copying OLE objects, 396–397
  objects, 382, 394
  pasting, 386
ClipHeight, 372
ClipWidth, 372
ClipX property, 366
ClipY property, 366
Close button, 112
Close command, 315

Index

Index

Index

Index

Index

Index

Index

Index

F

facts. *See* database
Favorites list, 460
field
    database queries, 254
    database table, 252
    Random Access file, 294
File control, 168–171
file extensions
    components, 118
    design files, 126
    forms, 126
    graphics, 164
    Project Explorer, 20
    project files, 126
    properties, saved, 122
    rich text file, 138
file formats
    bitmaps, 176
    incorrect, 265
    limiting view, 186
    opening files, 186
    projects, 126–127
File menu
    Add Project, 428
    compiling menu, 412
    described, 12–13
    Explorer, 54
    fonts dialog boxes, creating, 184
    New Project, 111, 113, 410, 416
    OLE objects, 384
    Open Database, 247
    Open option, 186
    Save, 126
    Save As, 140
    SDI/MDI, 54
    Standard toolbar, 16

File System controls
    described, 175
    error handling, 272
File System Objects (FSO)
    binary files, 304
    described, 290-291
File Transfer Protocol (FTP), 448, 449, 504
file types. *See* file formats
FileListBox, 18, 102, 118
filenames
    animation, 320
    browser, 448
    prevent loading, 188
files
    accessing, 175
    animation, playing, 320–321
    binary, 304–305
    bitmaps, loading from, 333
    database, 243
    display, 18
    drag and drop, 96
    errors, trapping, 300–303
    filtering, 186, 188
    FTP, 448
    help, 182, 510, 514
    input/output (I/O) described, 289
    managing, 20
    MAPI DLL, 466
    missing, 265, 266, 272–273
    printing from, 306–307
    Random Access, 294–299
    resource, 406
    saving, 188–189
    sequential, 292–293
    setup, 498
    sound, playing, 318–319
    text, 186
    types, 290–291
    Windows Explorer, dragging, 392–393

Index

Index

Index

Index

Index

Index

Index

M

Index

Index

Index

N

name

  ActiveX project, 436

  Add -In Designer, 52

  Add-In Manager, 412

  buttons, 298

  constants, 68

  identifiers, 39

  labels, 156

  menu, 132, 134

  objects, 64

  objects in procedures, 76

  project, 20, 30

  toolbars, 36

  variables, 67

Navigate method, 456

navigating

  KeyPress event, 98

  UserDocuments, 440

negation (-), 75

NegotiatePosition box, 134

Netscape, 449, 474, 486

NetShow, 328

network, 502

New Project window, 8, 414, 452

Next command, 315

non-European languages, 144

not equal (<>), 74

Not operator, 74

Notepad

  ASCII files, reading, 126, 292

  DHTML files, 476

  files, opening, 186

  Help files, 510

  HTML files, 474

  VBScript, 480

Notify property, 318

Now function, 218, 490

null error, 300

null-checking routine, 303

numbers

  arrays, 204

  Binary files, 304–305

  converting to dates, 72

  drawings, random-number generated, 344, 346

  error, 276, 278, 282, 284

  generating, 350

  random, generating, 220

  Random Access files, 294, 298, 300

O

Object box, 22

Object Browser

  constants, 68

  described, 6, 8

  flags constants, 188

  reference library, 194

  Standard toolbar, 16

Object Linking and Embedding (OLE), 118

  applications, adding from, 386–387

  Automation servers. *See* ActiveX documents

  control, 250

  Copying from the clipboard, 396–397

  database access, 46, 244–245, 252, 256

  described, 381, 382–383

  dragging from external applications, 392–395

  dragging-and-dropping, 382, 390–391

  inserting objects at runtime, 388–389

  servers. *See* code components

  tool, 18

  using OLE objects, 384–385

Index

Index

P

Package and Deployment Wizard
    described, 45, 498–499
    starting, 496–497, 502–503

packaging
    described, 495
    Graphics applications, 500–501
    Help Workshop, 510–511
    HTML Help, 512–513
    installing with Setup program, 506–507
    online help, 514–515
    Package and Deployment Wizard, 496–499, 502–503
    Setup programs, creating, 508–509
    Web server, deploying to, 504–505

packets, 448

pag extension, 20

Page Designer, 476

Page Down key, 100

Page Up key, 100

pages. *See also* **Web pages**
    navigating, 100
    printing, 192
    Property, 122

paint programs, 194, 362, 382

PaintPicture method
    animation, 324
    bitmaps, 176
    changing parameters, 338–339
    described, 333, 334, 336–337
    random drawing, 344
    vector graphics, 340–341

palette, color, 190

Paradox, 244, 245, 246

parameters, 238

parent form, 140

parentheses (()), 212

password, 56, 462

Paste, 16, 386

path
    directory, 170
    display, 18
    drive, 170
    error, 265
    file, 170
    graphic files, 502
    VBD file, 440

patterns
    collisions option, 352–353
    matching operator, 74

Pause command, 315

Pause Loop, 59

pencil, graphic, 289

percentages function, 214

Perl, 447

Personal Web Server, 484–485

phone line, 447

photographs
    bitmap, 176
    editing programs, 322, 362
    Image controls, 164, 370–371

PhotoPaint, 381

Pick a Design menu
    mnuColli option, 352
    mnuMagic option, 350
    mnuRings option, 354

picture
    forms, 112
    loading, 170–171
    in a picture, 180
    PictureBox, 176–177
    runtime, 164
    screen saver cycling, 178–179

Picture control, 250

PictureBox control
    animation, 322
    copy to the Clipboard and Paste, 396–397
    described, 175

Index

Index

(Continued)

Index

T

Index

U

(Continued)

Index

Index

Index

Index

Index